MASTERPLOTS II

POETRY SERIES
REVISED EDITION

MASTERPLOTS II

POETRY SERIES
REVISED EDITION

6

On Poetry: A Rhapsody–
Sketch for an Aesthetic Project

Editor, Revised Edition
PHILIP K. JASON

Project Editor, Revised Edition
TRACY IRONS-GEORGES

Editors, Supplement
JOHN WILSON   **PHILIP K. JASON**

Editor, First Edition
FRANK N. MAGILL

SALEM PRESS

Pasadena, California   Hackensack, New Jersey

Editor in Chief: Dawn P. Dawson

Project Editor: Tracy Irons-Georges *Research Supervisor:* Jeffry Jensen
Production Editor: Cynthia Beres *Research Assistant:* Jeff Stephens
Copy Editor: Lauren Mitchell *Acquisitions Editor:* Mark Rehn

Some of the essays in this work originally appeared in *Masterplots II, Poetry Series*, edited by Frank N. Magill (Pasadena, Calif.: Salem Press, Inc., 1992), and in *Masterplots II, Poetry Series Supplement*, edited by John Wilson and Philip K. Jason (Pasadena, Calif.: Salem Press, Inc., 1998).

∞ The paper used in these volumes conforms to the American National Standard for Permanence of Paper for Printed Library Materials, Z39.48-1992 (R1997).

Library of Congress Cataloging-in-Publication Data

Masterplots II. Poetry series.— Rev. ed. / editor, Philip K. Jason ; project editor, Tracy Irons-Georges
    p. ; cm.
  Rev. ed.: Masterplots two / Frank Northen Magill, 1992-1998.
  Includes bibliographical references and indexes.
    ISBN 1-58765-037-1 (set : alk. paper) — ISBN 1-58765-043-6 (vol. 6 : alk. paper) —
    1. Poetry — Themes, motives. I. Title: Masterplots two. II. Title: Masterplots 2. III. Jason, Philip K., 1941-   . IV. Irons-Georges, Tracy.

PN1110.5 .M37 2002
809.1—dc21

                                                                    2001055059

Second Printing

TABLE OF CONTENTS

TABLE OF CONTENTS

TABLE OF CONTENTS

MASTERPLOTS II

POETRY SERIES
REVISED EDITION

ON POETRY: A RHAPSODY

Author: Jonathan Swift (1667-1745)
Type of poem: Satire
First published: 1733

The Poem

Jonathan Swift's *On Poetry: A Rhapsody* consists of 494 lines of iambic tetrameter couplets that satirize the relationship of poetic inspiration, vocation, and flattery of those in positions of political power, both kings and prime ministers. The poem dramatizes the corrupting results of misplaced human ambition that ignores one's true aptitudes and that transforms poetry from an inspired art form into a debased and chaotic utterance.

In the first verse paragraph of the poem, animals are presented as wiser than people because animals follow their natural abilities. A human being is "the only Creature,/ Who, led by *Folly*, fights with *Nature*." This human folly involves seeking work where one's "*Genius* least inclines." The first seventy lines of the poem examine this destructive desire to reject one's proper vocation by presuming to become a poet. Swift insists in the second and third verse paragraphs that all other careers, whether in government, law, or science, require less "heavenly Influence" than poetry. However, if poetry is a heavenly pursuit for true poets, who receive little or no money or public respect, for those who have misjudged their abilities, writing poetry involves a series of trials that cannot be won and a curse from which there is no escape. This dire "Fate" comes from Apollo, the god of poetry and prophecy: "whom *Phebus* in his Ire/ Hath *blasted* with poetick Fire."

Beginning in verse paragraph 6, the narrator refers to himself as an "old experienc'd Sinner" who will give advice to new poets. They are told to choose the genre that moves them most; to revise carefully; to print the poem in a "modish Dress"; to observe, anonymously, how it is judged at coffeehouses such as "*Will's*"; and to try a second and third time if their first attempt is unsuccessful. If still unsuccessful after a third poem, the narrator urges honest poets not to throw away their pens but to forget fame and artistry and to become poets for sale. Such poetasters are transformed into hack writers by learning that the "vilest Verse thrives best at Court" and that flattering kings and prime ministers will "never fail to bring in Pence."

The rest of the poem, like the attitude expressed in fellow poet Alexander Pope's *Dunciad* (1728-1743), satirizes hack poets, in a line in which Swift echoes Pope, as "Dunces, Fools, and Sons of Whores." The narrator complains that these deluded poets refuse to admit what they are: "O, *Grubstreet!* How do I bemoan thee,/ Whose graceless Children scorn to own thee!" Also like his friend Pope's *Dunciad*, Swift's poem includes personal attacks on poet laureate Colley Cibber and many other bad poets but is not limited to satiric poetry of personal abuse. Swift attacks the poetic vices of flattery and "*Lewdness*" not only because they degrade poetry, for him in its true form the most divinely inspired kind of writing, but also, most important, because it leads to the atheism with which the poem ends.

Forms and Devices

Swift's admiration of the first century B.C.E. Latin poet Horace, a father of satire in English literature, is revealed in a number of important ways in Swift's poem *On Poetry: A Rhapsody.* Horace's persona or narrator in his satires was often mocked, along with the people at whom the satire was aimed. The narrator in Swift's poem, an "old experienc'd Sinner," receives his share of savage, if understated, irony.

A second and major influence on Swift's poem is the prescriptive poetics of Horace's *Ars Poetica* (17 B.C.E.; *The Art of Poetry*). In this work the Roman poet teaches the arts of poetry and criticism and instructs writers about how to know their poetic strengths and how to revise copiously and strenuously. An example of a poetic structure that needs revision is "*Similes* that nothing fit." Soon after this line, Swift uses three similes that satirize the use of combined epithets, which are in practice mere lists to fill up space, "Like stepping Stones to save a Stride," or "like a Heel-piece to support/ A Cripple," or "like a Bridge that joins a Marish/ To Moorlands." In this section of the poem where the narrator, speaking in his satiric voice, is telling poets how to improve poetic technique after producing three failed poems, the list of simile epithets is used to lead to and provide comparison with lines of discordant animal sexuality: "So have I seen ill-coupled Hounds,/ Drag diff'rent Ways in miry Grounds." Both the nature and ancestry of failed poems by false poets are discordant and illegitimate.

The metaphor that unifies the poem is illegitimacy. A poet is compared to a "Bastard" child, and a poem is called a "Bastard." Poets are described as "Sons of Whores"; readers are told that poets have no "filial Piety" and that they "prostitute the Muse's Name." This metaphor of illegitimacy and debauchery functions in the poem to dramatize the corruption at the heart of the narrator's advice. To reduce art and human life to animal sexuality like "ill-coupled Hounds" is to take Horace's famous advice about how to write and how to improve society through writing and to destroy all the distinctions between good and bad art and selfish and generous behavior on which that advice rests.

The poem is also unified by circle imagery, which serves to show just how widespread corruption in art and life is in the world Swift satirizes. This imagery appears in many lines and represents human civilization in small groups of people, in towns, and ultimately in the whole country, "taking *Britain* round." The circle is the symbol of the "universal Passion, *Pride.*"

On the matter of language, Swift's most illuminating word choice is "Rhapsody" in his title. Its meaning in the eighteenth century, as the *Oxford English Dictionary* indicates, was such that Swift uses the word to suggest an emotional overstatement in which intellectual balance is lost. The advice of the "old experienc'd Sinner" pretends to be rational and realistic but constitutes instead a dangerously emotional fantasy that separates people from divine reality.

Themes and Meanings

In this poem, Swift emphasizes the need to follow one's true vocation, especially if that vocation is not poetry. Does he do this simply to promote personal satisfaction or a sense of individual well-being? The clear choice as Swift presents it in this poem is either to put one's own will first, which eventually leads to moral disaster and atheism, or to put God's will first. To choose one's true vocation is to be in harmony with God's will and to contribute to God's kingdom on earth by pursuing God-given work as directed by one's natural abilities.

The poem ends in atheism because the "old experienc'd Sinner," who becomes narrator of the rest of the poem after line 70, and who at first seems to be Swift's playful way of referring to himself as a sixty-six-year-old poet, is instead Swift's satiric antithesis. The new narrator, in effect replacing Swift, is introduced with these lines: "How shall a new Attempter learn/ Of diff'rent Spirits to discern"? Swift, as a Christian minister, believed that only God can discern spirits. Anyone claiming this ability is engaging in blasphemy. The lines that follow seem to limit the reference to spirits simply to the writing and judging of poetry: "And how distinguish, which is which,/ The Poet's Vein, or scribling Itch?" The new narrator's real point of view is revealed throughout the poem by his perpetually advising hack poets to put their own wills before God's will. This "old experienc'd Sinner" speaks the voice and point of view of Satan, who eternally wants to put self before God. Swift wants readers to ask who is the oldest and most experienced sinner, and whether one should follow his advice.

In the worldview of Swift's poem, how many people are being foolishly willful in trying to be poets when they are not? Line 282 gives a specific number. The hack poets "Amount to just Nine thousand Souls." This number, as large as it is, would seem to amount to a small percentage of society as a whole. Yet, reminding oneself about the size of the reading public for even the most popular literary works of the first three decades of eighteenth century England, it seems clear that Swift intends to say that all readers are trying to be writers.

How many people tend to put their will before God's will? The poem begins with these lines: "All Human Race wou'd fain be *Wits*,/ And Millions miss, for one that hits." He immediately follows these opening lines with a reference to Edward Young's satiric seven-part poem *The Universal Passion* (1725-1728): "*Young's* universal Passion, *Pride*,/ Was never known to spread so wide." Finally, then, *On Poetry: A Rhapsody* is important in the body of Swift's writing not because it attacks hack writing as disrespectful of the divine source of true poetry but because it intends to show each reader that selfishly putting one's will before God's, especially in the matter of life's work, is a disaster for humans and for the world.

Robert Eddy

ON PRAYER

Author: Czesław Miłosz (1911-   )
Type of poem: Lyric
First published: 1984; as "O Modlitwie," in *Nieobjęta ziemia*; English translation collected in *Unattainable Earth*, 1986

The Poem

"On Prayer" is a short poem, twelve lines long, written in free verse. The title suggests a meditation on the nature of the act of prayer, which immediately signals the presence of a number of potential issues: the question of God's existence, the nature of one's relationship to God, and explorations of the ideas of faith and belief.

The poet adopts a first-person voice in this short lyric, written in the form of a direct response to a problem: "how to pray to someone who is not." The first line, in effect, announces the problem by restating a question asked by an implied listener, here assumed to be the reader. Czesław Miłosz's concise poem retains the immediacy of a personal response to the query, even to the point of a brief schoolmasterly aside in line 9 to make sure readers are paying attention. Without relying on the language of doctrine, Miłosz establishes his own quietly authoritative tone.

The first line raises the question of reconciling prayer, a desire for belief, with the contemporary context of disbelief or skepticism. How does one describe the act of prayer in such circumstances, and what function can it perform? Immediately, Miłosz has focused his readers' attention on a central paradox of spiritual expression in the twentieth century.

The next four lines make up the initial stage of the speaker's response: a description of what prayer does in his experience. The act of prayer builds a "velvet bridge," establishes a connection, and this bridge elevates people in some sense, creating a new perspective on reality. The image—softness capable of sustaining strength—touches on both the ephemeral and the substantive nature of the act. Miłosz's use of the simile of a "springboard" quickly following underscores this as a point of departure—an image that highlights both the act of prayer itself and his own poetic, imaginative foray into its description. The next two lines complete the idea by providing an image of this higher perspective in the form of magically transformed landscapes. It is worthwhile to note that the viewpoint remains materially focused. The image of light, traditionally indicating illumination and greater consciousness, is linked to a suspension of time and an epiphanic vision of richness and fecundity.

Line 6, beginning the second stage of the speaker's response, provides readers with the destination of the bridge: "the shore of Reversal." The capitalization of the noun gives the name a heightened significance, investing it with the kind of abstract quality found in allegorical representations. The formal placement of the naming appropriately marks the middle of the poem and suggests a shift in direction, an alteration in the nature of the vision or a limitation of its scope. Miłosz, by highlighting the quasi-allegorical nature of the place, suggests a complication of the simple correspondence between prayer and bridge established in the first half of the poem. Reversal implies an inversion as in a mirror or turning back in direction. The onset of abstraction immediately is linked to ambiguity of interpretation, re-creating in the poem the same limitation of verification to which all belief is subject. Miłosz takes his readers to the edge of belief but refuses to push the vision into a fixed depiction of the other.

The final section of "On Prayer" begins with the speaker's admonition "Notice: I say *we*." The scope of the explanation has moved now from abstraction to a very immediate personal relevance. The effect of reversal implicates everyone, changes the focus from the singular to the plural, and moves the altered vision back into the human sphere. With this plurality comes a consciousness of corporeal existence, a compassion and empathy with "others entangled in the flesh." The poem embodies the process it describes: prayer being the individual means toward faith, hence incomplete in a generic sense, yet offering a validation of the endeavor on moral and imaginative grounds.

Forms and Devices

One of the most striking features of Miłosz's exposition on the nature of prayer is his elaboration of the image of the bridge. Miłosz's use of metonymy (the substitution of one term for another), in this case prayer and the bridge, fixes in very concrete terms an extremely intangible subject. The description admits no merely linguistic connection, but functions as an element of fact; thus, the poet maintains the materiality of the image while using it to describe an extremely abstract and metaphysical religious concept. By this means, Miłosz retains a balance between his sense of human desire (goodness) and human limitations (the existence of evil). To leave aside the material nature of humans would be to invalidate the process, to render an untrue vision.

In an early section of *Unattainable Earth*, Miłosz remarks, "The language of literature in the twentieth century has been steeped in unbelief. Making use of that language, I was able to show only a small bit of my believing temperament." His use of the concrete reality to balance the metaphysical in "On Prayer" reflects this ongoing difficulty and incorporates the thematic material of the poem into its formal presentation. The deliberate simplicity of the diction and the generally proselike syntax is another way to keep his concerns firmly grounded in this world.

Another representative element of this short lyric is the studied, balanced tone. More extended lyrics in this volume give an indication of Miłosz's tendency toward a polyphonic voice to render the rich textures and variety of experience. Even in this short lyric, however, one gets an indication of the balances created by juxtaposing images of great poetic power (the illumination, for example) and his more prosaic, earthbound, and directive tones.

Themes and Meanings

"On Prayer" is part of a sequence entitled "Consciousness" in a volume that is organized as a single sequence—a pastiche of poetry, prose reflections, quotations from various sources, and fragments of letters. Central to the volume as a whole is Miłosz's sense of the ongoing struggle, through the limitations of mind and language, between the knowledge of God's presence and the existence of evil in the world. The historical realities of the twentieth century—war, genocide, and oppression on a scale never before known—underscore, for Miłosz, the paradox of belief. As he suggests, "While respecting tradition and recognizing analogies, we must remember that we are trying to name a new experience"—that of finding a moral position compatible with the experience of the present.

Miłosz's position is reflected in his dual perspective, which brings the abstract into continual, and necessary, conjunction with quotidian reality. "On Prayer" illustrates this in a number of ways. On one level, there is the description of prayer in material terms, the embodiment of an act of faith in the language of unbelief. On another level, Miłosz presents his desire to move away from this existence, to transcend the things of this world; then he links this irrevocably with the limitations of "the shore of Reversal," an image that turns the transcendent impulse back toward humanity. In "On Prayer," one can observe this paradox in the formal construction of the poem, in the concrete and lyrical nature of the imagery, and in the argument itself. In the nature of the reversal upon which the poem hinges, one sees a desire never to leave the reality of this world behind. Explorations into the nature of one's relation to God must always, for Miłosz, involve an incorporation of the entanglements of the flesh, must reconcile the realities of the human condition with the sense of a divine order.

While "On Prayer" shares with many other Miłosz poems this sense of an epiphany, an unexpected revelation of the nature of being, it is balanced by a recognition that this vision ultimately leads back to humanity. The emphasis in line 6 on the word "is," the singular present form of the verb "to be," indicates Miłosz's acknowledgment of the human experience of individuality, the fixation with the present, and also the element of hope that being involves. Notably, the redefinition at the center of this consciousness is not imposed from without, but rather entails a recognition of one's essential nature. Giving being an anthropomorphic focus instead of an otherworldly one, Miłosz maintains his human-centered vision.

James Panabaker

ON SHAKESPEARE

Author: John Milton (1608-1674)

Type of poem: Lyric

First published: 1632, as "An Epitaph on the Admirable Dramaticke Poet, W. Shakespeare," in *Mr. William Shakespeare's Comedies, Histories, and Tragedies*; collected in *Poems of Mr. John Milton*, 1645

The Poem

"On Shakespeare" is a sixteen-line epitaph written in iambic pentameter and divided into heroic couplets, an unusual meter for John Milton's poetry. In English verse, the heroic couplet was not a smoothly honed stanza until after Milton's poetic career had concluded. The poem was originally published under the title "An Epitaph on the Admirable Dramaticke Poet, W. Shakespeare," though the title Milton used in the 1645 edition of his lyric poems has been accepted ever since. The epitaph is related to the classical epigram, a brief lyric that includes pithy wit and polished verses. An epitaph, usually a brief poem, deals with a serious or philosophical subject in a witty manner. The poems were often written on the occasion of a death, as in Milton's "An Epitaph on the Marchioness of Winchester." The genre designation suggests a tombstone inscription, though few known poetic epitaphs actually served that purpose. William Shakespeare's own four-line epitaph, inscribed on his gravestone in Stratford's Holy Trinity Church, represents a notable exception. In Milton's lengthy epitaph on the marchioness of Winchester, he describes her family background, details the circumstances surrounding her death, and proclaims her heavenly reward for suffering. However, since Shakespeare's death occurred fourteen years before the composition date, Milton makes no allusion to death and mourning in the poem commemorating him. Instead he centers upon the immortality that art offers.

An occasional lyric (one written for a specific event), "On Shakespeare" was composed in 1630 to appear among the many poems prefatory to the second folio of Shakespeare's *Works*. In all likelihood, Milton was invited to contribute to the collection, possibly by his friend Henry Lawes. Commendatory poems were designed to set a tone of celebration for the event and to praise the author for his artistic achievement. Appropriately, the poem assumes an audience of readers rather than theatergoers. Like other contributors to the collection, Milton celebrates the power of poetry and the fame it brings its creators by endowing them with a form of immortality.

The opening six lines pose questions concerning Shakespeare's need for a monument. Initially, the poem implies that "my Shakespeare" needs no conventional monument such as a pyramid. Laboriously piled stones and pyramids, Milton proclaims, are not needed to cover or house Shakespeare's "hallowed relics." The usual monuments, however elaborate, can offer only "weak witness" of Shakespeare's name, whereas his works make him a "son of memory" and "heir of fame." Still, these exaggerated images of elaborate memorials are fictional, and Milton would have known that Shakespeare's actual grave was below ground, covered by a marble slab bearing a modest inscription. Milton's second question implies that Shakespeare is preserved through memory and fame, and the imagery of relics and the hint of succession distance the poem from the poet's death.

Shakespeare's works are responsible for the immortality that assures undying fame. The second portion of the poem (lines 7-14) opens with the ambiguous line "Thou in our wonder and astonishment," whose meaning is clarified within the context of subsequent lines. Initially, it would appear to mean that the bard has created his own monument to arouse the "wonder" of readers. However, "astonishment" is proleptic, foreshadowing the idea that the works affect the readers and thus create Shakespeare's genuine monument. Before the works' effect can be celebrated, however, the poem praises the creative power of the author. Milton asserts that the bard has surpassed "slow endeavoring art" to produce the fluent, easy numbers of genius. This achievement places him in a class above that of ordinary writers.

Having characterized the seeming ease of Shakespeare's art, the poem shifts its focus to concentrate on the effects of poetry on the audience. Shakespeare's art, it asserts, leaves an impression on hearts like that of an engraving on marble. Readers are so deeply impressed by the works, the "unvalued [invaluable] book," that their imaginations are suspended as if rapt in meditation. The effect has been a kind of ecstasy that suspends all thoughts and transforms them into marble. This power to move the emotions and overwhelm the imagination ("fancy") represents the important monument and Shakespeare's lasting achievement. Through art, Shakespeare has attained the ability to move or transform his audience, a feat associated from antiquity with divine power. In effect, his art has become the poet's monument, and this outcome is of greater significance than sepulchral pomp. In a witty, paradoxical conclusion (lines 15-16), the poem proclaims this ability so rare that, for a similar monument, even kings would wish to die.

Forms and Devices

In a poem concerned with fame and immortality, Milton appropriately employs an impressive number of images relating to death and monuments: "bones," "relics," "pyramids," "monument," "stones," and "marble." Thus the images create a sense of tangible durability associated with lasting parts of the person ("relics" and "bones"), with the materials that form monuments ("stones" and "marble"), and with the monuments themselves. They fittingly remove the tone from the immediacy of death to focus on posthumous fame. The concrete images, however, subtly shift to metaphor when the poem attributes everlasting qualities to Shakespeare's works and their effects, denying the view that fame rests upon tangible objects. The enduring "monument" created by Shakespeare consists of his works. Thus the imagery reinforces Milton's early denial of the need for conventional aids to fame. By contrasting the concrete images of fame to the metaphors that suggest a greater fame, the poem asserts that the more important kind of monument assures memory through successive generations.

The achievement is reinforced through an allusion to Greek "Delphic lines" (line 12), intimating that Shakespeare's artistry rivals that of the Greek classics. The allusion may well hark back to Milton's earlier epithet "great heir of fame," suggesting that the bard either writes in the immortal tradition of the classics or that he merits the respect accorded classical poets. At the very least, Milton recognizes that Shakespeare, like the ancients, has staying power. For any contemporary poet, this was high praise indeed. Furthermore, references to "pomp" and "kings" in the final lines accord Shakespeare a magisterial place among poets.

The subdued point of view moves from first person singular to the plurals "our" and "us" as the poem shifts to the effects of reading the poetry. By identifying himself with others, the poem's persona effectively becomes a spokesman for numerous readers. By the same token, through limiting and subordinating the role of the speaker, Milton achieves a tone of assurance and majesty appropriate to the power he celebrates in the subject.

Themes and Meanings

"On Shakespeare" develops the primary theme of immortality through artistic creation. A commonplace idea in Renaissance and seventeenth century poetry, it is pervasive in Shakespeare's sonnets, which celebrate a poet's power to endow the subject with immortality. The theme also commonly appears in the poems prefatory to various folio editions of Shakespeare's poetic works. Its widespread use, however, does not mean that it lacked special meaning for Milton. From his student days at Cambridge University, Milton made fame through art a motif in his lyric poetry, and he later introduced the theme into his prose works as well. As one who sought fame through poetic achievement, he found it congenial to proclaim that Shakespeare had already attained it. However, Milton surpasses the conventional treatment of the theme by adding another minor but pervasive motif in Renaissance poetry, that of metamorphosis or transformation. Evidence of Shakespeare's genius is to be found in the bard's ability to transform readers, to take them out of themselves with wonder and admiration and, metaphorically, render them marble. Milton realized that the power of transformation traditionally represented a divine attribute and a source of inspiration.

A further significant theme emerges from Milton's characterization of Shakespeare's creative imagination. Though his references to Shakespeare are limited, Milton became an early proponent of the view that Shakespeare was a naturally gifted genius, more a product of nature than of art. At its extreme, it depicted the bard as a pure and unlearned genius surpassing all the dicta of art. As applied to Shakespeare, the point of view can be traced to the writings of Shakespeare's contemporary Ben Jonson, though Jonson, the consummate artist, suggests in *Timber: Or Discoveries Made upon Men and Matter* (1641) that Shakespeare's ignorance of the classics and canons of art is a flaw. With Milton, however, there is no hint of disapproval. Milton celebrates Shakespeare's "easy numbers" and, in "L'Allegro," refers to Shakespeare as "Fancy's child" who warbles "his native woodnotes wild." In the epitaph, Milton draws a sharp contrast between art and nature: "For whilst to th' shame of slow-endeavoring art/ Thy easy numbers flow" (lines 9-10). Shakespeare thus achieves the effects of ease while ignoring the canons of art.

Stanley Archer

ON THE DEATH OF DR. ROBERT LEVET

Author: Samuel Johnson (1709-1784)
Type of poem: Elegy
First published: 1783; collected in *The Poetical Works of Samuel Johnson*, 1785

The Poem

"On the Death of Dr. Robert Levet" is a poetic elegy that celebrates the life, while mourning the death, of Robert Levet (1705-1782), a "lay" physician who for many years lived in Samuel Johnson's London house and tended the local poor, seldom asking a fee for his services. Johnson, the eighteenth century's greatest man of letters, was a scholar, a moralist, and a poet of limited range but genuine abilities. When Levet died in 1782, Johnson was near the end of his own long life—a life that brought him the fame and success his talents merited, yet was filled with illness, poverty, and great personal disappointment. It is hardly surprising, then, to find Johnson compressing so much life and thought within a relatively few lines occasioned by the death of a poor, awkward man unknown to the "greater" world of art and letters.

Johnson's poem is divided into nine four-line stanzas. The meter is iambic tetrameter; the rhyme scheme is *abab*. Each stanza is a grammatically self-contained unit that makes a statement not only about Levet and his life, but, by extension, about humanity and the human condition in general.

At a time when poetic diction was tending more and more toward the ornate, "inane phraseology" of which William Wordsworth later complained, Johnson instead chooses a language that is simple, direct, and "common"—a language wholly appropriate to its subject. In a like manner, Johnson foregoes the kind of elaborate imagery that so many earlier elegists had employed to "elevate" their subjects. Johnson's crowning artistic achievement, completed only a few years before, was a series of biographies of English poets now known as *Lives of the Poets* (1779-1781). Among the poets Johnson treated was the great John Milton, and one can easily imagine how, following Levet's death, Johnson's thoughts would naturally turn to the lofty language and grand images of Milton's "Lycidas," thought by many to be the finest English-language elegy ever written. Levet was not what the progressive-minded eighteenth century would call a "great" man, however, and Johnson surely must have felt that a series of highly wrought, "artificial" images would be sadly unsuited to what he saw as the eloquently sincere and uncomplicated statement made by Levet's life.

Instead, Johnson turns to the kind of simple, concrete imagery that he had employed successfully in his most famous poem, "The Vanity of Human Wishes" (1749). Moving from "Hope's delusive mine" in the first stanza to "Misery's darkest caverns" in the fifth, and on to the moving scene of the breaking of life's "vital chain" in the ninth, he gives spare, solid images that function to underscore, rather than overwhelm or obscure, Levet's accomplishments.

Johnson's strategy is straightforward. Following a general statement about the human condition that is traditionally Christian in its "philosophy" (though certainly not what one would call optimistic: people are all "Condemn'd to Hope's delusive mine"—a vision of earthly reality as a kind of purgatory), he begins to lay out Levet's life and character in a way that consistently obliges readers to look beyond the particularities of his existence—a way that obliges readers to see themselves in Levet and, significantly, to ask themselves just how their lives measure up to his.

Forms and Devices

"On the Death of Dr. Robert Levet" is traditional. It is, in fact, among those poems that anyone familiar with English poetry would immediately assign to the eighteenth century—and probably to Johnson. The consistent use of adjective-noun combinations ("sudden blasts," "useful care"); the presence of several key personifications ("fainting nature," "hopeless anguish"); and the carefully balanced phrasing ("The busy day, the peaceful night," "His frame was firm, his powers were bright") all indicate Johnson's commitment to order, form, and tradition.

Yet to speak of Johnson's poem as traditional is not to devalue it. One must remember that neither the eighteenth century in general nor Johnson in particular embraced the ideas about poetic originality that are valued in the twentieth century. (In Shakespeare's day, fools or eccentrics were often called "originals.") To be original was to veer away from the common stream of life; it was, in essence, to abdicate one's primary responsibility as a writer, which was (as Johnson put it in his celebrated "Preface to The Plays of William Shakespeare") to present "human sentiments in human language." Thus, a desire to reach out to as many men and women as possible, not just to a privileged few, can be seen in Johnson's firm commitment to poetic tradition.

In practical terms, this means Johnson commits himself to rendering Levet's story as "universal" in scope as possible, in the hope that it might function for all his readers as a moral lesson—indeed, as precisely the kind of biblical parable of which Johnson was so fond. (The parable of the "single talent," referred to in line 28 and taken from the biblical account in Matthew 25:14-30, was one of Johnson's favorites. Levet's story is ultimately an illustration of "The single talent well employ'd.")

Johnson searches out the most universal, the most "human" concerns—concerns all readers are likely to have shared at some time in their lives. He speaks of life and death, of human cares and anguish, of human virtues and accomplishments, of faith, duty, and compassion, and—though the word is never mentioned—of love.

Themes and Meanings

It is not unusual for an elegist to move quickly beyond his or her subject in pursuit of grander things. In "Adonais," for example, poor John Keats is soon forgotten as Percy Bysshe Shelley takes off on an exalted tour of the universe (which turns out, essentially, and not without some irony, to be Shelley's own mind). Johnson, however, never forgets Levet. The meaning he seeks inheres in Levet, in a sense *is* Levet.

What Johnson saw so clearly in this reserved, humble, and uncouth man may puzzle readers. It certainly puzzled Johnson's friends, most of them upper-class literati who wondered, for example, what pleasure the greatest conversationalist in England could possibly find in taking morning tea–*every* morning—with a man who seldom said a word.

Answers to such questions can only involve speculation, but it is probably safe to say that Johnson—a man whose entire life can be regarded from one perspective as a continual search after spiritual truth—saw spiritual truth in Levet. Three days after Levet's death, Johnson concluded a diary entry briefly describing the funeral with these telling words: "May God have mercy on him. May he have mercy on me."

What Johnson saw—or hoped to see—in the parable of Levet's life was the possibility of God's mercy and the hope of heaven. Throughout most of his life, Johnson was plagued by what his contemporaries called melancholy and what we would describe as depression. In his darkest moments, and in spite of his strong Christian beliefs, Johnson was tortured by religious doubts, not so much about the existence of God, but doubts about his own worthiness as a beneficiary of God's mercy. His doubts compelled him to weigh continuously his own spiritual worth (his journals and diaries are full of moments of painful self-examination), but his own immense honesty stopped him short of reading the world only in terms of his own doubts. Instead, he searched the lives and experiences of others for confirmation that life not only had meaning, but was also, in a sense, a spiritual pilgrimage with an attainable goal.

Levet's humble pilgrimage through life was for Johnson a meaningful example, a kind of *Pilgrim's Progress* (1678, 1684, by John Bunyan) in miniature, that was able to bolster his faith and bring him spiritual comfort. As readers see Levet work his way day after day through the London slums ("misery's darkest caverns"), selflessly dispensing his "useful care," they see he is walking a "narrow round" that is actually an upward spiral: When death "frees" his soul, it is called home "the nearest way."

Michael Stuprich

ON THE MORNING OF CHRIST'S NATIVITY

Author: John Milton (1608-1674)
Type of poem: Meditation
First published: 1645, in *Poems of Mr. John Milton*

The Poem

"On the Morning of Christ's Nativity" was written in 1629, while John Milton was still a student at the University of Cambridge. In some ways it is clearly an "apprentice" work, in its often naïve tone, youthful idealism, and occasional quaint conceit. In other ways, however, it shows an already clear control of the poetic medium, verse structure, and overall design. Its central concerns anticipate quite remarkably those of *Paradise Lost* (1667, 1674), written some thirty years later. The poem is thus of interest not only intrinsically, but also in that it indicates the contours of Milton's imagination and his concerns at the start of his poetic career.

In the introduction, the poem is seen as a nativity offering to the infant Christ. Milton uses the conceit of running before the three wise men in order to deliver his gift first. The poem is both gift and prophetic word, joining with the angelic choir.

In the main section of the poem ("The Hymn"), which becomes the gift itself, Milton describes first the time and place of the nativity. He is determined to move away from traditional depictions, which center on mother and child, the stable, and Joseph in an intimate, enclosed scene. Instead, his imagination soars, moving into the cosmic and universal realms, adopting a bird's-eye (or an angel's-eye) view and reaching into heavenly glory. The setting is depicted in terms of the whole of nature being at peace (an ancient belief held that at the time of Christ's birth there were no wars being waged anywhere); thus, the earth is at harmony with its Creator—since the Fall, a unique occurrence.

He returns briefly to the immediate locale, to describe the shepherds and the angelic choir they hear. This is the harmony made audible. Normally the sign of creation's harmony, the music of the spheres, is inaudible to human ears; on this night, that music blends with the angelic harmony in a transforming power, which gives a promise of a restored golden age.

Before this could happen, the poet realizes, Christ must die and be raised to glory, to judge the conquered Satan and his evil agents. Already their power is broken, however; the religions of Greece and Rome, which previously may have contained shadows of the truth, lose their prophetic and priestly power. Other pagan religions, such as those condemned in the Old Testament, also lose their evil hold: Their strongholds are overthrown. Milton catalogs those pagan gods in detail, from Peor and Baalim to Moloch and Typhon. Like ghosts, the false gods must return to the underworld at the dawn of the new Sun of righteousness. In the final stanza, the poem returns to the Nativity scene; the final image is not of the Christ child and Mary, but of "Bright-harnessed Angels"—that is, angels wearing armor—sitting about the stable in battle formation.

Forms and Devices

The poem is difficult to classify generically. Although the main section is entitled "The Hymn," it is clearly not a hymn in any traditional sense: It is not addressed to God, nor has it any explicit exhortation to fellow believers. It has features of an ode; although the Nativity is never addressed as such, it does have the elevated language associated with that genre. It also contains pastoral elements. It is best seen, perhaps, as a meditation on the transfiguring power that Christ's birth had over the created world.

"The Hymn" consists of twenty-seven eight-line stanzas, rhyming *aabccbdd*, although the last two lines never work as a couplet. The stanzas are basically one-sentence units, and they already prefigure the long sentence structures of Milton's later verse. The complex metric structure seems to have been entirely of Milton's making, showing a youthful ingenuity and mastery. The *a*- and *c*-rhyming lines are trimeters; the *b*-rhyming lines are pentameters; and the final two lines consist of a tetrameter followed by a hexameter. The meter is basically iambic, but not rigidly so. There is also a very flexible use made of syntactic structures within the metric ones. Milton exploits a wide dramatic range, from the quick, soft smoothness of stanza V, to the slow elegiac lament of stanza XX, to the dissonances of stanza XXIV.

The introduction consists of four stanzas of seven lines of iambic pentameter, apart from the final line, which is hexameter; it rhymes *ababbcc*. The complete poem thus consists of 244 lines.

One of its more remarkable features is the cyclic nature of the hymn. It consists of three cycles: stanzas I-VII; VIII-XV; and XVI-XXVII. The first two cycles begin at the Nativity scene itself, then soar away into glory, reaching powerful climaxes. The final cycle works the other way round, finishing on a dismissive note as the false gods troop off to the underworld like ghosts. The final stanza then leaves readers with the sleeping infant in an effective closure. In this cyclic structure, Milton keeps close control over his imagination.

There are two predominant trains of imagery. The first is of light and darkness; from the glory of "that Light unsufferable/ And that far-beaming blaze of Majesty" (lines 8-9) to the "greater Sun" (Christ) outshining the "bright Throne, or burning Axletree" of the sun (lines 83-84). Similarly, darkness depicts first the human condition—"a darksome House of mortal Clay" (line 14)—then the underworld, where "Th'old Dragon Swinges the scaly Horror of his folded tail" (lines 168, 172), and the sites of pagan religion: "twilight shade of tangled thickets" (line 188); "left in shadows dread/ His burning Idol all of blackest hue" (lines 206-207).

The second train of imagery is of music, especially of harmony: The music of the spheres and the angelic choir both suggest triumph; the weeping and lament suggest old powers broken and passing away. The poem itself becomes its own image of integrated music. Other images are pastoral and rustic, and even sexual—nature is a fallen woman, needing snow for a covering to restore the appearance of innocence (stanza II).

Themes and Meanings

Milton's imagination is cosmic. The central two stanzas of the introduction establish this. He wants to depict the full cosmic and spiritual significance of the Incarnation. This is his prophetic calling, similar to Isaiah's (line 28). He is also a humanist,
however—a lover of classical literature. There is thus a conflict posed for him as a
Christian poet: What values can be put on classical myths and belief systems now that
Christ has come to give full revelation? One traditional answer was to dismiss such
myths as lies and deceptions (the Augustinian solution); the other was to accept them
as partial revelation, as types and foreshadowings actually pointing the way to Christ.
This is the answer Milton adopts. Christ becomes the fulfillment of the nature god Pan
(stanza VIII); he is the new infant Hercules strangling the snake (Satan) in his crib
(stanza XXV). Thus the prophetic oracles at Delphos did utter truth, but their power is
now withdrawn and put on Christ (stanza XIX). This is how Milton states his Christian humanism, and how he establishes a basis for a transformed Christian pastoral.

When it is a question of Middle Eastern mythologies, as of Phoenicia, Canaan, or
Egypt, however, his condemnation is complete, since the Old Testament condemns
them utterly, and as a biblical Christian he needs to do the same. The position he
adopts is the same one he retained in *Paradise Lost*: The pagan gods worshiped falsely
are, in fact, not lifeless idols but real spiritual forces that need binding and defeating.
The transition from the treatment of one set of beliefs to the other occurs in stanza XX,
the tone of which is rather poignant and ambivalent, suggesting perhaps some lingering regret that something beautiful has been lost at the same time as the sordidness of
pagan ritual.

The nativity is seen, then, not as a celebration of a personal story of a virgin birth in
a humble stable, but as a breaking in upon Creation by its King: a reclaiming and a
moment of glory, anticipating the final glory of the Second Advent (stanza XVI). Milton collapses time here, as he does in Book III of *Paradise Lost*. Past, present, and future all exist within his incarnational language; however, he avoids any centering on
the Crucifixion, which one might expect more orthodox treatment to do (later, the Pu-
ritans actually abolished Christmas as a celebration). In fact, at no point in his poetic
career did Milton ever focus on Christ's death and suffering. This lacuna is already in
evidence here: The appearance of Christ foreshadows not his rejected humanity and
redemptive sacrifice but his appearance in final glory and judgment over the dark
falsehoods of satanic forces. That is the second climax of history; this Nativity is the
first.

David Barratt

ON THE MOVE

Author: Thom Gunn (1929-   )
Type of poem: Lyric
First published: 1955; collected in *The Sense of Movement*, 1957

The Poem

"On the Move" is composed in five eight-line stanzas, with the rhyme scheme *abaccddb*. The poem begins by observing the movement of birds in their natural surroundings and comparing their movement to human action. Whether driven by natural "instinct," acquired "poise," or some combination of the two, the birds seem to have some "hidden purpose" to give meaning to their motion. The "One" of the poem who observes them wonders whether his own "uncertain violence" of motion is driven by the same forces. Until now he has been bewildered equally by both the instincts of "baffled sense" and "the dull thunder of approximate words." The rest of the poem tries to make words yield their precise meaning in relation to the experience of motion.

In the second stanza, the motorcyclists are introduced. They mediate between birds and man, their movement seeming half instinctual, half pilgrimage. First the reader sees the machines on the road, then, from a distance, "the Boys," who look "Small, black, as flies" in their leather jackets and goggles. Suddenly, "the distance throws them forth" and they look and sound huge and heroic. Like knights in armor with visors, they wear impersonal goggles and "gleaming jackets trophied with dust." The observer questions their attitude of confidence, however, suggesting that goggles and jackets not only protect them from the elements but also "strap in doubt" to make them appear "robust."

The third stanza continues this line of thought. Their "hardiness/ Has no shape yet." They are undefined, their course unknown. Like Don Quixote following his horse's steps, the motorcyclists go "where the tires press." They are different from the birds that they "scare across a field," whose instinct gives them direction. They have only the manufactured "machine and soul," which they "imperfectly control/ To dare a future from the taken routes." Yet the will "is a part solution, after all." They are not damned because they are only "half animal" and lack "direct instinct." By joining "movement in a valueless world" one can approach one's goal, even if it is only "toward, toward."

The final stanza invokes the brevity of the interval one has to define oneself. "A minute holds them, who have come to go: The self-defined, astride the created will." Like birds and saints, the motorcyclists cannot stop in "the towns they travel through"; they must "complete their purposes," whatever they may be. Even if they do not reach the "absolute, in which to rest,/ One is always nearer by not keeping still." The worst that can happen is that "one is in motion." The physical engagement in the activity for its own sake is its own excuse.

Masterplots II

Forms and Devices

"On the Move" can be compared to Jack Kerouac's novel *On the Road* (1957), published the same year. Both titles suggest a restless detachment from society typical of the Beat generation of the 1950's. Early versions of the poem included the dateline "*California*" and an epigraph, "*Man, you gotta Go*" (both later dropped). The epigraph's colloquial address, hip informality, imperative urgency, and capitalized verb emphasize the poem's relation to the contemporary scene.

In contrast to the urgency of the title and epigraph, the tone of the poem is meditative. The narrator is an observer, his voice detached and philosophical; it is the still voice within that asks questions in the midst of action, though the questions about the "hidden purpose" of movement are implicit.

In this poem about "the sense of movement," Thom Gunn suitably exploits the flexibility of verbs. Action words become nouns and adjectives. A "gust of birds," for example, "spurts" across a field, and there is "scuffling" and "wheeling." When the motorcyclists arrive, these images yield another set of meanings, having to do with wind resistance, acceleration, roughhousing, and tires on the tarmac. In the same way, "baffled sense" can mean that the senses are bewildered or that the forward progress of meaning is thwarted. (A baffle is also a motorcycle muffler.)

Through a series of analogies, Gunn sustains the epic simile of the motorcyclists as existential heroes on the road of life, daring "a future from the taken routes." Like gods, they control the "thunder held by calf and thigh." Like knights in lowered visor and armor, they wear goggles and "gleaming jackets trophied with the dust" as they ride "Astride the created will." Unlike the inhabitants of the towns they travel through, they are never at home. They are rebels without a cause, heroes without a purpose, except the purpose of "not keeping still."

The poet and the motorcyclist undertake a similar action. Both must balance the reckless power of their vehicle. Gunn's technical control over the machinery of traditional verse is necessary to get him to his destination, but it is also satisfying in itself. Unable to rely on "direct instinct," the poet rides "the created will" to "complete [his] purpose." On a purely technical level, this purpose is to find the "poise" of the "noise" in "the dull thunder of approximate words."

The authority of the narrator's speculations on "the sense of movement" depends upon the similarity of his action to that of the motorcyclists. Speaking from an interested objectivity, he is not speaking for an egotistical "I" but for an indefinite "One." This raises the poem from the specific and personal to the general and universal experience of thought and emotion.

Themes and Meanings

"On the Move" is a poem about how one defines oneself through actions. Driven by instinct or will, one is able to articulate one's purpose only en route, through the act itself. This is as true of the motorcyclists as it is for the poet.

"On the Move" is the opening poem of *The Sense of Movement* (1957), which Gunn said was inspired by the existentialist philosopher Jean-Paul Sartre. A major tenet of

Sartre's existentialism is that one derives authentic meaning in one's lives not from any preconceived notions of what one should be, but from one's own actions. One cannot know what one is except through what one does. Because one is, as Sartre says, "condemned to be free," one must take full responsibility for one's actions and, thus, for one's existence.

Self-definition through engaged action is the ultimate existentialist act. If one could rely on instinct, as birds do, there would be no question of authenticity. Since the individual has free will, however, he or she must exercise it and take the consequences. The myth of the American motorcyclist is one of Gunn's favorite figures for the restless, searching, often inarticulate existential hero. His doubt is part of his charm. His restless motion, instinctual or willed, is, consciously or unconsciously, a creation of meaning through "movement in a valueless world."

The articulation of that meaning is no more the task of the motorcyclist than it is the task of birds. Just as the birds are the pretext for asking questions about the human activity of the motorcyclists, the motorcyclists are the pretext for the poet's articulation of the meaning of movement. More important than where they have come from, or even where they are going, is why. What drives them? What are they seeking? These questions are only rhetorical for all but the poet, whose authentic action is to capture "the dull thunder of approximate words." Like the motorcyclist, the poet "strap[s] in doubt—by hiding it" behind a confident pose so as to appear "robust," even though he "almost hear[s] a meaning in [his] noise." This is not hypocrisy, however, because the pose is a necessary protection, like goggles and jacket; it is not an end in itself, but the gear that gets him to his destination.

One of the paradoxes of the poem is that the motorcyclists, who pretend to be individualists, run in packs. They are always referred to as "they." They think of themselves as unconventional, yet they are locked into a uniform and a posture. They think they act on instinct, yet they travel "the taken routes." They are "the Boys," who "almost hear a meaning in their noise"—but not quite. Their group "impersonality" is in strict contrast to the "One" of the poem, who is able to interpret their motion precisely because he stands apart from their group mentality and outside their action. The poet may identify with them, but he must also articulate his difference from them. "Exact conclusion of their hardiness/ Has no shape" until the poet makes it. "They burst away," but "One is always nearer by not keeping still." The ambiguity of the poem's last line suggests that the motorcyclists may or may not create what they are looking for, while the poet, in the action of the poem, has.

Richard Collins

ON THE SONNET

Author: John Keats (1795-1821)
Type of poem: Sonnet
First published: 1836; collected in *Life, Letters, and Literary Remains of John Keats,* 1848

The Poem

John Keats's poem "On the Sonnet" examines that poetic form, especially its structural demands and restrictions. The poet begins by positing the necessity of "dull rhymes," which he feels chain "our English" and "fetter" the sonnet. He offers next the image of Andromeda, or "pained loveliness"; Ovid tells of this beautiful maiden being chained to a rock by Jupiter to pay for her mother's excessive boasting. Here Keats compares the confinement of the lovely and innocent Andromeda with the sweet beauty of poetry being fettered by the demands of rhyme. The poet seems, however, resigned to rhyme's fetters but insists that rhyme, like an intricate sandal, be more "interwoven and complete/ To fit the naked foot of poesy." The poet offers this interweaving as a solution to what Keats in his letters calls "pounding rhymes." He wants rhyme to be more subtle and intricate, complementing the content of the poem as a whole and not drawing attention to itself.

His next concern is the sonnet's need for a metrical pattern that is carefully handled: "Let us inspect the lyre, and weigh the stress/ Of every chord." The assumption here is that the sonnet should be music, but not music of a breezy or vague sort. The sonneteer should "inspect" and "weigh" the sound with "ear industrious, and attention meet," concerned that the meter and stress pattern enhance the sound of the poem. Traditionally, the sonnet is in iambic pentameter, and the poet's message here is that this standardized versification must be made to bring the poem beauty and vitality. Keats underscores this point with another reference to Greek mythology: Even as Midas was a miser of gold, so should the sonneteer be attentive to the metrical pattern. A "[Miser] of sound and syllable," the poet should not allow any "dead leaves," or useless syllables, "in the "bay-wreath crown." Every syllable and word should be apt and vital to the sonnet as a whole.

Keats closes his sonnet with a tone of cheerful inevitability: "So, if we may not let the Muse be free,/ She will be bound with garlands of her own." The sonnet, he acknowledges, presupposes certain structures and strictures. The poet cannot discard these but must accommodate them. Keats ends with both a note of respect for these forms and restrictions and the requirement that a poet work to subordinate these constrictions to the charms, the beauties, and the powers of poesy.

The closing balance achieved in this sonnet reflects the pattern of maturation that marked Keats's brief career as a poet. He began with youthful ardor and eagerness by writing effusive, lush, and loose verse after the example of his mentor, Leigh Hunt. The young poet decried the barren rationalism of the eighteenth century with its focus on form and structure; thus, he began by writing with slack structure and versification. As he matured, he came to tighten his metrics, vary his rhyme, and firm his rhythm. He confirms in the closing of "On the Sonnet" that he is now cheerfully reconciled to poetry's binding garlands.

Forms and Devices

Keats admired poet William Wordsworth, who had also written a sonnet on the sonnet: "Nuns Fret Not at Their Convent's Narrow Room" (1807). As in Keats's sonnet written twelve years later, Wordsworth announces that limitations and restrictions do not bother nuns, hermits, students, maids, or weavers; even bees crawl comfortably into the narrow foxglove florets. Therefore, Wordsworth decides that he, as a poet, will work within the sonnet's confines.

It is noteworthy that Wordsworth chose the English countryside of his day to illustrate his resolution; Keats, by contrast, reaches back to images from classical times. In the early nineteenth century, Romanticism was revitalizing mythological lore. In fact, Keats's best-known early sonnet expresses this delight: "On First Looking into Chapman's Homer" (1816). In this sonnet, he writes of the joys of discovering George Chapman's more vital translations of Homer, having only known that of Alexander Pope, which he had read as a schoolboy. In his entire poetic career, Keats treasured Greek lore, legend, and myth.

In "On the Sonnet," Keats not only mentions sandals, lyres, Muses, and bay-wreath crowns but also incorporates two more specific allusions to Greek myth. First, he refers to Andromeda as analogous to the sonnet's chained, "pained loveliness," both being a combination of restriction and beauty. Then, in line 11, he alludes to Midas as a miser, in an effort to remind sonneteers to be careful with sound and syllable. By exercising this concern and carefulness, he continues, the sonneteer will neither ignore nor downplay the careful inspection of the poem's metrics; he will ensure that there are no "dead leaves in the bay-wreath crown."

Few other poets are as aware as Keats of the artistic legacy of the past. For example, in his own poetry, he especially absorbed and revered the artistry of other sonneteers: Edmund Spenser, William Shakespeare, and John Milton. An overview of his poetry shows that Keats's inspiration also derived from various other art forms: the Elgin Marbles from the Parthenon, an engraved gem of Leander and Hero, and a Grecian urn. He memorialized—all with sonnets—Chapman's translation of Homer, Dante's *La divina commedia* (c. 1320; *The Divine Comedy*, 1802), Chaucer's poetry, and Shakespeare's *King Lear* (pr. c. 1605-1606). He also used the sonnet to write tributes to poets as varied as Thomas Chatterton and Spenser, George Gordon, Lord Byron, and Robert Burns. He even wrote a sonnet on the occasion of ". . . Seeing a Lock of Milton's Hair."

The overall tone of "On the Sonnet" is one of resignation and resolution. The resignation springs from the conviction that rhymes can be dull and restrictive, for they chain "our English" and constrain a sonneteer's expression, never allowing the Muse to be free. However, the poet does not complain, but rather cleverly adapts: He keeps the rhymes but makes them less poundingly regular and more "interwoven." He also carefully examines the stress in the meter pattern and allows for no dead weight. With this resolution, the poet closes, content that his sonnet will no longer be harmed by external, arbitrary constraints of form.

Themes and Meanings

Keats's central theme in "On the Sonnet" is the poet's successful handling of the demands of form. He wrote in many forms: songs, romances, epistolary poems, epics, hymns, ballads, and odes. He also composed more than sixty sonnets. Here he had inherited two different traditions. The first was the Italian form of Dante and Petrarch, which consisted of an octave with an *abba* rhyme scheme followed by a sestet, which allowed for a variety of possible rhyme schemes: *cde, cde*; or *cdc, cdc*; or *cd, cd, cd*. This Italian form required an eight-line development, allowing only two rhyme patterns and ending in a complete stop; this was then followed by the slightly more flexible sestet. Overall, this form of the sonnet prescribed four, or perhaps five, rhyme sounds, and no more.

The sonnet form in England established a new rhyme pattern, ultimately labeled "Shakespearean": *abab, cdcd, efef, gg*. Here, instead of an 8/6 division, there is a 4/4/ 4/2 pattern; also, instead of four or five rhyme sounds, there are seven. In May, 1819, Keats wrote to his brother George expressing dissatisfaction over the "pounding rhymes" of the Italian form and over the hurried snap of the concluding Shakespearean couplet. He then included "On the Sonnet," which illustrated his continuing experiments with the form. This sonnet's rhyme scheme is completely irregular: *abc, abd, cab, cde, de*. It follows neither the Petrarchan octave nor the Shakespearean quatrains and concluding couplet.

Keats's sonnet addresses his theme of the necessary but troublesome traditional stanza patterns and their rhyme schemes. The poet freely experiments with both, leading directly to the triumphant odes of Keats's *annus mirabilis*. These odes of 1819— "To a Nightingale," "Ode on a Grecian Urn," "Ode on Melancholy," and "Ode on Indolence"—display the fruit of Keats's sonnet experimentation, for this experimentation led directly to the new lyric form used in the great odes. Here Keats conserves some of the elements of both sonnet forms: the quatrain of the English form (*abab*) and the sestet of the Petrarchan sonnet (*cde, cde*). However, he organically extends these forms, makes them more malleable, "more interwoven and complete/ To fit the naked foot of poesy." In his odes, he successfully prunes out the "dead leaves" in the bay-wreath crown, avoiding monotony and gaining new freedom. Thus he develops the perfect genre he had been seeking in "On the Sonnet."

Marie J. K. Brenner

ON THE WOUNDS OF OUR CRUCIFIED LORD

Author: Richard Crashaw (c. 1612-1649)
Type of poem: Meditation
First published: 1646, in *Steps to the Temple*

The Poem

"On the Wounds of Our Crucified Lord" is a twenty-line poem divided into five stanzas of four lines each. The meter is predominantly iambic tetrameter, and the rhyme scheme is *abab*. Richard Crashaw's title suggests that the narrator is viewing a painting or a sculpture depicting Christ either on the cross or at the moment when his body has been lowered from the cross, a standard subject of Renaissance artists. Such images were often placed in alcoves or recesses in churches as objects for meditation; it is such a meditative process that the poem traces.

The narrator of the poem begins with an apostrophe, or direct address of an inanimate object. As his eyes scan the painting or sculpture, they focus on the bleeding wounds of Jesus caused by the nails pounded through his hands and feet at Crucifixion and by the torture of the crown of thorns and the spear wounds inflicted while he was on the cross. The sight of the wounds moves the speaker, especially in their paradoxical appearance of life ("wakefull wounds") on a corpse.

At first, he simply exclaims over their horror; then, he tries to find a suitable descriptive analogy for their existence. The comparisons he uses involve, appropriately, body parts: mouths and eyes. The rest of the poem draws out an elaborate comparison of wounds/mouths/eyes that, because it is strange, farfetched, and extended throughout the poem until its resolution in the final stanza, might be called a metaphysical conceit. The last line of the first stanza indicates how involved each watcher becomes in the spectacle of the crucifixion. Even though the wounds are in actuality neither mouths nor eyes, the community of observers, which includes all humankind, must apply the transformative metaphorical process to a sight too horrible to bear realistically.

The second stanza continues the metaphysical conceit by interpreting both images. Now, the body of humanity is implicated in observing and feeling and reading the spectacle along with the narrator. He addresses them, accepting and then expanding on both metaphorical readings of the wounds. Behold, he cajoles them, a wound that appears to be a mouth. The ragged edges of the wound transform it once again, from a mouth to a rose. Roses are standard symbols and metaphors, especially in love poems, yet here the comparison is scandalous, almost perverse. That God should sacrifice his son so that humans may find poetry is too extravagant a cost. Similarly, those who perceive the wounds as eyes find the tears (the blood of Christ, which will ultimately save humankind) to be wasteful weeping: the ultimate loss.

In the third stanza, the narrator projects himself out of his time and place to imagine others, the worshipful, who have similarly meditated before the image. Moving from the horror of the real wounds to the scandal of the metaphors that transform them, he now finds a redemption of the pain in the salvation that the wounds ultimately bring. Ironically, the steadfast worshipers have offered their kisses and their tears to the image, in empathy for the suffering that they perceive there. In the same way that Christ's wounds (as eyes and mouths) offered up the saving blood for humanity, so do the tears and kisses (from the eyes and mouths) of the worshipers redeem the poem and its metaphors from horror and scandal. There is a reciprocal relationship between Christ and his flock that hinges on metaphor and is revealed here, fittingly, in the center of the poem.

The imagination of the narrator begins to run wild in stanza 4. As he stares at the image of the foot, which has received the kisses and tears of the devout, he visualizes the wounds again as mouths and eyes, almost as if they had been placed there by the worshipful. This image may indicate the guilt of all humankind, which entailed the sacrifice of Christ. The mouths and eyes of the foot will repay the devotion of the worshipers with its own gems.

The last stanza reveals the victory of the poem, involving both the theme and the poetic figures. This victory is heightened by the altered meter of the lines: Here, the second and fourth lines are in trimeter rather than tetrameter, a foot short of what the reader has been led to expect. A tear may resemble a pearl and a drop of blood may resemble a ruby—human faith is the less-valuable form of homage (human tears, or pearls), which Christ exchanges for the more-valuable gem (his blood, or rubies) that grants forgiveness, salvation, and eternal life to those who believe.

Forms and Devices

The poem's technique is difficult to separate from the actual meanings and impact of the poem because they are so skillfully intertwined. The poem contains a baroque excess of emotion and an intense concentration on the two major tropes: mouths and eyes. Because the poet employs only these two figures, he must extend their comparisons and interrelate them. The simultaneous concentration and expansion, along with the ultimate resolution of paradoxes within the poem, renders the center of the poem a metaphysical conceit.

The comparison of wounds to mouths and eyes is not a typical one. It contains within it many suggestions that relate to the theme; for example, during Communion mouths accept the wine and wafer, which are the symbolic blood and body of Christ. The act of Communion re-creates and both laments and celebrates the sacrifice of Christ for the sins of humankind, which actually, in the poem, brings the worshipers to the time and the scene of the Crucifixion. It is kept constantly alive by human belief and devoutness and by its continued power to save.

The poem works toward a reconciliation of the oppositions inherent in the metaphysical conceit. The eyes that offer the tears (pearls) for Christ's suffering will be rewarded with the blood (rubies) of salvation. The major principle is one of exchange, yet the use of the image of a contract is not sacrilegious. Typically, God lends life to people with an implicit contract, which they then must fulfill by giving good account of that life on Judgment Day. This poem suggests the miracle of the God-human relationship: If humans give a good account, then they will receive the ultimate exchange—eternal life for temporal life, perfection, and a release from a fallen world given over to sin.

The contemporary reader must avoid modern preconceptions regarding taste in poetic language. The comic effect of a meter of iambic tetrameter rather than pentameter, which is usually reserved for serious subject matter, combines with an excess of explicitness for what seems a sordid focus that makes the reader want to laugh or to avoid such a poem. Crashaw, however, uses such excess and relentless focus to render the miracle of salvation more strongly.

Themes and Meanings

The poem reveals two miracles simultaneously: that of eternal life and that of the transformation of the profane into the sacred. For ordinary people to understand what God offers through the sacrifice of His son, they must work with what they know, which are things of this world. The poem shows how even the most minute of earthly details reveal God's plan. It focuses more narrowly as it progresses, from the statue or painting to the wounds to the fluids emanating from the wounds. Such a complete immersion into earthly details emphasizes Crashaw's view of the glory of creation and redemption. Similarly, the humor and bathos of the poem are balanced by the miracle of salvation.

If the poem offers a direct lesson, it is that of Crashaw's belief that the devout believers in Christianity will without doubt receive their just rewards. The poem makes the reader think of the little miracles that happen daily in life and suggests that they are purposeful reflections in miniature of the great, ultimate miracle of life after death. The poet mimics God's plan by working within a similar scope. The word "poet" means "maker," and each poem is a replica of the world, a cosmos of the poet's own fashioning.

Sandra K. Fischer

ON THINKING ABOUT HELL

Author: Bertolt Brecht (1898-1956)
Type of poem: Meditation
First published: 1964, as "Nachdenkend über die Hölle," in *Gedichte*, vol. 6; English
translation collected in *Bertolt Brecht: Poems, 1913-1956*, 1976

The Poem

"On Thinking About Hell" is a relatively short poem written in free verse without rhymes. It consists of twenty-one lines divided into three stanzas, each of which is a different length. The words of the title also form the beginning of the first stanza and are repeated in its fifth line. They set the tone of the poem, which is a reflection, a meditation on the earthly representation of hell. The work "Hell," capitalized in the English translation of the poem, thus emphasizing the biblical allusion, is repeated in the first line of each stanza; each repetition, however, hits at a different aspect of Bertolt Brecht's vision of hell. The poem is written in the first person, which poets often use to speak through a persona whose outlook and experiences may be quite different from their own. Here, however, no distinction is implied between Brecht the poet and the speaker of the poem. The poet reflects on his own impressions of Los Angeles, where he lived during part of his exile from Nazi Germany (from 1940 until 1945). To Brecht, the city appears strangely suspended in time and place. Attractive at first glance, its illusive nature quickly becomes apparent under his scrutiny, and Los Angeles turns into a repulsive urban sprawl.

In the first stanza Brecht declares his kinship with the British poet Percy Bysshe Shelley, who had likened the city of London, England, to the place of human damnation. The speaker of the poem, however, feels that Los Angeles is more like hell than London. The second stanza elaborates on this theme and deepens the contradictory feelings of superficial lure and deeply felt disgust. It is a study of the slow destruction of illusions fostered by the appearance of abundance and an easy life. However, this semblance of natural wealth in Los Anglese is superficial. The second stanza ends with the notion of aimlessness and emptiness that neither the unceasing movement of automobiles nor the "jolly-looking people" can mask. The first line of the third stanza continues the theme of beauty in hell, albeit in its negative form ("not . . . ugly"). The last three lines of the poem talk about the specter of homelessness that lurks behind the mask of affluence and security. Brecht leaves the reader to imagine the various reasons for being thrown out into the streets, a fate that can catch up with the inhabitants of villas as well as with those of the shanty towns.

Forms and Devices

Present participle constructions (such as "on thinking" in the English translation) abound in the original German version of the poem. This linguistic construction depicts an action suspended in the present tense. It is found six times in the poem and underlines the mood as it describes a state of unchanging sameness and immutable but ongoing monotony that holds the poem in limbo. This stasis consists of contrasts that hold the structure of the poem and its content in a precarious balance. Brecht uses exaggerations and contrasts to emphasize his point, a device that can also be found in other poems about his experience of exile in the United States. Even the lines of the second stanza are symbolic of this exuberance: They are so long that they must be printed on two lines.

"On Thinking About Hell" describes "flowers as big as trees" brought forth by the wasteful use of expensive water. There are "fruit markets/ With great heaps of fruit" that have "Neither smell nor taste," their appearance promising delectable delights that they cannot keep. Furthermore, the reader sees an endless procession of cars moving "faster than/ Mad thought" without any destination. To Brecht, the artificial growth and constant movement signify stasis rather than change and development. The passengers of the cars, however, keep up a jolly appearance. Coming from nowhere and going nowhere, they are caught in the vicious cycle of an adopted lifestyle that they are unable to change.

The hiatus of the juxtapositions is found in lines 16 and 17: "And houses, built for happy people, therefore standing empty/ Even when lived in." These lines hint at a past during which life still had meaning and provided contentment while the people who now live in Los Angeles can no longer fill space with life because they are no longer happy. Just as the fruit of the overgrown plants has no flavor, their houses remain hollow. In the last four lines, Brecht attempts to break any illusions that the reader might still hold about this washed-out paradise: The word "Hell" is now complemented by the adjective "ugly" and the nouns "fear" and "shanty town." The illusions and lures that masked the reality of life in the fast lane are ripped away. The poem ends by depicting psychological hell—the fear of homelessness—and thus comes full circle: The reflections at the beginning have been realized, and they will foster more thoughts and continue the cycle.

Themes and Meanings

Brecht and other refugees from Nazi Germany—authors, composers, and artists—moved to Los Angeles because of its reputation as a safe haven. Despite this positive, lifesaving function of the city, the poem conveys Brecht's feelings of dislike for this sprawling metropolis on the West Coast of the United States. According to a published note on Shelley, Brecht felt akin to the British poet in his awareness of the plight of the lower classes. Brecht expands this notion to include people of all social strata. Taking up Shelley's theme of the modern city as a manifestation of hell, Brecht believes that Los Angeles provides a more appropriate model of hell than London because it is no longer the smoky (yet productive) city of the Industrial Revolution that was hell mainly to the workers. Instead, the lush, overripe city of Los Angeles alienates people of all classes. The semblance of riches, of nature blown out of proportion, of houses that are empty shells, and of people apparently pursuing an idle life merely signify decadence that hovers on the edge of decay. The individual no longer plays a meaningful part in the life of the city but is swept through it as an isolated being, engulfed by the raging river of the masses. The American tendency to "keep smiling," exemplified by the "jolly-looking people" in their cars, is no longer a sign of happiness but rather of emptiness. Society's goal is no longer the contentment of people occupied with purposeful work. On the contrary, it appears to Brecht that its hectic movement is reduced to complete idleness that continues moving only to serve itself. Without its unabating motion, symbolized in the poem by "the endless procession of cars/ Lighter than their own shadows, faster than/ Mad thoughts," society might collapse. However, it would be mad to think about change. In the original German version, the word for "mad" is *töricht*, which carries the meaning of folly rather than of madness. *Töricht* implies that entertaining thoughts of changing the cycle would have disastrous effects: Once questioned in its function, this nonstop movement might collapse into itself, leaving behind a ghost town that is already envisioned in the empty houses.

In the last stanza, Brecht shatters all appearances by hinting at reality in the form of social conscience. The fear of being thrown out into the street carries with it the association of economic hardship, a logical contrast to the villas and the abundance described in the previous stanza. Brecht is probably also alluding to the experience of having been driven out of his home by the ruling powers in Germany. After all, he had to flee from the persecutions of the Third Reich, which stopped at neither villas nor shanty towns.

Karin Schestokat

ONCE

Author: Alice Walker (1944-   )
Type of poem: Narrative
First published: 1968, in *Once: Poems*

The Poem

"Once" is a poem consisting of fourteen numbered sections in free verse. The sections range from fifteen to forty-one lines, each presenting one image or short narrative from Alice Walker's work in the 1960's with the American Civil Rights movement. Together, the sections add up, like the pieces in a stained-glass window, to a complete picture.

"Once" opens with Walker in a Southern jail. Her companion points out the irony of the pretty lawn and flowers outside the jail, while Walker dryly comments on the irony that "Someone in America/ is being/ protected/ [from me]." This ironic tone informs most of the poem. At this point, the reader knows only that someone, assumed to be Walker (although no name or gender is specified), is in jail in the South. There is no reason given and no mention of when this happened.

In the next two sections, hints of the Civil Rights movement and the 1960's begin to emerge. The speaker appears carrying a sign as she runs through Atlanta's streets, and there are daily arrests. The fact that there is a "nigger" in the company of "white folks" is observed. By the end of the fourth section, the setting for the poem is clear. As soon as the reader becomes aware that this poem is about the Civil Rights movement, it is time to contemplate the title, "Once." Does Walker intend to conjure up the atmosphere of a fairy tale, to say that this happened "once upon a time" in a land long ago and far away, or does she want to emphasize that this movement is only one fight for justice among many? The answer is that she intends both meanings.

The reader is introduced to Walker's associates as the poem unfolds: the white friend who has been shunned by her family for her activism (section 4); Peter, a Jewish worker in the movement who is killed at seventeen (section 6); the arrogant black man with a smart mouth (section 2); the woman who smiles at little ironies (section 1). Introduced in the poem as well are an assortment of bigoted white Southerners: the absurdly "liberal" white woman and the stripper, who insist they are not prejudiced (sections 10 and 12); the driver who hits a young black girl with his truck and makes it seem to be her fault (section 13); the "understanding cops." The Southern blacks presented in "Once" tend to be powerless in one manner or another. They are poor and hungry (section 8); arrested (section 11); struck down (section 13). The term "nigger" is used throughout the poem, spoken both by "liberals" and by bigots.

The anecdotes are presented simply, with no interpretation. Many lines are direct quotations. Walker expects the reader to notice the ironies, to feel anger or sadness, based on the facts alone. Because most of the characters, including many speakers, are identified only by gender, race, or type, each image becomes more universal: These terrible moments are typical; they could have happened to many people, in many lands, at many times. Yet the poem ends on a hopeful note. The final scene finds a young black girl waving an American flag—timid, but just daring enough to celebrate the freedom that someday may be hers.

Forms and Devices

"Once" is written in very short lines that combine to form generally straightforward sentences. Often, a numbered section will contain only one sentence, as section 14, which closes the poem, does: "then there was/ the/ picture of/ the/ bleak-eyed/ little black/ girl/ waving the/ american/ flag/ holding it/ gingerly/ with/ the very/ *tips*/ of her/ fingers." Some commentators have wondered whether, in fact, this is poetry at all. Clearly, this poem is neither as substantial nor as sophisticated as those in Walker's later collection, *Revolutionary Petunias and Other Poems* (1973). There is much to recommend "Once," though, and its simplicity is essential to its beauty and power.

One effect of the very short lines is that they force the reader to slow down, to notice each element in the stanza. A child holding a flag is a common enough sight—so common that people tend not even to see it. Walker presents simple images in a simple style, but alters the typography so that the reader is forced to notice, to ponder. Thus, "american" is spelled with a lowercase letter and set off in a line by itself. The reader cannot help but pause over that line, stopped for a moment by the lowercase *a*. By forcing the reader to pause, Walker emphasizes the word so that the irony (this integration battle is going on in America) is not lost in hasty or careless reading. Walker creates similar effects, drawing attention to particular words and phrases, by using italics ("*tips*/ of her/ fingers"), dashes, and eye-catching alignment on the page. The short lines also help bring out sound effects that might otherwise be missed. In the stanza quoted above, the assonance of "bleak-eyed/ little black" is heightened by the way in which the words are arranged on the page; the sound effect calls attention to those two essential characteristics of the girl.

Walker does not use many common poetic devices, such as rhyme, meter, metaphor, or simile, which create a heightened but artificial language for poetry. "Once" and the other poems in this collection are written in a very straightforward style—the language that people actually use when they speak. The occasional obscenity is intended not to shock but simply to be realistic. If the words sound harsh, it is because the reality of racial hatred is harsh.

Walker does not use much figurative language in her poetry either. She does not say, "This is like that"; she says, "This *is*." By presenting images simply and honestly, Walker forces the reader to look.

Themes and Meanings

"Once" deals with Walker's own involvement in the Civil Rights Movement in the South during the 1960's. The collection of poems in which it appears, *Once: Poems*, was published in 1968, the year of Martin Luther King, Jr.'s assassination. In the collection, "Once" is followed by six more poems dealing with civil rights. This poem, informed by a strong black consciousness and a somewhat youthful didacticism, shows universally bigoted and inhuman white Southerners confronted by witty and courageous black and white activists from the North. Each numbered section is another image or event Walker remembers from her own experience: She appears in ten of the fourteen sections, if only to say, "I remember."

The effect of Walker's continually putting herself in the scene is to make it clear that the horrors she presents are true: She can verify that they are true because she was there. For young readers, this is especially important because they do not remember what went on in this country during the days of segregation and struggle. Walker is not concerned only with her own experiences. Although she writes about what she has seen or heard herself, she avoids making this a poem about particular people or events. Only one person, activist Dick Gregory, is precisely identified, and one of the poet's friends, Peter, is identified by first name only.

The rest of the people in the poem are identified by type or by their relationship to the poet: "my friend," "a Negro cook," "a little black girl," "the blond amply boobed babe." In fact, the speaker of the poem need not be the poet at all. The "I" could be any of hundreds of black "nice girl[s] like her" who participated in the Civil Rights movement. Walker's purpose in all this is to help readers experience another time and place. By not specifying the details too much, she leaves ample room for readers to use their own imagination to supply the details—the names, faces, feelings—that will make it real for them.

Once the reader is dwelling firmly in that time and place—the American South in the 1960's—Walker hopes that he or she will begin to realize why the Civil Rights movement had to happen, what the anger and frustration was all about, and what the dream was like. She does not tell readers what to think about each scene—she simply places them in it. There is little sense here that the activists believe they are winning the fight or that victories are what matter. There are tales of arrests and confrontations, but no scenes of voters registering or walls tumbling down. Instead, the poems focus on the humanity of the activists and the bigots.

For all its vignettes of hatred and conflict, "Once" ends on a hopeful note. The picture of the young black girl timidly waving the flag stands for all the dreams of all the activists. Although the girl is "bleak-eyed," although she holds the flag "gingerly," she is a symbol that appears again and again in Walker's work—she is the hope for the future.

Cynthia A. Bily

ONE BONE TO ANOTHER

Author: Vasko Popa (1922-1991)
Type of poem: Poetic sequence
First published: 1956, as "Kost kosti," in *Nepočin-polje*; English translation collected
  in *Selected Poems*, 1969

The Poem

"One Bone to Another" is a cycle of seven short poems. The title of the cycle establishes the mood and alludes to the personae of the poems, two bones that engage in an
intimate dialogue about the human condition in their subterranean *mise-en-scène*. The
titles of the individual poems indicate the setting and order of the events in the cycle.
These events are depicted as occurring in the immediate present; and the bones express their reactions to them in the first-person plural or first-person singular. As the
events unfold, each poem marks a shift in the mood of the bones, from smug independence and delight after being freed from their prison of flesh, to terror and helplessness at the realization that they must submit to the forces of human fate, and finally to
bewilderment and despair when confronted with the inevitable transience of human
existence.

The first poem, "Na početku" ("At the Beginning"), expresses the bones' relief and
newfound sense of independence after freeing themselves from the "flesh": "Now we
will do what we will." In the second poem, "Posle početka" ("After the Beginning"),
the bones gleefully begin to ponder the possibilities of their new existence; they will
"make music," and if any hungry dogs should come along, they plan to trick them:
"Then we'll stick in their throats/ And have fun." This delight in the prospect of mischief turns to a delight in each other in the charmingly romantic mood of the third
poem, "Na suncu" ("In the Sun"), as they sunbathe naked and declare their love for
each other. In the fourth poem, "Pod zemljom" ("Underground"), having concluded
that "Muscle of darkness muscle of flesh" are "the same thing," the personae contemplate what they will do about it. They decide to call together "all the bones of all
times"; they will all "bake in the sun" and "grow pure," and so they will become "eternal beings of bone" who wander about as they please.

This sense of independence is abruptly arrested in the fifth poem, "Na mesečini"
("In the Moonlight"), when, bewildered, the bones begin to realize that they are
slowly being covered in flesh and filled with marrow, "As if everything were beginning again/ With a more horrible beginning." Their bewilderment turns to despair in
the sixth poem, "Pred kraj" ("Before the End"), as they attempt to find a means of es-
caping the inevitable: "Where shall we go nowhere." This despair is tinged with resignation and defeat in the seventh and final poem in the cycle, "Na kraju" ("At the
End"), in which both bones express the fear that they have been swallowed by each
other, and that now they can no longer see or hear or be sure of anything. The sense of
freedom that preceded has vanished: "All is an ugly dream of dust."

Forms and Devices

The cyclic form is a hallmark of Vasko Popa's poetry. It enables the poet to maintain a free philosophical inquiry and thus promotes his artistic objective: the distillation of truth. As Ted Hughes writes in his introduction to *Selected Poems* (1969),
"Each cycle creates the terms of a universe, which [Popa] then explores, more or
less methodically, with the terms." A central theme is presented, and the poems within
the cycle explore various facets of that theme (although the number of poems varies,
Popa evidences a partiality for the number seven). This circular mode of inquiry
enables the poet to meditate on the theme from a number of imaginative angles so that
all of its cosmic conditions and possibilities are revealed. The result is disclosure of
the cosmic drama, and this phenomenon is reinforced by the way the cyclic form
mimics the nature of the cosmic structure: While each poem can stand alone, its
meaning is always amplified in the context of its relationships to the other poems in
the cycle.

The terse, economic style evinced in this cycle is a second regular feature of Popa's
poetry. In Popa's case, however, reductionism is more than simply a poetic style;
rather, it functions as a technical device which, like the cyclic form, promotes his
philosophical and artistic aims. Typically, Popa's poems are forty to fifty words in
length; they run ten to fifteen lines, with three to five words per line. They are arranged in somewhat uneven stanzas of single lines, couplets, tercets, and, more rarely,
quatrains. Thus the compression is visual as well as verbal. This compression also
contributes to the strong rhythm of his poetry; the meter is irregular but distinct. The
majority of Popa's poems are written in the present tense, which amplifies the terse-
ness and intensity. His syntax is highly compressed and frequently ambiguous, the
lexicon lean and concrete, the diction inordinately concise, and the neologisms frequent. He uses a minimum of connecting particles and transition words, and punctuation is altogether absent. By adhering to this economical style, Popa is able to sustain
the distillation process even as he develops a theme.

The functions of these features, however, are not mutually exclusive. While the cyclic form promotes a revealing, comprehensive inquiry by containing the thematic aspects in workable segments, it also implicitly participates in their reduction and consequent distillation. Conversely, just as reductionism exposes and reinforces the
multifarious cosmic relationships inherent in the poem, it contributes to the development and enrichment of the theme. The versatility of these features, then, enhances
the collective effect. Thus, the structure itself participates in the philosophical development and becomes an essential part of the meaning of the poem.

While Popa's linguistic code may seem austere, it finds a lively counterbalance in
his humor, as illustrated in "One Bone to Another." Popa's wry, ironic humor is most
closely related to the irrational humor of folklore. This kind of humor is distinguished
by its functionality: It is understood that the folktale, or the riddle, is a kind of verbal
play which attempts to account for reality by temporarily suspending the limitations
of "the real world." It is a product of instinct rather than of intellect. It is humanistic
and tends to suggest rather than define, it comments without judging, and it opens

rather than closes the circle. This humorous tendency is most dominant in Popa's first three poetic collections–*Kora* (1953; *Bark*, 1978), *Nepočin-polje* (1956; *Unrest-Field*, 1978), and *Sporedno nebo* (1968; *Secondary Heaven*, 1978)—in which it is manifested in the delightfully unself-conscious activities of the archetypal beings, such as the "bone couple" in the present cycle, who inhabit the primordial environment of Popa's poetic world.

Popa's folkloric orientation is apparent in his imagery as well. For example, while at first glance, an image such as "The backbone of a streak of lightning" seems to reflect the kind of incongruous juxtaposition of unlike objects which is the touchstone of surrealist texts, it is in fact typical of the kinds of anomalies which regularly occur in Yugoslav folklore. Moreover, such images, though rich in dramatic associations, are often tempered—just as in folklore—by a playful, childlike tone. The humorous escapades of the personae in "One Bone to Another," for example, make readers forget that they are eavesdropping on a conversation between two bones about the wonders and frailties of the human condition.

Themes and Meanings

The central theme of "One Bone to Another" is as old as poetry itself: the apparent futility of human existence. Popa's approach to this problem is unique, however, in that he examines it in cosmic terms. He does not speak for the world; rather, it speaks through him, and his ability to see things from its point of view is remarkable. He becomes the vehicle of communication for those other mysterious worlds that exist undetected and interact in the ongoing drama of cosmic life.

A second, more subtle theme that Popa touches on here is the place and function of the psychic realm in daily life. In "Underground," the fourth poem in the cycle, Popa writes, "Muscle of darkness muscle of flesh/ It comes to the same thing." This seems to indicate that conscious life—that is, the life of the "flesh"—tends to blind people, to keep them in "darkness" about the true nature of existence. Further, it implies that the meaning which people seek to fulfill their lives can be found only by awareness and investigation of the subconscious world of the psyche, for it is the true foundation of being. Conscious life, with all of its demands, tends to obscure inner, psychic life, so that, inevitably, a person is "swallowed" by it. This preoccupation with the psychic plane and the need to maintain contact with it is a recurring theme in much of Popa's work. As Charles Simić remarks in the introduction to his translation of Popa's *The Little Box* (1970), Popa seeks to penetrate "the truth that lies behind the forms and conventions."

This cycle reflects another level of meaning. It must be remembered that this text was written during the post-World War II period and, like so much of Popa's early work, reflects the anguish and turmoil of the time. The tone of frustration and despair that characterizes the poems parallels the emotional climate of postwar Europe. The goals to which the personae aspire—freedom, understanding, and, ultimately, survival—mirror those of many Europeans of that era. In addition, the personae exhibit characteristics which would appear to optimize the possibility of achieving those goals. They are tough, alert, and cynical—admirable qualities in any period, but essential in order to overcome the tragic, tumultuous aftermath of the war.

If there is an ultimate message in Popa's poetry, it is that if one wants to understand and preserve humankind, one must attend to the cosmos of which it is an integral part. One must listen to the cosmos as Popa does and try to see things from its perspective, for only by maintaining contact with it can one understand one's place in it. One's inner psychic life is the instrument through which one can make that contact; it is the "telephone" which enables participation in the collective cosmic conversation.

Maria Budisavljević-Oparnica

THE ONE DAY

Author: Donald Hall (1928-　　)
Type of poem: Poetic sequence
First published: 1988

The Poem

The One Day is a book-length poem of sixty-three pages divided into three major sections: "Shrubs Burnt Away," "Four Classic Texts: Prophecy, Pastoral, History, Eclogue," and "To Build a House."

Donald Hall bases *The One Day* on the "house of consciousness"—the idea that one mind might express many contradictory voices and different points of view. Its tripartite organization roughly corresponds to French moral essayist Michel Eyquem de Montaigne's *Essais* (1580, 1588, 1595; *The Essays,* 1603), traditionally held to exhibit three stages of human development: Stoicism giving way to philosophical skepticism and concluding in a moderate Epicureanism. Such an outline, however, fails to account for Hall's powerful statements about love, preparation for death, building a house as metaphor for living, and the emergence of self-knowledge and social order. Like James Joyce's novel *Ulysses* (1922), *The One Day* explores the thoughts of the poet over the course of a single day. As a poetic sequence, Hall's work invites comparisons to Robert Lowell's *Notebook 1967-1968* (1969) or John Berryman's *77 Dream Songs* (1964).

The poem begins with aphorisms, or concise statements of principles, taken from Montaigne ("Each man bears the entire form of man's estate"), from Pablo Picasso ("Every human being is a colony"), and most significantly from Abbé Michel de Bourdeille: "There are other voices, within my own skull I daresay. A woman speaks clearly from time to time; I do not know her name." The first and third sections of *The One Day* are spoken by a male farmer who "speaks" in roman typeface and a female sculptor who speaks in italics. A general consciousness narrates from an objective point of view. The three voices quote others, and Hall freely intermingles their narratives, speculations, and poetic effusions; sometimes two stories develop simultaneously, conflicting, supporting, and commenting indirectly on each other. Multiplicity and imaginative richness inform the poem from beginning to end, giving the book a dreamlike and intuitive ferocity.

In section 1, "Shrubs Burnt Away," the reader learns that the male struggles with his middle-aged complacency and looks forward to the only major event left for him: death. He thinks about his father, the values his father attempted to teach his son, his marital distress, lovemaking without emotion, and his memories of World War II. The male introduces other "colonists" of his mind, such as a homosexual actor, a retired man watering his lawn, a drunk who died after he fell from a parking structure, and a boy who read the complete works of Edgar Allan Poe. The poet states that the colonists enjoy building this house in his mind because it alleviates some of the stress of impotent, idle feelings that plague him.

The female voice tells of discovering creative talent as a girl sculpting dough in her mother's kitchen; her father's sudden death, however, subverts her artistic yearnings. Her mother then becomes an alcoholic, and her sister suffers from nervous breakdowns and requires constant hospitalization. A cycle of failure and mental instability seems destined to repeat itself in the lifetime of this woman. Later, in section 3, she suffers from nervous breakdowns and drug addiction herself. The male and female speakers approach death with different backgrounds, but they are united in the search for peaceful self-acceptance, meaningful relationships, and satisfying work.

Section 2, "Four Classic Texts," develops the poetic modes of prophecy, pastoral, history, and eclogue. New characters emerge: Elzira, Abraham, Marc, Phyllis, Senex (who is related to Roman Stoic philosopher Lucius Seneca), and Juvenis (who is related to classical Roman satirist Juvenal). This section attempts to reject modern material culture and work toward restoration of the whole human being: soul, family, and society. Hall says that many borrowings in this section come from classical Roman poet Vergil, Amos and Isaiah in the Old Testament, Roman historian Titus Livy, an anonymous German soldier in World War I, and stories from *The Boston Globe*.

Hall shows how these four timeless themes apply to today's fragmented world, often juxtaposing ancient history with modern idiom taken from kitchen and bedroom. Through a chaos of competing ideas, Hall forges an evocative statement about returning to a peaceful state of mind through the therapeutic art of building. Hall attempts to reverse the damages done by a modern, disassociated consciousness by looking through the eyes of ancient poets.

Section 3, "To Build a House," returns to the male and female speakers. This concluding section focuses on praise, artistic renewal, celebration, and the purifying work of farming. It resolves the conflicts of earlier sections in a passionate, triumphant declaration of order. The male and his wife concentrate on restoring an old orchard, logging, gathering maple syrup, and enjoying the pleasures of this paradise of work. Their lovemaking once again becomes an act of celebration of the spirit. Together they build their house, carefully manage their land, and look toward the end of the day. Both male and female voices desire to approach death in a house wrought of their own hands, sheltered from fragmentation and violence.

The female speaker finds a renewed ability to work at her craft of sculpture, seizing each hour to chisel away at alabaster. The female looks back on her troubled past of failed relationships, psychiatric treatment including electroshock therapy, and drug addiction. She realizes that a singleness of mind is the most prized goal in her life. Through a fresh commitment to her art, she finds old grudges against her father and mother disappearing. She can now sleep without disturbing dreams, enjoy the company of old friends, and spend meaningful time with her children. Both male and female realize that their final determination to build a house means they want to leave this world as happy, fulfilled, whole people who enjoy the support of family and friends.

Forms and Devices

In its conception, *The One Day* resembles a sonnet sequence, wherein a poet writes a series of concise poems linked to one another and dealing with a single, unified theme. In addition to the contemporary poetic sequences by Lowell and Berryman, Hall may be looking back to Dante Gabriel Rossetti's "The House of Life," a sonnet sequence published in 1881 that explores the poet's love for his dead wife and records events in their life together.

Donald Hall's skill with poetic structure is evident in *The One Day's* use of free-verse lines varying in length from ten to fourteen syllables, arranged in ten-line stanzas. Sections 1 and 3 have approximately the same number of stanzas, just as the four subheadings of section 2 are equally balanced. Hall says that the surface of the poem should appear smooth, but that—like an enormous electronic device—if one looks behind the smooth exterior, one sees a byzantine array of wires, tubes, and transistors. The organization is so precise that the reader may view each stanza as an independent lyric; however, the book is best appreciated through close attention to its uniform metaphors.

Five metaphors run through the poem, by which Hall illustrates the many pitfalls and conflicts each person must face over a lifetime. First, the dominant metaphor of the house of consciousness and building one's own home allows Hall to introduce the two main voices. The original title of the book, *Building the House of Dying*, shows that Hall looked at the work of building as necessary preparation for death; people cannot die without first leaving something of value behind, be it farmhouse or sculpture.

Second, one day in a person's life becomes a microcosm or mirror of an entire life. During one day, the male and female speakers look back to their past, living their lives over again. Thus Hall develops the concept—which also interested William Wordsworth in his poem "Lines Composed a Few Miles Above Tintern Abbey"—that a person constructs reality by the process of thinking and remembering. The poem follows Hall's thought processes as he seeks to understand his life, although much of the narrative material is pure fiction.

Third, Hall uses the metaphor of the bed as a universe. All thoughts about self, family, society, love, and death take place on this piece of furniture common to all homes. The bed both unites and divides, reflecting life's larger struggles in why people make love: for the satisfaction of lust, for companionship, for procreation, and for communication. The bed becomes another mirror of the soul in *The One Day*. In fact, one might imagine the whole "action" of the poem taking place as the poet reflects in a reclined position on his bed.

Fourth, the poem makes frequent references to airplanes. The male remembers the stories of Wrong-Way Corrigan, Amelia Earhart, Will Rogers, and a Pomona fireman, who all disappeared flying various kinds of aircraft. The female recalls with vivid clarity the stub-winged pylon racers of her youth, daredevil pilots, and tragic commercial airline crashes. The theme of flying as an escape from necessary work on earth becomes linked to pilots who attempt to build their houses in the sky.

Finally, Hall uses the metaphor of work as a restorative activity. Humanity will save itself only if men and women can find meaningful commitment to work that nourishes the soul.

Although *The One Day* contains strong unifying themes, the subdivisions of section 2 can also be approached as independent poetic genres. "Prophecy" is the poet's inspired declaration of divine will and prediction of future catastrophes. Isaiah prophesies that obstinate nations such as Babylon and Egypt will suffer from flames and plagues of God's wrath because they refuse to worship in the proper way. Similarly, the poet of *The One Day* states that he will strike down false buildings and reject materialistic values because they corrupt the human will.

"Pastoral" is a dialogue between Marc and Phyllis. Traditionally a poet uses this mode for a treatment of shepherds and rustic life, sometimes in the form of a discussion about the virtues of country living. Hall looks back to Vergil, who made his pastorals a vehicle for social comment, and uses this dialogue to describe the emptiness felt by many contemporary married couples. Hall's characters are firmly located in modern suburbia; they lament the stultifying order, sense of restraint, and dishonesty of middle-class American ways. The husband feels incapable of the most basic emotion or defensive action. The wife feels claustrophobic in her perfect home entertaining perfect friends for a game of bridge.

"History" takes up the character of president-emperor Senex and explains the nature of his rule through ancient, medieval, and modern times. Hall brings into question the idea of recorded history. If history books tell of enslavement, executions, trench warfare, and tyranny, humankind needs to reject history in order to restore the human mind.

The last subsection, "Eclogue," returns to the pastoral formula of the love-lay, in which a shepherd sings a song of courtship. In Hall's case, this song concerns renewed love relations and the building of a new history. In order to build the future properly, the poet must concentrate on the restitution of mothers, fathers, and faithful sexual relations. Greed and dishonesty must be replaced by self-respect and the enjoyment of real labors.

Themes and Meanings

Donald Hall wrote the various sections in *The One Day* over seventeen years, but it seems to be one continuous, energetic utterance. This unity of mind and purpose drives the book toward its inevitable conclusion: Hall's statement about ecstatic renewal and the resolution of past conflicts. It is a poem about the cycle of life and about how, in declining years, one attempts evaluations about beginnings and endings. Hall's most important summary statement comes near the end of the book: "We are one cell perpetually/ dying and being born, led by a single day that presides/ over our passage through the thirty thousand days/ from highchair past work and love to suffering death."

Hall emphasizes the need to build a house in one's mind—to come to an understanding of the various conflicting voices and disappointments that life offers. The poem concerns a search for order both within and without. People need to deal with sorrow and suffering on the way to building the shelter of personal acceptance. Building this house of understanding also involves social order, because once one has established shelter, one can relate fully to others and feel that life has meaning, mostly achieved through work. The poem is both spiritual and temporal because Hall discusses the failures of marriage, family, and career. The tone of expansiveness and resolution puts an optimistic ending on this sophisticated, elegant book. The poet has been able to follow the advice of his father, who told him to do only what he wanted to do.

Hall challenges the reader to search personal and social history as he has done to listen to the otherwise silenced voices inside. In order to survive, according to Hall, one most construct a house, a place of solace that gives one the room to interpret and evaluate experience. The metaphor of building necessarily involves human understanding.

People cannot merely shuffle passively through life without attempting to grapple with a fundamental question: For whom did they live their lives? At times, *The One Day* stretches the reader's ability to grasp the main point because of the stream-of-consciousness technique and complex allusions to history, literature, and religion. Sometimes Hall is prone to the dropping of names only casually related to his theme; however, his desire for a reevaluation and reordering of American society leaves the reader in a state of awe, knowing that he is absolutely right. Society and individuals must resist entropy, the natural tendency of things to go from a state of organization into decay. Man and woman must each build a house and find satisfying work to which a life is committed.

Looking back through history, one can see how often violence and tyranny caused people to die without ever having a feeling of home or emotional shelter. At ninety years old, when the female speaker goes to the White House to accept a presidential medal for her art, she realizes that this late-won public fame means almost nothing. The real work of building the internal house of self-acceptance and order has already been done.

If people spend adequate time preparing for death, life does not have to be characterized only by fragmentation and melancholia. The male surveys his farm and reflects on taking Communion, looking toward Christ's ascension as another pattern for the renewal in his life. Hall's plea is for the living not to allow life to defeat them but to fight back by building a house, making art, working an apple farm, and loving each other with final determination. In the end, the poem celebrates, restores, and prophesies leaving this world in a happy frame of mind.

Jonathan L. Thorndike

OPEN CASKET

Author: Sandra McPherson (1943-   )
Type of poem: Lyric
First published: 1978, in *The Year of Our Birth*

The Poem

"Open Casket" is a free-verse poem in which the poet describes and moves through various California landscapes. The identity of the speaker is muted, and the personal pronoun Sandra McPherson uses is the plural "we," which de-emphasizes the individual in the scene and focuses the reader's attention on the landscape itself.

Although the title suggests a funeral at which there is an "open casket" viewing of the deceased, the poem itself seems to go off in a different direction, depicting vacation entertainments, rural landscapes seen from a bus, a field trip for school-children, and other diversions. The school trip, in particular, suggests that the sights in the poem are seen from the viewpoint of a child.

The tone of voice in the poem is calm and understated, conveying a cool sweetness that contrasts ironically with other statements about the poor, going "back where we belong," or overpopulation, "Certainly too many people."

The first stanza begins with the sort of recommendation one might find in a travel brochure, describing as it does a ride in a "glass-bottomed boat," a tourist attraction in Monterey Bay near the town of Pacific Grove, on the California coast. The onlooker marvels at how clearly she can view the sea anemones and other underwater life. Presumably, this boat trip takes place on a vacation excursion.

The following, indented stanzas turn by association to other trips, or perhaps to other parts of this same one: riding a bus "between Santa Barbara and San Jose" or going to the state capital in Sacramento on a school trip to see the "gold and white capitol." She speaks of reading "the Gospel of John/ in a little red pocket version" on the bus, perhaps a child's edition or perhaps the sort of missionary publication one might find distributed in a bus station or some other public place. She also thinks of crowds of children being brought to the capital, where they learn about the state; its state flower, the golden poppy; and its mountains.

Although the speaker does not seem to have been dealing with death or a funeral, at this point the crowds of children and the Gospel of John, which deals with the life, death, and resurrection of Christ ("the friend who comes back"), make her think generally about the fact that each person will live "beyond another" and will thus have to deal with the meaning of death.

The poem moves to images of dry riverbeds seen from the bus between San Jose and Sacramento. The speaker's vision of "colored pencils" seems oddly out of place "in the grass" and "Thin wildflowers," as if the pencils had been dropped or left by someone interrupted while sketching, evidently a personal recollection that connects with the wild poppies.

These images lead into ellipses, and then, as if her attention turns back to the present from uncompleted thoughts of other times, she returns once more to the description of what it is like to look into the tidal pools and waters of the bay. The last stanza, like the first, deals with the boat trip and the image of sea life underwater. The first and last stanzas bracket the rest of the poem, which seems to be a series of memory associations in which the poet connects the present experience with thoughts of childhood, religion, beauty, and death.

Forms and Devices

McPherson uses indentation and stanza breaks to provide structure for her free-verse poem. The first and last stanzas serve as a frame for the others, but otherwise the poem is very open in form. Although the reader can occasionally hear rhymes, such as "brine" and "design," they are rare and almost incidental.

Strong visual images are very important in the poem. The poet describes things vividly and accurately in a few words, and as she does so, her observations and descriptions evoke layers of association and meaning. Although her images become metaphorical by association, McPherson's descriptions are also strongly physical. The world she describes is very concrete and real, and the connections she makes between objects and events follow channels of physical experience. In "Open Casket," the boat trip evokes feelings of peacefulness and awe and the sense of looking into another world, but the boat itself is a real object in a real world. It is associated visually with the funeral casket by the boat's shape, the flowerlike sea anemones, and other images. An interesting poem to compare and contrast with "Open Casket" is Emily Dickinson's poem numbered 712, which depicts death as an endless carriage ride. In Dickinson's poem, the dreamlike ride evokes feelings of depression, anxiety, and resignation associated with death, but the carriage ride itself, unlike McPherson's boat ride, is imaginary.

Other important images in the poem also work visually. The bean fields seen through the bus window and the purplish blue display of amethysts in the jeweler's window are like the underwater sights seen through the window of the glass-bottomed boat, momentary glimpses of another world. These images suggest how the mind works in trying to understand and absorb things. Together, these images of looking from one world into another take the reader into the experience in a dramatic and evocative way and provoke insight by their coincidences and parallels.

The tone that McPherson uses to achieve this effect is one of wise innocence, although she uses a somewhat impersonal point of view in the poem. There is never an "I" speaking, with her "we" referring perhaps to family members or to other schoolchildren. This plural pronoun brings the reader into the experience and also emphasizes the somewhat-passive feeling of the child as onlooker, part of a crowd, always being transported by one means or another, watching and remembering it all.

Themes and Meanings

The title of the poem gives the reader a hint that the poem deals with death and associated thoughts about an afterlife. It would be difficult to determine more about what gave her the ideas for the poem, but McPherson herself has explained that the poem was in part the result of her childhood experience of attending the "open casket" funeral of her grandfather. In an essay, McPherson says, "I was twelve; it was my first and only open casket funeral. Seeing down into death, I thought, was like being in the glass-bottomed boat I took also as a child in Monterey Bay."

Yet, she does not make the funeral the focus of the poem. Rather, the poem deals with other examples of seeing into some other dimension. With the aid of the glass-bottomed boat, which the reader is advised to take, one sees into an orderly and harmonious world, akin to heaven, were the reader actually able to see it.

From this harmonious vision, however, the reader is forced to return to the world of poverty and labor, heat and dust. Wanting something more, "we read the depot literature/ of miraculous healing." Only the jeweler's window, containing expensive and unattainable objects, precious bluish violet stones, reminds the reader of that vision of heaven in the sea.

The fact that San Jose and Santa Barbara are named for saints and that Sacramento means sacred or having to do with the sacraments reinforces the idea that the poem concerns itself with religion, particularly questions about death and resurrection and the mysteries of an afterlife.

Water is typically a symbol of life and the sacrament of baptism. Water appears here as the medium through which one looks into another world, the underwater world. Where people struggle to make a living in the bean fields, the surrounding hills are "hard dust." The riverbeds of the landscape are dry with "White salts and rusts and mires/ where the rivers used to be. . . ." This dry world lacks the perfection of the underwater world, which exists in "water-oiled harmony," that is, in a state of grace.

It is difficult to tell why McPherson evokes the image of colored pencils except as one more version of the image of looking down into something where colors and forms attract the eye. Perhaps the scene is part of the lesson on the state flower and the mountains, perhaps it is some other time when she tried to capture the beauty she saw in nature by sketching wildflowers.

In any case, whatever the shortcomings of the world, there is always Monterey Bay and the glass-bottomed boat to provide a vision of eternal life and beauty. McPherson has said that the word "vacation" in the last line made her think of the body vacated by the living person. The soul or spirit of the person whose body is being viewed is literally on vacation, that is, gone. Yet, the word "vacation" also suggests something happy and entertaining, a welcome relief from the everyday world of work. Looking into the underwater world and at the life there is like looking into a paradise where it is always "summer and/ vacation." The poem ends with a sense of hopefulness, as if the trip in the glass-bottomed boat has provided insight and spiritual relief.

Barbara Drake

OPEN HOUSE

Author: Theodore Roethke (1908-1963)
Type of poem: Lyric
First published: 1941, in *Open House*

The Poem

"Open House" is the title poem of Theodore Roethke's first volume of poetry. Friend and fellow poet Stanley Kunitz proposed the book title before Roethke actually had written the poem. Then, upon completing the poem, Roethke placed it at the front of the manuscript, suggesting that both the poem and its theme were to serve as an introductory promise for the poet's first work as well as for his entire career.

"Open House" is a terse, lyric definition of the speaker's poetics and, simultaneously, of his methods for the discovery of the self, indicating that for Roethke, these are one and the same. The title resonates with meaning. Upon first opening the book, the reader is welcomed into the poet's world, a place invented by the poet out of his search for self-knowledge and truth. Thus, the reader comes to the open house on a similar search, seeking to learn from the poet by following his lead in a parallel spiritual quest. The conceit is saved from mere cleverness by the poem's forthright tone and its concluding dark discovery.

In the first stanza, the poet establishes the connection between his self and the self's labor of love, his poetry. Although his art is natural, it is so difficult that it is painful. His secrets do not speak; they "cry aloud." They are expressed without the use of a corporeal voice ("I have no need for tongue"), since the poet's expression is all spiritual. Any reader may enter the poet's life, as his "heart keeps open house" and his "doors are widely swung." His love, poetry, is "an epic of the eyes." That love is simple, without "disguise," plainly visible on the page.

In the middle stanza, Roethke shows an awareness that his self-revelatory communication is a mystical and universal act. Saying that his "truths are all fore-known," he acknowledges a personal clairvoyance, as though he has meditated on the self many times. Such prior knowledge is made humble by welcoming public inspection of his house. Nor is he the first poet to discover the kinds of "truths" poetry offers.

At the very center of the poem, Roethke declares, "I'm naked to the bone,/ With nakedness my shield." It is a lovely pair of lines, affirming that the poet's open vulnerability is his strength and protection. As the fulcrum of the poem's advancing mystery, the second stanza is less descriptive, and more prophetic, than the first. It begins the poem's assertion that such personal mystery is not without serious psychic danger. For example, what in the first stanza had been a "cry," in the second develops into "anguish."

The third stanza continues the progression of the mystic journey into the self. Nearing what seems to be the deepest recesses of the house, there is a shift away from the personal control that was evidenced in the first two stanzas. In the first stanza the poet refers to himself with the personal pronouns "I" or "my" five times; in the second, six times; but in the third stanza he refers to himself only twice, and these two referents are used as brakes after the poet's journey has taken him near the white-hot center, where violent creativity reigns. Significantly, in the last stanza Roethke uses definite articles where one might expect pronouns. He writes: "The anger will endure,/ The deed will speak the truth." He is prevented from writing "My anger," "My deed," and "my truth" at this point in the poem specifically because he no longer seems in control of his own feeling ("anger") or his own action ("deed"). The journey through his own house, the self, has taken him inward to a place of universal mystery, a deep room of dangerous creativity.

Finally, for the good of his poetry the poet must retreat from his own psychic center. He must "stop" the journey. If he does not, the creative "anger" and "Rage" that the poet discovers within himself will ultimately consume him, reducing his "clearest cry," his poetry, to a state of uncontrolled "witless agony."

Forms and Devices

"Open House" is a brief poem of eighteen lines, composed in three sextains, or six-line stanzas. The English language gets the word "stanza" from the Italian, meaning "room," so that in this "house" there are three "rooms." In each stanza, the rhyme scheme unites an alternating rhymed quatrain with a final rhymed couplet (*ababcc, dedeff, ghghii*).

The rhymed quatrains in each stanza create a sense of tension and release, as if there were a rise in pitch followed by a corresponding drop, which is then further enhanced by the finality of the rhymed couplets. Two slant rhymes appear: the first in lines 1 and 3 of the first stanza ("aloud"/"house") and the second in lines 2 and 4 of the third stanza ("truth"/"mouth").

Every line scans into a regular iambic trimeter. As a result, the poem swings with a perfect cadence, which, in the beginning of the poem, seems light and airy, but which becomes frighteningly ironic in light of the "anger," "rage," and "agony" of the poem's conclusion.

One of the interesting developments in "Open House" is how Roethke uses sentence constructions to present his theme. The poem is initiated with two brief sentences, each of which is one line long. Then Roethke moves through the remainder of the first stanza and completely through the second in sentences of two lines, the paired lines singing like voice and echo. Finally, the cadence of the third stanza is slowed as Roethke stretches two sentences through three lines apiece. Consequently, the poem begins much more lightly cadenced than it ends. It is as if the reader's ear is at first attuned to a quick point-counterpoint rhythm that is later replaced with a more lethargic beat. The overall rhythmic effect is thus in keeping with the poem's movement from light to dark.

Themes and Meanings

As critic Peter Balakian notes in his book *Theodore Roethke's Far Fields* (1989), the phrase "To keep open house with one's heart" is philosopher Friedrich Nietzsche's. Balakian explains that maintaining an open house "is fundamental to Roethke's essential way of knowing reality and measuring truth. The title proclaims the need to search the self for the truth."

"Open House" is a poem about the poetic process of self-discovery, a theme common in the Romantic tradition. As the first poem in Roethke's first volume, it stands as a declaration of Roethke's allegiance to Romanticism, which stretches back to William Blake. One might even note that the poem's spare language, simple diction, and strict rhythms are indebted to Blake's *Songs of Innocence* (1789) and *Songs of Experience* (1794). Furthermore, in its originating metaphor, "Open House" is very similar to Robert Browning's poem "House," which begins:

> Shall I sonnet-sing you about myself?
> Do I live in a house you would like to see?
> Is it scant of gear, has it store of pelf?
> "Unlock my heart with a sonnet-key?"

Like Blake and other Romantics (especially William Wordsworth, Walt Whitman, and William Butler Yeats), Roethke believed that poetry is a mystic art quite contrary to, and more trustworthy than, reason. As "Open House" shows, however, the pursuit of self-knowledge through poetry can be dangerous and painful.

The poem might be easier to grasp if it were not so violent and oracular. The final stanza is clearly the most troublesome, particularly as the diction is more abstract, imitating the "strict and pure" language of high emotion. As the poem momentarily shifts to the future tense, the anger that "will endure" beyond the poem is as essential to Roethke's creative imagination as are notions of eternal reverie for other poets. Roethke only approaches rage at the end of the poem, as if pure creativity is like fire— life-enhancing or all-consuming, depending upon one's distance.

The poet must "stop the lying mouth" when the heat of creative rage "warps" his poetry to "witless agony." The word "witless" is especially well-chosen. Whereas its common meaning includes "stupid" or "foolish," to be without "wit" is also to be unable to perceive the metaphoric connections between words and the things, ideas, and feelings they stand for—a state, for any poet, that must indeed be close to "agony." In other words, the poem asserts the need to explore the open house of the self until that point where the exploration becomes self-defeating.

"Open House," as a journey to the center, is archetypal. Its theme is not Roethke's alone, nor is it a theme from which Roethke ever moves away entirely. For example, the first line of the title poem in Roethke's last volume of poems, *The Far Field* (1964), reads: "I dream of journeys repeatedly." Another poem in that book is entitled "Journey to the Interior."

William Hoagland

ORANGES

Author: Gary Soto (1952-   )
Type of poem: Narrative
First published: 1985, in *Black Hair*

The Poem

In "Oranges," Gary Soto conveys an achingly accurate portrayal of adolescent angst involving a young boy's first date and first love. As with many of his poems, such as "Home Course in Religion," "Black Hair," "The Plum's Heart," and "Walking with Jackie, Sitting with a Dog," Soto relies more on images and the repetition of images—in this poem, oranges—and short, succinct phrases to unify his poem rather than a particular rhyme scheme.

This short narrative poem chronologically follows a twelve-year-old boy's journey to meet his first date. By using first-person point of view, Soto personalizes this particular experience and establishes an immediate intimacy with his audience, as they recognize the inherent affinity with the subject. The audience experiences the young person's timidity, apprehension, and sense of joy as he prepares to meet his first date.

With a tone that is more reflective and gentle than in many of his earlier poems, especially those in *The Elements of San Joaquin* (1977), Soto conveys the poignancy and frailty of first love, articulating this frailty by juxtaposing the warmth and temerity of the young boy's feelings with the cold, external environment of December. This contrast between humans and nature begins as the boy sets out to meet his date: "frost cracking/ Beneath my steps, my breath/ Before me then gone." Despite the cold and sometimes harsh environment, it does not impede his quest.

In this somber, bleak setting that is not conducive to love, the young boy seems more vulnerable as he struggles with his own insecurity and doubts. His qualms, however, begin to diminish when he reaches "Her house," a feeling that is mirrored by his external environment: "a dog barked until/ She came out." Surrounded with bright images of light, she dispels his fears and insecurity and reinforces his strength and determination to continue. Confidently, he leads her down the street, and they enter the candy store, their destination.

Once inside the candy store, he faces a dilemma bigger than the cold: how to pay for the 10 cent candy she chooses when he only has 5 cents. He reaches inside his pocket, takes out a nickel and one of the oranges he has kept hidden in his jacket, and sets "them quietly on/ The counter." Stanza 1 ends with the saleswoman's compliance because she knows "what it was all/ About" and accepts his payment. The saleslady becomes his co-conspirator, allowing the boy to avoid embarrassment, validate his feelings, and complete the special purchase.

With the aid of the saleswoman, the young boy triumphs over the cold harsh environment that mirrors his insecurities and foreshadows his potential embarrassment. His reward: the love of the young girl. The poem concludes simply, poignantly with the innocence and beauty of first love. Through juxtaposition, Soto effectively and convincingly reminds the reader of the impact, innocence, and apprehension of first love.

Forms and Devices

Soto is at his best when he delves into particular events and universalizes them for the reader in language that is simple and direct rather than abstract and honest rather than pretentious, and it is this structural form that dominates and influences the success of "Oranges." The language and the form of the poem—brief, succinct lines with very few dashes and commas and even fewer periods—emphasize the brevity of the experience: a moment in time, a brief slice of life. The structural technique that reinforces the brevity of the moment is called enjambment, the process of continuing a thought from one line to the next without stopping or pausing. The form also reinforces the young boy's apprehension, excitement, and innocence and the purity of the situation. While Soto uses many images to portray the thrill and angst of a first date, the dominant images are those associated with cold and warmth.

From the very first line of the poem, Soto contrasts the pervasive power of the cold, external environment with the vulnerability and warmth of the twelve-year-old boy. It is a cold December day; frost cracks beneath his feet, and "dogs bark," yet he carries something warm and bright within him as symbolized by the two oranges he secretly keeps hidden and protected from the cold, unfeeling environment.

Because the oranges are not in season, they, too, like the boy's feelings, are vulnerable to the cold. If taken out and exposed too quickly to the elements, they would wither and lose their warmth. Just as his pocket protects the oranges, so, too, does he guard his feelings for the girl. Therefore, this fruit symbolizes the boy's latent spirit, his sensitivity, which he has to protect. Unconsciously, the oranges seem to provide him with the strength and warmth to continue on his journey, and prepare him to face his most difficult predicament. If he can overcome the cold and his own feelings of doubt, he can overcome anything.

His fears are assuaged as soon as he sees the young girl's home. The light on her front porch functions like a beacon: Her "Porch light burned yellow/ Night and day," perhaps suggesting the potential constancy of her love. As she runs out to greet him, her "face bright/ With rouge, he overcomes his shyness, smiles, "Touche[s] her shoulder" and walks her "down the street" to their destination: the drugstore.

Now assured of her reciprocal feelings from the "Light in her eyes" and the smile on her lips, the young boy unknowingly is ready to face his most serious contest: paying for a piece of candy she wants when he does not have enough money. He overcomes the dilemma by taking a nickel from his pocket, "then an orange," and placing them "quietly on/ The counter." Even though the saleslady accepts his offer, realizing the importance of the moment and not wanting to embarrass him, the moment is truly his. He controls the situation; he has reached deep within him, made himself vulnerable, and has triumphed over his fears.

As he leaves the store, he is oblivious to the "cars hissing past" and the "Fog hanging like old/ Coats between the trees." Now, he takes his "girl's hand" in his "for two blocks." He releases it only when she unwraps her chocolate and he peels his orange "That was so bright that. . . . Someone might have thought/ I was making a fire in my hands." Indeed, the fiery brightness of the orange visually symbolizes the spark of romance that now exists between him and his young girlfriend. The symbol of the orange reinforces the poignancy of the poem: The young boy's feelings are small and vulnerable and need to be protected against the harshness of the environment. Yet he also now knows he can create fire with nothing but his own hands.

Themes and Meanings

Soto's ethnic consciousness, his sense of himself as a Mexican American, permeates but does not impede the multicultural appeal of much of his poetry. By providing a cultural context to many of his poems, Soto enriches the meanings of his poems. While the incident he focuses on in "Oranges" is not particular to Mexican Americans, the predominant symbol in the poem does reflect his childhood and work experiences of picking fruit. Fruits, whether apples, plums, or oranges, become important symbols in some of his poetry. For example, in "Walking with Jackie, Sitting with a Dog," Soto articulates a couple's sense of hope for the future and, ultimately, life with oranges: "we . . . quarter an orange . . ./ We lick our fingers and realize/ That with oranges now and plums four months away,/ No one need die." Again, in "Home Course in Religion," the young protagonist struggles to survive on a diet of Top Ramen and cold cereal when his girlfriend brings him "a bag of oranges," which satiate his physical hunger and initiate a sexual encounter that provides him with a life-affirming vitality.

In "Oranges," oranges symbolize a young boy's awakening to the power and potential he holds within him. During the young man's physical journey to meet his girlfriend, he undergoes an emotional, almost spiritual journey within himself. This archetypal journey leads him to an epiphany: He has a life-affirming power within him. The brightness he creates when he peels his orange visually reinforces the spark of love between he and his girlfriend. It is an ordinary, almost banal moment, yet in Soto's hands it becomes a universal slice of life that is delivered poignantly and poetically.

Sharon K. Wilson

ORCHARD

Author: H. D. (Hilda Doolittle, 1886-1961)
Type of poem: Lyric
First published: 1912, as "Priapus"; collected in *Sea Garden* as "Orchard," 1916

The Poem

First published under the title "Priapus" and often referred to as "Spare us from Loveliness," "Orchard" is a short poem. Containing thirty-one lines, it is written in free verse and divided into four stanzas of unequal length. As its title suggests, its setting and focal point is an orchard in autumn, replete with epicurean treasures that inspire both awe and apprehension in the first-person narrator.

Unlike many poems in which orchard or garden imagery is used simply to suggest fecundity, fertility, or abundance, for this narrator the splendor of the orchard sets up a dilemma. This dilemma is the source of conflict within the poem: The orchard contains hazelnuts, figs, quinces, and "berries dripping with their wine"; however, like many people with puritan sensibilities, the narrator is wary of being seduced by its aesthetic and sensual appeal and leaves it "untouched."

On entering the orchard, the narrator is profoundly moved by its opulence. A falling pear serves as a reminder of the resplendent blossoms that preceded it, and the narrator is overcome with emotion and reverence. Because of the seemingly unbearable beauty of the orchard, the narrator falls to the ground and begs for mercy, wishing to be spared its intoxicating effects. In contrast to the bees who take no notice, the narrator feels vulnerable to the allure of the orchard and must struggle to overcome its aesthetic appeal. However, the narrator feels obliged to reject the orchard's beauty for reasons ranging from veneration to disdain. Rather than taking pleasure in its gifts, the narrator repeatedly entreats the god of the orchard to "spare us from loveliness."

In comparison to the orchard, the god appears coarse. He looks on impassively. Like the bees, he is unimpressed by the surroundings. But his plain appearance and indifferent demeanor make him a less threatening, more deserving object of adoration. By making an offering of the orchard's treasures, the narrator subordinates the aesthetic appeal of the orchard to authority of the "unbeautiful" (and therefore less suspect) deity. By using the immoderate bounty to supplicate a more meaningful ideal, the narrator satisfies both the impulse to revere the fruit of the orchard and the compulsion to reject it. By taking pleasure in the fruit by proxy, the narrator minimizes the risk of falling under its intoxicating spell.

Forms and Devices

Probably the most conspicuous form in "Orchard" is that associated with a style H. D. is credited with helping to invent: Imagism. Tenets of this literary movement included a propensity for short, concrete descriptions of naturalistic scenes, as well as an inclination to focus on images in and of themselves, rather than more elusive or enigmatic meanings. Much of this poem's meaning depends on its success in depicting images in unfamiliar ways, attributing characteristics to objects with which they are not normally associated. For example, instead of picturing pear blossoms as delicate, white, fragile, or ethereal, the poem implies that they are cruel, flaying observers with their beauty. Bees, instead of their familiar buzzing, "thundered their song."

By rejecting conventional portrayals, H. D. forces readers to reconsider the effect and meaning of everyday objects. However, the objects themselves are less important than the relationships among them. The narrator competes with the bees, realizing too late that they do not share her interest in the wonder of the orchard. The god of the orchard becomes more remarkable for his unpolished simplicity because he presides over a place of aesthetic enchantment. By juxtaposing disparate elements, H. D. calls attention to how contexts can determine how situations are likely to be interpreted.

Another way that H. D. brings attention to selected elements within the poem is by reducing them to their characteristics instead of referring to them directly. Thus, the bees become "golden-banded" and "honey-seeking." This technique serves a number of purposes. It allows the poet to direct readers toward the characteristics she feels are most important. In this case, the bees' stinging ability is less significant than how they follow sweet scents that lead them to flowers and fruit. Moreover, her reducing of the bees to certain familiar activities invites associations that might otherwise be overlooked. Human visitors to an orchard may well find little in common with the insects flying about them; however, "honey-seeking" may be an activity with which they have something in common.

H. D. also uses other devices to portray the scene in ways at once selective and complete. Repetition highlights the most significant occurrences in the poem: The pear falls, the narrator falls, the hazelnuts have already fallen, marking a succession of descents. The narrator flounders, then remains prostrate, symbolizing humility as well as a misstep. The narrator repeats the plea "spare us from loveliness," drawing attention to the ongoing struggle that occurs throughout the poem. In each instance the significance of the event is stressed through repetition, and the repetitive elements increase in importance exponentially.

Themes and Meanings

The poem's central theme is the tension, most often associated with Puritan ideology, between that which is beautiful, pleasurable, or sensual and that which is moral, ethical, or "good." The questionable nature of the orchard's bounty is addressed throughout the poem, from the opening lines in which the pear falls through the last stanza, in which the narrator makes an "offering" of the succulent fruit, rather than enjoying it in a more self-indulgent way. Is earthly pleasure inherently immoral? For the actors in "Orchard," the answer seems to be a qualified "yes."

The god of the orchard is, presumably, above the kind of corporeal temptation that plagues the narrator. For the bees, "honey-seeking" represents not joy, but gainful activity, rendering it unproblematic for them as well. However, what about the orchard's human visitors? Certainly the narrator of "Orchard" feels compelled to reject the orchard's gifts; less certain is whether the poem suggests that readers should follow suit. There is little to suggest that H. D. meant to offer advice; however, the narrator does seem to offer a warning to those who place material loveliness above moral or spiritual goodness: Be careful, cautions the narrator, the beautiful pear blossoms have the power to distract, to enchant, to render one helpless.

The appreciation that the narrator feels upon entering the orchard makes it all the more difficult to steel oneself against the impressiveness of the physical surroundings. Indeed, although the narrator succeeds in avoiding the sinful pleasures of the orchard, ceasing to desire them is another matter. This raises another question: Is it more virtuous to renounce worldly pleasures completely, or does true virtue depend on denying those things that tempt oneself? In this poem, rather than lessening, the temptation of the orchard seems to increase, as evidenced by the thick description of the tempting verdure that occurs in the last stanza. Even while resolving to dedicate the fruit to the god of the orchard, the narrator describes the offerings in appreciative detail, envisioning the wine that might flow from the grapes and the auspicious disrobing of the hazelnuts. Even as it is consecrated, the treasure of the orchard is secretly idolized by the narrator, who can renounce but not completely free herself from its allure. In this case, when the narrator repeats the phrase "I bring you an offering," the repetition is an essential part of mustering the resolve necessary to complete the sacrifice.

Like many of H. D.'s poems, "Orchard" observes a microcosm more complicated than a casual examination might suggest. It contains a multilayered interplay among the various elements of the poem, allowing readers a polychromatic glimpse of the carefully depicted imagery within. The question of whether one should be suspicious of earthly enjoyments might now appear dated or irrelevant; however, in view of the extent to which Puritan ethics inform modern American Judeo-Christian beliefs, perhaps the question posed by the poem is more topical than it seems. Certainly because it is one of the underpinnings of society's belief systems, the role that aesthetic pleasure, and the rejection of it, plays in life deserves a thoughtful reexamination.

T. A. Fishman

OREAD

Author: H. D. (Hilda Doolittle, 1886-1961)
Type of poem: Lyric
First published: 1916, in *Sea Garden*

The Poem

"Oread" is a six-line poem. In Greek mythology, an oread is a wood nymph. By giving the poem this title, H. D. (Hilda Doolittle) frames it as an address by the wood
nymph to the sea. Although there is no "I," the poem's first-person point of view is
further suggested by many of the descriptive words themselves. For example, the second line orders the sea to "whirl your pointed pines," and the third line repeats the image with "splash your great pines." Clearly, the ocean has waves, not pines, yet the
waves could be referred to as trees if the oread was speaking and transposed the objects with which she is familiar onto something different. Similarly, the last line uses
the image "pools of fir"; again, the reader has the sense of the oread addressing the sea
through her frame of reference.

Through this action of speaking, the poem creates a picture of the wood nymph
standing on the rocks, addressing the sea. What is important, though, is that the oread
is not speaking in singular terms; for example, line 4 states "on our rocks" rather than
"on my rocks." This plural form is not only consistent with the first person point of
view (that is, it is "our rocks" rather than "their rocks"), but also adds another visual
element to the poem. Although it is only one oread speaking, the plural possessive implies either many oreads or many trees. Either way, the picture created is one of thick
forests and jagged coastlines, the oread standing on the rocks, the sea pounding below
her, the salt spray splashing her. This is a picture of elemental nature.

Adding to this elemental picture is the fact that the verbs are all declarative in form:
"whirl," "splash," "hurl," and "cover." It would be more accurate to say that the oread
is invoking, not asking, the sea to perform these functions. That invocation adds to the
poem's elemental nature.

Finally, this image is one of enormous unleashed energy, an impression that is further developed by the poem's brevity. Because it is so short, every word carries an importance that it might not carry in a longer poem. Not only are the actions in the poem
dramatic, but the length of the poem itself suggests that everything extraneous has
been stripped away, exposing the core of the experience. The reader is left with this
immediacy.

Forms and Devices

H. D. is well-known for her use of ancient Greek imagery. Many critics have suggested that this imagery is a metaphor through which the poet discusses other issues
of either emotional or political import. Therefore, the images of trees and water,
and by extension, the entire landscape, can be seen as metaphorical. Since the poem

lends itself so heavily to an imagistic reading, the entire poem can be read as metaphor.

This sense of the poem—and the poetic landscape—as metaphor is suggested by the metamorphosis that the images undergo. When one approaches the poem, he or she has an image of trees as a category and an image of ocean as a category; those two categories are clearly separate. By the second line, however, when the oread invokes the sea to "whirl your pointed pines," the poem is beginning to blur those seemingly distinct categories. If one wants to maintain that trees and ocean are still separate, it is possible to say that the sound of waves crashing onto the rocks is similar to the sound of wind whipping the trees, or that the image of a wave rising has a shape similar to that of a tree. What is clear, though, is that the poem is, at the least, making connections between objects that are normally seen as having none.

In lines 2 and 3, even if the oread sees the waves as pine trees, the reader still sees waves and pine trees as separate. In line 5, however, the oread directs the sea to "hurl your green over us." Green is the color of pine trees, but it can also be the color of the sea; these two categories, thus, are moving closer together. This combining of categories culminates in line 6, where the oread names the water "pools of fir." This image can refer either to the frothy texture of the water or to the liquid texture of the motion of trees. Either way, what were separate at the beginning of the poem are, despite the poem's brevity, much less separate by the poem's end.

This blurring of categories gives the trees and water a metaphorical quality. Clearly, this is no ordinary landscape, for in the day-to-day world objects may be similar, but they do not take on qualities of each other. Furthermore, in the day-to-day world, it is difficult to see how trees and water are at all similar; any coastline, for example, clearly delineates where water begins and earth ends. The poet, though, is weaving a very different world, and seems to be pushing the reader to look beyond the surface of things into a landscape where objects that are normally distinct take on similar attributes, or even become each other.

The title also works on a metaphorical level to suggest a look into another world—or, at least, another way of looking at this one. Because the poem is in the first person, it would seem as if the reader is merely viewing everything through the oread's eyes. If this were so, however, there would be no need for the poet to shift the boundaries between objects from the poem's beginning through to the end; the oread's view of those objects would remain the same throughout. The fact that the categories do shift suggests that the oread herself is merely a metaphorical distancing device through which the poet can lay claim to her deeper vision.

Themes and Meanings

"Oread" is a poem through which H. D. calls into question traditional constructs that she sees as being inherently bipolar and unequal. The poet accomplishes this questioning by establishing several dualities and then blurring the basis by which those dualities are established. By the end of the poem, the reader is in a world where traditional ways of seeing and thinking have begun to break down.

Clearly, one duality is that of trees and ocean—or, perhaps, land and water. Yet as already seen, that duality, which was distinct at the beginning of the poem, is much less distinct by the poem's end. Another duality is between passive and active; this distinction also becomes rather murky. The oread can be seen as passive and the sea as active, for the sea is crashing onto the oread. The oread can also be seen as active, for she is the one invoking the sea to do that crashing. Yet is she really? Is the sea crashing because the oread has invoked it to do so, or is the sea crashing because that is what it does, and the oread is merely attempting somehow to personify an action that would happen anyway? It becomes difficult to tell which party is being active and which is being passive.

A third duality established is between violence and nonviolence. Although much of what the oread is addressing to the sea is fairly violent both in its declarative form and in the specific actions invoked ("whirl," "splash," or "hurl"), the poem ends on a non-violent gesture ("cover us with your pools of fir"). Is this that moment of quiet eddying after the waves have crashed, or is it that what seems violent through most of the poem is not as violent as one would think?

The poem clearly does not answer these questions but only raises them. This seems to be the poet's intent: to question the basis on which bipolar thinking is established. H. D. herself was a strong feminist; this poem was written early in the twentieth century, before women even had the right to vote. Much scientific and medical research at that time was done with the intent of proving the natural superiority of men to women. Traditional thinking had set up a very clear category of polar opposites—male and female—with men having social power and women having almost none.

In the poem, the poet is questioning both a society that subordinated women and, by further extension, the entire concept of bipolar thinking, which she sees as a social construct that is inherently unequal. Through the blurring of traditionally distinct categories, H. D. is suggesting a different way of viewing the world, one in which traditional, bipolar thinking falls away and a more egalitarian and fluid world emerges.

Robert Kaplan

THE OTHER ALAMO

Author: Martín Espada (1957-   )
Type of poem: Narrative
First published: 1993, in *City of Coughing and Dead Radiators*

The Poem

Martín Espada's "The Other Alamo" takes place in 1990 in San Antonio, Texas, the location of the Alamo. The poem's five sections move through several layers of time: from the present event of a veterans' gathering to reflections on Texas race relations since the Alamo siege in 1836. Its central event takes place in 1949, when the poet's father was refused service at a local diner. "The Other Alamo" refers to his father's protest against overt racism. To appreciate the poem, one must consider the Alamo's import.

During the siege of the Alamo, 187 Texans held off 4,000 Mexican troops led by General Antonio López de Santa Anna. The Texans were fighting to gain their independence from Mexico. On March 6, when the Mexicans punched a hole in the adobe wall, they entered and killed all the Texans, including the American frontiersmen Davy Crockett and James Bowie. The names "Crockett" and "Bowie" are mentioned in Espada's first stanza.

The poem begins at a gathering in the "Crockett Hotel dining room," where a veteran leads others in prayer. Subsequent lines concern the city's devotion to religious shrines and to the Alamo historic site. Tourists can purchase a "replica" of the Bowie knife, a hunting knife used extensively by American frontiersmen. Its design—a strong, single-edged blade and a horn handle—was attributed to James Bowie. Espada juxtaposes the military references with the religious, ending his first stanza with a reference to "visitors/ in white Biblical quote T-shirts."

The second stanza places the Alamo into the context of Anglo-Mexican relations in Texas. Independence won, and Texans soon dominated and denigrated Mexicans. Tourist brochures depict "Mexican demons,/ Santa Anna's leg still hopping/ to conjunto accordions." The only Spanish word in the poem, *conjunto* refers to a musical group featuring accordions; Santa Anna lost his leg in battle subsequent to the Alamo. Texans, the ultimate victors, used the law to appropriate Mexican land and exploit "Mexican peasants." Espada concludes with an image of "vigilantes" hunting men "the color of night." This catalog of offenses culminates in a single word: "Alamo," as if the deeds Espada recounts were in retribution for that massacre.

With no transition, stanza 3 takes readers to 1949, when three Air Force men in uniform, including one from "distant Puerto Rico," enter a diner where only whites are served. Stanza 4 expands upon the incident in which a waitress, the manager, and the police try to get the men to leave, citing "local customs." The men refuse and are finally served food cooked by a "black man unable to hide his grin." Ignoring the food, the airmen leave an enormous tip for the cook. At this stage, Espada interjects: "One was my father; his word for fury/ is Texas."

The final section of the poem returns abruptly to the present. The son of that Puerto Rican airman discovers that the diner no longer exists. Protest, however, continues: "Vandals," according to a newspaper account, have damaged the Alamo doors, "scarring" them "in black streaks of fire."

Forms and Devices

The accessibility of Espada's poem belies a sophisticated poetic intelligence and subtle effects in word choice and in the ordering of details. Assuming that readers are familiar with the Alamo event, he presents a fast-paced set of images in the two opening sections.

The first stanza refers to "a chalk-faced man in medaled uniform." Denoting exceptional paleness, the word "chalk" also works alliteratively and in assonance with "Crockett." This military man "growls a prayer." Mixing religious and military detail, Espada develops an ironic tone that borders on the scathing. The city may be "saint-hungry," but the saints are those brave Texans who gave their lives at the Alamo. Instead of a holy relic, tourists can grasp "the talisman of a Bowie knife replica." The color white returns in the tourists' "white Biblical quote T-shirts." The images accumulate a sense of a holy war having been enacted when Texas won independence. "White" represents good; dark represents evil. The whole movement of Espada's poem disputes this dichotomy.

Stanza 2 moves directly to the Alamo, where "The stones in the walls are smaller/ than the fists of Texas martyrs." This image chiefly functions to allow the mention of the "martyrdom" of the Alamo heroes while reinforcing the poem's religious irony. "Their cavernous mouths could drink the canal to mud" is a reference to the enormous thirst of the Texan defenders as the siege became prolonged. Not interested in elevating the heroism of the Texans, Espada makes even their thirst seem damaging.

Damage done to the Mexicans concerns Espada more. He refers to "the cotton growers who kept the time/ of Mexican peasant lives dangling from their watch chains." Colonialism was rampant. The damage, however, is cloaked in an aura of goodness. Even "the vigilantes [are] hooded like blind angels," and they gather "at church." The rule of the Anglo-Americans over the Mexicans is sanctified as retribution for the savagery at the Alamo: "all said this: Alamo."

In stanza 3, Espada's descriptions of the three airmen are precise. One is black, one blond, the third Puerto Rican. The black man heard the word "nigger" in his hometown Baltimore "more often than his name." Racism is an old story to him. The white man is "blond and solemn as his Tennessee/ of whitewashed spires." Espada's simile gives dignity to this white man. The Puerto Rican's skin is brown, a dangerous color "in a country where brown skin could be boiled for the leather of a vigilante's wallet." The image is hyperbolic—-or at least one hopes so. The repetition of the word "vigilante" recalls the second stanza and the threat of lynchings or worse.

Themes and Meanings

"The Other Alamo" provides a contrarian view of a pivotal event in Texas and American history. It asserts that there is an "other Alamo" of defiant protest against

Anglo-American tyranny, which needs to be recognized and applauded. While Espada does not dispute the valor of the Alamo defenders, he despises its effects both on present-day Texas and on the city his father visited in 1949. His main point is that Texas independence from Mexico led to the subjugation and oppression of the Mexicans who remained. This bias extended to other people of color. Espada is the champion of his father's protest against racism in San Antonio, an action taken in concert with a black and a white companion. Sadness creeps in, however, when he notes that the site of that protest, the lunch counter, "was wrecked for the dump years ago."

Espada's poem commemorates "the other Alamo" and points to continued protest in the news of the defilement of the Alamo's doors. His poem is important because it raises questions about the interpretation of a historical event. It is a risky poem because it challenges the traditional view of the winning of Texas independence. When the poem claims it was also traditional to treat Mexicans as "peasants" and to portray them as demonic, readers are pressed to question the value of certain traditions.

"The Other Alamo" is a passionate poem fueled by three strong emotions: the poet's pride in his father's refusal to be treated as inferior, his love for that young serviceman with his "cap tipped at an angle," and his anger that any human being could be the object of blatant discrimination. In this respect, Espada is similar to his father, whose "word for fury/ is Texas." The senior Espada was a photographer whose subject matter influenced his son's choice of poetic material—in both cases, the experience of migrant peoples, the places they live, and their struggles. In a sense, this poem is a kind of dialogue with Espada's father and an affirmation of his rebellious spirit.

It is also more than that because it reaches out to include other forms of protest against embedded oppression. The poem's final image of the Alamo doors scarred "in black streaks of fire" speaks of such protest. There is an inflammatory quality to Espada's work as a whole. His poems are in the Puerto Rican tradition of *bomba*, or whirls of high-pitched singing giving way to statements of personal or collective truth; *bomba* also means bomb. Clearly, Espada's intended audience is not the mainstream either poetically or culturally. His poems tell the stories of migrant peoples, and their most obvious purpose is empowerment.

Claire Keyes

OUR DAILY BREAD

Author: César Vallejo (1892-1938)
Type of poem: Lyric
First published: 1917, as "El pan nuestro"; collected in *Los heraldos negros* (1918);
English translation collected in *César Vallejo: A Selection of His Poetry*, 1987

The Poem

Though struck by its vivid imagery, readers of "Our Daily Bread" are often uncertain about its story and message. This imagery conveys a strong sense of existential guilt as well as a desire for redemption and social justice. The context of the poem becomes clearer as the reader progresses through its five irregular stanzas, the later stanzas clarifying the earlier ones. The importance of context in establishing the poem's meaning contributes to the nonlinear nature of the poem and is consistent with its overall message that human communion, that which overcomes the existential despair of the individual, is possible only if the divisiveness that categorizes language and thought is surpassed.

The poem conveys the notion of the poet facing the dawn of a new day, and yet the earth is "sad" and the poet, in his guilt, is asking for absolution. It begins with the vague third-person reflexive tense ("One drinks") to describe one drinking one's breakfast—probably just coffee—on a somber, cold morning. References to morning throughout the poem include "breakfast," "damp," the "morning eye" that still sleeps, the speaker "drinking this coffee," and lastly, the title of the poem and the request in the third stanza, both of which refer to the request in the Lord's Prayer: "Give us our daily bread."

The dreariness of the new day is established with the words "damp," "winter," "mordant," "enchained," and "fasting." Death is omnipresent, as the cemetery smells of the blood of loved ones. In the second stanza, the poet expresses a wish, perhaps as a result of this bleakness. This wish is also vague, as if the speaker does not know exactly what is wrong or how to remedy the situation: "One would like to knock on every door/ and ask for I don't know whom." The wish gets more precise as the religious imagery becomes clearer: one wishes to give the poor—who are presumably not able to break their fast—pieces of bread and to take vineyards from the rich "with the two holy hands" that "flew unnailed from the Cross."

The last two stanzas enlarge upon the poet's sense of guilt and switch to the first person, thus connecting the poet to the universal experience of facing each new day as an alienated being, knowing that social injustice and death are inevitable. The speaker feels estranged from his own body ("Every bone in my body belongs to another") and guilty ("maybe I stole them!"). Although readers are not informed of the cause of this guilt, it is so acute that the poet feels not only that he has stolen but also that if he had not been born, "some other poor wretch would be drinking this coffee."

The stanza ends with the speaker condemning himself as "a wicked thief" and asking the poem's fundamental question: "Where am I to go?" The answer to this question involves the wish for redemption, which is repeated in the last stanza. This time, however, it is repeated more emphatically in the first person:

> I would like to knock on every door
> and beg forgiveness of I don't know whom,
> and make him morsels of fresh bread
> here, in the oven of my heart . . . !

Forms and Devices

Written early in César Vallejo's career, "Our Daily Bread" bears the influence of the Romantics, whom he studied at the University of Trujillo, Peru, and wrote about in his 1915 bachelor's degree thesis, entitled *El romanticismo en la pesía castellana* (romanticism in Castilian poetry). The poem's fervent expression of emotion and despair is furthered by its seven exclamation points. Just as Romantic poets, such as José Espronceda and José Zorilla, often play with the porous boundary between life and art, Vallejo also conveys the Romantic notion that the poet's goal is to somehow overcome that despair through the poem itself. Art is thus an answer to life's difficulties, and it follows that the poem itself is a morsel of bread offered to readers.

The poem also reveals Vallejo's debt to the Spanish American modernists—Rubén Darío and Julio Herrera y Reissig in particular—especially in its emphasis on the senses, such as the dampness of the earth, the smell of blood, and the sound of the passing cart. Such vivid imagery, often uncontextualized, is a technique used by the modernists and the French Symbolists, whom Vallejo had also read.

In the first stanza, the nonlinear nature of the poem is achieved by the use of images that move like photographic flashes from "breakfast" to "Damp cemetery earth" to "City in winter" and, finally, to "The mordant passing/ of a cart." The most powerful image in the poem describes the taking of the vines from the rich by "the two holy hands/ which in a flash of light/ flew unnailed from the Cross!" This strong image of the cross maintains the poem's focus on religious imagery in that it echoes the "mordant passing" of the first stanza, a more literal translation of which would be "mordant crossing" (*mordaz cruzada* in Spanish).

Unlike the poetry of the Spanish American modernists, however, "Our Daily Bread" refers to a reality that is far from harmonious. Here the world is awry, as is suggested by one's drinking rather than eating breakfast. Furthermore, the first stanza ends with "an enchained emotion of fasting," as if to underscore the idea that this is a world where logic does not apply. The unexpected use of the adjective "enchained" to modify "emotion" in this phrase is a technique that Vallejo used with increasing frequency as his poetic career progressed. This kind of catachresis is borrowed from the poets of Spain's Golden Age, as well as from the Spanish American modernists and the French Symbolists, but instead of using the technique to somehow capture the sublime or to create a particular sound, Vallejo uses it convey his existential angst, as well as to suggest the limits of language itself.

Themes and Meanings

The importance of bread in "Our Daily Bread" begins with the title, which refers to the Lord's Prayer and which foregrounds the religious symbolism throughout the poem. In addition to providing spiritual nourishment in the form of Communion, bread also provides physical nourishment, and the poem plays with these two meanings.

Throughout his career, Vallejo consistently manipulated symbols. Rather than emptying them of their traditional meaning, he showed how they can hold many meanings. In effect, Vallejo exploits symbols to show the simultaneous ambiguity and creative capacity of language, which is one of the primary themes of Vallejo's well-known collection of poems *Trilce* (1922; Eng. trans., 1973). Thus in "Our Daily Bread," one breaks one's physical fast in the morning by drinking coffee, yet the sound of the cart introduces spiritual fasting. The wish to give pieces of bread to the poor combines the physical and the spiritual senses of bread, suggesting that the body and the spirit are not divisible. Here, spiritual nourishment is inseparable from physical nourishment just as, ultimately, religious justice is inseparable from social justice. The insurrection that the poem alludes to foreshadows much of Vallejo's later poetry, especially in *España, aparta de mí este cáliz* (1939; *Spain, Take This Cup from Me*, 1974) and *Poemas humanos* (1939; *Human Poems*, 1968).

One of the main themes of *Los heraldos negros* (1918; *The Black Heralds*, 1990) is the poet's sense of existential despair in a world abandoned by God. Existence itself condemns humans as "wicked" because it necessarily entails some sort of injustice at the expense of the dead and the poor. In this poem, the poet feels he may have stolen his very bones, and he thinks that if he did not exist, someone else would be in his place. The poem suggests that people are alienated from one another because they are ultimately alone in facing death, which pervades everyday life ("the earth/ reeks of human dust"). Thus, the poet wishes to remain asleep.

Nevertheless, "Our Daily Bread" finally reveals a glimmer of hope because, like much of Vallejo's later poetry, one of its central preoccupations is poetry itself. While Vallejo at first suggests that living in communion with others is impossible, he nonetheless seeks to provide others with communion made "in the oven of [his] heart." Despite the somber mood of much of the poem, its ending is positive because the poet has become Christlike in sacrificing himself for the sake of true spiritual communion and true social justice. Vallejo suggests that poetry, like "our daily bread," nourishes both body and soul, atones for existential guilt, and exalts humanity.

Elise Bartosik-Vélez

OUT IN THE OPEN

Author: Tomas Tranströmer (1931-   )
Type of poem: Lyric
First published: 1966, as "I det fria," in *Klanger och spår*; English translation collected in *Tomas Tranströmer: Selected Poems, 1954-1986*, 1987

The Poem

"Out in the Open" has thirty-three lines divided into three sections of uneven length. The poem takes place out in the open air, away from town and the town's evil; the poet attempts to bring things normally hidden out in the open. Each of these readings is problematic, partially because of the poem's fragmented nature.

The second and third sections are written in the first person, but the first section has only an implied first-person narrator. In all three sections, there is no distinction between the speaker and Tomas Tranströmer; one must assume that he, following the norms of the lyric poem, is the "I" in this poem.

The poem begins with a fragment, as if a stage direction were being given in a play: "Late autumn labyrinth." The idea of a labyrinth is appropriate for this poem because of the mystery in it as a whole and because of the abrupt and sometimes baffling changes in direction that take place, especially between sections. This first section of the poem follows a thin narrative: Someone waits at the edge of the woods, then decides to enter the woods, and then leaves. While in the woods, he hears a few sounds, notices the mushrooms "have shriveled up," and decides to get out and find his landmarks again before it gets dark. The scene is somewhat frightening, mainly because of the associations the reader might have with woods and darkness; the reader has no idea, however, why the person is in the woods or why exactly he needs to find his landmarks again. The section is evocative and startling in its metaphors, but it is certainly also opaque.

Section 2 begins with a statement that seems to connect logically the first two sections: "A letter from America drove me out again, started me walking." Perhaps our questions from section 1 are being resolved here. Tranströmer, however, does not provide instant gratification; he continues in the labyrinth. The letter from America drives him out not during late autumn but on a June night, and he walks not in the woods but "in the empty suburban streets." This section also shifts from the private, solitary thoughts that surfaced as he walked in nature to larger public themes as he walks among the new buildings with America on his mind.

This section addresses the presence of evil in the world. In America, according to Tranströmer, "evil and good actually have faces," but in Sweden—"with us"—things are more complicated. Tranströmer does know that those "who run . . . errands for" death "rule from glass offices" and "mill about in the bright sun." The section ends not with an evil bang but with a transforming and momentarily saving image. Tranströmer, the seer, sees a building's window become a "mirrorlike lake with no waves" that reflects the night sky and the trees. Caught up in his vision, Tranströmer reflects, "Violence seemed unreal/ for a few moments." That closing line shows how briefly the moment of epiphany lasted.

The third section begins with an image that seems to come out of Alfred Hitchcock's film *North by Northwest* (1959). Readers turn from the dusk and night of sections 1 and 2 and face a burning sun. A plane comes out of nowhere in the poem and places its cruciform shadow on a man "poking at something" in a field. The poem then abandons the man and the plane and cuts, in a cinematic fashion, to the picture of a "cross hanging in the cool church vaults." The cross, in Tranströmer's eyes, resembles a "snapshot of something/ moving at tremendous speed." The poem, which also jumps and moves "at tremendous speed," does not end with any final statement that might wrap up the poem's meaning. It ends where it began, in a labyrinth of images.

Forms and Devices

Metaphors are often used by poets to give unity to a poem, especially one that stays away from the other more conventional unifying forces such as rhyme scheme or narrative structure. Tranströmer is no exception. The woods that the speaker enters in section 1 are described as "silent abandoned houses this time of year." When the speaker leaves the woods to find landmarks, he looks for a "house on the other side of the lake." He enters the house of the woods and leaves the woods to find a house. The metaphorical description of the house is both intriguing and odd. It is a "reddish square intense as a bouillon cube." The description helps the reader see the house, and serves as a link to section 2 when the "newborn" suburban blocks are "cool as blueprints." Readers leave the woods for the suburbs, the red of the rusty machine and the "reddish square" of the house for the metaphorical blueprints, and they abandon that "intense" bouillon cube-shaped house for the "cool" blocks of suburbia. The inversions and playful reshaping help keep the poem centered.

Another pattern emerges when the images associated with the city and the woods are compared. In the woods the near silence becomes mechanized. The few sounds the poet hears are compared to a person moving twigs "with pincers" or an "iron hinge . . . whining feebly inside a thick trunk." The same type of reversal takes place in the city: The constructed world becomes naturalized when the building windows are transformed into a "mirrorlike lake with no waves." These transformations do not seem to have thematic importance; they serve as structural aids only.

The most conventional figurative language in the poem comes in the second section when death is personified. As in so many other descriptions of death by both writers and painters, the abstraction becomes concrete: Death is a "he" who has people "run . . . errands for him." The conventionality of the image matches the simplicity of the concept: Evil seems external to Tranströmer. The bad people, death's right-hand men and women, "rule from glass offices" and "mill about in the bright sun." The good person—Tranströmer—stands outside the offices or in nature and walks around at night. It does not seem as if the poet implicates himself in the world's evil or its violence. He stands apart, the pure visionary.

Themes and Meanings

Any poem that has thirty-three lines divided into three sections and that begins with a man journeying through woods, nearly lost, and ends with the image of a cross must be, at least for an instant, compared with Dante's *The Divine Comedy* (c. 1320). Dante's epic, divided into three parts, with two of those parts divided into thirty-three cantos, begins with Dante lost in a dark forest and ends with a vision of God. Despite the similarities, the comparison is interesting mostly because of the differences between the two works. Tranströmer's poem is a modern journey through the hell of human violence and evil, but no hope is offered at the end. The cross of the plane's shadow or the cross in the "cool church vaults" might perhaps serve as a symbol of suffering, but there is certainly no hope of that suffering having any purpose. For Christians, the cross represents both suffering and hope, but Tranströmer's use of the image seems stripped of nearly all transcendent meaning. In the center of the cross made by the airplane's shadow lies no savior, but some nameless man "sitting in the field poking at something"; and the cross in the church not only appears to be empty, but also turns into something else, something stripped of value, "a split-second snapshot of something/ moving at tremendous speed." The camera eye and the speed of technology replace the formerly stable icon of Christianity.

What seems to be offered in the poem to replace the redemptive quality of the cross is the power of the poet's own imagination. Tranströmer is admired widely and has been translated by a number of poets because of the power in his lyrical voice. He banishes the normal hinges of a poem and creates a fresh vision that benefits from surprising metaphors and innovative transitions. Tranströmer, however, recognizes that all of his verbal pyrotechnics really end up not affecting the world in the least. His image of death's errands being run by office workers is horrifying; but equally horrifying is the idea that poetry does nothing to stop the devastation. A stunning image might make violence seem "unreal/ for a few moments," but the perception is false. Tranströmer admits that violence is real, suffering is always present, and poetry, like the speaker in the first section, can enter nature or a sheltered realm, but it also must return eventually to the central facts of life. As W. H. Auden once said, "Poetry makes nothing happen," but Tranströmer might counter this by saying that poetry lifts the reader, for an instant, from the realm of dull logic and violence to the pleasures of images "moving at tremendous speed" and metaphors operating with the logic of dreams.

Kevin Boyle

OUT OF THE CRADLE ENDLESSLY ROCKING

Author: Walt Whitman (1819-1892)

Type of poem: Narrative

First published: 1859, as "A Child's Reminiscence"; as "A World Out of the Sea," in *Leaves of Grass*, 1860; as "Out of the Cradle Endlessly Rocking," in *Leaves of Grass*, 1871

The Poem

"Out of the Cradle Endlessly Rocking" is a poem about memory—about the ways in which an adult poet remembers and understands his childhood, and the ways in which his childhood prepared him for his adult poetic life. Like other British and American Romantic poets, Walt Whitman was interested in this relationship between the formative years of youth and the creative years of adulthood. Thus, Whitman wrote this poem, which is similar to British poet William Wordsworth's "Lines: Composed a Few Miles Above Tintern Abbey" and American poet Henry Wadsworth Longfellow's "My Lost Youth."

The opening stanzas begin with the setting, describing the past, specifically, the past in Long Island (referred to by the Indian name "Paumanok") and the memory of the "bareheaded, barefoot" child—a popular theme of nineteenth century British and American artists. A musical motif, which continues throughout the poem, is introduced in the image of a bird whose singing enchants the narrator, reminding him of his past.

This memory, enlivened by the notion of song, is emphasized through an italicized stanza in which a pair of birds sings joyous songs, introducing two important ideas: the enlivening quality of music, and the power of the individual aria, which, in fact, is the kind of lyric this poem actually is.

The poem proceeds by announcing the death of the female bird, and the subsequent italicized arias move from a reference to waiting—"I wait and I wait till you blow my mate to me"—to despair: "We two together no more." Despite this "aria sinking," all else continues, and the boy poet realizes that he will be a poetic bard, a solitary bird, and a solitary singer.

The end of the poem focuses upon this image of the "solitary me"—the solitary poet—hearing the sea sing to him of death. Death, however, is not a terminal point. Instead, death is incorporated into life, just as the "old crone rocking the cradle" suggests that the entrance into life is similarly an introduction to death, which, in turn, prefaces more life. The cycle of life and death, important in all of Whitman's poems, is thus emphasized in the conclusion of this poem. The elder poet remembers his youth; the old crone rocks the cradle; and the sea whispers to the aging poet of past, present, and future.

Forms and Devices

"Out of the Cradle Endlessly Rocking" is notable for its use of free verse and imagery. Like the King James Version of the Bible, in which free verse is frequently found,

"Out of the Cradle Endlessly Rocking" relies upon the irregular rhythm of phrases, images, and lines rather than the conventional use of meter. Thus, in the first three lines of the poem, the emphasis is not upon feet or syllabic count, as it might be in other, more conventional forms of poetry, but rather upon the rhythm and repetition within the lines themselves:

> Out of the cradle endlessly rocking,
> Out of the mocking-bird's throat, the musical shuttle,
> Out of the Ninth-month midnight.

Whitman's use of imagery is similar to his reliance upon free verse in that the technique permeates, subtly yet pervasively, the entire poem. One such image is the rocking cradle, referred to in the title, in the first line, and then in the final lines of the poem, connecting all parts of this lyric by its reference to movement, to change, to the cycles of life.

Another image is that of the singing bird, introduced in the opening lines as "the bird that chanted" to the poet and used throughout the poem, culminating in the final lines, in which the song of the bird, as remembered from the poet's youth, is both recalled and transformed into the adult bard's song, sung to him by the sea and, in turn, metamorphosed into the poem itself.

Still another image is that of the youthful poet, described in traditional yet Whitmanesque terms as "alone, bareheaded, barefoot" in the first stanza of the poem. This image is recalled throughout the poem; the adult bard refers to his reminiscence of himself "with bare feet, a child, the wind wafting in my hair" in the middle section of the poem, and in the final stanzas understands that he will never again be that youth, that "peaceful child." The image of the singing bird that learns to sing alone (and as a mature voice) is a parallel to this image of the youth become adult, the boy become bard.

Another image that should be noted is that of the sea, reminder of both life's constancy and its changes. Like the bird that can transcend the death of its mate, and like the youth who can survive the change from boyhood to adulthood, the sea is represented in this poem as a body that answers the poet and that whispers to him. Its answer and whisper is the same—death—but it means more than simply death in that monosyllabic answer and whisper. It means death that ushers in life, that rocks a cradle of life and death.

Themes and Meanings

Walt Whitman was passionately in love with opera, and this passion is revealed in "Out of the Cradle Endlessly Rocking," with its reliance upon operatic techniques and references, in particular, the aria. Still another connection to the operatic form is the suggestion that apparent tragedy is cause for music, for hope, for a belief in the transcending power of life.

The first stanza of Whitman's poem ends with a line referring to the narrator's singing "a reminiscence." The reminiscence, in this case, is life that yields to death, which, in turn, ushers in new life. The arias sung by the birds present this cyclic view of life, as do the commentaries by the bard himself. It is not coincidental that the sea is critical in this remembering process and is the final image of the poem, for the sea is the image par excellence of change, of tides coming and going, of life continuing, despite storms and deaths, of songs sung by two that become arias sung by one. What comes out of a cradle endlessly rocking, in Whitman's view, is essentially life, then death, then more and endless life. The cycle, not the specific parts of the circle, is what finally counts.

Marjorie Smelstor

"OUT, OUT—"

Author: Robert Frost (1874-1963)
Type of poem: Narrative
First published: 1916, in *Mountain Interval*

The Poem

Robert Frost's "'Out, Out—'" describes a farm accident that unexpectedly and irrationally costs a young boy his life. The narrator of the poem sets the scene, seemingly from an outsider's perspective, reporting the incident with objectivity and restraint. Yet, as the narrative advances, underlying emotions and tensions surface as the persona builds to the poem's conclusion: the seemingly senseless, abrupt ending of the boy's life, followed by his family's subsequent return to their daily routines.

The first nine lines of the poem set the scene: the "snarl" of the saw and the "sweet-scented" smell of the wood as it is cut into "stove-length sticks." Beyond the farm, the late afternoon sun settles over "five mountain ranges" extending "far into Vermont." It has been an ordinary day on an ordinary farm, despite the exceptional beauty of its location: "And nothing happened: day was all but done." This section concludes with its foreboding note, its hint not just of nature's majesty but also its fearful possibilities for disrupting everyday life.

In the next nine lines of the poem, both the narrator and the boy sawing the wood are introduced. So, too, is the narrator's discomfort with the story he has to tell. The persona "wish[es]" that the boy's family had given him "the half hour" he craved to be a boy after a full day of work. Instead, the boy has toiled until his sister announces "Supper"—the very moment when the accident occurs. The narrator is unsure just how the boy's hand comes to be severed: whether the saw heard the word "supper," too, and "leaped out," or the boy did so, or both.

In the aftermath of the accident (the following eleven lines), the boy gives a "rueful laugh" as he "hold[s] up the hand," beseeching help in disbelief, while at the same time trying to prevent his own "life from spilling." Yet it is too late, as the boy suddenly realizes: "Then the boy saw all"; "He saw all spoiled." Being old enough to understand the adult world and do adult work, "though a child at heart," the boy knows how little value his life will have when he is missing a hand. What kind of farm work will he do? Of what use will he be? He begs, "'Don't let [the doctor] cut my hand off,'" but it is too late. His hand cannot be saved, and unexpectedly, it appears, neither can the boy himself: "And then—the watcher at his pulse took fright."

In the last four lines of the poem, readers are given the family's reaction—first shock; then a realistic acceptance of death, "that ended it"; and, finally, a seeming callousness: "And they, since they/ Were not the one dead, turned to their affairs." Life on the farm must go on. Now that the boy is dead, there is "No more to build on there"; they return to their daily chores, building what they can and living their own lives. There seems nothing more to be said or done, and the poem concludes abruptly.

Forms and Devices

"'Out, Out—'" is one of Frost's mid-length narrative poems, written in blank verse to convey natural speech rhythms. The poet uses simple, everyday language, words such as "supper," "buzz saw," "apron," and "big boy." However, the natural flow is broken by hard caesuras (abrupt breaks) in almost half the lines; these increase in number toward the end of the poem, where they occur often early in a line, rather than in the middle where a pause is more natural (for example, in line 27: "So. But the hand was gone already."). These breaks betray the emotionality underlying the narrator's restrained reporting style, as do the three exclamation points dotting the poem. The hard caesura interruptions also correspond to the accident's abrupt break in the day-to-day rhythms of farm routine and the boy's foreshortened life.

Frost immerses the reader in the scene of the poem by drawing on all the senses. He creates the sound of the "buzz saw" through the refrain of strong action verbs, "snarled and rattled," repeated three times in the first seven lines, and by using *s*, *t*, *d*, and *z* sounds early in the poem. He also re-creates for readers the "sweet-scented" smell of the shavings from the cut wood and the majestic view, as the sun sets over the five Vermont mountains that dwarf the farm below.

The narrator gives readers more than simple, realistic detail, however. Imaginative, fanciful commentary intrudes on the reporter's objectivity. The saw, personified through the words "As if to prove saws knew what supper meant," suddenly comes to life; it "seemed to leap" at the boy's hand. Here the speaker suggests the possibility of an inanimate object's becoming animate, of the tool's possibly human, and certainly unpredictable and destructive, qualities. The narrator's imagination allows for the possibility of such supernatural happenings, as it also enables him to empathize with the boy.

The speaker understands how reluctant the boy has been to take on adult responsibilities when he would rather have been playing. "I wish," the narrator admits, the boy's family might have been more sympathetic and allowed him to quit work earlier. Instead, it is the narrator who realizes the boy is still "a child at heart," not "they," his family, who should have been more understanding of his needs. Thus, tension is created between the narrator/outsider who reports the accident and the family insiders who turn away from it, despite their part in its occurrence.

The title underscores this narrative tension. It is taken from Macbeth's soliloquy at the end of William Shakespeare's *Macbeth* (pr. 1606), when his words "Out, out, brief candle!" express profound grief over the abrupt death by suicide of Lady Macbeth. Such an overt expression of grief is missing here on the part of the boy's family, however, though not on the part of the poet who has made Macbeth's anguished cry his title. The words also suggest Lady Macbeth's torment before her suicide, "Out, damned spot! Out, I say!" as she vainly tries to wash away the blood of murder from her hands. So, too, as the boy's relatives turn away to resume their chores, they may find themselves unable to wash his blood from their hands. They may only appear to have washed away their sense of responsibility (however unintentional) for his death and their grief over his loss through their traditional New England stoicism and reticence.

Themes and Meanings

Frost based his poem on an accident that had taken place six years before, which had taken the life of a sixteen-year-old boy, Raymond Fitzgerald, in nearby Bethlehem, New Hampshire. Frost focuses on this small event to suggest the larger themes of his poetry: the isolation of the individual, the mystery of human existence, the ambiguity of nature, and the need to create order and meaning out of chaos.

As in his poem "Design," Frost in "'Out, Out—'" asks whether the pattern of nature is an evil one or simply random, haphazard, and indifferent to human life. Is there a malignant force unleashed through the buzz saw and responsible for the boy's death—or one as unheeding and unfeeling as the distant mountain range that forms a breathtaking backdrop to this human tragedy? Is the boy's death simply an elemental fact of nature (as the family's response to their son's death suggests) or an aberrant tragedy to be pondered and dissected? Is the proper response the New Englanders' verbal restraint and quiet resignation to fate or a more emotional outburst, a refusal to accept what does not make sense? Perhaps nature should not be blamed at all but, instead, humanity's disruption of nature through the use of buzz saws and other technological developments.

As the narrative of the poem unravels, conflicts appear subtly between different perspectives on life: the boy's desire to play versus the family's insistence on work; the narrator's imagination and empathy versus his own report's simple language, realistic detail, and blunt ending; the family's seeming heartlessness versus their sense of responsibility for, and grief over, the boy's death; nature's glorious beauty versus its daily sordidness and cruelty; the boy's solitary fate versus his family's togetherness and ongoing communal activity; the New England "insiders'" acceptance of fate versus the narrator "outsider's" more emotional response; the meaning of existence versus its utter insignificance; technological development as a necessary advance for humanity versus its unnaturalness and destructive potential. Frost's poem gives no final answers to the issues it raises; despite the finality of the boy's death, the poem remains open-ended, its many questions unanswered.

For Frost, the craft of writing a poem, like that of expertly cutting and stacking wood, creates order out of chaos. Faced with the perplexity of life, its many accidents, mysteries, deaths, and dramas, Frost uses language to give shape to important life issues and ask significant questions. Through words, he both draws near and distances the tragedies of life, orders nature's constant disorder, and communicates the largely inarticulate and isolated nature of human existence. In "'Out, Out—,'" Frost both embraces and cries out against the vicissitudes of life, as he does in the final words carved on his gravestone in Bennington, Vermont: "I had a lover's quarrel with the world."

Susan S. Adams

OVID IN THE THIRD REICH

Author: Geoffrey Hill (1932-   )
Type of poem: Dramatic monologue
First published: 1968, in *King Log*

The Poem

"Ovid in the Third Reich" is a short poem in two quatrains (four-line stanzas) of accentual verse; that is, the line is governed by the number of stressed, or accented, syllables. It is a dramatic monologue in which the poet speaks in the persona of the ancient Roman poet Ovid. The title, however, places him in the Third Reich of Adolf Hitler's Germany, instead of the first years of the Roman Empire under the Emperor Augustus. It is clear from the title that Geoffrey Hill intends a parallel to be drawn between the two periods. They compare very clearly in several ways: First, both states were totalitarian; in both states there was such a thing as correct thinking; and deviation from general opinion was frowned upon and thought subversive in both. Second, both rulers tended to be puritanical in their habits and tastes. Women were expected to be mothers, cooks, and keepers of the state faith. Third, the expression of art, literature, and the free spirit essential to them were severely curbed to accommodate the purposes of the state. The question arises as to what a poet such as Ovid can and should do under a vicious, stultifying, and brutal dictatorship.

For the epigraph, Hill selects one of Ovid's own lines, from the *Amores* (c. 20 B.C.E.). Although variously translated, and ambiguous in itself, the meaning relevant to "Ovid in the Third Reich" can be paraphrased: He who refuses to accept himself as guilty is not guilty. Only those who are well-known (who have played a part in the affair?) must, of necessity, profess their guilt. Whereas the Roman poet historically was banished from his beloved city, Ovid in the Third Reich accepts a self-imposed banishment rather than take part in the madness about him. Both suffer fearfully. The Roman is exiled to the farther shores of the Black Sea to live his days among barbarous folk, as he complains in one of his poems; Ovid in the Third Reich is forced by banishment to endure limitations, is deprived of the life of the city, the joy of companions, and the freedom to love and create.

This Ovid is reduced to the essentials in his life: "I love my work and my children." As a poet, he bears witness to the terrible time. He has learned one thing, as he says, that the vicious are as tormented as the damned. Strangely, though, they are part of the divine plan. In the world of the contraries, they make the harmony of the world; if man does not see and hear the dissonant, he cannot know the vibrancy of concord and the good and love. As dire as the days may be, he knows himself to be part of the "love-choir," in which, as a poet, he will always sing.

Forms and Devices

There is an impression of completeness in Geoffrey Hill's "Ovid in the Third Reich" that comes from the perfect unity of the subject and the poetic devices he employs, namely, the poem's diction, its rhythm, and its form—three essentials in the craft of poetry.

In the first stanza, the fear and trauma of events have reduced the poet—usually of an expansive nature—to sentences that reveal little emotion and lines that are short and declarative: "God/ Is distant, difficult." A lack of coherent thought is apparent as he moves erratically from subject to subject, as if his emotion has been dammed at its source.

The diction, too, is denotative and literal, which suggests a tautness and a matter-of-factness, as though, like God, the poet would distance himself from the scene. All sensitivity to shades of meaning and feeling has been stripped from the poet's vocabulary, leaving him with only the most general and simplest words to describe the complexity of his impressions. "Things happen," he tersely comments. Exactly what things the poet perhaps dares not or cannot say. This uncommunicative tone is overwhelmed, finally, by the last two lines of the first stanza. Sentences that have been of the simplest construction (subject, verb, direct object), with monosyllabic words, suddenly expand to accommodate "Innocence is no earthly weapon" under the impact of his reflections. Not for the first time have the "ancient troughs" run with the blood of the innocent, revealing the darker side of man's nature. Primitive rituals demanded blood sacrifice then, and the cultism of the Nazis demands it now, as an extension of that barbarity into the twentieth century.

With this insight, the diction begins to expand, and the trip-hammer rhythms of the first stanza become less strident and insistent. The strict regular blows of the spondee in "I have learned one thing: not to look down" gives way to a gentler rhythm. The form itself opens like a floodgate, as if liberated by the recognition that the events the poet has witnessed "Harmonize strangely." This frees him for even greater speculation.

The poet alludes, finally, to the "sphere," a metaphor for the universe, recalling ancient Pythagorean cosmology, in which the contraries of the world are met in the music of the spheres and all seeming disharmony is reconciled in accordance with the laws of nature. The poet, however, presents the idea in a Christian context, in which the contraries of good and evil are alluded to in an image from Dante's *The Divine Comedy* (c. 1320). The damned, embodying the evil in human nature, are still part of the greater design of God and must be accepted—if not with charity, at least with forbearance. Man is free to choose his own path. The damned are their own hell.

Themes and Meanings

"Ovid in the Third Reich" prompts two questions in particular. What is a good man is to do when faced with such consummate evil? What is a poet to do?

The major philosophical basis of the poem is the belief that the world of nature is an eternal battleground on which good and evil, love and hate, and tyranny and freedom are in ceaseless conflict. Since there is nothing new under the sun, as the author of Ecclesiastes asserts, the drama of history will be repeated over and over.

Man confronts evil in many ways: He may choose direct action, thereby courting martyrdom. He may, on the contrary, retreat into the comfortable ease of the accepted views of the state, accepted by the mass of men; in this case, by his very passivity he gives his assent to the evil.

Customarily, and from earliest times, the role of the poet has been clearly understood and honored. He is, first, a historian recording the events of society. "Things happen," Ovid in the Third Reich avers. The poet, furthermore, must cultivate a clear perception and objectivity in order that he should be neither a propagandist nor an apologist; in effect, he must keep his distance, very like a god. He must also, finally, come to terms with his own emotional response. He must fully acknowledge the concentration camps, as others have acknowledged the "ancient troughs of blood." In an intuitive leap from experience, the poet comes to a philosophical or spiritual knowledge which satisfies or at least consoles. In "Ovid in the Third Reich," the consolation comes from the recognition that, in the biblical phrase, "one must render unto Caesar the things that are Caesar's and unto God, the things that are God's." Man cannot judge. Thus, the poet tries to wrestle with the age-old Christian problem: How can God be omnipotent and all good? If He is omnipotent, then He purposely allows evil to flourish; if all good, then He must be limited, for an all-good, omnipotent God would prevent the evil of the world. It is the individual who tips the balance, not nations, which are a construct of man. In this final representation, Hill confirms the meaning of the epilogue. As a poet, he knows—as did Ovid in the first century—that no tyranny, oppressive and limiting as it may be, can destroy man's thought and feelings, for the mind is a very private place. The individual, if he has not intentionally violated the laws of man, nature, and God, cannot be guilty. He is still part of the "love-choir."

Maureen W. Mills

OZYMANDIAS

Author: Percy Bysshe Shelley (1792-1822)
Type of poem: Sonnet
First published: 1818; collected in *Rosalind and Helen: A Modern Eclogue, with Other Poems*, 1819

The Poem

"Ozymandias" is a sonnet composed by the Romantic poet Percy Bysshe Shelley and named for its subject, with the Greek name of the Egyptian king Ramses II, who died in 1234 B.C.E. The poem follows the traditional structure of the fourteen-line Italian sonnet, featuring an opening octave, or set of eight lines, that presents a conflict or dilemma, followed by a sestet, or set of six lines, that offers some resolution or commentary upon the proposition introduced in the octave.

The poem is conventionally written in iambic pentameter (that is, ten syllables per line of coupled unstressed then stressed sounds), so the poem's subject matter is framed both by the structural and metrical constraints chosen by the poet.

The first-person narrator of "Ozymandias" introduces a conversation he has chanced to have with a "traveller from an antique land" in line 1. The reader knows neither the identity of the traveler nor the circumstances wherein the poet has encountered the traveler but may assume he is a source of information about a strange and unfamiliar world.

The remaining thirteen lines of the poem quote verbatim the tale that the traveler has borne from his trek into the desert. The intrepid explorer has encountered "Two vast and trunkless legs of stone," the vestiges of a statue in disrepair whose head lay as a "shattered visage" nearby. Despite its broken state, the "frown," the "wrinkled lip" and "sneer of cold command" of the statue's face bespeak its sculptor's skill in capturing the vanity and self-importance of its subject.

The traveler remarks that the artist has "well those passions read which yet survive"—that is, those indications of the subject's character, indelibly "stamped on . . . lifeless things": "the hand that mocked them, and the heart that fed."

The octave thus confronts the reader in its first movement with an ironic portrait of an ancient monarch whose fame and stature have been immortalized in a static gaze that connotes paradoxically both celebrity and dissolution. In the revelatory sestet which follows, the poet posits, through the testimony of the traveler, the fate of vainglorious men. On the pedestal, he finds written the great man's empty boast: "My name is Ozymandias, King of Kings,/ Look on my Works, ye Mighty, and despair!"

Yet "Nothing beside remains" but ruin, a "colossal Wreck, boundless and bare" against the lonely landscape of sand and cruel, penetrating sunlight. A double irony is at work; neither the great man nor the work of the artist remains in credible shape to challenge or delight the imagination of those who would encounter it. King and artisan, mover and maker, share the same destiny. The poem ends with the reader/observer's gaze fixed upon this pathetic legacy, contemplating his own mortality.

Forms and Devices

The Italian sonnet presents the poet with the challenge of using an utterly familiar form in an innovative or provocative way. The chief variables within this form involve rhyme scheme. The traditional Italian sonnet features an *abba, abba, cde, cde* rhyme scheme, each letter representing a different end rhyme that is repeated in pattern.

In "Ozymandias," Shelley chooses to forgo the conventional scheme and employs a more eccentric *abab, acdc, ece, fef* pattern that creates the immediate effect of a woven tapestry of sound and rhythm that helps to underscore the poem's essential irony. As the reader's expectations are unmet, the very syntax forced by the unusual rhyme of the poem creates tension that matches that of the theme.

Critics have long noted the "Chinese box" frame in which the story of Ozymandias has come to the poet and thus, indirectly, to the reader. Each line of the poem, from first to last, reveals successively one more layer of the narrative's essential irony.

One learns first something of the poet's conversation with the mysterious traveler "from an antique land." The poet, in turn, reports but one tidbit of that conversation, "Who said—," in the very words of the traveler. Laboriously, the speaker then moves through each wave of recognition and interpretation of what he has encountered, climaxing with the presentation of Ozymandias's inscription.

Shelley's sonnet is remarkable for its spare and stark imagery. The poet is determined to re-create the barren desert landscape, the poetic counterpoint to the morbid and deserved fate of Ozymandias, the pompous fool. To do so requires that he carefully circumscribe his choice of descriptors to connote neither grandeur nor panoramic vista, but rather singular loneliness and constrained, fragmented solitude. Hence such modifiers as "trunkless," "Half-sunk," "shattered," "decay," and "wreck" serve his purpose well.

Consequently, the compression of the sonnet form, the unconventional rhyme scheme, the point of view chosen for reader entry, and the carefully wrought diction of the poem achieve the effect the poet was seeking. Amid vast stretches of unbroken sameness, the traveler—followed by the poet, then the reader—comes upon a bleak personage whose severed limbs and head first shock and dismay, then elicit reluctant mockery for the egotism of its subject.

Themes and Meanings

"Ozymandias" is at first glance a sonnet about the transitory nature of life and its pretensions of fame and fortune. The decaying, ancient statue bears witness to the fact that the pursuit of power and glory for their own sakes are not only fleeting, but they are also illusory, unworthy ambitions even within the lifetime of their seekers.

The nineteenth century was filled with "discoveries" of ancient landscapes, built upon a historiography of "great men," who were to elicit the attention and admiration of a generation of scholars and writers. Shelley chose, however, to poke holes in the "great man" theory of history, questioning its validity and its rationality.

The poem also works on another level, however—as a candid, poignant confession by the artist that his work is also ephemeral, and that as style, manner, and fashion change, so do reputation and honor. Such a confessional spirit was particularly appropriate for Shelley and other Romantics, that clan of "rebel spirits"—among them William Blake; George Gordon; Lord Byron; John Keats; Samuel Taylor Coleridge; and William Wordsworth.

This new generation of poets flouted tradition, inventing their own vocabularies, subject matters, and poetic form, and generally laboring to raise the poet's consciousness of his own imagination to an unprecedented level. "Ozymandias" exemplifies both in theme and in execution these "rebellious" notions.

Often, the poet himself was the topic and focus of his poetry, rather than the grander themes of man and God or the courtship of ladies and gentlemen. Audiences for the first time were confronted with the artist's "personality," and not only his work. Autobiography, not history, was to become the focal point of literary endeavor—and literary criticism.

The Romantics revitalized the craft of poetry in the nineteenth century, rescuing it from the narrow constraints of "classicism" built upon elevated language, artificial form, and exaggerated dependence on tradition. The price paid for this departure was the risk of alienating themselves from public taste and private virtue. The Romantics, Shelley chief among them, constructed their own "traditions" in various manifestos about the components, meaning, and social utility of poetry, even offering advice about how their poetry should be interpreted.

More than that, Shelley, in works such as *Prometheus Unbound* (1820) and *A Defence of Poetry* (1840), attempted to create a public persona for the poet as an arbiter of morality, genius, and political order. Thus, the Romantic, as exemplified in Shelley himself, was peculiarly subject to the rather pretentious self-promotion of his vocation—not unlike the wizened Ozymandias of his sonnet.

The ancient king's narcissism, his relentless declarations of immortality and supremacy, might serve as warning also to the artist whose folly may lead him to similar vanity. Read this way, "Ozymandias" is a sober exhortation to poets and politicians alike to foster realistic assessments of their influence and worth; the disposition to make truth serve the selfish ends of vainglorious men is a theme of history Shelley discerned well in his own time and attempted to expose in his poetry. In that regard, "Ozymandias" remains a powerful antidote to artistic pretensions and political hypocrisy.

Bruce L. Edwards

THE PANGOLIN

Author: Marianne Moore (1887-1972)
Type of poem: Ode
First published: 1936, in *The Pangolin and Other Verse*

The Poem

"The Pangolin" is a long, unrhymed, syllabic poem of ninety-eight lines in nine stanzas; eight stanzas have eleven lines and one has ten. The title refers to the class of animals known commonly as anteaters.

In the first half of the poem, Moore offers a rich and intense description of the anteater. She is fascinated by the armor plate, comparing the scaly covering to the layers of an artichoke with its tough, spiny leaves that protect a delicate and delectable inner meat. She focuses attention on the animal's nocturnal habits, its night feeding, its walking on the edges of its hands to save its claws for digging. Nevertheless, for all its outer toughness, the anteater avoids fights; when threatened, it can wind itself around trees and curl up into a hard ball to protect itself against its enemies.

As day breaks, the pangolin withdraws into its nest of rocks, which it closes with earth from inside to shut out the light. In the third stanza, Moore pauses briefly to observe that both humans and pangolins have a splendor, an excellence, but in humans those qualities coexist with an innate vileness.

Returning to the anteater in stanza 4, Moore comments on the animal's courage, manifested in a struggle with the dread driver ant, notorious for its warlike ferocity. Protected by its armor, the anteater attacks with both tongue and tail, an instrument of great power. If not threatened, the anteater will climb down from a tree; otherwise it will drop and walk away unhurt.

In stanza 5, Moore switches direction. Although she begins with a rich description of the anteater's multipurpose tail, she introduces a new term that applies to this body part: "graceful." Moore finds this grace in the anteater's movements at night. She comments that the animal's movements are not made graceful by virtue of its condition in life—it has not had to deal with "adversities" and "conversities."

In stanza 6, Moore turns to a direct examination of grace. Yet instead of providing a definition of "grace," she compounds the issue by raising a question of its nature, proposing various ways of looking at the meaning. Appearing to return to the subject of pangolins in stanza 7, she veers off into a consideration of the moral nature of humankind. In the inquiry, humans come up lacking.

This comparison is continued in stanza 8, where Moore declares that humans, the writing masters of the world, do not like comparisons that are denigrating. Nevertheless, humans have the capacity of humor that helps alleviate the struggle of existence. Moreover, humans have the qualities of "everlasting vigor," the "power to grow," though they also have the power to create fear and anxiety.

In the final stanza, Moore considers humans as a species of mammal—fearful, limited, and dependent on the sun, the light of day, for completing their enterprises and rejuvenating their souls.

Forms and Devices

"The Pangolin" appears to be a sprawling, formless unrhymed poem with widely varying line lengths, irregular meter, and little or no stanza pattern. Indeed, the poem does not appear to resemble traditional poetry. This impression, however, is part of its method and its charm. As a radical modernist poet, Moore utilizes a variety of visual, typological, auditory, and stylistic devices to give the appearance that her poem does not conform to traditional expectations regarding the look, sound, and content of poetry. A more critical look at the poem quickly dispels this impression, however; the apparent formlessness gives way to highly formal and traditional elements.

The largest element of form is the nine stanzas that are identified only by the two line spaces separating them. Otherwise, the stanzas flow into one another, as the last lines of each run into the next stanza. Each stanza has eleven lines (with one exception, the fifth stanza has ten lines) that follow an almost regular pattern of line lengths, measured by syllable count.

The dominant pattern of line lengths is established in the first stanza (9-14-9-17-12-11-15-8-5-9-9). Although this pattern is not exactly adhered to, Moore tries to stick closely to it from stanza to stanza. Thus, in stanza 2, the pattern is 9-15-8-16-13-12-13-8-4-10-10. She takes similar liberties throughout the remaining stanzas, perhaps because it was impossible to do otherwise in order to use the words she wanted, or because she preferred to introduce variety.

Another element of the poem's form is its music. Moore makes exquisite use of the musical devices of assonance, alliteration, and consonance. These devices of sound substitute for the more rhythmical pattern of standard meter and end rhyme, and they create a pattern of sound that is full of wit, whimsy, and surprise. The first line of the poem employs all three of these musical devices. The *a* in "another" "armored," "animal," and "scale" all combine to form an assonant pattern of vowel sounds that is supplemented by the alliteration of *n*, *m*, and *r* sounds and the consonantal sound of *l* in the same words. The accumulation of these sounds creates a sense of the whimsical treatment of the subject. The pattern also helps bind the words one to another, and each to the larger structure of meaning. Such elements appear throughout the poem and contribute to the rich pattern of sound and meaning.

Moore also uses a technique of incongruous associations of images, much like the English Metaphysical poets of the seventeenth century, who developed with great power the "conceit," a device that telescoped images of widely different associations to create a startling and witty perception of reality. Such images appear in line 4, where Moore compares the pangolin to an artichoke, or in line 6, where she compares the pangolin to Leonardo da Vinci, who, as both artist and engineer, created a drawing of an armored vehicle. In the third stanza, Moore describes the pangolin in terms of the grace of the wrought-iron vine designed in 1290 by the famous smith named Thomas—from the town of Leighton Buzzard—for the tomb of Eleanor of Castile.

Themes and Meanings

"The Pangolin" is a manifestation of Moore's passion for observation and rendering what the Germans called the *ding an sich* ("the thing in itself"). She turned her keen eye to the pangolin for the purpose of creating a real anteater in an imaginary world. Above all, her aim is to provide the reader with such a rich and powerful description of this creature that it will become a living imaginary presence. Her training in biology and in the methods of science are put to excellent use, as stanza by stanza the pangolin takes on a more substantial existence.

The poet's frame of reference for bringing this creature to life is not rooted in biology alone, but rather in human culture. In the initial stanzas where Moore details the major characteristics of the pangolin, she makes three references to give the pangolin added dimension: In stanza 1, she refers to da Vinci; in stanza 3, to Thomas (the medieval smith); and in stanza 4, to the modern Spanish sculptor, Pablo Gargallo y Catalán.

These cultural references are part of a structure of meaning that evolves within the poem. Not content to rest with observation of the pangolin, Moore takes the reader on an imaginative flight into the consideration of the moral condition of humans. This transition occurs in the final four stanzas, in which the pangolin falls into the background and human behavior becomes Moore's focus.

In stanza 6, she begins with the question of "grace." Following her logic is no simple matter, but it appears that she asks why—given the fact that grace promises eternal salvation—those who developed the idea would confuse it with lesser meaning, such as a "kindly manner," the period in which to repay debts, the cure for sins, or the stone mullions that are part of the architecture of a church ceiling?

Her answer is no answer, but an image of the "sail boat," "the first machine," followed by the image of pangolins that also move quietly and are "models of exactness." These images are clues to the poetic and moral sensibility toward which this poem evolves. Poems can be "models of exactness," and the enterprise of the poet can be to create such models. Such activity has high moral value for Moore, who seems to subscribe to the Romantic idea that poetry has a high moral purpose.

Life, on the other hand, is far from exact—it is messy and confusing. In the next two stanzas, Moore presents an ambivalent view of humans, whom she sees as destructive of the natural world, but nevertheless industrious, and paradoxically, unemotional and emotional. Torn between these perceptions of humankind, she allows that among animals only "*one* has a sense of humor," which to her is clearly a mitigating factor, a saving grace in humans, whom she otherwise castigates for their failings.

In the final paragraph, Moore's attention shifts clearly from pangolin to human. Implicitly contrasting humans to the nocturnal pangolins, she presents humans as creatures—mammals—who inhabit the light and for whom the sun provides a constant source of renewal and strength. Despite her reservations, she concludes with a celebration of human existence.

Richard Damashek

THE PANTHER

Author: Rainer Maria Rilke (1875-1926)
Type of poem: Meditation
First published: 1907, as "Der Panther," in *Neue Gedichte*; English translation collected in *Translations from the Poetry of Rainer Maria Rilke*, 1938

The Poem

"The Panther" is a brief poem of twelve lines divided into three quatrains, each following the rhyme scheme *abab*. The title indicates the object of the poet's meditations.

From 1905 to 1906, the German poet Rainer Maria Rilke worked as secretary to the French sculptor Auguste Rodin. After studying a small bronze of a tiger sculpted by Rodin, Rilke visited the Jardin des Plantes in Paris to observe a captive panther. Conventionally, a panther suggests feral violence; however, the poem overturns such expectations. The reader's experience of the predatory creature climaxes in what critic Siegfried Mandel calls "the psychological terror of absolute inward stillness."

The first quatrain describes the captive animal's vision as having grown weary, so that all he perceives are blurs, or things without definition or significance. Such deterioration is a symptom of the animal's imprisonment. The bars that surround him multiply in his sight to a thousand; he can only glimpse fragmentary images of what lies beyond. His universe is thus rendered monotonous and meaningless.

The second quatrain reinforces this sense of futility by conveying the circularity of the panther's movement. His incessant pacing also suggests that the imprisoned animal harbors reserves of force and rebellion. The intensity of this contained energy is implied by the suppleness and massiveness of the animal's tread. The image the poet creates is of a coiled wire; the creature's awesome stride is restricted to a circle whose size and scope is "miniature." The focus on this "dance of strength" shifts at the quatrain's end to the circle's immobile center, the site of a "powerful" yet "benumbed" will.

The panther's vision also dominates the third quatrain, though this time the reader observes not from the outside but from the inside. The immobility that closes the previous quatrain extends now to the animal's "tense, quiet limbs" and climaxes with the death of the image that slips through his randomly open eyes. This image searches out the heart, or the center, where it is annihilated. The imprisoned consciousness has lost its power or will to grasp the reality beyond it.

Forms and Devices

Rilke's association with Rodin, as well as the painter Paul Cézanne, led him to develop what the poet called *Dinggedichte*, or "thing poems." Rilke considered "The Panther," an early example of this type, one of his favorite poems, because it had shown him "the way to artistic integrity."

Rilke strove to make his poems self-contained and compact with meaning, like works of visual art. Like a painter or sculptor, Rilke crafted concrete forms and perspective by means of what Mandel terms "the illusion of movement." The panther's concentric pacing gives it volume and dimension, as well as animating the poem with tension and balance and ultimately drawing the reader inward. Contrast ("soft pace" and "supple massive stride") and repetition ("pace," "stride," "dance") create patterns of motion, which, like ocean waves, produce a visual surface. It is this surface that reflects the poet's inner mood, as waves mirror the tide.

According to the poet W. H. Auden, Rilke was "almost the first poet since the seventeenth century to find a fresh solution" to the problem of "how to express abstract ideas in concrete terms." Auden wrote that Rilke thought with "physical" symbols, that he imagined the human "in terms of the non-human, of what he calls Things (*Dinge*)." The panther's repetitive motion and mechanical, cameralike registering of images emphasize his "thingness." Rilke reinforces the poem's effect of concreteness with his choice of plain, simple vocabulary. He rejects erudite and florid language in favor of unassuming speech. Complexity is achieved by the poem's imagery.

To ensure concentration of thought and feeling, Rilke develops the image of the caged panther into an extended metaphor. This device also produces the symmetry and self-sufficiency of visual art. Much of the richness attributed to Rilke's poetry derives from the coherence of his imagery. In addition, critics have commented on how Rilke's interplay of meter and rhyme create a subtle music, whose rhythm and internal balance help draw the reader into the poem's self-contained world.

Themes and Meanings

The philosopher Martin Heidegger claimed that his own work had been an attempt to articulate in philosophical language what Rilke had confronted symbolically in his poems. Heidegger's existentialist philosophy defined the human condition as "being exposed to nothingness." "Rilke's captive Panther," states critic Erich Heller, is a "Zoological relation of [Vincent] Van Gogh's Sunflowers, those rapacious 'things' that draw the whole world into their dark centers." Rilke wrote about nothingness in a strangely compelling, almost erotic way. The panther he evokes as a symbol of deadening loss attracts the reader with a horrifying magnetism.

Rilke, like William Blake, rarely lapsed into sentimentality about nature's primal chaos. At the same time, he yielded to its mysteries, unflinchingly following to their heart of darkness. In such sympathetic contemplation, he discovered a transcendence achieved through the imagination, which enabled him to overcome his despair at the spiritual bankruptcy modern life afforded him. For Rilke, the intensity of poetic vision provided him entry into the realm of the spiritual and the eternal.

Rilke's poetry reveals a man sensitive to the dualities of existence, creatively seeking to unify experience. Critics have noted in his work the complementary themes of lament and praise. In "The Panther," for example, even as he grieves over the animal's captivity, Rilke extols the power and elegance of its gait.

The poet presents the caged panther as a figure of tragedy, invoking terror and pity. Trapped by the exigencies of time and space and matter, it is emblematic of the terror of contingency. The captive animal attains transcendence, paradoxically, once it is captured in the poem, an eternally existing object of the poet's imagination.

Amy Adelstein

PARISIAN DREAM

Author: Charles Baudelaire (1821-1867)
Type of poem: Lyric
First published: 1861, as "Reve parisien," in *Les Fleurs du mal*, second edition; English translation collected in *Flowers of Evil*, 1963

The Poem

"Parisian Dream" is divided into two parts, the first consisting of thirteen quatrains, the second of two. The eight-syllable lines rhyme in a simple, alternating *abab* pattern. Composed in 1860, this poem was included in the second edition of *Flowers of Evil* in the section "Tableaux parisiens" ("Parisian Tableaux"). The title announces a dream, qualified by the location "Paris," the loved and hated city to which Charles Baudelaire devoted much of his verse and in which he lived most of his creative life.

Part I recounts a dream remembered on awakening. A first person narrator speaks in the past tense, recalling a terrible but fascinating landscape from which he succeeded in banishing the irregular forms of plants. As a painter proud of his genius, he savored the intoxicating monotony of metal, marble, and water. Not a "natural" landscape, but one determined by architecture, it is an infinite palace, a "Babel" tower reaching to the heavens, where water is present in cascades falling into golden basins, crystal curtains falling along metal walls. Instead of trees, there are columns surrounding pools where gigantic naiads mirror themselves. Sheets of water between colored piers extend to the bounds of the universe. Great rivers pour from the skies into diamond abysses. An air of magic and myth hangs over the landscape; naiads are drawn from classical myth, the Babel tower from the Bible, the Ganges river personification from India.

The narrator calls himself an "architect" and his world a fairyland; he shaped his world with his own will and tamed an ocean to pass through a jeweled tunnel. Even the color black took on rainbow lightness, and light was crystallized to hold liquid. There was no sun, no exterior source of light—all illumination originated within the miraculous constructions themselves. There was no sound—"All for the eye, nothing for the ears." The words, "A silence of eternity," end the first section and the description of the dream universe.

In the two stanzas of part 2, the poet returns to reality, opening flame-filled eyes on the shack in which the real man must live. Where he was exalted in dream, he is now horrified, his soul full of worries. There is sound in the waking world: A clock strikes noon, and the sky casts shadows on a sad, sleepy world.

Forms and Devices

"Parisian Dream" is extremely clear and simple in form. Its eight-syllable verses move along quickly. They are neither cut nor run on, and the regular rhyme scheme is equally smooth. The first person narrator enters the poem in the first stanza and remains consistent throughout the poem. There are no ambiguities in time; the description of the dream world is entirely in the imperfect tense, which implies a continued or habitual action in the past. Thus, the dream world exists in a past time with no hard and fast boundaries, yet clearly distinct from the waking world of the second section, which is marked by use of two past tense verbs, "I saw . . . and felt." The imperfect tense is also used for the clock and the sky of the outer world, the habitual limits of everyday existence.

In its vocabulary and images, "Parisian Dream" appeals to the visual world, first as a painting, then as architecture. It is a "tableau," a picture, and the elements it evokes are water, gold and metal, precious stones, and crystal and marble, all agents which reflect or prismatically divide light. The color qualities of light are important. Not only is there blue water between green and rose-colored piers, but black is polished, light, rainbow colored. Baudelaire, a lover of pictorial art, uses words to produce a visual illusion. In the waking world of part 2, the sky sends shadows, not light, on the world and the return of sound, in the stroke of noon, is harsh and funereal.

Many terms are borrowed from architecture, an art of pure form, and from its materials and its constructions: staircases, arcades, basins, colonnades, and piers. These constructions are preferred to natural growth; vegetable irregularity is banished and colonnades replace rows of trees. The eye meets the regular swoops and curves of arcades and basins rather than unformed mountains or living beings. Water is architectural form in motion as well as an agent of light; cascades, cataracts, pools, sheets, and ice are all sculpted and tamed by the poet-architect. Unlike "real" water, it is purely, eerily silent.

Within the context of images of light and architectural form, the use of a vocabulary of magic and miracle is striking. Parallel with the objective world of the technical arts is the world of myth, dream, and emotion. The "monotony" of metal, marble, and water is "intoxicating." Naiads are beside the colonnades and pools, waves are magical, and rivers become the divine Ganges. The vision is qualified as a "miracle," "fairyland," "prodigy," and "moving marvel." The use of the first person narrator ensures emotional involvement in a dream world from which life and its irregularities are banished. The use of magical, emotional vocabulary ensures the complication of the mineral landscape with the qualities of human feeling.

Themes and Meanings

Baudelaire's collection of poems, *Flowers of Evil*, explores the dissonance between poetic sensitivity and the realities of life, both in people and in nature. The poet constructs many ideal landscapes, among them the erotic paradise of "Invitation to the Voyage" and the rooftop idyll of "Landscape." Where his visions may include living beings and combine delights of all the senses, "Parisian Dream" is austere and exclusive, lifeless, sunless, soundless.

There is no movement in the dreamscape except water in fountains, rivers, waves, oceans, and cataracts. This water is present in both liquid and crystal states, but not in foggy or obscure forms. There are no "misty skies" or "moist suns," as in "The Invitation to the Voyage." All edges are clear. The eternal rush of water duplicates the effect of stillness; cataracts fall like curtains, unendingly hung on metal walls.

Although the moving waters of the first twelve stanzas are described uniquely in visual terms, it is a shock to realize that they are all soundless, so strong is the habit of associating water in any form with some kind of characteristic sound. The poet announces this silence as a "terrible novelty." Ultimately, the reader hears only the murmur of words as they fall in their pattern of rhythm and rhyme.

It is equally unsettling that the light that flashes from the surfaces of the dreamscape is not sunlight but a "personal fire" from within. Unlike sunlight, this inward illumination casts no shadows. It is all brilliance without darkness. Even black is polished light in rainbow hues, not absence of light. The poet strives to reach a world so intensely personal that, although infinite and eternal, it is wholly controlled and internal. When he returns to the waking world, his eyes are still "full of flame," his own personal fire.

The suppression of the sun is an escape from time and mortality. The return to the waking world, with its harsh noontime shadows, is deathly. "The Clock," the last poem of the "Spleen and Ideal" section of *Flowers of Evil*, develops the theme of the tick of a clock as perpetual memento mori or reminder of mortality. In "The Sun," the second of the "Parisian Tableaux," the sun is "cruel" but also a "nourishing father" who "like a poet" descends into the life of cities and ennobles the vilest things. "Parisian Dream" attributes the creative power and illuminating beauty of the sun to the poet, liberated by the magic of sleep from death and shadow.

The world of the dream is also liberated from organic life, "irregular vegetable nature." The sonnet "Beauty," found in the "Spleen et idéal" ("Spleen and Ideal") section of *Flowers of Evil*, evokes the "dream of stone," where timeless, static beauty is given a voice and describes her relation to poets. The love she inspires is "eternal and mute as matter." This "beauty" never laughs or cries but hates movement, an essential quality of life, because it "displaces lines." Here, as in "Parisian Dream," the poet dreams of a mineral world where life is banished and eternal light shines from within the great mirror eyes of beauty itself.

"Parisian Dream" is built upon an essential paradox. In it, the poet plays with his own negation, affirming his power to create a world in which his own poetry is invalid. The poet works with sound, yet his dream world is silent. The dream precedes the poem. Waking, suffering the shock of return to poverty, sound, and time, is the only means by which the poet can capture his dream and fit his vision to a verbal architecture.

Anne W. Sienkewicz

PARISIAN NOCTURNE

Author: Paul Verlaine (1844-1896)
Type of poem: Lyric
First published: 1866, as "Nocturne parisien," in *Poèmes saturniens*; English transla-
tion collected in *Poems,* 1961

The Poem

"Parisian Nocturne" is a poem of 106 lines, divided into seven stanzas of unequal
lengths. The title suggests a musical composition, perhaps a peaceful evocation of
Paris by night. Instead, however, one finds a macabre reflection on the winding progress of the river Seine. This is the thirty-sixth and longest in a collection of forty poems ostensibly written under the influence of the planet Saturn. In keeping with the
coldly pessimistic title of the collection, "Parisian Nocturne" describes only negative
aspects of the river.

The poem addresses the Seine (a rhetorical device called apostrophe). The first
stanza (of six lines) serves as a brief introduction, in which the author calls upon the
cold, corpse-laden river to continue its flow through Paris while equally icy thoughts
of the poet flow into the lines which follow.

In the second, twenty-eight-line stanza, Paul Verlaine describes a catalog of rivers,
all of which possess graceful, musical, or majestic attributes. These rivers include the
Guadalquivir, a chief river in Spain, the Pactolus in Asia Minor, the Bosporus strait,
the Rhine, the French rivers Lignon and Adour, the Nile, the Mississippi, the Euphra-
tes, and, finally, the mysterious, exotic Ganges. Several elements of the descriptions
recall interests of the Romantic movement, which had preceded the era in which
Verlaine lived.

The third stanza, of twenty lines, contrasts the squalor of the Seine and Paris to the
rivers described in the preceding stanza. The author gradually evokes the night by describing sunset, the disappearance of swallows and emergence of bats, along with the
emergence of dreamers from "dens in slums." He invites the reader to experience the
hush of evening but also to see it as a time of illicit love and crime.

In the fourth stanza, of twenty-two lines, Verlaine describes the sudden discordant
music of an organ grinder. This is a surprising nocturne, "desperate" and "shrill."
Verlaine also describes the thoughts evoked in listeners such as himself. Readers are
moved to tears, because the music is a reminder of the longing for harmony. Sight
mingles with sound in a poignant, self-created synthesis of fulfillment.

In the shorter fifth stanza (of twelve lines), however, the music dies; "dull" night
descends; by gaslight the river becomes "blacker than velvet masks"; happy thoughts
are dispelled in "panic flight" and the persona of the poem is alone with "Seine, Paris
and Night."

The next-to-last stanza (of fourteen lines) addresses these three as doom laden, like
the mysterious writing on the wall at Belshazzar's feast in the book of Daniel, and as

"ghastly ghouls." The poet asks by which means it is better for "wretched man" to die: by darkness, drowning, or in the arms of Paris itself. In any case, humans are all offerings to the river, a mighty "Worm."

The final stanza (of four lines) continues the idea of the ancient river-serpent, flowing indifferently through the town, carrying "cargos of wood, coal and corpses," a much-admired formulation. "Parisian Nocturne" is a despairing poem, conveying the feeling of the helplessness of the individual in the face of implacable forces, represented by the city and the Seine.

Forms and Devices

"Parisian Nocturne" is written in the traditional French poetic units of Alexandrine couplets, with alternating masculine and feminine endings. The Alexandrine line, consisting of twelve syllables, most typically with a caesura, or pause, after the sixth syllable, is not only the most classical unit of French versification but also an apt choice for a poem of this length and narrative weight.

"Parisian Nocturne" is thought to be Verlaine's earliest extant poem, written not only while he was at school but actually in the classroom, according to his lifelong friend, Edmond Lepelletier, who kept the much-corrected original until Verlaine prepared the first volume of his poetry. It is understandable that a young poet would use the dominant French verse form. Furthermore, Verlaine was enthused at that time by the Parnassian group of French poets, for whom emotional detachment and formal excellence were positive values.

The complex French rhyme system classifies ends of words according to how many elements in them are identical. The most desirable rhyme is designated as "rich." "Parisian Nocturne" is full of "rich" rhymes. These, too, correspond to the expectation for formal excellence typical of the author's time. More detailed formal aspects of this poem could be considered, such as the use of enjambment, rhetorical devices, vowel choice for sonority, in imitation of the rolling river, and the use of exclamation points to punctuate the surprising turns of the narrative. These are pertinent aspects in considering the poem's effect in French, but translation cannot duplicate them.

The dominant metaphorical qualities of this "tone poem" are those connected to exoticism, music, and death, all attributed to rivers, some also to the sounds of the city. In his use of image, even of resonant phraseology, Verlaine is frankly derivative. For example, the first line in French, "Roule, roule ton flot indolent, morne Seine," is reminiscent of the line in George Gordon, Lord Byron's *Childe Harold's Pilgrimage* (1812-1818, 1819), "Roll on, thou deep and dark-blue Ocean, roll!" (noted by Jacques Henry Bornecque, in *Les poèmes saturniens de Paul Verlaine*, 1952). The evocation of the world's rivers, too, is replete with borrowings from Victor Hugo, Théophile Gautier, François-Auguste-René de Chateaubriand, and others.

Adjectives such as "icy" and "putrid," metaphors such as "Worm" and "serpent," as well as the reiteration of the word "corpses" serve to create a sense of despair in the reader. This feeling is reinforced by the adding of discordant music, which symbolizes modern life in the crowded city. The piling up of disparate images and negative similes to a crescendo in succeeding verses is a further musical effect. The last four lines imitate the river itself, because the use of repetition, where the second and third lines flow into the last line, carries the reader, as the words describe, to unity with the river, where he or she becomes one of the cargo items with which the poem so callously ends.

Themes and Meanings

"Parisian Nocturne" is an impressionistic poetic journey through the city of Paris and, by extension, through life, to its inevitable conclusion in anonymous death. The river serves to remind the poet of unpleasant verities concerning the life of each person as well as life in Verlaine's century and in this particular European city.

The poem has a paradoxical sense of concrete times of day, such as afternoon and evening, in identifiable parts of Paris, such as the Pont de la Cité and Notre-Dame (stanza 3), while it also universalizes these experiences to encompass the times and places of each reader's individual life.

The discordant song of the organ grinder, heard at night, although it would not be appreciated by a real musician, such as the composer Gioacchino Antonio Rossini (stanza 4), serves the poet again as a summarizing device. He describes the evocation of each person's dearest hope for harmony and for the benediction "of setting suns," which symbolize a happy ending to one's life. In the dream state, the reader or poet is capable of creating a beautiful "mingling" of visual and auditory impressions with inner recollection to make a positive whole, one that would transform death into a fulfillment.

The poet destroys, however, the synesthesia and the dream called forth, as in the Romantic period, by sensory stimulation, even if it is the discordant, populist, gypsy stimulus of street music. This process is analogous to the rejection of the Romantic worldview by the nineteenth century, where realism soon passed over into a naturalism emphasizing the ugly aspects of human experience.

Verlaine ends the poem (in the last three stanzas) with loneliness, fear, lack of consolation, and intimations of suicide. The fact that he mentions the implications of the Bible and shows Orestes without his consoling sister, serves to remind the reader of the dual heritage, Greek and biblical, of Western culture. That heritage, the poem implies, is negated by the awful reality of the soulless material world, represented here by the city and the river.

The last four lines give a dull, hopeless impression. The double use of the word "agèd," particularly, takes the reader to a world outside historical time, the world after Eden, lost because of the treacherous "serpent," which still snatches people back from Paradise, as reality snatches them from the dream of harmony, and deposits them, lifeless and unredeemed, among the flotsam carried by forces they cannot overcome.

"Parisian Nocturne" is a dramatic first poem for Verlaine, whose sensibility Clive Scott describes as "a floating sensibility, operating in the ill-defined space between sentiment and sensation, between self-surrender and anxious interrogation of the physical world" (*The Riches of Rhyme: Studies in French Verse*, 1988). In "Parisian Nocturne," Verlaine used the experience of the modern city-dweller to describe the wretchedness of the human condition.

Erlis Glass

PARSLEY

Author: Rita Dove (1952-   )
Type of poem: Narrative
First published: 1982; collected in *Museum*, 1983

The Poem

"Parsley" revisits a horrific moment in Caribbean history and, in doing so, highlights the manner in which language and ideology can combine to produce political violence. The poem dramatizes the slaughter of thousands of migrant Haitian sugarcane workers by troops following orders from Dominican Republican dictator General Rafael Trujillo on October 2, 1937. (Rita Dove's notes to the poem erroneously indicate the date of the massacre as October 2, 1957.) In Dove's poem, the Haitians are killed because they could not pronounce the letter *r* in *perejil*, the Spanish word for "parsley." They are slaughtered at the behest of a dictator who, as historical documents show, was obsessed with removing influences of neighboring Haiti from Dominican culture. The first section, a villanelle titled "The Cane Fields," is narrated in the voices of Haitian workers as they are murdered. The second section, titled "The Palace," takes as its subject the psychological and sociological dimensions of Trujillo's motivations. The narration in this section shifts from first person to third person as Trujillo arrives at the decision to murder the cane workers because of the way they speak.

The poem opens with a contrast of original and unoriginal modes of language. The general's parrot, with its "parsley green" feathers, offers the first articulations of the poem by imitating human language and human convention but signalling, through this imitation, the appearance of nothing new. This section establishes Trujillo's absolute authority and the Haitians' unmitigated oppression. The sugarcane, a dominant image for the livelihood of the Haitians and the economic power of Trujillo's government, appears ghostly, an image of the blood sacrifice demanded by the general. Dove pivots the villanelle on repeated lines that emphasize the conjunction of unoriginal language and bloody violence: "there is a parrot imitating spring// Out of the swamp the cane appears."

Section 2 portrays how Trujillo's murderous decree finds its origin in his psychological equation of desire and death. As section 2 progresses, it becomes clear that Trujillo's desire to "purify" the workers' Spanish is linked to his desire to resurrect his dead mother. He keeps his parrot in his mother's old room and feeds it elaborate sweets, memorials to his mother who collapsed and died one day while preparing pastries for the Day of the Dead, an Aztec festival assimilated into contemporary Dominican culture. "Cane" again serves as a dominant image in this section, as it does in section 1. Yet the phantasmal sugarcane of section 1 becomes, in section 2, the mother's walking cane "planted" by Trujillo at her grave and perceived by him to flower every spring. When Trujillo hears the workers mispronouncing "Katarina," a local mountain, as "Katalina," he perceives this as an affront to his dead mother, who, he says, "was no stupid woman" and "could roll an R like a queen." Remembering the parsley sprigs that the men of his village wore to signify newborn sons, the general closes his equation of desire and death begun when the parrot opened the poem: He orders the Haitians "to be killed/ for a single, beautiful word."

Forms and Devices

The villanelle is one of the most complex forms in English poetry; therefore, it is ironic that Dove chooses this form for the Haitians' voices, since the general considers their speech inferior to his Spanish. The dancelike circularity of a villanelle pivots on five tercets that lead to a final quatrain. The first line of the opening tercet is repeated as the final line of the second and fourth tercets; the third line of the opening tercet is repeated as the last line of the third and fifth tercets. These two repeated lines form the last two lines of a villanelle. In section 1, this complex, rigorous repetition contrasts with the empty repetition of the general's parrot. While the Haitians work the cane fields, they are denigrated by the general, who lavishes luxury upon his parrot in the palace. The Haitians speak a rough Spanish wholly their own; the general, however, privileges the imitative repetitions of his parrot over the original hybrid tongue of the workers. In this upside-down version of linguistic authority in which the imitative is privileged over the original, the general "searches for a word" that will signify that "he is all the world/ there is." As the section closes, the blood of the Haitians is framed by the "parrot imitating spring."

Personification dominates the narrative of section 2 as, for example, the workers personify the mountain in their songs while they hack at the fields. The dominant image of the sugarcane becomes the sugared pastries that spoil the parrot, which is the general's replacement for his dead mother. Trujillo sees his mother's walking cane in the sugarcane, the parrot resides in the mother's former room in the palace, and the parrot imitates even the voice of his mother. Desire and death are linked in those images. Symbols of life and creativity are twisted in this section: The original song of the Haitians inspires Trujillo to kill them, he corrupts the life force of his mother into an occasion for massacre, and his memory of artillery fire is dramatized as a song of war in his flashback to the violence of his military career.

Themes and Meanings

Like many poems situated at the crossroads of politics and culture, "Parsley" assumes that political ideology and cultural practice intersect most vividly in language. Dove's poem exposes the violence inherent in attempts to control the dynamic, creative changes that transform all languages over time. Trujillo understands his language to be authentic. Yet at the same time, the most important speaker in his life is a parrot that only imitates language. Trujillo's parrot merely repeats and does not create. In contrast, the Haitian workers re-create language (in this case, the Spanish language) to reflect their dual cultural position as migrant workers. As much as their language might seem to be an unauthentic derivative of "pure" Spanish, Dove makes sure to cast their voices in the elite form of the villanelle. The parrot's imitations evoke the wounds of the mother's death to the point of even imitating the voice of the mother. The Haitians create a new language but suffer death at the hands of a dictator who believes that the imitative language of his parrot is more authentic. Trujillo declares, "Even/ a parrot can roll an R!"

These issues of authenticity, language, and violence are enacted against a ritualistic background that fuses love and death. From the beginning, the parrot's language is described as "imitating spring," which stands in direct contrast to autumn, the season of the mother's death. The parrot's language is part of an endless circularity that, for Trujillo, brings the mother back to life in the same way that spring cyclically revives the natural world. The cane, too, is part of such a cycle: The Haitians are killed cutting cane in the fall, but the walking cane planted at the mother's grave "blossoms" for the general each spring.

As much as the poem seems to partake of the impersonal verity of seasonal change, the violence of the poem instead is occasioned by the general's personal stake in such change. Trujillo's "thoughts turn/ to love and death" in the fall. The Haitians are the innocent victims of Trujillo's violent fusion of desire and domination and his location of this violent fusion in language itself. As a child, Trujillo was nicknamed *chapita*, Spanish for "bottle cap," because he was a fervent collector of bottle caps. When he became dictator, he banished *chapita* from the language. "Parsley" describes Trujillo's attempt to extend such political control to the cycles of nature itself. His parrot can only imitate spring, but Trujillo orders a slaughter in October to reenact spring. His slaughter of the innocent workers is an attempt to "purify" the language of outside influence and cleanse autumn of its associations with his mother's death.

Usually, ritual is evoked in culture to revive authenticity. Rituals are meant to reacquaint a culture with the epic memory of its past. Yet in "Parsley," rituals such as the yearly cane harvest, the cycles of nature, national holidays (the Day of the Dead), and childbirth are reduced to images of individual obsession and mass murder. Most of all, the cyclic pattern of the villanelle, which evokes ritual in its creative circularity, is understood by the general as a threat to authenticity. Dove dramatizes Trujillo's motivation in the form of the poem itself; the shift from villanelle (section 1) to free-verse narration (section 2) portrays Trujillo's purification strategy as a misreading of language. Trujillo prefers individual memory to cultural verity and thereby produces a series of misreadings in the poem: He elevates imitative language over original language, free-verse narration over the centuries-old villanelle, and the parsley colors of his parrot over the greenery of spring.

Tony Trigilio

A PART OF SPEECH

Author: Joseph Brodsky (1940-1996)
Type of poem: Poetic sequence
First published: 1977, as "Chast' rechi," in *Chast' rechi: Stikhotvoreniya, 1972-1976*;
 English translation collected in *A Part of Speech*, 1980

The Poem

Joseph Brodsky's sequence comprises fifteen sections, each twelve lines in length (with the single exception of section three, which is sixteen lines). The sections are written in accordance with formal metrics and employ a variety of rhyme schemes and sound patterns to underscore the thematic concerns. Alternating between a first-person singular and a more impersonal, omniscient voice, the individual poems create a collage of perspectives around the central themes of time, exile, and alienation.

The title, "A Part of Speech," indicates two of the sequence's primary concerns. One is the sense of an incomplete and fragmented vision arising from the condition of displacement, loss and alienation; the second concern relates directly to the notion of language as a continuum and the poet's sense of his partial voice, of the difficulties inherent in speech and expression under these conditions.

The first section introduces the speaker's biographical situation and its relation to poetic expression. The section becomes an *ars poetica*, an explanation of his poetics, and an invocation to the muse, tying the nature of his temporal and spatial condition to language and creativity itself. Of particular interest is the stress on sound—the importance of articulation (voice) and the emphasis placed on reception (hearing), the two components necessary for successful speech and poetry.

Section 2 begins the process of elaboration, picking up on the initial geographic and climatic references. Here, the effects of the climate, the power of bitter cold to destroy and the desire it engenders for warmth and inclusion, become analogies for the speaker's psychological and political situation. Brodsky is mapping the condition of a psyche at odds with its environment, grappling with the displacements of time and space, and using the structures of the language itself to embody this reality.

The next section provides a more extreme example, linking exile and loss to linguistic indeterminacies and mental instability. Here, language cannot fix meanings and memory cannot reconstruct or revive a lost reality. The fourth section develops on this idea of indeterminacy and presents an exploration of the fallibility of observation. This examination of how reality is shaped by the observer plays on the concept of altered perspectives by introducing images of distorted vision, of reading and misreading.

Section 5 shifts the focus back toward the poet-seer, illustrating how he recognizes (re-thinks, or re-formulates) images of nature, finding in their naturally determined situations parallels for historical and political determinisms. By doing so, he is moving outside these temporal spheres and shaping experience in accordance with his muse—language.

The next section provides another perspective on consciousness with its illustration of recollection. A glimpse of dawn stimulates memories of a childhood classroom, boredom and ennui—of an early alienation. Section 7 is constructed around the opposite trait: forgetfulness. In this poem, the speaker re-creates memories of a northern village to replace the emptiness of a lost love.

The eighth section expands the theme of memory by relating a prosperous post-war Munich and the realities of its immediate past. The images of present material comfort and sensual enjoyment are ironically undercut by resonances from the imperial and Fascist past. The poet is indicting the failure of memory to protect humankind from tyrannies. The association of this forgetfulness with summer, a time of freedom and pleasure, creates an ironic perspective on the complacencies of the West—an image reiterated in the final poem of the sequence.

The next two sections shift toward a more pastoral vision, where the poet links the natural images of order and continuity. In both instances this entails the recognition of balances and limitations—in section 9, between time and space, and in section 10, between the forces of life and death. Under these strictures, in the context of an eternal present, connection with the Other seems possible.

Sections 11 and 12 continue this exploration of natural imagery in relation to the role of the artist. Both postulate the idea of completion, the added dimension of language. Section 11, by drawing on Immanuel Kant's notion of synthetic judgment, suggests a potential for meaning and a hope of futurity. The poet, in the following section, comes to embody this synthesis by assuming a hybrid form, that of the centaur.

The last three sections of "A Part of Speech" draw together elements of the speaker's alienated condition, the potential offered by vision and language, and a warning about the dangers of freedom. Against the silence of repression, the erosion of meaning and the assault upon language, Brodsky sets the poet's part: "his spoken part . . . a part of speech." The last poems function as warnings against the seductions of freedom, the assault upon memory and the dulling of vision inherent in the endless summer days of the West.

Forms and Devices

One of the most striking features of Brodsky's work is his unstinting allegiance to formalism. He understands traditional metrics to be one of the greatest challenges for a poet, the discipline of creating a vibrant, unpredictable expression within the strictures of strict metrical forms. Commenting on the formal verse of Anna Akhmatova, a Russian poet he very much admires, Brodsky suggests she avoided the comic or redundant echo of the metrics by a "collage-like diversification of the content." The meter, set against this wealth of seemingly unrelated material, acts as a "common denominator" binding them together, becoming a part of the act of speech, the means of articulation. His emulation of this practice can be observed even in the translated version of "A Part of Speech," in how the rhyme scheme works in tandem with the emotional or intellectual flow of the verses, how the qualities of assonance and alliteration highlight or comment on the material. As he suggests in the first section, his verse was formed by the "zinc-gray breakers that always marched on/ in twos. Hence all rhymes, hence that wan flat voice/ that ripples between them." This respect for the lineage and traditions of poetry permeates all of Brodsky's poetics, both in terms of his use of formal metrics and in his intertextual references—for example, the use of elements from Nikolai Gogol's story "Diary of a Madman" in section 3, or an oblique reference to Robert Lowell at the beginning of section 10.

A more specific example of Brodsky's attention to form can be found in a brief examination of section three. Here, the poet employs a variety of devices to delineate the psychological turmoil of the speaker; whether it is the passionate anguish of the lover, the despair of the exile, or the complexities of an artist's relation to his muse. Aside from its deviation from the standard lengths of the sections, this is also the only poem to adopt an epistolary form, playing on the associations of letter-writing with direct personal address. But these expectations are undercut by an onslaught of indeterminacies: the place is nowhere, the addressee is irrelevant, and the date uncertain. The lack of punctuation, coupled with the complicated clausal structure of the syntax, gives this poem a sense of breathlessness and creates a stream-of-consciousness effect that fits perfectly with the subject matter of passion, loss, and madness. A further accent to the heightened emotion of the speaker is the progressively stronger nature of the rhymes, becoming more pronounced as the tension of the poem builds. The cloistered, confined perspective of the speaker finds its mirror image in the bracketing of individual lines by repetition, assonance, and alliteration. The sound quality of the verse is extremely important to Brodsky, remarking as he has that "sound . . . is the seat of time in the poem, a background against which its content acquires a stereoscopic quality." The immediacy of the connection between subject and self, the image of the double so central to the poem, is reflected in these echoes, in the very textures of the verse. Throughout the sequence Brodsky brings the metrical voice of the poetry into play.

Themes and Meanings

"A Part of Speech" re-creates the condition of a fragmented consciousness, of loss and alienation, by exploring the mind grappling with apparently irreconcilable aspects of time and space. The lightning shifts between past and present, memory and projection, here and nowhere, compress a universe of possibility into the sequence. At the same time, the strong undercurrents of the forms and meters suggest the healing potential of the poetic vision and the myriad resources of language. What he hopes to reflect is his sense of "the graspable degree of arbitrariness" in the relation of language and experience. Two main elements that Brodsky brings together are the psychological condition of exile, reflected in feelings of loss, anger, displacement, and isolation, and the exile's relation to language and expression, how language itself forms and informs the nature of his condition.

One of the central concerns of the sequence is its ability to convey the sense of a mind searching for a firm vantage from which to view experience. As he remarks in the opening essay of *Less Than One: Selected Essays* (1986), relating the act of memory and writing: "Memory . . . directs our movements, including migration. . . . [T]here is something clearly atavistic in the very process of recollection, if only because such a process never is linear. . . . [I]t coils, recoils, digresses to all sides . . . so should one's narrative." In keeping with this, the movement of "A Part of Speech" is forward and back in time, unsettled and shifting between the present, the recent past, millennia, and the future; similarly, the spatial dimension of the individual poems keeps changing, some set in extremely confined areas, others covering great sweeps of space in a few lines. The sequence, although read in a consecutive fashion, builds on a nonlinear process that captures in language the speaker's attempt to "manage the meaninglessness of existence . . . to domesticate the reprehensible infinity by inhabiting it with familiar shadows."

One way Brodsky accentuates the nature of the fragmented experience is his construction of the sequence itself. Each section is geared to providing a part of experience, one element connected through language with the others, remaining independent yet creating resonances. For example, the image of the North in section 2 introduces ideas of inclusion and exclusion, of an isolating wasteland, and of a stifling or burial. Later poems return to these images to elaborate or provide another context for them. Section 6, for example, picks up the winter image and links it to the suffocating dreariness of a school classroom. Section 7 translates the wasteland into a remembrance of rural poverty and isolation. Section 8 and the last poem reverse the winter image to summer and redefine the wasteland in the context of political and material freedoms. The onset of time, the limitations of mind, memory, and language, all contribute to this sense of unavoidable fragmentation. As he remarks in section 14: "What gets left of a man amounts/ to a part. To his spoken part. To a part of speech." The method of the sequence is to gather together diverse parts and, using the synthetic and associative processes of the poetic imagination, fashion that part of speech.

James Panabaker

PASSAGE TO INDIA

Author: Walt Whitman (1819-1892)
Type of poem: Lyric
First published: 1871, in *Passage to India*; collected in *Leaves of Grass*, 1876

The Poem

"Passage to India" was first published in 1871 as the title piece in a book of seventy-five poems (twenty-three of them new) that were subsequently incorporated into the 1876 edition of *Leaves of Grass* as a separately paginated supplement. Slightly revised, the poem became an integral part of *Leaves of Grass* in 1881 despite Walt Whitman's having conceived "Passage to India" as well as the poems he planned to add to it as marking a new and quite different direction. *Leaves of Grass*, he contended, was the song of "the Body and Existence"; "Passage to India" was to be the song of "the unseen Soul," as the "ardent and fully appointed Personality" that had been the subject of the earlier collection entered "the sphere of the restless gravitation of Spiritual Law." The decision to incorporate the later intention into the earlier work reflects Whitman's willingness to expand, revise, and even reshape *Leaves of Grass* over the years. That decision also reflects, for all the overt optimism of "Passage to India," the poet's dissatisfaction as the United States, the nation that he believed was itself the greatest poem, failed to live up to his expectations and failed as well to accept him as "affectionately" as he had accepted it. (Any lingering hopes he still had to make *Passage to India* the successor to and equal of *Leaves of Grass* were put to rest by the stroke and partial paralysis he suffered in 1873.)

In its final form, "Passage to India" is a 255-line poem in nine sections, parts of which Whitman conceived as separate, shorter works. This "song," or "chant," of "free speculations and ideal escapades" begins by pointing to three recent engineering feats: the laying of the transatlantic telegraph cable in 1866, the joining of the Union Pacific and Central Pacific to form the country's first transcontinental railway in May, 1869, and the opening of the Suez Canal in November of the same year. Whitman envisions these technological achievements propelling humankind not only ahead into the future but back as well—linking the West with the East, the modern with the ancient, America (and Europe) with India and all that it represented. Whitman sees in the myths and fables of India the very origins of that spiritual quest of which the above achievements are only the most recent manifestations. More than scientific feats, they serve as metaphoric means. As those technological achievements connect the world materially, Whitman's poem connects the world spiritually. The sights seen from the deck of a ship passing through the Suez Canal or from the window of a railway car crossing the American West (lines 43-47, 48-64) please but do not completely satisfy. More than an ordinary observer or traveler, the poem's narrator adopts a wide perspective, unfettered by either time or space. "Resuming all," he becomes engineer, explorer, and time traveler, moving back to Adam and Eve, then ahead through the course of history, paying special homage to the "gigantic, visionary" Columbus, "chief historian" on history's vast panoramic stage.

The passage to India (which Columbus sought and which the narrator now resumes) becomes the voyage of the "repressless soul" to "primal thought," to "reason's early paradise." The speaker's desire to circumnavigate the now metaphorical globe in an effort to return to this Transcendental utopia of intuitive wisdom and poetic creation takes on added urgency in the poem's eighth section. Saying farewell to the weepers, doubters, and deprecators, the narrator sails off over the seas of Time, Space, and Death to a "Thou transcendent,/ Nameless," a human as well as divine "other" that is also the narrator's "actual Me."

At the very thought of this "Thou,"—at the very thought of God, Nature, Time, Space, and Death—the "I" shrinks to insignificance, only to grow (like the hero of an American tall tale) as vast as Space itself. The "gigantic, visionary" figure of the poet-explorer-savior (Whitman-Columbus-Christ) emerges only to depart, "bound where mariner has not yet dared to go," to the unmapped shores of the oldest, most impenetrable "enigmas."

Forms and Devices

Much of the cohesiveness and intelligibility of "Passage to India" derives from Whitman's elaboration of the conceit introduced in the poem's title: that of passage or voyage. The poem's greatness stems from a less obvious and more potent source: Whitman's artfully artless style. More spoken than written, it is a style at once intense yet diffuse, expansive yet elliptical. Drawing everything into its democratic embrace, it nevertheless tends to blur every "each" into a nearly indistinguishable "all" and seeks to convince the reader by virtue of a logic beyond or perhaps prior to reason. At once ahead of its time and primitive, it sends its "ceaseless" and "repressless" (though "varied") message via an elaborate system of rhetorical devices.

Whitman's style is orphic in form and ecstatic in effect. Parenthetical asides and purely rhetorical questions play their parts; more important are the frequent, urgent exclamations and the apostrophizing of everything from architects, engineers, and explorers to generalized facts, abstract truth, the year itself, the planet Earth ("Rondure"), unspecified "enigmas," and a "Comrade perfect" who may be friend, lover, God, or all three. The repeated apostrophizing is one of several factors that contribute to the poem's cumulative power. The repetition of individual words is another: In section 3, for example, the word "I" is used twenty-one times in only twenty-seven lines. There is also the breathless rush of Whitman's long pseudo-sentences rife with commas and syntactically parallel constructions, including the frequent use of participles to create the odd blending of motion and stasis that is one of the hallmarks of Whitman's Transcendental, oral-oracular style. Insistent in tone and repetitive in structure, "Passage to India" achieves a nearly liturgical intensity which, like the world it describes, has its own "hidden prophetic intention."

Themes and Meanings

"There is more of me, the essential ultimate me, in ['Passage to India']," Whitman explained to his friend and follower, Horace Traubel, "than in any of the [other] poems. There is no philosophy, consistent or inconsistent, in that poem . . . but the burden of it is evolution . . . the unfolding of cosmic purposes." In addition to underscoring the value the poet himself placed on the poem, Whitman's comment establishes the poles within which the poem operates: the cosmic and the personal.

"Spurning the known" and giving himself over to "unloos'd dreams," the poet (or, more accurately, an anonymous but nevertheless autobiographical narrative "I") attempts to make the "voiceless earth" speak in order to clarify ("eclaircise") God's "inscrutable purpose." As Transcendentalist and as cosmic evolutionist, Whitman takes as his aim something more than Puritan poet John Milton's efforts "to justify the ways of God to men" in the seventeenth century Christian epic *Paradise Lost* (1667, 1674). Neither God's apologist nor His amanuensis, the Whitmanic persona is God's alter ego and democratic equal. His self-appointed task is not so much to justify God's ways as to explore them and to engineer the overcoming of doubt and death through the mystical fusion of time and space, self and other.

Against the poem's great outpouring of cosmic energy and optimistic expectancy runs a strong undercurrent of frustration and disillusionment (or at least disappointment). Because he too has felt—indeed continues to feel—the weight of this "mocking life" and the hunger of the "unsatisfied soul," Whitman longs to give shape and direction to the "restless explorations" of all men and women of all ages as they "grope" their way through life, grappling with their sense of separation from "nature." Not content to play the poet's usual role, Whitman plays the parts of explorer and engineer, prophet and savior (Moses leading others to the Promised Land that he himself could not enter and Christ saving others by sacrificing himself). Above all, Whitman projects himself ahead by looking back to Columbus, praised here as much for the neglect he suffered as for the country he discovered.

An entry in Whitman's notebook on the poem's "spinal idea" helps clarify Columbus's role in "Passage to India": "That the divine efforts of heroes, and their ideas, faithfully lived up to will finally prevail, and be accomplished however long deferred." Having already waited sixteen years for America to accept its own Transcendental role (as envisioned in the 1855 edition of *Leaves of Grass*) and to acknowledge the author as its bard, Whitman seems to have grown doubtful regarding the outcome. In "Prayer of Columbus," published three years later, after Whitman had suffered a stroke, the title figure, now depicted longing for death, is unsure whether his dream of future fame and vindication is the vision of a prophet or the raving of a madman. A similar though clearly more muted self-doubt propels "Passage to India" away from the pains and disappointments Whitman actually suffered and toward cosmic evolution, universal brotherhood, and a "Comrade perfect" who patiently waits, listens, and understands—the poem's ideal reader, or perhaps only its idealized, self-projecting author.

Robert A. Morace

THE PASSIONATE SHEPHERD TO HIS LOVE

Author: Christopher Marlowe (1564-1593)
Type of poem: Lyric
First published: 1599, in *The Passionate Pilgrim*

The Poem

"The Passionate Shepherd to His Love" is a love poem that contains six quatrains of rhyming couplets in iambic tetrameter. In marked contrast to Christopher Marlowe's plays about heroes and kings, this lyric poem purports to be the words of a shepherd speaking to his beloved. Its simple, musical language and fanciful imagery create an idyll of innocent love. The version of the poem that was printed in 1599 contained four stanzas attributed to William Shakespeare; the poem was printed again in 1600, in *Englands Helicon*, with only the six stanzas attributed to Marlowe.

In this poem, the shepherd persona speaks to his beloved, evoking "all the pleasures" of a peaceful springtime nature. He promises her the delights of nature and his courtly attention. The first quatrain is the invitation to "Come live with me and be my love." Next, the speaker describes the pleasant natural setting in which he plans that they will live. Their life will be one of leisure; they will "sit upon the rocks," watch the shepherds, and listen to the birds.

The shepherd does not refer to the cold winter, when herding sheep becomes difficult. He does not suggest that his work requires effort or that he may need to go off into the hills away from his beloved to herd his flock. Instead, he imagines their life together as a game enjoyed in an eternal spring. He promises to make clothes and furnishings for his beloved from nature's abundant harvest: wool gowns from the sheep, beds and caps of flowers, dresses embroidered with leaves. Even the other shepherds seem to be there only to entertain the beloved, to "dance and sing/ for thy delight." The poem ends by summing up the "delights" of the pastoral idyll and repeating the opening invitation.

Forms and Devices

Marlowe was a university-educated dramatist who might have rivaled William Shakespeare had he lived longer. His plays probed the tangled passions of heroism, ambition, and power. He led an active theatrical life and frequented taverns: Indeed, he met his death at the age of twenty-nine in a tavern brawl. Yet he chose to write this poem in a shepherd's voice, using a pastoral convention that was frequently employed by Elizabethan poets. The pastoral tradition of courtly love poetry idealized the beloved and ennobled the lovers, using idyllic country settings and featuring shepherds as models of natural, unspoiled virtue.

The poem's images are all drawn from the kind springtime nature of the pastoral tradition and from music. This imagery creates a gentle fantasy of eternal spring. The poem appeals to almost all the senses—sight, sound, smell, and touch—as the speaker tells his love that they will watch "shepherds feed their flocks" and listen to birds singing madrigals (polyphonic melodies). He promises to make beds of roses, and clothing of flowers and wool for his beloved. Images of "shallow rivers," "melodious birds," "roses," "pretty lambs," and "ivy buds" evoke a nature that is pure, simple, blooming, and kind to innocent creatures.

To complement the pastoral imagery, the poem blends alliteration, rhythm, rhyme, and other sound patterns to create a songlike lyric. The labial *l* sound is repeated in words such as "live," "love," "all," "hills," "shallow," "flocks," "falls," and "myrtle." The sibilant *s* recurs in "Seeing the shepherds feed their flocks," in "shallow rivers," "roses," "sing," and "swains." The *m* sound appears in "mountain," "melodious," "madrigals," "myrtle," "lambs," and "amber." This combination of sounds creates a soft, harmonious, gentle tone.

The poem is written in regular four-line stanzas with rhyming couplets. Most of the rhyming words are words of one syllable, and most of the lines are end-stopped, thus emphasizing the rhyming words and the rhythm of the poem. The rhymes include such appealing words as "love" (repeated three times), "roses," "flocks," "fields," "sing," and "morning." There are frequent internal rhymes and partial rhymes in words such as lambs/amber, may/swains, seeing/feed, and finest/lined. The meter is iambic tetrameter with little variation. All these factors—short, regular lines, repeated simple rhymes, frequent internal rhymes and partial rhymes, and alliterative patterns—turn the poem into a song, with a melodious appeal that echoes the music of nature that it describes; the poem has been set to music by several different composers.

Themes and Meanings

Marlowe's "The Passionate Shepherd to His Love" is a celebration of youth, innocence, love, and poetry. The poem participates in an ongoing tradition of lyrical love poetry. It casts the lovers as shepherds and shepherdesses who are at home in a beneficent natural setting. According to the conventions of pastoral poetry (which began with the Greek poet Theocritus in the third century B.C.E.), shepherds are uncorrupted and attuned to the world of nature. Such pastoral poems are the work of urban poets who idealize the simplicity, harmony, and peace of the shepherd's life.

This idealized vision has often been subjected to satire. Sir Walter Raleigh, a contemporary of Marlowe, wrote "The Nymph's Reply to the Passionate Shepherd," in which the young woman replies somewhat cynically. The third stanza reads:

> Thy gown, thy shoes, thy beds of roses,
> Thy cap, thy kirtle, and thy posies;
> Soon break, soon wither, soon forgotten,
> In folly ripe, in reason rotten.

Three centuries later, in 1935, responding to the economic devastation of the Depression, C. Day Lewis wrote, "Come, live with me and be my love":

> Care on thy maiden brow shall put
> A wreath of wrinkles, and thy foot
> Be shod with pain: not silken dress
> But toil shall tire thy loveliness.

The many parodies of "The Passionate Shepherd to His Love" render a kind of tribute to its enduring vitality and power.

Marlowe's poem is an outstanding example of the pastoral lyric tradition. It succeeds because of its musical quality, its direct, conversational language, and its freshness of imagery and tone. It continues to be widely anthologized.

Karen F. Stein

PATROCLEIA

Author: Christopher Logue (1926-   )
Type of poem: Epic
First published: 1962; revised and collected in *War Music: An Account of Books 16 to 19 of Homer's "Iliad,"* 1981

The Poem

"Patrocleia" is a free adaptation of book 16 of Homer's epic poem about the siege of Troy (c. ninth century B.C.E., first transcribed in the sixth century B.C.E. by the Greeks after the Trojan prince, Paris, seduced Helen, the wife of Menelaus, one of the Greek chieftains, and fled with her to Troy (the fortress kingdom of his father, King Priam).

The Greeks and their allies have had limited success in attacking Troy; the war has gone on for more than nine years, and their efforts have not been helped by the fact that their finest warrior, Achilles, has quarrelled with Agamemnon, the king of Mycenae, the leader of the expedition, and now refuses to fight. In addition, difficulties for both sides lie in the intrusion of several gods of varying powers and eccentric inclinations. Achilles (whose mother is a deity) has asked the gods to deter the Greeks so long as he is at odds with Agamemnon. His absence has led to the Trojans being more successful in battle: The Greeks are backed up to the shore, where they are hard pressed to protect their ships.

Patroclus, Achilles' closest friend (Logue uses his name as a basis for the title of this section of the poem), chides Achilles for his stubborn inaction and suggests that if Achilles will not fight, he should at least allow his troops, the Myrmidons, to go into battle. Patroclus offers to lead them; to ensure their success, he suggests that he be allowed to wear Achilles' distinctive armor to frighten the Trojans. Achilles consents, but only on the condition that once Patroclus has driven the Trojans back he will stop his advance. Only Achilles is to have the glory of finally defeating the Trojans.

Patroclus agrees, and the attack on the Trojans is so successful that in the confrontation several leading Trojan warriors are killed. Patroclus is elated. He ignores Achilles' instruction and presses the attack on Troy itself. This action enrages the god Apollo, who stuns Patroclus with a godly blow. Patroclus is then wounded by a Trojan soldier. Disabled, he is caught and killed by Prince Hector, the greatest of the Trojan fighters. The section ends with Patroclus, in his dying moments, warning Hector not to rejoice, since it took the attacks of others to slow him down before Hector could strike the fatal blow. He predicts that Achilles will avenge his death, and a surly Hector acknowledges that possibility. This section is the turning point of *The Iliad*. The death of Patroclus devastates Achilles, who returns to the battle and kills Hector. Hector's death ultimately leads to the destruction of Troy.

Forms and Devices

Perhaps the best way to consider this work is to remember that it is only one part of an adaptation of a major poem and is best read with an accurate translation of Homer's original *Iliad* at hand. Logue has no ambition simply to translate the poem, but to filter parts of it through his twentieth century artistic sensibility. He makes use of motifs common to all epics, but with the difference that metaphor, narrative, language in general, and, perhaps most significantly, the facts of the original, are artistically, morally, and psychologically influenced by his own time and place.

The poem is laconic, the tone is cool, the voice of the third-party narrator distanced and uncommitted. The free verse is sometimes hardly verse at all, but informal, conversational, often little more than a kind of shorthand aside. The romance and the excitement of triumphant male endeavor, however deadly and cruel it may be, is celebrated in the Homeric work. The same events happen in Logue's poem, but the victories are sour, and poetic expansiveness and rhetorical flourish are avoided. The epic similes, so wide-ranging and poetically extravagant in the original, are rarer and shorter. Patroclus attacks a terrified warrior, cowering in his chariot: "And gracefully as men in oilskins cast/ Fake insects over trout, he speared the bog,/ And with his hip his pivot, prised Thestor up and out/ As easily as later men detach/ A sardine from an opened tin."

Logue does not set the action in the present, but he often uses language that would not—could not—have been used in the original. "Cut to the Fleet," for example, comes from instruction in a film script. The poem is closer to the modern short story than to the epic in structure, tone, and its ambiguous ending.

Themes and Meanings

The elements of the original that Logue abandons in his version give some indication of how he wants the poem to be read. There is considerably less spiritual meddling in the poem, save for the rescue of Sarpedon's corpse and Apollo's attack on Patroclus late in the work. Logue focuses the poem on the conduct of the men without having the constant diversion of the gods manipulating the action. The same desire to narrow the field of vision is behind the tendency in the poem to abandon the very long poetic passages of description and involved, detailed accounts of the battles. In the original much is made of the other warriors and their struggles; here the Patroclus tale is really the only story being told. For instance, little is made of Hector's desertion from the battle and his later return in Logue's version, since he does not want the story to wander, and the narrative is sharply cut back to concentrate on the Achilles-Patroclus-Hector triangle of mutual destruction.

Logue is primarily interested in the ironic nature of how men make their own fate, whereas the Homer poem makes more of how much they are the playthings of the gods. The heroes of the original are Achilles and Hector, who set the standard of heroism for their respective societies. Logue's poem shows how little power they have over their destinies. Patroclus takes the place and costume of Achilles, and in such is killed by Hector, who strips him of the armor that he should not be wearing—and is not worthy of wearing. Hector in turn will be killed by Achilles for so doing, and Achilles, in turn, will die young, since his fate has already been decided by the gods.

This sense of inevitability and disdain for military prowess is peculiar to the late twentieth century. Logue turns the Homer poem upside down, stripping it of its triumphs in the face of the grim reality of mindless slaughter and the waste of life occasioned by the male enthusiasm for egotistical, deadly conduct. Logue seems to suggest that even at their best, the men are there to kill and be killed. People of the twentieth century, with its loss of spiritual connection, cannot blame the gods for their bloody conduct.

Charles Pullen

PATTERNS

Author: Amy Lowell (1874-1925)
Type of poem: Dramatic monologue
First published: 1915; collected in *Men, Women, and Ghosts,* 1916

The Poem

An eighteenth century Englishwoman walks through an elegantly patterned garden. The carefully arranged garden paths and flower beds cause her to reflect that her society has similarly arranged her, seeing to it that she will passively endure her stiff, brocaded gown, her powdered hair, and a jewelled fan after the fashion of the day. Although her pink and silver gown and high-heeled ribboned shoes are decorative, the woman feels imprisoned, sealed off from the softness and passion of her heart, her true self.

At first she feels that both she and the flowers are locked into rigid patterns, but she begins to realize that her situation is mocked by the wider liberty of nature. Inspired by the greater freedom of the flowers and trees, she passes a marble fountain and sees herself bathing nude in the basin, all the while imagining that her lover is hiding in the nearby hedge, observing her. Continuing the fantasy, she imagines the water sliding over her body as would her lover's hand. The sensuality of summer makes her wish to shed her restrictive, conventionally feminine clothing for a newly liberated body whose nudity expresses a more desirable combination of pink and silver.

She imagines herself running fluidly through the maze of paths, laughing, pursued by her lover, who will eventually catch and embrace her, the buttons of his military uniform pressing sensuously against her flesh, allowing her to achieve the erotic release she has been seeking. Her desire is to be free and, by exposing and then contrasting her nude body to his military uniform, to free him as well. In reality, the woman's body is still in its heavy, fussy clothing, and she can release herself only in dream and wishful thinking.

Her sense of frustration is explained more fully when the reader learns that in her bosom is a letter brought that morning which informs her that her lover, Lord Hartwell, has died in action while serving under his commander, the duke, in Flanders. This revelation further explains the entrapment and despair she has felt while walking in a seemingly beautiful and tranquil garden. Although in another month they would have been man and wife, the woman now regards the future as a meaningless cycle of seasons in which, winter or summer, she will pace her manicured garden forlornly, her body stiffened by the stays, bones, and buttons of her repressive clothing. In addition to the constraints of her patterned garden and of her clothing, which reflect her society's regulation of her sexuality and personal freedom, she realizes that the business of war is an even more crushing pattern that has intruded into her life. Reflecting on war's official and socially sanctioned pattern of aggression, the woman reaches a catharsis by taking the name of Christ in vain. This daring profanity is followed by a defiant questioning of the meaning of all the societal patterns that have controlled her life and shaped her destiny.

Forms and Devices

"Patterns" is a poem composed in the light of the Imagist movement in modern poetry, for which Amy Lowell had great sympathy. She eventually became one of its major proponents and leaders. Imagists sought to break with the traditional forms of poetry, preferring unrhymed and unmetered ("free") verse and a more colloquial, economical diction closer to prose or to the rhythms of speech. In "Patterns," her best-known poem, Lowell used an irregular rhyme scheme to suggest that expression must follow the movement of the natural speaking voice rather than customary poetic diction. The lack of formal constraints in "Patterns" creates a free-flowing style that passes effortlessly from verse to prose and back again, according to the mood or emotional needs of the narrative voice.

Although Lowell employs recognizable poetic devices, she is also using her poem as a way to tell a story—complete with a heroine and a supporting set of characters—as a piece of prose would. This story of a woman in crisis is facilitated through the technique of dramatic monologue, which allows the poet to explore the psychology of her narrator. In addition, dramatic monologue reinforces Lowell's conviction that poetry is an oral art that should be heard to be completely understood. The woman's unaffected but impassioned human cry of pain at the end suggests a speaking voice breaking out in anguished spontaneity.

The lack of a formal rhyme scheme in "Patterns" does not mean that Lowell is simply writing a form of cut-up prose. While not following a strict meter, the lines in "Patterns" can be defined as loosely iambic and as having from two to four accents a line with varying numbers of syllables. More important, the poem is composed of interweaving sound patterns that establish a musical or cadenced rhythm. This musicality is one of the attributes of "Patterns" that distinguishes it from that of a prose narrative. In addition, Lowell uses such formal poetic devices as internal rhymes (quills, daffodils), end rhymes (brocade, shade), assonance (paths, patterned, daffodils), and consonance (gown, fan). It is this interplay between formal devices and freer verse that is also germane to the poem's theme of the necessary balance between freedom and constraint.

A final important aspect of "Patterns" is Lowell's selection of vivid images. Readers must draw their own inferences from her images, however—she feels no need to supply an extended explanatory commentary. When the narrator is brought the letter announcing the death of her lover, for example, the letters on the page are compared to writhing snakes. This image may call to mind the serpent in the Garden of Eden, bringing sin and death, but Lowell does not provide this interpretation herself, instead letting the image resonate in its own way for each reader. The poem's economical but sensuous images especially concern the garden and the gown, and when these images are carried from stanza to stanza, one begins to understand that they are also being deployed as symbols. For instance, the imagery of the woman's gown, with its stiffness and its stays, develops into a symbol of society's cruel repression of healthy instinct.

Themes and Meanings

"Patterns" centers on the unmet needs of a love-starved woman. While the woman in the poem yearns for an ecstatic eroticism, her civilization has denied her a sexually responsive identity. Her unbearably constricted clothing articulates the theme of a world that has instituted a set of social controls that do not accommodate or recognize female sexuality. She is trapped in a system that has deprived her of her inmost identity as a passionate, sensual, and free-spirited young woman. Psychologically, her emotional state suggests suppressed hysteria, the result of a society that requires female passivity and affords few opportunities for spontaneous expression of feeling. A corollary of this theme is that of the female body. Although her social mask is that of a decorous product of her society, the socially constructed femininity represented by her gown and the formal garden acts as a prison for her body, which yearns to be free. This awareness of her own body is an inherently enlivening one, leading her to think of the fulfilling experience of sexual love.

Like her garden, which is perfectly pruned and arranged after the custom of the day, the lady is likewise beautifully organized. However, as she paces along the mazelike patterns of her garden, she feels imprisoned in a social system and in a false identity that denies her what she truly wants. A woman's capacity for passion and its cruel restriction becomes a figure for yet another theme—the general denial of personal freedom in a repressive society. Just as the form of the poem contains both free-flowing elements and formal poetic devices, the image of the woman's nude body pressed against her lover in uniform indicates an eroticism based on the balanced interplay of nature and cultural order. It is the one-sided, overly masculine and puritanical dominance over both the natural world and women's lives that is the problem; the poem suggests that it is necessary to permit the sense of freedom and guilt-free sensuality, associated here with the female body, to act as a welcome counterpoise to the claims of civilization.

The final theme in the poem is of war. The sharp cry of pain that concludes the poem can be interpreted not only as a defiance of conventional morality but also as a protest against the inhumanity of war. The woman becomes a tragic figure, victimized by male-dominated modes of aggression that leave her languishing in an unvisited garden. The profane invocation of the deity at the end is not only a protest against war—it is also an opposition of the war by connecting the women's passions with what is truly sacred. It is her celebration of the body and its erotic life that preserves what is holy in the face of the misguided patterns of her culture.

Margaret Boe Birns

PAUL REVERE'S RIDE

Author: Henry Wadsworth Longfellow (1807-1882)
Type of poem: Narrative
First published: 1861; collected in *Tales of a Wayside Inn*, 1863

The Poem

For generations of readers, Henry Wadsworth Longfellow's poem "Paul Revere's Ride" has defined the beginning of the American Revolution, and Revere has become an American hero. Longfellow's primary concern was not historical accuracy, however; he portrays Revere as the only messenger, ignoring the equally important roles of William Dawes and other riders. From beginning to end, the poet consciously attempts to create a legend. Thus, in the first stanza, he adopts the persona of an older person transmitting a significant oral tradition to a younger generation ("Listen my children") as he recounts events of eighty-six years earlier that influenced the course of American history. This stanza, the shortest in the poem, serves as prologue, a parallel to the patriotic epilogue in the final stanza.

Subsequent stanzas detail the events of "the eighteenth of April, in Seventy-five." The second stanza continues to develop the title character's role as protector of his community; though Revere's name is not mentioned here, Longfellow explains Revere's scheme to alert the populace if the British initiate military action. The third stanza focuses upon the situation in Boston, emphasizing the intimidating power of the British military as embodied in the *Somerset*, a man-of-war that seems to dominate both the harbor and the city.

In the fourth stanza, Longfellow further emphasizes the vigilance of the colonists. The unnamed "friend," who has been delegated to watch the British soldiers, discovers movement but waits until he determines that the invaders will travel by sea. The friend remains central through the sixth stanza. The subject of the fifth stanza is his climb to the North Church tower. From the highest window he surveys the city he is trying to protect. The sixth stanza adds to the myth as he briefly muses on the nearby dead and his own loneliness but soon concentrates on the soldiers' movement and his role in warning his fellow citizens.

With the seventh stanza, the focus shifts to Revere, who waits impatiently on the opposite shore. He strides back and forth, pats his horse's side, and tightens his "saddle girth." As he watches the church steeple, he too thinks about the adjoining graveyard and the danger inherent in the task before him. For him as well, these musings end with greater concentration upon his mission, and he cautiously watches until he is certain he sees the second lamp.

The eighth stanza uses the sights and sounds of his ride to emphasize its significance to "the fate of a nation." Longfellow implies that, without the patriotism and courage of people like Revere, the American Revolution might have failed. In the ninth stanza, Longfellow begins to trace Revere's progress through the countryside.

Stanzas 10-12 describe his intrusion upon the essentially pastoral setting in towns such as Medford (10), Lexington (11), and Concord (12).

The concluding stanzas return to emphasis upon America's legendary past and Revere's relationship to the future. In stanza 13, Longfellow develops the contrast between the "British Regulars" and the American "farmers" who successfully oppose them, forcing them to retreat. The final stanza establishes Revere as the embodiment of American independence; Longfellow suggests that his spirit of "defiance" will reappear to defend Americans whenever the nation is threatened.

Forms and Devices

Common criticisms of Longfellow's poetry involve its conventional diction, trite imagery, and excessive metrical uniformity. This poem contains some such flaws, especially in diction and syntax. For example, Longfellow refers to "the tramp of feet" and "the measured tread of the grenadiers" (stanza 4). Likewise, stanzas 9-12 contain such clichés as "the tramp of his steed," "the crowing of the cock," "the barking of the farmer's dog," the "spectral glare" of the meetinghouse windows, "the bleating of the flock," "the twitter of birds," and "the breath of the morning breeze." Sometimes Longfellow also sacrifices syntactic clarity to rhyme scheme. The inverted syntax at the end of the first stanza may be justified by the need to establish an archaic tone, but a similar inversion in stanza 2 ("I on the opposite shore will be") clearly is not realistic dialogue.

Much of the poem's imagery also seems somewhat trite. For instance, the simile of the warship's shadows as prison bars (stanza 3) is a bit heavy-handed. Likewise, repeated references to the moonlight (stanzas 3, 5, and 11) are a bit forced, especially in stanza 11, where the moonlight is described as gilding the meetinghouse's weathercock. A similar objection could be raised concerning the metaphor of "the spark struck out by that steed, in his flight" as the beginning of the Revolution, and Longfellow's physical descriptions often consist of various sensory images in rapid succession.

On the other hand, it is important to remember the poet's purpose and the era in which he wrote. Longfellow deliberately chose conventional imagery and diction because he was developing an American legend; moreover, some elements of the poem may appear trite, primarily because they have become part of American national consciousness. Most important is the fact that, despite these flaws, the poem still appeals to American readers and inspires patriotism.

Certainly this poem is not excessively uniform in stanza length (ranging from five to sixteen lines). Narrative flow seems to determine stanza length; for example, stanzas describing the actual ride (8-12) are shorter than those (6 and 7) in which the characters contemplate their mission. These shorter stanzas create a sense of urgency and rapid movement. Varying stanza lengths also lead to inconsistent rhyme schemes. Most stanzas contain couplets, but none consists entirely of couplets. Likewise, several stanzas include quatrains, but these quatrain patterns also vary.

As in most nineteenth century poetry, true rhyme dominates, but some rhyming syllables are further linked by consonance. For instance, stanzas 5 and 6 employ three rhymes ending in "-ll" ("tall," "hill," "well"). Scansion of individual lines is difficult because Longfellow customarily uses many compressed or slurred syllables; inversions (dactyls for iambs) and substitutions (anapests and dactyls) are frequent, but the iambic tetrameter line is the most common.

Themes and Meanings

Decades before the Civil War, the North and the South vied for the dominant role in America's Revolution. Each claimed to have originated the idea of independence, and their writers commemorated specific battles as proof of these assertions. Apparently, Longfellow originally intended "Paul Revere's Ride" as part of this literary war; he had actually written this poem slightly earlier, but coincidentally *The Atlantic* published it as the Civil War began. Both Longfellow and editor James Fields recognized that the poem could build support for the Union, and supposedly Fields suggested the reference to "the hour of darkness and peril and need" in the final stanza.

The patriotic message is only one reason for emphasis upon the Revolutionary past. Longfellow is the prototypical poet of American Romanticism, whose work incorporates most Romantic conventions. For example, Longfellow's attempt to create a legendary American hero is philosophically compatible with the Romantic emphasis upon the importance of narrative poetry, especially that which recounts significant events in a culture's political or social history. Further, Romanticism required that such narratives be set at least sixty years in the past, and Longfellow describes events that took place eighty-six years earlier.

Also typical of Romanticism is the theme of individualism, especially the effect of one person whose heroism elevates him or her to mythic significance. Longfellow portrays Revere as essentially a colonial American Everyman, whose cleverness and courage earn him a place among Revolutionary War heroes. The infrequent references to Revere by name increase this sense of the messenger as a representative American citizen-soldier, the type of individual that might appear in response to the nation's needs, at any time or place. Since Romantics saw past, present, and future as interrelated, Longfellow probably would have made Revere the guardian spirit of American sovereignty, even without the impetus of sectional conflict.

Romantic individualism was also closely associated with melancholy musings on loneliness and death. For example, when the friend climbs the tower (stanzas 5 and 6), he feels separated from the citizens he is trying to save, his loneliness leads him to contemplate the danger and death represented by the church graveyard, and he is momentarily distracted from his mission. Revere echoes this lonely, somber mood as he too observes the proximity of the graveyard and the church (stanza 7).

The most obvious examples of the death theme occur as Revere nears the end of his ride (stanzas 11 and 12), however. In Lexington, the meetinghouse windows are as "blank and bare" as the eyes of the dead, and Longfellow suggests they are contemplating with horror "the bloody work they would look upon." As Revere enters Concord, the peaceful pastoral setting is marred by his reflections that someone now "safe and asleep in his bed" will become the first casualty of the coming battle.

Romantics were strongly influenced by the literature of other cultures. Longfellow began his career as a professor of comparative literature, but his studies extended beyond traditional familiarity with English, French, German, and Italian literature to include knowledge of Scandinavian literature as well. Narrative genres like the saga and the romance were compatible with his temperament and his purpose. Certainly one major influence during this period was Geoffrey Chaucer's *Canterbury Tales* (1387-1400); Longfellow adopted a similar framework for *Tales of a Wayside Inn*, in which he incorporated "Paul Revere's Ride," assigning this tale to Squire Howe, the innkeeper. In this way, Longfellow seems to remind readers that the poem is a literary construct, not a historical account.

Charmaine Allmon Mosby

PEARL

Author: The Pearl-Poet (fl. in latter half of the fourteenth century)
Type of poem: Elegy
First transcribed: Latter half of the fourteenth century

The Poem

Pearl is a poem employing both alliteration and end-rhyme, with 1,212 lines arranged in 101 stanzas of 12 lines each. It originally bore no title but has long been known by its first word. Its anonymous writer is usually referred to as either the Pearl-Poet or the Gawain-Poet after his or her two most widely acclaimed works, *Pearl* and *Sir Gawain and the Green Knight.*

Pearl narrates a dream, a common strategy for medieval poetry, which incorporates elements of allegory and elegy. The first-person narrator of the poem visits a garden where he lost a valuable pearl. The reader soon realizes this "pearl" is a two-year-old girl, presumably a daughter, whose grave is marked by many flowers. Overcome by their rich scent and his own grief, the narrator falls asleep on the spot where the pearl was lost. The girl appears to him in a dream, at first rebuking his despair as self-indulgent, but then consoling his sorrow. The girl stands across a river from the narrator; although the latter sleeps in a sheltering garden, the dream landscape features a river, cliffs, hills, forests, and meadows.

Early in her conversation, the girl encourages the narrator to abandon self-pity for a more positive view of life, within the context of Christian teaching. After this, she tells him about her existence in New Jerusalem, the heavenly city of the biblical Book of Revelation. Finally, she grants the narrator a vision of her home to comfort him. When he sees the beautiful city, he wishes to join her there, but he cannot cross the river. He concludes the living must remain in the world until their own times come, preparing their "pearls" (themselves) for the prince of the city, Christ.

Forms and Devices

The central image in the poem is that of the pearl. It represents the girl, who was a pearl pleasant enough for a prince's delight ("Perle, plesaunte to prynces paye"). The pearl also serves as a symbol of Mary. The girl lives as a queen, like all women in New Jerusalem, under the influence of Mary, their empress. To medieval perception, the round pearl was an image of perfect grace, for it has no sharp edges or corners but is beautifully smooth. It also is spotless, pure, and incorruptible, and so represents both Mary and all heavenly maidens: When the girl appears, she is arrayed in pearls. Her dress is ornamented with them, she wears a crown set with them, and a large pearl shines on her breast, the Pearl of Great Price, from a New Testament parable representing heaven.

In addition, pearls are mentioned in Revelation as constituting the gates of the New Jerusalem, which description the poem amplifies, describing vividly the glowing colors of the gems that make up the walls in section 17. Even the paths upon which the girl and the narrator walk boast pearls as gravel (section 2).

In contrast with the other gems, pearls (as the paths and gates to New Jerusalem) are white. The poet mentions whiteness many times, including the color of the child's dress, as well as that of all the other maidens of New Jerusalem, where each shines more perfectly than the moon. Like perfect pearls, they have no spot, while the moon is marked by craters and seas. Similarly, the white flowers growing over the girl's grave show brightly among the red and blue ones. The mixture of colors suggests the glow of New Jerusalem's walls. Most important for the poet is the whiteness of the Lamb of God, another biblical image of Christ, to whom the maidens are all wed. The repeated whiteness emphasizes their union.

The poem's rhyme scheme is technically demanding, since only three rhyme sounds are used in a stanza, arranged as *ababababbcbc*. Moreover, the stanzas are arranged in twenty sections of five each, except for section 15, which has six stanzas (in a climax leading to the narrator's request to see New Jerusalem). In these sections, the *c* rhymes are shared among all stanzas. They do not dominate as much as do the *a* and *b* rhymes but only assert themselves as multiple stanzas are read. In addition, the final line of each stanza in a section repeats the word or words used in the final line of the others, as in section 1, which repeats "perle wythouten spot" (pearl without spot). This pattern produces a reassuring rhythm in each section, like the refrain of a song.

In addition to the complex rhymes, the poem also uses alliteration based on Old English tradition, with four stressed syllables in each line. *Pearl* displays many patterns of poetic alliteration, in which anywhere from two to all four stressed syllables could begin with the same letter. The individual lines generally run from eight to ten syllables each but vary considerably, since the length was dictated by the sounds of vowels and consonants, rather than by the number of syllables.

Also, there is a strong sense of symmetry produced by abundant echoes of phrasing and idea throughout the poem. For instance, the opening line refers to a pearl worthy of a prince's pleasure ("paye" or "pay"), and the final line calls readers precious pearls for Christ's pleasure ("precious perles vnto His pay"). Repetitions of ideas include the spice scents that dominate the grave (section 1) and the fruit scents that fill the dreamland (section 2), or the flawlessness of the lost pearl (section 1) and that of the immaculate heavenly crowd (section 16). The imagery and language exhibit a neatness lacking in many medieval works of comparable length, as the poem ties everything together with a balance and elegance suggestive of a string of well-chosen pearls.

Themes and Meanings

Pearl is considered a part of the Alliterative Revival, a rebirth of old poetic styles in the midlands of England during the fourteenth century. However, it employs the old structures with greater flexibility and skill than most works associated with that movement. The language of the poem is that of the northwestern midlands, although enriched with creative phrasing as well as borrowings from Latin and French. The poet is generally assumed to have been quite well read, in view of what seem to be echoes not only of the Bible but also of contemporary authors from Great Britain, France, and Italy. However, conjectural attempts to reconstruct the poet's library differ widely. It is safest to say simply that the poet participated in the intellectual and artistic life of the time.

Critics debate over the extent to which the poem probably reflects the life of the poet, who some speculate may have lost a two-year-old daughter named Marjory or Margaret, both of which mean "pearl." Early scholars even tried to identify the writer based on such an assumption. On the other hand, some critics aver that the little girl is an image of purity, of the baptized soul, or of comparable religious abstractions. Still others suggest that the situation of a grieving parent visiting the garden grave of the child is simply a dramatic way to begin a poem that speculates about heaven. Whatever is true, much of the charm of *Pearl* lies in its combination of the loveliness of setting, the sadness of loss, and the splendor of heaven shown by a gracious little girl.

The description of the child herself suggests the poet's philosophical view of the afterlife expressed otherwise through her statements and the images the narrator relates. Drawing from the New Testament concept of the Christian church as the "Bride of Christ," the girl's dress with its pearls and high collar resembles a contemporary aristocratic bridal gown; she is also called a bride. As such, she seems more than two years old. Similarly, although the narrator recognizes her as the lost child, she behaves as an adult. The details suggest that in the timelessness of eternity, the soul is forever childlike but also fully mature, belonging to no earthly age but embodying all the best of life.

The poem also asserts what was a potentially controversial point, that infants, though unaware of religion, are acceptable to God. The narrator expresses surprise that the young girl, who had not yet learned her prayers, is accepted alongside saints and martyrs. She answers that all in heaven are equally happy, even though some receive special honor for their trials in earthly life. Like all the poem's major points, this is repeated in another form, as the joyful maidens file through New Jerusalem.

Apart from its historical and scholarly interest, *Pearl* presents a believable psychological portrayal of grief and of one way people may find release from emotional pain. It is grounded in Christian belief, although other readers may enjoy the poem as an exploration of mental healing and as a summoning of visionary experience. For those who do not read Middle English, most of its artistry survives translation well. *Pearl* is a masterwork, memorable for its beauty of imagery, grace of language, and evocation of feeling.

Paul James Buczkowski

PEARL HARBOR

Author: Robinson Jeffers (1887-1962)
Type of poem: Meditation
First published: 1948, in *The Double Axe and Other Poems*

The Poem

Robinson Jeffers's poem "Pearl Harbor" expresses the poet's perspective on America's response to the December 7, 1941, Japanese attack on the U.S. fleet in Oahu, Hawaii. Jeffers begins the first of the two sections of twenty-four and twenty-six lines, respectively, that make up this poem by belittling the attack, calling it no more than "fireworks."

The attack, which signaled the entrance of Japan on the side of Germany and Italy in World War II and the entrance of the United States on the side of the Allies, is for Jeffers the result of men who "conspired" to "embroil this republic in the wreck of Europe." Jeffers feels that, in a sense, the Japanese attack is a fitting punishment for these men. Jeffers wonders what he can do as a response to the attack. He feels the only thing he can do is to fly the national flag from the top of the tower that is his home. Only the flag, as a symbol of the entire nation, can express America, for America does not have a single race or religion or language.

Jeffers's attention then turns to his "little" tower, which stares "Confidently across the Pacific." He built the tower at the end of World War I, "the other war's end." Calling the interwar period a "sick peace," Jeffers suggests he built the tower to express his contempt for a sick "Civilization." By contrast, the tower is built of living granite. Jeffers believes the gray stones, which are "quiet and drink the sea-wind," will "survive/ Civilization."

Unlike the granite of the tower, however, Jeffers himself is old and must be more modest. His tower is a "little tower" after all. Yet, World War II is also a little thing, only "dust" of the passage of the British Empire, "torn leaves" of Europe, wind of propellers, and smoke of Tokyo. Jeffers sums up these wars in the image of a nameless "child" with a "butchered throat." He tells the tower to "look no farther ahead," as if the human race has no future other than world war.

Jeffers begins the second section of "Pearl Harbor" by pointing out that since America had provoked war "carefully" for years, it is ironic it should have been surprised when its fleet and planes were destroyed. He views the public panic on both coasts and its leaders' orations with contempt. He finds the American plan to impose peace on the entire planet similarly overblown. At the same time, he bets America will win this war of its own making just as Jonathan Swift's enormous Gulliver could overcome his adversaries as long as he had his big "horse-pistols."

Looking out at an ocean authorities have cleared of ships and planes following the raid on Pearl Harbor, Jeffers finds it empty of humanity and hence a "great beauty." Machines are gone save for one plane flying high above on patrol at dawn and at dusk.

Walking at night, Jeffers notices that a blackout ordered by authorities has doused all lights along the shore. He celebrates the return of "the prehuman dignity of night" which "was before and will be again." In the beauty of darkness and silence, humanity fades away, and it becomes possible for Earth to see God and even God's great staring eyes.

Forms and Devices

As a child, Jeffers read ancient Greek tragedy and biblical tales under the guidance of his father, a theologian and scholar. Many of his poems rework these sources. Jeffers's stance as a poet is that of prophet, large-scale philosopher, doctrine-giver, and seer in the tradition of Percy Bysshe Shelley. Jeffers's poetry, like biblical poetry, has no concept of rhyme. One senses that the language of "Pearl Harbor," like Old Testament verse, is organized as verse, but it still seems to be missing something essential to verse, which is hard to define. Semantic parallelism is a prevalent feature of biblical verse and also of Jeffers's poem.

As lines of biblical verse are composed of two or three "versets," or members which parallel each other in meaning, so too, is the first section of Jeffers's poem. The poet says "Here" in the first verset, "Stare" in the second verset, "Look" in the third verset, "Look, little tower" in the fourth verset, and "Look no farther ahead" at the close of the first section. This parallelism of meaning is joined with a balancing of numbers of rhythmic stresses between versets and sometimes by parallel syntactic patterns as well. Jeffers may follow this underlying formal model or he may modify it or abandon it altogether. In the second section of "Pearl Harbor," he eventually returns to the pattern he established in the first section with the phrases "Make a great beauty," "Watch the wide sea," "Watch the wide sky," "High on patrol," "Walk at night," and "Stands, as it was before."

The structure that predominates in all genres of biblical poetry is a kind of semantic pressure that builds from verset to verset and line to line, intensifying and finally reaching a climax or a climax and reversal. The two sections of Jeffers's poem "Pearl Harbor" are built this way, the first beginning with "fireworks" and ending with "the child with the butchered throat," the second, beginning with ships like "sitting ducks" and "planes like nest-birds" and ending with the "great staring eyes" of God.

Hyperbole or deliberate exaggeration for effect and irony are also common in biblical writing. Jeffers's poem, while employing irony in that America, by trying to enter the war in Europe has found itself at war in the Pacific, belittles rather than exaggerates the war, particularly in the shocking contrast between the title of the poem, "Pearl Harbor," and its first line, "Here are the fireworks." Jeffers was not noted for technical ingenuity in his poetry, but he did develop a style drawn from Greek and biblical models that meshed with his philosophy, and "Pearl Harbor" is a good example of this practice.

Themes and Meanings

A legacy from an uncle allowed Jeffers to move with his wife, Una, to Carmel, California, where he built for himself a granite house and an observation tower overlooking the ocean. This tower figures as a central image in his poem "Pearl Harbor." Robinson and Una Jeffers's own Irish ancestry, their interest (Una's particularly) in Irish round towers, and their admiration for the Irish poet William Butler Yeats led them naturally to build Hawk Tower, which ultimately incorporated a stone from Yeats's own tower at Thoor Ballylee. In Jeffers's later poetry, Hawk Tower became a symbol of sanctuary in ways that related it to Yeats as well as earlier Romantics, though Jeffers looked forward to the day it would be reabsorbed into the coastal shore from which it had been quarried.

"Pearl Harbor" expresses Jeffers philosophy of "pantheism" or "inhumanism," which he characterized as a shift of emphasis from human to not human or the rejection of human-centered concerns in favor of transhuman magnificence. Like philosopher Arthur Schopenhauer, Jeffers held that a superior reality exists behind appearance, a reality that is hidden but still discoverable. Jeffers, like D. H. Lawrence, was elated by the new physics and theories of evolution on one hand and disgusted with historical humanity on the other—in particular, with Christian, self-important, warring humanity. This led both poets to a religion of the inhuman universe. Look without, look within, and people will find the one thing needful—an extra-human greatness of reality.

Jeffers and Lawrence went beyond their fellow modernists to transform the beautiful into something inhumanly sublime. For Jeffers, this sublime, superior reality can be summed up as "God." Images of hawk and stone, representing fierce consciousness joined with final disinterestedness, were for Jeffers the ideal human perspective on existence. Jeffers's pessimism was reinforced by his reading of Greek tragedy and the Hebrew Bible. He found violence intrinsic in human history and believed that this unpleasant truth must be faced rather than repressed.

Jeffers's "inhumanist" philosophy characterizes the way he thinks about the American disaster at Pearl Harbor. From Jeffers's perspective, Pearl Harbor is an unimportant event, something one would expect of violent human beings. As a patriot, Jeffers flies the American flag, but he counsels the stones of his tower to pay little attention to events in Britain, Europe, and Asia. World War II will end with an American victory because America is richer and stronger than its adversaries. That too is not important, however. What is important is that the blackout imposed on the California coast after the attack makes it possible to see what is really important: the shore at night, dark and silent as it was before humanity's appearance obscured the sight of God.

Elaine Laura Kleiner

THE PEASANT WOMEN FROM CUÁ

Author: Ernesto Cardenal (1925-   )
Type of poem: Epistle/letter in verse
First published: 1984, as "Las campesinas del Cuá," in *Vuelos de Victoria*; English
   translation collected in *Flights of Victory*, 1985

The Poem

Ernesto Cardenal's "The Peasant Women from Cuá" consists of seventy lines of
free verse in the reportorial style of a vivid yet unadorned chronicle of the Nicaraguan
civil war. The poem is based upon actual events during the President Anastasio
Somoza García era and serves as a telling account of the tumultuous events. It is representative of oppression of peasants in the mountainous regions of Nicaragua, in which
insurrection brewed and initiated a popular revolution.

This documentary poem evokes the trauma and agony of women who are left to
deal with soldiers of Somoza García's government after their men have fled. It appears in part 1 of *Flights of Victory*, "Flights of Insurrection." A responsorial poem entitled "Llegaron las de Cuá" ("The Women from Cuá Arrived") is in part 2, "Flight of
Victory and Celebration." It recounts the testimonies of a delegation of Cuá's women
at a mass pro-Sandinista rally after the overthrow of the Somocista regime. Their testimonies serve as affirmations of survival and spiritual triumph.

The narrator chronicles several women's accounts of their experiences while they
were imprisoned for three months in a mountain barrack. Recurring images of their
boys in hiding are juxtaposed with the gruesome fates of other captured boys. Another
image recurs throughout the poem: "pangs of birth." The women's cries at the death
and loss of their men ironically evoke their birth pains upon giving life. The cyclical
nature of human experience emerges from the siege, crisis, and spiritual triumph of
the village of Cuá. Descriptions of women giving birth, nursing their young, or aborting reinforce the message that the cycle of life continues despite oppression and imprisonment.

In the second half of the poem, poignant repetition of the women's visions and
dreams shifts the focus from their present reality to the hope that their boys are safe in
their mountain hideouts or triumphant in their guerrilla attacks against the military.
The optimistic tone impacts the second half of the poem. The transition from the focus
on the forces of oppression and its deadly consequences to the power of the human
spirit to overcome adversity delivers the poem's message that freedom emerges from
spiritual triumph over earthly evils.

Forms and Devices

Cardenal's style is devoid of artifice. It utilizes prosody in poetic structure. No consistent metric pattern dominates. The English translation resembles a prose poem
with irregular line breaks. Some names of victims are isolated on separate lines or in

short staccato lists to heighten their impact. Women are listed by name with their testimonies, concise and unelaborated accounts of their traumas. The simplicity of their speech heightens its impact. Their voices return as they are again identified in the continuation poem "Llegaron las de Cuá." This structural aspect resembles techniques of film documentary in which reality is edited, interpreted, and underscored by linguistic choices.

The poem focuses on "María Venancia, 90 years old," "Amanda Aguilar, 50 years old," and "Angela García, 25 years old." Some lines focus acutely on a woman's agony: "Matilde aborted sitting down/ when they questioned her all night long about the guerrillas/" and "Worse ones came in an army truck/ Three days after they left Cándida gave birth." Other images reveal cruel irony: "A guardsman called to Cándida/ come here and wash my pants/ but he wanted something else/ (Somoza smiled in a picture like/ an Alka-Seltzer ad)." The portrait of President Anastasio Somoza García as a benevolent overseer contrasts with the soldiers' brutality. Commonplace icons of the political regime and consumer culture alternate with the women's visions of their men's triumphant return.

The poem's vocabulary is markedly unpoetic, originating in the vernacular and the consumer culture. Cardenal's poem presents reality directly through its objects and images rather than through abstractions and symbolic analogies. Its language is at times prosaic. The women's denial of "I haven't seen any boys" and "We know nothing about them" recurs with emphasis on reportorial stylistics. Their speech is clear and concise in its structural simplicity. Repetition reinforces the women's message of defiance.

The interplay of life and death is also repeated. When one of the boys is taken away or killed, another one is born or raised to take his place. Stark realism marks this cycle: the Cándida suckles her baby, "very tiny and underfed." After listing the nightly disappearances of Esteban, Juan, Saturnino, and Chico, Matilde aborts her child and Cándida gives birth.

The overt political message does not detract from its intensity and clarity. Lines 49-70 digress from factual reportage to a suspension of reality. Elements of political ugliness combine with the purity and beauty of a spiritual vision as prosaic and poetic language merge. The narrator describes the women's dreams in which inexpressible hopes become hazy visions: "their dreams are subversive."

This final section is the only digression from the harsh chronicle. Utilizing vocabulary and line structures more analogous to traditional poetic language, this dream state liberates the women from their imprisonment structurally as well as thematically. Repetition of "mist," "mountain," and "at night" distance this section from the preceding explicit reality. Elderly María Venancia reappears. Rather than her defiant contest to the soldiers' interrogations, she sees the boys in misty mountains. She joins the village women, empowered by their unified vision crystallized in their silent defiance. Cándida, Amanda, and Emelinda return in stark contrast to their torturous experiences with the soldiers. In their dreams, they are free, climbing mountains, wearing knapsacks and singing "happy-go-lucky songs." Their joint creation of a dreamworld strengthens their belief that their boys will come home. The repetition in the final lines concretizes their resolve: "so often at night in dreams/ they see the boys."

Themes and Meanings

Vivid and explicit language conveys the tragedy and pathos of the women who endure the exile, torture, and death of their Sandinista sons and brothers. It does not compromise its political ideology with euphemisms or extraneous poetic language. The narrator begins the poem as a continuation of an account, another chapter of a chronicle written by a human rights observer. The first line begins "Now I'll tell you. . . ." The speaker serves as a reporter, a focused intermediary illuminating the experiences of several women as they survive atrocities. From the honesty and integrity of the language emerges a poetic voice speaking from life. It serves as a contemporary epistle, alluding to the biblical letters of the early apostles and disciples as they evangelized and recorded their experiences. The oppression, exile, persecution, and torture of early Christians correspond with the women's experiences during the siege of Cuá.

The poem also demonstrates that dreams and visions spun by the magical realism of the traditional Nicaraguan peasants defy and defeat the brutal regime that governs them. Shared dream sequences return the embattled peasants to their inherent dignity and power so that they may determine their own destiny. The women's imaginations seek out their men. The power of their shared imagination blends their visualization of a peaceful and free village life with the poignant reality of their torture and imprisonment. The women's "subversive" thoughts cancel out their oppressors' control. Their faith and tenacity enable them to envision their men's triumphant return. In their dreams, where night mist shrouds distant mountains, the Cuá women find freedom. This is where they return in their nightly spiritual journeys to "see the boys." Through their hopes manifested in dreams, the Cuá village survives. The poem chronicles their struggle, and their victory is later proclaimed in "The Women from Cuá Arrived."

"The Peasant Women from Cuá" serves as a rallying cry for liberation theology, a political and religious movement in which Nicaraguan peasants seek justice and self-determination. The concept of theology in practice as well as theory as means of liberation is not limited to Central American peasants. By transcending the siege of Cuá without minimizing its significance in the Nicaraguan struggle for freedom and justice, the poem serves a greater spiritual mission of conversion and enlightenment. It elicits political consciousness on the part of the reader, as its intense and explicit language reveals the poet's penetrating focus, committed compassion, and acute insight into humanity's strengths and frailties. Above all other messages that the poem conveys, it restores dignity to the oppressed. The Cuá women poignantly speak with honesty and integrity as they discover their own language of empowerment.

Carole A. Champagne

THE PERFUME

Author: John Donne (1572-1631)
Type of poem: Dramatic monologue
First published: 1633, in *Poems, by J. D.: With Elegies on the Authors Death*

The Poem

Although designated an elegy in its original title, "The Perfume" is really better considered a seventy-two-line Renaissance imitation of a classical form. John Donne called it an elegy because he composed it in closed couplets, consecutive lines of end-stopped iambic pentameter, a verse pattern that roughly corresponds to the Latin *elegia*. He used the same pattern for his satires, but unlike those, this is addressed to a particular lover, as a commentary on their relationship: The two lovers are being separated by the girl's parents, and this poem is written after the two had been caught together.

The poem is in two parts: The first part details the lovers' attempts to avoid the parents' vigilance; the second investigates the properties of perfume, the agent that gave them away. The speaker begins by complaining that ever since their detection, her father has blamed him for all her escapades. Still, despite the father's close supervision and his threats (even to cast her out of the will), they usually have been successful in their deceit. They even have managed to escape the scrutiny of her mother, ancient in the lore of female wiles. The girl's parents bribed her brothers and sisters to spy on them, but to no avail. The couple also managed to elude the serving man who was commissioned to shadow her. One thing alone betrayed them: They were smelled out by the perfume he was wearing.

To be betrayed by a fragrance was ironic and unjust. Had it been an evil odor, her father never would have noticed it, assuming that it was merely his feet or breath. Just as everyone becomes suspicious of things not native to his or her environment, though, so her father immediately detected something that smelled good. Notwithstanding all his precautions with all other possible giveaways, the lover forgot the one thing that would at once proceed from and be traced back to him.

The speaker proceeds to revile perfume. Compounded of the excretions of plants and animals, it is, like cosmetics, used to disguise the real physical state of the user. Prostitutes concealed infections with it and thus spread them through the population. When men used it, they ran the risk of being labeled effeminate. It was treasured only by courtiers and placeseekers, those who dealt primarily with the insubstantial and the apparent rather than the real. The use of perfume as incense and burnt offerings offers little evidence of intrinsic excellence; the gods simply are flattered by the act of sacrifice.

Furthermore, all perfumes are blended, suggesting that the individual ingredients, taken separately, are offensive. How can a health-giving whole be made out of unwholesome parts, though? Even if one concedes that perfumes are intrinsically good, they vanish, so that they are not good for long. The speaker offers to donate all of his perfumes as embalming fluids for her father—and then suddenly realizes that there is hope of his death, for in noticing a scent he is giving signs of erratic behavior, perhaps a sign of impending collapse.

Forms and Devices

The principal device used by Donne in this poem is the Metaphysical conceit, a kind of forced metaphor joining two terms by exploiting an otherwise obscure relationship that turns out unexpectedly to be illuminating, often on different levels of meaning. In many of his poems, Donne uses this technique to fuse widely separated orders of experience, for example, by linking the sacred with the profane. Here he simply is demonstrating wit, the kind of intellectual and imaginative agility highly prized in fashionable Elizabethan-Jacobean circles. On the simplest level, it is merely clever wordplay, the kind reflected in puns; but with Donne, it is usually much more sophisticated, involving irony, multiple ambiguity, and paradox.

This device first appears in "The Perfume" when the writer refers to his lover's father as "hydroptique," referring simultaneously to bloated, swollen, dropsical; unsatisfied, like an unsaturated sponge; alcoholic; and suspicious, not easily satisfied. The first and third meanings then are reinforced by his "glazed eyes," which glare "as though he came to kill a Cockatrice." This is a fabulous monster with a death-dealing glance; supposedly the glazed eyes will like a mirror reflect the deadly look back to its source. In a similar vein, her mother is described as "immortal" because she spends so much time in bed that she might as well be dead, but resolutely refuses to die. She also proves immortal in her encyclopedic knowledge of female deviousness, which she tests by "sorceries" that suggest she really is a witch.

Donne also uses more conventional devices, especially through the central part of the poem. A significant one is hyperbole, not usually considered part of Donne's repertoire. Hyperbole appears in "the grim eight-foot-high iron-bound serving-man," who appears to be the Colossus of Rhodes to the less formidable suitor, but who will not really be the worst punishment of hell. Donne also employs synesthesia, or the representation of one sense by another: The traitorous "loud" perfume "cryed" at the father's nose; and the "opprest" shoes—because they both are walked on and muffled—are rendered "dumbe and speechlesse." He even anticipates modern marketing strategy and twentieth century taste in coining the phrase "bitter sweet."

Donne returns to more complex figures, especially paradox, toward the end of the poem. The perfume, for example, has at once "fled unto him, and staid with me." Deceived by it into confusing the sweet-smelling with the wholesome, the "seely Amorous"—where "seely" means simultaneously silly, innocent, and gullible—finds death where he should find life; he "suckes his death/ by drawing in a leprous harlots breath." At court, "things that seem, exceed substantiall"—appearance, pretense, and gesture count more than competent performance.

A series of paradoxes ends the poem. The gods accepted burnt offerings simply because they were offerings; they were indifferent to smells, as gods should be. Perfumes defy logic: A combination of independently offensive scents should not be sweet smelling. Their cost exceeds the value of the benefit they provide. Finally, the lover voices a paradoxical hope: Perhaps the perfume that undid him will be the agent of the father's death.

Themes and Meanings

The dramatic situation Donne chooses here, that of young lovers separated by protective parents, is easy for most readers to identify with, as are the emotions of the male persona. The young lovers embody the urge to generation, fertility, and the hope of the future. Opposed to them is the old-fashioned, obsolete, repressive world of the parents, dedicated to maintaining order and controlling the rate of change. Since parents basically attempt to preserve the past and prevent change, they furiously work to keep things the way they are. Looking only ahead, the lovers in no way can see through their parents' eyes. In fact, the parents become foreign, alien, even monstrous.

This accounts for the hostility of tone and the distorted characterization of the parents: the hydroptique father and immortal mother. Yet it is far short of being rancorous. In fact, the focus on witty phrasing and verbal dexterity mutes the hostility, diverting it toward playfulness. This competition between generations is far from final or deadly. Although it is waged with intensity and urgency on both sides, some of the apparent seriousness merely is assumed.

The recognition that humor tempers intensity is the central focus of the poem. Nothing is quite as it seems here. The contest is only semiserious. When the lover teases about the old lady's refusal to die, or when he breaks off the poem at the end with the abrupt "What? Will hee die?," he actually is not contemplating their death. He is merely voicing the lover's final consolation: The old man and woman cannot live forever. Yet those deaths are in the background of the action; in fact, they create much of the tension in this situation because he will die. The older generation must give way, if only at death. Normally, and more beneficially, it occurs earlier. Furthermore, easing the transition benefits both generations, hence the function of humor here. Humor lubricates transitions.

At the core of the poem, the lover declares his commitment to his mistress, despite the temporary setback of his discovery and ejection. By rallying her spirits and expressing his antagonism, he indicates his intention to stay the course, regardless of the opposition he must overcome. He is confirming the pact they have made already. His humor also cements and reinforces his decision. He shows his recognition that he occupies the favored position. He can afford to wait, and thus he can afford to make fun. In this poem, Donne makes splendid fun.

James Livingston

PERSEPHONE IN HELL

Author: Rita Dove (1952-   )
Type of poem: Poetic sequence
First published: 1995, in *Mother Love*

The Poem

"Persephone in Hell," a sequence of seven poems, forms the third of seven sections in Dove's collection *Mother Love*. The sequence and the collection explore the Greek myth of Demeter: With almost no witnesses and with the permission of her father Zeus, the supreme Olympian deity, Persephone has been abducted and raped by Hades, the ruler of the underworld and her uncle, who subsequently makes her his queen. Unable to find her daughter, an angry and inconsolable Demeter wanders among mortals, disguised as an elderly woman. She comes to Eleusis, where she meets the four lovely daughters of Celeus, king of Eleusis, and his wife Metaneira. Demeter, at Metaneira's urging, becomes nurse to the couple's only son, the infant Demophoön. Determined to make the boy immortal, each night Demeter secretly places him in the fire. One night Metaneira discovers this and screams in terror, thus thwarting Demeter's plans. An angry, radiant goddess reveals herself and disappears, but not before ordering the people of Eleusis to build a temple and altar in her honor and promising to teach them rites that became known as the Eleusinian Mysteries. Still inconsolable, Demeter lets the crops die and refuses solace from the other Olympian gods and goddesses. Eventually Zeus agrees to return Persephone, but because she has eaten pomegranate seeds offered by Hades, she must spend fall and winter with her husband and spring and summer with her mother, thus ensuring the seasons, agriculture, and partial consolations.

The focus of "Persephone in Hell" is the riveting episode with which the ancient account of the myth, the "Homeric Hymn to Demeter," begins: the abduction and rape of Persephone by Hades. Dove's treatment of this episode is innovative and complex. The former U. S. poet laureate (1993-1995) announces its complexity in the section's epigraph by American expatriate poet H. D. (Hilda Doolittle): "Who can escape life, fever,/ the darkness of the abyss?/ lost, lost, lost . . ." In the sequence's opening poem, radical innovations appear, including a modern Persephone, a nineteen-year-old American "Girded . . . with youth and good tennis shoes." Her first-person voice ushers the reader into the sequence's setting: Hell is a bone-chilling October in Paris, the City of Lights; the city, Persephone notes, of detritus and neon-lit underground sewers; and the city of Our Lady (Notre Dame Cathedral) to whose heavy presence, like the mental presence of her mother Demeter, Persephone keeps turning her back. In the fifth poem, another innovation appears: Hades is a sardonic, older Frenchman, a habitual seducer whose character borders on caricature.

The mood of the sequence's first six poems combines ennui and irritation. Both underscore the detachment with which Persephone thinks of her mother who "with her frilly ideals// . . . couldn't know what [Persephone] was feeling;// . . . I was doing everything and feeling nothing." Ennui characterizes the way in which Persephone and Hades individually assess their surroundings and people. Both are especially irritated by ineffectual artists and intellectuals, whom Hades compares metaphorically to a "noisy zoo"; Persephone responds, "let this party/ swing without me." Within this dissatisfaction, Dove reconstructs their encounter.

The sequence is crafted as a three-stage rite of passage for Persephone: fledgling initiatives/waiting, the contact, the life-defining initiation. In the first four poems, Persephone experiments with sexual and social relationships, which remain superficial. She is curious but detached, a young woman who knows only "seven words of French," the language of Hell and adulthood. The one who will teach Persephone that language appears in the fifth poem, a monologue delivered by a bored Hades whose *"divertissement"* (Persephone, as it turns out) will be a matter of chance: "The next one through that gate,/ woman or boy, will get/ the full-court press of my ennui." The sixth poem captures Persephone and Hades's first meeting and conversation. Both realize that Persephone does not belong there, but, as she inadvertently points out, the "Midnight./ The zero hour" of their encounter has arrived. In the sequence's final poem, Dove alternates their voices as each approaches their pivotal sexual encounter. Persephone, for example, recognizes that a part of her "had been waiting," to which Hades counters, "I am waiting/ you are on your way."

Forms and Devices

The "Persephone in Hell" sequence is linked by theme rather than form. Dove gives each of the seven poems a distinctive format, using the varied forms, lines, quotations, and typography for crucial purposes. They identify multiple voices and personas that move in and out of the poems. They also intensify a driving sense of order that moves below the seemingly random surface of Persephone's experiences and responses. The result is an intense unit. While none of the seven poems of "Persephone in Hell" is in the sonnet form, the closely linked thematic unit suggests that Dove may have had in mind a seven-poem form known as a "crown of sonnets." Whatever the case, "Persephone in Hell" ends with Persephone being claimed sexually as the queen of the underworld.

Surprising appearances of formal language in the dominant informality of the sequence support its unsettling effect. In addition, although Dove occasionally uses irregular end or internal rhymes, most of the lines are unrhymed. This decision, as well as the poet's mixtures of other devices, emphasizes the poems' nuanced informality. For example, Dove frequently sets up terse catalogs of details. Just as often, she uses a consonant emphasis, such as *s*, to carry a barrage of details and partial and irregular rhymes: "Through the gutters, dry rivers/ of the season's detritus./ Wind soughing the plane trees./ I command my knees to ignore the season/ as I scuttle over stones." Similes, used sparingly but strategically, combine tension and details. Typical examples include Persephone's description of Paris's sewer system ("like some demented plumber's diagram/ of a sinner's soul") and her initial impression of Hades ("He inclines his head, rather massive,/ like a cynical parrot.") A more important device is Dove's repetitions of images and emphases. To trace, for example, her use of Africans, "way," light/dark, Mother/Our Lady, food and drinks, and autumnal references is to study the poet's craft and the poems' themes.

Themes and Meanings

The "Homeric Hymn to Demeter," even in its disturbing account of Persephone's rape, gives the starring role to the goddess of agriculture. Dove expands Demeter's role, adding psychological layers to the goddess-mother's love and loss. The poet, however, also develops Persephone's and Hades's characters, giving them prominent first-person voices throughout the collection. These revisions of the myth serve Dove's thematic purposes. With this triad, the poet can emphasize contradictions in and pressures on maternal love, mother-daughter relationships, and adulthood.

One such contradiction, the narcissism of all three characters, is Dove's covert psychological gesture to the account in the "Homeric Hymn to Demeter" in which a narcissus flower attracts first Persephone and then Hades to Persephone. Certainly, Demeter's maternal pride matches the self-absorption of both Persephone and Hades. The result is a triangle of willfulness, uneasiness, and power struggles. Demeter, for example, will not accept her daughter's sexuality or autonomy. The goddess is also a chronic worrier. Persephone, even as she gains independence and tries to shake off her mother's worry, is bored and numb. The latter problem also characterizes Hades and the detachment with which Hades and Persephone approach each other. In fact, all three characters in this sequence reflect numbed states of waiting: "*It's an old drama, waiting./ One grows into it,/ enough to fill the boredom . . ./ it's a treacherous fit.*"

Finding a way out of this treacherous, three-way fit is the goal of Dove's account of the myth. Dove allows Persephone to articulate that difficulty: "For a moment I forgot which way to turn"; "*Which way is bluer?*"; and "*And if I refuse this being/ which way then?*" The quest is for light and enlightenment, and, ironically, Persephone approaches it when she raises to Hades the glass of chartreuse that he compares to "*un mirage,*" which she coyly translates as "a trick of light." As their sexual encounter begins, she reflects confusion in whispered questions to herself ("if I whispered to the moon,/ if I whispered to the olive/ which would hear me?"), which are patterned on the opening line of German poet Rainer Maria Rilke's 1923 *Duineser Elegien* (*Duino Elegies*, 1930): "Who, if I cried out, would hear me among the angelic orders?")

By invoking (in whispers, not screams) the virgin goddesses of the moon (Artemis) and the olive (Athena)—both with contradictory roles, both cruel when offended—Persephone confirms her divided mind. Still, in her charged last question—"who has lost me?"—she moves toward an unexpected nexus where selfhood, sexuality, an adult relationship, and her mother's advice ("be still she whispers/ and light will enter") meet and where understanding can begin.

Persephone is on her way to becoming the perennial traveler-mediator between darkness and light, fragmentation and harmony, and interior and exterior worlds. However, she must begin with an interior journey. As Dove explained in a 1996 interview, "I would like to remind people that we *have* an interior life . . . and without that interior life, we are shells, we are nothing." The "Persephone in Hell" poems demonstrate Dove's wise advice. The reader is pulled into a modern interior of the Demeter myth, into its underworld of change, chance, sexuality, grief, willfulness, violence, and love. It is only within the interior that poetry and myth reveal their secret: The underworld teaches the reader the way back to the seasons of life, seasons transformed by the journey.

Alma Bennett

PERSIMMONS

Author: Li-Young Lee (1957-   )
Type of poem: Narrative
First published: 1981; collected in *Rose,* 1986

The Poem

"Persimmons" consists of eighty-eight lines of free verse. The speaker is clearly Li-Young Lee himself, who immigrated to the United States from China as a small boy. The poem begins with Lee in trouble with his sixth-grade teacher because he cannot hear the difference between the words "persimmon" and "precision." This scene is the first of several episodes Lee recalls in "Persimmons," each of which involves a verbal ambiguity, misconception, or blunder of some sort. In the course of the poem these encounters involve Lee and four other people: Mrs. Walker (the teacher), Lee's wife Donna, his mother, and his father.

After recalling his punishment in school, Lee jumps ahead many years to a scene in the backyard, where he and his wife are making love. Here, too, words seem to fail the poet; he can teach Donna the Chinese for crickets, but cannot remember the words for dew and naked. He does, however, "remember to tell her/ she is as beautiful as the moon." The love between them quickly eliminates the awkwardness Lee feels.

Next he recounts other words "that got me into trouble" as a boy, "wren and yarn" most poignantly. His mother seems to have contributed to his confusion, but she also helped him to see the underlying unity of things: "Wrens are soft as yarn./ My mother made birds out of yarn." She also made a rabbit and "a wee man" as Li-Young watched, toys for her child, acts of love that taught him to see how rich words might be if they were not tied too tightly to single meanings. From his mother the toy maker, Lee takes the reader back to Mrs. Walker. She has brought a persimmon to class "and cut it up/ so everyone could taste/ a Chinese apple." The boy can see that the fruit is not ripe, but he says nothing and only watches the faces of his classmates.

Two brief verse paragraphs follow in which the poet describes the persimmon more fully and compares it with the cardinal on his windowsill, which sings to him, "The sun, the sun." The remainder of the poem focuses on Lee's father, who has gone blind. His relationship with the persimmon is the most complex and has the most to teach the poet.

Forms and Devices

"Persimmons" opens with the scene in Mrs. Walker's sixth-grade class. The incident is recounted in the flat language of simple narrative, but the stage is set for a more complex, stream-of-consciousness account of the poet's coming of age, both as a poet and as a man. "Persimmon" itself constitutes the strongest current in that stream: The sound of the word, the taste, feel, and appearance of the fruit, and the symbolic significance it has for the poet and his parents all contribute to the design of the poem.

"Persimmon" and "precision" may not sound much alike to a native English speaker, but that same speaker may also lack the "precision" Lee has learned from his Chinese mother in distinguishing ripe from unripe fruit, a difference he can trace as he watches the faces of his classmates as they sample pieces of an unripe persimmon Mrs. Walker has imprecisely chosen in the market. This kind of wordplay is the dominant poetic device Lee employs in "Persimmons," a kind of play that continues with wren and yarn and fight and fright. In each instance, the poet finds in the memories of his childhood something that connects the words with each other.

It is not only the sound of these words that engages Lee's attention but also the sense impressions they evoke. Lee uses imagery of taste and touch as well as sight and sound, among them rich images like the touch of a wolftail brush on silk, the sounds of crickets and the feel of dew in the yard where Lee and his wife lie naked in the moonlight, and especially the taste of a genuinely ripe persimmon. (The sense of taste is something of a Li-Young Lee trademark; see especially "Eating Alone" and "Eating Together," collected in *Rose*, the volume in which "Persimmons" appears.) Lee's imagery often employs synesthesia, whereby one sense is described by evoking another; thus, the persimmon tastes like sunlight, and the backyard shivers with the sound of crickets.

The persimmon also carries a kind of symbolic weight for the poet and his family. When Mrs. Walker calls the fruit a "Chinese apple," she points to a meaning of which she is almost certainly unaware. Lee's father is a political refugee whose pursuers have driven his family far from home. They can never go back, it would seem, but they have brought knowledge of the persimmon with them; what is exotic to the American teacher and her students is familiar to Lee's family. Further, the more his mother and father tell him about the fruit, the more mysteriously potent it becomes: It has a sun inside, it is "heavy as sadness/ and sweet as love." Lee has been granted a kind of power through knowing the secrets of the persimmon.

Other objects carry similar weight in the poem. Lee finds three of his father's paintings: "Hibiscus leaf and a white flower/ Two cats preening./ Two persimmons, so full they want to drop from the cloth." All of these subjects seem to have been ones that Dr. Lee could still paint after going blind, suggesting that blindness and vision are no more remote from each other than wren and yarn. This stress on the thing rather than an idea links Lee to older modern poets such as Wallace Stevens and William Carlos Williams.

One more point should be made about the structure of "Persimmons." Until near the end, the poem moves from episode to episode as sounds and images carry the poet from one place in time to another. When he asks his father the "stupid question" about his blindness, however, the nature of the movement changes. With his painting of the persimmons in hand, Dr. Lee takes over. He describes painting blind, with the physical sense of brush in hand and the strength and "precision" in the wrist substituting for sight. The last episode is narrated not by the son, but by the father, who at this point sees more effectively, even though he is blind. This situation is an ironic twist familiar to readers of Sophocles and John Milton, but it seems less painful here, as Dr. Lee emphasizes how much remains to him.

Themes and Meanings

"Persimmons" is a poem about ways of knowing and of expressing what one knows. The most obvious form of expression for a poet is words, but Li-Young Lee learned early that words can mean very different things and that without love, including the kind of love a patient teacher might display toward a slow student, words may carry more confusion than understanding.

Lee's experience as an immigrant provides him with a novel perspective on this familiar theme. Because English was not his first language as a child, he readily confused one word with another in ways a native speaker could hardly imagine. To his teacher, he simply seemed stupid, and she punished him. There was no love between them and therefore no understanding. Later in the poem, when she brings a persimmon for the class to share, Lee merely watches the faces of his classmates as they bite into the unpalatable fruit. Neither student nor teacher is prepared to teach or to learn from the other.

In contrast, when Lee tries to share the language of his childhood with his American wife, he finds that much of the understanding between them is nonverbal. It does not really matter that he cannot think of particular Chinese words because they share a complex set of physical and emotional sensations. Love, which is in part a deep sharing of such experience, creates and maintains understanding in the absence of the exact word.

Similarly, his relationship with his mother is also charged with love. Although the confusion between wren and yarn got him into trouble with his teacher, he was learning a new way to look at the relationships between word and thing and between one thing and another. The yarn can become a wren in the hands of the knitter or in the language of the poet. For both kinds of artist, reality is more fluid, the possibilities more creative, than a literalist such as Mrs. Walker could ever imagine.

This is the point the poet's father makes. Dr. Lee can still paint even though he is blind because he has never lost certain sensations: the taste of a persimmon, the scent of a lover's hair. Seeing, feeling, hearing, tasting, loving, imagining, by the end of the poem, the persimmon comes to stand for all these things.

William T. Hamilton

PETER QUINCE AT THE CLAVIER

Author: Wallace Stevens (1879-1955)
Type of poem: Lyric
First published: 1915; collected in *Harmonium*, 1923

The Poem

"Peter Quince at the Clavier" is made up of four lyrics of differing formal properties, and through them one senses that the poem has "movements," as a musical composition often does. As in a sonata, the distinct parts involve changes of mood, tempo, and emphasis. This is one of the best-loved and most often recited poems of Wallace Stevens's long career, perhaps because it handles, both playfully and seriously, ideas about art that are as suggestive as John Keats's famous "Beauty is truth, truth beauty—that is all/ Ye know on earth, and all ye need to know."

In William Shakespeare's *A Midsummer Night's Dream* (c. 1595-1596), Peter Quince is a comic character—an overachieving, self-conscious, aspiring director of the stage who brings his unskilled actors into the woods to rehearse a short play for the Duke and Duchess's impending nuptials. In Stevens's poem, the "Peter Quince" speaker is a serious thinker on the relationship between music and feeling, beauty and desire. To make his point, Quince ventures into an unusual account of Susanna and the elders, a story of beauty and lust in the Old Testament Apocrypha. In the apocryphal account, Susanna fails to be seduced by court officials who spy upon her bathing; in their outrage, they try her as an adultress and she is put to death. In Stevens's account, the violence is only suggested. He places the emphasis on music and beauty. The speaker, in an unusual way, associates himself with the elders. Like those who lusted for Susanna, he says, he sits "here in this room, desiring you"—his beloved in part I.

In part II, the reader is taken into Susanna's point of view by a free-verse song in which Susanna, bathing, hears music and senses a unity in everything around her. Only the last two lines of her song hint at the cruel authority about to destroy her complete accord. In the five tightly rhymed couplets of part III, the poem shifts to the point of view of Susanna's weak-willed attendants, who arrive too late to help their mistress. By the time they respond, she has already been accused by the noblemen. Susanna is abandoned to her fate.

The last part (IV) takes a tremendous jump from the elliptical nature of the Susanna narrative to the deeply reflective and almost philosophical tone of the ending. The sixteen lines of this self-contained poem are rhymed and have the tight, rhymed argument and reasoned logic of a sonnet. The difficulty in the argument has somewhat to do with a conundrum: Beauty is momentary in our minds, while in the physical body it is immortal. One would have expected the poet to say just the opposite—that beauty is immortal in the mind and merely fleeting in the flesh. Thus, the poem carries the burden of explaining how flesh and immortality are not at odds as is normally thought. The poet explains it four times until one accepts the subtle truth of the argument.

Bodies do die, but other bodies take their place; evenings die but produce a succession of evenings; gardens and maidens die, only to set up an eternity of gardens and maidens, and one maiden celebrates the whole. The last six lines argue, in difficult but lyrical language, that Susanna's music lives in the "you"—the beloved mentioned at the beginning of the poem—and lives in Peter Quince's musical attempt to consecrate Susanna by retelling her story. Some consider these last six lines among the most gorgeous in the English language; they place Stevens in the company of Sappho, Shakespeare, and Keats.

Forms and Devices

References to music abound in the poem. Some musical references are stated obviously, and others lie embedded in puns. On the narrative level, the word "music" is repeated four times in the first six lines of the poem, in which a speaker is seated at a keyboard. Other direct musical references ("melody," "chords," "choral," and "play," as in play upon a violin) combine with a host of musical instruments—clavier, viol, basses, cymbals, horns, and tambourines. These references are further compounded by "strains," "pizzicati," "pulse," "springs," "winds," "breath," "refrain," "flowings," and even "scrapings" (as of a violin badly bowed). The poet says outright that "thinking of your blue-shadowed silk/ Is music."

A reader's awareness of all these compounded references, however, does not make the poem easier to understand. In fact, awareness can add to the complication and bewilderment readers feel when they try to make sense of it. The poem's opening narrative takes place in a parlor, where a lover is making love at the keyboard. Immediately, the poem jumps to a mythic time (part II) in which a woman is made love to by bawdy, red-eyed elders (later, "white elders"). The poem seems to guide readers to a reconciliation of these two opposing images. Such reconciliation is not found in the immediacy of a story line or in the argument at the end. Stevens elsewhere stated his beliefs in "new ways of knowing." On the simplest level, this poem requires that readers find in its formal elements, involving associations of words and narratives, a new way of knowing an old story that, in the Apocrypha at least, seems to be about lust and treachery. Formally, one is presented with a way of knowing Susanna's story by the juxtaposition of a modern lover (presumably young) with those ancient thin-blooded, lecherous old men. He seems to hint that he is somewhat like these old men in the tale. His puns help him explain himself.

All lovers feel the "strain" of love, whether they feel it in a genteel way (as a strain of music) or in a more physical way—the strain in copulation and sexual performance. Lust in the old is less of a physical strain than the act itself is; lust for the young is more of a musical strain, and lovemaking is easier. Stevens was a master of serious puns. His pun on "strain" allows readers to suppose (in III) that the old men may have tried and failed at rape; they resorted to accusations when their own desire failed. The "uplifted flame" of passion reveals only the shame of lust, not the act itself. When the simpering attendants flee the scene, their tambourines make no music, only noise. Without true feeling there can be no music. When readers understand this, Peter's first puzzling statement (in I) becomes much clearer: Music is not sound; music is feeling.

Susanna herself (in II) seems to intuit what Peter knows without speaking a word on her own behalf. A repeated subject/verb refrain forms a kind of scaffolding for section II: "Susanna lay./ She searched// And found// She sighed,// . . . she stood// She walked . . .// She turned." Balancing these subject/verb constructions are the less active and more tentatively worded lyrical phrases—the quavering of a different sensibility in Susanna's reality—the music felt beyond sound. She is counterpart to male certainty and forced entry—the crashing cymbals and roaring horns. These cymbals and horns are the noise of desire that can be heard if Susanna's complement of music is overridden.

Stevens takes a phrase such as "touch of springs" in Susanna's section (II) and replays it in part IV as "touched the bawdy strings." Stevens relies on the reader hearing from phrase to phrase the various plays in his puns and associations and repetitions. This is part of the tremendous formal pleasure of the poem; every reading turns up more and more sound.

Themes and Meanings

The salient themes and meanings of the poem seem to be in the unraveling of "Beauty is momentary in the mind" but immortal in the flesh. One way to read this puzzle is to put the young poet together with the lecherous old man, much as one might prefer to keep them apart—the one loving, the other violent toward his object of desire. In such minds (young poet/old lecher), Susanna (the beauty) is only able to last momentarily, since these individual minds die away. Susanna is independent. First, her flesh lives on in other flesh. Susanna, as a beauty in body and soul, survives people's weaknesses—moral and physical. Second, her flesh is immortal in the whole scheme of nature and of change. One knows evenings both in their multiple and in their individual returns. There is no way for one to know an evening without knowing constant change from day to evening, nor is there any way to forget. Susanna lives in the perception of beauty always with people in the flesh. Her body dies, but that dying is only an escape from desire's pitiful scrapings. When the speaker says that after all this time Susanna is still remembered, readers must remember that the "now" of the poem is at the beginning, when Peter Quince plays "in this room" to his Susanna and tries, by placing his fingers on the keys, to connect the two beauties and thus participate in a constant music, a "constant" (or immortal) sacrament of praise.

Beverly Coyle

PEYOTE POEM

Author: Michael McClure (1932-   )
Type of poem: Meditation
First published: 1958; collected in *Hymns to St. Geryon and Other Poems*, 1959

The Poem

Peyote Poem is a long serial poem of 242 lines divided into three major parts. The three numbered parts are further divided into stanzas or sections. Part 1 consists of seven sections of various lengths, part 2 is divided into two sections, and part 3 into seven. None of the sections or stanzas are numbered but are separated from each other by long, horizontal lines. The poem is written in the first person. The occasion of the poem is a record of Michael McClure's first experimentation with the hallucinatory drug peyote, a form of mescaline used by some North American Indian tribes in religious ceremonies. The mystic painter/photographer Wallace Berman, who was an active member of a small cult of peyote eaters in the San Francisco Bay area, was McClure's guide during his first peyote experience in 1957. McClure considered this experiment to be one of several alchemical tools that he used to explore the boundaries of consciousness. McClure, who is both a Beat poet and a member of the San Francisco Renaissance group, treated the use of such drugs as a serious vehicle for developing and expanding spiritual states. McClure and some other poets made these experiences the content of some of their poetry.

The setting of part 1 is the living room of McClure's home in San Francisco, and the poem records what he experiences as he looks out of the window. After ingesting the drug, he becomes acutely aware of pain in his stomach, a recurring image that becomes a metaphor for what Buddhists consider the center of consciousness. The stomachache recurs over twenty times during the course of this twelve-page poem. The first revelation of his peyote experience is that there is no time, only space; he also realizes that he is "separate." Throughout the poem, the speaker defines his fall as a fall into the knowledge that there are only two facts of existence (consciousness and empty space) and that they are connected only by the speaker's imagination. This traumatic cleavage becomes the cause of his "!STOM-ACHE!" as he views the world from his window. The window becomes a metaphor for the separation of the artist from a world he can only view from the outside; he can never participate in it. At the conclusion of part 1, he has a terrifying vision of a frozen osprey, an echo of a feathered Satan in Dante Alighieri's *Inferno* (c. 1320; English translation, 1802).

In part 2 the osprey, which is a bird of prey (a fish hawk), glares at the speaker ominously, an act that brings him into the full realization of the nature of reality: "I have entered the essential-barrenness/ . . . I face the facts of emptiness." The osprey grows more gigantic and fierce and terrifies the speaker into an even deeper awareness that he is utterly alone: "The fact of my division is simple I am a spirit/ of flesh in the cold air . . ./ . . . I am separate, distinct." Part 3 documents the speaker's increasing sense of isolation but further intensifies the pain in his belly by the growing discovery that "There is nothing but forms/ in emptiness." That sense of terror overwhelms him from within: "I AM AT THE POINT OF ALL HUGENESS AND MEANING," a foreboding that spreads from his stomach to the rest of his body. From this knowledge, he realizes in the poem's climactic section that his peyote trip has reduced him to "a bulk/ in the air" in a world devoid of categories, justifications, and, therefore, meaning.

Forms and Devices

The formal requirements of the serial poem dictate to some degree the structure of this long, complex poem. However, the movement of the poem comes not from intellectual analysis but rather from information that his senses, especially his stomach (that is, his literal "gut" feelings), reveal to him. The persistent metaphor of the stomach as the center of consciousness pervades all three parts of the poem. The peyote's effect is to clarify the speaker's perceptions to such a degree that mere sight is transformed into cosmic revelation (that is, visionary experience). The recurring motif of stomach pain signals the next development in the speaker's expanding awareness of the emptiness of existence, which is embodied in the repetition of the word "space."

A result of the speaker's knowledge of the world's emptiness (another recurring image throughout the poem) is his deeply disturbing discovery that he is separate and distinct from it. Another revelation in part 1 is that time is an illusion created by the imagination, and without time the cosmos literally has no point or reason. Empty space is transformed into a dragon surrounded by clouds, mists, and vapors out of which emerges the principal image of part 2, the dragonlike figure of "an osprey frozen skyhigh/ to challenge me," a metaphor more than a little reminiscent of Satan in Dante's *Inferno* and French Symbolist poet Stéphane Mallarmé's recurring "frozen swan" motif.

Many of the images running throughout the poem (aching stomach, space, emptiness, timelessness, and separateness) culminate in the controlling metaphor for the whole poem: the fall into consciousness. However, that knowledge creates only weariness, a sense of ennui best expressed in one of Mallarmé's most brilliant lines: "Alas, the Flesh is sad/ And I've read all the books." Many of the poem's images attest McClure's familiarity with the work of the French Symbolist poets of the nineteenth century, such as Mallarmé, Arthur Rimbaud, and especially Charles Baudelaire, whose influences are evident throughout the poem.

In part 2, the metaphor of the stomach as knowledge and the seat of consciousness nears the bursting point: The speaker says, "MY STOMACH IS SWOLLEN AND NUMB!" as he realizes that "measurement is arbitrary" and that metamorphosis and transmutation are spiritually alchemical processes that are irrelevant in the "essential-barrenness" of the world. In part 3, however, McClure juxtaposes the brutal images of empty meaninglessness with images of memory, warmth, and love that are centered in his voice: "The answer to love/ is my voice" and "I am caught in reveries of love." Though experience is intractably solipsistic, the speaker finds some consolation in the knowledge that though his experience is private, it does, nonetheless, belong to him.

That knowledge momentarily assuages the pain of ennui and isolation: "My stomach is gentle love, gentle love."

Themes and Meanings

Peyote Poem is about discovering that the cosmos is essentially empty and meaningless without the structuring capacity of the human imagination. However, McClure came to that knowledge only with insight gained from his peyote experience. As one of the principal Beat and San Francisco Renaissance poets, he recognized that there were very few avenues for transcendence available to artists and poets in the spiritually empty and excessively materialistic United States of the 1950's. He also realized that he could not attain a clear vision of reality that was not distorted and conditioned by cultural and societal preconceptions. By taking part in the rituals of a small peyote cult in the San Francisco Bay area, he hoped that the hallucinatory visions of peyote might somehow expand his consciousness beyond the mundane world of mere time and space. Linguistic philosophers such as Ludwig Wittgenstein and Ferdinand de Saussure, as well as phenomenologist Edmund Husserl, had been addressing similar problems earlier in the century. They all found it virtually impossible to get beyond the conditioning nets of perception and language. McClure and his fellow peyote eaters utilized the pre-Columbian religious practices of some American Indians, who attained spiritual transcendence through drug-induced visions, but only within the regulating contexts of ritual.

What McClure discovers in his peyote vision is not a unified, harmonic vision of the cosmos but rather the opposite. He discovers that time is arbitrary and is the product of the imagination, and he is left with only space: "I have entered the essential-barrenness/ . . . I face the facts/ of emptiness." Concurrent with the "facts of emptiness" comes the corollary proposition: "The fact of my division is simple I am a spirit/ of flesh in the cold air . . ./ . . . I am separate, distinct." From his discovery that he is alone and utterly unconnected to anything, he also begins to understand the true nature of the universe: "There is nothing but forms/ in emptiness." The poet has descended into Hades, his own "dark night of the soul," similar to those experienced by earlier visionary poets such as Dante, Saint John of the Cross, and Saint Teresa of Avila. Though his response to the essential emptiness of the cosmos gives him little cause for celebratory ecstasy, the dark vision does produce feelings that authenticate his existence: "I KNOW ALL THAT THERE IS TO KNOW/ feel all that there is to feel."

The final revelation of *Peyote Poem* produces a mixture of despair and hope because the poet has found within the painful recognition of the world's emptiness and meaninglessness that he must rely on the only evidence available: "My feelings real to me. Solid/ as walls.—I see the meaning/ of walls—divisions of space,/ backgrounds of color./ HEAVEN AND HELL THIS IS REACHABLE." He had earlier discovered that "The answer to love" is his voice. What the speaker understands after his nightmarish vision is that "The room is empty of all but visible things./ THERE ARE NO CATEGORIES! OR JUSTIFICATIONS!" The cosmos is, then, the product of his imagination and, as a poet and painter, McClure has redeemed the emptiness of the cosmos with the power of his imagination to define himself with utter precision: "I am sure of my movements I am a bulk/ in the air." The recognition that the cosmos does not possess any inherent categories, justifications, and, therefore, meaning, releases him to celebrate the fact that the world is inexorably his own solipsistic world. However, that evidence is authenticated solely by his deepest feelings.

Patrick Meanor

PHILHELLENE

Author: Constantine P. Cavafy (Kōnstantionos Petrou Kabaphēs, 1863-1933)
Type of poem: Dramatic monologue
First published: 1912, as "Philhellene"; in *Poiēmata*, 1935; English translation collected in *The Poems of C. P. Cavafy*, 1951

The Poem

"Philhellene," which means "a lover of things Greek," is a short dramatic monologue spoken by a king of one of the puppet monarchies on the edge of the Roman empire in western Asia. "Beyond the Zagros" (mountains that straddle the border between Iraq and Iran), this imaginary kingdom is far from the center of what the king regards as civilization. The time is not specified, although one can assume that it is sometime in or after the first century C.E. The king is addressing either his coin designer or one of his courtiers, a man named Sithaspes, about the design on a planned coin. The poem is in (in the original Greek) a very loose iambic meter, with line lengths usually from eleven to fourteen syllables; such a varied pattern allows the speaker to seem informal and colloquial, but the language is still highly controlled.

The king commands his listener to be careful with the design. Above all, it must be in good taste—that is, Greek. For example, the "diadem" on the coin must "be rather narrow." Otherwise, it would be too extreme, opposed to the classical Greek ideal of "the middle way." Indeed, the king adds, almost sneeringly, in an attempt to establish his own Greekness, that the bad taste, the excessiveness, of the neighboring Parthians, at that time a real antagonist of the Romans, does not please him.

The very vehemence of his words reveal the king's insecurities. He goes on to say that the "inscription" must be in Greek, not the native language of the kingdom, and it must be restrained, "nothing hyperbolic, nothing pompous," especially because that might also be a political error, since the Roman proconsul could perhaps misread it and report to Rome. At the same moment, the king, trying to hang on to his dignity, says, "It should be, however, honorable."

For the reverse side of the coin, the king wants something carefully artistic, perhaps "a handsome young disk-thrower." With that, though, the poem comes to the real concern of the king—how to make the world know that he is truly civilized. "Above all," he says to Sithaspes, make sure that after the words "King" and "Savior" on the coin there be added the term "Philhellene." Above all, he is a lover of things Greek—especially the restrained taste of the Greeks—and so indeed is a kind of Greek himself.

As in most dramatic monologues, there are implied reactions by the listener, and here the king must see some hint of a smile on Sithaspes' face, for he says: "Don't make your jokes, your remarks about 'Where are the Greeks?' and 'Where is the Greek culture here beyond the Zagros Mountains, beyond Phraata?'" (Phraata was the summer capital of the Parthian empire.) On he goes, suggesting that they have a right to be considered somehow Greek: "People who are far more barbarian than we write such things [on their coins], therefore we will also write them." Moreover, occasional sophists, versifiers, and other such "wiseacres" from Syria come here. Therefore, "we are not non-Greek, I think," he concludes.

Forms and Devices

Constantine Cavafy, especially in the poems he regarded as his real poems, avoided language that was flowery, hyperbolic, or expressive of self. Indeed, one could say that his choice of the dramatic monologue as a common device was an attempt to control the language so that it did not become excessive.

One finds few figures of speech in Cavafy's poetry—especially in this poem—no striking similes or metaphors, no obvious images used as symbols. Even rhymes are rare, if not accidental, here, although he does make use of them elsewhere.

The whole purpose of the poem, at least on the surface, is to create the character of the king, not to be a personal expression of the poet. The poem is not presented as a beautiful object in itself, although in its very restraint it does achieve a kind of beauty. The poem's language must be simple, within limits, in order to make its effect. Indeed, the essence of Cavafy's poetry is not in external elaboration or ornamentation, but in a precise control of tone and structure, elements that shift subtly, letting the reader know much more than the speaker says.

Therefore, the king is direct, seeming simply to give orders. He is revealing himself, however, revealing what he regards as beautiful and wise but also aspects of his own ego that perhaps he does not know himself. For example, when he describes the front of the coin, where his *own* profile will be, he immediately warns Sithaspes about being careful with the inscription, so that the Romans who are the real power will not be offended. In the next line, however, he turns to the design of the coin's back and once more emphasizes the beautiful—the figure of the discus thrower. Then he returns to his own insecurities, his knowledge that he is not really Greek. It is with this insecurity that the poem ends. Indeed, the last line, with its poignant negatives, emphasizes this: "So we are not un-Greek, I think."

Themes and Meanings

To read Cavafy, one must know how he viewed himself. He once said that he had two abilities: to write poetry and to write history. The history that he used allowed him to objectify the world he lived in and was of interest in itself, for it was the history of Greek civilization. After Alexander the Great's conquests in Asia, despite the collapse of his empire, there were for many years small and large Greek-ruled states as far away from Greece as the borders of India; political power was also cultural power. Greek culture did not, however, die with the loss of political power.

The history that Cavafy uses is largely the history of the Hellenistic world after the end of Greek independence. Even before the Romans conquered the eastern part of the Mediterranean, however, the prestige of Greek civilization had a powerful effect on the Empire. After the conquest, the high culture of that eastern half of the Mediterranean was Greek, and everywhere Greek culture was regarded as the epitome of cultural achievement. Although in one sense Cavafy is satirizing the philhellene king, in another he is in agreement with him. They both love the Greek language and Greek culture; these things give meaning to their lives.

For Cavafy, history is not simply the recounting of events or the examination of an underlying economic or social substructure. Indeed, one of the reasons for Cavafy's use of the dramatic monologue was that it served his idea that it is the "dramatic" in history that matters. He admired historians who wrote history as drama, since drama is lived, not merely experienced intellectually.

"Philhellene" is not merely a poem about history. The king is also an aspect of Cavafy himself. Therefore, despite its appearance of objectivity, one must admit that the poem is an expression of the poet. The poem is, in essence, the examination of an insecure soul who is seeking some sort of dignity and identity in being part of a greater civilization, not merely a king without power. It is, in short, an examination of a kind of alienation. Cavafy, who was a homosexual, was a Greek who was born in Alexandria, Egypt; he was an outsider in both his sexual orientation and his nationality.

In a sense, the king's idea of the work of art expresses the aesthetic belief of Cavafy that a work of art is to be judged by the quality of its workmanship. The king wishes for a thing of beauty, which is perhaps a way of overcoming his sense of being outside. There is one more connection between Cavafy and the king: Cavafy was a man who believed in the life of the body—in pleasure—both artistic and physical. The king's insistence upon the discus-thrower figure for the back of the coin suggests something about his idea of living—that it be pleasurable, and not only to the eye.

Cavafy remarked that his talents were those of a poet and a historian, but one must note that "poet" comes first. Cavafy was first a man of letters, an artist; second, a historian; and, finally, an outsider.

L. L. Lee

PHONEMICS

Author: Jack Spicer (1925-1965)
Type of poem: Lyric
First published: 1965, in *Language*

The Poem

"Phonemics" is in serial form; it consists of six related poems, varying in length between eleven and twenty lines. The title alludes to the study of language sounds, and it helps bring to the foreground the materiality of language in this poem as in other works of Jack Spicer.

Spicer was a professional linguist, and "Phonemics" is one of seven such serial poems in a 1965 book entitled *Language*. The book jacket of *Language* consists of the title page from an issue of a linguistics journal of the same name, an issue that contains Spicer's sole professional publication. Obviously, the poet wanted to remind his readers that poems, whatever their sentiments, consist of language, that the words one uses govern the way one thinks, and that the ways that one's culture provides for putting words together delineate the boundaries of what it is possible to "say" with words.

It would be misleading to term this a first-person poem, for three of the six sections do not contain the word "I." The form of address is rather that of a lecturer who is being objective concerning a situation. That said, however, it should be noted that the voice remains thoroughly idiosyncratic, completely identifiable as Spicer's idiolect, so that even though the first-person pronoun, in either subjective or objective case, seldom occurs, the presence of a single speaker can be felt throughout—the presence, as the poet and critic Ron Silliman has remarked, of a felt absence.

"Phonemics," in common with much other poetry by Spicer, examines, poetically rather than academically, the matter of distance—its role in communication, the ways in which speaking or writing causes it to be felt and discerned between would-be communicants. "The lips/ Are never quite as far away as when you kiss," he writes, offering a paradox that can exemplify this condition. The double role that lips play—kissing and speaking—in human interaction also informs the following lines from the ensuing section:

> Tough lips that cannot quite make the sounds of love
> The language
> Has so misshaped them.

For Spicer, the struggle to be authentic involves a deep mistrust, if not a downright rejection, of any language that convention assigns to various duties. Those clichés predict behavior, whereas love requires freshness, the use of inventive and playful language, spontaneity—the kind of use that this poem embodies, with an irregularity which is that of life and not the predictable pattern of death.

People are always looking for shortcuts, Spicer implies, but true love has a course that is not only rough but also lengthy:

> On the tele-phone (distant sound) you sounded no distant than
>   if you were talking to me in San Francisco on the telephone
>   or in a bar or in a room. Long
> Distance calls. They break sound
> Into electrical impulses and put it back again. Like the long
>   telesexual route to the brain or the even longer teleerotic
>   route to the heart. The numbers dialed badly, the
>   connection faint.

It might not be too much of an exaggeration or a simplification to say of Spicer that he wrote antipoetry and was against love—love, at least, as commonly lived (and voiced) by those around him. It should be added, however, that he took those positions for what he perceived to be the good of poetry and of love.

Forms and Devices

The free-verse sections—poems in their own right, really, which make up the poem "Phonemics"—are united by a number of qualities found throughout. In the first place, their sentence structure is unorthodox: Many of the sentences are actually sentence fragments; phrases are left dangling, unattended by the normal considerations of verb or subject; there is considerable underpunctuation and heavy reliance upon ellipses; quotations are interpolated without attribution; words are broken into their phonemic parts with total disregard for customary procedures. All these violations are deliberate and serve again to highlight the language; the awkwardness and out-of-the-ordinary quality they lend to the writing are calculated to remind the reader that language has a primary, privileged role in one's thinking about reality, and indeed in the creation of that reality.

These sentences and sentence ruins often comment upon one another, so that the progression through a Spicer poem is less linear than crablike or sideways. Take, for example, the following passage:

> Wake up one warm morning. See the sea in the distance.
> Die Ferne, water
> Because mainly it is not land. A hot day too
> The shreads of fog have already vaporized
> Have gone back where they came from. There may be a whale
>   in this ocean.
> Empty fragments, like the shards of pots found in some
>   Mesopotamian expedition. Found but not put together. The
>   unstable
> Universe has distance but not much else.
> No one's weather or room to breathe in.

This, the second section of "Phonemics" in its entirety, illustrates a number of the devices referred to above. Intrusion of the scholarly sounding "Die Ferne," German for "distance," may also occur to the poet because it contains the English word "far" half hidden in it; Spicer interrupts what had been promising to be a bland beginning—just the kind of "poetic" language he abhorred, with the heavy alliteration of the first sentence, the platitudinous rhyming of "sea" and "see"—with a pedantic-sounding footnote, which he follows with a second academic pun, "main": another word for sea, half buried in "mainly." The poem then loops back to further landscape evocation, quite accurately characterizing the conditions of that portion of Northern California in which Spicer lived, and quite neutral in tone—although the lack of punctuation at the end of lines 3 and 4 sends a characteristic signal, as does the apparent afterthought qualifying the fog, a phrase more often applied to unwanted visitors. The speculative assertion that ensues concerning the possible whale leads only to a sentence apparently summarizing the poem thus far, although it might, at the same time, refer to the poet's feelings about the depicted scene.

While "Found but not put together" lacks explicit signs of value, there is a suggestion in the context of "Phonemics" and *Language* that it is a good thing to leave such shards "as is" and not to try to force or contrive unity, not to glue things back together. The poem itself partakes of this condition of shards incompletely welded to one another. It does so, Spicer implies, because reality is also shardlike rather than unified, and because the poem owes a debt to reality, if only by creating what one calls the real out of our words.

Themes and Meanings

Baseball provided Spicer with many figures of speech. "The poet," he wrote, "thinks he is the pitcher. But actually he is the catcher." People may think they initiate what, in actuality, they only participate in. The ego-strong poet (or person) thinks he is deciding the course of his poem (or his life); in reality language, or life itself, is dictating the course of things, and one can only attend. The poet, Spicer said elsewhere, is a radio, receiving first, and only then transmitting. What he or she receives are messages from all over, messages that are simply "in the air," and which the poet sits down to sort out whenever he or she writes. While this procedure has affinities with the automatic writing practiced by André Breton and other Surrealists, Spicer did not believe in accepting wholesale whatever was delivered; he believed that one still had to discern between false and true senders and messages.

In "Phonemics," one sees Spicer's beliefs embodied in two ways: in the very form of the poem, with its sudden gaps (as though another transmitting station had broken in on one's radio), its many puns (as though two stations were transmitting and being received simultaneously), and its indecipherable passages (as though heavy static interfered with a message); and in the semantic content, with its warnings of an unreliable, uncommandable, ungovernable universe, its reiterated cautions about distance, and its passages concerning the double role of language as creator and betrayer of human intentions. In "Phonemics," the dynamics and mechanics of language use are constantly being brought to the foreground, and people are forever appearing to be embedded in these dynamics and mechanics of language, rather than being language's lords and masters.

David Bromige

PIANO

Author: D. H. Lawrence (1885-1930)
Type of poem: Lyric
First published: 1918, in *New Poems*

The Poem

"Piano" is a lyric poem reflecting the thoughts and feelings of a single speaker as he listens at dusk to a woman singing a song that brings back childhood memories of sitting at his mother's feet while she played the piano. It is a short poem of twelve lines divided into three quatrains, rhymed *aabb*. The poem contains vivid images, and specific and concrete details provide a clear embodiment of his memory.

In the first stanza, a woman is singing softly to the speaker. The song takes him in memory back to his childhood, where he sees a child sitting under the piano, surrounded by the sounds of music and pressing "the small poised feet of a mother who smiles as she sings." The scene is one of homely comfort and ease, of childlike innocence, of intimacy and peace.

In the second stanza, the speaker realizes that he is being sentimentally nostalgic. Yet in spite of himself, the power of memory sweeps him back into the familiar scene of a Sunday evening at home, with the cold and storms of winter kept outside. Inside, his mother is singing and playing the piano in the cozy parlor, leading the family in the singing of hymns. It is crucial that the speaker does not give in easily to his emotion; it is "in spite of myself," he says, that "the insidious mastery of song/ Betrays me back" (lines 5-6). The speaker, now an adult, realizes the gap between his childhood perceptions, which are idealized and romanticized, and those that he has as a mature adult.

In stanza 3, the reader discovers that he is no longer listening to the current singer and the current piano; he is so overcome by his memories that he weeps like a child for the past. Again, he struggles against this retreat into the past before he finally succumbs. He recognizes that what he sees is nostalgic and sentimental, the "glamor of childish days" (line 11)—deliberately not "childlike" days—that reduces him from being a man to being a child once again, and he weeps like a child for the past.

D. H. Lawrence in this poem does a convincing job of seeing from a child's perspective, while juxtaposing it with the point of view of an adult. Though the *abab* rhyme scheme is perhaps a strained choice for this theme, and though the diction is somewhat trite, especially in the second stanza, the concrete detail and clearly visual images reproduce effectively the experience of an adult who knows that his own childhood eyes cast an aura of illusory beauty over that time. Stanza 2 is weakened for some readers by lines 7 and 8: Lawrence's word choice here, "the old Sunday evenings at home, with winter outside/ And hymns in the cozy parlor, the tinkling piano our guide," seems too ordinary to carry the burden of nostalgia created by the speaker's memory earlier in the poem. There is, however, enough detail in the first and third stanzas to keep the poem as whole from becoming blurry or sentimental.

Forms and Devices

Lawrence centers much of his writing, both poetic and fictional, on the creation and development of a central metaphor. In "Piano," it is the image, with all of its associations, at least in Western European Christian culture, of Sunday evenings at home with one's family. No matter that most people's experiences were seldom so peaceful and harmonious—Lawrence's certainly were not either. It is the idea of a cozy and warm parlor on a cold winter's evening, with a family gathered around a piano singing hymns and enjoying one another's company, that is the important factor. The setting and the music combine to invoke the myth of the ideal family at home: warm, loving, reverent, and peaceful. Lawrence effectively juxtaposes this with the singer and the piano in the speaker's present, a speaker who is about to "burst into clamor" (line 9), accompanying a piano which is reaching a crescendo with a "great black" apassionato. Notice that it is the present experience which is large, dark, and noisy; the speaker's remembered experience is small, warm and "tingling" (line 3).

The ironic tone in the poem, and the clear ironic distance between the poetic voice and his memories of childhood, are central to the poem's success. Without them the tone might become maudlin, but with them one sees and experiences the clear disjunction between a child's and an adult's eye—between a child's perspective that all is well in the world and the adult's knowledge, after the fact, that this was not really the case.

Lawrence's poetic forms and devices, then, echo and reinforce the ironic gap between the original experience of the child, now transformed through the power of memory and imagination, and the current experience of the adult, which acts as trigger and catalyst for his descent into his own past.

Themes and Meanings

"Piano" is a poem about the power of memory and about the often disillusioning disjunction between the remembered experience of childhood and the realities of adult life. The poem is nostalgic without being sentimental; that is, it captures the power of one's experiences as a child without ignoring the facts that one's adult memories are selective and one's perceptions and perspective as a child are severely limited by lack of experience, ignorance, and innocence. Lawrence does, however, provide adequate reason for the intense feeling, and he supports it with concrete, physical detail about the piano and the child's mother.

The theme in "Piano" is a common one in much of Lawrence's writing, from short stories such as "The Rocking-Horse Winner" to novels such as *Sons and Lovers* (1913). How do adults make their peace with the memories they have of their childhoods, and how do they separate memories of actual experience from imagined and invented moments? The speaker in this poem knows that his memory casts a romanticized and sentimentalized glow over the actual events that occurred, yet the power of the past, and his deep need to recapture a similar sense of the peace and protection he felt as a child, overwhelm his rational mind. In Lawrence's world, the power of emotion is almost always too potent for the power of thought; what one feels intrudes on one's thinking, even at times one does not wish it to.

It is important in the poem that the speaker believes that the singer is singing to him, for this reflects the egocentric world that is captured in his childhood memory. This is an experience with which most readers will identify; one can remember times when one believed that some piece of art, music, or literature was created or delivered especially for oneself, and perhaps times when a parent seemed to belong to oneself alone. It is even more important that the speaker (and his audience) recognizes the ironic gap between what he wished (and perhaps believed) were the case, and what the case was in fact. This tension between the heart's desires and the mind's qualifications, between hope and experience, creates a necessary if paradoxical balance in the poem. It seems as if D. H. Lawrence is suggesting finally that one should listen more to one's deeply feeling heart than to one's perhaps overly analytical mind; yet the tension between the two is for him an essential part of being human.

Clark Mayo

PICTURE BRIDE

Author: Cathy Song (1955-   )
Type of poem: Meditation
First published: 1980; collected in *Picture Bride*, 1983

The Poem

"Picture Bride" is the title poem of Korean American writer Cathy Song's first book, one that earned the Yale Series of Younger Poets Prize in 1982 for its Hawaii-born author. It is a meditative poem in thirty-four lines of free verse.

To present-day Euramerican readers, the title may conjure up the vision of a stereotypically picture-perfect bride decked out with veil, lace, and train. If so, this vision would contrast ironically with the historical Asian American reality of the term. The title refers to a matchmaking practice common among many Asians who immigrated to the United States during the late nineteenth and early twentieth centuries. As part of this practice, intermediaries and family members arranged a marriage between an Asian immigrant man in the United States and an Asian woman in Asia. Usually, the only contact between the bride and the bridegroom during the courtship, if it can be called such, was an exchange of letters and photographs—hence the term "picture bride." Often, the wedding was solemnized by proxy in Asia, after which the bride proceeded to the New World to meet her groom in the flesh and to consummate the marriage.

The picture bride of Song's poem is the grandmother of the poem's speaker. The grandmother is the object of meditation for her granddaughter, a persona who closely resembles the author in age, gender, and ethnic background (Song's father and mother are of Korean and Chinese ancestry, respectively). The speaker of the poem is thus a third-generation Asian American woman, a twenty-four-year-old who imaginatively projects herself into the thoughts and feelings that the now-matriarch of her family must have had when she first crossed the Pacific Ocean to establish a family with a "stranger" (line 26) she had never met, in an unfamiliar new land.

The speaker marvels at the notion that her grandmother was only twenty-three years old, a year younger than the speaker herself, when she left her family in southern Korea to assume her destiny in the United States. She wonders how her grandmother must have felt as she left the familial protection of her ancestral hearth and her native city, the port of Pusan, to set sail for the distant Hawaiian Islands, a place she had learned about only a short time before. She also wonders how her grandmother regarded the husband whom she had never met. All her grandmother knew was that he was a Korean immigrant laborer thirteen years her senior who worked for the Waialau Sugar Mill. The speaker is curious about how her grandmother felt and acted when this stranger took her from the dock to their new home, where she had to undress for the sudden intimacy of their nuptial bed.

Throughout, the poem maintains a tone of admiration for the grandmother's upbringing and strength of character, which armed her with the acceptance and fortitude to undergo the shock of marrying a stranger chosen for her by other people. In different ways, her grandmother's act is as extraordinary to the speaker as it was strange to the grandmother. The grandmother's performance is seen as a paradoxically self-denying yet self-defining act; it is this act that bears fruit by giving life to her more freely choosing granddaughter, who now pays tribute to her grandparent. The grandmother's act is also one that originates within a cultural and historical context vastly different from that of the speaker. Mingled with admiration, the poem's tone also suggests that the speaker herself would shrink from an act as demanding and self-denying as her grandmother's. However much the speaker may admire her grandmother, to whom she is connected by family, ethnicity, and gender, the two women are estranged by the gaps of generations, socialization, and implicit notions of individual freedom of choice—the grandmother's generation and culture socialized her to disregard her individual prerogatives, whereas the granddaughter's viewpoint has been shaped by her upbringing as an American woman of the late twentieth century.

Forms and Devices

To consider this poem as a meditation, it might be useful to note that meditation is a serious, imaginative, and time-honored practice advocated by several religions. Usually, the purpose of a religious meditation (such as that encouraged by Saint Ignatius of Loyola) is to bring the meditator into closer understanding and communion with a sacred text, a divine mystery, or a moment in a saint's life. For example, one purpose of a Christian meditator could be to think and imagine oneself as being present during a crucial moment of Christ's life, such as the Crucifixion—in such a sense is John Donne's seventeenth century metaphysical poem "Good Friday, 1613. Riding Westward" a meditation.

The object of meditation in Song's poem, however, is a secular rather than a religious one, although the grandmother is, nevertheless, highly esteemed and even revered. It is common in several Asian cultures for ancestors to be regarded in a worshipful manner. One could then read the poem as a meditation in which the speaker thinks and imagines herself into the situation of her revered grandmother at a crucial moment in the latter's life, thereby achieving an understanding and communion with her.

That the speaker chooses to honor a female ancestor in her meditation rather than a male one seems natural, given the speaker's sex. Within an Asian context, however, it could be considered a rather unusual choice, for within the highly patriarchal Asian hierarchy the place of honor and reverence would normally be accorded to the male ancestor: the grandfather. Song's meditator, however, salutes the matriarchal figure of her family and devalues the grandfather into a "stranger." This choice by Song may thus be read as a feminist one.

The poem makes extensive use of contrasts in situations and imagery. Some of the more noticeable situational contrasts are those between the speaker and the matriarch: the younger, freer generation and the older, more-constrained generation, the turn-of-the-century Asian and the modern American, the bride and her husband, the long-familiar and the suddenly strange. These contrasting situations serve to highlight the matriarch's strength of character and the speaker's sense of wonder.

The poem's imagery creates immediacy and lends it a dramatic quality; it also furthers the impact of the poem's situational contrasts. For example, the bittersweet quality of the grandmother's experience is reflected in the sensory contrast between the implied sweetness of the sugar "cane stalks" (line 22) and the bitterness of the "burning . . . cane" after the harvest (line 34—a line that was added in the 1983 version of the poem). There is the dramatic imagist contrast between the bride's disciplined self-control as she "politely untie[s]/ the silk bow of her jacket" to undress (lines 29 and 30) and a thirsting passion implied by "her tent-shaped dress/ filling with the dry wind" (lines 31 and 32). Most striking perhaps is the contrast between the dark of the night and the light of the lantern (lines 16 to 21), which suggests a parallel between the grandmother's risky journey from Asia to the United States and the moths' risking death in "migrating" from their natural habitat of the dark "cane stalks" toward the artificial light of the lantern.

Themes and Meanings

"Picture Bride" is about immigration, generational differences, women, and individuality. By imaginatively recovering her grandmother's experiences, Song reconstructs the experiences of an entire subgroup of Asian American immigrants: the Korean Americans and the Japanese Americans. Picture brides were uncommon among Chinese Americans because American immigration laws were enforced between 1882 and 1945 to exclude Chinese women from American shores; however, female subjects of the militarily powerful Japanese empire, which included Korea, were grudgingly allowed to migrate to the United States. (A knowledgeable account of the Asian American experience of immigration is to be found in Ronald Takaki's 1989 book *Strangers from a Different Shore*.) Although Song's poem focuses on the psychological and emotional impact of immigration on a single individual, it also hints at the economic hard times facing these Asian immigrants as well as the cultural reservoirs of endurance that enabled them to survive such an alienating experience.

The poem juxtaposes an American woman of the twentieth century and an Asian woman of two generations earlier. Their assumptions about what it means to be a woman and their assumptions about self-fulfillment are worlds apart—so far apart as to provoke a wondering near-incomprehension from the younger woman. The woman of the past generation was schooled to negate her individual prerogatives, to allow others to determine her destiny, and to accede without argument to male authority. The modern woman is hard put to understand this attitude, and by implication she would assert her individuality, control her destiny, and abhor submission to arbitrary male authority.

The contrastive structure of the poem tempts the modern reader to an evaluation of the grandmother's experience of immigration and notions of individuality. One may well wonder how much of one was positive, how much of the other negative. Perhaps an answer lies in the key image of the photograph of the bride. After all, a photograph is a developed picture that is the bright positive print of a dark negative film. Print and film, dark and light, positive and negative—their contrasting existences are inextricable in the same way that the final sum of human experience is.

C. L. Chua

PIED BEAUTY

Author: Gerard Manley Hopkins (1844-1889)
Type of poem: Sonnet
First published: 1918, in *Poems of Gerard Manley Hopkins, Now First Published, with Notes by Robert Bridges*

The Poem

"Pied Beauty" is a rhymed "curtal" (shortened) sonnet divided into two stanzas, consisting of three full tercets and a truncated fourth. The title refers to the variegated beauty of the world that first may appear ugly or chaotic. Though "pied" suggests at least two tones or colors, it also suggests a blotched or botched effect, as when in an earlier era, a printer spilled a galley of set type, creating a printer's "pie."

Though traditional sonnets are fourteen lines, Gerard Manley Hopkins, in his experiments with poetic form, line, and meter, altered the shape of the sonnet. In the case of "Pied Beauty," he "curtailed" or shortened the sonnet's traditional fourteen lines to eleven; in some other cases, he lengthened the form and wrote sonnets "with codas," or tails.

The poem celebrates God for the beauty in a varied creation. Hopkins, a devout Jesuit priest, isolates a number of instances of this "pied" or dappled beauty in the first stanza (lines 1-6). He finds it in two-toned skies as well as on cows, on spotted trout, and on the wings of birds. He also sees variety and unity in the contrasts between all these life-forms, for he sees echoes of plants on fish—"rose-moles . . . upon trout," echoes of the dying embers of fires in the chestnuts falling from the tree.

In fact, the first stanza catalogs God's infinite variety in creation in instances that symbolize all life as well as inanimate forms, from the heavens to the seas, from plants to animals, from animals finally even to humans. The fifth line observes the pied quality of the landscape as humans have altered it. The landscape is a pied checkerboard with pens for animals (such as sheepfolds), plowed fields, and those fields lying unplowed (fallow). The human pied effect on land is then juxtaposed against the variety of human mercantile activity or trades.

As in most sonnets, the second part or stanza generalizes, summarizes, or abstracts from the particular details observed by the poet in the first part. Therefore, the next three lines (lines 7-9) point out the general patterns of contrast. The word "counter" suggests this contrariness: The beauty of God's creation grows out of oppositions. Many of the adjectives—such as "fickle"—Hopkins uses to describe the pied beauty may seem in themselves unappealing or ugly. "Fickle" usually connotes unpredictability, disloyalty, perhaps even immorality. In the context of a vast creation, however, these strange, pied qualities are amalgamated to the overall beauty. The ninth line itself reiterates this effect of balanced and beautiful contrast in a series of paired oppositions. Having described the pied beauty of the Creation in the first nine lines, or first three tercets, Hopkins turns to the Creator or "father" (God) in the last two lines and concludes by directing the reader to "Praise him."

Forms and Devices

Characteristic of Hopkins is his use of a variety of intricate sound devices, each heightened or altered in some untraditional way. Hopkins's idiosyncratic and innovative techniques perhaps explain why the majority of his poems were published only in the first decades of the twentieth century, nearly thirty years after his death. "Pied Beauty" consists of patterns of such idiosyncracy in its alliteration, assonance, neologism, archaism, end rhyme, and rhythm. All these patterns interconnect and contrast with one another so that the poem itself is an example of "pied" beauty, or mixed elements.

Thus the alliterative *g* sounds of the first line ("Glory . . . God") give way to the *l* sound, which echoes in "dappled," "couple," "colour," "moles," and "stipple," interconnecting the patterns of the first three lines with the entire first stanza. The alliterative pattern of sounds connects the "couple-colour" of the sky to the skin of the "cow." The *c* sounds are thus "pied" or combined in contrast with the *l* sounds.

At first glance, a word such as "rose-moles" seems both odd and hard to pronounce because the assonance of the *o* sounds contrasts with the following consonants of *s* and *l*. It is a near rhyme or off-rhyme that occasionally turns a Hopkins lyric into a near tongue twister. Even a sympathetic reader may wonder what a rose-mole is, for it is indeed one of Hopkins's neologisms (or invented words) to describe the colored pattern of a trout's skin. It is not surprising that in the same line he employs the archaism "brinded" to described a pied pattern of grey flecks or streaks on a cow's hide. Also, normal associations with rose, usually an image of perfection or beauty, contrast radically with traditional associations with mole, usually seen as a beauty defect or unpleasant growth. Yet the phrase, the sound, the very unusualness of the concept suggest the exciting variety of a universe constantly changing and contrasting.

In addition, the structure of the poem is itself an example of pied beauty, since the expected patterns established by the rhyme schemes of the first six lines (*abcabc*) are broken in the next five (*dbcdc*). The poem's tercet pattern ends abruptly in a line and a half (lines 10 and 11) instead of three full lines. This last shift marks the radical difference between God's creation and God. Hopkins thus dramatically reminds one that God, unlike the dappled things, is powerful and unchanging and has a beauty of oneness or integrity. He also simultaneously shows one that the relation of God (unchanging) to his Creation (fickle, changing) is itself an example of pied or mixed, contrasting beauty.

The abrupt ending also forces the last two words ("Praise him") to bear enormous weight; because of the established pentameter rhythm of the preceding lines, they enjoy the supposed five-beat stress typical of that pattern. This makes those two words both momentous and simultaneously humble, like a quiet prayer.

The stunted end is what makes this a "curtal" or curtailed sonnet. One misses the patterned, traditional beauty of a fourteen-line sonnet but finds instead another beauty in an odd form Hopkins created particularly for this occasion.

Themes and Meanings

In Hopkins's poetry it is virtually impossible to separate device and form from meaning since he is constantly at work molding lines, words, and sounds to create an intricate pattern, making one feel that the poem one is reading is nearly a synesthetic version of the aspect of creation or theology on which he is commenting. Thus this analysis of theme may seem somewhat repetitive of comment on forms and devices. In effect, that is part of the point of the poem.

"Pied Beauty" is essentially a list reminding us again and again, in a variety of ways, that the visible universe and human creation is varied and beautiful even in its ugliness and contrast, and all is a hymn of praise to God the Creator. In this list, Hopkins isolates details that reveal his perceptiveness as a poet and that invite the reader to see the world and word anew and more carefully. Thus the strategy of the poem's first part is that of enumerating unique details conveyed in unusual words, such as "stipple" or "brinded." Each detail is like the brush stroke of a great painter, and for Hopkins, God is the careful painter mixing and matching, putting all into a whole. Though individual details are striking, unusual, unique, or even initially ugly, the overall effect is one of massive pattern, reiterated by the echo of the word "all" at the end of one stanza and beginning of the next.

God's Creation is beautiful because the seeming variety and contrast conceals a principle of unity that links all living things to one another and to God—sky to earth, fish to cow, the dying embers of a fire to the fall of a chestnut from a tree. Though most of the first examples come from nature, and even the first human examples of pied beauty are from agriculture, Hopkins finds beauty also in mercantile work—in all the trades, often despised by other religious writers for being nonspiritual, and even in the equipment used in trade. Perhaps one can also see that the "tackle" used to catch the trout is as beautiful as the trout itself—and beautiful by contrast.

In Hopkins's vision, God is the creator of beauty, traditionally the father, the divine spark. He is "past change" in that he is eternal, omniscient, a fixed and absolute entity. He encompasses the variegated creation simply as mention of him both begins and ends the poem.

Hopkins remarks upon this beauty, announces it, embodies it in the intricate interwoven complexity of his words, but he does not purport to understand it. The mystery of how the variegation occurs and how or why it is beautiful is announced in the very conversational, almost nonpoetic "who knows how?"—a rhetorical question of amazing power and honesty.

"Pied Beauty" is an ironic paean to God for not creating a perfect universe, but for creating one that is beautiful because of apparent imperfection. The odd locutions and abrupt stuntedness of the poem itself embody the pied quality Hopkins discerns in the external world.

Jonathan L. Price

LA PIETÀ

Author: Giuseppe Ungaretti (1888-1970)
Type of poem: Lyric
First published: 1933, in *Sentimento del tempo*; English translation collected in *Selected Poems of Giuseppe Ungaretti*, 1975

The Poem

"La Pietà" (the pity) is a poem of seventy-four lines arranged in four sections. The English translation is generally very close to the Italian original in meaning and identical in arrangement of line. Most stanzas are composed of only one line, although several contain more; moreover, the poem is divided into four parts, the first being composed of thirty-nine lines, the second of twenty, the third of only four, and the fourth of eleven. The lines are of irregular length in the original, and the translation follows the line length of the original as much as possible. For instance, in the second stanza, composed of four lines, the English translation has two lines of six syllables each, one of five, and one of four; in the original, each line has eight syllables. The lines, in both languages, are unrhymed. In both the original and the translation, the poem is written in grammatically correct, complete sentences, but with a simple, conversational style.

The poem takes the form of a monologue, which occasionally becomes a prayer. The speaker begins by saying "I am a wounded man," expressing a desire to "reach" pity, as if he were trying to journey to a place where he might be healed. In a sense, the rest of the poem describes a journey through various aspects of the speaker's profound dissatisfaction with his existence. Ungaretti wrote "La Pietà" in 1928, when he was forty, and in it he reassesses life—as do many thinkers at that age—but in ways specifically his own.

Forms and Devices

The poem shares its general sentiment with some biblical psalms, as a lamentation over the human inability to find ultimate certainty or fulfillment. Like many psalms, it is a first-person meditation in which both personal grief and the fate of humanity are lamented. Also like biblical poetry, "La Pietà" repeats ideas in different words, as in the first section's "You have banished me from life./ And will you banish me from death?" In both lines, God has somehow chosen to isolate the speaker from the world around him, and the lines repeat the thought, forming a pair that is more memorable than either line would be on its own. This biblical rhetorical strategy gives a traditionally religious feel to the poem.

Also, like the four movements of a classical symphony, the parts of the poem complement one another. Although each portion reflects the same general state of unhappiness with worldly life, each portrays a different aspect. The first section, which constitutes just over half the poem, recounts the poet's disillusionment in detail. He compares himself to leaves being blown by the wind and claims he has been crying without an audible voice, suggesting total futility. In section 2, the poet speaks directly of a lack of joy and of an awareness of death in the midst of the bustle that is contemporary life. He once was joyful and knew purpose in life, but now is convinced his activities belong to a world already dead.

In the third section, the shortest of all, the speaker pleads for "light," a renewed presence of the divine in his life. He begs for the light as being the greatest happiness possible, for it gives certainty and meaning. In section 4, he describes humanity as being cut off from the divine, from light and certainty. The speaker concludes that human attempts to think about God are only blasphemous, and that all men and women can truly do is mark the decay of the universe.

The message seems at first to be entirely of despair, and yet in the careful balancing of elements Ungaretti shows his readers an example of the richness of human thought. Perhaps the best example is in his title, which is also a term for traditional artistic images of the Virgin Mary holding the dead body of Jesus, such as the famous sculpture by Michelangelo (although neither Mary nor Jesus are referred to in the text). The association evokes ideas of both grief and compassion, more than a specific reference to Christ, and adds one more dimension to the speaker's attempt to cry out to God, for the speaker becomes a reflection of the same intensity of feeling the artists show in the image of Mary.

Themes and Meanings

Ungaretti was one of the most influential figures in twentieth century Italian poetry and a founder of a poetry movement called Hermeticism. This movement was an effort to establish a newer, simpler form of poetry unencumbered by traditional ornamentation, such as rhyme, and based more on a dreamlike association of ideas than on logical order.

Ungaretti published "La Pietà" in its first collection as part of a series of poems termed "Inni," or hymns, which marked his return to a predominantly Christian view of life and literature, after he had explored less overtly religious modes of thought in his earlier work. Many writers and artists of the 1920's saw life as bleak and unfulfilling; the return to religious faith was Ungaretti's own response to a common perception.

The poem expresses disillusionment and discouragement with life in general and implies that the speaker is very much in need of mercy from God. This mercy would assuage the painful emptiness he has discovered in his life and renew the "light that goads us" in section 3, the sense of the divine which Ungaretti found missing from much European intellectual activity in the decades between World Wars I and II. The pity the speaker seeks is not expressed in traditional Christian terms of forgiveness for sins, but instead as redemption from the transitory and unsatisfying life in which he feels the human race is burying itself.

Ungaretti expresses the recurrent thought that the individual exercises a kind of dominion over his or her own life, but one which disappoints, suggesting that egotism is pointless. In section 1, the speaker parallels Adam, naming the animals in Genesis, but the speaker's naming the "silence" of his life is an attempt to fill a void rather than to establish order in a new and promising world. He asks, carrying this image further but also reflecting his work as a poet, if he has become a slave of words which have no meaning, and finally concludes that he reigns "over phantoms." In other words, his poetry is without value, substance, or significance. This image is brought back in the fourth section, where humanity ("Man, monotonous universe") is compared to a demigod building an insubstantial world, one which only results in tombs and blasphemies. The speaker has progressed from seeing himself as an Adam presiding over a dead world to seeing humanity as a mockery of God's creative power, and therefore implicitly in need of pity.

Another theme running through the piece is the suggestion that God could act to end the speaker's spiritual stagnation. In section 1, the speaker pleads with God either to pity the human race or to mock it, as either would be better than the self-centered void in which even "those who implore" God only know the "name," but not the reality, of the supreme being. In section 2, again, the speaker asks if God is "no more than a dream" and comments that at least the dream of God is the "clearest madness," the closest approach to sanity, that contemporary people have. In the third section, he begs to be dazzled by light from the divine. At the very end of section 4 the speaker finds that humanity has only blasphemies—in this case, vague images—through which to think about God.

Ungaretti's poem provides a glimpse of an individual who is weighing belief and unbelief, time and eternity. It can be painful to read, because the author describes the painful crisis of confidence involved in having the foundations of one's life suddenly opened to doubt. It also is esthetically balanced between these extremes, giving it power. On one hand, God seems remote, but on the other hand, human effort to reach out to the divine seems useless. People cannot solve the dilemma on their own but must wait for God to do it for them. In the end, the journey suggested in the opening lines is an illusion—the only activity is that of a mind cataloguing its miseries and inabilities. Any meaningful occurrence must come from the divine.

Despite its Christian basis, the poem at times may remind readers of the *Dao de Jing* (late third century B.C.E.), as everything which human beings can speak, think, or do is revealed to be empty, while truth eludes them constantly. "La Pietà" marked Ungaretti's own reexamination and ultimate affirmation of Christian belief, although the longing and emptiness the poem conveys may be appreciated by readers of any or no faith; like the grief in artistic depictions of la Pietà, the emotions are more universal than any one creed.

Paul James Buczkowski

PIKE

Author: Ted Hughes (1930-1998)
Type of poem: Narrative/meditation
First published: 1960, in *Lupercal*

The Poem

"Pike" is written in free verse and consists of forty-four lines divided into eleven stanzas. The title focuses immediate attention on the creature under scrutiny and on the natural world, which informs most of Ted Hughes's work. The poem can be divided into three sections or perspectives.

The first section, stanzas 1 and 2, sets the scene, depicting the voracious, ruthless nature of this fish and establishing its green water world. In these first stanzas, Hughes maintains an objective narrative perspective in which the fish and its environment occupy the center of attention.

The next section, the third through seventh stanzas, begins a consideration of the predatory nature of the pike and describes it as it moves through a green, gold, shadowy habitat. No sounds disturb the quiet of the fish's waiting expectation beneath the water's surface. In stanzas 3 and 4, Hughes graphically describes the fish's "jaws' hooked clamp and fangs" and makes the reader sense the pike's ruthless nature as it lurks silently waiting in the weeds for its prey. In stanzas 5 and 6, he heightens this vision by describing what happened when he kept three small pike captive in an aquarium: The ruthless fish preyed upon one another until only one remained, "with a sag belly and the grin it was born with." Hughes juxtaposes a second scene of the pike as unstoppable predator by concluding this section with the image of two dead, six-pound, two-foot-long pikes lying on a river bank, one jammed down the gullet of the other. Even in death these fish are portrayed as grimly determined.

The final section, stanzas 8 through 11, brings the narrator into direct contact with this coldly grim predator. Here Hughes describes the evening encounter he had while casting for pike on an ancient, quiet monastery pond. Set in the waning twilight, this section recapitulates the skulking, waiting nature of the submarine predator and makes the reader experience the fear that the pike engenders, even in the man standing safely on the bank—afraid to fish for what he imagines to be monstrous pike, yet unable not to.

The last stanza of "Pike" concludes with an image of the silent fish slowly surfacing to consider the fisherman who has dared disturb its nighttime lair with his puny fly casting. It is clear from Hughes's choice of detail that this world, both pond and bank, belongs to the menacing pike and that the narrator violates the fish's domain at his peril.

Forms and Devices

The conversational tone of "Pike" serves as an effective device for Hughes to heighten the tension and impact of the poem's violence. Hughes's choice of language is simple, with few polysyllabic words; his phrases are stark, almost bare—without the frills that people seem to need in order to escape from the brutal realities of living. Such simplicity allows Hughes to make "Pike" a highly visual poem; his descriptions evoke sharp images for the reader in which the fish becomes tangible. One can see the water, see the weeds, and sense the presence of the pike as it blends in, waiting to lunge at its unsuspecting quarry. The descriptions are rhythmic, lulling the reader and allowing the final stanzas to take on additional sinister import.

Hughes skillfully juxtaposes the natural with the human world, pairing the images of the fish floating patiently in its natural element with those of an artificial world that imprisons the creature for the cruel or whimsical purposes of the human that has captured it. Because Hughes contrasts what he regards as naturally appropriate, such as the pike's very existence, which he describes as "A life subdued to its instrument," with the next section in which the pike eat one another in the tank, the poet is able to call into question the behavior of the people who captured the fish in the first place.

By focusing on the expression of the pike—as a grinning set of hungry, vicelike jaws—Hughes increases the uneasiness that many people feel when they must witness the raw hunger and power of natural impulse. Repeatedly, in each section of "Pike," Hughes draws his readers' attention to the fish's mouth: a grin, open and waiting in the weeds, smiling with a full belly—still determined in death, locked around the body of its kin. Because the fish is depicted as lurking, shadowed, and mysterious, the choice of the word "grin" to describe its expression is jarring and disconcerting. Nothing about the pike, which Hughes clearly respects and even admires, makes this image one with which the reader will be comfortable.

Finally, Hughes leaves the reader with the impression that the fisherman, not the pike, is the real intruder, perhaps even the only source of true violence in the natural world. By doing so, the poet invites the reader to examine his or her attitudes about the natural world, about who or what has the "right" to behave in a particular way. It is the narrator, not the pike, who feels fear; the pike, on the other hand, rises to the surface prepared to stare down this intruder.

Themes and Meanings

As in most of his poetry, in "Pike" Ted Hughes uses the natural world to its fullest advantage as a stage where humans are only one species among many and are clearly not as powerful as they would like to believe. Hughes's poetry dwells on the innate violence in the natural world and on instinctive predatory behavior; yet, because this behavior is presented in such a manner as to seem uncontrived and natural, Hughes seems to view it as appropriate. Nature as depicted in a poem such a "Pike" shares the perspective of other British poets such as Alfred, Lord Tennyson, who described nature as "red in tooth and claw" (*In Memoriam A. H. H.*, 1850). These writers—Hughes included—attempt to reconcile what at first appears to be a horrible violence in nature. Their concern reflects a conflict that has troubled people since Charles Darwin's theory of evolution offered an explanation for human development that appeared to omit the hand of God. Perhaps humans are no different from a creature such as the pike, driven by impulse and appetite in a universe that follows no moral law but eat or be eaten.

Hughes clearly views the pike as a creature that belongs in its water world, an animal that exemplifies survival of the fittest. The fish is a part of, rather than apart from, the natural world in which it feeds. The pike shares the colors of the water, the weeds, the pond bottom, and the shadows; it is in harmony with and a necessary part of this world, but it is a type of creature—like the shark—that many will view as unwholesome because of its very drive to survive. Hughes clearly believes that the pike belongs where it is and has a "right" to behave as it does, no matter the violence, for it follows a naturally preordained path, instincts that drive it even when the fish is only a three-inch fry: Pike are "Killers from the egg." Those who find the fish's appetite and killer instinct unsettling do not see the world as Hughes does; to them, killing to survive is repugnant. Hughes, on the other hand, expresses subtle admiration for the one pike out of three that remained alive in his aquarium prison, having outlived—and eaten—its kin.

If anything, it is the narrator of the poem, the voice that emerges in the last half of the poem, who is out of place in this natural world. This person has not only removed young fish from their natural habitat and imprisoned them in a glass cage but also invaded the pike's sanctuary to fish for creatures that have outsmarted fishermen for generations, pike that Hughes describes as "too immense to stir." Gradually the narrator is overcome by fear; the violence that the pike direct at their prey seems to be turned toward him as the fish rises slowly to the surface of the bottomless pond to regard the man who foolishly thinks he will catch the natural killer. By his use of a monastery as the site of this particular pond, Hughes implies that the violent, hungry pike has a divine right to live where it does and, by extension, to behave in the way that it does. By equating the pike with the legendary nature of the monastery pond, he makes it a creature of myth like the dragon: powerful, haughty, and impervious to human needs. It is the narrator, not the fish, who must learn a lesson—that pike behavior is "good" and that nature exists for nature's sake, not for humankind's.

Melissa E. Barth

PITCH PINES

Author: Brendan Galvin (1938-   )
Type of poem: Lyric
First published: 1980, in *Atlantic Flyway*

The Poem

Brendan Galvin's "Pitch Pines" is a forty-four-line poem divided into nine stanzas of four to six lines each. Each stanza presents a series of images that culminate in the stanza's final image. In stanza 1, for example, the trees are described as assaulted by winds and other natural forces; they are bent and twisted. In the final line of the stanza, readers see the trees as a jumble, leaning in all different directions. Stanza 4 gathers images of sourness and acidity until the final line states that the pines' pollen "curdles water." The cumulative effect is one of harshness, of forces constantly attacking the pitch pines and the pines barely able to withstand the attack.

Although the predominant images in the poem are those of assault and death, the overall impression crafted by Galvin is one of awe and respect. Despite the inhospitable environment and indifferent treatment by nature (storms and fires), the harvesting of forests for human needs, and the pitch pines' own sometimes thwarted efforts to survive (they pollinate windows and water), they do survive. While other varieties of trees—cedar, birch, elm, beech, and oak—are harvested for specific purposes, the lowly pitch pine stands neglected; it may be knocked down by accident or as a matter of course. Nevertheless, they have developed ways to hold on. The poet is as interested in looking at previous generations of trees as he is in the trees standing in front of him.

In Galvin's landscape, trees are nearly anthropomorphized; they perform deliberate, though treelike, actions: They "loft their heads," "rattle maroon clusters," and "pollinate windows." However, the poet stops short of personification. The trees do not whine, weep, or stretch; rather, they do what trees do, only more deliberately. In this way they begin to people the reader's world.

The poem encompasses a sweeping historical panorama. From a present-day vantage point, the reader is moved back in time to the specific historical moment when the forest was first being "civilized" and its natural abundance was being gathered to build ships and meeting houses, to make shingles, and to build fires for smelting and other activities that required huge amounts of concentrated heat and energy. Images of industrious human endeavor predominate, but the unspoken reaction of the poet is one of wonder at how, amid unthinking industry and human activity, anything of the natural world survived. Galvin does not dwell on the sins of the past, however; he is fascinated by how the trees have evolved and learned to adapt. The poem concludes: "the grandfathers/ of these pines held on until/ heat popped their seeds/ to the charred ground."

With that closing image, the poem moves outward to encompass not only the sturdy, common pitch pine but also the early colonists who settled in the New World.

They too were common stock, and many fell to storms, fires, and the vagaries of nature. What has survived best in the New World, Galvin reminds readers, is not the exotic or the rich and high born, but the common, dependable, and adaptable.

Forms and Devices

Galvin does not depend on conventional devices such as rhyme and meter to shape and control his poems. Readers must look for subtle devices that are closely tied to the subject matter and the cadence of the lines. He writes in vernacular English at its best, firmly in control of the words and how they will be read. The conversational tone of the poem holds readers' attention as they await the next phrase, the next image. The brief lines waste no syllables. Each contains three or four stressed syllables in conversational rhythms. The no-nonsense lines and clear images command attention. Powerful, sometimes unexpected, verbs propel the lines along: Winds are "salted out of the northeast," old branches are "knotted" and "mingle . . . and rot," a shower of pollen "curdles water," and the cape is "timbered to its shores."

The diction that shapes the terse lines and stanzas is also forceful. Repeatedly in Galvin's work, poetic structures gather power from the transforming power of nature. In this poem a particular "[verb] to [noun]" structure is used no less than a half dozen times; it propels action and emphasizes the transformation and use of the elements involved. Three examples are "limbs flaking and dying/ to ribs," "a shower/ that curdles water to golden scum," and "hardwood that fell to keels." In these very brief, consistent structures, massive natural and artificial forces are shown at work. Like much that is American, there is little time for the decorative—the elaboration of phrase, the prettification of an image or action.

Unlike the landscape that is clear-cut in the process of harvest, unlike the gigantic wastefulness that Galvin depicts, the poem itself is economical. The poet demonstrates, without explicitly lecturing his readers, that the best approach for humans is to conserve, to trim—in a sense, to edit their actions. Just as humans have the power to "[boil] the Atlantic to its salts," they have the power to reduce and concentrate their efforts when it comes to nature. Galvin subtly advises his readers to see how the pitch pines have learned to hold on, to clutch their threatened seeds inside cones.

Themes and Meanings

"Pitch Pines" celebrates all forms of life that exhibit the will and the tenacity to survive even when the odds are stacked against them. Just as the common, yet sturdy, pitch pine has survived all that nature and humankind have hurled at it, so have the people who inhabit the pines' native ground. The unheralded American ancestor appears through these images. It was from these early generations that America emerged and continues to emerge. The image of the seed-bearing cone is also the image of the seed of America grasped tight in the minds and wombs of colonists and pioneers.

Galvin's poems in general contain an elaborate and powerful sense of respect for nature, its objects and its forces. Galvin, along with a handful of other contemporary poets, has been an environmentalist since long before it was fashionable to be one.

These poets are cut more from the cloth of Aldo Leopold and Henry Beston than from that of Robert Frost. Frost certainly knew nature intimately, but he ultimately rejected its calling. The environmentalist poets, Galvin significant among them, engage as well as respect nature. Natural objects are beheld, not from a distance, but through the intimate closeness of eye and hand, nose and ear. One need not anthropomorphize the natural world in order to make it interesting: Closely observed, all things in nature may be seen to do the unexpected, the wonder-causing, the awe-inspiring.

"Pitch Pines" does not attempt to elevate the common tree above its station; it merely seeks to observe and fix it in its natural place. For the poet, respect for nature arises from the act of recognizing the dignity of the thing, beholding it, and setting it down in words. "Pitch Pines" contains an understated sense of wonder and even something very akin to joy in the illustration of the beaten and threatened marshaling against indifferent nature, uncaring humankind.

H. A. Maxson

PITY THIS BUSY MONSTER,MANUNKIND

Author: E. E. Cummings (1894-1962)
Type of poem: Sonnet
First published: 1944, in *1 x 1*

The Poem

E. E. Cummings's brief lyric "pity this busy monster,manunkind" is a fourteen-line poem and is thus a sonnet, at least in Cummings's deliberately broad definition of that poetic form. Though the punctuation (and certainly the capitalization) is unconventional, the poem clearly breaks into four sentences. This grammatical division is not reinforced by the line or stanza breaks, however; stanzas vary from one to four lines and begin in mid sentence. In many respects, the poem is typical of Cummings: It presents some of his favorite poetic devices and themes.

The opening sentence urges the reader not to pity the "busy monster" of humanity, or, rather, in Cummings's invented term, "manunkind." The next sentence describes progress as a disease of which humanity is the victim unaware. Then the poet asserts the distinction between natural and artificial: "A world of made/ is not a world of born." The reader is thus invited to pity, instead of humankind, the defenseless things of the organic world—from trees to stars—which are, presumably, victims of the increasing artificiality of progress. The disease metaphor is invoked again in the concluding sentence of the poem where doctors declare the modern world to be a "hopeless case" and invite the reader to join them in the "hell of a good universe next door." The force of the concluding line is ironic; the reader knows that there is no alternative universe to which one can escape.

Cummings's poem, like so many of his lyrics, is an eloquent protest against what he saw as dehumanizing trends of contemporary culture. Its eloquence resides not in complex argument or traditional poetic elevation, but in the value-laden wordplay that strives to expose the myths of modern society as life denying. Thus humankind is rendered as a self-important monster, spreading incurable disease and worshiping false gods ("electrons deify one razorblade/ into a mountainrange"). The term "monster" calls to mind the frightening perversion of the natural; the conglomeration of innocent and natural individual beings forms a whole ("this busy monster") that is neither innocent nor natural. Cummings's humor and playfulness, however, keep the poem from becoming a tract or a tirade. Amused irony tempers his righteous indignation.

Forms and Devices

Readers are struck first by Cummings's unorthodox use of lowercase letters. Indeed, he even signed his poems "e. e. cummings." His avoidance of initial capital letters takes one step further the modernist tendency to capitalize only the first words of sentences, not the first word of each poetic line. In this poem, Cummings does use initial capital letters for new sentences, except in the title and first line. In any case, his unconventional punctuation (including the absence of spaces after commas and semi-colons) reflects essentially the same tendencies throughout his career. First, the typo-graphical idiosyncrasies call attention to the poem as the product of the typewriter, a machine-age self-consciousness apparent (through different means) in the poetry of William Carlos Williams and Marianne Moore as well. In addition, the typographical unconventionality asserts a larger unconventionality of values that the poet wishes to reflect in the poem. "I oppose the staid and traditional" is what Cummings's poems seem to say by their very look on the page.

Similarly, Cummings invents his own comic compound words—in this poem as in many others. These compounds assert a desire for linguistic freedom and a willing-ness to play with forms of contemporary rhetoric: from advertising lingo to political neologisms to scientific coinages. A phrase such as "hypermagical/ ultraomni-potence" mocks the pretensions of science to magic and religion in form as well as content. The prefixes "hyper-" and "ultra-" parody the typical exaggeration of adver-tisements and reinforce the poet's deflation of pretension. Cummings's reliance on coined compounds is apparent in the following lines: "lenses extend/ unwish through curving wherewhen till unwish/ returns on its unself." Here, context helps clarify a po-tentially baffling line. "Unwish" suggests the social tendency to bring about negative change: Even though no one wishes for the decline in the quality of life, progress may bring it about in the future's here and now (the "wherewhen") because the nameless force of change (the "unself") has a self-perpetuating power. Cummings's point is ad-vanced as much by the playful absurdity of the language itself as by this sort of analyt-ical paraphrase.

The most dramatic use of a compound coinage occurs in the opening lines that form the poem's title. "Manunkind" clearly puns on the lack of kindness in mankind con-sidered as a whole. The force of the opening command, however, is intensified by the poetic syntax that moves the damning negative, "not," not only to the final position in the sentence but also to the next line and stanza. What first appears as a call to pity hu-manity is deflated by the strategically placed "not."

Traditionally, a sonnet is defined as a fourteen-line poem in iambic pentameter with a regular rhyme scheme. By that definition, this poem is not strictly a sonnet. Cum-mings, however, was drawn to the brief controlled utterance of the sonnet form throughout his career, and he wrote hundreds of fourteen-line lyrics. "Pity this busy monster,manunkind," however, is carefully structured. Though the meter is rarely strictly iambic, each line is ten syllables long. There is no clear rhyme scheme, but some decidedly slant rhymes connect words ending lines (hypermagical/hell, unwish/ this, know/go). Cummings's use of the sonnet form reflects the idiosyncratic mix of conventionality and rebellion characteristic of his verse. Cummings is attracted to the controlled form of the sonnet—both in the overall length of the poem and in the disci-pline given to line lengths. At the same time, the deliberate resistance of iambic meter and rhyme shows that Cummings is not interested in the metrical balance of the son-net form or its tendency to divide the lyric into sections of an argument (as in three quatrains and a couplet or an octet and a sestet).

Themes and Meanings

Cummings's poetry is essentially a poetry of oppositions, and this poem dramatizes two of the most important of those oppositions: the individual against the collective, and the organic or natural against the artificial. Cummings deplored the trends in modern society toward the conquest of the natural environment by the human-made and synthetic and toward the destruction of the individual by the mass. The busy monster of "manunkind," is pictured as a society frenetically engaged in subverting the natural ("poor stones and stars") in the name of progress. This progress that supposedly advances the good of the collective, however, ignores the vitality of the individual and thus fails miserably. Such is the motivation behind the incipient metaphors of the body politic pictured as terminal patient: "your victim (death and life safely beyond)/ plays with the bigness of his littleness." Society has moved "beyond" life and death because, in treating the mass, the individual has been dehumanized (an experience Cummings witnessed in both world wars).

This metaphor continues in the glib talk of the experts—the doctors—that concludes the poem. The body politic, stripped of the individual and the organic, becomes "a hopeless case." Faced with the reality of death, the technology-driven doctors seek, in imperialist fashion, to find new territories to conquer, and they set off for the universe "next door." The final invitation—"let's go"—works in two ways. First, it forms the ironic conclusion of the progress worshipers faced with the corpse of a society: They go off into the optimistic utopia of tomorrow that will prove to be (as "utopia" suggests) nowhere. The poet is also a doctor of sorts here, diagnosing the ills of society, and his invitation to move to another universe may be a serious call to reimagine the world through poetic sensibility. If people follow the poet's advice and save their pity for the natural world and learn to cherish it, then their future might indeed promise a "hell of a good universe." Such is the faith that Cummings extolls throughout his poetry.

Christopher Ames

THE PLACE FOR NO STORY

Author: Robinson Jeffers (1887-1962)
Type of poem: Lyric meditation
First published: 1932, in *Thurso's Landing and Other Poems*

The Poem

"The Place for No Story" is a short free-verse lyric of twelve lines varying in length from ten to two words. Despite its brevity, the poem is one of Robinson Jeffers's most important, expressing succinctly and in concentrated form a major theme of his poetry: the supremacy of unconscious nature over the human social worlds of culture and civilization. In this poem, Jeffers returns to the majestic coastal California landscape of his long narrative poems but without the tragic passions of their human characters. That is the significance of the poem's title; in this lyric, the rocky California coast which provides setting for most of Jeffers's narrative poems and for the actions of his human characters is now treated as a subject in its own right.

In both *Thurso's Landing and Other Poems* (1932) and *The Selected Poetry of Robinson Jeffers* (1938), "The Place for No Story" immediately follows the long title narrative of *Thurso's Landing*, an especially sanguine story of infidelity, insanity, and murder. This positioning suggests that "The Place for No Story" is to be understood as a kind of palinode, a poem of apology or recantation, offered by Jeffers as a partial corrective for the fury and violence of his narrative.

The poem begins, as many of Jeffers's poems do, with the place name of a real site along the California coast—in this case, Sovranes Creek, south of Monterey. Jeffers believed that poetry should conform to physical realities, and he expressed a reverence for the spiritual significance of specific places that recalls in its intensity the pagan worship of local deities (genius loci) in sacred groves and streams. Jeffers intends his lyric to be the evocation of the spiritual significance of this specific place.

The poem's speaker, whom it is reasonable to accept as the poet himself, immediately begins a description of the estuary landscape where Sovranes Creek meets the sea. The poet first describes the area's treeless upland pastures with their thin covering of soil stretched above granite bedrock. The striations and contours of this underlying rock are likened to flame, a simile suggesting their volcanic and molten origin. From these upland pastures, the poet draws one's attention westward to the scarp and the ocean below, where a plunging surf appears as a line of "long white violence" bordering an enormous gray expanse of open sea fading to the horizon. From there, one's gaze is lifted upward to a dark mountain slope dotted near its summit with a distant herd of grazing cattle and, above all, the sky itself, overcast and "haunted with hawks." The description of hawks as haunting the sky may suggest that in the heavy cloud cover they can be heard but not seen or that they are riding rising thermals of warm air in arcs so high as to be only dimly visible. This descriptive passage conveys a sense of tremendous distance and isolation.

At this point, the speaker of the poem declares simply that "This place is the noblest thing I have ever seen." The poet's curious ascription of a human quality, nobility, to an aggregate of inanimate and animal phenomena composing a landscape is immediately reinforced by the claim that any "human presence" in this wild scene would only detract from its nobility, its "lonely self-watchful passion." The descriptive adjective "lonely" in this final line expresses a normal human response to a landscape of this kind. This response had been suspended in the descriptive passage opening the poem. Now that a subjective word is used, the reader is surprised to learn that "lonely" is meant as praise for the conditions making this landscape's nobility possible: the absence of humans. The landscape's loneliness, at first neutrally described by the poet, is now embraced and contrasted, implicitly and negatively, with the social world of humans and human-centered concerns.

Forms and Devices

A distinguishing aspect of Jeffers's poetic style is his extensive use of a form of personification called the "pathetic fallacy," which is the ascription of human characteristics and emotions to material things such as trees, water, and rocks. This kind of personification, especially characteristic of Romantic poets, is evident in "The Place for No Story." Jeffers describes the ocean surf as "violent" and credits the landscape with both "nobility" and a form of consciousness which makes possible its "self-watchful passion."

For many poets, this form of personification is only a convention, a bit of poetic license not to be taken seriously. For Jeffers, however, and for his Romantic predecessors such as William Wordsworth, this use of the pathetic fallacy is seriously meant. Like the Romantics, Jeffers was something of a pantheist—one who believes that consciousness, even a divine consciousness, is distributed throughout the whole of nature. Jeffers describes the landscape of the Sovranes estuary as "noble" because for him it is, in a real sense, alive and aware. Jeffers bases this belief upon a combination of mysticism and science, arguing that since all things are composed of the same material (atomic) constituents, they must all share a fundamentally common nature. This aspect of Jeffers's poetic vision, sometimes called panpsychism, is likely to seem most strange to a reader unfamiliar with the philosophical backgrounds of his work.

In addition to the use of personification, Jeffers incorporates two important symbols common to his poetry: the rock and the hawk. They represent the fierce integrity of nonhuman nature; both are embodiments of impassive and impersonal forces dividing between them the animate world of focused energy and the inanimate world of stolid calm. Elsewhere in his poetry, Jeffers frequently contrasts humankind, with its anxiety and doubt-ridden consciousness, unfavorably with the unitary strength and simplicity of the rock and hawk. The consciousness of nature, the pantheistic sentience of things, is symbolized for Jeffers in the bird and stone. Nature's consciousness, which they share, is whole, while the human consciousness is divided. Rock and hawk in harmony with natural forces possess an organic completeness, a "nobility," that humans lack. In "The Place for No Story," humankind is only significant by its absence; neither the soaring hawk nor the ocean beaten stone need it; they are sufficient in themselves.

Themes and Meanings

Late in his career, Jeffers suggested that many of his poems were expressions of a philosophical outlook that he provocatively called Inhumanism. Jeffers defined the basic tenets of this creed in various ways, but its essence is simple: Humankind has exaggerated its importance in the scale of natural creation and now invites disaster. Only if humankind recovers a sense of its insignificance in the face of transhuman nature can it regain balance and dignity. As it is, humankind is self-absorbed and self-obsessed, cutting itself off from the strength of natural order in favor of artificial powers derived from technology and bureaucratic organization. Jeffers owed something of his philosophical outlook to the pessimistic German philosopher Oswald Spengler (1880-1936), who argued that civilizations grow old and decadent as part of an inalterable historical process resembling the biological processes of birth, aging, and death. According to Spengler, symptoms of this coming social decay in Western civilization included the rise of metropolitan cities, mass production, and rampant population growth—all of which Jeffers notes and deplores in his poetry.

In the face of this coming collapse of civilization, Jeffers suggests that the best way to retain courage and integrity is to look away from humankind and toward nature. The speaker of "The Place for No Story" does exactly this; he gazes into the "self-watchful passion" of a landscape empty of human turbulence and strife. If it contains violence, it is only the great cyclical violence of crashing waves and the balancing "nobility" of isolation and endurance.

Jeffers is, as many of his critics recognize, a moralizing poet, a man with a message. Didactic poetry of the kind favored by Jeffers, which seeks to instruct or admonish its readers with forthright statement and a lofty, prophetic tone, lost favor among the ironical poets of the modern and postmodern era. Jeffers, once lionized, is now seldom read. For some readers, the poet's verses are little more than misanthropic rant filled with irrational hatred of democracy and rational progress. For others, a fiercely loyal minority, the verses are prophetic visions of humankind's current predicament, and Jeffers himself is a voice crying in the wilderness.

Whitney Hoth

PLANETARIUM

Author: Adrienne Rich (1929-   )
Type of poem: Lyric
First published: 1971, in *The Will to Change*

The Poem

"Planetarium" is a forty-five-line poem in free verse that was prompted by a visit to a planetarium during which Adrienne Rich read about the work of astronomer Caroline Herschel (1750-1848). Herschel had worked with her brother William, the discoverer of Uranus, and later worked on her own. The poem is in "free" verse only in that its groupings of lines and phrases are irregular; they are actually carefully arranged to emphasize the progression of observations and thoughts that make up the poem.

The opening lines refer to the constellations, their shapes identified since ancient times with mythological beings; among them is "a monster in the shape of a woman." Then Rich moves to a real woman, Caroline Herschel, and quotes from a description of her working with scientific instruments; Herschel, she notes, discovered eight comets. In seven words, Rich deftly points out a kinship among Herschel, herself, and all women: "She whom the moon ruled/ like us." In a description that sounds like a metaphor but is based on the fact that astronomers often observed from cages that were raised high in the air within the observatory to allow them to see through the telescope, Herschel is seen "levitating into the night sky" and "riding" the lenses.

Rich links the mythological women in the heavens with all women; all are serving "penance," and it is implied that the penance is being demanded by the men who created the myths and named the constellations. Another quotation appears, this one of astronomer Tycho Brahe speaking of his own observations. Brahe, in 1573, discovered the "NOVA," the "new star" in Cassiopeia (actually a star that, in the final stage of its existence, had expanded to thousands of times its original size). Rich relates the nova to women ("us"), the life exploding outward from them.

The poem then shifts subtly in tone, as the speaker (presumably Rich herself) gradually moves into the foreground, leading to the forceful declaration of personal vision that concludes the poem. "What we see, we see," Rich states, then, crucially, "and seeing is changing." She sees a paradox of power and delicacy; she sees a joining of the cosmic and the minuscule (and the inanimate and the animate). Light can destroy a mountain yet not hurt a person; the pulsar and her own heartbeat combine in her body.

Line 34 stands alone in the poem, and it acts as both a pronouncement of strength ("I stand") and a pause before the final section—eleven lines that run together, broken only by brief pauses within the lines. In the final section, Rich attempts to define herself anew, apart from history and old mythologies. She is a deep galactic cloud; she stands in the path of signals, an "untranslatable language." Discarding the ancient celestial monster/woman of line 2, she declares herself "an instrument in the shape of a woman." That is, she is a writer, a creator of "images," trying to make sense of her own observations and experiences; moreover, since "seeing is changing," she is reconstructing—as she realizes she must—the way she views herself and the world.

Forms and Devices

The groupings of lines in "Planetarium" are too irregular to be called stanzas; they are clusters of lines grouped according to separate thoughts, observations, and quotations. The fact that the words "An eye" have a line to themselves, for example, hints at the importance of vision (and re-vision) in the poem. The poem is dated 1968 (Rich regularly puts the year of composition at the end of her poems), and a number of poems dated 1968 in *Leaflets* (1969) and *The Will to Change* use structures similar to that of "Planetarium." The poems also have spaces within the lines that add to the fragmentation of the thoughts being expressed. The reader senses hesitations, directions being pondered, options being weighed:

> Galaxies of women, there
> doing penance for impetuousness
> ribs chilled
> in those spaces   of the mind.

The density of the poem's closing group of eleven lines presents a rush of thoughts, with occasional pauses in midline that seem to be pauses for breath as well as momentary breaks in the sudden forward movement of connected ideas. The density also reflects the content, mirroring Rich's depiction of herself as an "involuted" galactic cloud through which it has taken light fifteen years to travel.

In many of her poems of the late 1960's, Rich combines the cosmic and the personal; the words that unite the two can often be applied to astronomy, physics, and communication. In "Planetarium," one finds impulses of light, a "radio impulse" from Taurus, "signals," and "pulsations." In "The Demon Lover" (1966), in a figure similar to the one in "Planetarium" that unites heart and pulsar, a "nebula/ opens in space, unseen,/ your heart utters its great beats/ in solitude." Immediately preceding "The Demon Lover" in *Leaflets* is a Rich translation of a Gerrit Achterberg poem named for the Dwingelo observatory in Holland: "signals" are coming from constellations, "the void" whispers in the radio telescope, and "the singing of your nerves is gathered." In "Implosions," Rich offers the "word" of her pulse and asks the person she addresses to "Send out your signals."

Astronomy for Rich is, in one sense, a metaphor for the search for truth—particularly for the attempt to discover a new truth. The night sky, with its constellations (in the poem "Orion" and the "Dwingelo" translation as well as here), contains both the old myths and the potential for overturning those myths. The fact that astronomy involves studying pulses and signals also unites it with both the physical body and communication—and therefore with language, the instrument of the poet.

Themes and Meanings

Through its allusions to mythology, anecdotes from the history of astronomy, and final personal declaration, "Planetarium" depicts a moment of awakening consciousness. Rich states, in metaphorical terms, that she is at last seeing things clearly and is consequently taking a stand.

During the late 1960's, Rich was struggling to learn truths about herself and about the traditional female roles—wife and mother—that she had filled in the 1950's and early 1960's. In those earlier years, she experienced intense feelings of anger, conflict, and failure that she sought—desperately sought, she says—to understand. The "mad webs of Uranisborg" in "Planetarium" echo the "dark webs" (as she herself put it) that she groped among in those years.

Beginning with references to the women shaped like monsters that inhabit the sky—representing the distorted identities that men have given to women who refuse to fit into prescribed social roles—the poem moves to its closing declaration of independence both from those limited roles and from the old wrongheaded perceptions of those who refuse those roles. The power to change things begins with awareness. Astronomy, concerned with "observing" the sky—with vision—here embodies the struggle for that awareness. Rich frequently speaks of "instruments," of objects that can assist in the struggle to gain knowledge or freedom; sometimes, as here, the instrument and the person become one.

In a 1971 essay entitled "When We Dead Awaken: Writing as Re-Vision," Rich discusses the necessity for women to view society and history in new ways. "Revision," she says, is "an act of survival" that can enable women to refuse to participate in the "self-destructiveness of male-dominated society." She also notes the power of language in this process: "Writing is re-naming." Because seeing anew and writing anew are part of the same process, "Planetarium" concludes with the image of the woman being bombarded with "untranslatable" signals and pulsations that she must translate "for the relief of the body/ and the reconstruction of the mind."

In the 1965 poem, "Orion," Rich gazes at that constellation, first remembering how she thought of it as a child (her "cast-iron Viking"), then seeing it in the present as her "fierce half-brother" who "burns" like a defiant pirate. In "When We Dead Awaken," she writes that Orion represented the active part of herself; that is, she saw two alternatives, the female (various types of love) and the male (creative egotism), and saw no way of combining the two. In retrospect, she sees those as false alternatives. Rich calls "Planetarium," written three years later, a companion poem to "Orion." In the later poem, she says, "at last the woman in the poem and the woman writing the poem become the same person."

H. McCrea Adams

PLAYBOY

Author: Richard Wilbur (1921-   )
Type of poem: Lyric
First published: 1969, in *Walking to Sleep: New Poems and Translations*

The Poem

Richard Wilbur's "Playboy" consists of seven quatrains written in iambic pentameter. The first and fourth lines of each stanza rhyme, as do the second and third, constituting an *abba* pattern with differing sounds occurring in each stanza. Thus, while the rhyme pulls the poem through its dramatic stages, the sounds themselves do not repeat from one stanza to the next. Through the use of rhyme, each stanza illustrates the self-absorbed young man who is the focus of the poem, as well as the claustrophobic nature of his world.

The poem opens with a reference to the young "stock-boy," sitting high above the floor on a ladder, perusing the glossy page of a magazine which features pictures of scantily clad women posed in sexually charged settings. The title of the poem itself suggests one such magazine, popular around the time this poem was written. The reader realizes that the title, therefore, is ironic, as the poem centers on a young man who longs for a woman he cannot have, a woman he encounters in the magazine's pages. Wilbur does not reveal the stock-boy's age, suggesting his youth and inexperience by never referring to him as a man. Wilbur is not describing, therefore, the sensual response of a mature man. Instead, Wilbur seems to have fun at the stock-boy's expense.

The poem proceeds to answer three questions the poet addresses to the reader, as if poet and reader were quietly eavesdropping, observing the scene unbeknownst to the stock-boy. Indeed, the tone of the poem suggests an awareness that the reader and the poet share, but which escapes the stock-boy. With the first question, Wilbur asks, "What so engrosses him?" Specifically, he wonders what so captivates the stock-boy that he is oblivious to his own surroundings. In lush description that forms the second question, Wilbur paints a picture of the answer. The setting in which the woman is posed is geared to enhance the dreamlike quality of the experience. Each element of decor suggests a romanticized notion of feminine sexuality—the scatter of furs and pillows on the floor, the raised goblet, the rose in a crystal vase, the vermilion tablecloth.

The second question runs for three stanzas, attempting to suggest an answer to the first question by elaborating on the luxuriant setting. The description emphasizes the opulence of the surroundings, even speaking of a tablecloth as being such rich fare that a moth would shrivel if it tried to eat the cloth. Is the setting, therefore, that which so captivates the attention of the stock-boy?

Wilbur concludes stanza 5 with the one-line question, "Or is he pondering her perfect breasts?" Such a closure at this point balances the three-stanza sentence that precedes it. Wilbur's economy of language serves to emphasize the corporal fixation that the stock-boy encounters. The placement of this question as the last elevates it, in the rhetorical argument of the poem, to the highest level of importance.

With the exception of the woman's pose—her physical placement relative to her world—Wilbur's description of the woman never becomes specific. Although he describes with great detail the room in which she is placed, he does not give the reader any sense of her as an individual. Such details as hair color, for example, are entirely absent. The reader only learns that she is a smiling nude. The reader therefore participates in the same kind of stereotyping that subjugates the stock-boy. He knows nothing of this woman as a person; indeed, in the past, such magazines carried very little information about their nude models.

The last two stanzas go beyond the stock-boy's fantasies to comment on the nature of art itself to transform perceptions. Although the stock-boy certainly stares at the woman's body, allowing the setting itself to draw him into her realm, her face holds the key to his problem as well as to the key to this poem. From the point of view of the stock-boy, the photograph captures her face just as the woman is on the verge of yielding to his desires, his "inexorable will." This woman, whom he has never seen, now accepts him, according to his trust in a still picture published in a magazine that thousands of other men buy. This playboy can only succeed in the realm of the imagination, with women he cannot possibly possess in real life.

Forms and Devices

Wilbur's poetry develops its rhetorical argument through the use of formal stylistics. This poem consists of seven quatrains, using rhyme that does not interlock from stanza to stanza. The effect of such independent rhyme is to heighten the questioning stance that describes the stock-boy. The iambic pentameter works to provide a conversational meter, as if the poet were conspiring over the stock-boy's predicament.

Other devices of sound also play a part in elucidating the sense of this poem. In the first three stanzas, for example, consonantal sounds predominate. In the first stanza, there are *s* sounds; in the second, *f*, and in the third, *p*. The fourth stanza, however, takes on a softer sound as if to heighten the dreamlike quality of the description. In that stanza, *o* sounds move the ear and eye to the fifth stanza, which carries *a* sounds through the sixth stanza, culminating in *o* sounds in the final stanza.

Wilbur frequently utilizes classical allusions in his poetry, and this poem is no exception. In the first stanza, the stock-boy is "As lost in curves as Archimedes once." Wilbur's elegance and subtlety can detract a reader from the very dry, often bawdy, wit that some of his poems express. For example, Archimedes invented a tubular helix, or screw. The stock-boy is lost in thought over a different kind of curve.

Through the simile, Wilbur illustrates the naïveté of the young man. As the youth feeds himself, his left hand brings the sandwich to his mouth "like a mother-bird in flight." Such a comparison underscores the stock-boy's lack of maturity. He is, in effect, still a child needing the care of his parents, or at the very least, a male mentor who can instruct him in the ways of the heart. Likewise, by comparing the stock-boy to a dunce as he sits on a stool eating, Wilbur portrays him as being so enrapt with the pictures that he feeds himself without looking at the sandwich. Although the stock-boy has the fixed concentration of a sage, he sits like a dunce.

The one clue to the woman's identity emerges through Wilbur's use of the rose as a metaphor. While picturing her in static poses, within the context of an unbelievable boudoir, she lifts a goblet using the hand most distant from the observer. She seems to toast "an exploding rose." Wilbur compares the still, controlled sensuality of the created setting to the possibilities that make up this woman's true self.

Themes and Meanings

Using formal stylistics, Wilbur contrasts the reserved, controlled world of the stock-boy's everyday life, a world over which he has little authority, with the highly imaginative, sensually charged world of the magazines he reads when he thinks no one sees him. The stock-boy believes that he can possess the woman, although he cannot. Her smile is studied, her skin is "strangely like a uniform." The woman offers him nothing that she does not similarly offer anyone who has the money to purchase the magazine. Although Wilbur risks having a knowing laugh at the stock-boy's expense, the poet does not ridicule him. Instead, Wilbur uses great tenderness in describing the helplessness of the young man.

Wilbur suggests that the world of the imagination contains lessons that each person must learn. The imagination is a safe place for the stock-boy, as no one is harmed by his self-absorbed musings. By contrasting the two worlds, Wilbur heightens the boy's need to pass through one world in order to fully grasp whom he must become in the next. As a poet, Wilbur owns both sources of knowledge—that which youth is eager to find out through the energy-driven need to conquer the world, and that which age supplies through experience.

Martha Modena Vertreace-Doody

PLAYER PIANO

Author: John Updike (1932-   )
Type of poem: Lyric
First published: 1956; collected in *The Carpentered Hen and Other Tame Creatures*, 1958

The Poem

"Player Piano," a quirky example of light verse from the early works of John Updike, demonstrates the well-known novelist's penchant for showcasing the musical nature of language. The three-stanza poem, primarily in dactylic tetrameter (a form reminiscent of that of the limerick), describes a melody played by the mechanical "fingers" of a player piano:

> My stick fingers click with a snicker
> As, chuckling, they knuckle the keys;
> Light-footed, my steel feelers flicker
> And pluck from these keys melodies.

The "speaker" of the poem, the player piano itself, relates to the reader the processes it experiences while it is playing the tunes recorded on its paper rolls. The poem, while seemingly lighthearted and amusing on the surface, gives the reader a rather disconcerting look into the mind of a machine. Even though the player piano is performing an essentially human task—the playing of music is usually regarded as a creative art, not a mechanical science—the machine contemplates its tasks much differently than would a human musician.

The player piano's execution is nimble and light, but any human listener would not be able to forget that the player piano, a machine, lacks any sense of what it is playing; "My paper can caper; abandon/ Is broadcast by dint of my din." Although it is technically proficient when it plays the tunes on its paper rolls, the player piano is also, regrettably, inhuman in its playing: "no man or band has a hand in/ The tones I turn on from within." The rollicking tunes, while pleasant and musical to the listener's ear— "At times I'm a jumble of rumbles,/ At others I'm light like the moon"—betray the demanding regularity inherent in the working of any machine: "never my numb plunker fumbles,/ Misstrums me, or tries a new tune."

The rhythm is insistent and ruthlessly regular, the expression of every note is precise, and the melody perfectly duplicated each time it is rendered because the player piano can never alter any aspect of its playing. The absolute regularity of the player piano's tune, like the meter of the poem describing it, is reflective of the expression of a purely mechanical musician and imparts a sentience quite unlike that of the rather slipshod, but essentially creative and expressive, playing of a human musician.

Forms and Devices

The Carpentered Hen and Other Tame Creatures, the collection in which "Player Piano" first appeared, is prefaced by a quote from Boethius' *De consolatione philosophiae* (523; *The Consolation of Philosophy*, late ninth century), which celebrates the two-fold nature of poetic endeavor: the poem as lesson as well as entertainment. At times, it seems as if Updike repudiates Boethius' sentiment, creating poems that are merely flights of fancy rather than imparting any great philosophy of life, but it would be a mistake to assume that the whole of Updike's poetry is fanciful and superficial. Under Updike's many puns and wordplay is a deep respect for the power of language.

"Player Piano," in particular, seems to delight in verbal patterns; "click with a snicker,/., . . . steel feelers flicker," for example, demonstrates both internal and end rhyme and the combination of dactyls and iambs in "At times I'm a jumble of rumbles" is an auditory delight that is echoed throughout the work's three stanzas. The constancy and regularity of such rhyme and meter, difficult in any tongue, is particularly admirable in English, which has fewer rhyming words and less natural meter. Such facility of language seems to suggest the poet's confidence in his wordplay, but it must not be assumed that the levity of the poem's form is the whole of the poem's substance.

As a rule, the form of light verse tends to buoy the poem's subject—"lightening," literally, the gravity of any deeper theme. Theoretically, a weighty poem should lack excessive rhyme and an overly regular metrical structure—the presence of both features in "Player Piano" tends to designate the poem as frivolous in topic. On the other hand, Updike's very insistence on verbal play seems to suggest his disdain for such inflexible definitions of verse.

On the surface, "Player Piano," with its intense rhythm and rhyme, uses onomatopoeia to suggest the very ordered, mechanical nature of the piano rolls. Beneath the surface, however, is the suggestion that the machine's reliance on order and structure limits it from the pleasure of musical "accidents" or even playing another tune—the very structure that prevents "misstrums" also prevents creativity. On the surface, "Player Piano" uses a rigorous meter to imply the demands of the mechanical form (the piano's mechanical workings) upon the creative medium (the music). Beneath this meaning, however, is the less obvious theme of all creative works—that a strict form (meter and rhyme for poetry, like mechanical keys and paper rolls for a player piano) can alternatively assist a creative medium like poetry or music from verbal mistakes or restrict its meaning. The dual nature of the player piano, then, reveals Updike's ambivalence for the poetic form and, perhaps, why he chose to largely abandon the poem in favor of the greater expression available to him as a writer of prose.

Themes and Meanings

Critics have often remarked that Updike, as a novelist, writes works that engage both the mind and the emotions. His most famous character, Rabbit Angstrom, has occasioned many a column of praise from the literary-minded. On the other hand, Updike the poet has garnered only a fraction of the notice applied to his prose writing.

It is a specialist in poetry who recognizes such works as "Player Piano" as the equally fine handiwork of Updike. A lighthearted tone, present in both poetry and prose, is the primary key to identifying Updike's hand, a trait that is anything but exclusive to Updike.

Perhaps the difficulty in seeing the novelist behind the poems is that it is hard to find good novelists who also write good poetry. The combination was far more common among the Victorians—William Makepeace Thackeray, Charles Dickens, and Emily Brontë had an equal fascination for both prose and light verse (Thackeray's "Little Billee," for example). Born well after the Victorian period, Updike nevertheless betrays many of the literary quirks of his Victorian forebears, particularly the tendency toward creating deep philosophical musings in the guise of a humorous ditty.

On the surface, "Player Piano" seems to be conventional in its adherence to the strictures of light verse; the work seems to be solely descriptive, neither despairing nor jubilant and establishing no logical nor rhetorical treatises. On the initial read, "Player Piano" seems to have been meant solely as an enjoyable and yet highly erudite poem. Yet these surface details fail to convey the deeper, inner messages within the poem.

"Player Piano" is detached in tone, lacking the intimacy of a "human" meditation, but it does reveal to the careful eye a private world beyond the surface pleasantries. The poem presents the shared human experience of the slightly twisted world, which all people at times must face—the most ordinary situation becomes extraordinary and alien: "My paper can caper; abandon/ Is broadcast by dint of my din." It is the universality of this kind of disturbing experience—the jarring disjuncture of surface and internal "realities"—that makes Updike's poems so engaging. Just as with Edgar Allan Poe's "The Raven" (1845), anyone who picks up Updike's "Player Piano"—both those who find poetry incomprehensible and tedious and those few who find poetry addictive—will find themselves reading and rereading the lines in an effort to figure out why such a light poem engenders such inward unease.

The combination of accessibility and readability makes "Player Piano" such an interesting work. Clever and yet also comfortable, the work is appealing. Moreover, Updike's writing has the rare ability to evoke laughter at one moment and solemn philosophical contemplation at the next. "Player Piano" celebrates a simple tune played on a mechanical piano and yet also leads one to contemplate the odd juxtaposition of music and machine—if the making of music is the most human of endeavors, how then can it be so easily duplicated by a rigorously and inhumanly scientific machine as a player piano? How does the music of the player piano express the jarring eccentricities of the mechanical world in which modern humanity must live? Under the guise of light verse, Updike's "Player Piano" addresses such compelling concerns and reveals readers' own, human, discomfort with the answers.

Julia M. Meyers

POEM ABOUT MY RIGHTS

Author: June Jordan (1936-   )
Type of poem: Narrative
First published: 1980, in *Passion*

The Poem

"Poem About My Rights," written in free verse, juxtaposes the personal odyssey of one black woman facing oppression in the United States with the political struggle of nations against oppression in southern Africa. The poem's title is ironic, as the narrator chronicles the "wrongs" that exist within the person she is as well as the external conditions that impact her. Society's edicts infringe upon and impede any rights that author June Jordan feels are hers. She is a product of her people's heritage and, as such, must live according to contemporary cultural suppositions.

Using first person throughout, Jordan details the wrongs that she perceives in herself: wrong color, wrong sex, and living on the wrong continent. She is the potential victim of any man who would physically force himself on her. The rape victim becomes the wrongdoer because the law assumes implied consent in cases of rape and brutality. Burden of proof is also left to the victim in order for justice to be served. Personal, consensual rape is then transferred to the broader area of southern Africa: South Africa's forced penetration into Namibia and Namibia's subsequent penetration into Angola are detailed.

Jordan then shifts the scene of "Poem About My Rights" back to the United States and cites both national and personal wrongs. She highlights the use of power by the government and the Central Intelligence Agency (CIA), the killing of black leaders, and the treatment of blacks on college campuses. The poet was even rejected by her parents, who wanted to alter both her behavior and her physical appearance. The latter third of the poem culminates in the poet's realization that she is very familiar with all of the problems elucidated: "the problems/ turn out to be/ me/ I am the history of rape/ I am the history of the rejection of who I am/ I am the history of the terrorized incarceration of/ my self." She is also the "problem everyone seeks to eliminate" by forced penetration. In a dramatic ending, Jordan avows that this poem is not her consent to anyone: "*Wrong is not my name//*. . . my resistance/ my simple and daily and nightly self-determination/ may very well cost you your life."

"Poem About My Rights" is a pessimistic poem. However, the work ends on a somewhat hopeful and optimistic note. Throughout the poem, the individual is seen as a victim of society. Near the beginning of the work, Jordan asks, "who in the hell set things up/ like this?" The phrase is repeated again near the end of the poem as Jordan calls on the reader to resist and to take an active stance in order to guarantee individual freedom and rights. The poem is reflective of the storytelling tradition. Readers feel as if they are at the scene with Jordan as she shares her thoughts and beliefs and implores them to comprehend her situation from her point of view.

Forms and Devices

The individual human condition is juxtaposed with national and global conditions. Victimization of the black female by society is compared to the victimization of African countries by more powerful African countries. Jordan has said that when she writes a poem, she searches for the most harrowing or superlative way to express her feelings and get her point across. The rape image in "Poem About My Rights" reflects this practice. The poem's shocking and violent images are used to make comparisons among individual, national, and global situations. The forced gang rape of an unconsenting female in France is deemed by law as consent since male penetration did not include ejaculation, and therefore there is no proof. It is determined that the individual is wrong because of who and where she is at the time of the incident. To Jordan, this is analogous to the penetration of African nations by more powerful countries. Jordan also applies the rape image to her current situation as a black female: "I am the history of rape"; "I have been raped because I have been wrong"; "I have been the meaning of rape"; and "I have been the problem everyone seeks to/ eliminate by forced/ penetration with or without the evidence."

In Lauren Muller's *June Jordan's Poetry for the People* (1995), Jordan defines poetry as "a political action undertaken for the sake of information and the exorcism that telling the truth makes possible." She goes on to say that poetry should achieve a maximum impact with a minimum of words. Punctuation should be omitted. Vertical rhythm may be used to move the reader from one line to the next. Jordan also notes that a poem should not depend solely on the distribution of stressed and unstressed syllables but should incorporate musical qualities such as assonance and dissonance. Written in free verse, "Poem About My Rights" has little punctuation but is divided into four segments. In the first segment, Jordan's personal situation and viewpoint are introduced. The section ends with the word "silence" and a colon. In the second segment, the rape images of both the individual and the globe are presented. The idea of implied consent by the victim and a semicolon end this section. The third section is introduced with the capitalized comment "Do You Follow Me." This section recounts the wrongs inflicted upon blacks and upon Jordan by her parents, the government, and the world. Jordan is at the same time the product of her history and a member of current society. It is in this section that Jordan states, "I do not consent." The final section, briefer than the first three, is set off by the italicized words "*I am not wrong: Wrong is not my name.*" It is here that Jordan becomes an active and self-determined resister. She becomes proactive rather than reactive.

The ending of the poem is unsettling. Jordan writes that her "self-determination/ may very well cost you your life." The poem concludes on a dramatic and implied violent note without punctuation. The poem begins with the tranquil notion of taking a walk so the poet can clear her head and think. This calm setting gradually fades as images of oppression, brutality, and loss of freedom emerge. Rather than reverting back to the calm beginning, the ending portends more violence as the oppressed begin to take action.

Themes and Meanings

Violence toward and oppression of individual African Americans and countries in southern Africa are the overriding themes of "Poem About My Rights." This treatment is inflicted by those with power who choose to abuse that power. The misuse of power by those who are now empowered and the need to take a stand by those who are seemingly without power are themes to which Jordan repeatedly returns. The American culture as perceived by Jordan is antifemale, antiblack, and cruelly and unfairly violent. Victimization and oppression are unavoidable in Jordan's everyday life. This is also true of the victimization of Third World countries by neighboring countries. Both individually and globally, burden of proof is essential. In an essay in *I Know What the Red Clay Looks Like* (1994), Jordan decries this practice of blaming the victim.

"Poem About My Rights" is a passionate, emotional, and personal poem. Jordan's view of the world serves as a mandate for change. A bleak and violent society's condition becomes a vehicle for change both by the individual and by society. "Rights and wrongs" and "right and wrong" are subjects of the poem despite the fact that the words "right" or "rights" are never mentioned except in the title. Jordan is never right and never has rights in the narrative, but, by the poem's end, at least she is no longer wrong. She is her own person, ready to act. To Jordan, consent is not equivalent to having rights, and she consents to no one: not to family, not to school, and not to the country's bureaucracy.

"Poem About My Rights" serves as a testament to the belief that the individual can make a difference even though doing so requires an ongoing struggle. Near the end of the poem, Jordan avows, "my name is my own my own my own." The strength to meet challenges head-on is evident. The ending, however, portends violence: Individual action may cost participants their lives. While people do have the power to alter the course of oppression and correct the loss of rights, they must take action to make a difference. Indeed, this proactive position is the only hope for altering the current scenario.

Lynn Sager

POEM ABOUT PEOPLE

Author: Robert Pinsky (1940-   )
Type of poem: Lyric
First published: 1974; collected in *Sadness and Happiness*, 1975

The Poem

"Poem About People" is composed of thirteen unrhymed quatrains with no imme-diately obvious metrical pattern. Its title establishes its subject; written in the first per-son, the poem is the speaker's quiet meditation on what people are in appearance and in actuality and how they relate to one another.

It opens with the "I" speaking of the people he sees at grocery stores. In particular, he notes apparently middle-class, middle-aged, but still attractive women, and polite, fattish young men. Although they are all strangers to the speaker, they are people whom he believes he could like. Indeed, he says, one could "feel briefly like Jesus," referring to the New Testament (as well as Old Testament) command "to love thy neighbor as thyself."

The first three quatrains are concrete and almost cheerful; by suggestion, it is broad daylight. As the fourth quatrain opens, the tone and the images begin to change. The speaker feels "a gust of diffuse tenderness" that seems to link him with these people, but this gust is "crossing the dark spaces" between him and them. The poem is no lon-ger about the sunlit world of people at the market, about human relationships; it moves within and is now about what the speaker is seeing and remembering, there where "the dry self burrows."

The remainder of the poem is given over to showing how people do not connect with one another despite this "gust." The third line of the fifth stanza begins with a "but" that signals the change. The speaker says that "love falters and flags" whenever a person is asked to face squarely another person in need. The poem now develops both by discursive statements and by two expanded images.

The people at the grocery store were strangers, easy to love in the abstract or to re-ject, but now the speaker remembers a friend. This friend, divorced and alone, hangs up the pictures he had painted; his wife had kept them hidden in a closet. He says, rue-fully, that she was probably right, yet he puts them up. He asks too much of others, asks for their approval and their love. Then the speaker presents an image drawn from movies that depict the development of love and its triumph over hatred. It is a rather obvious story of a young Jewish soldier attempting to save the "anti-Semitic bully" drowning in a river as they are raked by "nazi fire." The image represents the type of symbol that modern culture provides when attempting to teach forgiveness and love.

The first of these two images shows an actuality: The divorce itself suggests that love can come to an end, and the man's situation shows how the fact of being alone makes one more needy. The second image, the movie scene, sentimentally depicts how love and forgiveness (and, therefore, connection) between seemingly irreconcilable people win out. Movies are not actualities, however, so this image becomes deeply ironic. The last three stanzas, in a way, shift the scene again, for, although the reader is still in the mind of the speaker, the speaker gives a description of the external world again—this time of a world of full night and rain-filled wind. The images have progressed from bright, calm day to black stormy night, from images of possible love to the recognition that people's own desperate selves keep them from one another.

Forms and Devices

The critic Ian Hamilton, in the *Oxford Companion to Twentieth Century Poetry*, calls Pinsky a discursive poet—that is, one who is more likely to deal with statements and abstractions than with images. This is true in that Pinsky's subject matter is usually more than expressions of mood or feelings: His poems are also explorations of ideas. "Poem About People," however, is filled with images and subtly metaphoric language, as, for instance, those that bring out human commonalities with animals—animals that are, in the end, alone. The young men have a "porky walk," and "the dry self burrows." More important, these deep selves are connected by a simile (a comparison using "like") to the robin on the lawn and then evolutionarily back to the robin's "lizard" ancestry. The only other simile in the poem is the moment when the speaker speaks of momentarily feeling "like Jesus." These two similes are opposites, with the second one, leading from self to robin to lizard, cancelling out the first, which speaks of love.

Sound is very important to Pinsky and to this poem. Sound is an essential element in the meaning. Although the poem lacks an obvious meter, most of the lines are built on three- or four-beat measures and are so arranged that the poem continually hesitates on the edge of becoming iambic tetrameter. In short, there is a traditional music in the background, but there is also a tension between the finely rhythmical beat that is actually there and the understood, traditional meter. The structural contrast reinforces the thematic contrasts of the poem's ideas, the otherness of others.

Equally important, Pinsky makes extensive use of alliteration, repeating the beginning sounds of words to emphasize those words. Examples include the related *b*'s and *p*'s of the second and third stanzas in the description of the young men. The last *p* and *b* in the third stanza are in the line "possible/ To feel briefly like Jesus," and so connect the young men with the idea of love. One more alliteration (of *f*) signals the change in the fifth stanza of the poem, for as the images change, the speaker tells how "love falters and flags."

This alliteration also emphasizes the language of the poem. The language is almost solidly drawn from Old English roots and has many single-syllable words. The sound itself comes at times close to the emphatic beat of Old English alliterative verse. Such a beat hammers home the statements of the poem. More subtly, Pinsky uses contrast in language roots that also adds to the emphases: "my friend/ In his divorced schoolteacher/ Apartment" has two words, "divorced" and "apartment," derived from French, separated by the Germanic "schoolteacher." There is also the strange uses of "divorced schoolteacher" as a kind of compound Old English adjective for "apartment," which calls the reader's attention to the oddness and separateness of the friend.

Themes and Meanings

The major thematic concern of the poem is, as previously noted, that people are separate from one another, but that they need one another. This need is deeply egoistic and destructive. The people whom the speaker describes in the first lines are, by implication, not too different from the speaker himself, the point being that he should be able to relate to them if one can relate to others at all. Pinsky is, by using these people and this speaker, emphasizing the difficulty. "Only connect," the English novelist E. M. Forster wrote, suggesting that individuals, by coming truly together, could perhaps create a better world. Pinsky's poem questions whether this coming together is possible.

Even the title emphasizes this theme in stating that the poem is "about" people. It is not a lyric effusion about one person, not a communication to a particular person. Rather, it stands outside people, even when the reader seems to be inside the mind of the speaker. The poem is saying that people cannot quite leap the gulf that separates them, one from the other. They cannot because people are all essentially egoistic, incapable of real love for others: *"Hate my whole kind,* but me,/ Love me for myself." People want to be loved simply because they are "selves," not because they are human beings.

Human beings have thought of themselves as different from other species because humans are supposed to be capable of altruism—selflessly loving others. Yet humans are animals, concerned primarily if not exclusively with themselves. At the end of the poem, the speaker says that one can only "dream" of the gust of wind that connects everyone, for it has become a "dark wind." These words are set against the earlier reference to a "gust of diffuse tenderness." Perhaps the dark wind can cross "the wide spaces between us," but those spaces are indeed wide. Oddly, the poem is in the end not entirely pessimistic. The speaker regrets that people do not, perhaps cannot, love one another, yet such a regret suggests that at least they can try. In addition, a poem about a failure to connect is paradoxically a way of connecting, for art is one way that human beings do communicate beyond simply presenting facts.

L. L. Lee

A POEM BEGINNING WITH A LINE BY PINDAR

Author: Robert Duncan (1919-1988)
Type of poem: Ode
First published: 1958; collected in *The Opening of the Field*, 1960

The Poem

This is an "open" poem drafted according to new writing principles developed in the mid-twentieth century, aimed at breaking up the repetitive structures of argument and discourse in so-called closed or conventional poetry. Content of various sorts flows into the poem constantly, demanding close attention to the winding course of its plot. The advantage of openness is the unpredictability of outcome that keeps the reader guessing at each new turn in the poem. This mode of suspense depends on the poet's ability to synthesize all that is introduced into the argument.

The ode, ancient or modern, is a form in which a poet takes up the theme of death and allows the mind to wander over many experiences before responding. The Romantic ode explores the emotions aroused by reaching middle life, as in William Wordsworth's "Ode: Intimations of Immortality," and Samuel Taylor Coleridge's "Frost at Midnight." Robert Duncan is thinking in particular of John Keats's "Ode on a Grecian Urn," with its theme of eternal innocence and desire set against the ravages of time. Duncan approaches the subject of aging similarly, regarding the innocence and desire of various lovers from his vantage point at a corrupt, degraded moment of history: "Only a few posts of the good remain."

The poem opens with a "misreading" of a line from an ode by the Greek poet Pindar (522?-443 B.C.E.), known for his sensuous lyricism. In the Pindar line, one hears a light foot with a lover's expectancy, but Duncan misreads the line as "the light foot hears." This error generates a new line of thought which the poet then follows through four numbered sections, each organized around the premise that what is meant by love is the mind's longing to flesh itself in a material form, or for the body to embrace the immortal ideal with its aging flesh. Mind and body are the ultimate lovers whose passion is never satisfied, and which art celebrates in the guise of male and female figures.

Duncan considers various depictions of classic lovers; after Pindar, he turns to Francisco Goya's portrait of Cupid and Psyche, which he interprets as "carnal fate that sends the soul wailing." Soul and mind are interchangeable terms; carnal fate is the eventual death of the body. Part II begins by noting that the gods prevent aging in these lovers; they are principles, or archetypes, more than figures representing actual life. Psyche, whose name stands for mind (as in psychology) "is preserved." Mind is eternal, its powers passing from one generation to the next, while the body lives, dies, and is buried. Hence, the "old poets" have died but their minds live on in texts.

Duncan shifts from ancient poets to American presidents, sarcastically referred to as the "*Thundermakers*," the opposite of poets in their self-interest, their violent political goals. The succession stretches back from Dwight D. Eisenhower, in his second term of office as the poem is being written, to Andrew Johnson, Abraham Lincoln's vice president, who came to power after Lincoln's assassination in 1865. Duncan is thinking of Walt Whitman's lament for Lincoln in his poem "When Lilacs Last in the Dooryard Bloom'd," in which the themes of love and death emerge.

The mind knows mainly despair in its life as spirit; it witnesses death in all its forms, Duncan says in part III. This brings Ezra Pound to mind, who wrote *The Pisan Cantos* (1948) at the close of World War II and lamented the death of all his friends in Europe. He, too, writes of profound despair at the breaking up of a cherished ideal. Part IV returns to the footfall, now equated with the presence of any image in the mind waking it to the world around it. Other ill-fated lovers are introduced—Jason and Medea who turn against each other over the "golden fleece," and Orpheus and Eurydice, separated by the underworld. The poem closes on the image of sacred mountains where spirit is enshrined in nature, the religious form of expressing the mind's yearning to embrace the physical world.

Forms and Devices

Duncan tells the reader in his prose note in part IV that Pindar's art is "mosaic," composed of small units of language instead of being a "statue," composed of one material in a single form. This is an apt description of the ode in general, made of smaller thoughts joined by perceptual links to form a larger recognition. Duncan's poem shifts back and forth between pithy lyrics rich in metaphor to longer, digressive passages in which he lists items under a general heading, as with the American presidents who form a monotonous tradition of warriors linking periods of war.

Duncan was a careful student of sacred literature, and he copied many of its devices into his poems. Among liturgical techniques is the chant, with its repetitive syntax, which Duncan reproduces here to create a sense of magic and incantation and to remind readers of one of his poetic sources, the poetry of Walt Whitman, which also used repetitive phrasing throughout *Leaves of Grass* (1855). Repetition is found in prayer, lamentation, spells, children's songs, even states of madness, and thus leads to the threshold of the inner realm of dreams and spirits. Set against this tendency is the more prosaic language of political diatribe against the presidential line, with its strident tempo and anger.

Notable are the indented passages emphasizing the lilting rhythm of song, or used to "map" the process of ideation as Duncan struggles to clarify his understanding of love. In other passages, the language is compressed to gnomic density as Duncan reworks ancient myths. In part III, dedicated to the experimental poet Charles Olson, Duncan imitates Olson's method of spacing out lines and letting paragraphs loosely sprawl; the language here forms complex echoes as it recalls not only Olson but also his mentor, Pound, as it quotes directly from passages of *The Pisan Cantos*. Here, too, style advances argument; drawing on the words of other poets is a merging of spirits (minds) as all despair over the fate of Eros and the body.

Themes and Meanings

Duncan's poetry is a modern extension of Romantic themes—the love of beauty, the meaning of death, the sacred function of the poet, the role of vision in imagination. In this poem, Duncan explores the historic preoccupation with representing love. His interest in the subject is principally to grasp how this archetype of lovers yearning to possess one another in countless works of poetry, painting, and sculpture contains a deeper truth about the painful divisions lying within human nature. The poet is struck by the fact that the fable of unrequited or sundered passion stretches across the length of Western culture down to his own time. His allusions cite Pindar's poem from fifth century Greece, Goya's painting in the eighteenth century, Keats's ode in the early nineteenth century, Whitman's lament for Lincoln in the 1860's, and Rainer Maria Rilke's love poetry at the beginning of the twentieth century.

Duncan's view of poetry and the arts is that they express the same truths in a tradition not unlike that of the prophets of the Old Testament, as a heritage of sacred wisdom passed from one mind to another through the ages. Love lies at the heart of sacred wisdom: It expresses the irreconcilable relation between body and soul, divine and mortal beings, between the pure idea and the vagaries of nature, the image in the mind and the erratic powers of the artist to express it. Despair is thus the true voice of art, since vision can never be fully captured in language.

The presidential succession in the United States comes into the argument as a representation of the part of society that turns its back on vision. This is the materialistic dross of society, with its refusal to reach for the divine or the ineffable. Love is an ennobling form of despair, an elevated suffering in which the divine order of things is partially revealed.

The poem closes as it opened, with Duncan reading Pindar at his desk, having digressed into his own response to a line misread; it ends with the light of dawn spreading around him at the end of this meditation. The final three lines present the reader with the image of children turning in a circle, Duncan's metaphor of innocence prior to the divisive knowledge of adults. The dawn reminds him of youth, the beginning of life. The children's rhythmic turning in a game is both with and against time as they sing songs, uttering truths that will outlive them.

Paul Christensen

POEM FOR AN ANNIVERSARY

Author: Cecil Day Lewis (1904-1972)
Type of poem: Meditation
First published: 1935, in *A Time to Dance and Other Poems*

The Poem

"Poem for an Anniversary" is a brief poem of twenty-four lines divided into four sestets. Each stanza is made up of a pattern of short and long lines; the first and last lines are terse and repeat a sentencelike format, and each stanza is, in itself, a complete thought. The poem gives the reader a command ("admit then and be glad") at the onset of each stanza, and each order is reminiscent of an action associated with an anniversary celebration: admit, remember, admire, and survey.

The anniversary of the title is never specifically indicated, yet the reader is left with a sense of worldwide chronology. There are references to boiling lava, storms, and "giant lightning" that evoke images of the beginning of time. In fact, the beginning of the poem notes the end of a prehistoric age: "Our volcanic age is over." The second and third stanzas introduce ages "made for peace" in which religious and philosophical thought exists. These lines eschew former times, times in which "foul" love existed, times of evil, thoughtless procreation. The final stanza leads the reader through a new world with a balmy climate in which plants and people flourish. This new world is "Love's best," a fecund place and time with fields of grain harvested by a community of people with "linked lives." These inhabitants are the survivors of fire and storm. They know the value of the rain clouds for engendering fertility and growth rather than causing havoc and wanton destruction. Each anniversary, each harvest, is important because it marks the continuance of stability.

Forms and Devices

The first two stanzas contain striking imagery of violent earthquakes, tidal waves, and "terrible lava" flows. Then clouds appear that reflect "the fire below," and "Shuddering electric storms" unleash a cooling water that tames the lava's deep furrows with peaceful streams. This rather pedantic, at times frightening, picture is broken up by Cecil Day Lewis's use of alliteration. Much like an Old English poet, he makes use of a repetition of sounds to reinforce the imitating message in each stanza. Thus the reader is dually instructed to "admit then and be glad" that the pre-Jurassic period, with its "bedrock boiling," has come to a close. Similarly, the fire storms that form the earth's cooling crust are to be remembered without regret as a necessary evil, a coupling of "foul or fair" nature that destroys as it creates.

In the second half of the poem, the countryside becomes a place to admire. Plants provide shade, and dangerous boulders lie at rest, providing "landmarks" for travelers. The earth's vista is no longer a fearful place but rather a "contour fine" ready for the plow and the seed. This is an area where the waterways go "Hotfoot to havoc" to provide an aquifer for future fields where before only "the lava went." Finally, the earth has "grain to grow," tilled by the "linked lives" of those who have taught the "lightning to lie low." Yet the author also uses puns and personification to allow the poem a little laughter amid its serious story. The "rent" the earth must pay for its fertility is its own destruction. Initially, seas leap from the ocean floor, clouds dream, and storms "shudder," but finally lightning crouches in obedience to humankind.

There is a curious rhyme scheme in the poem: The third and sixth lines of each stanza end with an *o* sound. This does not seem particularly significant until it is observed in relation to the overall subject of the poem: the destruction and re-creation of "The little O, th' earth" (William Shakespeare's *Antony and Cleopatra*, 1606-1607). With its repeating *o* sounds, the poem reverberates with the message that the resurrection of society is a continuous process, one that must be endured if humankind is to advance rather than decay. Indeed, that image is echoed in the choice of *o*-rhyming words. In the first stanza, the earth is shaken "from head to toe," but only temporarily. The poem goes on to assure the reader that this tremor did not last. The second section is a reminder of the "fire below" that all "used to know" but that is no longer evident. In fact, where there was once fire and molten rock, now "Cooler rivers flow." By the close of the poem, the awful discord on earth has lain "low," leaving time and space for a harvest to "grow."

Themes and Meanings

Echoing the dominant images of fire and fertility, "Poem for an Anniversary" is an anthem of destruction and creation. Espoused by his politically leftist comrades, Day Lewis promotes in this poem the paradox of total dismemberment of a state in order to rebuild it under a new regime. The persistent vision of volcano and fire reinforces an image of the phoenix of a new government rising from the ashes of the complete destruction of the old order. The volcano itself is a symbol of both debacle and miracle. Its eruption and the resultant lava and spume of ash set the earth aflame and choke out all life; but it is that same volcanic action that creates midocean atolls, providing a resting place for birds and animals that eventually settle on them to create an island of life where before there were only seas.

Images of living and mating are evident throughout the poem, except in the opening stanza in which the seas leap "from their beds" and the "World's bedrock" is deemed "terrible" in the light of the abundance of lava. Yet the persona assures readers that "Now it is not so." Soon there is a "mating in air" that is evaluated as neither "foul" nor "fair" love but rather as a natural phenomenon. Soon, however, prayers are raised, perhaps signifying the onset of enlightened thought and action. An "us" appears, the advent of rational life, and soon humanity experiences "Love's best," resulting in their "linked lives," a people joined in tending the new crop of ideas in a fine and cogent climate. Even though these changes are wrought under violent circumstances, the reader is instructed to admire, not fear, the incipience. They may seem terrifying at the beginning, but they should be remembered for their reproductive qualities, much like the farmer who burns his field, not to destroy it but to make way for the next year's crop.

Jennifer L. Wyatt

A POEM FOR BLACK HEARTS

Author: Amiri Baraka (Everett LeRoi Jones, 1934-   )
Type of poem: Elegy
First published: 1965; collected in *For Malcolm*, 1969

The Poem

Amiri Baraka, a leader and inspiration within the Black Arts movement, opened the Black Arts Repertory Theater/School (BARTS) in 1964, which, in combination with the Black Arts movement, promoted an interest in music, poetry, art, and drama in Harlem, New York. During the 1960's, Baraka began to distance himself from mainstream white American culture while aligning himself with the politics of Black Nationalism. Baraka wrote "A Poem for Black Hearts" to eulogize Malcolm X, a separatist leader of the Civil Rights movement, who was assassinated in 1965. While iconizing the political figure of Malcolm X as a symbol of African American masculinity, dignity, and self-consciousness, the poem's speaker urges "black men" to "avenge" Malcolm's death.

The poem, written in free verse, consists of twenty-seven lines that build an image of Malcolm X, which immortalizes him as a "black god of our time" while encouraging African American men to continue the struggle for civil rights. Malcolm's body and essence are fragmented by the speaker; each part of Malcolm's body is given significance so that the created image of the fallen leader becomes an image for all "black men." While the poem is "For Black Hearts," it is also "For Malcolm's eyes," which, according to the speaker, have the ability to break "the face of some dumb white man" by challenging his authority, his bigotry. The poem is "For/ Malcolm's hands," which "blessed" everyone in the African American community (the speaker included), "black and strong in his [Malcolm's] image." The speaker asserts that the poem is "for Malcolm's words," which are descriptively and figuratively renamed "fire darts" to show that his flaming words included the rhetoric of war and were carefully aimed at the enemy.

The speaker feels that Malcolm was assassinated "for saying, feeling, and being/ change," believing that Malcolm was murdered for speaking out against racism and encouraging political action by "any means necessary." In addition, the poem is "For Malcolm's/ heart," his love for his fellow "black men" and his "pleas" for African American dignity, life, and education. Finally, the poem is "For all of him [Malcolm] dead" and all of him remembered, which "clings to" African American political and cultural rhetoric.

The speaker incites his intended readers, "black men," to "quit stuttering and shuffling," "whining and stooping" and to "look up." Instead of hanging their heads in defeat, "black men" should raise their heads in dignity and look to Malcolm as an example of African American pride, masculinity, and political activism. In the closing lines, the speaker, while aligning himself with and including himself in the African

American community, challenges "black men" to "let nothing in [them] rest" until Malcolm's death has been avenged. He furthers his vow of vengeance by pledging that "if we fail" to avenge Malcolm's death, "let us never breathe a pure breath." It is clear, at this moment in the text, that the speaker wants "black men" to internalize Malcolm's eyes, words, heart, and dignity as well as his desire to change the world so that the voices of "black men" can continue to speak and act within the space Malcolm helped create.

Forms and Devices

Baraka utilizes enjambed lines to carry syntax over from one line to the next, as well as unconventional punctuation and repetition to stress particular words and phrases. In addition, he creates a mood of urgency in his layout. This urgency in combination with the fast and forward moving rhythm works to persuade and rally his intended readers, "black men," to continue Malcolm's battle: to challenge the dominant orders that disenfranchise and exclude African Americans.

Throughout "A Poem for Black Hearts," enjambment and unconventional punctuation control reading speed. Commas instigate light stops in the progression of the poem's narrative. Intentionally, Baraka places commas after he introduces an aspect of Malcolm. This use of the comma creates both a slight pause and a stress, which becomes apparent in the first two lines of the poem. The comma between "eyes" and "when" functions to stress the word "eyes," appearing before the comma, while preparing the reader for the symbolic significance of "Malcolm's eyes," in particular, the shattering gaze, which follows after the comma.

The poem is "For Malcolm's eyes," which were significant, powerful "when they broke/ the face of some dumb white man." In addition to the arrangement of the clauses, the fact that the first line ends with the word "broke," which is not followed by punctuation, pushes the reader into the first two words of the second line, "the face." This is an example of how Baraka initially sets the pace of his poem with enjambment. Rather than employing a comma at the end of the first line to designate a pause at the end of the first line, the reader is forced to quickly begin the second line while carrying the syntax (all the words and clauses of the first line), into the second line.

In the second sentence of the poem, which includes lines 2-19, enjambment is of particular interest because it speeds the reader through the poem to the climax. Enjambment complicates the lines and poetic layout because it does not support a conventional meter or rhyme scheme. Following this long series of clauses, Baraka begins the resolution, which relies on repetition, particularly of the phrases "look up" and "black man" in lines 20-22, to chastise his readers for defeatism before calling on them to "avenge" Malcolm's death. Thus, the relationship between the words and clauses in previous lines flows into the following lines and gives the poem continuity.

Themes and Meanings

The struggle for a dignified and collective African American identity, the self-conscious recovery of African American manhood, and the urgent need for continued political activism are all addressed within this poem. The main purpose of "A Poem for Black Hearts" is to incite awareness and self-consciousness in African American men so that they will actively continue to struggle for civil rights, which is also articulated as a struggle for African American masculinity.

While Baraka's poem asserts that racial oppression emasculates the African American man, it also suggests that a solution to racial oppression includes reclaiming and redefining African American masculinity in the image of the martyred leader "Great Malcolm." The speaker of Baraka's poem encourages and unites his intended audience, "black men," with images of Malcolm, symbolizing African American manhood. The speaker suggests that while Malcolm's image can serve as a representation of African American manhood, masculinity must be earned through a struggle for vengeance. These images of a strong masculine leader, a "black god" slain, are contrasted with a pejorative for emasculated African American males: "faggots." Vows of vengeance and an effort to reclaim African American masculinity in Malcolm's image will, according to the speaker, prevent "black men" from being called "faggots" and oppressed by "white men . . . till the end of/ the earth."

This poem's concerns link African American masculinity with the struggle of the Civil Rights movement. Moreover, it displays prominent characteristics of Black Nationalism, in which the responsibility of political leadership rests upon the shoulders of "black men." "A Poem for Black Heats" represents the urgency of the Civil Rights movement, which relied upon and articulated Enlightenment notions regarding human rights: rights of individuals to self-governance and the pursuit of knowledge, freedom, property, and happiness. African Americans were excluded from many of these basic rights because of categories of race and gender, which constructed them as "Others" within the social consciousness. As a prominent figure of the Black Arts movement and Black Nationalism during the 1960's, Baraka expressed his political views while capturing the African American community's struggle for equality within his poems, dramas, and nonfiction works.

Trisha M. Brady

POEM OF THE END

Author: Marina Tsvetayeva (1892-1941)
Type of poem: Poetic sequence
First published: 1925, as "Poema kontsa"; collected in *Izbrannye proizvedeniya*,
   1965; English translation collected in *Selected Poems of Marina Tsvetayeva*, 1971

The Poem

"Poem of the End," composed in 1924, is a poetic sequence of fourteen lyrics describing the end of an affair between the poet, Marina Tsvetayeva, and her lover Konstantin Rodzevitch. Although the poem is autobiographical, it is not necessary to know much about the relationship to understand the poem, which is universal in the intensity of its emotion. As the lovers meet, walk along a river, and pass places they once frequented, the poet struggles with her lover's decision to break off the relationship, and the structure of the poem reflects this struggle. Much of the poem is written in first person, and the "I" functions as referent to both the poet and the persona. It is often difficult to tell who is speaking, the poet or her lover, indicating that the parting is difficult for both; the two are still very much in love, but the lover is driven away by the intensity of the poet. The ambiguity of the speaker's voice, however, also suggests that their conversations may be imagined or remembered.

In the opening lyric, the lovers meet, and the poet becomes suspicious of her lover's demeanor, the "menace at the edges of his/ eyes." When the lover suggests going to a movie, the poet insists on going home, but, in the second poem, "home" turns into "houses/ collapsing in the one word: home," and the lover's house on the hill appears to burst into flame as the poet finds her love self-destructing. The third lyric provides a contrast in imagery as the couple walks along the river and the poet notes her affinity for water, in which she will not drown because she was "born naiad," a reference to the poet's given name (Marina). The fourth poem presents a striking shift in tone and structure; in this segment, Tsvetayeva imitates a popular ballad form to ridicule ordinary people going about their daily activities, "snout-deep in the feathers of some/ business arrangement." The poet reveals both a disrespect for common people and her sense of alienation as a poet, a theme that recurs in the twelfth lyric as the pair walks through the Jewish ghetto of Prague: "In this most Christian of worlds/ all poets are Jews." In the fifth poem, the lovers begin a painful discussion of their relationship, and the awkwardness of their conversation is reflected in the spacing between words, the speech interrupted by parenthetical remarks and abrupt shifts indicated by dashes.

There is little action after the fifth poem, and the remaining segments explore the poet's inner thoughts. The poet grapples with her emotions; she is angry at her lover's cowardice in making a clean break and at his superficial gestures—he has offered her a ring as a symbol of parting rather than commitment; still, she does not want to leave and determines to cling more tightly in order to force her lover into a violent separation: "I bite in like a tick/ you must tear out my roots to be rid of me." Finally, the lover is reduced to tears and is ridiculed by a trio of prostitutes passing by. The poet marks the contrast between the intimacy of her affair and the casual, commercial sexual exchanges of the laughing women, but the cycle ends on a somber, pessimistic note as "without trace—in silence—/ something sinks like a ship."

Forms and Devices

"Poem of the End" is not easily translated because Russian is an inflected language and because Tsvetayeva uses many innovations that cannot be rendered into English. Russian, unlike English, employs case endings so that meaning is more independent of placement than in English, in which objects regularly follow verbs that are preceded by subjects. Tsvetayeva takes advantage of Russian inflection, deviating from standard word order, a feature that cannot be translated. English translations cannot adhere to the rhyme schemes and metrical patterns of the original either. Therefore, some of the power and innovation of the poem are lost in translation.

Structurally, "Poem of the End" is very complex. Tsvetayeva employs a stream-of-consciousness technique to take the reader into the poet's psyche. Her style is characterized by dashes, refrains, spaces between words, odd line breaks, and enjambment (run-on lines) to create new, jolting meters. For example, in the sixth section, she imitates the struggle to control her tears with the lines "So now must be no/ so now must be no/ must be no crying" and continues to repeat "without crying" in the next six stanzas. Although she does not repeat the phrase in the final stanza of the section, the reader expects to hear the phrase and is invited to supply it. Such refrains connect the poetry yet provide a contrast to the pervasive ellipses of her style. Additionally, Tsvetayeva varies the meter from section to section to show mood swings and shifts in focus. Such stylistic contrasts and variations maintain both syntactic and semantic tension throughout the work.

Tsvetayeva's metaphors contribute to this tension, jolting the reader from one image to another, as in the following line, which begins as a rhetorical question but ends with a startling comparison: "who shall I tell my sorrow/ my horror greener than ice?" She frequently shifts between colloquial and formal diction, between classical allusions and description of her surroundings, often ending with a disturbing image. In the third section, for example, she alludes to the lush hanging gardens of the Assyrian princess Semiramis, then describes the river along which she and her lover walk as "a strip as colourless/ as a slab for corpses."

Themes and Meanings

On the surface, "Poem of the End" is a journey, a simple walk along a river in Prague, but it is also a psychological journey, and this is where the meaning of the poem resides. For Tsvetayeva, who believes the poet holds an exalted position, ordinary life means death; she is incapable of conventional emotion, and it is her intensity that has caused the break with her lover. The end to which the poem refers is both the ending of the affair and the poet's rejection of ordinary life. As the cycle moves between detailed descriptions of Tsvetayeva's physical surroundings and her mental landscape, these endings become apparent.

The poem reveals its meaning through images of banality and death, which are introduced in the first poem. In the opening line, the poet waits for her lover beneath a sign, "a point of rusting/ tin in the sky," and when her lover arrives, he is as "on time as death is." In the seventh stanza, these images combine: "life is/ at death point." This repetition of the word "point" suggests that the rusting tin signifies not just a shabby café but death as well. In the third and fourth segments of the cycle, Tsvetayeva again juxtaposes themes of death and tawdriness, this time using separate poems for each. In the third poem, the river, traditionally a symbol of life, is described as "a slab for corpses," and references to death recur throughout the third lyric. In the next poem, the locale shifts abruptly to a café, perhaps a flashback to the café where the lovers met; here the poet examines the banality of ordinary people. She returns to this juxtaposition in the twelfth poem, saying "Life is only a suburb" and, four stanzas later, "Life is a place where it's forbidden/ to live." The poet goes on to identify herself with the Jews: As a poet she is an alien, an outsider, and to live she must exile herself from ordinary life and its ordinary affairs. Her love must fail because she is a poet, someone too intensely emotional to succeed at conventional love.

Tsvetayeva's break with the conventional is reflected throughout "Poem of the End" in her innovative structure, which also functions thematically. In order to rise above the deathlike river and the deadly towns and suburbs, she must not follow "a path for/ sheep." Instead, she must soar beyond traditional modes of expression. By employing stream of consciousness, using unconventional punctuation and line breaks, and varying the meter, Tsvetayeva demonstrates that she has rejected the conventional: ordinary love, ordinary life, ordinary verse.

In spite of the poet's commitment to existing on a higher plane, the poem ends somberly: "And into the hollow waves of/ darkness—hunched and level—/ without trace—in silence—/ something sinks like a ship." This final stanza suggests that the poet fears failure, that her voice will not be heard, that she herself will disappear in silence without a trace. In fact, when "Poem of the End" was first circulated, it was not well received by critics, perhaps because of its stylistic innovation. However, it has since come to be considered one of Russia's finest psychological poems and the best example of Tsvetayeva's mature style.

K Edgington

POEM ON HIS BIRTHDAY

Author: Dylan Thomas (1914-1953)
Type of poem: Lyric
First published: 1952, in *In Country Sleep*

The Poem

"Poem on His Birthday" is composed of twelve stanzas of nine lines each. It was written to mark Dylan Thomas's thirty-fifth birthday, and is the fourth and last of Thomas's birthday poems. In the first four stanzas, the poet looks out at the real and imagined scene from his house overlooking the bay on his thirty-fifth birthday. As he gazes at the river and sea illumined by an October sun, he "celebrates" but also "spurns" his birthday, likening the passage of his life to "driftwood."

The first stanzas abound with images of sea birds and fish—cormorants, flounders, gulls, curlews, eels, and herons—as they instinctively go about their appointed tasks. The poet is acutely conscious that the scene he observes, apparently so full of industrious life, is in truth a steady passage toward death. He realizes that all nature is a vast killing field: "Finches fly/ In the claw tracks of hawks." He applies this insight to his own life. In his inner ear he can hear bells tolling, not only in celebration but also in anticipation of his own death. Yet, although the natural scene is filled with the omens of death, it is also holy. The herons, with which each of the first three stanzas closes, are "steeple stemmed" and "bless."

Stanzas 5 to 7 switch from the natural scene to the landscape of the poet's own mind and his anticipation of a rejuvenated life after death. Once again he hears the tolling of thirty-five bells, one for each year of his age, but each bell is a reminder of death and loss. He imagines the terror of death and sees a flash of flame; then divine love "unbolts the dark," and he inherits a more joyous life "lost/ In the unknown, famous light of great/ and fabulous, dear God." This is not a conventional Christian heaven. The poet imagines his soul wandering with the spirits of all the sea creatures and birds that inhabited the "horseshoe bay," every one of them now a priest of God.

In stanza 8, the poet returns to the present, realizing that the liberating experience of death is a long way away. As long as he is alive, he must pray with the living. He knows that death is inherent in all things, and ultimately, all things will return to God. This awareness leads him, in stanza 9, to plead that he may be allowed, in his middle age, to mourn "the voyage to ruin [he] must run," but with full realization of the holiness of the process.

In the final three stanzas, the poet puts his anguish aside and exultantly celebrates his life. His five senses are undergirded by a spiritual sense that propels him through the world of "spun slime" to his "nimbus bell cool kingdom come." The closer he moves to death, the more holy the entire creation appears, and the more wholeheartedly he is able to praise it. Angels bestride every human soul, and this is a consoling thought for the poet as he "sail[s] out to die."

Forms and Devices

Throughout the poem, the most conspicuous poetic device is alliteration. "Bent bay," "birthday bell," "finches fly," "seizing sky," "dolphins dive," "boulders bleed," "midlife mourn," "secret selves," and "black base bones" are only some of the many examples. Less immediately noticeable is the assonance in such phrases as "mustard-seed sun" and "driftwood thirty-fifth wind turned age." Sometimes Thomas combines alliteration with assonance, as with "tumbledown tongue," "This sandgrain day in the bent bay's grave," "livelong river's robe" and "Herons, steeple stemmed, bless." These devices, when combined with subtle variations in rhythm that occur throughout, give the poem a charming, incantatory quality, especially when read aloud, that works quite independently of the poem's meaning.

"Poem on His Birthday" is one of the last poems Thomas wrote; like most of his later poems, it is much less dense than his early work. It gives an impression of spaciousness and openness, unlike the taut intensity of many of the early poems. The result is greater lucidity and less obscurity. Some of Thomas's characteristic tricks with language can still be observed, however; he forms compounds to create new expressions, such as "cloud quaking," "wind turned," "tide daubing," and "steeple stemmed" (although Thomas does not hyphenate them). He creates expressions with more than one meaning, often employing an unusual syntax in the process, as in "I hear the bouncing hills/ Grow larked," "larked" being a way of saying "full of larks" but also implying a playful frolic (a lark), which reinforces the sense of triumph and exultation in the last stanza. Sometimes Thomas will surprise his reader by substituting an unexpected word, as in "the dew larks sing/ Taller this thunderclap spring," where "taller" replaces the expected "louder" and appeals to a different sense. The technique can also be seen in the synaesthetic line "The louder the sun blooms."

The image of the sea voyage toward death, derived in part perhaps from D. H. Lawrence's poem "The Ship of Death," underlies the poem. The sea is the sea of life, the all-embracing ocean from which life emerges and to which it returns. This image pattern is first suggested in stanza 1, in which the poet compares his life to a piece of driftwood. It can be sensed in the next two stanzas in the poet's observation of sea creatures and comes to the foreground in the references to shipwreck in stanzas 3 and 5. After going underground, it emerges again much more explicitly in stanza 9, in which the poet mourns "the voyage to ruin [he] must run." The image then dominates the remainder of the poem, culminating in the vision of the poet sailing out on a turbulent sea to die, accompanied by angels.

Themes and Meanings

While he was writing the poem, Thomas made a manuscript summary of the meaning he was trying to convey:

Now exactly half of his three score and ten years is gone . . . he looks back at his times: his loves, his hates, all he has seen, and sees the logical progress of death in every thing he has seen & done. His death lurks for him, and for all, in the next lunatic war, and still singing, still praising the radiant earth, still loving, though remotely, the animal creation also gladly pursuing their inevitable & grievous ends, he goes towards his. Why should he praise God, and the beauty of the world as he moves to horrible death? He does not like the deep zero dark and the nearer he gets to it, *the louder he sings, the higher the salmon leaps, the shriller the birds carol.*

The idea that every breath of life is also a movement toward death and that humankind is intimately involved in the same processes that operate throughout the natural world is not a new thought for Thomas. He stated it in an early poem, "The Force That Through the Green Fuse Drives the Flower," and repeated it many times over. In "Poem on His Birthday," however, he draws a distinction. The creatures of the animal kingdom are all "Doing what they are told"; as they "Work at their ways to death," they have no self-consciousness and therefore suffer no mental anguish, unlike the poet, toiling at the "the hewn coils of his trade" in full awareness of what awaits him. Seen in this light, the poem is a successful struggle by the poet, who carries the burden of mortality, toward a heroic affirmation of the sacramental nature of the universe.

From the outset, the poet attempts to read the deeper realities in the natural scene. He watches as the "herons, steeple stemmed, bless," a phrase which builds on the religious connotations discernible in the phrase "Herons spire and spear" in stanza 1 ("spire" suggesting the spire of a church in addition to its primary meaning of "to rise upward"). When Thomas writes of herons, he draws on symbolic meanings that he has established in earlier poems. In another birthday poem, "Poem in October," he refers to the "heron/ Priested shore," and in "Over Sir John's Hill," the heron is also a central image of the holiness to be found in nature.

The poet's affirmation of life even in the face of death becomes even more impressive when it is realized that he has no firm intellectual basis for his faith. Although he possesses a vague sense of the divine realm as a *coincidentia oppositorium*—a harmony between the light and dark elements in creation—the stanzas which describe the heaven that awaits all creatures, human and nonhuman, are full of contradictions and uncertainties. God is described as "fabulous" and "unborn"; the latter may mean "eternal," but it could equally mean "not present." The priestlike souls are "gulled," which suggests that they may be fooled, and the "cloud quaking peace" that envelops them does not sound very peaceful.

The doubts and ambiguities make the poet's ringing celebration of life in the final stanzas even more impressive. It does not seem to matter that this is an emotional rather than a carefully reasoned response. The poet has come to feel that his life is more than the piece of driftwood he described in the first stanza. He realizes that he is aflame with divine love and that this unites him in spiritual communion with every other human soul in its perilous, seaborn pilgrimage.

Bryan Aubrey

POEM WITHOUT A HERO

Author: Anna Akhmatova (Anna Andreyevna Gorenko, 1889-1966)
Type of poem: Meditation
First published: 1960, as *Poema bez geroya*; English translation collected in *Requiem, and Poem Without a Hero*, 1976

The Poem

Poem Without a Hero is subtitled "A Triptych." Each of the three parts consists of a series of lyrics which together amount to about 750 lines. The poem was composed over a period from 1940 to 1962, in three Russian cities (Leningrad, Tashkent, and Moscow). The poet continually came back to the poem, revising and changing her work under conditions of war, personal danger, sickness, and severe government censorship during the darkest of the Stalinist years. The complicated fate of the poem—fragmentary, frequently revised, and with a complex and fugitive publication history—is a mirror of the unsettled circumstances of its composition. Indeed, in her foreword Anna Akhmatova herself reports that she had been advised by readers to make her poem "clearer." She replies, "This I decline to do. It [*Poem Without a Hero*] contains no third, seventh, or twenty-ninth thoughts. I shall neither explain nor change anything. What is written is written."

Poem Without a Hero is Anna Akhmatova's protracted meditation on the fate of St. Petersburg/Leningrad, her beloved adopted city, a fate that is intricately bound up with the fate of herself and of those she loves and remembers. Many of the details of the life she shared with her compatriots are obscure to those not intimately familiar with that long vanished world, but the poet turns those intimate details into parables with which the contemporary reader of an English translation can identify.

The poem as a whole contrasts the creativity, youth, and passion of St. Petersburg (the city of Alexander Pushkin and many other Russian artists and poets) with the war-torn suffering of postrevolutionary Leningrad. The renamed "Leningrad" is a site of the silencing of poetry and of poets; it is the place where many of the heirs of the earlier cultural heritage, as well as the visionary promise of the Revolution, have been arrested and executed by the state. Although the poem has no "hero" in the conventional sense, the city itself, in both its romantic and its tragic incarnations (particularly as these qualities are embodied in the friends Akhmatova knew as a young woman), is the sustaining image of the heroic.

In the dedicatory poems that precede the first part of the poem proper, the unhappy love affair between two of Akhmatova's friends—a young officer named Vasevolod Knyazev and a beautiful dancer named Olga Glebova-Sudeikina—becomes the background for Akhmatova's exploration of her youthful aspirations at the St. Petersburg hangout for young artists named the Roving Dog. Akhmatova's focus of attention is on the consequences that follow from the fact that the dragoon's love for the lovely dancer was not returned. When he discovered her entertaining a rival, the officer shot himself and died outside her door. The death this young man chooses becomes entwined with the political, unchosen deaths of many of Akhmatova's associates, including her husband and the poet Osip Mandelstam, both of whom perish in the hands of the state police.

The dedication and foreword, however, were written long after the crystallizing event that triggered the poem. One learns about that event in the first part, entitled "Nineteen Thirteen": On New Year's Eve, 1940, Akhmatova is packing to flee to the relative safety of Tashkent just as the German army is about to begin the siege of Leningrad. She is "visited by shadows from the year 1913, disguised as mummers." At first she wishes to repel the masqueraders: "You're wrong:/ This isn't the Doge's Palace./ It's next door." The revelers insist, however, and the poet ultimately welcomes them, saying, "It's you I celebrate."

The guests are more than costumed celebrants. They are the dramatization of the literary, spiritual, and personal experience that is now practically gone. They are Faust, Don Juan, John the Baptist, Dorian Gray, figures from Greek mythology and Russian folklore, Hamlet, the Man in the Iron Mask, and the Prince of Darkness. Being able to see the past so clearly (she compares its vividness to Francisco de Goya's painting) is more upsetting than consoling. She asks, "But by what necromancy/ Am I living and they dead?" The black art of communicating with the dead (necromancy) is less potent than the art of the poet, and she exercises her greater power when she writes that "As in the past the future is maturing,/ So the past is rotting in the future—/ A terrible carnival of dead leaves."

The first part of the triptych ends with the poet back in the terrible present of 1941. Akhmatova, speaking through the poem, claims the right to be the "ancient Conscience" who lives to remember and speak of the death of the young lover. The persistence and power of the poem is validated in the emphatic capitalized words that conclude the first part: "WHAT IF, SUDDENLY, THE THEME ESCAPES/ AND HAMMERS ON THE WINDOW WITH ITS FISTS."

Part 2, subtitled "Obverse," is set in the same house in Leningrad on January 5, 1941. Akhmatova's editor is displeased with her work: "It's got to be simpler!/ You read, and when you've finished/ You still don't know who's in love/ With whom and why . . . who's/ Author and who's hero." It may well be that these questions and others of the same sort that follow from the editor's mouth are the very ones a contemporary reader might ask. Akhmatova's ironic strategy is to allow the reader to hear the banal words from a contemptible Soviet party functionary. She is able to imply a critique not only of those who censor art from a political perspective but also of those who expect it to be nothing more than ordinary transparent communication.

The ongoing meditation of the section is broken into numbered stanzas. At stanza 10, Akhmatova includes several lines of ellipses. At stanza 12 there is only blank space. Following Alexander Pushkin, Akhmatova includes these absences to indicate the poetry that could not be written, the life that could not be lived in the historical turmoil of the Soviet Union. Unlike the "heroic" figures of English Romantic poets, Akhmatova cannot transcend history. She alludes to Percy Bysshe Shelley "dead on the shore" while Lord Byron "held the brand [which was Shelley's incombustible heart], and/ All the world's skylarks shattered/ The dome beneath eternity." These lines refer to Shelley's "Ode to a Skylark" and to "Adonais," his elegy on the death of his young fellow poet John Keats. Akhmatova here conflates two powerful confirmations in English of the poetic imagination against the ravages of suffering and death. She does not possess, she says, "that English muse . . . I have no ancestry." She refers to the thoughts of T. S. Eliot in *Four Quartets* (1943), spoken from a London under the threat of German invasion. Akhmatova endeavors both to connect with such an endangered traditional and personal past and to assert her specific and historic uniqueness.

"Epilogue" is part 3 of the poem, its final element. Akhmatova speaks from the point of view of, and on behalf of, the many exiles from the city of Leningrad. She is in Tashkent, but others who suffer exile, from New York to Siberia, feel with her that the "Bitter air of exile/ is like poisoned wine." Leningrad itself is nearly abandoned and the "witness of all in the world,/ at dawn or twilight" is an old maple that both inhabits the external world and looks into the room where Akhmatova began the poem some time before the devastation. The maple not only sees but bears auditory witness. It is neither the "first nor the last dark/ Auditor of bright madness." The sound it hears was the "red planet . . . streaking/ Through my still unbroken roof." The red planet is Mars, named for the god of war, and represents the ideological "redness" of Soviet repression. The maple tree outside Akhmatova's house registers both the foreign invasion by the Nazi army and the brutal domestic destruction of life and art by the Soviets. More significant than either its witnessing and auditing, its seeing and hearing the historical crisis, is the fact that the maple endures.

In the early part of the poem Akhmatova is "doubled" by the dancer Olga in her romantic entanglement with art and love. In this last part of the poem Akhmatova is doubled by an unnamed inhabitant of the gulag "In the dense taiga's heart." That the prisoner is nameless does not mean that he or she is depersonalized for the poet. On the contrary, the vivid personalities enduring terror and death in the subarctic forests, reduced to "a pile of camp-dust," are individuals—her former husband, her son, and her friends, especially the poet Mandelstam. Her memory of these people is so intense that she virtually becomes them. She writes that as her "double goes to interrogation,/ With the two thugs sent by the Noseless Slut" the sound she hears answering the thugs is "The sound of my own voice."

As the poem comes to an end, and as the poetic doubling that had begun as the romantic entanglements of youth ("Love, betrayal and passion") is completed in the tragic entanglements of the historical present, "Where there's no end to weeping/ The still fraternal graves," Akhmatova is able to say, "my city is shrouded but standing." The reader of "Poem Without a Hero" is left with the image of Akhmatova herself, looking down on the panoramic landscape of Russia from the window of the airplane that brings her back from exile to her city: "Knowing the calendar/ Of vengeance, having wrung her/ Hands, her dry eyes lowered, Russia/ Walked before me towards the east."

Forms and Devices

The conditions of censorship, betrayal, and imprisonment under which Akhmatova wrote and rewrote *Poem Without a Hero* are tangibly present in the form and technique of the poem. Critics point out her use of the characteristic Russian device known as *tainopis*, or secret writing: When a poet could not be named or quoted for reasons of censorship or discretion, lines from an officially permitted poet would be used instead as an ironic or secret reference to what the state had declared to be forbidden. Akhmatova said that this practice of *tainopis* enforced a subtlety on her poetry that would not otherwise have been possible.

The English-speaking reader of the Russian *Poem Without a Hero* is struck with the abundant presence—through direct quotation, indirect influence, and subtle allusion—of Romantic and modernist English poetry. Byron, Shelley, and Keats—the most conspicuously present—can be freely quoted and alluded to. Their association with freedom and the value of the individual is not seen to be threatening, although the work of contemporary Russian writers such as Mandelstam or Boris Pasternak would be. T. S. Eliot can express his sense of despair and recovery at the bombing and destruction of London when his counterparts (Akhmatova and her circle) in the Soviet Union could not do so in reacting to the siege of Leningrad.

Akhmatova employs "secret writing" not only in regard to English poets. Even classical Russian and other European poets and artists are enlisted in this subversive truth telling. Pushkin can speak of his sense of the endangerment of the city of St. Petersburg when Akhmatova cannot. Akhmatova can present Wolfgang Amadeus Mozart referring in *Don Giovanni* to the cruel and literally petrifying force of the Stalin-like "Commandatore" when no one in Soviet Russia would be allowed to make the same presentation. Russian-speaking readers of Akhmatova's poem must feel that *Poem Without a Hero* is a sanctuary of the forbidden heritage and treasures of Russian literature.

Themes and Meanings

The overarching theme of *Poem Without a Hero* is introduced in the frivolous harlequin and masquerade of the opening section and brought to conclusion in the ghostly prisoner-double of the poet in the last section. Put simply, the theme is that of the enduring personal power of poetry (especially Russian poetry) itself. This is a *Poem Without a Hero* in the usual sense—the hero is poetry itself. The anonymous brutality of fascism and communism operating in the name of the collective good are only a mockery of the true community, one that endures in the land, the people, and the language of which the poet is the steward.

The stewardship of the poet, her reverent salvaging of the poetry and culture of the past, is her memory. Her memory is the sanctuary that protects and preserves the living consciousness of her race; *Poem Without a Hero* is a record of that consciousness. The symmetry between Akhmatova's personal memory and the poem is established very early, when she describes the "absent Companionship" with which she will "hallow/ The coming forty-first year." This companionship takes the form of the mummers who invade her room as she packs for her evacuation from the city, as well as being seen as traces of the lost past. The sense of absent companionship is the ghostly presence of the dead, the preserving companionship of those who can live only in the imagination of the poet.

As the Russian critic Viktor Zhirmunsky observes, "the poet is both hero and author of the poem, contemporary and guilty along with the people of her generation but at the same time a judge pronouncing a verdict over them." In attempting to fathom the meaning of this intricate poem, the reader can keep in mind the ways that Akhmatova is committed to being at once a commentator on and an impresario of her life. She is determined to live deeply in the historical reality in which she finds herself. *Poem Without a Hero* attempts to mirror in every ambiguous and terrifying detail the events of the first forty or so years of the twentieth century. The meaning for which it strives is the meaning of the time during which it was written and which it reflects. To experience the poem is to experience the devastation of meaning itself in completely personal and at the same time completely historic terms.

Sharon Bassett

THE POEMS OF DOCTOR ZHIVAGO

Author: Boris Pasternak (1890-1960)
Type of poem: Poetic sequence
First published: 1957, in *Doktor Zhivago*; English translation collected in *Doctor Zhivago*, 1958, and *The Poems of Doctor Zhivago*, 1965

The Poems

The Poems of Doctor Zhivago is a collection of twenty-five poems that Boris Pasternak appended to his novel *Doctor Zhivago* (1958). Some were published individually in various publications; others appeared for the first time when the novel was published in Italian in 1957, in many other languages (including English) in 1958, and in the first Russian edition in Paris in 1959. The significance of the title lies in Pasternak's insistence on the authorship of Yuri Zhivago, the protagonist of the novel. The poems are not simply appended to the novel without being connected to it. Their most important characteristic is the fact that they correspond to the novel closely and therefore must be considered an organic part of it. In fact, in the original volume, the poems are designated as the final, seventeenth, chapter of the novel.

One-half of the poems are told in the first person, that of Yuri Zhivago. One-fourth are in the form of a third person, often Christ, and an equal number are descriptions by an omniscient observer.

The opening poem of the collection, "Hamlet," is perhaps Pasternak's best-known poem. It can also serve as an introduction or prologue to the rest of the collection. The main reason for invoking Hamlet is his famous soliloquy in which he muses about his dilemmas and his indecision in solving them. Pasternak's Hamlet finds himself in a similar situation except that he is addressing Pasternak's own predicaments, time, and place. In this sense, "Hamlet" is the most autobiographical of the poems.

The collection follows a pattern of seasons, not chronologically within the novel but harmonically, starting with spring, the most natural symbol of a beginning. The first of the five poems of the spring cycle, "March," depicts the hustle and bustle of annual renewal, ending with the metaphor of a pile of manure, a source of the nutrients that are necessary for new life. "Holy Week" moves from renewal to resurrection, the foundation of Christianity. As it wakes up and rejuvenates everything, spring also awakens love feelings in the young man ("White Night"). "Bad Roads in Spring" recalls Zhivago's abduction by the partisans on his way home. The last poem in this cycle, "Explanation," refers to the three women of Zhivago's life—Tonya, Lara, and Marina—and the different appeals that they hold for him. As love is awakened, the light tone of the poem corresponds to the awakened sensuality in life and nature.

The summer cycle is short (only three poems), as is the Russian summer. "Summer in Town," "Wind," and "Hopbines" all picture the ripening stillness of the summer, sometimes interrupted by storms, while the two lovers, Zhivago and Lara, blissfully share their love amid the intoxicating fragrance of the summer idyll.

That idyllic atmosphere carries over into the autumn cycle, which consists of five poems. Many of these poems are connected in some way with Lara. The first, "False [Indian] Summer," exudes the contentment of family life amid the homey winter preparations from the bountiful harvest. This time, the woman in the poem is Tonya, Zhivago's wife. "Wedding" expresses earthy joys and affirmation of life in the fullest sense, but it also represents symbolically the spiritual wedding of Lara and Zhivago. In a highly lyrical fashion, "Autumn" depicts their happiness under the cloud of impending disaster, which makes their love even more fateful and passionate. At the same time, Yuri laments the departure of his wife, whom he still professes to love. "Fairy Tales" is the linchpin of the entire collection. It portrays a fearless knight who slays a dragon and saves a maiden—a reference to Yuri and Lara. The final poem in the autumn cycle, "August," bemoans their final parting at "this predestined hour," ending "years of timelessness."

The winter cycle also has five poems. The opening poem, "Winter Night," refers to the moment when Zhivago saw in a window a candle which had been lit by Lara. He had not met her yet, and the moment exemplifies the theme of predestined coincidence that runs through the novel. The next two poems, "Parting" and "Encounter," deal with Lara's departure from Zhivago and his pining for her, as he is unable to "draw a line" between her and him.

The remaining poems in the collection deal with the life, death, and resurrection of Christ as they influence Zhivago's life. "Star of the Nativity" celebrates the birth of the Child (Lara and Zhivago's?) in all its splendor, renewing Yuri's hopes after Lara's departure. The atmosphere of gloom that threatens to return in the city poem "Dawn" is relieved by the poet's rediscovered faith in God and by his identification with every human being and creature in nature. The poem seems to refer to the last years of Zhivago's life.

In the last six poems, Zhivago returns once again to spring. The second spring cycle points to life's new beginnings, as if to underscore the certainty that there is no end, only renewal. References to Christ continue. Through an episode in Christ's life, "Miracle" broaches a problem of artistic sterility and the need for God's patience and faith in the talented. "Earth" is related to "Dawn," except it takes place in the spring and shows the poet communing with friends, which is reminiscent of the early days of Christ and his disciples. The final four poems deal with the last days of Christ. "Evil Days" depicts Christ's thoughts and reminiscences as he was being betrayed and condemned. The two poems of "Magdalene" and "Garden of Gethsemane" are self-explanatory. In all these references to Christ, Zhivago sees parallels with his own destiny in his final days.

Forms and Devices

The Poems of Doctor Zhivago are of different forms and length. They are almost equally divided among trochaic and iambic meters, while only one is in anapest. The stanzas are mostly rhymed quatrains, but some show varying lines.

Metaphors and images are the most important and powerful devices that Pasternak uses in these poems. Furthermore, metaphors are often used together with images, which tends to strengthen the impact of the metaphors. With the metaphor of Hamlet in the introductory poem, as Zhivago seems to reflect Pasternak's views and sentiments and Hamlet's thoughts parallel those of Zhivago, it can be assumed that Hamlet speaks for the author as well. While translating William Shakespeare's *Hamlet* (c. 1600-1601), Pasternak noted that the play is not a drama of weakness but of duty and self-denial. Accordingly, "Hamlet" emphasizes those two traits of Zhivago's character. Hamlet's lament "I stand alone" implies that Zhivago is weak. Yet, Zhivago often shows a surprising strength of character. Thus, just as Hamlet is a victim of his sense of duty and sacrifice, often too weak to defy fate and at times unable or unwilling to act toward the solution of his dilemma, so is Zhivago a victim of the events and forces that he cannot control. The depth of Zhivago's precarious position is seen in the image of thousands of binoculars staring at him in the murky night. He is ready to admit defeat because someone else has set the order of the acts and "nothing can avert the final curtain's fall." The only thing left for him to do is to beg the Father to remove the cup from him. Herein lies the answer to his prayers. For, by frequently using the metaphor of Jesus Christ as the only salvation, Zhivago steels himself enough to strengthen his sense of duty and sacrifice, thus transforming himself from a weakling into a strong man.

Another set of metaphors is connected with the perennial change of seasons that symbolizes the endless passage of life to death and death to life. There are numerous images reinforcing the seasonal changes of humanity and nature and their constant rejuvenation. Spring is "that corn-fed, husky milkmaid," and the pile of manure—the source of fertility—"is pungent with ozone" ("March"). During the summer, linden trees "have a glum look about them/ Because they haven't slept themselves out" ("Summer in Town"). In the autumn, Yuri's woman sheds her garments as a grove sheds its leaves ("Autumn").

"Fairy Tales" is a metaphor containing the central theme of the novel, that of the knight saving a maiden from a dragon. Although the knight is anonymous, it is not hard to see in him the legendary Saint George slaying the dragon. A variation of the name "George" in Russian is "Yuri." From the plot of the novel, one can easily see Yuri saving Lara from her demon Komarovsky, thus affirming his love for her and the sense of duty and sacrifice proclaimed in "Hamlet."

Lara is also referred to metaphorically. She is the symbol of beauty and freedom, standing for Russia itself. Zhivago dreams about her as if "she had been cast up from the depths/ By a high wave of destiny." In the Orthodox mythology, Larisa (Lara) stands for a seabird or a sea gull. Lara is thus a force in nature, rather than merely a woman.

Many metaphors are connected directly with Christ. One depicts Christ's encounter with a fig tree full of leaves but barren of fruit which is destroyed by God for its uselessness. The poet likens this situation to artistic sterility and pleads with God for patience ("Miracle"). Another metaphor relates to Mary Magdalene, in a clear reference to Lara. Both women are sinful, yet they play consoling roles: Magdalene washes Christ's feet on the eve of his death, and Lara offers Yuri the true love that he craves.

Finally, in "Garden of Gethsemane" Zhivago sees similarities between his troubles with his "Judas" and "Pharisees" with those of Christ. Yet, as Christ did, Zhivago will live again (the meaning of the name "Zhivago").

One of the strongest devices of Pasternak's artistry is imagery. His image of the nightingale that enthralls with its singing but also heralds approaching danger with its frantic song ("Bad Roads in Spring") is a beautiful one. Another striking image is that of a candle burning in a window, which seems to fascinate Yuri even though he knows nothing of its origin ("Winter Night"). A flickering light in the dark winter night adds an aura of mysticism. It also points to predestination at work because Lara, the woman who had lit the candle, will become the woman of his life.

Themes and Meanings

The Poems of Doctor Zhivago have several meanings that parallel closely those of the novel proper. In fact, almost all the poems can be traced to events in the novel. Questions arise, however, as to whether these poems are necessary and whether they provide something that the novel does not. The poems are not concerned with the plot, and they do not refer openly to the characters of the novel. What they do provide is additional emphasis on important aspects of the novel. Moreover, they offer a deeper insight into the psyche of Yuri Zhivago in a condensed poetic form.

The central theme of *Doctor Zhivago* is the struggle of a Russian intellectual to preserve his individuality amid revolutionary changes and to fulfill his artistic destiny in service to truth, goodness, and beauty. By representing a window into Zhivago's soul, the poems allow the reader to follow his heroic struggle to preserve his self, which eventually leads to a triumph of individualism over collectivism.

Another important theme of the novel is the idea of the immortality of the human spirit, and the poems express this idea much more effectively than the prose. As well-constructed, compact works of art, they celebrate a constant renewal of life through the regular change of seasons, thus crystallizing the triumph of life over death.

The novel shows that humans are spiritual beings in a constant struggle with forces attempting to rob them of their spirituality. By displaying a deeply felt, although somewhat unconventional, religiosity and communion with Christ in some of the best poems in the collection, Zhivago's spirituality triumphs over the materialism that is rampant around him.

Individuality, immortality, and spirituality are unthinkable without personal freedom. Zhivago fights to preserve at all costs his freedom and the freedom of those he loves, thus bringing about a triumph of freedom over slavery, as best illustrated in "Fairy Tales."

Finally, the novel is basically a love story in several variations. Zhivago's love for the three women, each in his own way, coupled with his love for his fellow human beings and for the wonders of nature, is demonstrated in the poems. Some of the poems can be considered apotheoses of love—both pure and down-to-earth love.

The novel tells of Zhivago's life and mission but also of his poetic talent. Yet, there is little tangible evidence in the novel of his poetic achievements. The poems bolster

Pasternak's assertion that Zhivago is a great poet, which gives the character added importance and his life deeper fulfillment.

In the last analysis, both the novel and the poems belong to their creator, Boris Pasternak, and they enhance his already well-established stature, not only in Russian letters but also in world literature. As one of his last works which, more than anything else, garnered for him the Nobel Prize in Literature, *Doctor Zhivago* and *The Poems of Doctor Zhivago* occupy a special place in Pasternak's opus.

Vasa D. Mihailovich

THE POET'S COURAGE

Author: Friedrich Hölderlin (1770-1843)
Type of poem: Ode
First published: 1801, as "Dichtermuth"; collected in *Gedichte*, 1826; English translation collected in *Poems*, 1943

The Poem

Friedrich Hölderlin's "The Poet's Courage" consists of seven four-line classical hexameter stanzas that examine the relationship of the poet to nature, lament the loss of the poet to natural forces beyond the poet's control, and exhort the reader to take both courage and caution from the poet's costly struggle. The poem begins by posing a rhetorical question to the reader, asking if the reader understands that human beings are kin to all that is alive and asserting that humans exist ultimately to serve "Fate." Based on these assertions, the poem directs the reader to travel without fear though life.

This idea of accepting "all that happens there" continues into the second stanza as the reader is once again provided with affirmations that neither harm nor offense should be found in the progression of that which must be. The images of the third stanza support this representation of human existence in service to nature's larger forces, in the "quiet near shores" or over "silent deep/ Water" through which the "flimsy/ Swimmer" travels. The fragile poet loves to be among these living, teeming creatures, and it is this union that makes possible the poet's song. Moving from the general human condition to that of the poet in particular, the fourth stanza establishes the relationship of the poet to all "those alive, our kin" for whom "we sing his god." The poet is developed as nature's spokesperson, one who exists in a "glad" state, open and "friendly to every man." Additionally, the idea of trust is introduced and carried into the fifth stanza, in which the poet, the "brave man . . . trusting, . . . makes his way" only to be dragged below the waves at times; thus submerged and overwhelmed by the forces of nature, he falls mute.

After the poet's death, as the sixth stanza explains, his "lonely" groves lament the loss of "Him whom they most had loved" even though he died with joy and gladness. His message has not been lost, though, since a virgin, an appropriately uncorrupted listener, often still hears his "kindly song" in the "distant boughs." Ironically, the song of nature sung by the poet is now echoed by nature after the poet's loss. The last stanza presents a final image of "a man like him," another poet who passes the place where the forces of nature submerged the first poet and who contemplates this "site and the warning." As the poem concludes, however, this warning does not deter the other poet from his task since the final line explains that the poet, "more armed," walks on. "The Poet's Courage" provides a cautionary example for the reader and for those poets who trust all and speak for nature: While nature may overwhelm and silence a single voice, other voices will draw on that courage and continue the refrain.

Forms and Devices

Hölderlin's modernity lies in his reliance on particulars, on the invocation of a person or thing, while more conventional poets have felt obliged to present a sequence of arguments or metaphors. Hölderlin's poem "The Poet's Courage" proceeds by flashes of perception or allusion, true not to the laws of argument but to expressions of feeling and thought. From the first two stanzas' spirited illumination of the human traveler who ought to vanquish fear and thoughts of defense in the light of Fate's directing hand, the poem moves into the particular images of powerful nature in contrast to the precarious position of the poet who is at one with nature yet is overwhelmed by the magnificent forces to which he gravitates. This extraordinary combination of concrete imagery and visionary breadth, this fusion of spiritual intensity and sensory details, gives the poem its impact. Hölderlin provides glimpses of water images (quiet shores, silvery floods, the silent deep, overwhelming waves, and teeming sea life) then carries the trusting poet under, swallowed up by the very object of his devotion. The reader is thrust into the company, then, of the virgins and the other poets who observe the first poet's passing and learn from his song.

"The Poet's Courage" relies on the personification of nature: The wave is "flattering" when it draws the poet below, and his "lonely" groves "lament" his loss. This representation of nature further reinforces Hölderlin's notion of the poet's union with nature, especially since his song can be heard "in the distant boughs." The poem describes all of nature as "our kin," and by recognizing, developing, and trusting this close relationship with nature, the poet is able to sing for "Each of them . . . his god." Even the trees echo the poet's song, and the site of his passing carries a warning.

In addition, the poem's structure reveals Hölderlin's admiration for classical Greek poetry since his experimental verse forms are adapted from the fifth century Greek poet Pindar. Even in translation, his lyric rhythms pull the reader like a forceful current guided by laws of the form but flowing with an energy of their own. Hölderlin's use of inversions, too, creates the illusion of antiquity ("Glad he died there"), as does the creation of the lost poet as the vanished classical tragic hero whose fatal flaw (his trusting union with the very nature with which he is one and of which he sings) is also his priceless gift.

The inversions also serve to create a sense of suspension since Hölderlin often builds a series of clauses and phrases preceding a concise, emphatic, main statement. For example, the third stanza's construction defies sequential syntax, opening with three prepositional phrases that increase the intensity of the eventual subject, which is further suspended in the inversion "travels the flimsy/ Swimmer." These radical departures can lead to ambiguity, but Hölderlin himself asserted that "much greater effects can be obtained" via the use of these devices.

Themes and Meanings

In his tragic odes, especially "The Poet's Courage," Hölderlin's pantheism, his desire to be at one with the cosmos, continually comes up against his awareness not only of the essential differences between humans and the rest of nature but also of the isolation into which individual people are precipitated by their consciousnesses. The poet who possesses the great gift of knowing, of being at one with nature, suffers alienation from the rest of humanity, those who do not have the courage or the vision to recognize and embrace this relationship. In the fifth stanza, the poem describes "One such brave man" who stands apart from the masses and who is mourned in his passing not by his fellow human beings but primarily by the forces of nature and the virgins who have been uncorrupted by the general human retreat from nature. This tragic poem, then, provides a metaphor of an intellectual point of view that can be none other than the awareness of being at one with all that lives and an assertion of the courage that is required to embrace that awareness. This representation of the tragic is mainly based on what is monstrous and terrible in the coupling of God and humanity, in the total fusion of the power of nature with the innermost depths of humankind. Hölderlin said, "There is only one quarrel in this world: which is more important, the whole or the individual part," and, in "The Poet's Courage," his message is clear: Individuals who acknowledge their place in the whole of nature, who sing of the union with joy and trust, will eventually cease to exist as individuals, becoming one with the whole and surviving only in the message that they have fused with nature.

Hölderlin bases his vision on a belief that nature, history, and art are part of a larger scheme that transcends individual existence; he speaks as a poet-seer, looking forward to the possibility that opposites can be harmonized. In addition, Hölderlin, who believes that the poet's mission is to educate through art, emphasizes the value of the poet's work. This air of the heroic poet, this tone of noble idealism and exalted transcendence, permeate the poem. Ultimately, the poet must make the great sacrifice and cultivate this marvelous, mysterious knowledge even though these gifted individuals come to grief. They are heroes, these poets, who represent humanity's honorable and hazardous attempts to ennoble itself, and their fate is shrouded in a heroic, tragic atmosphere.

The feeling in much nature poetry seems to derive from the conviction that something is to be found in nature that is absent from civilized urban life. In "The Poet's Courage," however, Hölderlin goes beyond the assertion of nature's grandeur, release, beauty, and ability to inspire, into an emphatic representation of nature as a power asserting itself and expressing itself in manifold forms, a power at once material and spiritual, comprehending all creation. This power of nature is so all-encompassing that once poets reach this awareness they cease to exist, and it takes a special kind of courage, "The Poet's Courage," to seek that awareness.

Kathleen M. Bartlett

POETRY

Author: Marianne Moore (1887-1972)
Type of poem: Lyric
First published: 1921, in *Poems*

The Poem

Marianne Moore's "Poetry," one of her earliest lyrics, is written in free verse. It is so subtle in its arrangement on the page as to seem almost fragmentary, a quality frequently found among Imagist poets of the early twentieth century. The Imagist movement, by which she was much influenced, proposed in their manifesto to discard the shopworn and hackneyed diction of the previous generation. They intended to free poetry from the strictures of metrical patterns so as to approximate more closely the rhythms of colloquial speech.

Moore begins her poem with an astonishing confession for a poet: She says about poetry that "I, too, dislike it." The assumption is that most people do not like poetry simply because it has ceased to reflect the world they know or the speech they use. She hints slyly that the writing of poetry is only fiddling, thus voicing the frustration of many poets who take pains in the search for the *mot juste*, the "right word," to express their feelings, impressions, and ideas.

Having nothing but "contempt" for "all of this fiddle," and questioning the value of the whole process, she can still maintain that poetry is valid, but only insofar as it is "genuine." As long as a poem is a mirror of reality and is exact in its detail, as opposed to presenting idealized preconceptions, there is much to be said for poetry. Moore would insist on the real "hands that can grasp," as opposed to the lily-white and delicate hand of the idealized woman. Similarly, she would prefer the "hair that can rise" to the silken tresses so much admired by the Victorians.

Moore counsels her reader and other poets to look clearly and steadily at the object or subject; when they do, she notes, they will see a most "unpoetic" scene of "wild horses taking a roll," or perhaps an "immovable critic twitching his skin like a horse that feels a flea." By looking at things anew, one finds a much more substantial body of subject matter to be explored. The poet and the reader are not confined, then, to the traditional themes of poetry which have become tiresome with overuse; nor are they confined in their treatment of such subjects. In effect, there are as many subjects as there are things in the world, all of which are equally fit and proper for poetry. Moore would not even exclude the most banal of "business documents" or the most boring "school-books" as too prosaic for consideration.

She concludes by insisting that "all . . . phenomena are important" and speculates as to why, in the "imaginary" constructs of the mind, such as a garden, poets cannot present to the reader a real "toad." In all of its ugliness and with all of its curious features, she implies that the toad may be much more interesting than the prince. If "you" are interested in the honest and "genuine" toad, and in that which shows you, in all its rawness, the material of the physical world, and if, furthermore, you are not offended by his intrusion into the garden, then "you are interested in poetry."

Forms and Devices

Certainly one of the most notable aspects of "Poetry" is the sense of liberation of thought and expression that the free-verse form allows. The natural, colloquial diction, almost intimate and companionable, encourages trust as Moore leads the reader into territories in which the familiar is viewed in an uncommon way, and the unfamiliar (that is, to the topography of poetry) is viewed with all the precision of a scientist's eye.

Her own surprise at the riches that her careful observation brings to her is conveyed by her images, which are vigorous in detail, and her sound devices, which are traditional though barely perceptible in the context of her free-verse.

She is particularly skillful in her use of the internal rhyme. Rhyme, as used in "Hands that can grasp, eyes/ that can dilate, hair that can rise," holds together the poetic line internally, although it scarcely presents a familiar poetic image. She uses a half-rhyme as well on several occasions, most notably when she observes that we "do not admire what/ we cannot understand: the bat" ("what" is half-rhymed with "bat"). Far from being accidental, the half-rhyme indicates how tenuous the relationship of humans to bats is.

She links much of her world of nature in a curious and exciting way by this use of sound. Images of another sort appear which, although strange and startling in themselves, are given an added vividness by the sound used in describing them. The "elephants pushing," for example, fairly imitates the lumbering visual image of the beasts. Although she has a fondness for such imagery, the ridiculous in human behavior does not escape her attention. Moore declares that although all these phenomena are important, a "distinction" must be made; humorously, she envisions a situation in which ponderous and solemn ideas are promulgated and "dragged into prominence by half poets"—perhaps, half-baked ideas by "half poets." The alliteration and explosive consonants emphasize their self-importance.

Frequently, too, her humor is displayed in her juxtaposition of images. Although she provides no verbal link of comparison, it is clear that the "wild horse taking a roll," and the "critic twitching his skin like a horse that feels a flea" bear more than a passing resemblance; both suffer from a minor aggravation of a perpetual itch.

In "Poetry" the animal world provides the source of much of Moore's imagery, and its appearance is a disquieting departure from the more frequent traditional views of animals, where the wildest might be a tiger, hand painted by the poet himself. Moore's are very real creatures in a very real world.

Themes and Meanings

The main theme of "Poetry" is simply what poetry is, what a suitable subject is, and what approach should be taken by both the poet and the reader.

It is clear that Moore has some difficulty, as do most readers, in defining poetry. She comes as close as she can to a definition through the negative. It is easier, in this case, to define the subject by realizing what it is not and, by eliminating those characteristics, to understand it.

Poetry is not intended to be informational. In effect, the purpose is not to disseminate knowledge as "business documents" are so intended; although, as Moore observes, they cannot be totally excluded as part of the raw material of experience. Nor is poetry intended to inspire with a "high-sounding interpretation" of experience, thus abstracting it to fit a mold of thought. Poetry is not intended, furthermore, to teach like the "immovable critic." It may do so, but that is not its essential purpose. Above all, poetry is not intended for simple self-aggrandizement on the part of the poet, with all its attendant "insolence and triviality."

What, then, is poetry? Moore insists, above all, that poetry must be "genuine" for both the poet and the reader. The response of both must not be colored by preconceptions or learned responses. The ideas and emotions cannot be, she believes, "so derivative as to become unintelligible," because "we do not admire what we cannot understand." Moore also demands that the subject be firmly grounded in reality, that the images, sounds, and rhythms mirror life as people know it, in all its "rawness." By "rawness" the poet means both the data of life and the recognition that life is not ideal, that there is much ugliness but that poetry is certainly no sermon to proclaim high moral values.

The raw material—that is, the data—should find its way into an artistic structure which is the poet's own particular "garden" of impressions, of feelings, of ideas absorbed in a given time and place—that is, the "imaginary garden" which is created by the art of poetry. It must be honest, and it must be "genuine."

When Marianne Moore edited a subsequent collection of her work (*Collected Poems*, 1951), she ruthlessly deleted from "Poetry" all but the first three lines. One can only speculate as to the rationale for her doing so. Perhaps she believed that she had violated her own dictum by teaching in "Poetry."

Maureen W. Mills

POLITICAL POEM

Author: Amiri Baraka (Everett LeRoi Jones, 1934-   )
Type of poem: Meditation
First published: 1964, in *The Dead Lecturer*

The Poem

"Political Poem" is a fairly short poem of twenty-eight lines, divided into three stanzas, written in free verse. Despite the title, it is no more political than most of Amiri Baraka's poems; rather, it is a poem about the politics in American poetry.

The first six-line stanza is by far the most easily accessible. It is a short meditation on the effects of luxury on thought. Basically, Baraka is saying that luxury is a way of avoiding thought. Living in luxury is like living under a heavy tarpaulin, protected from information and ideas. In such sheltered conditions, theories can thrive easily, because they do not have to contend with unpleasant ideas or with facts which might contradict the theory.

Although there is no explicit first-person identity in the first stanza, there is no reason to think that the speaker is anyone other than Baraka himself. In the second stanza, though, a first-person narrator appears. The stanza begins with the opening of a parenthesis that never closes. This seems to be a way of signaling that the poetic voice is about to shift, and in fact, the first word of the stanza is "I," indicating that a definite persona is now speaking. The speaker says that he has not seen the earth for years, and now associates dirt with society; the implication is that he is cut off not only from the earth but also from people. He goes on living as a natural man, but he knows that this cut-off existence is unnatural.

When a second parenthesis opens, it seems to be the same speaker still. The parenthesis shows how the small interruptions of answering a phone and getting a sandwich prevent him from even following through on the thoughts he has been pursuing. More important, however, his poem has been undone by his "station," as one of the people living in too much luxury. When the parenthesis closes, he ruminates on the mistake that people such as he make by trying to fill their lives with an unclear ideal of love.

The third stanza begins with the thought that the speaker's poetry is also undone by "the logic of any specific death"—meaning that any individual death can have more power than any poem. Then another parenthesis begins, which also remains open. The speaker refers to "Old gentlemen/ who still follow fires," perhaps meaning professors and critics of art and poetry. They ask the poet, "Who are you? What are you/ saying?" In their eyes, "you" are "Something to be dealt with." Their rules and guidelines of art and poetry are poisonous; they say "No, No,/ you cannot feel," unlike the poetry of the Beat generation, with which Baraka was associated, which values emotion highly. The "fast suicide" of the last line, similar to the message of the "old gentlemen," is the suicide of renouncing feeling.

Forms and Devices

Amiri Baraka was greatly influenced by the Surrealist movement of the early part of the twentieth century, particularly by the Dadaist movement which flourished in France in the 1910's and 1920's. Surrealism in general was a movement in all the arts that disdained conventional forms. The Surrealists tried to create images directly from the unconscious mind, without putting them into any conventional framework. The Dadaists took this one step further, and tried deliberately to subvert conventional forms in art.

Baraka was not trying to write Dadaist or Surrealist poetry in "Political Poem," but the influence of these movements can be seen in, among other things, his unconventional grammar and punctuation. He used such devices as opening two parentheses that he never closes, and he wrote much of the poem in a series of sentence fragments. The use of fragments demands that the reader find the connection between the individual images for himself or herself; the reader must re-create the associations that Baraka saw.

Much of the meaning of this poem is created by its images, and each image may suggest several meanings. For example, when near the end of the first stanza he talks about theories thriving "under heavy tarpaulins," the reader might picture these tarpaulins as covering the clearly negative "open market/ of least information" of lines 3 and 4. When taken together with the opening of the next stanza, however, in which the speaker talks of being cut off from the earth, dirt, and seeds, a reader might get the sense that theories are like mushrooms, which grow in dark enclosed spaces, while ideas are seeds, which need the fertile "dirt" of society to take root. Both interpretations are suggested. Similarly, there are many possible interpretations of an image such as "The darkness of love,/ in whose sweating memory all error is forced." It refers not only to the dark and unclear ideal of love but also to two people making love in the dark.

To appreciate Baraka's poems fully, one must read or hear them read aloud; "Political Poem" is no exception. Baraka works closely with the sounds and rhythms of his poem. A simple phrase such as "Gettin up/ from the desk to secure a turkey sandwich" begins with almost waltzlike rhythm, which is broken at the end. This rhythm has a light, singsong quality to it that is noticeably missing from the lines immediately before and after the parenthetical material in the middle of the second stanza, and it sets up a similarly singsong quality in the next lines, "the poem undone/ undone by my station, by my station." Although the speaker here is lamenting that his poem is "undone," the music seems to suggest that the interruption from his weighty meditations comes as a relief—indicating that the relief he feels is the real problem.

Themes and Meanings

"Political Poem" is a cautionary statement about the danger of separating poetry from real-world society and politics, but also about the danger of putting it at the service of political beliefs that are out of touch with society. Although it would be a mistake to identify the first-person speaker of the poem with Baraka himself, it would also be a mistake to miss such things as the reference to Newark, where Baraka lived when he wrote this poem. The speaker who declares, "I have not seen the earth for years," seems to be a version of Baraka—that is, the poet he would be if he did *not* write poetry that actively engaged the political issues of his day.

As such, because this poet is trying to write a type of poetry that can only thrive "under heavy tarpaulins," his poem is easily interrupted—by a phone call, by a turkey sandwich, and by the "bad words of Newark." The real world undoes his poetry.

In the course of his ruminations on this dilemma, however, this poet's position evolves. He realizes the futility of trying to create poetry in isolation from the world and cannot help but see his efforts in a wider context of trying to fill the breech of "this/ crumbling century" with "the darkness of love." Yet this position—of trying to create a bridge of love with his poems—is insufficient and is "undone by the logic of any specific death." More must go into the poetry; anger as well as love has a place in poetry, because there are some things which must be rejected.

When, in the third stanza, a parenthesis opens (it will remain open), it marks the completion of the change of the persona that was presented in the second stanza. That is, the speaker who was presented as the type of poet Baraka would be if he avoided political themes in his poetry has been transformed into the poet that Baraka was at the time he wrote this. This is the poet who knows that theories are worthless without ideas and that reason cannot replace feeling in either politics or poetry.

The second stanza concerns itself specifically with the creation of a poem, but a second meaning emerges if the reader understands that Baraka is also addressing the dangers of formulating political theories while out of touch with society. When a theory of politics tries to substitute sterile reason for feeling, it becomes politically as noxious as the poem that makes this substitution. For either a poetically or politically inspired person, this substitution is suicidal to the cause. Another point the poem makes, then, is that poetry should not serve the reasons of politics, but that good poetry is nurtured by the same ground from which healthy politics grow.

Thomas J. Cassidy

POPPIES IN JULY

Author: Sylvia Plath (1932-1963)
Type of poem: Lyric
First published: 1965, in *Ariel*

The Poem

"Poppies in July" is a short poem written in free verse. Its fifteen lines are divided into eight stanzas. The first seven stanzas are couplets, and the eighth consists of a single line. The title presents an image of natural life at its most intense—at the height of summer. It evokes a pastoral landscape and suggests happiness, if not joy or passion. The title is ironic, however, because the poem is not a hymn to nature but a hallucinatory projection of the landscape of the speaker's mind and emotions.

Sylvia Plath begins the poem innocently, even playfully, as the speaker addresses the poppies, calling them "little poppies." The tone changes immediately, however, as the poppies become "little hell flames," and the speaker asks if they do no harm. She can see them flickering, but when she puts her hands into the imagined flames, "nothing burns." She feels exhausted from watching the poppies, but she imagines that their "wrinkly and clear red" petals are like "the skin of a mouth." This introduces an erotic element into the poem, but it is followed by an image of violence—"A mouth just bloodied." Immediately, another change occurs, as the poppies become "little bloody skirts." This shocking image marks the exact center of the poem.

Aside from the obvious implications of bloody skirts, another meaning is suggested by the fact that "skirt" is a slang term for a woman, and in England, where Plath was living, "bloody" is a curse, a profanity. Combined with the word "marry," which occurs later in the poem, these details suggest that the speaker is responding to her husband's marital infidelity. In anger, she has bloodied his mouth, and her invocation of "hell flames" indicates that she would like to see the adulterers punished for their sin against her. The speaker feels like she is in hell. As thoughts of the situation surface in her consciousness, she turns away from images based on the color, shape, and texture of the poppy, to images based on its smell and the drugs that are extracted from it.

The poppies smell like "fumes" to her. In a derangement of her senses, she confuses smell with touch and says she cannot touch them, as she could not touch the earlier "flames." She asks the poppies where their opiates are and thinks of "nauseous capsules." She thinks she could achieve relief if she could "bleed, or sleep," but an emotional wound does not bleed, and her state of mind will not let her sleep. An alternative is to "marry a hurt like that," but she cannot accept or tolerate the situation. She wants the "liquors" of the poppy to "seep" to her in what she calls "this glass capsule." She feels separated from reality; this is why she cannot touch anything. She wants the liquors to be "colorless," with everything suggested by the color of poppies to be refined away.

Forms and Devices

The couplet form traditionally exemplifies order, balance, harmony, and reason. Each line exhibits the same grammatical and metrical structures. Each couplet forms a complete unit of meaning, and often the lines rhyme. Plath draws on this tradition by writing the poem in couplets, but she violates the form by writing free-verse lines. Her couplets represent the speaker's effort to control her thoughts and feelings, which are expressed in the lines of free verse. The length, rhythm, and grammar of these lines vary with the ebb and flow of the speaker's emotions. For example, the longest line in the poem evokes the image—"the skin of a mouth"—which precipitates the speaker's anger in the next couplet, which in turn refers to the bloodied mouth and bloody skirts. This is the shortest couplet in the poem, each line having only five syllables. It concentrates and releases the speaker's anger, like the blow of a fist.

The free-verse couplets also facilitate the presentation of the images of the poem. These follow one another according to the speaker's associational process in a logic of emotion, rather than the couplet's usual logic of reason. The images advance leap by leap, each suggesting the next by a shared characteristic, such as color, shape, or texture, in a series that is increasingly disturbing. Plath transforms the images, one into another, in a manner characteristic of motion pictures, in which one image dissolves as another forms to take its place. The poppies fade into flames; the petals dissolve and the skin of a mouth replaces them. This technique contributes to the hallucinatory quality of the poem.

The poem exhibits instances of parallel grammatical and metrical structures, but the parallels do not usually appear together. The word "little" prefaces the images of poppies and flames in the first line, then is repeated in the eighth line in a phrase which is parallel to the first two—"little bloody skirts." When the three images prefaced by the word "little" are considered together, they form a complex of associations— poppies, flames, skirts—suggesting sexual passion. The first image of a mouth is in the sixth line and the second is in the eighth line, but the third does not occur until the twelfth line, where the speaker thinks she could achieve relief if her mouth could "marry a hurt like that." The hurt refers back to the mouth bloodied in the seventh stanza. Likewise, the phrase "nauseous capsule" finds its parallel in "this glass capsule."

Many other examples of parallelism occur in the poem. It is as if a poem written in traditional couplets has exploded, and the speaker is trying to put the parts back together. This effectively expresses what has happened to the speaker's marriage. A couplet is a pair of lines. The one-line stanza that ends the poem may signify the separation of the speaker from her marital partner, perhaps through loss of consciousness or even death.

Themes and Meanings

The term "Konfessional" has been applied to the poetry of Sylvia Plath. It refers to a poem in which the poet speaks in her own person, not as the impersonal poet or through a persona. Subjects and themes of confessional poetry are usually intensely personal, often disturbing, experiences and emotions. "Poppies in July" has sources in Plath's life, and its meaning is strongly implied by its place in a sequence of poems Plath wrote during a three-month period in the summer of 1962: "The Other," "Words heard, by accident, over the phone," "Poppies in July," "Burning the Letters," and "For a Fatherless Son." Sylvia Plath committed suicide on February 11, 1963, by inhaling fumes from her gas stove.

In her autobiographical novel, *The Bell Jar* (1963), published under the pseudonym Victoria Lucas just before her death, Plath depicts the schizophrenic episode that preceded her first suicide attempt, when she was twenty. Esther Greenwood, the heroine, imagines that a great bell jar has descended around her, enclosing her in an invisible and colorless barrier between herself and the world. She attempts to kill herself by taking sleeping pills. The bell jar parallels the "glass capsule" of "Poppies in July."

Although the poem reflects events in Plath's life, it transcends purely personal experience and stands on its own, communicating its meaning without the need for references to outside sources. The poet speaks not only for herself but for all who have experienced the mental and emotional torment accompanying the infidelity of a partner in marriage.

The speaker of the poem is alienated from life, represented by the blood-red poppies. When she transforms the image of the bloody mouth into the vaginal mouth implied by "bloody skirts," she expresses an emotion close to revulsion for all of the blood of female experience—menstruation, loss of virginity, giving birth. The image may also suggest rape; Plath hemorrhaged as the result of a date rape when she was a student at Smith College. When the poppies become flames, they represent sexual passion, which the speaker's husband did not control and which she cannot feel. The alienation expressed through these images causes her to desire the oblivion represented by the opiates that can be derived from the poppy, "dulling" her senses and "stilling" her mind.

Most of the poems collected in *Ariel*, including a companion poem to "Poppies in July"—"Poppies in October"—were composed after "Poppies in July." In the companion poem, poppies are a "love gift/ Utterly unasked for," representing the exhilaration of life. Poetry itself, for Plath, is "the blood jet," as she expressed it in "Kindness." "This glass capsule" from "Poppies in July" can also represent the poem, as well as imply the detachment necessary for the poet to create art out of life.

James Green

PORPHYRIA'S LOVER

Author: Robert Browning (1812-1889)
Type of poem: Dramatic monologue
First published: 1836, as "Porphyria"; collected as the second of two poems titled "Madhouse Cells," in *Bells and Pomegranates, No. III: Dramatic Lyrics*, 1842; subtitled "Porphyria's Lover" in the collected edition of *Poems*, 1849

The Poem

"Porphyria's Lover" is a sixty-line poem of irregular iambic tetrameter with an *ababb* rhyme scheme, a pattern which continues through the poem's twelve five-line divisions. It is believed to be Robert Browning's earliest study in abnormal psychology. It is perhaps more accurately termed a soliloquy or an inner monologue than a dramatic monologue, since it identifies no specific auditor. The term "dramatic" more aptly describes many of Browning's later poems, in which the tension arises from the drama that builds as the speaker unwittingly reveals himself to a specifically identified listener present in the poem. The fact that Browning called the poem "dramatic" is probably explained by his reaction to reviews that had ridiculed his earliest work as too subjective. After these, he insisted that readers see his poetry as objective by distinguishing between his personal self (the poet) and the voices of his fictive speakers in his monologues. He did not want critics to think these created speakers expressed the poet's personal emotions.

The title leads one to expect a love relationship, perhaps two lovers in a cozy cottage retreating from the storm described in the opening lines. However, the perceptions reported by the speaker (the "lover") soon alert the reader to his unbalanced perspective. This speaker attributes attitudes and willful actions to the wind: It is "sullen," it has torn the elm trees "for spite," and it has tried to "vex the lake." These opening lines reveal the speaker as fearful, as a passive listener, and as one who seems to project his own emotions onto the external world. He appears to be an unreliable reporter.

He then describes the entrance of Porphyria, whose actions and words contrast with the speaker's passivity: She has "come through wind and rain" to "shut the cold out and the storm." She then warms the cottage, an action that the speaker has lacked the will to perform for himself. He seems to lack any awareness that he has a will or a voice of his own: He reports that his arm and his cheek are placed by Porphyria around her waist and on her shoulder. He seems to experience himself as being without an active, directing center of his own being, since he has only "debated" possible action, being too engrossed in his own feelings to initiate action. When he can finally act, prompted apparently by a drive to preserve the moment of Porphyria's surrender to him, he murders her by strangling her with her own hair. In the remaining lines, the speaker clinically describes opening Porphyria's eyelids, loosening her hair around her neck, kissing her dead cheek, and propping her head on his shoulder in an act that mimics her earlier placement of his head. As he had projected his own attitudes and emotions onto the external storm in the opening lines, he concludes by attributing his murderous act to Porphyria's "utmost will" and "one wish." The final line suggests a complete lack of conscience in the speaker: "And yet God has not said a word!"

Forms and Devices

Browning's forte and his principal formal strategy in this early poem is a monologue through which an unaware speaker reveals character disorders. It is the speaker's diction and syntax as he reports his perceptions and inferences that reveal his moral character. The first four lines are simple, flat, four-measure statements, end-stopped and regular in meter until the spondee of line 5, "heart fit." After the speaker's personification of the wind, which suggests his own helplessness and suppressed emotions, the ambiguous grammar of the emphatic spondee suggests both a heart ready to break and a heart that is having a fit. Lines 6-15, which describe Porphyria's movements, are correspondingly more fluid, with enjambment and midline clause breaks. The effect is a contrast between Porphyria's action and the speaker's unmoving passivity. Lines 15-30 show the speaker overcome by Porphyria's presence. He has lost even the weak "I" of line 5 and has become so dissociated from himself that he reports his inability to reply to Porphyria's call as "no voice" being heard, as though he is outside himself listening. The word "displaced" (line 18) suggests the displacement of the speaker's center of being, a kind of moral paralysis. This self-alienation continues with the speaker's sense that Porphyria is the one who moves his arm and head. The word "stooping" (line 19) is, again, grammatically ambiguous, this time as a dangling modifier, since the speaker, not Porphyria, is the one who must bend over to reach her shoulder (line 31 shows that he is the one who must look upward). Lines 22-25 seem to indicate the speaker's judgment more than Porphyria's "murmuring," as they continue his merging, or confusing, of their identities.

Still seeing himself through Porphyria's eyes, the speaker regains his sense of "I" in lines 31-35, but the descriptive phrase "happy and proud" is ambiguous, referring either to "I" or to "her eyes." He feels that he has become her god or idol, although he is in the position himself of the worshiper, looking up as his elation further severs his swelling heart from his debating judgment. Lines 36-41 reveal the speaker's intense need to capture the moment, to possess Porphyria permanently in a kind of aberration of an erotic consummation, the act of strangulation reported in the emphatic first half of line 41. The speaker's certainty that she "felt no pain," which he repeats, is further evidence of a bizarrely delusional personality. The simile of the bud mocks epic grandeur and, through grammatical ambiguity again, may refer to the speaker or the dead Porphyria, just as the laughing blue eyes may be his own or his hallucinative perception of hers. With Porphyria reduced to an unthreatening corpse and after having asserted his will by murdering her, the speaker is able to act part of the role of a lover as he kisses her dead cheek. It is clearly a demented lover, however, who takes possession of the corpse and interprets its expression as "glad" that its "will" is fulfilled since his love is "gained." Use of the passive voice is significant throughout the poem, indicating a speaker who cannot feel responsible for what he does. Is the "one wish" (line 57) a "darling" wish because it is hers, or is it the wish of her "darling," the disordered speaker? Does the speaker await, during and after the night vigil, blame or commendation from God?

Themes and Meanings

This poem enacts the behavior of a distorted personality and mocks, pointedly, the attribution of the capacity to love to such a personality. Browning would not have used the term "schizophrenic" because it did not come into psychiatric parlance until the twentieth century. He could, however, present the disordered thinking of one suffering from personality dissociation, experiencing alienation from self and from what is normally perceived as reality, exhibiting inappropriate emotion and behavior, and unable to feel responsible for his emotions or his actions. This "lover," so dubbed ironically, obviously cannot love or even affirm himself as an autonomous being who could generate love. In Browning's moral perspective, this speaker would be another jealously possessive and tyrannical male similar to the duke who speaks in the more widely known poem "My Last Duchess." The theme is a frequent one in Browning's poetry.

A possible additional thread of meaning may be derived from the knowledge that the poem was first published with another poem, "Johannes Agricola in Meditation," and that the two poems were later grouped under the heading "Madhouse Cells." Browning clearly believed that both poems represented forms of madness. Johannes Schneider (Agricola) was associated with German religious reformer Martin Luther, but they did not agree on all points of theology. He was the founder of the Reformation sects of antinomianism, a belief labeled heretical by the orthodox because it taught that those among the elect (that is, those predestined for salvation, according to some forms of Calvinism and Wesleyanism) could not sin regardless of the apparent evil of their acts. The periodical in which Browning first published the two poems, the *Monthly Repository*, was edited by W. J. Fox, who was a friend of the Browning family and who rejected Calvinist ideas of election in favor of Unitarianism. Either he or Browning prefaced the poems with a note explaining that antinomianism maintained that God would not chastise one that he had chosen to save even if that person broke the moral law by committing murder or other heinous crimes. This context of early publication seems to offer the best explanation of the final line of the poem. Browning's characterization of his speaker as a lover can thereby be read as his satiric exposé of a religious fanatic so convinced of his predestined salvation that he feels himself to be beyond divine retribution for his murderous act and subsequent necrophilia.

Carolyn F. Dickinson

PORTRAIT OF A LADY

Author: T. S. Eliot (1888-1965)
Type of poem: Dramatic monologue
First published: 1915; collected in *Prufrock and Other Observations*, 1917

The Poem

The title of the poem is drawn from two sources: Henry James's novel *The Portrait of a Lady* (1881) and Ezra Pound's poem "Portrait D'une Femme" (1912). The lady in question in this poem and in Pound's is based upon Adeleine Moffatt, who lived in Boston and invited T. S. Eliot and other selected undergraduates to tea and conversation. She was described in Conrad Aiken's fictionalized autobiography, *Ushant: An Essay* (1952), as "the *précieuse ridicule* to end all preciosity, serving tea so exquisitely among her bric-a-brac."

The epigraph is taken from Christopher Marlowe's play *The Jew of Malta* (published 1633) and is important for setting a mood of betrayal, though, by comparison, the persona in Eliot's poem appears to be much less culpable than the character in Marlowe's play. This character, Barabas, accuses himself of certain lesser crimes in order to disguise his poisoning of a convent of nuns.

The poem, in three sections of approximately forty lines each, follows for a year the relationship between the male persona and the lady. In free verse, the young man (clearly much younger than the lady) quotes his hostess, at least as he remembers her words, and offers his highly judgmental, apparently detached, introspective reaction.

In the first section, situated in midwinter, the two are returning from a concert of Frédéric Chopin's piano music. In this very brief space, the lady refers to friendship five times. Friendship seems a bit of a letdown, though, since the young man has begun his account by describing the room as looking like Juliet's tomb. This allusion to the romantic double suicide that concludes William Shakespeare's *Romeo and Juliet* (c. 1595-1596), like the violent and repulsive epigraph from Marlowe, makes this harping upon "friendship" seem unattractively bland. The young man's response is proud rejection of the lady's interest—though he says nothing of the sort to her. The section ends with his escape from her parlor to the male habitat of a bar, where he can remain untouched by her emotions and, in conversation, can dissect her with his comrades.

The second section is set in spring, but the only thing blooming (apart from the mention of lilacs) appears to be the young man's increasing discomfort in the lady's presence. The lady recognizes in the lilacs an example of the fleeting beauty of youth and alludes to her earlier life and to her present comparative old age and fragility. She describes the young man as embodying, like the lilacs, the perfection, beauty, and strength of burgeoning life, to which, she confesses, she can add little. The last stanza of this section offers the youth's embarrassed reaction to the lady's observations and his confused reflection upon this embarrassment. Why, he wonders, should this woman's problems upset him more than the tragedies he reads about in the newspaper—and why should he still be upset when a particular melody or the fragrance of flowers reminds him of her?

The third section takes place in autumn, a time of dying. The young man's emotional discomfort in visiting the lady is now felt in his whole body—it is as though he is walking, perhaps like an animal, on his hands and knees when he mounts the stairs. The two discuss his going away on a permanent basis to Europe, and she recognizes that he has remained as distant emotionally as he soon will be physically. Her clear insight forces the youth to even greater attempts at deception: He does not want to lose "control" of the situation by letting her understand how disturbed he is. In the last stanza, he imagines her death and frames the questions that will plague him even after she is gone.

Forms and Devices

Eliot claimed that the form of expression in this poem and in much of his early writing drew upon the conversational style of later Elizabethan drama and upon the French Symbolist, Jules Laforgue. The latter's influence on him is evident especially in "Portrait of a Lady," which marks the development in Eliot's style from that of a romantic to a postromantic. There is in the diction and tone of the language, in other words, a sense of greater detachment and irony, a tentativeness and a general sense of disillusionment.

Rhyme is scattered throughout the verses, and the rhythm is frequently close to iambic pentameter, but both rhyme and rhythm follow no set pattern. Instead, they are used to establish a languid and even haltingly self-conscious tone, close enough to ordinary speech to convey the scene and characters convincingly, but musical enough to render these few chosen moments of memory as special and unusually significant in the mind of the persona.

Music is, in fact, the principal metaphor in the poem, representing the fluid movement of emotions between the older woman and the younger man. Beginning with a reference to a Chopin prelude, identified with the lady, the poem is interrupted by the "false note" of the young man's own prelude, beating in his head in rebellious counterpoint. As the relationship fails to develop and harmonize, the jarring music from the two players leads inevitably to a "dying fall" and an early, disastrous collapse of their concert. In the concluding stanza of the first section, for example, the movement from the delicacy of violins, through the harshness of cornets and drums and on to the dubious "music" of clocks in watchtowers, demonstrates the young man's insistence on getting away from the highly strung world of the lady's tea parties and back to his pedestrian world of beer and pretzels. Along with an emphasis on music, the poem makes insistent reference to the passage of time, with careful allusion to the specific season in each section, as well as an indication of various timepieces.

Themes and Meanings

This early poem already sounds themes that were to obsess Eliot throughout his career, reaching its fullest expression in his late *Four Quartets* (1943). The passage of time, its effects on the body and human emotions, the individual's consequent search for some sense of permanence, history, and personal significance—all are present even in an early poem such as "Portrait of a Lady." One sees their expression principally in the older woman's quiet but somewhat desperate attempt to craft a meaningful relationship with this younger man, finding in his relative youth the energy and hope that seem to be slipping from her grasp.

The poem, however, seems finally to focus attention not on the lady but on the youth. The reader is made quite aware that the woman is being viewed through the youth's rather haughty eyes, and one gradually recognizes the speaker's own discomfort not only with the lady's "advances" but also with his own timorous retreats. He is resentful of her attempt to treat him as an equal, as simply one who, were it not for their arbitrary differences in age, shares personal needs and fears.

Ultimately, his retreat from the woman is not a sexual rejection. To the extent that there may be a sexual overtone to their "friendship," it suggests simply another manifestation of the limitations placed on the human condition by time: a literal embodiment of the yearning for completion that continues on even into physical frailty. As perverse and sad as it may appear to the younger man, readers who are observing both characters with a more objective eye may be able to view the woman's ongoing interest in the relationship itself as far more positive than the younger man's paralysis. It is not until the concluding stanza of the poem that the young man allows himself consciously to ponder his own advancing years, when he too will face the loneliness and regret that seem so important in the life of the woman. Where, he wonders, will his air of superiority have taken him by then?

Like the James novel to which Eliot's title refers, this poem is about incompletion, attenuation, and half-sentences left hanging in midair. It is a poem of "what-ifs": What if these two characters had been the same age? What if he had been more forthcoming, either in rejecting the woman outright or in revealing to her his own fears about mortality and individual isolation? What if, in later life, he were to learn of her death and become plagued by his youthful lack of response to another human being's obvious pain? Like a melancholy musical prelude that is suddenly interrupted, the questions remain.

John C. Hawley

A POSTCARD FROM THE VOLCANO

Author: Wallace Stevens (1879-1955)
Type of poem: Elegy
First published: 1935, in *Ideas of Order*

The Poem

"A Postcard from the Volcano" is a short elegy written in three-line verses of un-rhymed tetrameter. The title image captures the theme and perspective of the poem. It suggests a small or compressed message from something big and violent, conveying a loss that is too huge for the tiny means chosen for the communication.

The poem is written from a first-person plural viewpoint. The speaker projects into the future, referring to another generation ("children") looking back at the present one. There appears to be a significant gap between what they will see and what currently exists. One senses the inadequacy of the small "postcard" to express proper feelings of loss, or death.

The first half of the elegy, assuming the perspective of a future generation, expands on what they are missing—it is a loss that comes with the absence of first-hand experience. Hence, the poet employs images that betray action ("foxes"), sensual involvement ("smell" of grapes ripening), and feeling as a way of seeing. Yet all imply death ("breathing frost"), since they will be lost in the future.

At the center of the message there is a significant shift of tense—a transitional sentence connects yet separates the two generations. Now the poet uses images of distance ("spring clouds" beyond a "mansion-house") to illustrate a "literate despair." In abstract terms, he seems to make a judgment on language itself as a "limited" vehicle to convey meaning across time and space. It may be a comment on poetry itself as subject of the elegy.

In the last half, the poem picks up again the subject of the future children. The focus continues to be on language, spoken and written, as a means of knowing ("Children,/ . . . Will speak our speech . . ./ will say"). The present generation appears symbolically as "the mansion" that the children can never completely know or understand any more than people can understand an erupting volcano from afar.

The conclusion of the poem adds another dimension. The children not only see (that is, know, understand, and appreciate) the mansion (the past) in a limited way, but also actually change it in the process of knowing. Here the poet introduces colors (white and gold) associated with the imagination—or, as in Wallace Stevens's "The Man with the Blue Guitar," the imagination's action on the external world. The mansion is "peaked" and "smeared"—in a way, destroyed—indicating a new or double sense of loss.

The final note of "A Postcard from the Volcano," however, indicates more than loss. The poem is also a tribute to the power of the imagination to change things creatively. In the end, the reader sees three worlds. One is the current generation's—"what we felt/ At what we saw." This world, however, is "A tatter of shadows" (an outworn scarecrow) to the second world—the children's. The third is a brighter, "opulent" world that the children have redone in their own image.

Forms and Devices

This poem is in itself a kind of "postcard from a volcano." Stevens uses a short piece of writing (the poem) to convey a wealth of feeling and thought (the volcano) to the reader. As a poet, he senses all the limitations of such an effort, yet he attempts it. He uses the language of poetry—such as colorful images, different kinds of rhythms, repetition, and finally alliteration—to send his message.

The key image used to convey loss is the rural Southern setting—the "mansion-house" over which hang "spring clouds" "Beyond . . . the windy sky." The poet connects two generations, separate and removed. The house is a mansion, suggesting a bygone aristocracy, and it is "shuttered"—protective of its mysterious, inner sanctum. Indeed, it becomes symbolic of a prior tradition, or old ways of thinking and acting—what "we felt/ At what we saw" and "said of it."

Children are active in their way, yet within the rural scene connecting them to tradition. If the older order sees itself as "quick as foxes" (referring to an old Southern sport), the children are now "weaving budded aureoles," not recognizing the foxes whose "bones" they are "picking up." Indeed, there are "walls" between the "look of things" and "what we felt/ At what we saw"—between appearance and reality.

Into the rural scene the poet then injects the changing seasons—images and rhythms which capture the loss that comes with time and are natural to the country. Children pick up the bones in the spring, but what they do not reflect upon is the autumn. That is when the grapes are most ripe, alive, and pungent, although they are also "breathing frost." Life and death are coextensive in the country, something that may be lost on the children, but not on the poet—or on "us," the readers.

To enhance further his rural changing scene, with its traditional ways, the poet employs changing rhythms. The poem starts out briskly, emphasizing vivacious country life, as the enjambment (run-on lines) of the first stanza captures the action of the foxes. Then the pace slows; the sentences are shorter and broken with clauses, as the poet becomes more reflective, even approaching "despair." The fragmentation of the lines also matches the sense of loss—both between generations and in the poet's inability to communicate fully.

As the poem moves toward a conclusion, the tempo again changes, this time reaching a steady but mounting crescendo. The rhythm underpins the new theme of confidence (will) as the children take the words of the older generation (tradition) and recreate them ("speak our speech"). The word "will" is repeated twice, giving new and definite direction to their action. Now "never know" and "seems as if" disappear as the poet generates new hope and confidence with a steadily mounting pace, forceful repetition of key words, and the bright, colorful images—"white" and "gold"—of the last lines.

Themes and Meanings

If in "The Man with the Blue Guitar" Stevens examines the relation between the poet and the present world, in "A Postcard from the Volcano" he adds the dimension of time—the relation between future and present generations. In the former poem, he speaks of a "nothingness" that results when a person imagines the world, as if smell and taste are lost in imagining a baked pie. The latter adds the further gap of time, and therefore a double loss, when children try to experience, or imagine, the life of past generations.

At the center of this poem is a "literate despair"—the inability of words (written or oral) to convey the total (contextual) meaning of another time or place. This gives one cause to mourn, and for this reason the poet, along with the children looking back at the present, "Cries out" in frustration. Yet there is more to this elegy than loss.

The poem is rooted in irony. Death and life are closely connected in this piece. The "bones" of the foxes are juxtaposed with foxes that are "quick" (alive). The dying of the grapes ("breathing frost") is directly associated with life at its height, having made "sharp air sharper by their smell." Autumn can only give birth to spring.

It is the spring that most excites or "springs anew" for Stevens. For the older generation (the "we" of the poem), the "mansion's look," once articulated, "became/ A part of what it is." These people, too, are imaginative. The mansion got its being from their view, perspective, and feelings, not necessarily from any essential being apart from them. Though this will be lost on their children, that loss will generate new life or imaginings. Death and life are coextensive, part of the natural flow of things. Stevens is above all a poet of the present, not of romantic or theistic systems.

The last part of the elegy, therefore, is ironically a celebration of life. The children may "never know" what "we," their forebears, meant when they "speak our speech"; tradition is never fully understood, and that is tragic. Yet, all things considered, it does not really matter. The house may seem "dirty," bathed in "shadows," its walls "blank" (meaningless), the whole thing "gutted." These things imply death, but they also represent a point of view that is necessary to regeneration. Out of this dark, empty shell, the children make the most of their old house (their ancestors) by re-creating it imaginatively.

The poem's final phrases, like "spirit storming," are important, for they suggest vivacious internal action, an ironic contrast to the "gutted" and "blank" house. "Smeared" is also double-edged; it may mean disfigured, but here it suggests something totally covered with life—"the gold of the opulent sun." This is Stevens's final message, that life follows death and that the best instrument for creating the highest type of life is the human mind, as full of potential ("opulent") as the sun itself.

The "volcano," therefore, need not be limited to the past, and this is the final irony. The poem becomes a tribute to the future generations that the poet initially seems to criticize. Ultimately, it is the children who are not afraid to imagine—to feel deeply, explode verbally, and spew emotion in controlled blasts. That is also the job of the poet in all generations, and to fulfill that end Wallace Stevens sends his postcard.

Thomas Matchie

A PRAYER FOR MY DAUGHTER

Author: William Butler Yeats (1865-1939)
Type of poem: Lyric
First published: 1919; collected in *Michael Robartes and the Dancer,* 1920

The Poem

Anne Butler Yeats, the poet's first child, was born on February 26, 1919, only a month after William Butler Yeats completed "The Second Coming," his apocalyptic vision of violence and anarchy. Four months later, he composed "A Prayer for My Daughter," in which he expanded his belief that a return to tradition and ceremony remained the single means of avoiding the earlier poem's "blood-dimmed tide" now "loosed upon the world." Yeats prays that his daughter may cultivate self-regard and independence and that she may marry into a home that respects ritual and ceremony. Only in these ways, he believes, can she find the innocence and peace to transcend the impending cataclysm of physical and spiritual chaos that he had foreseen in "The Second Coming."

"Things fall apart; the centre cannot hold;/ Mere anarchy is loosed upon the world," he had written in "The Second Coming," prophesying the rise of fascism in Europe and recalling the bloodshed of both the Russian Revolution (1917) and the Irish Easter Rebellion (1916). These powerful images refer as well to the emotional, psychological, and spiritual disintegration that accompanies international and social crisis. If Yeats's vision of the violent and lawless modern world had prompted "The Second Coming," it was the possibility of transcending such a world that prompted "A Prayer for My Daughter"; the two poems can be read as companion pieces.

It is well acknowledged that the bulk of Yeats's great work drew upon the events of his life. "A Prayer for My Daughter" is one of his most exquisite personal poems, for here Yeats prays that his daughter may shun those very qualities that characterized the woman he loved throughout most of his life. Maud Gonne, whom he had met when he was twenty-two, and whom he wooed unsuccessfully for nearly thirty years, was both an actress and political activist. Yeats not only shared some of Maud's political and professional interests but also, because of his unabating love for her, wrote a body of love (and political) poems about the exaltation and dejection incumbent upon wooing "a proud woman not kindred of his soul" ("A Dialogue of Self and Soul").

Yet if Yeats celebrated Maud's beauty and nationalistic fervor, he also immortalized her unhappiness and single-mindedness—those personal qualities that ultimately destroyed Maud and many others who had similarly fought for Irish freedom in the early years of the twentieth century. It was only in 1917, and at the age of fifty-two, that Yeats turned to another woman, Georgie Hyde-Lees, and married. Georgie was a woman of decidedly less beauty and flair than Maud, but she was also a woman who, as one sees in "A Prayer for My Daughter," was worthy of celebration. Her "charm" finally "made [him] wise," as did her virtuous "glad kindness." Georgie, it would appear, embodied those qualities of generosity and self-sufficiency that he hoped to see perpetuated in their daughter.

The first two of the poem's ten stanzas describe the violence of the outer world. "Once more," he begins, "the storm is howling," and nothing can stop the "screaming" wind that threatens to level nature (the woods and haystacks) and civilization (the roofs and his tower). He listens to the howling "sea-wind scream," along with the storm in the "elms above the flooded streams." He then imagines "in excited reverie" that his daughter has grown to adulthood. The prayer begins in the following, third stanza: "May she be granted. . . ." First, he would have her granted physical beauty— but not Maud's excessive beauty, for this not only makes men "distraught," but, more important, leads its possessor to vanity and indifference to others. Overly beautiful women ignore the cultivation of natural kindness and thus lose the capability of recognizing and retaining true friendship.

Of her various personal virtues, he would have her cultivate ("learn") "courtesy." Yeats suggests that kindness and generosity breed trust and affection between people. Yeats would also wish his daughter a life of stability and deep-rootedness—that is, a quiet life away from noisy thoroughfares—an immersion in a world that is distant from intellectual, political, financial, or emotional struggle. Planted in such an environment, she might cultivate her own personal worth and, most important, her soul. Contact with the soul would give her a sense of self-measure, pleasure, and ultimate peace; she might thus transcend the chaotic external world and achieve a kind of existential triumph. She would realize that the soul's "own sweet will is Heaven's will." Many of Yeats's later poems repeat this notion that self-mastery is humankind's greatest achievement (when the "soul clap[s] its hands and sing[s]/ and louder sing[s]," as he expresses it in "Sailing to Byzantium"). This alone provides a means of transcending external contingency.

Forms and Devices

After first reestablishing the mood of "The Second Coming," Yeats builds a series of images that contrast the virtues he would wish for his daughter and a set of specifics associated with Maud. He sets "custom" and "ceremony" against "hatred" and "arrogance," and "radical innocence" against "murderous innocence." So too he opposes the "horn of plenty" and an "old bellows full of angry wind"; the "flourishing hidden tree" and "the wares/ Peddled in the thoroughfares"; the "linnet [firmly planted on] the leaf" and the screaming "sea-wind," along with "flooded stream"; and "magnanimities of sound" and "scowl[s] [from] every windy quarter."

In using the traditional image of the cornucopia, an emblem of bounty or fecundity, he says of Maud Gonne that although he has "seen the loveliest woman born/ Out of the mouth of Plenty's horn," she, like Helen of Troy and Venus, was overly beautiful ("chosen") and vain, and she lacked the necessary qualities to choose an appropriate man to love. ("Helen," although "chosen," also "found life flat and dull," and in preferring Paris to Menelaus, later "had much trouble from a fool.") Similarly, Venus, the "great Queen" who "rose out of the spray," who might also have chosen any man, selected the bandy-legged Vulcan for her husband. The erratic and eccentric behavior of such "chosen" women inevitably leads to their own undoing: "It's certain that fine women eat/ A crazy salad with their meat/ Whereby the Horn of Plenty is undone."

In wishing that his daughter live a life filled with tradition and that she have deep roots, he proceeds to another traditional image, the tree—in fact, the laurel tree, usually associated with victory. Yeats would want his child to entertain only magnanimous and beautiful thoughts, and he would have her "dispense" them "round" like the melodies of the linnet bird. The opposite kind of behavior, one filled with intellectual hatred, neither sustains itself nor soothes the tribulations of the external world. Again expanding images from "The Second Coming," he continues: "Assault and battery of the wind/ Can never tear the linnet from the leaf." Although people might "scowl" at her and "every windy quarter howl," she could remain "happy still."

Finally, Yeats would have a bridegroom bring his daughter to a traditional home, "where all's accustomed [and] ceremonious," rather than to a life in the "thoroughfares," for, as he explains in a rhetorical question, how can one be free to cultivate the virtues of selfhood and soul if she must worry about concrete matters of survival: "How but in custom and in ceremony/ Are innocence and [true] beauty born?"

Having thus far explained his two abstractions ("ceremony" and "custom"), and having established the metaphoric possibilities of the cornucopia and tree, he concludes the poem by connecting his images in a summary statement: "Ceremony's a name for the rich horn,/ And custom for the spreading laurel tree."

Themes and Meanings

"A Prayer for My Daughter" is concerned with surviving the chaos of the modern world—the separation of reason from passion, or the surrender of reason to one's own violence or the anarchy of the external world. The ascendancy of irrationality or animal instinct over reason and culture is vividly expressed in the widely quoted image of "The Second Coming" where "Turning and turning in the widening gyre/ The falcon cannot hear the falconer."

Yeats thus far in his career had celebrated the mighty Irish heroes of both legend and the historical past and present—those courageous men and women who sacrificed themselves for their ideals. Now, however, the poet expresses a certain ambivalence toward those heroes. He understands that in the necessary sacrifice for a cause, one may surrender "heart" ("Too long a sacrifice/ Can make a stone of the heart," he wrote in "Easter 1916"). In fact, any single-minded commitment—to political, social, or intellectual causes, even to beauty—may become obsessive and negate one's more important personal and humane concerns. "A Prayer for My Daughter" proposes the means of rescuing the self, heart, and soul—true beauty—from a world of growing disorder and increasing human misery.

Lois Gordon

PREFACE TO A TWENTY VOLUME SUICIDE NOTE

Author: Amiri Baraka (Everett LeRoi Jones; 1934-   )
Type of poem: Lyric
First published: 1961, in *Preface to a Twenty Volume Suicide Note*

The Poem

Dedicated to Kellie Jones, the author's daughter, who was born on May 16, 1959, Amiri Baraka's "Preface to a Twenty Volume Suicide Note" suggests a turning point in the poet's relationship to American society in the late 1950's. Written from a first-person perspective, the poem, likely a reflection of the poet's own concerns and personal experience, is autobiographical in tone, though the point of view could be that of a fictive voice struggling with the same issues.

Then known as LeRoi Jones, Baraka is one with the persona of the poem. In a confessional tone, he meditates upon his own existence and renders a number of observations associated with apparently daily actions of domestic life. The poet first describes becoming "accustomed to the way/ The ground opens up and envelopes" him as he is engaged in such a mundane activity as walking his dog. Immediately, there is a mood of repetition, the recurrence of daily chores or duties, but these actions are linked to more complex psychological states—the sensation of the "ground" opening up—and are beyond expected expressions of boredom connected to numbing repetition.

Certain ruminations occur at night, and the poem implies a spiritual awareness of personal vacancy associated with the thought processes set free by recognizing one's place in the cosmos. The "I" voice also observes the "broad edged silly music" of the "wind," which is linked to racing to catch a bus. These two activities, the walking of the dog and the catching of the bus, imply a routinized lifestyle, one which causes associations that are psychologically ironic and not necessarily linked to the actions described. The attempt to catch the bus also suggests lateness and an inability to keep pace with expected routine or with the times.

The line "Things have come to that" adds to the tension caused by a disassociation from the commonplace. The poet tells of a nightly activity, "I count the stars," and his arriving at the "the same number"; the practice is complicated by the admission that there are also occasions when the stars "will not come to be counted," at which time he records "the holes they leave." Though the third stanza is unified around the counting of stars, the line that follows it, a single-line stanza, suggests a complaint against the times, "Nobody sings anymore."

The final confession recounts "last night" and the poet's silent walk "up to" his "daughter's room," where he hears her speaking behind the closed door of her bedroom only to discover when he opens the door that she has been praying in "Her own clasped hands."

Forms and Devices

Written in a conversational style, the poem is structured in six stanzas, and there is minimal separation between the voice of the poet and the persona of the poem. The perspective is that of a psychologically complex individual, whose race, class, and occupation are unannounced. The poet has reached a juncture at which the usual activities of life are charged with deeper meaning and the need for self-assessment. Of the three longer stanzas—those of more than one line—the first and fifth are of five lines each, and the third is four lines long. These longer stanzas are each followed by a single-line stanza, which serves as a kind of response, an answer or summation, to the stanza preceding it. The line "Things have come to that" sums up the comments in the first stanza, which alludes to the walking of the dog and the running for the bus, and "Nobody sings anymore" is an oblique summary to the activity of star counting. The closing single-line stanza, "Her own clasped hands," is in actuality the final phrase of the preceding sentence. Furthermore, the poet uses ellipses as a minor device, one in the first stanza at the very end, and the other after the fourth line in the fifth stanza.

The poem does not employ rhyme but uses the straightforward language of everyday thought and reflection; there is an absence of traditional meter, though the lines within the longer stanzas are often "run-on," as in the first and second lines of the first stanza: "Lately, I've become accustomed to the way/ The ground opens up and envelopes me." The third stanza uses the word "And" to initiate the first three lines, a pattern of anaphora, which adds to the persona's sense of hopeless repetition and routinized daily experience.

Though the experience presented in the poem is deceptively simple, certain uses of language add to the complexity of the poet's presentation of isolation and uncertainty. The line "The ground opens up and envelopes me" is obviously metaphorical in its suggestion of death, suffocation, and containment. Other natural elements are employed such as the "wind," which makes "broad edged silly music," an ambiguous auditory image that uses synesthesia, intersensory modality, the idea that a "broad edged" shape can be paralleled to a musical sound.

In addition to the "ground" and the "wind," the poet employs the often conventional image of the "stars," used traditionally by poets to connote a host of possible meanings, from fate to aspiration to isolation to ambiguity, the latter meaning suggested in this poem. The hyperbole, the counting of stars, an act that is apparently undoable, is used to support the seemingly meaningless act, a search for the finite within the infinite. Ambiguity of imagery is further evident in the continuation of counting stars despite their inaccessibility; the poet says, "I count the holes they leave," in the absence of the stars themselves. The narrative style of the poem, its story like form, is suggested in the closing stanza and the description of overhearing the daughter's prayers.

Themes and Meanings

The poem ultimately expresses dislocation and political stasis, implicitly questioning the role of the poet as a social voice. The meaninglessness of routinized life engenders a literary death wish. The uncertainty of direction, the inability to take action, is suggested through the poet's construction of a "suicide" note as an ongoing literary act, a "twenty volume" discourse. The poem itself is a search for meaning and spiritual wholeness in the face of an existential quandary and malaise. Despite the personalizing of the context in the reference to his daughter, the poet also speaks for a generation of Americans facing an era of upheaval and doubt. When the speaker considers that the "ground . . . envelopes" him when he walks his dog, the emphasis is on the patterned regularity of the experience. Although there is little context around which to establish the speaker's lifestyle, there are hints as to its repetitiveness, as in "when I run for a bus," suggesting either hectic routine or keeping pace with the times.

The first stanza introduces a motif of music in a metaphorical and imagistic sense: "the broad edged silly music the wind/ Makes." Perhaps the notion of running for the bus connotes the rapid social transformations in American culture, a transition that entraps the poet as well. This theme is echoed in the second single-line stanza, "Nobody sings anymore," a comment that implies a turning point in an era or epoch and a loss of spirituality or emotionality. This expression of lost sensibility of song may be the poet's way of characterizing what was then the turmoil of the civil rights era, where lyricism as a trope for social harmony is no longer attainable.

The final long stanza, in which the poet describes overhearing his daughter speaking in her room, points to a spiritual dilemma; her praying might suggest Baraka's own inability to resolve his uncertainty about a political direction. The final stanza also implies that it is through the innocent petition of the daughter that the poet recognizes, though unstated, the irony of uncomplicated spirituality and hope. In Baraka's own life, his growing disaffection with white liberalism and the bohemian lifestyle may have generated the searching quality of the poem. Certain dilemmas might lead one to contemplate a metaphorical "suicide" but not necessarily an actual one.

Baraka's poetry of the 1960's and after was more obviously political, voiced in the language styles of urban black life, the blues, and jazz. Following his trip to Cuba in 1960, Baraka began to consider his role as a social poet and later in the decade wrote black protest poetry that challenged white liberalism. "Preface to a Twenty Volume Suicide Note" does not contain strident political protest or Afrocentric iconography of the Black Arts movement, which Baraka would later embody. The poem represents an earlier persona, that of LeRoi Jones, influenced by the themes, styles, and subjectivity of Beat poetry yet on the threshold of commitment to social relevance and action.

Joseph McLaren

PRELUDES

Author: T. S. Eliot (1888-1965)
Type of poem: Lyric
First published: 1915; collected in *Prufrock and Other Observations*, 1917

The Poem

"Preludes" is a lyric poem in free verse, divided into four numbered parts of thirteen, ten, fifteen, and sixteen lines. These sections were written at different times during T. S. Eliot's years of undergraduate and graduate studies at Harvard University and in Europe.

The title is appropriate if it suggests a type of short musical composition in an improvisational or free style. Since some of the images in this very early poem anticipate the barren, rubble-filled atmosphere of *The Waste Land* (1922) and other poems, it could be considered a "prelude" to Eliot's later works. The title may also be viewed as an ironic one, such as "The Love Song of J. Alfred Prufrock" and "Rhapsody on a Windy Night," because it creates expectations about the poem's contents that are not fulfilled. Although the first three sections or preludes move from evening to morning, the fourth returns to the evening hours without suggesting that anything in the poem is a preliminary to a more important or enlightening action or event.

The point of view shifts from an objective description of a city street on a "gusty" winter evening in prelude I to a more emotional first-person response to this scene in the middle of IV. The "you" in preludes I and IV could refer to the reader or to anyone who has walked the city streets. The scene moves from the dirty streets to dingy rooms at the end of II, with the transition introduced by the formal observation, "One thinks." A woman in such a room is addressed as "you" in III, which describes her actions and thoughts as she wakes up. Prelude IV contains three separate parts, beginning with a third-person description of a man's soul in relation to the street scene, followed by a more lyrical, subjective thought expressed in the first person. The closing lines use imperatives and second-person pronouns to direct the listener's or reader's responses, as the poem ends with an uncouth gesture, laughter, and a bleak image of "ancient women" in the "vacant lots" that were introduced in prelude I.

With this shifting and uncertain point of view, it is impossible to define a persona speaking in the poem. One catches glimpses of an inner life—of someone's familiarity with a woman and her thoughts—and discovers some tender feelings in prelude IV. Most of the poem, however, reflects Eliot's efforts to avoid the subjectivity of nineteenth century Romanticism in favor of a more objective technique using concrete images to create a mood and represent emotions.

The images in "Preludes" are more unified than those in most of Eliot's other poems because they all come from the city streets and all suggest the tedium and emptiness of modern urban life. Although this urban scene has been associated with St. Louis, Boston, and Paris—all cities Eliot knew as a young man—he selected images that would represent any modern city. One of Eliot's earliest poems showing his fascination with the squalid life of the slums, "Preludes" also reveals the influence of the French writer Charles-Louis Philippe. Two of his novels of Parisian life supplied images that Eliot adapted in "Preludes" and "Rhapsody on a Windy Night," including the details of the woman with sordid thoughts and "soiled hands" rising from bed in prelude III.

Forms and Devices

Although the line lengths and meters of "Preludes" are more uniform than those of many of Eliot's other poems, its forms show him experimenting with irregular and fragmented structures. The first two lines begin in iambic tetrameter, like the "Sweeney" poems and several other early poems, but the third line, with only three syllables, creates an abrupt interruption in the rhythm; there is frequent variation from the eight-syllable iambic line through the rest of the poem.

Rhymes are interspersed irregularly in each prelude. They often link parts of related images, such as "wraps" and "scraps," or "stamps" and "lamps" in prelude I, or "shutters" and "gutters" in III. Prelude II has the most regular rhyme scheme (*abcadefdef*), with the three rhymes in the last six lines connecting the two sentences that make up this section and marking the transition from the street to shabby "furnished rooms."

The syntax of the poem also mixes the regular and the irregular; its structures reinforce the perception that modern life is both fragmented and monotonous. The regular syntax and meter of the first two lines are followed by two fragments emphasizing the time—the end of the day. Next begins the first of many sentences and phrases starting with "and," several of them fragments, which contribute to the impression that this poem is an accumulation of images with connections and implications that are not always explained logically. Prelude III is one long sentence that contains sequences of parallel clauses beginning with "you" and "and." These repetitions of ordinary structures create a monotonous effect that emphasizes the tedious routines of daily life as the woman's morning actions are narrated.

Prelude IV contains the most irregular and confusing syntax. Its first section can be read as a series of noun phrases, but the relationships among them are uncertain. Is the soul, besides being "stretched tight across the skies," somehow "trampled by insistent feet" as well as by the fingers, newspapers, and eyes in the following phrases? Does "the conscience" refer to the eyes of the previous phrase, or is it also part of the image of "his soul"?

The relationship between these irregular forms and the images they contain shows Eliot's connections with the English and American Imagist poets in the first two decades of the twentieth century. Imagists used concentrated, concrete images, conveyed in simple and precise language, with no restrictions on the choice of subjects for their poems. As the fragments and the ambiguous syntax of prelude IV demonstrate, they were most concerned with conveying each image directly to the reader as it occurs to the mind. Gertrude Patterson observes that in doing so, the poet "will not take time to 'translate' it into the expository prose sentence with the normal grammatical rules of syntax" (*T. S. Eliot: Poems in the Making*, 1971).

Also influenced by the French Symbolist poets, especially Jules Laforgue, Eliot went beyond Imagism by constructing more elaborate sequences of vivid images that represent intense emotions and moods, demonstrating that physical sensations and thought are inseparable. Throughout "Preludes," the concrete images from the streets and glimpses of human actions, presented in plain language, become increasingly suggestive of some deeper significance; their associations with abstractions such as consciousness and conscience become more prominent in each prelude. The complex and ironic meanings of the poem are embodied in the connotations and symbolism of these images.

Themes and Meanings

Several critics have called preludes I and II Imagist poems. Their concentrated images of wet and dirty streets create a dreary atmosphere that permeates the explorations of mind and soul later in the poem. Prelude I consists entirely of physical sensations and actions, including the vivid image of wasted energy in its only metaphor, "the burnt-out ends of smoky days" (similar to the "butt-ends of my days" found in "The Love Song of J. Alfred Prufrock"). Symbols and themes introduced in I continue throughout this poem and many of Eliot's later works: the passage of time; smoke, wind and rain; the broken, decayed, and discarded objects and grime in the street; domestic smells that become stale by morning; and glimpses of the routine actions of city dwellers.

Isolation and depersonalization are themes represented by the scarce, fragmentary, and anonymous human images in this urban setting. The "lonely cab-horse" waits for someone while rain and wind sweep across vacant lots. "The lighting of the lamps" suggests a human action in nearly deserted streets, but it is expressed only as a fragment floating at the end of prelude I. Feet are the only specific human detail in I, "street" and "feet" being prominently repeated words in all four preludes. "Insistent feet" trampling muddy streets represent the crowds beginning and ending the "masquerades" of their work day, while the hands "raising dingy shades/ In a thousand furnished rooms" are reminders of the cramped and anonymous masses in the city.

The passive woman in prelude III is shown physically only through gestures involving her artificially curled hair and her soiled hands and feet. In IV, fingers stuffing pipes, eyes "assured of certain certainties," and a mouth engaged in derisive gestures mock human ignorance and futility. The brief moment of compassion inspired by these fragmentary images takes the vague form of "some infinitely gentle/ Infinitely suffering thing" rather than a definite vision of human romance or tragedy.

The images of "yellow soles" at the end of III and "his soul" in the first line of IV provide an ironic juxtaposition of the sordid and the spiritual, an apparent movement from the shabby and sensual to the profound. Yet since in Eliot's view no experience could be separated from the physical, the thoughts and soul of a woman or a man in this setting are "constituted" in relation to images from the street. Their "vision" of the world is limited to understanding the life around them, where morning light brings only the resumption of meaningless routines until night "blackens" the street again. The "I" who yearns for deeper significance also fears, like Prufrock, that his gentler feelings will be ridiculed by his listeners, so he ends by reducing the revolving of worlds to the image of "ancient women/ Gathering fuel in vacant lots."

Tina Hanlon

PRO FEMINA

Author: Carolyn Kizer (1925-   )
Type of poem: Lyric
First published: 1963; collected in *Knock upon Silence*, 1965

The Poem

The words *pro femina* are Latin, meaning "for the woman," and the opening line is an imperative sentence: "From Sappho to myself, consider the fate of women." This announcement of the topic is immediately followed by the exclamation in the second line, "How unwomanly to discuss it!" The implication is clear. Women are not to speak of their own history of oppression—or even to recognize it—for to do so might lead to a demand for change. That is precisely what the poem does demand: a change that will end patriarchal control of women's lives.

Forging unity among women to create this change is central to Carolyn Kizer's thesis, and throughout the poem she uses the plural "we" for the narrative speaking voice. "We" thus bonds the speaker and her audience ("real women, like *you* and like *me*") as parts of a whole: women, who together can change the world. The poem develops the thesis through numerous references to traditional societal attitudes about women's "place."

Part 1 addresses the narrator's anger at the way women have been treated. Women are entitled to the same freedom that men take for granted, but women who "howl" for "free will" are scorned and accused of being "cod-piece coveters." Ignore such epithets, says the narrator. Men have denounced women for their vices, but in fact such vices were caused by women being set apart as inferior. Women have traditionally forgiven men or acquiesced and "worshiped God as a man."

Now women are "freed in fact, not in custom," and they can begin to change the customs and lead the world in a new direction. As mothers, they have developed respect for life and place life above abstractions such as "national honor." If women are allowed to speak out and to be more than simply wives and mothers, they can teach society to adopt this attitude of caring; then "we might save the race." Meanwhile, if given the chance, women will change, develop, and grow as they struggle for liberation.

Part 2 addresses the problems that have arisen from man's treatment of woman. The poet announces her theme here as the "Independent Woman" (non-male-identified). Women have been "maimed" in their efforts to expand the roles allotted to them, for men disdain their unladylike behavior and choose instead the "full-time beauties" (as defined by men). Both women and men need "well-treatment," but men pretend that only women are dependent and use that as the excuse to keep women out of "the meeting," the decision making.

Women are fitted into roles designed for them by men, thus masking women's true selves and their true participation in humanity. The superficial obsession with women's physical appearance, with all the cosmetics and restrictive clothing (including "shoes with fool heels"), keeps women occupied with trivial vanity while men, in functional "uniform drabness," conduct the business of the world. If a woman refuses to play her male-assigned role, if she uses her mind instead of her looks, men reject her. If she acts out the role of posturing, ravishing sex object, she will not develop her talent and intellect. Women must escape this double bind; the independent woman will have to create herself.

Part 3 specifically addresses the problems that male dominance has caused for women writers. The narrator refuses to accept a continuation of this dominance and declares: "I will speak about women of letters, for I'm in the racket." The successes, she says, have been single women; the failures have been women who married for security, gave in to self-pity, played helpless to win men's favor, or disparaged other women "to stay in good with the men." Some are "traitors" who say with men that women should remain passive.

Women's writing should not be some "prettily-packaged commodity" but should speak the truth, for women "are the custodians of the world's best-kept secret:/ Merely the private lives of one-half of humanity." Men ignore or patronize women who speak this truth, and some women respond by aping the ways of men. Others use the positions they attain to "flog men for fun, and kick women to maim competition."

Change is underway, however; there is hope of ending the old roles that warped and bound women. If women work hard, join together to stand up for their rights, speak and write the truth they know, and take pride in their freely chosen lives, nothing can stop them. Men and children will share in the luck of living in a world with such women; all humanity will benefit.

Forms and Devices

Like much contemporary poetry in the second half of the twentieth century, "Pro Femina" is written in free verse. There are no syllabics or rhyme to use as a defense between the author and the material. As in any lyric poem, there is a clear sense of the author speaking through the narrative voice to express her own thoughts and feelings.

Kizer assumes an educated reader (audience) familiar with her allusions and references. She assumes, for example, that the opening mention of Sappho, the sixth century B.C.E. lyric poet, will suggest to the reader the long history of women writers and will also suggest their "fate"; Sappho's works were deliberately and systematically destroyed by men who equated "Sapphism" with lesbianism. The numerous references throughout the poem resonate with meanings and connotations that do not lend themselves to easy synopsis. They provide a compressed rhetoric that gives the poem its force and wit. The individuality of Kizer's writing style exemplifies her central argument that women have a right—a responsibility—to create their own works and their own lives.

Central to the thesis is the use of the first-person-plural pronoun "we." It is a shifting referent, variously meaning we feminists, we women writers, we women in general, but always in the sense of seeing women as the half of humanity whose emerging voices must be heard.

The tone is one of acerbic irony. Mixing the colloquial with suavely elegant phrases, the narrative voice is both tough and insistent. The word choices reveal the problems that rigid gender roles have caused: women maimed, scorned, neutered, turned into "cabbageheads"; women made into scabs (like the scabs who betray striking workers by taking their jobs) who "kick" other women "to stay in good with the men"; women whose lives and writings have been denigrated, denied, and destroyed.

Women have developed qualities that men should adopt: respect for life, caring for others, and "keeping our heads and our pride." Women are asserting the need for new attitudes, and if they "defect to the typewriter" and honestly tell their "secret," all humanity will benefit.

Alliteration, a caustic wit, and punning wordplay (paronomasia) add zest to the argument throughout. "So primp, preen, prink, pluck and prize your flesh,/ All posturings!" says the narrator, scornful of such superficial goals. She speaks of the "toast-and-teasdales," making alliterative and punning reference to Sara Teasdale, the American poet who wrote slight, "sensitive" verses expected of female writers. "But the role of pastoral heroine/ Is not permanent, Jack. We want to get back to the meeting," laughs the narrator warningly. When she says, "even with masculine dominance, we mares and mistresses/ Produced some sleek saboteuses," she at one stroke succinctly suggests that much more could be accomplished if women were given full opportunity, alludes to men's view of women as either wives or mistresses, carries out the image of horses and mistresses as sleek, objects to derogatory feminine endings (such as poetess) by coining the word saboteuse for saboteur, and makes fun of men who cannot even recognize when their beliefs are being attacked.

The poet uses vivid images throughout, as in the three stanzas which critically summarize the way women of the time were expected to dress. Lines such as "Strapped into our girdles, held down, yet uplifted by man's/ Ingenious constructions, holding coiffures in a breeze/ Hobbled and swathed in whimsy, tripping on feminine/ Shoes with fool heels" catalog literal restrictions and lead to the conclusion that such emphasis on appearance keeps women "in thrall" to their own surfaces and trivializes their lives.

The poem uses satire to show the cost exacted from women who insist on more than superficial beauty: "So, Sister, forget yourself a few times and see where it gets you:/ Up the creek, alone with your talent, sans everything else./ You can wait for the menopause, and catch up on your reading." Here as throughout the poem the elliptical allusions (being up a creek without a paddle, or waiting for menopause, when supposedly men would not choose you even if you tried to be a beauty) combine with the sharp and outspoken wit to give a rich texture that implies more than the words first seem to say.

The time to insist upon more is here, Kizer says. It is time to "stand up and be hated" if that is what it takes to break the cycle of devouring and being devoured.

Themes and Meanings

The poem is a feminist manifesto for change. The first-person narrator creates a feminist analysis of the history of women, focusing on women writers, which shows the ways women have been warped by trying to fit into the script that patriarchy has written for them and the challenges that continue to face women as they insist on equality, autonomy, and "free will." The liberation of women is a vital cause whose goal is nothing less than to save the human race. Women make up "one-half of humanity," and their new stories must be lived, spoken, and heard. Society as a whole will gain from this fuller definition of humanity. As Kizer says, "Relax, and let us absorb you. You can learn temperance/ In a more temperate climate."

Kizer is one of the generation of American women poets who were the first group to dismantle existing views of women and speak for a revolution against patriarchal control. Kizer and other poets such as Denise Levertov, Maxine Kumin, Anne Sexton, Adrienne Rich, and Sylvia Plath lifted the constraints on women writing the truth about their lives. They both refused to accept the place society had assigned women and refused to "write like a man." Above all, these poets and others who have followed them think of women as "we." They recognize the need for unity and love among women in the common cause of ending sexism. Carolyn Kizer and her sister poets, like all the most enduring writers, question their society and insist on the creation of a better world.

There have always been exceptional women who recognized and spoke against male dominance. In a 1984 author's note in *Mermaids in the Basement: Poems for Women* Kizer thanks the earlier French writer Simone de Beauvoir for inspiring "Pro Femina." Such thanks could extend back through the nineteenth century women who struggled for suffrage and women's rights, to Mary Wollstonecraft's *A Vindication of the Rights of Woman* in 1792, or back farther than male-dominated history has allowed women to see. Never, however, have so many women writers spoken out at the same time and gained such a wide and receptive audience as in the last third of the twentieth century. "Pro Femina" was published in 1963, half a dozen years before the contemporary women's movement gained widespread momentum or public attention.

Kizer's poetry was in the forefront of that movement; it served as a prototype of what subsequently became a rising tide of women's consciousness. "Pro Femina" is indeed "for the woman" in all senses of that phrase. Its message is for (directed toward) women; for women in the sense of seeing women as a category for discussion; for women in urging women to become fully functioning independent beings. It speaks for women, telling women's story with a directness that shocks and enlightens, and it urges women to tell their own stories. The message of the poem is female, political, and revolutionary.

In *Mermaids in the Basement*, the poem "Fanny," from Kizer's book *Yin* (1984), appears in sequence as "Four: Fanny" in the section entitled "Pro Femina." While not following the form of parts 1, 2, and 3, it can be said to present a specific example of the theme. Fanny, the narrator, took care of Robert Louis Stevenson in his last years of life on the island of Samoa. While Stevenson writes, Fanny endlessly plants trees and crops and vegetable gardens to sustain them. She tries to keep a journal, but finds that Stevenson is marking out passages and making changes. She starts censoring herself, then abandons the journal entirely. She is one of the "mutes," unable to write the truth of her life, like the "millions/ Of mutes for every Saint Joan or sainted Jane Austen" mentioned in part 1. Kizer re-creates Fanny's life through this poem and lets Fanny speak. The poem ends with Fanny's proclamation that now that Stevenson has died, she will "leave here" and "never again succumb."

Lois A. Marchino

THE PROBLEM

Author: Michael Collier (1953-   )
Type of poem: Lyric
First published: 1989, in *The Folded Heart*

The Poem

Michael Collier's "The Problem" is a colloquial lyric poem examining how as a young boy the poet faced the fear of his father's death. Writing as an adult, Collier offers mature insight into his childhood awareness of death. He implies that just as natural as the fear itself is his own compulsion, both as boy and adult, to come to terms with it, and he uses the poem for just this purpose.

The poem's setting is Collier's room as a boy of ten or so. World War II airplane models hang over his bed. Attached to the ceiling "by thumbtacks and string," the planes are the last objects he sees before falling asleep at night. He thinks of his father, perhaps because he has received his father's help in assembling the planes. Such thoughts, though, make him dread sleep because he fears his father will die before he awakens. The young boy succeeds in making "the world fair enough for sleep" only by assuring himself that his father will not die before he himself reaches the age of twenty-one, an impossibly advanced age for him to imagine. Lulled to sleep through this nightly "bargain" with death, with his adult wisdom Collier wryly notes that childish egocentricity projected his needs into a kind of "promise" made to him by his father.

Collier makes clear to the reader that his boyhood strategy of postponement, midway between "gamble" and "promise," like the fear of death itself, is a matter of the imagination. The poem's focus on the key role played by the imagination, the poet's contemplative tone, and the concentration on the unique, individual feelings of the boy place the work firmly within the Romantic tradition. At the same time, though, the underlying angst of the work makes Collier a postmodern artist.

As in many postmodernist works, the resolution that climaxes this work occurs through a dramatic act rather than being proclaimed as a transcendent vision, as in traditional Romantic poetry. The act is the way the youngster creates the airplane models themselves, accomplishing the difficult feat of attaching the wheels to the plane without freezing their movement by applying glue in just the right place. Possibly in a trick he has learned from his father, in the same way that one breathes air into a fire to make it burn, so the young Collier "blows" on each wheel to dry the glue and make the tire "spin." By analogy, the boy's ability to attach the axles and landing gear to the plane without binding the wheels suggests to the reader the notion that that the awareness of death is not only an attachment or halting but also a means of transporting and releasing human qualities and achievements.

Forms and Devices

In "The Problem," Collier creates a poem that falls neatly into two almost equal parts. The first ten of the twenty-one total lines consist of two unrhymed couplets of irregular meter in which the poet moves into "the problem" by bringing the planes that he built "out of their shadows." He does this by naming them. The names are appropriately exaggerated and violent in the manner of a cartoon: "Messerschmitt," "Spitfire" and "Hellcat." In a sudden contrast to these exciting words, the poet confronts "the problem" itself in plain English. He asks himself how old he would have to be to endure his father's death—"How old must I be before I am old enough for my father to die?"

The seemingly casual, conversational tone with which this question is broached is echoed in the structure of this half of the poem. Formatting it as dialogue, the poet follows the twin couplets, which pose a question or make an observation, with a one-line stanza summing up an answer or comment. At the end of the first half of the poem, when the "bargain" or "promise" is made that the father will not die until the boy reaches the age of twenty-one, the youngster believes he has overcome the fear that threatens to overwhelm him; he has "made the world fair enough for sleep."

The second half of the poem modifies the question-and-answer formula. Mirroring the profound release that comes with the boy's creation of the planes as moving, life-like objects, the one-line comments become the conclusion of sentences already started in the couplets, rather than existing as sentences in their own right.

Interestingly, as in the previous portion of the poem, here also the poet reveals ancient roots. For example, although deliberately experimenting with a postmodern dissonance at the end of lines, within lines Collier cultivates older accentual patterns and rhyme schemes through his unobtrusive use of both full and slant rhymes, such as "fear" and "gear," "fear" and "fair," and "plane" and "names." This assonance within lines counteracts and softens the dissonance between lines, the anomalous juxtaposition of "planes" with "ceiling," "twenty-one" with "night," and "protruding" with "careful."

In an additional effort to link this poem with the literary past, an aim expressed rather explicitly in other poems in the collection, Collier also puns modern and ancient meanings. "Fair" means not only "equal" but also "beautiful." "Plastic" means "synthetic" as well as "pliable." Finally, Collier's "bargain" with death not only invokes the contemporary three-stage approach to death—denial, bargaining, and acceptance—but also refers to the ancient imaginative and dramatic symbol of humankind's effort to postpone death through gambling, dueling, or playing chess or cards. Here the poet figures his adversary as the absolute necessity to apply "noxious glue" one drop at a time in a "difficult place." If he makes a mistake, the tires will not spin.

Themes and Meanings

Many of Collier's poems of this early period examine the fear of his own or another's death, usually envisioned as being buried, taken away, or, as here, falling or falling asleep. Almost always in these poems, however, juxtaposed to the fear of death is the affirmation of living that occurs in a creative act. Such acts can take the form both of an imaginative, verbal act, a "bargain" with death or a "promise"; or of a deliberate, dramatic deed that releases individual energies, as in diving into water, playing a guitar, breaking open a piñata, or, as here, constructing a model plane with wheels that move.

Because he works within the Romantic tradition, Collier's quest for a solution to "The Problem" also takes him back to his childhood experience of night terror, as he brings to bear the dual perspective of child and adult; childhood offers the raw material of experience, which the mature poet then interprets.

In many Romantic poems the poet emphasizes the loss implicit in growing up and fails to build a solid, reasonable resolution to the problem the poem establishes. Here, though, the poet mourns no loss and finds the resolution to the problem of death embedded within the childhood experience itself. This resolution embraces first the provisional answer of ruling out or postponing death on the grounds that death is just as unimaginable for a child as for an adult. This affirmation then moves on to a scheme that formulates the dramatic act of creation as a way of staying death's hand, even the creation of something so humble as a model airplane. In other words, going well beyond the conventional Romantic assertion of art as an antidote to death, here Collier validates any kind of meaningful act as a kinetic release from time, perhaps especially one that is not accepted as being artistic. In yet another significant departure from tradition, both the imaginative and dramatic acts that constitute the resolution to "The Problem" occur quite spontaneously, rather than being grounded in a sense of oneness with the renewal of nature, as is often the case in Romantic poetry.

Collier's handling of his material also differs from much postmodern poetry, however, in which the feeling is a conviction of being cut off from the past. Here, through the use of ancient accentual patterns, punning and the highly conscious use of literary symbols, Collier makes clear his indebtedness to the past. The result is a poem that looks simple but that actually operates on three different levels. The first is the way a preadolescent boy handles fears about his father's and, by extension, his own death. Just below that level is adult awareness and analysis of the twin imaginative and dramatic steps involved in allaying such fear. At the very foundation of the poem, however, is what literature and art has already said about death. At its base can be found the profoundly human, individual, and unique experience that both lies behind the fear of death and gives rise here to its imaginative and dramatic resolution.

Susan Tetlow Harrington

PROLOGUE

Author: Yevgeny Yevtushenko (1933-   )
Type of poem: Dramatic monologue
First published: 1957, as "Prolog," in *Obeshchaniy*; English translation collected in *The Poetry of Yevgeny Yevtushenko, 1953 to 1965*, 1965

The Poem

"Prologue" is a poem in free verse, its sixty-six lines divided into six stanzas of uneven length. Written in 1953, shortly after the beginning of Yevgeny Yevtushenko's career, the poem can be seen in retrospect as an introduction to his entire body of work, as the title indicates.

Like many of Yevtushenko's poems, "Prologue" serves as a vehicle of self-identification. In the very first line, "I am different," the poet makes a statement that would sound self-evident and redundant had it not been written at the beginning of a new phase in Russian poetry. A new generation, led by Yevtushenko and Andrey Voznesensky, was making its voice heard, replacing the officially approved old guard which had ruled the poetic scene for decades. In that sense, the above declaration is not only prophetic but also courageous, coming immediately after the death of dictator Joseph Stalin.

The poet also declares that he does not fit in—another statement that goes beyond its nominal meaning: He does not fit into the encrusted establishment of prescribed tenets and norms. He does not fit in because "much of everything is mixed" in him—his thoughts, his allegiance, his creeds—which would be acceptable under normal circumstances but was not in his country at that time. He denies that he lacks the "integral aim" for which he is criticized; on the contrary, there is great value in being different and individualistic. He believes that this is what makes him indispensable to his society, whether or not it wants to admit it. By "greeting all movement" he welcomes constant change in life, change that alone can guarantee progress.

The restrictions the poet is forced to endure blur his horizon and sap his energy. "Frontiers are in my way," he laments in the second stanza, feeling embarrassed at not being able to visit foreign cities such as Buenos Aires and New York, stroll in London and Paris, or speak with people in their languages.

The complaint about these restrictions is followed by an even stronger complaint about not being able to express himself freely as an artist. "I want art to be/ as diverse as myself" is another of the poet's creeds, perhaps the most important one. If the freedom he is seeking brings torments and harassments, he is willing to accept them, for he is "by art besieged." In the next stanza, he enlarges upon his domain, declaring that he feels himself akin to Sergei Yesenin, a leading Russian poet of the twentieth century, to poet Walt Whitman, to composer Modest Moussorgsky, and to the artist Paul Gauguin, thus placing himself in the company of giants in all the arts.

The fourth stanza gives expression to another Yevtushenko trademark, boldness and defiance, for which he is, perhaps, best known. "I like/ to defy an enemy to his face," he says openly in a way familiar to all of his "enemies." In the final stanza, he carries his defiance to the end, standing up to death itself. He sings and drinks, and he has no time to think of death; if it comes, "I shall die from sheer joy of living." It is in this joy of living that Yevtushenko finds the highest purpose of his life, for the attainment of which he is willing to defy all enemies and encourage all his brethren, in the arts and otherwise.

Forms and Devices

There is no one particular form or device that dominates "Prologue" but rather several, among which is the use of contrast. When he speaks of his frame of mind as well as his emotions, he uses contrast to underscore the complexity of human nature. He is overworked and idle at the same time, indicating that not all exertion is worth undertaking. He thinks he has a goal, yet he finds himself aimless, again pointing to the discrepancy between professed intentions and real aims. He is both shy and rude, nasty and good-natured, which is a more realistic appraisal of human nature than the insistence on either a black or white reading. He sways from West to East and back, alluding to the perennial dichotomy in the Russian mind and soul, to which he is not immune either, but whose expression has been officially suppressed. Finally, he sways from envy to delight, revealing that he is capable of a wide range of emotions. All these contrasts serve one main purpose: to show that in real life things are never black and white, as officials claim, but a combination of stands and moods often opposing one another.

Another device used in the poem, even if sparingly, is imagery. When he finds himself in a mood of exhilaration, the poet feels himself "heaped as high/ as a truck with fresh mown hay." He would "fly through voices,/ through branches,/ light and chirping,/ and butterflies flutter in my eyes,/ and hay pushes out of cracks." On another occasion, he would "love to crunch/ cool scarlet slices of watermelon" in August heat. The use of such striking images lends lyricism to Yevtushenko's poem, thus poeticizing his references to not-so-lyrical matters.

The form of the poem is consistent with the prevalent mode of Yevtushenko's poetry: free verse, its lines according to their rhythm, often in only a few words, sometimes in a cascading fashion, rhyming frequently but not according to any strict scheme. There is a built-in dramatic tension in the verses which lends itself well to Yevtushenko's powerful style of recitation.

Themes and Meanings

"Prologue" is an autobiographical poem, enabling the poet to express his beliefs and attitudes. Yet the poem is not exclusively personal. This may sound contradictory, but Yevtushenko has always been convinced of his mission as a poet speaking for his entire generation, not only for himself. Through his own declarations, he crystallizes a set of creeds for a coming generation ready to claim its own place in the sun and unwilling to accept the confines of the past. Perhaps for this reason, "Prologue" is almost like a manifesto, a programmatic poem that can be placed at the head of any collection of Yevtushenko's poetry.

The themes that pervade the poem all circle around the poet's need to be free to express himself as he sees fit. The fact that Yevtushenko has had to work for a long time in a highly confining environment has conditioned his approach to his art. For this reason, he is often coy in his allusions, despite his inherent boldness, perhaps so as to see his poems in print. One wonders how his poetry would seem had he been able to say exactly what he wanted, and in the way he wanted to, at the time it was written.

At the same time, it would be wrong to see "Prologue" primarily as an anguished outcry of a poet shackled by an oppressive system. Many of the themes in the poem—the insistence on being different, the ebullience of youth, a thirst for life and joy of living, the confusion of contradictory forces within oneself—could be applied universally. The universality of his themes, coupled with his artistic acumen, have enabled Yevtushenko to outlive the topics of the moment and remain a leading Russian poet for decades.

Yevtushenko's pronouncement of his kinship with poets Yesenin and Whitman is of interest not only to literary historians but to the general reader as well. That he would be akin to Yesenin is not surprising, for both poets remain faithful to their rural origins while becoming urban poets later in their careers. The kinship with Whitman, plausible though it may seem (primarily because of their mutual closeness to nature), is more surprising; it brings a poet from the American prairies close to a poet from the Siberian taiga.

Vasa D. Mihailovich

PROVISIONAL CONCLUSIONS

Author: Eugenio Montale (1896-1981)
Type of poem: Lyric
First published: 1956, as "Conclusioni provvisorie," in *La bufera e altro*; English
translation collected in *The Storm and Other Poems*, 1978

The Poem

"Provisional Conclusions" actually comprises two poems: "Piccolo testamento"
("Little Testament") consists of six sentences forming thirty undivided lines of free
verse, while "Il sogno del prigioniero" ("The Prisoner's Dream") has thirty-four free-
verse lines divided into four stanzas of various lengths. Each title plays upon alternate
meanings of "conclusion": "Little Testament" alludes to death, the final end, and
"The Prisoner's Dream" carries the political connotation of termination or liquida-
tion. Both are written in the first person, for they present the poet's "temporary judgment or conclusions" about contemporary life.

"Little Testament" opens at night as the poet contemplates his own kindled
thoughts. No ardent blaze ignited by political or religious reflection ("factory or
church . . . red or black" signify communism and Catholicism), the fragile "mother-
of-pearl" iridescence springs from recollections of love. As if present, the poet tells
his beloved to conserve the "powder" of these memories for the time when "every
other light's gone out" and "dark Lucifer" swoops down on the "wild," "hellish"
world to make the apocalyptic pronouncement, "It's time."

Hardly diminishing this frightening vision, the poet says his modest gift is "no in-
heritance, no goodluck charm/ to stand against the hurricanes." Yet to counteract the
gloom, he goes on to reassure his beloved that "the sign was right" and will be recognized, just as each individual will recognize the truth behind his or her own thoughts
and actions. Only by knowing oneself and acting according to that knowledge may the
"faint glow" of good slowly catch fire and blaze again in the world.

The second poem apparently presents the same narrator imprisoned in the dark, in-
fernal times foreseen in "Little Testament." Poignantly illustrating the persistent
"faint glow" of love and humanity, "The Prisoner's Dream" opens with an introduction to an unnatural world where "you can't tell dawn from night."

Opening with the prisoner's longing for freedom ("starlings over the watch-towers/ . . .
my only wings"), the second stanza then presents rapid, significant details of existence in the squalid cell. This dismal reality is escapable only through sleep and
dreams of the beloved.

Abruptly disrupting even this meager comfort, stanza 3 curtly opens: "The purge
never ends, no reasons given." The brutal, absurdist reality of ideologies and regimes,
reigned over by "gods of plague," replaces the meanness of confined existence. Only
by recanting, confessing, or "breaking down and selling out the others" may one be
saved and "get the spoon/ instead of being dished up."

In the final stanza, this brutal reality merges with the liberating dream-vision. Lying on "this piercing mattress," the prisoner imaginatively fuses with a "soaring moth" and "shimmering kimonos of light," conjuring "rainbows" and "petals" to combat prison bars and unending beatings. His thoughts rise, "only to fall back/ into the gulf where a century's a second." Physical suffering and mental delirium uncover moral crisis and self-doubt: "I don't know whether I'll be at the feast/ as stuffer or stuffing." The only certainty is that he must endure and dream, a realization which closes the poem.

Forms and Devices

The two poems are joined not only by poet Eugenio Montale's label as "provisional conclusions" but also by the similar forms and devices they share. Presented as loose, even sometimes incoherent ruminations, both open with references to the night, as the narrator ponders the perennial battle between darkness and light. Through various manifestations and images of these forces, each poem offers its own distinctive vision of the difficult, often tragic reality of modern life. In "Little Testament," this vision is structured around a nucleus of personal religious sentiment. In "The Prisoner's Dream," on the other hand, it is conditioned by the exigencies of political dogma. No doubt its focus on the public or social arena of contemporary times makes this second poem more accessible to most readers.

In large part because of their pessimistic visions, both poems are pervaded by gloom and obscurity, which the poet partially offsets through the device of symbolic imagery. Above all, Montale's images revolve around different types of illumination. In "Little Testament," for example, "flickering," "glass-grit," "faint glow," and "striking . . . match" all refer to brief, unstable fits of light, with an eventual and more constant brightness promised in references to the "tough log on a grate" and the "glow catching fire/ beneath" at the end of the poem. Images of light of equal significance can be found in "The Prisoner's Dream," such as the realistic "oily sputtering" of lamps or the fanciful "winey lantern," or even the prisoner's own metaphorical fits of mental lucidity. Through this figurative sense, especially evident in the fourth stanza, reality, dream, and hallucination become one.

Closely related to images of tenuous, shifting light are those of iridescent rainbows and spider webs. An evocative symbol of fragility and transience, "spiderweb" is present in both poems, although "Little Testament" additionally identifies it with the idea of memory. It is the rainbow, however, which is Montale's most symbolically charged image. In Italian, *iride* denotes both a rainbow and an iris; the poet uses both of these images as his own private token or emblem of fidelity, love, faith, and hope. The poet plays upon the word's multiple denotation in "Little Testament," for the second sentence associates the image with the biblical postflood rainbow representing God's covenant or promise, while in the next he treats it as a flower now crumbled to dust. This image has a much weaker presence in "The Prisoner's Dream," however, where it seems to function more as an illusion "conjured up" to transform the dingy here and now than as a complex emblem of faithful love.

The poet's vision of an ever-worsening world focuses on two equally powerful and ambiguous forces, religion and politics, which also offer their own share of imagery. Although "Little Testament" expresses an idiosyncratic form of belief, it is nonetheless full of allusions to traditional religion: Faith, hope, humility, pride, signs, Lucifer, apocalypse, salvation, and resurrection are all derived from Christian belief. Many of these same elements appear faintly and in a more abstract form within the strongly defined atmosphere of political evil in "The Prisoner's Dream."

Themes and Meanings

"Little Testament" and "The Prisoner's Dream" are complex poems about many things, all of which have multiple meanings. Montale approaches one of the major conclusions from these "judgments"—the theme of the prison world of human existence, especially in modern times—in two different ways. In "Little Testament," the prison world is represented as the general existential condition of humanity. The theme achieves cosmic proportions, both through its allusions to contemporary social and cultural crises of values and through its predominately religious-based imagery. In "The Prisoner's Dream," the theme is interpreted as a more concrete, specific condition, derived from the poet's own perception of the Cold War years. In both, the individual's "dark night of the soul" coincides with the world's own darkness, fanaticism, and inhumanity.

Alongside this realistic, powerfully expressed negative theme, the poet masterfully places another which is more positive but more tenuous and intangible. This theme is that of human significance, which he approaches by affirming modest, unheroic virtues such as dignity, morality, love, faith, commitment, and humanity. Montale's poems make it clear that he believes these all-important elements are no longer operative in today's society and are even in danger of being forgotten. The perceived fragility and impermanence of these significant values—indeed, even of civilization itself—is perhaps the essential message of "Little Testament."

While the poet is unable to change the threatening conditions beleaguering humanity, he can still affirm essential values in the language, images, characters, and events of his poems. Because he brings these elements to life, readers have the opportunity to experience vividly their significance and so can more readily remember and understand their importance. Also, the poet can capsulize his own personal strategy for affirmation—endure, bear witness, and create poetry out of this persistence—as he apparently does in "The Prisoner's Dream." Like the love token, his poetry perhaps "only survives in ashes," the pale vestiges of a vital, uncontainable reality, but it is valuable nonetheless. That is perhaps the central message of "The Prisoner's Dream."

Although Montale perceives all of life as "provisional" or inconclusive, he holds firm the belief that individuals must keep faith with themselves and with life. Only through decency, stoic endurance, and vigilant openness toward even the smallest signs of good can one's own humanity be realized. Montale's own self-realization occurs through communicating and transmitting, with his poetry, the human values he himself has received. Regardless of each's individual emphasis, both poems affirm the poet's own tenacious conviction that love is the refuge and shield of humanity, its only hope for enduring and transforming the prison of existence. Even though such "persistence" may only lead to "extinction," the flame still burns, the mind remembers, and the heart recognizes love, the ultimate and most enduring "sign"; humanity, like the "dream," "isn't over."

Terri Frongia

PSALM

Author: Paul Celan (Paul Antschel, 1920-1970)
Type of poem: Dramatic monologue
First published: 1963, as "Psalm," in *Der Niemandsrose*; English translation collected in *Paul Celan: Poems*, 1980

The Poem

"Psalm" is a short poem in free verse. Its twenty lines are divided into four stanzas, each representing a separate unit in the poem's movement. The title indicates the theme and sets the reader's expectations: This poem is a prayer, an evening song, a praise. God, whom traditional evening songs praise, is, however, repeatedly identified with "no one" and, eventually, the poem turns out to be a song in praise of the human spirit. The context of Paul Celan's poetry and the imagery of "Psalm" also suggest that, more specifically, this poem is about Jewish people who were murdered by the Nazis during World War II. This specificity nevertheless bears universal validity and human significance.

The poem is written in the first-person plural, and, thus, the persona is actually a congregation of people. As the first line indicates, however, this congregation is dead. In obvious reference to the story of creation in the Bible, the persona declares: "No one molds us again from dust and clay, no one conjures up our dust." The word "again" betrays that a chance to live, once given, has been irretrievably lost, and the people represented by the persona have lost all hope of coming to life again.

The three lines of the first stanza, in each of which the words "no one" are repeated, end on a note of desperation. The praise of the name of "no one" in the first line of the second stanza is therefore full of shocking irony. The shift toward an upward movement nevertheless begins here as the persona associates the congregation with a flower that wants to bloom for "no one" and even wishes to glorify and court "no one." Thus, the sense of devastation introduced in the first stanza is somewhat dissipated, even though bitterness is still betrayed by the voice.

The bitter self-awareness of the congregation is continued in the third stanza as it recognizes its own nothingness that informs its own past, present, and future. The self-identification with the flower is also continued, however, and the congregation is characterized as the nothing rose and the no one's rose. Whereas the image of the rose conveys beauty, lack of value is suggested by the first metaphor and an orphaned state by the second one. The fact that this rose is "blooming" contributes to the affirmation of an inner richness and force.

In the last stanza, parts of the rose are compared to human mental and physical states and convey both much suffering and transcendence. The reproductive parts of the rose as well as the implication of many petals of its "crown" convey dynamic growth of a people, a drive toward beauty and spiritual awareness. The inner core of the rose, the pistil, is as bright as the soul. The stamen is ravaged by heaven, as if laid to waste or burned by the sun. The head of the rose, which the poet calls a crown (rendered as "corolla" in the translation) is red with "the crimson word." The suggestion of blood in the colors red and crimson is unmistakable. It emphasizes suffering, martyrdom, and untimely death. The "crimson word," sung over the thorn, suggests cries of pain and complaint as well as beauty.

Forms and Devices

"Psalm" is a complex poem because it is built upon a movement from irony to paradox and is developed through an extended metaphor that fuses with several other metaphors. The tone of irony, bitterness, and an initial sense of nihilism are relieved by overtones of mystic imagery and symbolism, which render the poem ambivalent. This ambivalence is a source of the poem's richness, as it makes two contradictory interpretations possible. The duality that pervades the whole poem allows the reader to experience overwhelming pain and despair, as well as empathy with the people who suffered devastation and untimely death. Awe and respect for them is evoked through an awareness of their inherent beauty and loveliness. Even a trace of reconciliation redeems the poem from bitterness.

The repeated personification of "no one" emphasizes divine absence. The irony that results from the suggested relationship of a silent "no one" and a congregation that is full of praise disappears as the image of the rose begins to predominate. This rose, a symbol derived from Jewish mysticism, may appear forlorn, deserted, or lost—as suggested through the metaphoric combination of this image with nothing— but it gains significance through spirituality.

For Celan, the rose, along with the image of the crown, symbolizes the people of Israel. Whereas the pistil and the stamen represent reproductive principles and therefore organic growth—and, in the context of the poem, self-generation—the petals of the rose also symbolize the members of the community or the congregation. The crown, which also may be interpreted as an image of transcendence, unites the reproductive organs of the rose, whereas in the Neoplatonic and Jewish mystical tradition, sexual union symbolizes ultimate unity and harmony, the goal of all redemptive activities. To suggest a spiritualizing principle in the rose, Celan associates the pistil with the soul or anima on the basis of its light color. The stamen, representing the male principle and thus, in this mythical tradition, the physical aspects of a human being, is envisioned by the poet as torn by intense suffering. The combination of the two suggests transcendence.

The unifying effect of the "crown" is increased by the red color, which identifies the rose with the crown and conveys both vitality and an open, bleeding wound. This effect is reinforced by the metaphor of the "crimson word" sung by the congregation, for in this context the word implies both praise and a cry of woe.

An interesting analogy may be drawn between the negative reference to God's creating abilities as manifested in bequeathing human life through addressing the dust, or, as translated, "conjuring," and the "crimson word" or loud complaint. Whereas the divine creating force of the word has disappeared, the "crimson word" of the rose remains rich with beauty and suffering, as if capable even of creating God. Whereas this interpretation may appear ironical and shocking, in the mystical tradition creation or re-creation of God is identified with redemption.

Themes and Meanings

Celan—an East European Jewish poet whose parents and close friends were killed by the Nazis—never recovered entirely from the tragedy he experienced when barely twenty years old. He repeatedly expressed his utmost grief in his poetry and searched for a solution or answer to the extreme suffering of his people.

In "Psalm," Celan addresses the universally valid question of the relationship of the world and an infinitely absent God. Twentieth century European nihilism, frequently attributed to the German philosopher Friedrich Nietzsche (1844-1900), who declared that God was dead, also affected Celan, who, because of his traumatic wartime experiences, faced a spiritual crisis. Eventually, however, Celan came to use the resources of Jewish mysticism for probing questions raised by the suffering he witnessed and experienced. Celan nevertheless differs from mystic poets, because the mystical symbolic significance of his imagery hangs in balance with an all-but-unresolvable bitterness and despair. In "Psalm," he juxtaposes a sense of nihilism with tenets of his religion and raises a question that is hidden beneath a twentieth century convergence of cultures and tragic historical events: Can God be redeemed from the void of his infinite absence and indifference?

The poet approaches this question by fusing in the image of "no one" two different religious traditions of Judaism. In the biblical tradition, God is envisioned as being personally involved in the creation of human beings and a committed part of a covenant with Israel. For Celan, this God has disappeared. In the Judaic mystical tradition, which influenced rabbinical Judaism and was transmitted through the Cabala, the creator of the universe is an infinitely distant, nameless entity—a nonbeing who projected the chain of powers from which the world ensued. This God, envisioned as male, frequently is experienced as infinitely distant, but He repeatedly is sought out and courted by mystics, who have asserted that He is discoverable in the midst of emotional intensity. The skillful fusion of these two concepts in the image of "no one" renders "Psalm" poignant and touching: It is extremely painful to register the absence of God, and it is overwhelming to witness the immense effort of the congregation to personalize and beautify this apparently indifferent, absent nonbeing. The suggestion of the discoverability of God is nevertheless hidden in the image of the rose. As David Brierley points out in "*Der Meridian*" (1984), Gershom Scholem, Celan's primary source of Jewish mystical imagery, also traces the rose to its identity with the Shechinah, the mediator between humans and God in Jewish mythology, the anima of the world.

Ultimately, as the poem concludes with the image of the thorn, the song of the congregation remains a monologue, and the pain from which the poem derives both is transcended by vision and remains historical and real.

Marie Gerenday Tamas

PSALM

Author: Georg Trakl (1887-1914)
Type of poem: Lyric
First published: 1912, as "Psalm"; collected in *Die Dichtungen*, 1919; English trans-
lation collected in *Poems*, 1973

The Poem

"Psalm" ushered in what is known as Georg Trakl's middle period, in which his poems were longer and his imagery more complex than had been the case in his previous
work. The influence of the French poet Arthur Rimbaud is well documented. "Psalm"
is written in long, flowing lines of free verse. In the original German, it contains the
mellifluous language that ensured that Trakl would continue to be read, even if he was
not entirely understood.

"Psalm" has four stanzas of nine lines each, and a single, isolated line at the end.
Semantic associations between adjacent lines are not always readily apparent.

Although everything is described in the third person, the poem is highly autobiographical, as is all of Trakl's work. The title seems to indicate a devotional poem, but
"Psalm" is devotional only in that for Trakl, the act of writing was a means of atoning,
at least in part, for his sins.

The first stanza is a good illustration of the extreme contrasts that characterize
Trakl's poetry. Four consecutive subjects are operated on by negative forces. They are
extinguished, abandoned, burned, and misused. A madman dies and is replaced, exactly halfway through the stanza, by the sun god in an idyllic South Sea island paradise, an image qualified only by the closing observation that it is a paradise lost.

At first, the second stanza seems to consist of nine unrelated images. The sense of
danger, though, is omnipresent, and it is clear that something horrible is happening in
the last line. It is the female figures who are at risk. The nymphs have left their safe
place, perhaps out of a false sense of security, for no sooner is the strange man buried
than he is replaced by the son of Pan, whose strong body soaks up the heat of the midday sun. The following central line of the stanza portrays some very vulnerable little
girls who, one suspects, are also of central significance.

The sister who is mentioned in the middle of the poem dominates the beginning of
the third stanza. While she remains the constant focal point, there is now a fragmentation of the male personality. He appears in rapid succession as the someone of "someone's evil dreams"; the "student, perhaps a double"; his "dead brother" (in two
places); and the "young novice." What happened at the end of the second stanza
seems to have overwhelmed and destroyed the integrity of his personality.

Indeed, the remainder of the poem is anticlimactic, with images of ending, departure, decay, and desolation. The Church remains silent, as does the God portrayed in
the last line, a *deus absconditus* (hidden god). Only the opening of his eyes indicates
acknowledgment of the poet's penance.

Forms and Devices

The most conspicuous structural device in "Psalm" is Trakl's prominent use of anaphora. He employed this rhetorical device of repetition in only one other poem, "De Profundis." By setting apart consecutive subjects with the formula "It is a . . ." Trakl has heightened the evocative power of each image and has lent the poem the air of an incantation. Images that might be questioned in a more relaxed format tend to be accepted when stated so absolutely. Trakl has applied the technique to both negative and positive images. It is a compelling way of presenting the realities of his mind, and it is because his inner world is portrayed so convincingly that he is considered the foremost poet of German expressionism.

Trakl's poems are extraordinarily closely knit. He wrote them slowly, and his manuscripts show many revisions and alternative wordings. In the final version, everything is significant. Adjacent lines are associated, no matter how disparate their content may seem, and the more structurally important their position in the poem, the more interpretive weight may be placed on them. For example, the climax and turning point in "Psalm" occurs halfway through the poem, the key lines being the last line of stanza 2 and the first line of stanza 3: "A white steamer carries bloody scourges up the canal./ The strange sister appears again in someone's bad dreams." The first line suggests sadistic sex; the second line identifies the victim. Thus the peak of the poem "Psalm" captures the essence of Trakl's confession, the driving force behind all his poetry: He had an incestuous relationship with his younger sister Grete. The central significance of the sister is formally attested by her exactly central position in the poem. By adding the single extra line at the end, Trakl made her line the median, with eighteen lines before it and after it.

Numerous cross-references extend throughout the poem like long threads holding it together. The white steamer that carries "bloody scourges" at noon has its counterpart in an empty boat that moves down the black canal in the evening. There is an aural accompaniment to this event. The rooms in stanza 2 are filled with chords and sonatas, but the music stops in stanza 3 with the final chords of a quartet. Likewise, the shadows who, in the third last line of stanza 2, embrace before a blind mirror reappear in the antepenultimate line of the poem as the shadows of the damned, descending to the sighing waters.

The self-judgment implicit in the imagery indicates that this psalm was written by a poet who entertained no hope of redemption.

Themes and Meanings

The quality of Georg Trakl's poetry has never been disputed, but its meaning has eluded critics for decades. Attempts to interpret his work within the Christian context were necessarily selective. Studies of particular images found that they could mean different things in different poems. When the pieces simply did not fit together, the last critical resort was always to the biographical fact of Trakl's dependency on cocaine, which supposedly rendered the logic of his visions unreproducible. Certainly, the surface picture is often confoundingly complex.

It was not until 1985, more than seventy years after his death, that Trakl's work was decoded in a monumental psychoanalytical study by Gunther Kleefeld, *Das Gedicht als Sühne* (the poem as penance). His title, taken from one of Trakl's letters, emphasizes the highly personal nature of the poetry. Trakl did not consciously set out to construct a clever system of cryptic symbols. In fact, he himself may not have known why his poems took the shape they did. Images arose in free association out of the deep structures of a disturbed psyche, much as they do in dreams, and the psychoanalytical approach has proved to be the best method of deciphering their meaning.

The task of interpreting Trakl's poetry is simplified by the small size of the cast of characters who may appear (although in any number of forms). He deals with himself, his sister, his father, and his mother, and continually reworks his family situation.

In "Psalm," the first stanza shows (in psychoanalytical terms) Trakl's id (the unconscious, instinctual area of the psyche) yielding to the superego (the moral, social area of the psyche; seat of the conscience), the madman to the sun god, the bad boy to the good. In the second stanza, the id is buried as the stranger, but it resurfaces as the sexually charged son of Pan. The sister figure is represented by the nymphs, the little girls, and the sonatas (Grete used to play Franz Schubert pieces). They embrace, and the last two lines introduce Trakl's own verdict of sickness.

Stanza 3 shows Trakl as neither the id nor the superego, but as the very confused ego in the aftermath of the event. What has happened with the sister now seems like a bad dream, and it has had a negative affect on her as well, making her even more vulnerable than before. The music stops, and the little girl is now blind.

Trakl blamed his parents for his unhappiness, for the lack of attention and absence of control that led and allowed him to become involved with his sister. The father appears in "Psalm" as the gardener and the caretaker, and is portrayed as inept at both jobs. It is in his old asylum, in stanza 4, that dead orphans lie beside the garden wall. The orphans are Georg and Grete Trakl, who appear in the following line as fallen angels.

Finally, the mother is present in "Psalm" in the first and fourth stanzas as water, the universal female symbol. In an image with positive emotional resonance, she is the singing sea, the womb that gave rise to the sun god. This image belongs to the past; the paradise is lost. In stanza 4, she is the sighing waters to which the shadows of the damned descend. All that is left for them is the death wish, the desire to return to the inorganic state.

This poetry is not only about the troubled Trakl family. Trakl's intense imagery of psychic agony transcends his immediate circumstances and applies to all who find themselves drawn in directions that are not condoned by society.

Jean M. Snook

THE PULLEY

Author: George Herbert (1593-1633)
Type of poem: Meditation
First published: 1633, in *The Temple*

The Poem

Most of George Herbert's poems are profoundly personal. This is not to say that they are always autobiographical, although indeed one senses the force of lived experience in his most successful poems. Yet whether or not they describe Herbert's own experiences, they typically present an individual in the midst of some dramatic process of meditation, analysis, worry, or wonder. "The Pulley" is a remarkable exception, structured as an explanatory tale about the creation of humankind.

Herbert does not often operate on the level of myth, but "The Pulley" owes something to the classical story of Pandora's box. In Herbert's version, however, it is not all the troubles of the world that are loosed upon unsuspecting humankind by an overly curious Pandora but all the "world's riches" that are poured upon humankind by a beneficent God. In revising not only the Pandora myth but also the biblical story of Creation in Genesis, Herbert constructs a narrative that is charming and bold. The speaker imagines himself as a witness to the moment of Creation and gives an on-the-spot report of what transpired and what was on God's mind as He both gave and withheld certain gifts.

There is a touch of humor in the poem as God not only pours blessings out of a glass on his new creation but also quizzically examines and then rationalizes his own actions. When nearly all the blessings are out—secular blessings, it seems, such as strength, beauty, wisdom, honor, and pleasure—God pauses and decides to keep the one remaining treasure, "Rest." He explains himself in direct terms, and this explanation is central to the poem: God's purpose is not to mystify or torment but to instruct, and the story of Creation is intended to give insight into how one should lead one's life. If humans were given everything, including "rest," the highest jewel of all, they would become complacent and have a mistaken sense of their own self-sufficiency. They would, in short, pay devotion to "Nature, not the God of Nature."

So it is to anticipate and correct this devotional danger that God gives all the blessings but one to humankind. In a pun that is both playful and serious and is even dizzying in its meaning and effect, God concludes by saying that while the comfort of "rest" will be withheld, all the "rest"—that is, the remainder—of the blessings will be freely given. As a result, humankind will be "rich and weary." There is no sense of threat here, but the ending of the poem is somewhat sobering. Human's life will be one of "repining restlessness" and "weariness." Yet this will prove to be a way to God. Only in the last lines of the poem does Herbert provide enough information to understand why the poem is entitled "The Pulley": Human existence involves reciprocal forces pulling or pushing against one another, but the pull to earth will be more than balanced by the pull to heaven, and as is typical in Herbert it is not one's strength but fully acknowledged weakness, compensated for by divine strength, that sends one to God's "breast."

Forms and Devices

One of the great charms of "The Pulley" is its simplicity of language. There is an easygoing, conversational quality to the poem that turns a potentially overwhelming spectacle, Creation, into a comprehensible fable and similarly turns a potentially foreboding power, God, into a familiar friend. As in many other poems by Herbert, God speaks directly to humankind, and not in the form of puzzles or distant pronouncements, but in statements that are intimate, patient, and consoling. Without these latter qualities, the underlying message of the poem—that human life is invariably characterized by incessant restlessness and weariness—would not be so palatable.

The images of the poem are also simple and homely, despite the fact that the subject is potentially disturbing and complicated. God performs actions that are magical and bold: For example, in language that recalls Genesis, he commands, "Let the world's riches, which dispersed lie,/ Contract into a span." Herbert frequently plays with quick transformations of space, especially from large to small, and this sudden description of Creation as an event of tremendous concentration—the entire world, as it were, contracted into the size of a human hand, a span—is momentarily startling. Despite his astonishing power, God appears primarily as a humble artificer, working with a glass of blessings containing simple ingredients that he pours out, and there is something infinitely comforting about the fact that the divine mysteries of Creation can be understood in terms of a common tool, the pulley.

Perhaps to reinforce the consoling familiarity and simplicity of the narrative, the poem is not very adventurous technically. The four five-line stanzas uphold a regular rhyme scheme, and the few variations in the meter are not so much complicated inversions to add tension or intensity but rather (presumably) deliberate flattenings of the lines to make them sound prosaically familiar. God noticeably does not speak in elevated language. Sincerity, not sublimity or cool austerity, characterizes his style, and this makes his assurances to humankind disarming and compelling.

Beneath the simplicity of the poem's language, though, is a level of complexity added by the wordplay. God apparently likes puns—or at least it makes perfect sense for Herbert to imagine God's language as embodying verbal ambiguities. A pun is a perfect figure of speech to convey the simultaneous playfulness and philosophical seriousness of the theme of "rest" in "The Pulley." This word is repeated throughout the poem not only to toy with its various meanings but also to understand fully its consequences. Peaceful "rest" is at first glance obviously a blessing, much desired by humankind, but ironically, more than any of the other blessings poured upon humankind, it has the capacity to distract humankind from its true goals, heaven and intimacy with God. For this reason, God, with great wit, allows humans to keep the remainder of the blessings, knowing that they will not afford any "rest." True rest will come only as a result of "restlessness," which will toss humankind upward. Herbert's choice of a concluding word is particularly shrewd and completes the wordplay of the poem: Embedded in God's "breast" is one's final "rest" (a pun more obvious in the seventeenth century spelling of "breast" as "brest").

Themes and Meanings

"The Pulley" is both a myth of origins and a moral and spiritual fable; these two genres overlap because, for Herbert, one's devotional responsibilities are perfectly consistent with and flow inevitably from who one is. Despite the brevity and simplicity of the poem, several key facts are affirmed. For example, this version of the Creation myth emphasizes the dignity of humankind, bestowed by a God who is thoughtful, generous, and kind. The story of Creation in the Book of Genesis is astonishing: A spiritual breath raises dusty clay to life in the form of Adam. In Herbert's poem, the Creation seems even more splendid, as humankind is described as the sum and epitome of all the world's riches, and God is a being who communicates easily and cordially with His creation.

Simultaneous with this emphasis on the dignity of humankind, however, is a carefully drawn distinction: Strength, beauty, wisdom, honor, and pleasure are necessary and vital components of humankind, but they are not sufficient to guarantee spiritual health. For this humans need rest, the one quality held back by God. Human independence, then, is qualified, but not undermined completely. "The Pulley" does not suggest that humankind is disastrously flawed and impotent, or that life in the world of Nature is insignificant and useless: Life can, after all, be "rich." It does show the limits of human powers and the liabilities of earthly existence: The inevitable human fate is restlessness and weariness.

Perpetual desire serves two extremely important purposes. First, it is an important devotional corrective, saving one from an undue concentration on Nature, the things of this world, and what is in fact only the illusion of human independence. It is all too easy to be distracted and "adore" the gifts rather than the giver, Nature rather than "the God of Nature." Since the former provide no lasting peace, however, one is thereby always redirected to the latter.

Life may thus be a series of postponed gratifications, even afflictions, but this will ultimately take one to God, the second purpose served by perpetual desire. "The Pulley" is not a poem of advice about how to change the focus of one's devotion from the things of the world to God, the author of those things. It is rather a dramatic, even magical poem that envisions a climactic union of humanity and God accomplished not by human intellectual power or will but simply by desire. Much like the poem "Love" (III), which concludes Herbert's sequence of lyrics in *The Temple*, "goodness" is somewhat beside the point when it comes to intimacy between humankind and God: Not worthiness but "weariness" tosses one to God's breast and secures rest.

Sidney Gottlieb

THE PURPOSE OF ALTAR BOYS

Author: Alberto Rios (1952-   )
Type of poem: Dramatic monologue
First published: 1982, in *Whispering to Fool the Wind*

The Poem

"The Purpose of Altar Boys" is composed in free verse. Its forty-five lines are held together in a single stanza. The title appears to be straightforward and serious, preparing the reader for an account of the function of altar boys in the Catholic church. Alberto Rios, however, looking back from the point of view of adulthood, assumes the voice of a mischievous altar boy who has created innovations in the performance of his duties when he assists the priest during the sacrament of Communion. As the poem progresses, the word "purpose" of the title takes on the meaning of intention.

The altar boy begins by explaining the way in which the human eye is constructed for perceiving good and evil. He says he learned this from his friend Tonio at catechism, where the boys were being taught the principles of their religion. Tonio learned about the eye from his mother. The altar boy explains that "the big part" of the eye "admits good" and the "little/ black part" is for "seeing evil." He believed this because Tonio's mother was a widow and, consequently, an "authority" on such things. Because the dark part of the eye sees evil, the altar boy associates evil with darkness. He explains that this is why children cannot go out at night and why girls sometimes undress at night and walk around their rooms or stand in their windows with nothing on but their sandals.

The narrator claims that he was the altar boy who "knew about these things." Therefore, when he assisted the priest at Communion on Sundays, he believed he had his own mission. One of an altar boy's responsibilities during Communion is to hold the communion plate under the chin of each person receiving the consecrated bread of the Eucharist, called the Host, so that it cannot accidentally fall to the floor and be defiled. As the narrator expresses it in the poem, his job as altar boy was to "keep Christ from falling." While performing this duty, however, he had opportunities to accomplish his own purposes.

On some Sundays, he says, his mission was to remind people of the night before. Holding the metal plate beneath a communicant's chin, he would drag his feet on the carpet, stirring up static electricity. He would wait for the right moment, then touch the plate to the person's chin, delivering his "Holy Electric Shock" of retribution. The right moment would be when "Christ" had been taken safely into the communicant's mouth. The narrator says that the shock caused a "really large swallowing and made people think." He adds that he "thought of it as justice." On other Sundays, however, the "fire" in his eyes was different, and his mission was changed. On these days, he would hold the plate too hard against the same nervous chins, pressing upward, so he could look with "authority" down "the tops of white dresses."

Forms and Devices

In "The Purpose of Altar Boys," Rios adopts the persona of a young boy, whose essential innocence attracts the reader and contributes to the humor of the poem. This persona affects the poem's language and structure. The diction is simple and colloquial, as exemplified in "kids can't go out" and in the boy's references to the iris as the "big" part and to the pupil as the "little" part of the eye. This voice also accounts for the absence of such literary devices as simile, metaphor, and rhyme. These would give the poem a self-consciousness that the altar boy does not have. He narrates his story in a linear structure and without the interruptions of stanza breaks, as his mind moves quickly from thought to thought, image to image.

The sense of ease and speed in the narration is also facilitated by the poet's use of a relatively short poetic line, usually containing six or seven syllables. Although the lines are short, the sentences are long. Five of them take up six or more lines, and one of these extends through twelve lines. The other three sentences in the poem take up one, two, and three lines, respectively. The combination of short lines and long sentences creates a sense not only of speed but also of breathlessness—these features express the altar boy's excitement as he tells his story of good and evil, judgment and temptation.

His excitement is also conveyed by repetition. Fascinated by darkness, he repeats "at night" three times in four lines. Speaking about things that happen at night, he begins two of three consecutive lines with "That's why." The most significant occurrence of repetition, however, is the boy's use of the pronoun "I." It increasingly dominates the poem. The pronoun does not occur until line 17 and does not appear again until line 24. In the remaining twenty-one lines, however, it occurs six times. Toward the end of the poem, the word "I" ends one line and begins the next. The increasing appearance of the word reflects the altar boy's self-assertion and reveals the pride he takes in fulfilling his missions.

The poet achieves special effects with punctuation and line breaks. He uses one dash in the poem, following the word "evil," overemphasizing the word, as a boy would do. He uses a colon in "the precise moment: plate to chin" to indicate the gap across which the static electricity will jump. Line breaks also mirror the action: "To keep Christ from falling/ I held the metal plate/ under chins." The poet places "under chins" beneath "I held the metal plate," as the plate would be held under a chin. On the other hand, he places "from falling" on the same line as "To keep Christ," indicating that the boy does not allow such a fall. Another significant line break occurs in "and I/ I would look," where the first "I" represents the altar boy in his official role, and the second reflects his personal impulse. The boy's eyes move down, just as the "I" does. This is where he lets "Christ" fall.

Themes and Meanings

Alberto Rios explores the relationship between authority and experience in "The Purpose of Altar Boys." The narrator says that Tonio's mother was an "authority" because "she was a widow." As a woman, a mother, and a widow, Tonio's mother had considerable experience. She was once a virgin, a girl no older than the altar boy. Perhaps an altar boy looked down the top of her white dress. She has fallen in love, been married, experienced sex, given birth, suffered the death of her husband, and raised Tonio. Her authority derives from her experience. She told Tonio the story about the parts of the eye to protect him from temptation, to preserve his childhood innocence.

The narrator claims that he also had experience. He "knew" about girls standing naked in their windows, although he does not say how he learned this. He believed that this experience gave him the right to punish those girls with his electric shock, as well as the "authority" to look down their dresses. The altar boy's experience does not compare with the experience of Tonio's mother. He also based his authority on his position as an altar boy, presuming to derive the right to judge and punish from being the helper of a priest. He considered himself superior to the other altar boys, claiming to be "the" altar boy who "knew," and he thought of his electric shock as "Holy," although he was not vested with the authority of a priest.

The ultimate authority in the poem is the Catholic Church. It is ironic, but appropriate, that the altar boy heard the story of the eye at catechism, where he was learning the church's views of good and evil. The Catholic Church has some two thousand years of experience, including experience with altar boys. It knows that boys are liable to create mischief and, entering adolescence, likely to be curious about the bodies of girls. It knows that altar boys are human. Is this the purpose of altar boys: to exemplify human nature, to remind people that there is a bit of the devil, as well as the angel, in everyone?

The altar boy is a comic character, a prankster whose mischief is essentially harmless. What is harmless in a child, however, may be evil in an adult. A voyeur is not an attractive person. Far worse are people who commit murder and claim that God told them to do it; the altar boy was flirting with the sin of pride when he took upon himself the authority to judge and punish others. It is important that the poem is written in the past tense. The adult narrator has experience that he lacked as a boy. His concepts of good and evil are no longer naïve. Evil occurs during the day as well as at night, and the sin of pride is far more serious than stealing a glance down the top of a girl's dress.

James Green

THE PURSE-SEINE

Author: Robinson Jeffers (1887-1962)
Type of poem: Lyric
First published: 1937, in *Such Counsels You Gave to Me and Other Poems*

The Poem

"The Purse-Seine" is typical of many of Robinson Jeffers's short poems. As is characteristic of lyric poems, the poet shares his personal experiences, thoughts, and opinions directly with the reader, using beautifully rendered scenes of nature to illustrate his point. It is written in Jeffers's unique verse form: a type of free verse with very long lines. The poem's twenty-four lines are divided into four unequal stanzas. The first stanza presents a scene of commercial sardine fishermen working with a particular kind of net known as a purse seine. The reader is told that this kind of fishing must be done at night when there is no moon so that the schools of fish can be located by their phosphorescent glow. Thus readers are presented with the image of a small boat at sea in nearly total darkness. The narrator then focuses in more closely with a description of the lookout man pointing out a group of fish. The helmsman circles the boat around the fish, setting the net. The bottom of the net is pulled closed, or pursed, and the trapped fish are hauled aboard.

The second stanza is a more artistic interpretation of the same event. The poet begins with a disclaimer, "I cannot tell you/ how beautiful the scene is" and then proceeds to describe it. He says it is a "little terrible" as well as beautiful because of the panic of the trapped fish as the net tightens. The beauty is in the phosphorescent glow that the fish make as they swim and thrash, churning the water into a "pool of flame." Then, in contrast, sea lions slowly rise from the darkness of the sea, separated from the sardines, their normal prey, by the net. A mention of the night studded with stars closes the scene, locating the activities described within the context of the entire universe.

The third stanza shifts to a new scene in which the narrator describes the view of a city from a hill at night. He tells the reader that the lights of the city remind him of the fish in the net. He explains that because humanity has become cut off from nature and has become dependent on the artificialities of the cities, each individual is helplessly trapped by whatever future civilization has to offer. According to the narrator, the shine of the city is the same as the glow of the fish, indicating that the net of doom is tightening around it. He predicts that "inevitable mass-disasters" will come in a few generations: Civilization will decline through political repression, revolution, or anarchy. In the final short stanza, the narrator, now identified as the poet by speaking of "our verse," asks if the reader can blame him for writing poems that are "troubled or frowning." He claims that his poem "keeps its reason" instead of becoming hysterical about such predictions of doom by accepting the fact that "cultures decay, and life's end is death."

Forms and Devices

One of the most striking aspects of the poem is the verse form. Jeffers has been praised and criticized for his unusual verse form consisting of long lines that seem to be divided arbitrarily. Some lines in this poem are twenty-two words long and take up three lines on the printed page. The lines are without rhyme, and often the rhythm is not immediately apparent. It is not quite free verse, however, and the poet himself claimed to use a system of meter and stress suggestive of the rhythms of the tides and the blood, and the patterns of everyday speech. Many critics have attempted to discover the key to this system by counting accents and lines; however, the structure of the poem seems to be driven by its meaning and the sound of its words rather than by an arbitrary, mathematical arrangement of syllables and stresses.

Jeffers's short poems usually involve the description and interpretation of a particular experience. From this basis, he goes on to comment on the experience and use it as a symbol or an analogy for some aspect of the human condition. "The Purse-Seine" follows this pattern, describing the capture of the fish and comparing it to humanity's entrapment by civilization. Jeffers's lessons are rarely left hidden: The messages are stated quite clearly. The instructional or moralistic nature of the poem is achieved through the unique narrative voice that Jeffers uses. It becomes obvious that the poet is speaking directly to the reader, especially by the time the poet refers to his own verses in the last stanza. He also speaks plainly, describing the scene in conversational language and then bluntly stating that he is comparing the purse seine net to the confining civilization of the city. The poet's tone is prophetic and admonitory, warning humans of the doom that awaits them if they follow their present course.

Jeffers is able to take this "moral high road" without offending the reader by his use of a distant perspective: He becomes an omniscient narrator as well as an individual speaking to the reader. He describes the fishing scene from an indefinite point of view that even knows the actions of the sea lions in the deep, dark water. He observes the city from a specific place on a nearby hill but also from a great psychological distance. He speaks of humanity as "them" rather than "us." This perspective gives his opinions and warnings some validity: Readers are led to believe that he can see things that they, mired in the immediate present, cannot see. The poet's conversational tone also helps readers to believe him. He uses words rooted in science and politics that readers may not be accustomed to hearing in poetry: phosphorescence, interdependence, government, and anarchy. He speaks directly to readers, saying "I cannot," "I was looking," and "I thought." At the same time, he disarms readers with beautiful descriptions of nature and metaphors of fish as rockets and cities as galaxies of stars.

Themes and Meanings

Jeffers was as much a philosopher as a poet, and no discussion of his work would be complete without mention of his philosophy of Inhumanism. This perhaps unfortunate term, coined by Jeffers himself, is often misunderstood. It has nothing to do with cruelty or meanness, though those human failings are common in his long narrative poems. Instead, it refers to a detachment that allows the poet to step outside the human condition for a more cosmic viewpoint. The poet's way of dealing with the suffering and other negative aspects of humanity and modern civilization is to see them in the context of geological or cosmological time and space. From the perspective of billions of years and the infinite distances of the universe, humankind is really a brief and perhaps not very important phenomenon. This cosmic viewpoint is underscored by the images and metaphors used in the descriptive passages in the poem. The phosphorescent fish are described as rockets and comets, and the first scene ends with the walls of night and the stars, which places the small, confined world of the fish in the net in the context of the limitless expanses of space. The city, too, is described as confined and even claustrophobic, yet it is compared to the light not only of stars but also of galaxies.

Inhumanism is the key to another of Jeffers's major themes: the beauty of the natural world. The poet is in awe of what he calls in the title of another poem "divinely superfluous beauty." This is beauty that exists for its own sake, usually unseen by humans, from the starry wheels of the galaxies to the phosphorescent glow of the fish in the sea. He even finds beauty in the violence and apparent cruelty of nature. In other poems, he praises the violence of weather and the sea, and the ferocity of hawks; in "The Purse-Seine," he praises the seemingly cruel work of catching fish. The fishermen in this poem are not part of the city and civilization; rather, they are making their living close to nature and are not condemned for killing the fish any more than the sea lions would be. They are part of the pattern of life and death and thus contribute to the beauty to be found in the natural world. From this detached, Inhumanist viewpoint, the poet sees the tragedies of civilization and its estrangement from nature, as well as its eventual decline into chaos and darkness, as acceptable or even beautiful. These things all play their small parts in the inevitable evolution of the grand ways of the universe.

Joseph W. Hinton

THE QUAKER GRAVEYARD IN NANTUCKET

Author: Robert Lowell (1917-1977)
Type of poem: Elegy
First published: 1945; collected in *Lord Weary's Castle*, 1946

The Poem

"The Quaker Graveyard in Nantucket" is one of the noisiest poems in the English language. Robert Lowell employs a multitude of harsh sounds, broken rhythms, and recurring patterns of alliteration to reflect the poem's preoccupation with the violence and turbulence of the world it depicts.

The poem is divided into seven parts, differing in length and tone. It begins with an evocation of the violent death of Warren Winslow, one of Lowell's cousins, who was lost at sea when his ship sank during World War II; the poem is dedicated to Winslow's memory. Borrowing heavily from a description of drowning victims in Henry David Thoreau's *Cape Cod* (1864), Lowell presents a grim image of the drowned man and describes a burial at sea. He also mentions Ahab, the mad whaling-ship captain in Herman Melville's *Moby Dick* (1851), who took his ship and crew with him to a watery grave in his pursuit of the white whale.

The second section depicts the bleak site of the Quaker graveyard on the island of Nantucket, where markers record the deaths of many of the island's men who were lost at sea on nineteenth century whaling expeditions. The nearby ocean is violent, noisy, and menacing, and the gulls' cries seem to echo the cries of drowning sailors. Humans, however, are the purveyors of violence, as well as its victims, as evidenced by the "hurt beast" (the harpooned whale slaughtered by Ahab's crew).

The third, fourth, and fifth sections of the poem continue to depict the wild and violent world of the ocean in which the Nantucket sailors, including Ahab's men as well as the real Nantucketers, wreak their violence on the creatures of the sea and are violently killed themselves. Lowell introduces a religious theme, first in an ironic passage in which the drowning Quaker sailors say, "'If God himself had not been on our side,/ When the Atlantic rose against us, why,/ Then it had swallowed us up quick.'" Clearly, they are about to be swallowed. The theme of religion is developed through references to the crucifixion of Christ, which the poem relates to the biblical Jonah, who spent three days in the belly of a whale. Jesus, Jonah, and the whale are all depicted as crucified and speared by the harpoons of the whalers.

The violence of the poem is put aside in the sixth section, entitled "Our Lady of Walsingham." At the time he wrote "The Quaker Graveyard in Nantucket," Lowell was a recent convert to the Roman Catholic faith, and this section of the poem borrows from a book describing an old English Catholic shrine in order to evoke a mysterious peace that is in sharp contrast to the violence of the rest of the poem. The sailors of the earlier segments are replaced by pilgrims who walk humbly to the shrine of Mary. The medieval image of Our Lady is neither beautiful nor expressive, but it presents an image of submission to a God whose purposes encompassed both the innocence of the crib at Bethlehem and the violent death of Christ at Calvary.

The final section is the most dirgelike. The winds are "empty," and the ocean is "fouled with the blue sailors." Humans kill and die, but the violence is ancient and somehow part of God's purpose. The last line asserts: "The Lord survives the rainbow of His will."

Forms and Devices

The violence that the poem depicts is reflected in many of the devices Lowell uses. The rhythm, for example, combines a basic iambic measure with many variations, producing a kind of ground swell that is interrupted violently on many occasions, as if suggesting a stormy sea. The lines are of varying lengths, and although all the lines of the poem contain end rhymes, there is no regular rhyme pattern.

The most noticeable aspect of the poem is the use of a variety of sound devices, ranging from alliteration to assonance and including echoes of various sounds as well as end rhyme. Most of these sounds are harsh, with hard vowels and plosive or stop consonants, but such sounds may be preceded by softer sounds. This can produce sudden sharp changes, as in the lines "ask for no Orphean lute/ To pluck life back."

The noisy quality of the poem resounds throughout, as in the hard vowel sounds and the *k* consonant sounds in lines such as "As the entangled, screeching mainsheet clears/ The blocks: off Madaket." Piled-up alliteration and echoing sounds show in the following: "This is the end of them, three-quarters fools,/ Snatching at straws to sail/ Seaward and seaward on the turntail whale,/ Spouting out blood and water as it rolls,/ Sick as a dog to these Atlantic shoals."

The poem contains a wealth of other devices, including allusions, primarily to *Moby Dick* and to Christian symbols, but also to classical mythology. There is personification of the sea; "the high tide/ Mutters to its hurt self." Lowell makes considerable use of metaphor—for example, in an image of the beach "Sucking the ocean's side"—and simile: "We are poured out like water." Such devices, however, are less important than the sounds that create the tone of the poem and provide its unique characteristics.

Themes and Meanings

Lowell's clear intention in "The Quaker Graveyard in Nantucket" is to depict the harshness and violence that he sees as conditions of all life and to provide an understanding of how religious faith can reconcile humans to the harsh conditions of life. The death of the author's cousin is related to all violent deaths at sea, and through the allusions to *Moby Dick* and the biblical appearances of whales, those deaths are connected to the deaths of other creatures—destruction that is caused by humankind.

The final two sections of the poem are intended to convey the "peace that passeth understanding" that is promised by Christianity. It is presented in the section entitled "Our Lady of Walsingham," and this peace is not easy or pretty: The image of Mary has neither beauty nor expression, and the will of God, referred to in the final section, is not easy to understand. The reference includes the sobering reminder that "the Lord

God formed man from the sea's slime" and that death has always been part of life. Worship of the Judeo-Christian God requires unquestioning faith.

The poem's final meaning, however, is anything but simple, in large part because of the variations in tone of the poem's different parts. There is a vigor and vitality implicit in the loudness and harshness of the first five sections that is muted in the final two sections. The shift to the reverence of the sixth section is almost an anticlimax, and when the poem moves from the shrine at Walsingham back to the ocean in the final section, there is a sense of fatigue almost amounting to depression. This is to some extent dissipated by the surging grandeur of the final nine lines, but the sense of exhaustion is very strong in the closing section.

The result of this is that the poem's intention to show religious faith reconciling humans to their harsh fate is subverted to some extent by the poet's fascination with what he can express in language. Lowell seems to have been in love with words and with the sounds of words, especially in his younger years, and this shows more clearly in "The Quaker Graveyard in Nantucket" than in any other poem. More vitality is instilled into the depiction of the terrors of this world than into portraying the consolations of religion, so that the fascination of the struggles of life and death outweighs any attempt to reconcile humans to their fate.

John M. Muste

THE QUALITY OF SPRAWL

Author: Les A. Murray (1938-   )
Type of poem: Lyric
First published: 1983, in *The People's Otherworld*

The Poem

Sprawl commonly denotes an unevenly extended spatial position lacking visual order, as in "urban sprawl." This fifty-line free-verse poem adapts the usage to identify
a behavioral stance in which individuals exceed the limits of conventional behavior
to achieve an end. The poem contains eight stanzas, each of which is an independent
unit of illustration. The word "Sprawl," which begins each stanza, is the subject of a
present-tense statement of what sprawl is or does contrasted with its negative image.

Many of the characters and incidents representing sprawl have the exaggerated
quality of social "tall tales," but are offered in a straightforward and definite tone that
invites belief. The opening incident shows sprawl to be a farmer cutting down a Rolls-
Royce to make a pickup truck. The reaction of the company in trying to reclaim its image is predictably routine and bespeaks a lack of sprawl.

In the second set of illustrations, a farmer sows his fields by plane, a hitchiker is
driven "that extra hundred miles home," and someone concentrates on internal being.
These are acts of "sprawl" because they exceed accepted norms for a purpose that can
be seen as practical. Wasteful and useless gestures such as "lighting cigars with ten-
dollar notes" are not acts of sprawl.

A contrast is also drawn with "style," which has display as its goal. Sprawl extends
the rules, as when racing dogs are fed "liver and beer," or when a "dozen" bananas are
actually fourteen.

Acts of sprawl become expressive or powerful when words and conventions are
powerless. When logger Hank Stamper, a hero figure in a film drawn from a Ken
Kesey novel, faces a powerful lumber conglomerate, his eloquence consists of using
his chain saw to dissect a bureaucrat's desk.

The fourth illustration turns to historical information. Sprawl is always on the side
of the individual but "is never brutal," as was Simon de Montfort in his revolt against
Henry the Third.

All human activities leave room for sprawl. Among those parts of poetry that qualify as sprawl, the poet humorously includes the nonexistent fifteenth to twenty-first
lines of a sonnet. He continues to tease the reader, stating that, though he is familiar
with paintings possessing sprawl, "I have sprawl enough to have forgotten which
paintings."

Sprawl is a semiheroic stand against authority that may be seen as "criminal pre-
sumption" by those with a group identity. The sixth stanza mentions the Borgia Pope
Alexander proclaiming the division between the Spanish and the Portuguese "New
World" as such a questionable example.

The actors in the next-to-last stanza are Australian eccentrics, such as Beatrice Miles. A street person, she reputedly traveled by taxi from Sydney to Melbourne on coin donations from impromptu recitations. Sprawl is thus elevated to a state worthy of public pride. The poet applauds the independence of spirit that leads such people to follow their impulses.

The final stanza discusses sprawl and its possible effect on society. Sprawl is subversive in a mischievous way. It endures only if it is not taken seriously by those it mocks. The poem ends in a somber warning: "people have been shot for sprawl."

Forms and Devices

Stanzaic organization is a conspicuous element in the framework of "The Quality of Sprawl." Free verse is often organized according to word and line placement that avoids recurring patterns in favor of rhythmic effects and visual configurations. In many unrhymed poems, stanzaic division is irregular or nonexistent.

By comparison, the discursive content of this poem is presented in eight orderly stanzas of roughly equal informational importance. The basic component of all stanzas is the complete grammatical sentence. Phrases do not dangle or drift loosely. Most are integrated within sentences as clauses. Word groupings in longer sentences are regulated by means of the correct use of commas and parentheses, though some internal quotation marks are left out.

A large variety of sentence length and structure is used. The five lines of the first stanza are a single, elongated compound-complex sentence with three clauses. A short, simple sentence, "Sprawl occurs in art," opens the fifth stanza. While the stanzas range between five and nine lines, the number of grammatical sentences in each varies from one to five.

Every stanza can be read independently. No sentence or idea is continued from one stanza to the next, nor are there intricate transitions between the stanzas. In place of such links, a basic internal organization is repeated. Each stanza contains one central statement about sprawl followed by a discussion focusing on an example of this aspect of sprawl. An internal balance is formed with a corresponding glimpse of what is never sprawl. The word "sprawl" is used to begin each new stanza, producing a visual uniformity that further connects the individual stanzas. The final stanza alone breaks this pattern by adding "No" to its first line.

Despite this reliance on the conventions of written composition, Les A. Murray maintains the liveliness of natural speech. He sustains a tone of congeniality, choosing vocabulary that is never didactic or argumentative, creating an impression of immediate understanding between reader and author. This is necessary to ensure that sprawl is accepted as an existing human characteristic, not a function of Murray's reactive imagination. The audience is, therefore, addressed in language that is specific rather than general, with examples that are concrete rather than abstract. The car that is turned into a utility vehicle is identified by brand name. The "lighting" of a cigar "with ten-dollar notes" is called an act of "idiot ostentation and murder."

The few places where language is distilled beyond the commonplace stand out. The first instance (stanza 6) is the use of a Latin term, "*In petto*," in place of more everyday words such as "secretly" or "to himself." An ordinary reader would need to look up this term, especially since it is the hinge on which the example of Pope Alexander's act of sprawl turns. Another atypical line, "And would that it were more so" (stanza 7), is notable for its fervor as well as its poetic syntax.

The overall good humor with which Murray entertains as he informs offsets the more serious tone that surfaces at the poem's conclusion. The poem remains a light handling of a theme that Murray believes is worth serious consideration. He accomplishes this by using a lively and diverse array of subjects—from folk wisdom to British painting, from Catholic history to the author's own kinfolk—that provide pictures of sprawl in action.

The anecdotal approach, rather than one of full narrative richness, presumes acceptance and precludes close analysis. Vignettes are offered in a quick succession of cartoonlike drawings of sprawl. These are focused by means of a contrasting negation of sprawl within each frame. The overall effect is that of a good-natured piece of entertainment with a serious theme.

Themes and Meanings

The theme of this poem is the resilient spirit of the individual who refuses to be rendered helpless by the norms of society. Despite Murray's disclaimer that "Sprawl is really classless" (stanza 7), this poem is very much about class. The hero is the "little person," the average citizen who does not normally control fate but who, on occasion, seizes a chance to make a forceful personal statement. The unspoken villain is the establishment, which evokes conformity to rules even when they are meaningless or makes decisions on a scale that negates individual preference.

Murray presents sprawl as inherent in certain types of actions regardless of motive or consequence. The first story, for example, is clear, but many details are left out. One can imagine that there is some reason, such as a dispute or the age of the vehicle, behind the transformation of the luxury motor car into a mundane truck, but such background detail remains unnecessary. The degree of success achieved by Hank Stamper's response is similarly irrelevant. The emphasis is on the largesse of spirit that connects such diverse acts as "farming by aeroplane" and going far out of the way to take home a hitchhiker.

From the outset, there is no attempt to offer a concise, dictionary-style definition of "sprawl" as used by the author. No exact synonyms are given. Such a verbal approached is avoided. In its place, a lively, often satirical, extended definition is formed, example by example.

"Sprawl" here is a noun of adjectival fullness, describing and defining a certain group of actions and reactions that will seem immediately familiar to most readers, even those who do not engage in such behavior. Its application is to any nonroutine human response that blends the grandly inelegant with the forcefully expressive once-in-a-lifetime gesture. "Sprawl" colors human actions in glaring neon hues that break through the routine sameness and the dull everyday necessity to "fit in."

Murray begins and ends by applauding sprawl. Sprawl is noticeable but not showy. It may be inelegant, but it is not disgusting. Inventiveness and practicality merge with stubbornness and independence in sprawl. It endures because it encourages action and makes people feel good about themselves.

Karla Sigel

QUEEN-ANN'S-LACE

Author: William Carlos Williams (1883-1963)
Type of poem: Lyric
First published: 1921, in *Sour Grapes*

The Poem

Written in nonmetrical verse, "Queen-Ann's-Lace" is a single-stanza, twenty-one line poem. Its title suggests it is about the common field flower also known as the wild carrot. A wide, white flower about a hand's width in size, Queen Anne's lace contains scores of tiny blossoms and, in the center, a dark spot. In *I Wanted to Write a Poem* (1958), William Carlos Williams said that he used "straight observation . . . in [his] four poems about flowers, 'Daisy,' 'Primrose,' . . . 'Queen Ann's Lace,' and 'Great Mullen.'" He "thought of them as still lifes . . . . [and] looked at the actual flowers as they grew." Indeed, the poem's speaker might be observing a field of Queen Anne's lace as the sun's rays touch it.

The poem's opening line, however, announces a much different subject: the whiteness of a woman's body, which the speaker contrasts briefly in the first three lines with "anemone petals." He finds "Her body is not so white," "nor so smooth—nor/ so remote a thing." Then, throughout the remainder of the poem, he compares her body's whiteness with a commonplace "field/ of the wild carrot." With this comparison, there is "no question" of too much "whiteness," for at each flower's center rests "a purple mole."

Initially, the wildflower exerts its power, "taking/ the field by force," not allowing the grass to "raise above it." In the second half of the poem, however, the woman's body responds to her male lover, "a blossom under his touch." "Wherever/ his hand has lain there is/ a tiny purple blemish." Ultimately, his touch erotically transforms and purifies her (and the whole field of Queen Anne's lace), first into "a/ white desire," then "to whiteness gone over." Just as such a field of wildflowers would respond to the light and warmth of the sun and could not live without them, the woman responds to her male lover.

Clearly, Williams moved well beyond his "straight observation" of actual flowers, the still life which was the starting point for this poem. Rather than being simply a poem about a flower, "Queen-Ann's-Lace" represents an intense human experience, a moment during which the poetic imagination transforms straight observation of a common wildflower into a sensuous—and sensual—moment of awareness. Focusing, at this point in his career, on the essence of physical things, Williams later explained, "Emotion clusters about common things, the pathetic often stimulates the imagination to new patterns."

Forms and Devices

At the time Williams wrote "Queen-Ann's-Lace," he had been, for several years, a member of the Imagists, a small group of early twentieth century poets that included

Ezra Pound, H. D. (Hilda Doolittle), John Gould Fletcher, Amy Lowell, and Wallace Stevens. Rejecting Romantic idealism and Victorian moralism, the Imagists advocated, instead, the use of common speech and concrete images, the freedom to choose any subject matter, and the need to create new rhythms. "Queen-Ann's-Lace" exhibits all of these principles. With only one word that might puzzle some readers ("anemone," a flower in the buttercup family), its language is simple. The poem, furthermore, presents, in detail, an image of a common wildflower that most readers have already experienced or easily can. Likewise, its subject is not the typical rose of Romantic and Victorian poetry but a wild carrot and a woman's body, both energized with sexual meaning.

Although Williams begins the poem with a simile that contrasts the whiteness of a woman's body with the anemone, it is mainly through metaphor that he transforms his straight observation, his still life, into a dynamic field of action that reveals the life and energy hidden in Queen Anne's lace. To create this dynamic field, Williams uses a central metaphor: Her body "is a field/ of the wild carrot taking/ the field by force." He then extends the analogy throughout the remainder of the poem. Forceful, but *not* "white as can be" and certainly *not* virginal, the woman (and the flowers) respond to the lover's caresses with increasing intensity marked by changing color. Thus, instead of the "remote" whiteness of anemone petals, "Wherever/ his hand has lain there is/ a tiny purple blemish," then "a/ white desire," and finally "whiteness gone over."

While the poem's movement from beginning to end may seem circular, from "white as/ anemone petals" to "whiteness gone over," it is actually spiral. It does not return to where it began but moves to a different plane. The "white desire," the "pious wish to whiteness gone over" are not "remote"; they depend upon the lover's touch, just as the transformation of the flower depends upon the poet's subjective observation and interpretation. As critic Peter Halter notes in *The Revolution in the Visual Arts and the Poetry of William Carlos Williams* (1994), "Throughout his life Williams was to remain diffident with regard to too facile use of metaphors and similes, but throughout his life he was to use them as a poetic device for making the energy in things manifest."

In "Queen-Ann's-Lace," as in many of his other poems, Williams does not employ traditional metrical or stanzaic patterns. As critic Stephen Cushman notes in *William Carlos Williams and the Meanings of Measure* (1985), Williams's prosody is "based not on time, accents, sounds, or recurrent phrases, but on lineation" marked by enjambment (run-on lines). Thus, to create the "new rhythms" called for by his fellow Imagists and his own particular form of "free verse," Williams systematically used enjambed lineation, carrying rhythmical and grammatical sense from one line to the next without pause or punctuation. As a result, the lines of "Queen-Ann's-Lace" often do not begin or end as the reader might expect. Only three of six sentences, for instance, begin at the start of a line, and only three end at the conclusion of a line. Likewise, only eight of the poem's twenty-one lines end with pauses or stops; conversely, eleven lines contain one or more internal pauses or stops. Ultimately, however, the dominant run-on lines of Williams's nonmetrical verse establish rhythm between lines and connect line to line.

Because enjambment appears so frequently in Williams's poetry, its absence—a change in the fundamental pattern—becomes noteworthy. In "Queen-Ann's-Lace," the last four lines are end-stopped, not enjambed. Significantly, these lines describe, in a series of images, what the poet's "touch" has caused the field of flowers to become "white desire, empty, a single stem,/ a cluster, flower by flower,/ a pious wish to whiteness gone over—/ or nothing." Arresting and emphatic, the punctuation and rhythm here parallel each striking, powerful, and discrete image. These effects would be blunted if the images were broken up and carried over from one line to another.

Themes and Meanings

In his personal epic, *Paterson* (1946-1958), and in several other places, Williams writes, "No ideas but in things," declaring that the poet's role is to perceive and express through "immediate contact with the world" the objects which surround him. The poetic imagination can make a poem of anything, even a field of common wildflowers. Precisely such a poem, "Queen-Ann's-Lace," appeared in *Sour Grapes* (1921), a book of verse whose title reflected Williams's mood at the time, one filled, as he writes in *I Wanted to Write a Poem*, with "disappointment, sorrow. . . . [for he] felt rejected by the world." This very positive poem and several others like it in *Sour Grapes*, however, embody his delight in physical things, and his ability to discover their hidden beauty. Beginning with straight observation, he transforms the wild carrot and makes a poem which is a woman.

In *Poets of Reality* (1969), critic J. Hillis Miller observes that "Queen-Ann's-Lace" also admirably represents "Williams's power to charge a whole scene with sexual meaning," a "constant mode of his relation to the world" that is demonstrated throughout his work. Indeed, the poem reflects the relaxed sexual mores of the 1920's in the United States, for Williams openly depicts the flower-woman's sensual arousal and rapture under the sun-poet's touch. The poem does not, on the other hand, embody the era's new freedoms for women (for example, the right to vote guaranteed by ratification of the Nineteenth Amendment in August, 1920). Displaying his opposition to such freedoms, Williams portrays the woman and the flower in "Queen-Ann's-Lace" as both earthbound and submissive. In contrast, the sun and the man that touch them are unrestrained and dominant. The flower may thus prevail over "the grass/ [which] does not raise above it" and take "the field by force," but it blossoms only wherever the male sun's "hand has lain." Likewise, the woman can only respond to the man's erotic touch, which fulfills her "pious wish to whiteness," purifies her, and makes her more than "nothing." She (and the flower which represents her) may be lovely and sensual, but she owes her existence to the poetic hand and imagination that created her.

Joseph M. Nassar

QUESTION AND ANSWER IN THE MOUNTAIN

Author: Li Bo (701-762)
Type of poem: Lyric
First published: wr. c. 753, as "Shan zhong wen da"; in *Li Taibo chuanji*, 1717; English translation collected in *The Penguin Book of Chinese Verse*, 1962

The Poem

There are two other alternative titles for this poem in some existing editions, but neither is as apt. The first, "Answer to a Question," is too general, whereas the second, "Answer from the Mountain, to a Worldly Person," is too explicit.

The poem begins with an innocent question, which can be translated differently depending on which of the two variant texts is used. According to one text, the line can be rendered as: "You ask me what I am doing dwelling in the Emerald Mountain." In the second text, the line would be: "You ask me why I intend to dwell in the Emerald Mountain." The first reading specifies dwelling in the mountain as a fact, whereas the second suggests that the poet is contemplating doing so. The distinction between the two readings will have a significant bearing on the rest of the poem.

To answer the question, the poet writes that "I smile but make no reply, for my heart itself is at leisure." In the variant text, the poet simply says nothing instead of making no reply. Although the wording "make no reply" echoes the title of the poem appropriately, saying nothing could be an interesting reading because it suggests that the poet does not wish to be bothered by the question at all. This reading is more consistent with the sense of serenity expressed in the phrase, "for my heart itself is at leisure."

Having handled the question in one way or another, the poet begins to muse upon the pleasures of the idyllic world. In the last two lines, Li Bo describes a locale with peach blossoms floating along the stream "into the distance." The variant text for line 3, which has the peach blossoms flow "in a meandering manner" instead of into the distance, is visually more pleasing but less meaningful, since the whole point of the stream is that it is a conduit into a horizon lost to the mundane world. In this realm, the poet concludes, there is a different heaven and earth not belonging to the world of human beings.

The relatively large number of varying texts and titles for this brief lyric suggests that the poem may have been popular enough to be widely circulated and thus corrupted in the process. The variant texts for the poem appear to be a minor issue, as in each of the three instances the difference involves one word (in Chinese) only. As pointed out above, however, the one-word difference in line 1 would require one to read the whole poem differently. If dwelling in the Emerald Mountain is already a fact, the poem would be a descriptive record; if it is only a matter of the poet's contemplation, then the whole poem would be a psychological projection.

Forms and Devices

"Question and Answer in the Mountain" is written in the seven-character, truncated-verse format. It does not employ the matched couplet usually found in "recent-style" Chinese poems. Although this is not an irregular practice, it gives one the impression of "craftlessness" and freedom from formal constraints—which are some of Li Bo's virtues as a poet.

The poem employs several rhetorical devices. The first is the question-answer situation commonly found in Chinese writings, including poetry and religious (Taoist and Buddhist) dialogues. The device is effective for writers who intend to demonstrate some sort of truth, and Li Bo's poem obviously has a similar purpose. The second rhetorical device is found in line 2, where a negation (not having words to say) is juxtaposed with an affirmation (having leisure at heart), with the latter being reinforced as the sharper focus. Because line 2 does not really answer the innocent question in line 1, a tension is suddenly created for the next two lines to resolve. Finally, there is also a paradox in the poem: Although the poet has no answer to offer his interrogator, he has in fact answered the question in the end.

More important than the rhetorical maneuvers mentioned above, an allusion is used in the last two lines. In general, allusions are an indispensable resource for Chinese poets because explicit or implied references to historical figures, places, or events could give the poem an ornamental texture or thematic accent. In Li Bo's case, he alludes to a tale by T'ao Ch'ien (also called T'ao Yüan-ming) entitled "The Peach Blossom Spring." The story describes how a fisherman, following the trail along a peach-blossomed stream, reaches a secluded farming community. The people of this land, thanks to their ancestors who escaped the turmoils of the Warring States era, have been left alone to enjoy their idyllic life for hundreds of years, undisturbed by the vicissitudes of the dynasties outside. Having been entertained, the fisherman leaves, but somehow his strange encounter becomes public knowledge, thus jeopardizing the lost horizon. In the end, however, no one is able to relocate the secluded community. In his poem, Li Bo not only compares the Emerald Mountain to the Peach Blossom Spring figuratively, but he also objectifies the desire to get away from the mundane world and lead the life of a recluse.

Themes and Meanings

In approximately 743, Li Bo served as a court poet (in effect a courtier) in the capital Ch'ang-an. Because of the scheming, the favoritism, and above all, the demoralizing intrigues that are part and parcel of courtly life, he resigned from his post. Between 744 and 755, he traveled around the country, visiting many places before reaching Hsüan-chou in 753, where he stayed for some time and wrote the famous poem, "A Farewell to Li Yun in the Xie Tiao Pavilion." During his tours, Li Bo could have seen foreboding signs of the An-Lu rebellion, which was to break out in 755 and decimate the country on a massive scale. "Question and Answer in the Mountain" was probably written shortly before 753 while the poet was visiting the Emerald Mountain, in modern day Anlu County, Hubei Province.

The poem is a classic example of how intellectuals in traditional China might have dealt with the frustrations of public life if they did not wish to be enmeshed in it, and this is the real question beneath the surface of "Question and Answer in the Mountain." In general, when times are favorable, intellectuals would go into public service and carry out their duties according to the precepts of Confucianism. Once the commitment proves impossible to sustain (because of the corruption of the court), however, they would abandon the official life in order to return to the fields and farms, or travel among the mountains and rivers—in effect becoming hermits. It should be noted that cultivating one's own gardens and traveling casually are important metaphors in Taoism, which is a central component of Li Bo's philosophy of life.

In the contexts outlined above, the first main theme is therefore the withdrawal from public life and its accompanying pleasures, particularly a sense of freedom and leisure. This is also the real answer conveyed by the smile and the silence in line 2. Considering Li Bo's experience with the court, it is no accident that his poem invokes the poet-recluse T'ao Yüan-ming of the Chin Dynasty, who set an example for intellectuals of integrity. The first two lines of the poem, indeed, seem to echo T'ao's fifth poem of the "Drinking Wine" sequence.

Because of the landscape setting associated with reclusive life, the congeniality of nature is another important theme in Li Bo's poem. Defining human experience positively, the landscape provides the poet with an alternative existence that is both cathartic and fulfilling. Furthermore, the allusion to T'ao Yüan-ming's fable makes it clear that the actual landscape of the Emerald Mountain and the fictional space of the Peach Blossom Spring eventually coalesce into a "utopia." Desirable as it is, this "utopia" is nevertheless characterized by an inherent irony of which Li Bo may have been aware: The ultimate truth about the Peach Blossom Spring is that the premise of its sole existence is the real world being torn apart by war. Although the An-Lu rebellion had not yet broken out when Li Bo wrote about the different heaven and earth in his newfound world apart from humanity, it would seem that he was diagnosing and divining the problem of his time accurately.

Balance Chow

RABBI BEN EZRA

Author: Robert Browning (1812-1889)
Type of poem: Dramatic monologue
First published: 1864, in *Dramatis Personae*

The Poem

"Rabbi Ben Ezra" is a long poem of 192 lines expressing Robert Browning's optimistic philosophy of life regarding both youth and old age. Youth is a time of struggle for glimpses of God's omnipotence in an imperfect world. Old age can usher in the wisdom of spiritual maturity that comes from recognizing divine perfection behind earthly imperfection and from perceiving God's unbounded love as well as God's omnipotence.

Abraham Ibn Ezra (1092?-1167) was a Spanish rabbi who, in his middle years, was driven by persecution from Spain into a life of travel and scholarship. He was a theologian, a philosopher, a linguist, and a scientist. A strong believer in immortality, he found the second half of his life much more productive and satisfactory than the first half. The ideas of the poem are Browning's, and they are not always in accord with the rabbi's actual sentiments.

The first stanza of the poem enunciates the philosophy of the whole work and begins a series of exhortations encouraging readers to look forward to the aging process that brings a mature faith in God's providence to take what is defective and partial in this world of seeming limitations and to make all right and whole.

Stanzas 2 through 9 refuse to chastise youth for the frustrated ambitions, doubts and confusions, and unsatisfying pleasures that serve the useful purpose of redirecting human striving for higher spiritual goals. Humankind was born to struggle and aspire and not to rest, as animals do, in a satiety of low material pleasures. A divine spark energizes the human heart into undertaking a quest for infinite satisfactions centered in God.

Stanzas 10 through 19 note that the experience of youth, with its glimpses of God's power and perfection, prepare for the greater wisdom of old age and the discovery of God's perfect love during the evolution of humans from brutes to spiritual beings whose struggle for oneness with God continues even in the hereafter. Therefore, let all that makes up humans—youth and age, body and soul—be cherished in their evolving spirituality and quest for the divine.

Stanzas 20 through 25 affirm that the perception of ultimate truth in old age transcends the disputations of youth, the disparate convictions of confused thinkers, or the voguish values of the masses. On the contrary, knowledge of the "Right/ And Good and Infinite" rests on our intimations of immortality and those faint "Fancies" or intuitions of something immeasurably greater, too often ignored by the vulgar populace.

Stanzas 26 through 36 elaborate on the biblical metaphor of God as the divine potter who molds the clay of a human's spiritual nature on the spinning wheel of the world of time and transient matter ("He fixed thee 'mid this dance/ Of plastic circumstance"). Under the divine fashioning of the struggling and striving human clay, humans are ultimately wrought into a heavenly chalice of spiritual perfection for the slaking of the thirst of their Creator. Thus, human life in youth, age, and death has a providential purpose of attaining spiritual perfection.

Forms and Devices

"Rabbi Ben Ezra" is a dramatic monologue of thirty-two stanzas, each consisting of six lines with an experimental rhyme scheme (*aabccb*). The prevailing meter is iambic trimeter ("Grŏw óld ălŏng wĭth mé!"), but the rhyming third and sixth lines in each stanza employ iambic pentameter ("Thĕ lást ŏf lífe, fŏr whích thĕ fírst wăs máde"). The musical effect of short and long lines of iambic beats is an alternating staccato and legato (smooth) sound system that parallels the sense of the poem's alternating concern with dynamic yearnings and divine satisfactions, where human yearnings have their ultimate rest. Consonance and assonance permeate the poem ("Grow old along with me!/ The best is yet to be").

The primary paradox of the poem is the reconciliation of the oppositions of earthly imperfection and divine perfection by affirming that doubt and limitation teach humanity faith in ultimate spiritual fulfillment ("For thence,—a paradox/ Which comforts while it mocks"). Metaphors abound. Human aspirations are implicitly compared to plucking flowers (lines 7-9), admiring stars (lines 10-12), and waging chivalric war (lines 79-84). Throughout the poem, the dichotomy of the material and spiritual sides of human nature is metaphorically expressed through the contraries of "clod" and "spark"; brutish "beast" and "god in the germ"; and "flesh" and "soul, in its rose-mesh." These metaphors, in turn, feed into the poem's climactic metaphor of the potter (God) molding clay (a human's spiritual nature) on a spinning wheel (the world of time and transient matter) to transform humanity into a heavenly chalice of spiritual perfection, slaking the thirst of the Creator.

Two biblical passages inspired Browning's metaphor of the potter. First, Isaiah 64:8, "But now, O Lord, thou art our father; we are the clay, and thou our potter; and we are all the work of thy hand." Also Romans 9:21, where Paul asks, "Hath not the potter power over the clay, of the same lump to make one vessel unto honour, and another unto dishonour?"

Browning was a modern master of the dramatic monologue, a poetic form in which a single person speaks, often at a moment of crisis, for the purpose of revealing both the self and the society conditioning the speaker. "Rabbi Ben Ezra" is not typical of Browning's best dramatic monologues, because the poem is less a revealing portrayal of the speaker and his age and is more a declamatory presentation of the author's optimistic, faintly Neoplatonic Christian philosophy of life.

The language and syntax are characteristic of Browning's elliptical, rough, and even grotesque style that so appealed to modernist poets of the twentieth century and that captured the dynamic incongruities of Browning's aspiring, struggling humanity in an imperfect world. For example, line 24 is typically difficult, rushed, compressed, and experimental: "Irks care the crop-full bird? Frets doubt the maw-crammed beast?" Its labored phrasing communicates the question: Do care and doubt bother the bird and brute whose bellies are full? The answer is no. Only a heaven-starved humanity needs more than finite satisfactions.

Themes and Meanings

"Rabbi Ben Ezra" is a poem about a Jewish thinker who sums up Browning's optimistic vision of an imperfect, heaven-starved humanity searching through youthful doubts and trials for mature intimations of immortality that come in old age as a prelude to optimum spiritual fulfillment after death.

According to Browning's philosophy of life, God created an imperfect world as a testing-ground for the full and final realization of human nature (with its immortal soul) in a heaven of spiritual perfection. Browning's optimism was not blind; it was continually being tested by his awareness and acceptance of the evils of the world and human nature ("Then, welcome each rebuff/ That turns earth's smoothness rough"). The optimism that once made "Rabbi Ben Ezra" a favorite of Victorian fans of Browning, however, eroded the poem's popularity among twentieth century readers accustomed to harsher cultural realities and put off by the bouncing exhortations and affirmations in the verses. Underlying the poem's theme of ultimate spiritual perfection behind apparent mortal limitations are three contrasting motifs of age and youth, godlike human and brute, and potter and clay.

The works of Abraham Ibn Ezra that Browning was most likely to have known were commentaries on the Old Testament. Although elements of Ezra's philosophy are expressed in the monologue, Browning did not attempt to capture the spirit of medieval thought, but rather to express his own vigorous optimism tinged with Neoplatonic Christian idealism.

"Rabbi Ben Ezra" explores problems of faith and doubt, spirituality and evolution (for example, Darwinism) that troubled Browning's Victorian contemporaries. In particular, the speaker's rejection of low pleasures in the human quest for true happiness may be Browning's dismissal of the hedonism in Edward FitzGerald's *The Rubáiyát of Omar Khayyám* (1859), which had similarly employed the metaphor of the potter and the spinning wheel.

Thomas M. Curley

RAGGED ISLAND

Author: Edna St. Vincent Millay (1892-1950)
Type of poem: Lyric
First published: 1954, in *Mine the Harvest*

The Poem

Edna St. Vincent Millay's "Ragged Island" is a twenty-four-line descriptive poem that expresses the poet's deep connection to the Maine island in Casco Bay where she and her husband summered for many years. She meditates on the distinctive attributes of this island and its beneficial effects. Intimate in its approach, the poem addresses an unspecified "you," most likely Millay herself, no stranger to Ragged Island.

The opening gesture of the poem is a fifteen-line segment punctuated as a single sentence. The first and last lines of this segment begin with the word "There" to emphasize the island itself. Its outstanding feature is a steep cliff at the top of which spruces grow. Because of the shape of this cliff and the way it plunges into the sea, there is no perceptible wave action—low tide or high tide makes little difference. Instead, the surrounding ocean simply "moves up and down" the cliff face. The speaker meditates on this feature. To her, it seems "as if/ All had been done, and long ago, that needed/ Doing." Ragged Island emerges from the first ten lines as an extraordinary, memorable place. Nothing clutters the aspect of "Clean cliff going down as deep as clear water can reach."

In the rest of the poem's first sentence, Millay draws a contrast between the "eastern wall" of Ragged Island and other, more ordinary seascapes. Because of the cliff and the lack of beach, there are neither people nor things here, only the ocean and that wall of rock. Whatever might have crashed up against the cliff has left no sign. With no seaside detritus to distract the observer, Ragged Island's cliff face offers a transcendental experience: "There, thought unbraids itself, and the mind becomes single." Overall, the effect of the island is peaceful and unitary.

Composed of nine lines, the second segment of the poem also begins with the word "There" but contains three sentences, each set apart yet all leading to the same conclusion. Departing from the description of the cliff, the speaker describes someone rowing a boat peacefully toward Ragged Island. The rower causes no unseemly disturbance; the ocean simply folds back over the place where the rower has been, and there is "no scar from the cutting of your placid keel." This delicate image is followed by statements underlining Ragged Island's effect: "Care becomes senseless there; pride and promotion/ Remote." Millay stresses the importance of observing well in order for the island's full effect to occur. Taken up by observing the place, the rower is free from the intrusion of ordinary feelings.

To clarify Ragged Island's effect, Millay contrasts it with experiences and passions of the world beyond this seascape. While she recognizes the importance of engagement with the world, Ragged Island makes passionate involvement in the world seem pointless. The island experience is definitely outside the ordinary realm; even "thrift is waste." What is the point of ordinary virtues in a place whose effect is so extraordinary and spiritual?

The poem culminates in an expression of deep longing to be in the island environment, mainly because the speaker can experience peace and quiet "under the silent spruces." Even the evening descends differently; without hurry, it simply gets dark. Thus there is no anxiety about time passing or about mortality. When death occurs, it does not sully the ocean, which remains intrinsically pure.

Forms and Devices

"Ragged Island" is loosely rhymed with a predominantly iambic rhythm, some of it strict, some fairly loose. In key places, the iambic foot is strong: "you row with tranquil oars" or "you only look; you scarcely feel." The last nine lines of the poem are rhymed in an *ababcdcdd* scheme. This is a poem composed in a traditional manner but with a lack of rigidity about rhyme and meter.

Syntactically, however, the first fifteen lines are tightly constructed. Through a series of independent clauses punctuated by semicolons, Millay creates a long, periodic sentence. The reader is propelled to the end point: "There, thought unbraids itself, and the mind becomes single." To achieve coherence, Millay employs a series of parallel phrases beginning with the word "no": "no wave breaks," "no driftwood there," "no beach," and, once again, "No driftwood." The "no" is understood in lines 13 and 14, where she simply mentions "Barrels" and "Lobster-buoys." She withholds the "no" in order to focus on the description of objects you'll find elsewhere than Ragged Island. The choice of "unbraids" as a verb reinforces her dropping of the pattern. "Thought" loosens; there is no intertwining with perceived strands coming together to make a whole. There is simply wholeness or oneness.

Millay employs alliteration in the middle of the poem, where she notes the "Clean cliff," the driftwood that gets "hefted home," and the "Barrels, banged ashore." The sounds here are percussive, the brevity of the syllables akin to the speaker's clarity and sharpness of vision. The clipped quality of the diction mellows somewhat in the quatrain about rowing "with tranquil oars." While there is alliteration in "Shows no scar," Millay employs a softer sound and reinforces it with the sibilance in "placid keel." "Scar" is a significant metaphor. The rowboat may "cut" through the ocean, but there is no division, no separation, no violence.

Lines 20 and 21 are notable for the assonance contained in the statement concerning "adventure" as "aimless ardour." Also striking is the paradox of "thrift is waste." In both instances, Millay views the values of the outer world—whether "adventure" or "thrift"—as being useless on Ragged Island. Her poetic devices heighten her meaning.

The imagery and diction of the final three lines introduce a somber, almost funereal tone. The speaker longs to be on Ragged Island "under the silent spruces." The preposition "under" suggests a burial. There is no more rowing, the evening is "quiet," and "the sea [is] with death acquainted." The element of eternity is introduced with the description of the sea as "forever chaste." With all its teeming life, the ocean hardly seems a pure place. Perhaps chastity has more to do with the speaker's ultimate state of being, no longer sullied by physicality but totally enveloped in the spiritual realm.

Themes and Meanings

The woman who wrote "Ragged Island" was not the darling of the New York literary world whose "candle burn[ed] at both ends," as she once was. Millay was aging, and her speaker sheds worldly concerns such as achievement or ambition and instead seeks spiritual union. "Ragged Island" was published posthumously in 1954. Millay had died four years earlier, and this poem could be read as a desire for a peaceful death. If so, its gestures and images take on an eerie quality. Not a simple poem about the desire for unity with nature, this poem anticipates the end of life. In it, Millay composes the preferred setting for her release from earthly concerns and from her physical being.

The speaker of "Ragged Island" is exhilarated by coming close to the chosen place. The opening repetition, "There, there," conveys her excitement. If "no wave breaks," there is no crash of surf, thus minimal sound. Here it is "as if/ All had been done, and long ago, that needed/ Doing." Millay knows that "cold tide" and how it moves differently here on Ragged Island's eastern edge. She longs for that "Clean cliff going down as deep as clear water can reach." One could read that plunge as Millay's perception about the end of life. If so, it is chilling.

The poem could be read simply as an expression of an old truth: Spiritual unification with nature is worth seeking. In Millay's austere "Ragged Island," this unification comes if one is willing to separate from worldly concerns and social intercourse: The rower is alone. Her theme is clearly articulated: "Care becomes senseless there; pride and promotion/ Remote." At the same time, the poem takes on more depth and poignancy when read as the poet's anticipation of her own death. She confronts it bravely and with clear vision.

Millay's best work often came when she wrote about her experiences in settings such as this Maine island. With its chiseled clarity and the formality of its devices, "Ragged Island" is typical Millay. She always preferred traditional methods of writing poems. Over time she wrote a looser stanza, as here in "Ragged Island," with its varied line lengths and flexible rhyme scheme. She paints a vivid seascape for her readers, who can appreciate the sonority of her rhymes, her alliteration, and her assonance. The energy of the poem, however, goes toward its series of negations, among them those "Lobster-buoys, on the eel-grass of the sheltered cove." In order to enter the full experience of the poem, one needs to learn how to shut out such tempting distractions. Most people avoid thinking about death; Millay imagines it coolly and without self-pity. This is the importance of her poem.

Claire Keyes

THE RAISING OF LAZARUS

Author: Rainer Maria Rilke (1875-1926)
Type of poem: Lyric
First published: 1934, as "Auferweckung des Lazarus," in *Späte Gedichte*; English
translation collected in *Poems, 1906 to 1926*, 1957

The Poem

Rainer Marie Rilke wrote his only novel, *Die Aufzeichnungen des Malte Laurids
Brigge* (*The Notebooks of Malte Laurids Brigge*, 1930, 1958), in Paris in 1910. It left
him emotionally drained and unable to write much in the ensuing years. He traveled to
North Africa and Egypt, then to Italy and Spain. From Toledo, where he studied the
art of El Greco (1541-1614), Rilke moved further south for the winter to Ronda. It was
there that he wrote "The Raising of Lazarus." Surrounded by beautiful landscape, he
enjoyed six weeks of prolific writing in early 1913. The poems he wrote in Ronda are
among his best but were not published together during his lifetime. Rilke had come to
the conclusion that only cohesive groups of poems should be published, and he was
already working on his *Duineser Elegien* (1923; *Duino Elegies*, 1930) at the time,
which would eventually become a cycle of ten complex poems. In June of 1913, he
would publish his cycle on the life of Mary, *Das Marienleben* (*The Life of the Virgin
Mary*, 1951), which he had written in January of 1912.

Rilke was raised in the Roman Catholic Church, and much of his poetry shows a
deep Christian influence. *Das Stunden-Buch* (*The Book of Hours*, 1941) was a major
early work, written in 1899, 1901, and 1903 and published for Christmas of 1905. Its
three books, *Vom mönchischen Leben* (*Monastic Life*), *Von der Pilgerschaft* (*Pilgrimage*), and *Von der Armut und vom Tode* (*Poverty and Death*), treat Christian themes in
a traditionally devout manner.

Something happened to change Rilke's outlook. "The Raising of Lazarus" is so
boldly secular that it hardly seems to have been written by the same poet. Rilke had, in
the interim, read the works of the Danish philosopher and religious thinker Sören
Kierkegaard (1813-1855), who was critical of conventional Christianity and emphasized the importance of individual choice.

To see just how far removed Rilke's poem is from the only account of the miraculous raising of Lazarus from the dead in the Bible, it is helpful to read John 11 for
comparison. Verse 25 is the one most often quoted, where Jesus said: "I am the resurrection, and the life." Rilke has chosen to cast the event in a different light, with a post-
Freudian focus on how Christ felt about what he was doing. And he leaves out God the
Father altogether.

Much remains unsaid in "The Raising of Lazarus." Rilke assumes the reader will
recognize the unnamed main character as Jesus Christ, who has already amply demonstrated his ability to heal the sick. It is useful, when reading the poem, to recall,
from John 11, what happened before the scene Rilke portrays and the consequences of

that scene. Christ deliberately delayed coming any earlier, and his raising of Lazarus was the ultimate provocation for the Pharisees, who then were determined to have him put to death. Rilke is fascinated with the individual who, following the dictates of an inner necessity, avoids an easier route and subjects himself to the stress of a supremely challenging task.

Forms and Devices

The poem itself deals only with the actual raising of Lazarus in Bethany. Narrated in the third person, it elaborates greatly on the Biblical observation that Christ "groaned in the spirit, and was troubled" (John 11:33). His reluctance is evident from the start, as is his critical detachment from humanity: "people need/ to be screamed at with proof." He briefly entertains the hope that at least his friends Martha and Mary, Lazarus's sisters, will believe in advance that he can bring Lazarus back to life. But not even they see his arrival in Bethany as the solution. Rilke effectively uses direct quotation so that one may hear, with Christ, what he has to contend with: "you come too late."

The next step is essentially a violation of nature and goes against Christ's own inclinations. Two extremely short sentences describe his intensely emotional reaction: "In anger" and "He wept." Even on the way to the grave, he has serious reservations. But as Christ begins to walk, Rilke's sentences begin to flow: eight verses before the full stop at "Move the stone!," then through to the end of the poem without a break. Since English sentences tend to be shorter than German ones, the contrast in Rilke's sentence lengths is not always retained in translation. In the original German, the syntactic units mirror the content. They show Christ stop and gather his energy, then set in motion a process that even he is unable to stop.

In the Bible, Christ talks briefly with God, then calls Lazarus to come out. Rilke's dramatic poem relies more on gesture than on words for its effect. He introduces the silent and suspenseful raising of Christ's hand, then the tightening into a claw, which in the German literally applies suction to the grave ("ansaugen"). Then he creates tension in the reader by revealing that Christ fears he might accidentally be raising many more than Lazarus, that "*all* the dead might return/ from that tomb."

Rilke keeps readers in suspense and expands his rhyme scheme as the tension builds. The basic scheme of the poem is rhymed quatrains, but, at the last, Rilke makes readers wait for a fifth verse before the rhyme, before Christ has the reassurance that he has raised only one and the life of the common people can go on as usual. The nightmarish elements of uncertainty and doubt make reading the poem an emotional experience.

Rilke's interest in existential questions places him outside expressionism in literary history, yet "The Raising of Lazarus" has much in common with the work of Rilke's expressionist contemporaries, whose influence cannot be ruled out. It was written in 1913, during a period of protracted inner crisis for Rilke that coincided with the unrest felt by many artists, particularly the expressionists, prior to the outbreak of World War I. Its unique approach to the familiar Bible story concentrates on Christ's inner feelings, giving precedence to subjective reality, as did the expressionists. Rilke's poem shows Christ strongly resisting what he must do, an attitude in keeping with the father-son conflicts in expressionist literature. And finally, in common with the innovative expressionists, Rilke uses the form itself as a means of expression: A basic pentameter propels the poem, and the lack of division into stanzas mirrors the inexorability of Christ's undertaking.

Themes and Meanings

Prior to writing "The Raising of Lazarus," Rilke had gone to Toledo for several weeks to see more works by the famous Spanish painter El Greco. The poem has strong visual components and the feverish intensity of El Greco's later works, even though El Greco is not one of the artists who painted the raising of Lazarus. The shocking moment Rilke captures so well is the moment of Christ's uncertainty. There is so much tension in his hand that it clenches like a claw as he begins to work his miracle, unsure of how it will end. This is Christ the man, not the god. The terrifying uncertainty he experiences is something everyone feels when doing something dangerous or unfamiliar for the first time.

Rilke's empathy with the figure of Christ, as he describes him, extends beyond the moment to Christ's whole situation. Even those closest to him do not understand him. They force him to defy nature in order to prove his deity but are incapable of grasping the continuity of life and death so evident to him. At the same time, there is a conspicuous absence of communication from above, from God the Father.

Christ's alienation in the poem is strikingly similar to that of the equally freely reinterpreted Prodigal Son in Rilke's autobiographical novel, *The Notebooks of Malte Laurids Brigge*. The final paragraph of the novel reads: "What did they know of him? He was now terribly difficult to love, and he felt that One alone was able for the task. But He was not yet willing." Both Christ and the Prodigal Son are misunderstood. Both contend with the excruciatingly difficult task of being true to their own natures, which place them quite apart from the average person. Rilke's extraordinary accounts of these biblical characters result from his identification with aspects of them, and they become representations of elements of himself. He was convinced that he must write and became frustrated when he could not do so. His works were produced at great personal cost. He could not live with other people for any length of time but needed human contact, and this led to a most unsettled lifestyle. Rilke's life is testimony to the difficulty of living with a creative gift that consumes the artist. His portrayal of Christ in "The Raising of Lazarus" focuses on the agony that accompanies the possession of exceptional powers.

Jean M. Snook

THE RAVEN

Author: Edgar Allan Poe (1809-1849)
Type of poem: Ballad
First published: 1845, in *The Raven and Other Poems*

The Poem

"The Raven" is a ballad of eighteen six-line stanzas with decidedly emphatic meter and rhymes. The ballad is a nightmarish narrative of a young man who, bereaved by the death of the woman he loved, compulsively constructs self-destructive meaning around a raven's repetition of the word "Nevermore," until he finally despairs of being reunited with his beloved Lenore in another world.

Narrated from the first-person point of view, the poem conveys, with dramatic immediacy, the speaker's shift from weary, sorrowful composure to a state of nervous collapse as he recounts his strange experience with the mysterious ebony bird. The first seven stanzas establish the setting and the narrator's melancholic, impressionable state of mind. Weak and worn out with grief, the speaker had sought distraction from his sorrow by reading curiously esoteric books. Awakened at midnight by a sound outside his chamber, he opens the door, expecting a visitor; he finds only darkness. Apprehensive, he whispers the name Lenore and closes the door. When the tapping persists, he opens a window, admitting a raven that perches upon a bust of Pallas (Athena).

In stanzas 8 to 11, the narrator, beguiled by the ludicrous image of the black bird in his room, playfully asks the raven its name, as if to reassure himself that it portends nothing ominous. He is startled, however, to hear the raven respond, saying, "Nevermore." Although the word apparently has little relevance to any discoverable meaning, the narrator is sobered by the bird's forlorn utterance. He assumes that the raven's owner, having suffered unendurable disasters, taught the bird to imitate human speech in order to utter the one word most expressive of the owner's sense of hopelessness.

In stanzas 12 and 13, the narrator settles himself on a velvet cushion in front of the bird and whimsically ponders what the raven meant by repeating a word he inevitably associated with thoughts of the departed Lenore. At this point, the grieving lover, in anticipation of the raven's maddening repetition of "Nevermore," begins masochistically to frame increasingly painful questions.

Imagining a perfumed presence in the room, the narrator, in a state of growing agitation, asks the raven whether God had mercifully sent him to induce in the poet forgetfulness of the lost Lenore; the inevitable response causes the narrator to plead with the raven—now addressed as a prophet of evil sent by the "Temptor"—to tell him whether there is any healing in heaven for his grief. The raven's predictable answer provokes the grieving lover, now almost in a state of maddened frenzy, to ask bluntly whether his soul would ever be reunited with Lenore in heaven. Receiving the horrific "Nevermore" in reply to his ultimate question, the distraught narrator demands that the raven, whether actual bird or fiend, leave his chambers and quit torturing his heart; the raven's unendurable answer drives the bereaved lover into a state of maddened despair. The raven becomes a permanent fixture in the room, a symbolic presence presiding over the narrator's self-inflicted mental and spiritual collapse.

Forms and Devices

"The Raven" is Edgar Allan Poe's most famous poem, not only because of its immediate and continued popularity but also because Poe wrote "The Philosophy of Composition," an essay reconstructing the step-by-step process of how he composed the poem as if it were a precise mathematical problem. Discounting the role of serendipity, romantic inspiration, or intuition, Poe accounted for every detail as the result of calculated effect. Although the essay may be a tour de force, informed readers of the poem—from the nineteenth century French poets Charles Baudelaire, Stéphane Mallarmé, and Paul Valéry to such twentieth century poets as Allen Tate and T. S. Eliot—have recognized the value of Poe's essay in understanding the poem's forms and poetic devices.

Poe's analysis of the structure and texture of "The Raven" is too detailed to consider at length (and some of it must be taken with several grains of salt, allowing for considerable exaggeration on Poe's part); however, his essay sheds light on three important aspects implicit in the poem's form: its conception as a theatrical performance; the narrator's anguished involvement in making meaning by obsessively asking increasingly self-lacerating questions; and the function of the maddening, incantatory rhythm and rhymes that help cast a mind-paralyzing spell over both the declaiming narrator and the reader.

Although the principles of brevity and unity of impression or effect that inform the poem rest on Poe's aesthetic theories, derived from the facultative psychology of his time (the world of mind separated into faculties of intellect, taste, and the moral sense with crucial implications for the form and substance of poetry and romance), it is more helpful to see the contribution of this severe economy of means to the histrionic qualities of the poem. The persona narrates the poem as a kind of dramatic monologue, carefully arranging the scene of his chamber and the stage properties for maximum theatrical effect: the play of light and shadow from the hearth, the esoteric volumes, the silken, purple curtains, the door and window opening onto a tempestuous night offstage. There is also the dramatic juxtaposition of the black talking bird perched on the white bust of Pallas over the chamber door, the velvet cushion on which the narrator sits facing the raven, and the lamplight throwing shadows over the narrator's soul "floating on the floor," at the frenzied climax of the poem. Even the pivotal refrain that keynotes the poem's structure contributes to the artistic effect "in the theatrical sense."

The most original device of the poem is the way the narrator unconsciously arranges his questions. He begins nonchalantly with a commonplace question; under the hypnotic influence of the raven's cacophonous, melancholic repetition of "Nevermore," and driven by both the human thirst for self-torture and a superstitious mind, the bereaved lover luxuriates in sorrow by asking more distressful questions until the inexorable answer becomes intolerable, and he melodramatically sinks into maddened despair.

The nightmarish effect of the poem is reinforced by the relentless trochaic rhythm and the arrangement of the ballad stanzas into five lines of octameter followed by a refrain in tetrameter. This combination, along with emphatic alliteration, allows for strong internal and end rhymes, resulting in a mesmerizing syncopation of redundancies as inescapable as the sonorous refrain. This incantatory repetition creates an aural quality that helps force a collaboration between the poem and the reader, a maddening regularity aptly conveying the speaker's disintegrating reason, while contributing to the theatrical effect of the poem as histrionic performance.

Themes and Meanings

"The Raven" objectifies Poe's belief that the artistic experiencing of a poem is an end in itself. As both poet and critic, Poe attacked two trends that he found equally disastrous: what he called "epic mania" (using the length of a poem as an index to its power and significance) and the "didactic heresy" (taking the explicit moral or philosophical meaning of a poem as its chief value).

Although Poe's aesthetic theories, set forth in such essays as "The Poetic Principle" and "The Philosophy of Composition," rely on a romantic theory of the imagination (as filtered through the writings of Samuel Taylor Coleridge and the temperament of Poe), the gist of his art is targeted toward the poem as experience. According to Poe, the intellect craves truth (the sphere of philosophical, rational discourse), and the moral sense craves duty (the domain of didactic writing), whereas taste thirsts for beauty (quenched only by poetry with its musicality and, therefore, its indefinite pleasure, and by romance with its more definite pleasure). Hence, a poem, in providing an indefinite, pleasurable aesthetic experience, requires a sense of complexity (all means including rhythm and sound adapted to a predetermined end) and a suggestive undercurrent of meaning.

In speaking of "The Raven," Poe declared that an intended undercurrent of meaning first becomes apparent in the metaphorical "Take thy beak from out *my heart*, and take thy form from off my door!/ Quoth the Raven 'Nevermore!'" The raven thus becomes "emblematical of Mournful and Never-Ending Remembrance." Fortunately, the poem's thematic significance transcends this limited intention.

The undeniable power of "The Raven" comes from the inexplicable, overwhelming sorrow at the heart of the poem, conveyed through the narrator's theatrical passion, grief, and, finally, insane desperation. The reader, involved in the complicity of the poem's design, sees the narrator as existing operatically, on a stage, outside the normal relations of space and time, and moving from the barely plausible to the realm of fantasy. The sensitive narrator's apparent passivity and the pounding rhythm create the emotional logic of a dream, in which things happened to him that he cannot change, only experience. Yet he is paradoxically involved in promoting his own psychological disintegration by posing a crescendo of self-destroying questions whose answers were the illogical repetition of a single word, croaked by a non-reasoning creature. Through his compulsions, he participates in constructing the unendurable meaning of eternal loss and separation from the one object of his desire. The drama of this loss of sanity is unforgettable as the reader surrenders to the histrionic performance which is the poem.

Clifford Edwards

READING LAO TZU AGAIN IN THE NEW YEAR

Author: Charles Wright (1935-   )
Type of poem: Meditation
First published: 1990; collected in *Chickamauga*, 1995

The Poem

"Reading Lao Tzu Again in the New Year" is a poem of middle length (forty-seven lines) written in free verse. The title is somewhat misleading, since neither Lao Tzu nor whatever work of his Charles Wright has been reading is mentioned in the poem. Instead, the reading of Lao Tzu's poetry and his view of nature seem to trigger a meditation on the end of the year and the absences or emptiness in nature and humankind. The speaker of the poem is the same speaker who appears in all the poems of *Chickamauga* and Wright's next book, the Pulitzer Prize-winning *Black Zodiac* (1997). He is an aspect of Wright himself, a seeker of some ultimate truth, some "essence," who never seems to find the answers he is seeking. Instead, in this poem, the search sets in motion a meditation on "essence" that deals primarily with time and the winter landscape. The poem is divided into three distinct sections and has a clear movement and development. The first two sections portray the world as dead and the speaker close to despair. The third section shifts from this gloom to affirmation.

The poem begins with the "Snub end of a dismal year." The focus is on winter and the dying of nature rather than on any suggestion of renewal provided by the new year. This sense of endings is further defined and intensified in the description of the landscape. The sky has an "undercoat of blackwash," and in his dead world the speaker must "answer to/ My life." The tone is morbid, nearly despairing. A new year may be beginning, but "nothing will change hands." There will be no revelation, only repetition.

The poem then meditates upon cycles of rising and falling: "Prosodies rise and fall./ Structures rise in the mind and fall." The speaker thinks only of "failure," and nature seems cut off from its own parts rather than being a unified and healing system. There is a more hopeful shift at the end of the second section, as all the "loss" the speaker sees becomes a "gain."

The last section of the poem is more description than meditation. It is "Four days into January," and tiny grass is growing "under the peach trees." The birds are singing, and the speaker now sees the place of humankind in a more hopeful light. People may be "between now and not-now," but they are "held by affection." They are connected by bonds of feeling, not merely adrift in a world of failure and dead ends.

Forms and Devices

One of the most important devices of the poem is Wright's use of free verse. It is not a free verse that arbitrarily breaks lines; there is, instead, a clear integrity of the line. Wright also sets one line off against another by indenting some lines far toward the right margin. He thus creates a counterpoint between lines, adds asides that comment on the previous line, and makes forceful caesuras between lines.

Wright uses a number of traditional poetic devices in the poem, but imagery is clearly the most important. There are images of emptiness or diminishment in the first section—the "dwarf" orchard and the sky with its "undercoat of blackwash." It is the "snub" end of a dismal year. There is also an interesting allusion in the first section: "this shirt I want to take off,/ which is on fire." These lines allude to the shirt of Nessus, which caused Hercules to go mad after putting it on. In that fit of madness, he killed his wife and children.

The second section continues the negative imagery. Failure "reseeds the old ground"—a brilliant image that reverses the renewal of "seeding" into a cycle of failure and hopelessness. The rest of the second section is more statement than imagery: "Prosodies rise and fall./ Structures rise and fall." There is, once more, a cycle that does not renew but only repeats. The references to prosody and structure are literary and suggest the problem of creating a meaningful poem in the midst of a meaningless cycle.

Images of nature follow these statements, but they are negative also. "Does the grass, with its inches in two worlds, love the dirt?/ Does the snowflake the raindrop?" Things that should be closely connected into structures instead have their parts cut off from each other; everything and everyone is isolated. There seems to be no solution to this problem, because "those who know will never tell us." The "word" that should illuminate instead "leads us another step from the light." At the end of the second section, however, the poem turns from its depiction of despair to the beginning of affirmation: "Loss is its own gain./ Its secret is emptiness." The "dark selves" of the poem move as "the tide moves." The acknowledgment of emptiness and the movement of self and nature together seem to point a way out of the dilemma.

In the last section, the images of nature are connected, in contrast to the isolation of the first section. "The grass grows tiny, tiny/ Under the peach trees." Although the growth is tiny, it does provide some hope, and the speaker seizes upon that hope. Birds are singing, and nature is growing; only humankind is isolated "between now and not-now." Yet even that displacement is "held by affection." This tenuous affirmation is supported by the poem's final, significant image: "Large rock balanced upon a small rock."

Themes and Meanings

The first important theme in the poem is that the change of the year does not produce change or renewal but a seemingly endless cycle: "Old year, new year, old song, new song." Nature is part of this repetitive cycle. The references to literary elements in the poem are worth noting, as they are also caught in an unrenewing cycle. "Prosodies rise and fall./ Structures rise in the mind and fall." The change in prosodies does not give the poet a useable metrical system but a sense of chaos in the displacement of existing systems. The imagination of the poet is caught in this dead end as well; Structures may rise in the mind, but then they disintegrate. Furthermore, words—and thereby the naming and placing of objects, the most elemental tools of the poet—do not provide an instrument for vision but take one further from illumination.

The "emptiness" of the second section is an important thematic shift in the poem. It reflects not a repetitive cycle but a closure. Although it does not provide renewal, it is a step toward change and a way out of the endless cycles of the poem. The "loss" that has filled the first two parts of the poem is now a "gain." Wright does not explain this paradox; he simply asserts it as a truth. In addition, there is a freedom of movement here that has not been seen earlier in the poem—"dark selves" move like bodies of water being moved by the tide. The darkness that has been so much a part of the poem is also altered in the last section as "Sunlight sprays on the ash limbs." The image finally proclaims an illumination of the dark world and dark selves.

The place of humankind, for which the poet has been looking since the beginning of the poem, is discovered and asserted at the end. The phrase "We're placed between now and not-now" seems at first to be merely a description of human displacement; people can never live truly in the present, only between two states. However, Wright adds another line to this formulation. People are also "Held by affection." Both words are important: "Held" suggests human contact and being sustained, while "affection" suggests the feelings, bonds, and gestures of everyday life. With this assurance, this balance, the speaker can stop his metaphysical speculations about humankind and nature. Where he is in time becomes less important than being "Held by affection." The last image is also important: "Large rock balanced upon a small rock." The differences are brought together in an equilibrium that closes the poem.

James Sullivan

READING THE BROTHERS GRIMM TO JENNY

Author: Lisel Mueller (1924-   )
Type of poem: Meditation
First published: 1967; collected in *The Private Life*, 1976

The Poem

"Reading the Brothers Grimm to Jenny" is a forty-six-line poem arranged in four stanzas. Jacob Grimm and his brother Wilhelm were well-known nineteenth century German collectors of fairy tales. As the title indicates, the poet is reading these fairy tales to her daughter Jenny. In later collections, the poem includes the subtitle "Dead means somebody has to kiss you," which shows that Jenny is young enough to form her image of death from a fairy tale, specifically from the story of Snow White, who was awakened from deathlike sleep by a kiss. Although the poet seems to be addressing the child, she is not speaking but thinking the poem while reading fairy tales aloud. In fact, the poet is arguing with herself. By implication, she is also arguing with her contemporary American peers, many of whom disapprove of fairy tales for children in the belief that they present a false picture of life.

In the first stanza, the poet contrasts Jenny's "black and white" world, in which things happen by magic, with the poet's "real world," which functions by negotiating ("gray foxes and gray wolves/ bargain eye to eye") and by doing what it takes to survive ("the amazing dove/ takes shelter under the wing/ of the raven to keep dry"). In the second and third stanzas, the poet asks herself why she lies to the child by allowing oversimplified fairy-tale values to seem real when she knows that one day Jenny will have to live in the adult world and "live with power/ and honor circumstance." In the fourth and final stanza, however, the poet recognizes that the creative power of belief can transform the world and says that she learns this "once more" from the child.

The poem is full of references to magic, including the stories of Snow White ("Death is a small mistake/ there, where the kiss revives"), Cinderella (who had the nearly impossible task of sifting lentils from cinders), Rapunzel (upon whose hair a prince climbed the tower in which she was imprisoned and whose pitying tears cured him after he was blinded), and birds that "speak the truth" (found in many fairy tales). In this magical world, life is divided into "kingdoms of black and white," both commanded by the mind; in the adult world, however, the "foxes" and "wolves" are gray and so are the values, and the mind must cope with power and circumstance outside the self. The conflict between childhood and adult views of the world and the conflict within the poet-as-mother about what she should teach the child creates and sustains tension throughout the poem. The recognition of this conflict allows transcendence of it at the end to become a credible answer to the question.

Forms and Devices

The imagery of the poem is vivid and physical: "you shoulder the crow on your left,/ the snowbird on your right." At the same time, imagery of equal intensity evokes scene after scene from fairy tales. Common metaphors (clichés) in this poem show how deeply fairy tales have become ingrained in everyday life. The reader is led to see the gray foxes and wolves not only in their metaphorical senses of clever (foxes) and devouring (wolves) people and not only as a mixture of good and bad (gray) but also as actual gray-haired businesspeople and politicians negotiating and making compromises.

When read aloud, the poem sounds like a ballad, yet the balladlike rhyme and rhythm are not arranged visually in traditional four-line stanzas; rather, they are set into four long stanzas: The first and fourth are of fourteen lines each, suggesting the fourteen-line sonnet, a reflective form that traditionally poses and then answers a question. Like the sonnet, this poem asks and answers a question. Unlike the sonnet, the question is not asked until the second stanza and is answered in the fourth and final stanza. The second and third stanzas have nine lines each. This symmetrical arrangement of stanzas further reinforces the idea of an ordered world. The progression of the poem is not narrative like a ballad but is an argument that makes use of ballad meter and rhyme to reinforce one side of the argument. As long as the poem deals with the magical and with the belief that everything is simple, the lines are end-stopped (their thought does not carry over to the following line) or the rhyme and meter themselves compel the stop: "gray foxes and gray wolves/ bargain eye to eye,/ and the amazing dove/ takes shelter under the wing/ of the raven to keep dry."

When the poet begins to recognize that the child's "truthful eyes" and "keen, attentive stare/ endow the vacuous slut/ with royalty," the lines spill over onto the next lines; then the form returns to the more structured end-stopped lines, even though the poem has shifted to include the idea of a less simple adult world. The rhymes begin with true rhyme (white/right, through/roo-coo), followed by slant (consonant) rhyme (wolves/dove, innocence/circumstance) and assonant (vowel) rhyme (climb/binds, is/ insist/bliss), eventually returning to true rhyme (see/key/be). This variation would also be found in a ballad. In this poem, the variation helps to prevent a sing-song effect, and the return to true rhyme reinforces acceptance of the magical view.

Themes and Meanings

The central issue of the poem is the conflict between the way things are and the way they should be. This is a conflict as old as the human hope for a better world. Realists refer to it as "reality versus illusion"; idealists refer to it as "the real versus the ideal." Lisel Mueller sums up the realist view in the lines "Jenny, we make just dreams/ out of our unjust lives." However, the poet is not content with labeling them only as dreams; instead, she finds that the ideal can serve a creative purpose: "Still, when your truthful eyes,/ your keen, attentive stare,/ endow the vacuous slut/ with royalty, when you match/ her soul to her shimmering hair,/ what can she do but rise/ to your imagined throne?" The poet sums up her balancing of the real and the ideal in the lines "And what can I, but see/ beyond the world that is// the world as it might be?" The poet recognizes that this is more than a conflict; it is a juggling act. With nothing but the fairy-tale ideal, a child is ill-prepared for the real world, in which there is no absolute right or wrong. On the other hand, with nothing but the real world in its present state, there is no hope for anything better. It is a temporary balancing, one that Mueller has undertaken in many of her poems. In this one, she relieves the didacticism of her conclusion—that people expand their limits when someone sees a creative possibility for them—by referring to it as something the child teaches her "once more."

Poets are especially concerned with balancing the real and the ideal, knowing that these are also the literal and the imaginative and that poetry needs both. Mueller's concern with the real and the ideal is made more poignant by the knowledge that she and her parents escaped from Adolf Hitler's Germany and took refuge in the United States in 1939. She grew up all too aware that the world is no simple fairy-tale existence. Yet many of her poems are filled with the fairy tales of her childhood, and her work shows that, despite discouragement, it has remained important to her to help make "the world as it might be." The intensity of her use of fairy-tale characters and motifs reflects the fact that, growing up in Germany, her idea of fairy tales differs from the American view that such tales represent mere wishful thinking. Rather, she inherits the European view that fairy tales, like myths, vividly present stock characters and situations people meet in everyday life, and she takes their power seriously, even though she recognizes their simplicity.

Helen Shanley

THE REAL WORK

Author: Gary Snyder (1930-   )
Type of poem: Narrative
First published: 1974, in *Turtle Island*

The Poem

"The Real Work" consists of a title, an italicized epigraph, and three stanzas: one of six lines, one of five lines, and one of three lines. The poem introduces the reader to citizenship in the environment, its ecosystems, its landscapes, and its water systems. This citizenship is to the continent, not to the political state, and the reader is shown that humans can live in harmony with the world and its creatures, even if some humans abuse the environment and its natural inhabitants.

The title calls attention to the choice that citizens of the world face. They can dedicate themselves to the work that is not the real work, losing themselves in the distractions of activities that offer money, fame, or power but afford no satisfaction to the soul and spirit. A life spent in this way is foolish and often abusive to the environment. However, the citizens of the world may also choose "the real work," in which humans explore the landscapes of their minds, reflect on relationships between the components of the landscapes, and discover an outlet, whether in art or labor, that protects and perpetuates nature's harmony and satisfies the human heart.

The epigraph, muted by being enclosed in editorial brackets, sets the poem in the present: "Today." The speaker is with his friends, Zach and Dan, and they are engaged in rowing on the San Francisco Bay, passing Alcatraz and circling Angel Island. They are small figures in a vast and powerful natural scene, and they pose no threat to the territory they explore.

The first stanza subtly reveals the threat that the environment faces. There are "sea-lions and birds," which seem friendly and appropriate, but the sun must force its way "through fog." Its light is "sun haze." This sun "looks" at the humans on the bay, staring at them "dead in the eye." The ominous image of "a long tanker" concludes the stanza, and this tanker is "riding light and high" because it has already discharged its cargo. The tanker is much larger than the rowboat, and the tanker's mission—very likely the delivery of a massive quantity of petroleum—makes some humans rich while the environment is exposed to the danger of catastrophic accidents and the consequences that follow from the use of fossil fuels.

Despite the danger posed in the first stanza, the next stanza presents the environment in its natural harmony. Along a "choppy line" two "tide-flows" combine, offering a location that provides abundant food for "seagulls." The rowers "slide" on the smooth water, appreciating "white-stained cliffs." In this stanza, humans, wildlife, water systems, and the massive features of the mainland are joined in peace, beauty, and harmony.

The final stanza—powerful yet mysterious in its brevity—reiterates the words of the title: "the real work." Referring to "washing and sighing,/ sliding by," Snyder explained in an interview that he is describing "the wash of waves on the island out in San Francisco Bay with the seabirds, and the feeding and schooling of the little fish." Snyder insists that "the real work" is "always here." One takes on the real work "without the *least* hope of doing any good." One aims to "check the destruction of the interesting and necessary diversity of life on the planet so that the dance can go on a little better for a little longer."

Forms and Devices

The poem seems to be open in form, with no capitalization, no metrical pattern, and no rhyme scheme. Nevertheless, the poem does consist of fourteen lines and appears to stand between the eight-and-six line division of the Italian sonnet and the twelve-and-two line division of the English sonnet. The first six lines function as a sestet, which in an Italian sonnet is usually the concluding portion of the poem. Taken together, the last two stanzas are an octet, but the separation of the last three lines gives them special weight. Like the concluding couplet of an English sonnet, the concluding three lines stand in opposition to the foregoing eleven lines, asserting the importance of "the real work." The concluding three lines comment on the contrast between the first two stanzas, favoring a gentle, cooperative, and appreciative engagement with nature. The form of the poem captures the seriousness and antiquity of the sonnet, yet Snyder's modification of the form keeps the poem fresh and light.

Snyder helps to create a connection among humans, natural phenomena, and wildlife through personification. The sun is made human because it is given the capacity to "look" with intensity into a person's eyes, as if the sun were another person. The seagulls are made human because they can "sit" at their meal, as if they were people. Conversely, Snyder makes the people in the rowboat similar to water as they "slide by."

At the center of Snyder's poem is the image. Borrowing from Chinese and Japanese writers, who compose poetry with epigrams or render ideas with the photo-flash impressions of haiku, Snyder stacks phrase upon phrase in "The Real Work," creating a series of visual effects. Snyder also borrows from the Imagists, such as Ezra Pound and William Carlos Williams, who abandon the rhythm of the metronome and present vivid mental pictures. The reader who demands that the images be perfectly explained is missing the point of the method, which is to allow things to express their inherent ideas. One does not need to say that the bay, birds, and cliffs are sources of beauty worthy of love; such an idea emerges from the environmental features themselves.

Reading "The Real Work" as an isolated poem is possible, but Snyder's method relies significantly on the interconnection of poems made possible through the series of poems that surround "The Real Work" in *Turtle Island*, as well as in the body of Snyder's collected works. Without a sense of Snyder's overall ecological outlook, the reader may not get the full impact of "a long tanker riding light and high." Similarly, one may not appreciate the mythic associations activated by the power of the sun.

Themes and Meanings

The idea of "the real work" is recurrent in Snyder's *Turtle Island*, which includes the phrase "the real work" in the poem "I Went into the Maverick Bar" and in the poem "The Real Work." The phrase recurs in a collection titled *The Real Work: Interviews and Talks, 1964-1979* (1980). The question "What is the real work?" follows Snyder wherever he goes.

On one hand, the idea of "the real work" is very simple. In an interview, Snyder declared that the North American continent is real, and the deepest human loyalty is really owed not to the United States, but to mountains, rivers, plant zones, and creatures. The real work is to discover a citizenship based on natural boundaries rather than the borders of political states. The real work is any form of human endeavor, be it wood cutting, truck driving, garbage collecting, or the making of art, so long as the human involved in the work discovers himself or herself in the work and is made whole by doing the work.

On the other hand, "the real work" is an idea that no one, not even Snyder himself, fully comprehends. He once admitted that the suggestiveness of the phrase allowed him to puzzle over its meaning ever since he wrote it down. He said an honest person might confess that he or she does not really know what "the real work" is. One might go to his or her death without knowing "the real work," and that unsolved mystery might be satisfactory, too.

If "the real work" has a special connection to poetry, then Snyder's ideas on writing poems may prove illuminating. Snyder insisted that poetry is based on real life and real feelings. He declared, "Poems are what you do when you want to talk about what really happened." If someone discovers "the real work" in the writing of poetry, he or she cuts through the levels of enforced correctness and invented pretenses in order to arrive at an authentic record of the human spirit.

William T. Lawlor

REAPERS

Author: Jean Toomer (1894-1967)
Type of poem: Lyric
First published: 1923, in *Cane*

The Poem

"Reapers" is a short poem of eight lines in iambic pentameter rhymed couplets, a form sometimes referred to as heroic couplets. It appears as the second piece in Jean Toomer's *Cane*, a collection of short stories, sketches, and poems intended to show the beauty and strength of African American life. The poem is spoken by a first-person narrator, but this narrator neither enters the action nor comments on it. This is typical of the work collected in *Cane:* The narrator usually selects particular details to present to the reader but trusts the reader to interpret the details wisely. Only rarely, and usually in prose pieces, does the narrator guide the reader more directly.

The eight lines divide neatly into two sections, each representing a different vision. In the first four lines, black field workers sharpen their scythes with sharpening stones. When they are finished, they place the hones in their pockets and begin cutting. The men are silent; the only sound in the scene is the sound of the steel blades being ground against the stones. The narrator, standing far away (physically or emotionally), dispassionately reports what he sees. In the second four lines, the narrator turns his gaze to another field or another day, and the silent black men are replaced by a machine, a mower, drawn by black horses. The mower has run over a field rat, which lies among the weeds bleeding and squealing. The mower blades, stained with the rat's blood, continue on their path.

Forms and Devices

"Reapers" is divided into two sections, two scenes, with no commentary from the narrator to help the reader interpret their meaning. That the two are meant as separate pieces is clear, both because of the fact that the only lines that are end-stopped are the fourth and the eighth and because of the pointed similarity of the openings of the two sections: "Black reapers" and "Black horses." However, the two pieces are closely linked; Toomer has not written the poem in two separate stanzas but as two pairs of paired couplets. The meaning lies simply in the contrasts between the two parts, and the poet uses careful arrangements of sounds in the two scenes to emphasize those contrasts. In the first scene, silent except for "the sound of steel on stones" and the suggested swishing of blades through grass, the poet uses repetitive sibilant sounds as seen in the phrase just quoted and in the second line: "Are sharpening scythes. I see them place the hones." The sounds and rhythms of the poem echo the sounds of the scene and direct the reader toward hearing the scene as peaceful and steady.

By contrast, the second scene features a noisy machine and a "squealing" rat, and the sounds of the lines are harsher, with consonants standing side by side to create cacophony. In line 6, the words "field rat, startled, squealing bleeds" must be read one at a time; the ending consonants of one word and the beginning consonants of the next word do not run well together and thus cannot be read aloud smoothly. The consonants in this section are more explosive. For example, the hard *c* of "continue cutting" is not found at all in the first section, and the insistent near-rhyme of "bleeds," "blade," and "blood" can only be intentional. Before turning to writing, Toomer had considered becoming a musical composer, and all of his poetry reveals a deep concern for the musicality of language. Critics have often commented on the lyrical cadences of his poems about natural beauty such as "Georgia Dusk" and "Evening Song" (also from *Cane*). "Reapers" is an example of his use of the same ear to echo the sounds of men and machines.

Themes and Meanings

For Toomer, one of life's essential truths was that industrialized society had ground humankind down, destroying people's natural goodness and sense of community. As industrialization increased, the world became more chaotic. In "Reapers" and in the longer *Cane* from which it is taken, Toomer explores the dichotomy between humans and machines and, by extension, between the human and the subhuman or nonhuman qualities of people. Humans can feel and care, they can make moral choices, but machines cannot. "Reapers" demonstrates this truth by setting two scenes side by side: a scene of men working in a field and a scene of a mowing machine. In the first scene, all the work is done by humans with hand tools. Notably, it takes more than one reaper to do the job; doing work by hand requires more workers and therefore builds or sustains a community. Toomer pointedly calls these men reapers rather than mowers or cutters. They are reaping, or cutting and gathering, with a purpose: to provide food.

The machine, on the other hand, is a mower cutting weeds. It is driven by two horses; the human driver, if there is one, is not seen and does not appear to be directing the action. Instead, the narrator presents only a mindless machine pulled by mindless animals with no sense of purpose and no human sensibilities. A machine cannot react to a squeal of pain or a stain of blood. It does not know what it destroys, and it would not care if it did know. Toomer believed that people who harm or oppress others do so because they have given up their human qualities and have become like machines.

The pessimistic tone of "Reapers" is typical of the section of *Cane* in which it appears. Just before "Reapers" is a short story, "Karintha," about a beautiful and innocent child of the South who is ultimately destroyed by the sexual mistreatment of the men around her. "Reapers" is followed by another poem, "November Cotton Flower," and a short story, "Becky," both about victimized and defeated women. Throughout *Cane*, images of machines and factories always hint of decay or destruction. For Toomer, modern life—and particularly modern Southern rural life—was doomed unless humankind would turn its back on mindless industrialization and reclaim its humanity.

Cynthia A. Bily

REASONS FOR ATTENDANCE

Author: Philip Larkin (1922-1985)
Type of poem: Lyric
First published: 1955, in *The Less Deceived*

The Poem

"Reasons for Attendance" is a short poem of twenty lines that is divided into four cinquains with regular rhyme scheme based primarily on slant rhymes. The title hints at Philip Larkin's multiple concerns in the poem. He ponders why the young couples with "flushed face" move "to and fro" inside the dance hall while he remains outside. Similarly, he considers why he, despite his protests that he does not need the happiness inside the hall, is drawn "To watch the dancers"—that is, to "attend" to them, in the archaic sense of "give heed to."

"Reasons for Attendance" begins with the speaker standing outside "the lighted glass" feeling compelled to watch the dancers inside. For the remainder of the poem, Larkin alternates between the perspectives of the observer outside and the dancers inside the hall. In the third line of the first stanza, he shifts from himself to the particulars of the dancers, who shift "intently" and "Solemnly on the beat of happiness."

The second stanza brings another shift in perspective, as the poet focuses on what he senses ("smoke and sweat" and "The wonderful feel of girls") as he attempts to penetrate the atmosphere inside. The first line of the stanza ("Or so I fancy") raises the possibility that the earlier sensations described inside the dance hall were only what the poet's "fancy" projected onto the scene.

Beginning with line 2 of the second stanza, the poet presents the two competing motivations that inform the poem—sex, seen by many as "the lion's share/ Of happiness," and the "lifted, rough-tongued bell" of art, which demands a separateness of its followers. In the third and fourth stanzas, Larkin seems to resolve the conflict by asking that the dancers and the detached observer be allowed to follow their own "voices"—the dancers to follow the "trumpet's voice" of communion and sexuality, and the speaker, the "individual sound" of his muse's bell. He concludes that "both are satisfied."

With the last line of the poem, however, the poet undercuts this apparent resolution by raising the possibility that neither party has found happiness: "If no one has misjudged himself. Or lied." This ambivalence saves the poem from the kind of easy truce between competing ethics that Victorian readers admired and contemporary readers may find too pat in Alfred, Lord Tennyson's "Ulysses": "He works his work, I mine."

Forms and Devices

In "Reasons for Attendance," the poet uses ambiguity and paradox to suggest his uncertainty over the choices he has made and his ambivalence toward the dancers. In the final line of the third stanza, the poet moves toward a clear declaration of his position concerning human choices: "It speaks; I hear." "It" seems to refer to the vague concept in the stanza's second line—"that lifted, rough-tongued bell." Sensing that the reader will not be able to understand the significance of the bell, Larkin parenthetically identifies it as "Art," only to withdraw certainty with his qualifier "if you like." If the bell is art, the statement bridging the third and fourth stanzas seems deliberately ambiguous: "others may hear as well,/ But not for me, nor I for them." May hear what? the reader might ask, since the "others" in the poem—the young dancers— have heeded the trumpet's call to communion, not the voice of art. When the poet concludes "and so/ With happiness," the reader can only wonder, and what with happiness? since "so" apparently refers to the preceding ambiguous statements about hearing.

The poet ends with a final instance of ambiguity, this time a pair of demonstrative pronouns presented in parallel positions, neither with a clear referent: "Therefore I stay outside,/ Believing this; and they maul to and fro,/ Believing that." The poet has worked himself into a state of confusion concerning his own motives and implies that the young dancers experience a similar confusion.

Larkin creates a sense of the uncertainty he feels about the world inside the "lighted glass" of the dance hall through a series of paradoxes. The young dancers move "on the beat of happiness," yet they shift "Solemnly." The poet juxtaposes the "smoke and sweat" inside the dance hall with the "wonderful feel of girls." He also creates a paradox in his use of a lion metaphor: The sexuality enjoyed by couples may be "the lion's share/ Of happiness," but the young couples "maul to and fro."

Instead of letting his confusion rage, Larkin remains detached, controlling his emotions through a number of poetic devices. In the second stanza, when the poet senses his own anxiety over the possibility that sex holds "the lion's share/ Of happiness," he distances himself by shifting to the purposely pretentious tone of the third stanza: "What calls me is that lifted, rough-tongued bell/ (Art, if you like)." Larkin also reins in his fears by using a consistent meter (iambic pentameter) and relentlessly adhering to his chosen rhyme scheme (albeit most often through less obtrusive slant rhyme). Finally, the poet guards against his own emotions by using understatement throughout the poem: "It speaks; I hear," "and so/ With happiness," "both are satisfied," "Or lied."

Themes and Meanings

The central concern of "Reasons for Attendance" is the choice between competing ways of life—a life of human connection and sexuality, and the detached, isolated life of the artist/misanthrope. In this poem (as in Robert Frost's "The Road Not Taken"), the decision-making process itself is dramatized for the reader. In Larkin's poem, the reader sees what Mikhail Bakhtin calls the "dialogic imagination" at work as separate "voices"—the "trumpet's voice" and the "rough-tongued bell"—struggle to present their competing claims.

After noting how he answers the trumpet call of the dance hall, the detached poet becomes more and more engaged by the movements of the "flushed face" dancers until he can actually "sense" the "smoke and sweat" beyond the glass. Finally seduced by thoughts of the "wonderful feel of girls," he is forced to ask himself, "Why be out here?" At this moment, the voice of individuality is compelled to counter with "But then, why be in there? Sex, yes, but what/ Is sex?"

Triggered by the mention of sex, Larkin the individualist plunges ahead to proclaim his judgment of the notion that supreme happiness is possible only through sexuality: "Surely, to think the lion's share/ Of happiness is found by couples—sheer/ Inaccuracy, as far as I'm concerned." Forced by the break in stanzas after the word "sheer" to wait to hear the poet's final assessment, the reader can almost feel Larkin struggling to choose the right word to express his disdain. Through the device of enjambment from one stanza to another, Larkin creates the turn of the poem. Poised at this moment of indecision, the reader has been led by the emphatic words "Surely" and "sheer" to expect an outburst of contempt for the notion that social contact is superior to individual happiness. Instead, either under the influence of his competing voice or in fear of the passionate crescendo of emotions in the preceding lines, the poet retreats to understatement—calling the notion "inaccurate"—and assumes the detached, pretentious tone that dominates almost until the poem's end.

In fact, from this turn in the poem until the final line, Larkin is able to create what Bakhtin calls a "centripetal force": The two voices seem to reach a resolution in which each accepts the beliefs of the other and both are "satisfied" with their own choices. Larkin even seems to underscore this controlled harmony by resorting in the final stanza to exact rhyme rather than slant rhyme for the first time in the poem.

The final line of the poem ("If no one has misjudged himself. Or lied."), however, destroys the poem's logical and formal harmony, setting off again what Bakhtin would call the poem's "centrifugal force." Larkin's honesty (the same unflinching clear-sightedness that pervades many of the poems in *The Less Deceived*, the monograph in which "Reasons for Attendance" appears) raises the possibility that either the dancers or the poet have been self-deluded in their happiness. Which of the two parties is "the less deceived"? Larkin's honesty at the poem's end might lead the reader to conclude that the poet is less deluded than the solemn, mauling dancers. Yet the use of the masculine "himself" (though ostensibly a generic pronoun) and the dramatization of the poet's self-deception in the course of the poem lead the reader to speculate that the poet, though less deceived than at the poem's beginning, is still deceived himself.

Janice Moore Fuller

RECESSIONAL

Author: Rudyard Kipling (1865-1936)
Type of poem: Meditation
First published: 1897; collected in *Recessional and Other Poems*, 1899

The Poem

"Recessional" contains five stanzas of six lines each, with the first and third lines and the second and fourth rhyming. Following each quatrain there appears a rhymed couplet, which remains the same in the first four stanzas, then changes in the fifth. The closing couplet issues an even firmer admonition to underscore the warning that is extended in the previous refrain.

A recessional is a hymn or piece of music that is sung or played at the end of a religious service. From one perspective, the title dictates the form of the poem, which follows the tradition of the English hymn. More significantly, though, the title may be taken ironically. The poem was written in 1897, the year of Queen Victoria's Diamond Jubilee, which turned into a celebration of the British Empire. "Recessional," seems to herald the end of the Empire rather than to assure its long life.

In the opening quatrain, the poet speaks to the "God of our fathers" and acknowledges Him as the Lord of all that the British control. The couplet that follows asks that God's spirit be with the poet and his proud, vain countrymen unless they fail to understand that permanence and salvation can be found only in "Thine ancient sacrifice," not in temporal things: "Lord God of Hosts, be with us yet,/ Lest we forget—lest we forget." The poet then continues what is essentially a prayer, and in each stanza he speaks more directly to the empire builders themselves. In the second stanza, for example, he reminds them that rulers depart and only God remains. This idea he reinforces in the third and fourth verses, which take up the fleeting nature of pomp, power, and pride.

The final stanza emphasizes even more strongly that such worldly accomplishments as the Empire, no matter how valiantly sought and guarded, transform into mere dust when placed alongside the eternal nature of God. The closing couplet, different from those that have ended the preceding four stanzas, warns the British of boasting and foolishness, and supplicates God for mercy: "For frantic boast and foolish word—/ Thy mercy on Thy People, Lord!"

Forms and Devices

Today Rudyard Kipling is not considered a fashionable poet, in part because of the even rhythms and rhyme that characterize his work, but those very forms and devices for which he is now often criticized make many of the poems pleasantly readable, especially when presented aloud. Certainly, he was neither an innovator nor a major influence on English poetry, but many of his varied poems provide an accessible and often amusing history of the British Empire. He was a master of the dramatic monologue, as illustrated in a poem such as "Gunga Din," and he could handle the ballad form with good effect.

From a technical standpoint, however, "Recessional" stands apart from the poems that record the brighter side of the Empire. In this poem Kipling departs from his usual methodology and adapts the form of the hymn to suit his own purposes. The English hymn owes its origins to the eighteenth century poet Isaac Watts (1674-1748), and those who came after Watts followed the patterns set down by him. Kipling also remains faithful to the established forms and devices.

First, the hymns were usually addressed to God, who is called by various set names. Kipling follows this format and employs many of the prescribed titles: "God of our fathers," "Lord God of Hosts," "Judge of the Nations." He uses the formal "Thy" and "Thine" throughout. An expression such as "awful Hand," which appears in the first stanza, is also typical, even though it jars modern readers who may not know that "awful" once meant "full of awe" and served aptly to describe God.

This stilted language, so characteristic of the hymn, is not only exercised to name the varied attributes of the divine being but is also used to describe material objects. For example, Kipling in the final stanza pictures a gun as a "reeking tube and iron shard." In the first stanza, rather than calling the Empire by name, Kipling chooses the metonymic device of "palm and pine" to represent the vast regions the British dominate; later he conjures up great stretches of the Empire by the simple words, "dune and headland."

Echoes from the King James Version of the Bible also find their way into the language and imagery of the hymn. Kipling follows this dictate as well by speaking of the "dust that builds on dust" and referring to an Old Testament city, Nineveh. The fourth stanza draws on a direct reference from Romans in the New Testament to point out how the British erroneously considered themselves superior to those they ruled.

Finally, the hymn requires what might be called stock words to depict humankind's folly in contrast to divine wisdom. Kipling fulfills this demand as well, when he damns the Diamond Jubilee of Queen Victoria for being full of "tumult," "shouting," and "pomp" and admonishes the celebrants, whom he sees as "drunk with sight of power," speaking in "Wild tongues that have not Thee in awe."

Kipling, then, has relied on the versification and diction of the traditional English hymn, which for the most part does not constitute great poetry. This undistinguished form and its devices—noble in their own manner—may give Kipling's poem an old-fashioned air and may even at first obscure its timeless truths. Once "Recessional" is seen as a subversion of the very pattern it employs, the irony becomes apparent and the poem gains resonance. Although the hymn tradition that serves as the basis for the poem is intended to praise, Kipling has done quite the opposite, condemning the excesses of Empire and those caught up in an orgy of nationalism.

Themes and Meanings

At the time that "Recessional" was written, the British boasted that the sun never set on their Empire, one of the most extensive, powerful, and prosperous exercises in imperialism that the world had ever known. That Kipling observed the celebration of an empire—surely thought to last a thousand years—by titling his poem "Recessional" suggests that he foresaw an end to British dominion over such far-flung places as great parts of Africa and the West Indies, Australia, Canada, New Zealand, and India. Even though this gloomy assessment disappointed those who thought of Kipling as a defender of the Empire and led to criticism, he was right after all. In fact, even at the time of the Diamond Jubilee in 1897, cracks had started to appear in the imperial shield. There had been the 1857 mutiny against the British in India, and the Boer War in South Africa would start in 1899; as well, nationalism was on the rise in settler countries such as Australia. World War I weakened the Empire further, and World War II brought about its dismantling—by the 1950's, the Empire was indeed only the "pomp of yesterday." Kipling predicts this collapse in his disparaging reference to the glorious exercise in dominion that occurred when bonfires were lighted simultaneously around the world to observe the anniversary of Queen Victoria's accession to the throne; the line that calls up this event is less than triumphant: "On dune and headland sinks the fire."

Two lines in the fourth stanza allude to the British attitude toward the subjects who populated their Empire: "Such boastings as the Gentiles use,/ Or lesser breeds without the Law." This allusion is not altogether clear without reference to its biblical source, Romans 2:14: In Paul's epistle to the Romans, he warns the Gentiles that they are not exempt from the holy law, but like the Jews are subject to the "judgment of God." Particularly appropriate is the earlier verse (2:11), where Paul states: "For there is no respect of persons with God." At the basis of Empire lay the idea that the British were superior to those they ruled and were not subject to the same restrictions as the "lesser breeds"—Kipling's ironic description of the British subjects, black and white, who dwelled in the stolen land on which the sun never set. The Anglo-Saxon superiority so cherished by the British had apparently been granted them by their Christian God. The spread of Christianity figured prominently in the business of Empire, but even the embrace of the official religion did not confer British superiority on the Indian or African.

While the poem may be read satisfactorily in its historical context as a death knell for the British Empire, it can also be approached as a religious poem that summons humankind to shun earthly delights and with "An humble and a contrite heart" direct attention toward eternal values. The Empire then becomes a metaphor representing worldly things that turn to dust, even if their glitter attracts a boasting and foolish people.

Robert L. Ross

THE RED WHEELBARROW

Author: William Carlos Williams (1883-1963)
Type of poem: Lyric
First published: 1923, as "XXII," in *Spring and All*; as "The Red Wheelbarrow," in
   Selected Poems, 1949

The Poem

"The Red Wheelbarrow" is a brief lyric written in free verse. It is composed of four stanzas, each consisting of two short lines. The entire poem contains only sixteen words, four words in each stanza. The lyric "I" does not appear, placing the reader in direct contact with the images of the poem. These are presented one by one in short lines, which slow the reading and focus the reader's attention on each bit of information in a sequence that suspends completion of the scene until the very last word. The surprise implicit in this arrangement is particularly present in the poem as it was first published, without a title, as poem number "XXII" in *Spring and All*. In that book William Carlos Williams alternates passages of prose expressing his theories of poetry with groups of poems illustrating those theories.

The poet begins with an impersonal statement, composed of abstract words: "so much depends/ upon." This stanza creates suspense by raising the question, What depends on what? This is partly answered in the second stanza: "a red wheel/ barrow." In contrast with the words of the first stanza, each word here, except for the article "a," evokes a sense of impression. By dividing the word "wheelbarrow" into its parts, "wheel" and "barrow," and by breaking the line after "barrow," the poet slows the reading, which helps to imprint the image on the reader's mind. It also makes a wheelbarrow less familiar than usual, its wheel separated from its barrow, a tray with two handles at each end for carrying loads. Implicit here is the original idea for the invention of a wheelbarrow.

In the third stanza the poet begins to provide a context for the wheelbarrow in the natural world with the information that it is "glazed with rain/ water." It might be thought that the word "water" is superfluous. By separating the word "rain" from "water" with a line break, however, the poet continues the slow motion and suggests that the rain has just stopped. The word "glazed" implies light shining off the film of water still present on the red paint of the wheelbarrow. The sun has come out.

The fourth and final stanza completes the scene. The wheelbarrow is "beside the white/ chickens." The color white contrasts with the color red, which intensifies both colors and suggests bright light. The sentient chickens contrast with the inert wheelbarrow. The chickens are moving, and the scene comes alive. Human beings do not appear in the poem, but they are implied, as it took people to domesticate animals and invent machines.

Forms and Devices

Williams has excluded most of the forms and devices traditionally associated with poetry in the composition of this poem. He rejects the convention of beginning each line with a capital letter; he does not employ a traditional form; he avoids writing in an established meter; and he does not use rhyme. He does not use words for their connotations or associations or write in elevated language. He excludes similes, metaphors, and symbols. Even the subject of the poem is mundane, a wheelbarrow not being the sort of thing likely to inspire aesthetic contemplation or reveal great truth. The term "anti-poetry," sometimes applied to Williams's work, is valid only in reference to characteristics such as these.

Williams relies almost entirely on images to communicate the meanings of "The Red Wheelbarrow," and the poem exemplifies the principles of Imagism, a literary movement originated in London by friends of Williams, the American expatriate poets Hilda Doolittle (H. D.) and Ezra Pound. Imagist poetry presents things directly, using only words essential to the presentation, and is composed in free verse. Although Williams sometimes used the term "Imagism" and "free verse" in reference to his work, he was intent on creating an American poetry distinct from English poetry, and he distanced himself from the expatriates, substituting the term "Objectivism" for "Imagism" and developing his conception of the variable foot to distinguish his versification from free verse.

Although the images in "The Red Wheelbarrow" refer to objects in the external world, Objectivism also applies to the poem as an object itself, made out of words and comparable to a painting made out of paint. Williams knew and was influenced by such visual artists as Alfred Stieglitz and Charles Demuth. He believed that a poem can be a painting and a painting can be a poem. "The Red Wheelbarrow" creates a visual scene in the reader's mind, and the first stanza, "so much depends/ upon," functions like a frame for the picture. It says, "Look at this." A painting is seen, however, all at once, while the poem occurs image by image, line after line, having a duration in time.

The poem is intricately structured in repeating patterns. For example, there are four words and three stressed syllables in each stanza. Stanzas are arranged in two lines each, the first containing three words and two stressed syllables, the second containing one word and one stressed syllable. The poem also exemplifies the variable foot. Each line is a poetic foot, and each foot is to be given the same duration in reading. This results in a pause following the second line of each stanza to make up for the extra stressed syllable in each of the first lines. Variations in rhythm also result from the number and placement of unstressed syllables. For example, the unstressed syllable in the third line of the poem, "a red wheel," comes before the two stressed syllables, while in the fifth line, "glazed with rain," it comes between the two stressed syllables.

Themes and Meanings

What "depends upon" a red wheelbarrow, white chickens, and rain? The reader is aware of the usefulness—in the case of rain, the necessity—of these things in the external world. The things referred to in the poem are also particular instances of types and classes of things—the wheelbarrow being a machine, for example, on which life also depends. Furthermore, sensations, feelings, emotions, thoughts, and ideas depend on such things. As the poet expresses it in his poem "A Sort of a Song," "No ideas/ but in things." The faculty of the mind that has ideas is the imagination. "The Red Wheelbarrow" is about the relationship between the imagination and reality.

In *Spring and All*, Williams explains that the imagination is the opposite of fantasy; it penetrates fantasies to reveal realities. It clears away personal and conventional associations and meanings that human beings have attached to things, and to the words that represent them, enabling human consciousness to perceive the things of reality as directly as possible. In *Spring and All*, Williams writes: "To refine, to clarify, to intensify that eternal moment in which we alone live there is but a single force—the imagination."

The poet creates such an experience for the reader in "The Red Wheelbarrow." The imagination is itself a force of nature that creates things like poems and wheelbarrows, just as nature creates rain and white chickens. The reader experiences the poet's imagination in the process of making the poem, making a thing out of words to stand in relation to the reader as would an actual experience of the scene represented in the poem. Williams does not employ the lyric "I" of the poet's personality or use the conventions and devices traditionally associated with poetry. This allows the reader to focus on the words and images of the poem. Williams's strategies also seek to dissolve the personal ego of the reader. Forgetting self, the reader achieves a moment of pure awareness.

It is the poet's mind that the reader experiences, as it selects and arranges the words of the poem, revealing the ideas implicit in them. The words depend on the things and the processes they name for their existence and meaning. In this light, the nonimagistic words in the poem are particularly interesting. The images name things and their visual qualities, but what is the difference between "a" red wheelbarrow and "the" red wheelbarrow? What ideas are referred to in the prepositions "on," "with," and "beside"? What is the meaning of "depends"? The ideas expressed by these words have been discovered by the human imagination in its contemplation of things and the relationships among them. Language depends on things, and civilization depends on language.

James Green

A REFUSAL TO MOURN THE DEATH, BY FIRE,
OF A CHILD IN LONDON

Author: Dylan Thomas (1914-1953)
Type of poem: Lyric
First published: 1945; collected in *Deaths and Entrances*, 1946

The Poem

"A Refusal to Mourn the Death, by Fire, of a Child in London," a poem of twenty-four lines divided into four stanzas of six lines each, follows the rhyme scheme *abcabc*. The title indicates the poet's rejection of conventional means of responding to death. The refusal takes on greater force as it confronts the senseless casualty of a child to war; the fire refers to the firebombing of London during World War II.

The poem is written in the first person, and more is revealed about the poet who speaks than about the child who has died. The poet declares that not until he himself dies will he declaim the child's death. He rejects somber elegies, with their toxic spirituality; in dying, the child has united with the elements from which life springs and therefore is no longer prey to death.

The poem opens boldly with an extended adjective—"mankind/ making/ Bird, beast and flower/ Fathering and all humbling"—that modifies "darkness." The image locates the origin of life in death. The poet thus evokes at the start the natural cycle of birth and death. The darkness signals the "last light breaking"—light indicating consciousness—as well as the stilling of the "sea tumbling in harness," or the blood surging through the body. Death, then, extinguishes both the psychic and physical signs of an individual life.

This loss is more accurately a transformation: Single life diffuses into universal life. After death, one must "enter again" the "Zion of the water bead" and the "synagogue of the ear of corn." Rather than personal immortality, humans are destined for incorporation into dynamic, elemental bonds or assemblages of freshly sprouting life. Once metamorphosed, the poet can convey the child's experience in death, embodying the substance and vitality of nature itself.

Gripped by this awareness, the poet views customary rituals of mourning as sterile and hollow. To presume to honor the child with such pieties is to "murder" her humanity; to dare to sanctify her "innocence and youth" is to "blaspheme" the Incarnate Christ. With the phrase "the stations of the breath," the poet alludes to "the stations of the Cross," a ritualization of Jesus' suffering—again fusing life ("breath") and death.

In death, the girl joins life—that is, the "long friends," those long dead and forever alive—the "grains beyond age," or the seeds and sands of time, and the "dark veins of her mother," or the earth, veined with rivers. The water of the "riding Thames," London's river as the child is "London's daughter," is "unmourning"; it is the water of renewal, vital and teeming with life. Water quenches fire and nourishes seed, and just as rivers pour into the sea—all water being one—individual life flows into universal life, all life being one.

The ambiguity of the poem's last line, "After the first death, there is no other," suspends contraries in a vision of wholeness. Nature is compelled toward regeneration; therefore, while a death is final, life itself is eternal.

Forms and Devices

Fellow poet Conrad Aiken has called Dylan Thomas a "born language-lover" with a "genius for word magic." Thomas's passion for words is revealed in his conjuring of their sensual appeal as well as their connotative power.

The texture of the poem is enriched by the sound pattern woven by the poet. Besides the tight rhyme scheme, alliteration, as in "mankind making," "last light," and "sow my salt seed," helps draw the reader's senses into the world of the poem.

The poet also chooses words for the richness of their associations: "Zion," "synagogue," "pray," "sackcloth," "blaspheme," and "first death" are all radiant with religious significance. Juxtaposition of such terms with natural imagery—"water bead," "ear of corn," "sound," "valley," "grains"—indicates Thomas's understanding of the sacramental force of nature: The symbols of religious myth and ritual owe their potency to a link with primordial, natural realities.

The poet communicates such visionary insight with his complex imagery. "Zion of the water bead," for example, merges a symbol from religious legend, "Zion," with an original metaphor inspired by nature, "water bead." The complexity of Thomas's imagery renders it dynamic; the image provokes a reader to resolve the tensions between its disparate parts. Readers' preconceptions of science and religion, nature and myth, and past, present, and future are dramatically challenged.

As envisioned by the poet, human and natural life are of the same stuff. He envisions the human body as a microcosm of nature; the circular system is "the sea tumbling in harness." At the same time, he personifies nature: "grains" are "friends," and London's earth has "dark veins."

Themes and Meanings

Thomas's poetry has an almost revelatory power, in which meaning is experienced in the act of either creating or re-creating (that is, reading) the poem. The sound, rhythm, and visual impact, as well as psychological force, of the words have a transforming effect on the imagination. The violent shifts of perspective that the poem achieves help make one receptive to its visionary, ultimately healing power.

Thomas's concern with the creative process is evidenced in his own description of his "dialectical" method:

> An image must be born and die in another; and any sequence of my images must be a sequence of creations, recreations, destructions, contradictions. . . . Out of the inevitable conflict of images . . . I try to make that momentary peace which is a poem.

The poet's struggle is that of the creative imagination attempting to name the unnamable—that is, the mysteries of existence. The poem confounds contradictory images of life and death, sacred and profane, human and nonhuman, and the one and the many in an attempt to capture the inexhaustible fecundity and resilience of life. It climaxes in a statement which is itself a paradox: Death is final and yet is not, ultimately, definitive.

The poem's vision of the protean unity of all things transforms grief into wonder. This insight is affirmed both by ancient belief that life has eternal regenerative power and by scientific theory that matter can never be destroyed but only transmuted—into energy.

Amy Adelstein

THE RELIC

Author: John Donne (1572-1631)
Type of poem: Lyric
First published: 1633, in *Poems, by J. D.: With Elegies on Authors Death*

The Poem

"The Relic" is a lyric poem consisting of three stanzas of eleven lines each. As with numerous other English Metaphysical lyrics, the stanza form and rhyme scheme are unusual and perhaps unique. The pattern of five rhymes in each stanza is *aabbcddceee*, while the meter of lines is complex and somewhat irregular but basically iambic and effectively supplements the poem's thematic development. The four weighty iambic pentameter lines that conclude each stanza reinforce a change of tone from flippant or cynical to serious.

John Donne relies heavily on a first-person speaker who comes across as both worldly and spiritual, each quality being carried to an extreme. At the beginning, the speaker projects himself into the future when, long after his death, his bones are disinterred to make room for another burial. The macabre image of a disturbed grave contrasts with another more pleasant image. The grave digger, Donne asserts, will discover a bracelet of bright hair about the bone of the speaker's forearm. The hair represents the mistress, the "she" of the poem, just as the bones represent the speaker. Once the remains have been discovered, the perspective shifts from the speaker to the grave digger. The sexton may leave the grave without further disturbance, thinking that the "couple" is a pair of lovers who used the device of the hair so that at Judgment Day their souls might meet at the grave and enjoy a visit. This conceit is understood only if the reader knows the medieval and Renaissance conception of Judgment Day, in which believers thought that souls would go about seeking their scattered body parts at the time of the Apocalypse in order to reunite them and experience the resurrection with both body and soul intact.

The second stanza introduces another possibility more in keeping with the poem's title. Donne suggests that the sexton may do his work during a time when "misdevotion" rules, that is, when worship includes the adoration of relics. If that happens, he will take the bones and the hair to the bishop and the king, who will make them objects of adoration. The woman's hair will remind a later age of Mary Magdalene, and the speaker's bones will suggest "something else." After they have become relics, they will be credited with miracles performed during their lives, and people of the later period will want to know what miracles they performed. At the stanza's close, the speaker promises to explain them. The third stanza represents the speaker's view of the miracles they accomplished, expressed for the enlightenment of a later age. He asserts that they loved well and faithfully but that their love had nothing to do with differences of sex. Their constant love was instead entirely chaste, subdued, and so mysterious that they themselves did not understand it. At the conclusion, however, another abrupt shift in thought occurs, changing the poem into a compliment. The speaker asserts that he would surpass all language if he told "what a miracle she was."

Forms and Devices

The devices of "The Relic" are complex and intricate, with brilliant imagery and characterization. The macabre beginning and cynical tone suggest a poem that will conclude with wry pessimism or cynicism. Instead, the lyric offers a positive affirmation upholding the value of love. Personification is perhaps the most ingenious device that the poet employs. Objects such as the grave are personified, but Donne goes beyond his normally strained meanings by making the bones represent the speaker's character and the wreath of hair represent the mistress. While the first-person speaker sees his bones becoming his character in a later age, he also retains his own authorial persona, asserting that his address in "this paper" (the poem) will explain the miracles they have wrought to the audience. The speaker's alteration between a tone of hard worldliness and a spiritual, idealistic side creates a vivid, dramatic contrast. The grave digger also becomes an important personage in the poem, for he reacts to what he sees in different ways. Even a generalized audience is conjured up as the two lovers become objects of devotion, adored by "All women . . . and some men."

The work reveals the typical obscurantism of Metaphysical poetry, including allusions to esoteric ideas and outmoded concepts such as the more extreme Renaissance concepts of the Apocalypse and the practice of removing bones from graves after a time and placing them in a charnel house in order to make room for a new tenant. Yet some allusions remain obscure to modern scholars. The reference to the chaste mistress as Mary Magdalene has led scholars to conjecture that the mistress may be Magdalene Herbert, Donne's patron and the mother of the poet George Herbert. What Donne means by having the speaker refer to himself as a "something else thereby" cannot be clearly ascertained. Another crux occurs in lines 29-30 ("Our hands ne'er touched the seals/ Which nature, injured by late law, sets free"), a passage that has puzzled critics and editors for many years. The lines clearly proclaim that their love was chaste, but the precise meanings of the metaphor "seals" or the personification "nature, injured by late law, sets free" remain elusive. A possibility is that Donne had in mind the innocent sexuality of Eden before the Fall contrasted with a later time of law when human sexuality became laden with the concept of sin.

The lyric is, above all, a poem of sharp contrasts. In an early analysis, poet T. S. Eliot refers to the intellectual agility required of the reader, using the alliterative sixth line ("A bracelet of bright hair about the bone") to illustrate the point. The imagery exerts special demands and offers special rewards. The initial image, a bracelet, is pleasant, and the phrase "of bright hair" that follows, though unusual and unexpected, still represents something pleasant. The completion of the image lends further surprise, even astonishment, for the expected "about the arm" veers into the macabre "about the bone." The reader finds it necessary to adjust the normal and expected responses to conform with the juxtaposition of diverse images. The entire poem places exceptional demands upon the reader yet offers pleasant surprises. The stanzas themselves illustrate the need for shifts in perspective. As they begin, the worldly speaker offers cynical asides, sardonic references, and a tone of hard realism. In the course of each stanza, a transition to a contrasting idealism or a suggestion of idealism occurs by way of conclusion.

Themes and Meanings

Although its title suggests a religious poem, "The Relic" is in reality a celebration of platonic love and a poem of compliment. The poem's pervasive religious diction and imagery establish a framework for celebrating a platonic relationship between the poem's speaker and his mistress. However, the complexity of both religion and love as themes invites multilevel meanings and ambiguities, and the poem is fraught with these. Donne is at his most ingenious and obscure as he develops the tropes and witty hyperboles of the lyric.

In his numerous songs and sonnets, Donne offers extremely varied treatments of love as a theme, from the most cynical and blatantly sexual to the most idealized, platonic form. "The Relic" employs a highly charged religious context to celebrate an ideal, chaste love. In the poems that reflect a positive attitude toward love, whether sexual or ideal, Donne frequently depicts the love as unique, special to the speaker and his mistress, even arcane and elevating, and apt to be misunderstood by ordinary people. The love celebrated in "The Relic" is mystical; not even those who share it can understand it. This hieratic view of love is implied by the sexton, who is puzzled by the remains he discovers, and then by the speaker's urge to explain it to a later age. The thinly veiled implication is that people in the later age, like those in the present, will be incapable of understanding the lovers' virtue because they cannot approach it.

It is a tribute to Donne's imaginative genius that he derives a transcendently noble theme from an initial, macabre image. In this regard, "The Relic" represents a sharp contrast with its companion poem "The Funeral," which employs similar macabre imagery. In "The Funeral," Donne uses the device of a woman's hair and a recently deceased corpse as a kind of consolation for unrequited love. The speaker, who proclaims that he will be discovered dead with a wreath of her hair about his arm, protests that he intends to bury some of her because she would have none of him. In contrast, the speaker in "The Relic" celebrates a long-enduring, chaste love that is comforting but too mystical to be fully understood.

Stanley Archer

RELIGIO LAICI

Author: John Dryden (1631-1700)
Type of poem: Verse essay
First published: 1682

The Poem

Religio Laici (a layman's religion) represents John Dryden's tentative and candid examination of major religious issues of his day. From the title, one might expect a personal confession of faith. Instead, Dryden examines the principal contemporary religious currents in England and, although he reveals only general points about his own beliefs, he clearly expresses his adherence to the Church of England. The poem, consisting of 456 lines of heroic couplets, divides into several logical sections.

In the beginning, Dryden eloquently points to limitations on the power of reason in religion, stressing that even the ancient philosophers, despite all their wisdom, could discover no adequate foundation for religion through their intellectual efforts. Because he shared with his contemporaries a profound respect for the intellectual attainments of the classical Greeks and Romans, this line of reasoning effectively prepares the groundwork for Dryden's rejection of Deism, the rational religion of his own day. A summary of basic Deistic tenets (lines 42-61) precedes a formal rejection of natural religion.

Dryden suggests that any light the Deist sees originates in revelation, not from man's intuitive knowledge as the Deists assumed, and that, in any case, a lesser being such as man cannot atone for his own sins through his own efforts (lines (62-125). Only an unfallen being, Dryden urges, would be adequate to the task. Defending the Bible as the true source of religious revelation (lines 126-167), Dryden cites specific factors that support its authority: its antiquity, its narrative consistency, the conviction and courage of its authors, external confirmation from other sources, its style, its success despite its demanding ethics, and its acceptance despite persecution.

The Deist renews the debate that it is unjust that so many who never had an opportunity to receive revelation have been lost. Dryden agrees that this is a grave charge, yet he thinks that through divine mercy many who never knew the true religion might yet have been saved (lines 168-223).

As this point, the poem takes a different approach to the question of scriptural authority by discussing Father Richard Simon's *Histoire critique du Vieux Testament* (*Critical History of the Old Testament*), first published in 1678 and translated into English in 1682 by Henry Dickinson. In a note in his text, Dryden explains that this portion is a digression, though it returns him to the authority of Scripture versus tradition, a central difference between Protestants and Catholics. Since he has already argued for the authority of the Bible, Dryden has laid the groundwork for parrying a newer and more recent challenge. Through meticulous scholarship, Simon demonstrated that translators had so loosely and inaccurately translated biblical books that their claim to serve as a basis for faith was seriously compromised. His purpose was to induce readers to turn to the authority of the Roman Catholic Church as an infallible guide. Dryden acknowledges that Simon's points are cogent in many instances but believes that the translations are sufficiently accurate on matters of genuine importance. He asserts that Scripture is clear on essential points and rejects the view that an infallible church exists. While Dryden does not entirely exclude reliance upon tradition, he points out that generally the most reliable is the most ancient. Thus, tradition should be considered, but more trust should be placed in the authority of the most ancient church fathers.

Excessive reliance on tradition, Dryden charges, has caused the Catholic Church to deny the laity access to the Bible (lines 356-397). Yet making the text available had the unfortunate effect of causing individuals to become overzealous and to run to extremes of contention and sectarianism (lines 398-426). Rejection of tradition thus led to extremes of private interpretation and ensuing religious strife.

In the conclusion of the poem (lines 427-456), Dryden recommends moderation based upon the realization that necessary points of faith are few and plain. He further suggests that disputed points might be settled through the authority of the earliest and least corrupt of church fathers and that an individual who differs from others on doctrine can promote the interests of society as a whole by keeping personal beliefs private.

Forms and Devices

In his lengthy prose introduction to *Religio Laici*, Dryden comments on the style appropriate to a poem of its kind:

> If anyone be so lamentable a critic as to require the smoothness, the numbers, and the turn of heroic poetry in this poem, I must tell him that, if he has not read Horace, I have studied him, and hope the style of his *Epistles* is not ill imitated here. The expressions of a poem design'd purely for instruction ought to be plain and natural, and yet majestic; for here the poet is presum'd to be a kind of lawgiver, and those three qualities which I have nam'd are proper to the legislative style.

Casting himself in the role of an instructor and teacher, Dryden is content to eschew poetic ornaments and figures in favor of a direct, plain style.

The poem employs the heroic couplet, Dryden's preferred verse form, with few variations. Major structural divisions are usually indicated through verse paragraphs. Although most of the couplets are end-stopped, the norm for this stanza pattern, a large number end with less than a full stop so that the grammatical unit carries over to additional lines. This extension of the grammatical unit enables Dryden to pursue a line of reasoning smoothly to its end, taking into account some of its complexities. Dryden's expansion of the normal limits of the couplet is one key to his skill at reasoning verse.

In Dryden's heroic couplets, metrical departures are limited to two major ones, and both can be observed in *Religio Laici*. By occasionally adding a line to form a triplet,

Dryden breaks the steady rhythm of the couplet. The break is even more effective when he makes the third verse a hexameter and creates a climactic effect, although among the seven triplets in *Religio Laici* few create an impressive rhetorical climax. The satiric tone of the following, expressing disapproval of excessive and individual reliance upon Scripture, may represent the triplet at its most effective in the poem:

> The spirit gave the doctoral degree;
> And every member of a company
> Was of his trade and of the Bible free.

The triplet's final verse, a hexameter for emphasis, achieves subtle poetic effects through balance and the use of zeugma, an unusual scheme for Dryden.

The second variation, use of a hemistitch or "half line," occurs only once in the poem. As a precedent for this metrical variation, Dryden cites Vergil, probably erroneously, for modern critics believe that the short lines in the *Aeneid* (c. 29-19 B.C.E.) are actually incomplete verses. Dryden uses the hemistitch to achieve an effective climax in the following passage:

> Those giant wits, in happier ages born,
> . . . .
> Knew no such system; no such piles could raise
> Of natural worship, built on pray'r and praise
> To One Sole GOD.

The final verse of only four syllables draws the reader up short; emphasis is further heightened by accents on three of its four syllables.

Throughout the poem Dryden uses schemes of repetition, such as balance and antithesis, yet his style remains for the most part simple and unadorned, at least by comparison with his other long poems in heroic couplets. In large measure, he assumes the stance of the debater, answering objections from the Deist on the one hand and the Catholic on the other. On occasion, Dryden personifies his adversary and gives him a direct quotation. The effect is clearly to stack the argument in Dryden's favor, since his opponents have no opportunity to attack his own moderate positions outlined near the poem's conclusion. When he presents his own views, he speaks in the first person, in a tone that is both reassuring and restrained. In both prose and verse, Dryden was a master of the art of taking the reader into his confidence.

Not all the diction is informal and colloquial, however; the most striking departure from the plain style can be found in the poem's opening twenty-two lines. In stately, slow rhythms, verses adorned with similes and metaphors and with schemes of repetition achieve a studied, majestic effect as Dryden explores the limitations of reason. The careful arrangement of sounds creates a tone of solemnity appropriate to Dryden's subject—the inadequacy of reason in religion. The verses remind the reader that Dryden is indeed capable of the heroic style that he has agreed to abandon. Paradoxically, while Dryden rejects reason as inadequate, he employs it as fully as possible in support of his major arguments throughout the rest of the poem.

Themes and Meanings

Although Dryden acknowledges the limits of reason in religious inquiry, his objective is to persuade the reader by presenting a rational, moderate argument. As he says in his preface, men are to be reasoned into truth. His portrayal of the Church of England and its theological stance reflects the longstanding view of the church as a *via media*, a middle way between extremes. Dryden is content to uphold general beliefs, such as the authority of Scripture and atonement, and leave other points vague.

The occasion for the poem is not known, though it is possible that, as poet laureate, Dryden thought it prudent to distance himself from the rising current of Deism, or rational religion, which appealed to his age. Like many Englishmen of the Restoration, he shared the view that extremes in religion brought calamity to society, though unlike the Deists, he was unwilling to distance himself from Christianity.

He disagrees with Deism on two basic assumptions. First, he rejects the view that basic religious truths are innate and articulable through reason. If that were so, Dryden argues cogently, the ancients would have discovered them. Second, he argues that following the fall, man's reconciliation with God cannot be achieved by man himself. The Deists, rejecting the idea of original sin, logically denied the need for atonement. On the other hand, Dryden agrees with the Deistic view that to condemn those who lived before or outside the Christian tradition seems unjust. Dryden's answer is to view the matter with tolerance and to suggest that divine mercy, in some manner, may well extend to everyone.

His eloquent defense of Scripture paves the way for rejection of the arguments raised by Simon's work on the Old Testament. Instead of attacking specifics, Dryden addresses the writer's motive, believing that the author sought to discredit the Bible in order to persuade men to accept Catholic oral tradition. While acknowledging some errors in biblical accounts, Dryden maintains that the text is adequate on essential beliefs and points out dangers in man's reliance upon tradition.

The rejection of extreme Protestant belief is brief by comparison. Dryden thinks that extremes of individualism have been the result of too much reliance upon individual interpretation of the Scripture, a condition that leads to sects, dissent, and strife. He suggests that men consult their own church's views on particulars of belief and ancient tradition.

Dryden is more concerned with defending a middle-of-the-road position in religion than with making any original contributions of his own. From this position, he discredits movements he believes to be socially dangerous, subversive, and disruptive. While attacking what he regards as dangerous extremes, he carefully avoids consideration of any specific doctrines of religion, as if to suggest that the Christian tradition permits many shades of belief and that tolerance of differences represents the best attitude.

Stanley Archer

RELOCATION

Author: David Mura (1952-   )
Type of poem: Meditation
First published: 1982; collected in *Breaking Silence: An Anthology of Contemporary Asian American Poets*, 1983; revised in *After We Lost Our Way*, 1989

The Poem

"Relocation," a poem of forty-seven lines, has four major sections separated by asterisks. Within each major section are three four-line stanzas, with the exception of the first section, which has only two stanzas, and an italicized haiku that concludes the final section. The poem's dedication reads, "for Grandfather Uyemura," the central character in the poem. It is his several "relocations" that the poem describes. The physical removals from Japan to America, within America, and back to Japan are sometimes voluntary and sometimes coerced, and they result in either exhilaration and freedom or depression and oppression.

David Mura uses the format of the poem to deliver a sketchy biography of his grandfather, recounting the most significant events in his grandfather's adult life. The poem also indirectly traces the emotions with which Mura's grandfather responds to those life experiences and, even more indirectly, Mura's own emotional reactions to those events that predate his own birth.

The first section begins with an expository stanza that makes reference to an Asian custom prevalent around the 1920's. Asian men who had immigrated to America to seek their fortunes would send to their home countries a picture of themselves as a way of advertising for a bride of the same ethnic background. They would pay the one-way passage to America of any eligible woman who would be lured across the ocean by the picture and promise of marriage. Because the couple would not have previously met, the woman thus based her entire future happiness on the merit of a snapshot, and there were often unpleasant surprises at the dock if the man had misrepresented himself. Grandfather Uyemura, however, was so handsome that he did not hide behind a picture but returned to Japan in person to claim a bride. He was able to sail back to America with his arms around his chosen mate.

In section 2, Mura recounts his grandparents' success in establishing a happy life in their new country. Through industry and hard work, Grandfather Uyemura has bought a greenhouse where he grows orchids and roses. He also has enjoyed a certain amount of luck in the gambling houses.

The mood shifts away from happiness and good fortune in section 3, however. World War II breaks out, and the Japanese people living in America, including Grandfather and Grandmother Uyemura, are herded by the government into various "relocation camps" for the duration of the war. Instead of their pleasant home and greenhouse, the couple now lives with other Japanese Americans in barracks surrounded by guards and barbed wire. Grandfather Uyemura is forced to plow fields and eat meals in a common mess hall with his wife.

The war has ended for some time by the final section, and the couple has a son whom they have named Kitsugi. He, however, adopts American ways with a new name—Tom—and a new religion—Christianity—which confuses and disappoints Grandfather Uyemura, a Buddhist. When his wife dies, Grandfather Uyemura returns to Tokyo and composes haiku in his old age.

Forms and Devices

Although all stanzas but the final haiku have a consistent number of lines that are roughly the same length, the poem breaks from conventional form because the lines do not rhyme. Grandfather Uyemura himself breaks from tradition in that he returns to Japan in person rather than trusting a snapshot to deliver a life partner to him.

His early adult life is lucky. His exuberance and good fortune are shown in the shining chrome of his Packard, at which he proudly beams. There is also an invincibility evident in the second stanza: After a lucky night at gambling, he greets even the thorns on the roses. He will not let hurtful things bother him. His imprisonment in the relocation camps with other Japanese does not defeat the spirits of either him or his wife. Their strength is that they have each other—for companionship and love—and their heritage.

At dinner, Grandfather Uyemura folds an origami crane out of a napkin, to the amusement and rapture of his wife. Besides signifying flight or freedom of spirit as any bird imagery would do, the crane has long symbolized for cultures ranging from China to the Mediterranean three other qualities: justice, longevity, and the good and diligent soul. The poem shows that Grandfather Uyemura possesses all three of those traits. Though treated with gross injustice, he unquestioningly does what he is ordered to do; he outlives his wife; and he is a good person who works hard. In Japanese, the name he has chosen for his son means "prince of birds."

An important poetic device that Mura uses is ambiguously purposeful enjambment (when the grammatical, logical, and syntactical sense of a poetic line both continues into the next line and also gains an additional meaning by pausing at the end of the first line). The first occurrence of this device is in lines 9 and 10. If one reads without pause to the first comma, the main idea is that Grandfather Uyemura was able to purchase his greenhouse through hard word and diligent saving. If the reader pauses instead at the end of line 9, the word "field" is sensed as a noun of location rather than an adjective. Imagining Grandfather Uyemura's greenhouse "on a field" emphasizes the concept of land that is important to the poem—specifically, the new land of America that challenges such immigrants as Grandfather Uyemura.

Another instance of enjambment occurs in the final four-line stanza in lines 42 to 44. At this point, Grandfather Uyemura's defiance has become resignation; his wife has died, his son seems more American than Japanese, and he himself is returning to Japan. If these lines are read with attention to the commas—not pausing at the ends of the lines—the picture that evolves is of Grandfather Uyemura, thin and cranelike, sitting in a chair and writing poetry. If, instead, the reader pauses at the end of line 43 and considers "spent" as an adjective rather than as a transitive verb, the implication is that old Grandfather Uyemura is himself spent, defeated by an unjust life in his new country. From such a stance, though, poetry finally emerges, and such a voice signifies a spiritual strength despite an emaciated physical body.

Themes and Meanings

Two important themes are central to an understanding and appreciation of the poem: movement or relocation and the larger issue of the clash of Japanese ethnicity with American culture.

The bird imagery in the poem, beginning with the screech of seagulls at the dock when Grandfather Uyemura meets his future wife, symbolizes the flight that characterizes the grandfather's life: immigration, return to Japan for a bride, return to America to seek his fortune, forced relocation in the internment camp, and return to his homeland. Putting down roots in a new country has not been possible for Grandfather Uyemura (although there are indications that it will be for his son), whose adult life has been marked by a continual pattern of flight. He is like the origami crane that he himself designs.

As the poem's title, "relocation" names what once must have been Grandfather Uyemura's sought-after personal goal. By the end of the poem some twenty years later, though, his return to his place of birth and to composing a verse form that is particularly Japanese indicate that American culture has not assimilated him and that he has settled on his culture of origin as his ethnic identity. As early as stanza 2, "pale ghosts" are gathering, which may be read as *hakujin*, or white people, that surround the Japanese couple in America. (The practice of labeling non-Asian people as "ghosts" is given extensive treatment in the works of another Asian American writer, Maxine Hong Kingston.) On a less literal level, the pale ghosts could symbolize the ghosts of the grandfather's Japanese ancestors who will not let him rest until he returns to his home and his heritage.

Confined by Caucasian guards in the camp, Grandfather Uyemura outwardly submits to hard physical labor on one hand, but on the other hand silently defies his imprisonment, which he will not allow to break his spirit. He keeps his gaze on the "west," toward Japan, and mutters under his breath "Baka" to the guard. Mura does not gloss this Japanese expression, which is slang for "idiot" or "dumbbell." The grandfather is not giving in, and Mura also seems resistant toward catering too much to a non-Japanese reader.

Grandfather Uyemura has long cultivated the earth—as a field hand working to buy his greenhouse, then in the camp working a mule-driven plow. He has perhaps pruned the bonsai tree, which he writes about in his haiku, as he has nurtured his American orchids and roses. It is ironic, Mura implies, that the grandfather, at the hands of white America, has not been tended and nurtured with equal care and respect. His belief that "the Buddha always ate well" is at once a retort to his son's Christian crucifix that bears a gaunt and dying Jesus and a justification for himself, emaciated and aged, to return to Japan.

Subsequent to appearing in *Breaking Silence: An Anthology of Contemporary Asian American Poets* (1983) as one of hundreds of poems written by fifty Asian American poets, "Relocation" appeared in Mura's first book of poetry, *After We Lost Our Way* (1989), under the title "Suite for Grandfather & Grandmother Uyemura: Relocation." The more recent version uses richer and more enigmatic imagery and shows Grandfather Uyemura contemplating remarriage after returning to Tokyo. The rest of the narrative lines, including the final haiku, are retained, however.

Mura discusses his own writing and concerns in his prose autobiography, *Turning Japanese: Memoirs of a Sansei* (1991). Awarded a writing grant that allowed him to spend 1984 in Japan, Mura describes his own search for cultural identity. The book is a meditation on difference and assimilation as well as a telling portrait of modern Japan.

Jill B. Gidmark

REMEDIES, MALADIES, REASONS

Author: Mona Van Duyn (1921-   )
Type of poem: Lyric
First published: 1970, in *To See, to Take*

The Poem

"Remedies, Maladies, Reasons" is written in a loose iambic pentameter form and is composed of fifty-eight couplets that rhyme obliquely. The last line in the poem, which rhymes with the previous couplet, stands alone. There are three sections in the poem: The first thirty-six couplets form the first part; couplets 37 through 58 compose the second; and the single concluding line is a separate section of its own. The title serves as a synopsis of the poem: The speaker searches for reasons why her mother was so obsessed with her daughter's and her own physical maladies, and she wonders, in part, whether her mother's remedies were effective.

Mona Van Duyn and her mother are placed at the center of this lyric poem written in the conventional first person. This is not a persona poem; the speaker is the poet, and she is reflecting on her own past. The first section records chronologically Van Duyn's personal history, but the history is limited to the speaker's health and how the mother and daughter respond to it. The first sentence explains the dilemma: Van Duyn "nearly died/ at six weeks from nursing a serum" her mother had taken, so her mother becomes extremely overprotective of her, even when she grows up. "Girl Scouts, green apples, tree climbs, fairs," everything the "other kids" enjoyed, were off limits to her. Van Duyn describes herself as her mother's "one goose" that refused "to fatten" despite her mother's attempts to poke food into her daughter's mouth until she gagged. Enemas, mucus, mineral pills, bowels, and sore throats are the subjects of the mother-daughter discussions; the seemingly unhealthy relationship focuses solely on the daughter's health.

Van Duyn behaved in a submissive manner, partially because she "was scared to die," until she finally fought back as a junior in high school when her mother, in disciplining her, was "Breaking/ another free yardstick from the drygoods store/ on a butt and legs still bad." She continued rebelling in college, learning "how to tear up the letters" in which her mother gave her the customary advice: "for my sake please don't do it . . . don't try it . . . don't go . . . !" Years later, after Van Duyn had married and begun her career, when she returned to her mother's house to tend her ailing parents, she still heard the same litany: "Don't you dare go outside that door without your sweater!" The poet imagines that her mother can see on her daughter's shoulders, only "the weak, rolling head of a death-threatened baby."

In the beginning, section 2 turns the focus away from the mother's obsessive fascination with her daughter's health and concentrates on the mother's self-scrutiny; the self-scrutiny is limited to the world of the senses. Van Duyn's mother apparently has little interest in struggling for spiritual or psychological truths. She charts the levels of "blood in the snot," marvels at the smell of her sweat or urine, chronicles "the gas that makes her 'blow up tight as a drum,'" and counts the times she vomits: "I puked four times, and the last one/ was *pure bile!*"

Despite listing all the obvious shortcomings of her parent, Van Duyn remains fond of her mother and, in her mind's eye, can "still see the mother [she] wanted, that [she] called to come,/ coming." The poem closes with tremendous tenderness after all the "suppurating, rotting, stinking, swelling,/ . . . shrieking, . . . oozing." The emotional warmth, in the end, outshines the body's powers and failures.

Forms and Devices

Poets often write in couplets to draw the reader's attention toward the pairing going on in the poem; in this case, Van Duyn is drawing together mother and daughter, life and death, grief and tenderness, sickness and health, youth and age, accurate vision and hallucinations. The couplets also serve a more grounded purpose: In a particular rhyming couplet, the poet often tries to join words or ideas that are meant for each other. Van Duyn is a master of this. She rhymes "ate" and "toilet" and thereby heightens the intake/outflow obsession of the mother. "Oil" and "bowel" are linked by sound and function. The mother "marvels" at the "smells" her stinking body makes. It is marvelous to rhyme and find beauty in the beastly flesh. Rhyming also points out oppositions: The young Van Duyn wanted to "hike," but she was denied permission and forced to wear the shoes of the "chronic" invalid.

Van Duyn also yokes disparate ideas or images through her metaphors and comparisons. The poet describes her mother as a "Homer of her own heroic course" whose catalog of maladies and remedies echoes, humorously, Homer's own examples of bloody encounters and noble endurance. Van Duyn stays with the epic journey motif and describes her mother as an Odyssean character: "Keeping her painstaking charts, first mariner/ of such frightful seas, she logs each degree and number." The metaphor is funny but not cruel; the mother is on an epic journey toward death, but she only charts the number of times she "pukes" or the number of units of penicillin her doctor prescribes. The classical allusions end with another mock-heroic picture: The mother consults an oracle (a mysterious and sometimes dangerous action in ancient Greece), but here she consults only "the eight shelves of the six-foot, steel,/ crammed-with-medication oracle."

The final coupling takes place between the two different pictures the poet has of her mother. Van Duyn says, initially, "I know what she is, I know what she was:/ a hideous machine that pumps and wheezes." Her mother is a disgusting, stinking machine for "students to learn/ the horror, the nausea, of being human." The poet, however, draws the poem to a close with a typical gesture: She counters the mood by saying, "And yet. . . ." The qualification comes in the form of a reversal: The mother, looked at now, is "an attractive woman" and is the kind of mother the poet actually wanted. The formal device of the couplets makes the reader anticipate some sort of yoking or linking, and Van Duyn delivers on the promise that her formal choice suggests: Her mother is terrible and tender, both a horror and a blessing.

Themes and Meanings

"Remedies, Maladies, Reasons" is a love poem. It examines a mother's overbearing love for her daughter and the daughter's attempt to come to terms with her memories of that, at times, misdirected love. It is also a poem of praise, however, a character study of a woman—warts, snot, bile, belches, mucus, gas, and all.

Van Duyn, in college, away from the cloying love of her mother, is able, for the first time, to bear "like a strange bubble the health of [her] body/ as [she] walked the fantastic land of the ordinary." In this poem she is able, perhaps for the first time as well, to appreciate her mother as a larger-than-life character, one motivated by love. She is able to see, by the poem's close, what it is like to walk in the land of love's hallucinations.

The third section of this poem is a single line that has a double meaning. The line simply says, "Do you think I don't know how love hallucinates?" This line explains how the mother can be both a "suppurating, rotting, stinking, swelling . . . machine" and an "attractive woman." The love the mother felt for her daughter forced her to hallucinate about all the horrors that could befall her once-sickly child; but, on the other hand, love also allows the daughter to see the mother as something other than a sick flesh machine. Love purifies vision; the warts and all, accented so terribly in the first fifty couplets, are removed by the power of love. The loving mother is loved. She is attractive because of that love.

These hallucinations of love could, however, have another meaning. The poet imagines her mother "armed with pills, oils, drops,/ gargles, liniments, flannels, salves, syrups,/ waterbag, icebag," doing heroic battle, over her daughter's bed, with the Enemy—death. Van Duyn imagines that the mother will always drive her Enemy "from every sickening place where he hides and waits," but this is the ultimate hallucination. The Enemy always must win eventually, and that is the final terror of the poem. The daughter must be separated from her mother by death, and Van Duyn must also be separated from "the fantastic land of the ordinary" by death. The love one feels from a mother and for a mother may allow one to imagine an escape from death's sting, but the fantasy cannot last long. Van Duyn knows that it is only a hallucination when she imagines death always defeated. She knows that life, regrettably, is coupled with death.

Kevin Boyle

REMEMBERING TITIAN'S MARTYRDOM
OF SAINT LAWRENCE

Author: Jorie Graham (1951-   )
Type of poem: Lyric
First published: 1982; collected in *The Pushcart Prize, VIII*, 1983

The Poem

Although American, Jorie Graham grew up in Italy and received much of her education in Europe. "Remembering Titian's Martyrdom of Saint Lawrence," like many of Graham's poems, comes from her Italian experience. The poem describes a religious painting by the Renaissance painter Titian, a painting that exists in two versions. In both versions, the painting's foreground features Saint Lawrence, who reclines on a grill with a fire burning beneath him. In the earlier version of the painting (completed about 1557), the martyrdom is set in front of a temple façade, while in the later version (painted 1564-1567 by Titian and his workshop), the martyrdom occurs in an open archway. Smaller differences between the two versions abound. (In the painting's second version, for example, the human figures that surround Saint Lawrence are more grotesque, and two cherubs holding a crown descend from the sky.)

As Graham remembers the painting, she seems to be blending details from the two versions. This conflation may be unintentional, or she may be repainting Titian's martyrdom to suit thematic purposes of her own.

"Remembering Titian's Martyrdom of Saint Lawrence" is very much like the many other poems about paintings in Graham's second volume of poetry, *Erosion* (1983). In these poems, Graham describes a painting in detail but often freely alters these details, perhaps fulfilling what she calls in an interview her "rage to change" what is fixed and finished. The poems about painting—fitting into a subgenre of lyric poetry called ecphrastic poetry—follow a typical pattern of description modulating into meditation. The clearly meditative sections of Graham's ecphrastic poems often involve sudden plunges into metaphysical questioning about time and eternity, for instance, or permanence and impermanence, or the relation between spirit and flesh. Many critics of Graham's poetry have called her a philosophical poet, a very apt description as long as it does not imply that her poems are abstract or unsenuous. Graham is, however, one of the few contemporary poets who acclaims abstractions because she feels that they are messengers of silence and implicitly mark the failures of language.

Forms and Devices

In "Remembering Titian's Martyrdom of Saint Lawrence," Graham remembers most vividly the roiling smoke of the painting and its dominating lights—red from the fire, which flickers eerily and searchingly over the helmets and breastplates of the soldiers and the body of Saint Lawrence; and a blue light, which streams from the heavens and penetrates smoke and flame to brand, as the poem says, "even the meanest/ twig or/ fingertip." The lights of the painting irradiate not only Saint Lawrence and every detail of the painting but also the painting's circumambient air and, most intensely, the viewer of the painting:

> See
> how the two lights
>
> twine, over my face,
> my hands.
> Every pocket will be
> found out,
> every hollowness
> forgiven.

It is the way in which the painting's lights search out the viewer that most amazes and troubles the speaker of the poem. The blue and red lights are so lurid and searching that it is the viewer rather than the saint himself that must suffer the painting. The saint is, paradoxically, untouched by his own martyrdom: "Even the excitements/ of the smoke/ glide over him/ unshadowing." It is the viewer who is touched, ultimately examined, and judged by the painting.

Graham uses this and other paradoxes to begin what finally becomes an argument with the painting, a deep objection to its intervention in the life of humanity, which is by nature impermanent and vulnerable, unlike the marble-bodied saint that Titian depicts. The saint in the painting ultimately becomes, for the speaker, an affront to humanness.

Besides the poem's use of paradox and its intensification of the imagery and lighting within the Titian painting, Graham reconfigures or figuratively displaces what she calls the "rivers" of light in the painting, turning these into a kind of Heraclitean, ever-changing river of the world. At the poem's structural crux in stanza 13, the speaker defies the saint, saying she would not want to be like him—untouched by the elements, impervious to the flames. Graham turns her devotions from the saint to the transitoriness and genuinely immolating qualities of the world. "I would not be that man/ in the fire," she says, then asks whether there is a stream "whose banks don't/ come away/ into its muscular spirit,/ whose love/ doesn't scour its own bed,/ roil its mud/ with sky."

This crux in the poem is structurally its most important feature. The aspects of poetry—stanzas, line breaks—that are usually used as formal controls or indicators of content are, here and in much of her work, employed by Graham in an almost nominal fashion. The free verse stanzas have great visual symmetry, but the logic of the poem typically straddles stanzas; similarly, line breaks often occur where sense would seem to militate against them. Formally, Graham's poems are often like a temple in ruins.

In the short line poems of *Erosion*, Graham's use of stanza and line seems to rupture deliberately both cadence and sense, a device that seems to call for a broken reading, one that cuts against the firmly articulated argument of the poem. The very short lines (ranging in this poem from one to, at most, six or seven words) also create a great blank space around the poem. Graham has said that poems need white space because white space, like abstractions, suggests silence.

Not surprisingly, she admires the versification of William Carlos Williams, whose sense of line may be a model for her own. In an essay called "Some Notes on Silence," Graham says that she likes to think of the poetic line as "otherwise skeletal notes rising in a very large empty cathedral." This description seems applicable to "Remembering Titian's Martyrdom of Saint Lawrence."

Themes and Meanings

Toward the end of the poem, Graham seems to be imagining the ascension of the saint into the heavens. As he rises on the blue river of light that flows from the sky, the speaker's feelings are of both awe and indignation, as she demands of the saint how he can know and judge humankind: "how can you know/ when you see us," she asks, "the terrible deficit/ we work into? . . ." These lines express the speaker's anger that this saint and his world could presume to exercise judgment over the living.

The postulate of the painting—that there exists an immutable world, an immutable body—is ferociously rejected. The speaker almost plunges her hands into flame to feel the human condition and to deny the argument made by the painting. Human life is not like the lives of the martyred saints, which can, so the painting suggests, be reconfigured and redeemed in the light of a flawless heaven. No, humans, for the speaker of the poem, work into a "terrible deficit." For humans, there can be no reparations or reimbursements, only, as the poem says earlier, the muscular spirit whose progess through the world scours its own passage, roils mud into the sky, and finally incinerates itself.

The thematic concerns of this poem echo, but interestingly vary, a perennial modern theme, the idea that perfection is grossly discordant with the life of humanity. Like William Butler Yeats, Wallace Stevens, and Sylvia Plath, to name only a few of her predecessors, Graham finally says that humans live in a world of changes, and most painful ones. The rebellious, muscular rejection of perfection is perhaps the distinctive tonalty that Graham adds to the music that surrounds this theme.

Anne Shifrer

REMEMBRANCE

Author: Emily Brontë (1818-1848)
Type of poem: Lyric
First published: 1846, in *Poems by Currer, Ellis, and Acton Bell*

The Poem

Except for its brevity, Emily Brontë's lyrical poem "Remembrance" contains all of the characteristics of an elegy. Its subject is the mourning of the death of a beloved; the poem is meditative; the poet attempts to come to terms with the death of her lover from the past; finally, there is some evidence that the poet accepts her loss and finds solace, at long last.

The persona of the poem may or may not be Emily Brontë herself. Biographers have tried unsuccessfully to identify a young man from her youth whose death could have later given occasion to the writing of the poem. Whatever the case, the first person narrator addresses her dead lover, mentally though not literally, at his graveside some fifteen years after his burial. She remembers and thus observes a "remembrance" as she comes to terms with his death, trying—still trying—to give him up.

The first two stanzas are each questions addressed to her only lover, many years dead. "Have I forgot to love thee?" she asks, after letting the reader know that he is "cold in the dreary grave." Her first problem is to determine if enough time has passed to "sever" her loss. Whether she has forgotten to love him is an ironic question, since the act of remembering him is in itself an act of love. She then, in the second stanza, asks herself if her thoughts still "hover" to his grave far away.

In the third stanza, she asks her dead lover to forgive her if she now forgets him. She indicates that her loyalty to him is in question because of her intentions to bury him at last. "Other desires and other hopes" beset her, causing her to recognize functional displacement of his love although there is no operative displacement. She next records that "No later light has lightened up my heaven." The poet, or at least the persona of the poem, has not in fifteen years genuinely reexperienced any aspect of her relationship with another person. The speaker of the poem does, however, indicate an acceptance of his death, and she tells how she has survived in a universe without his love. His death has caused her "golden dreams" to perish; she records that she proceeded in life "without the aid of joy."

In the last two stanzas, she recognizes that her passion for him is identifiably "useless." Accordingly, she has "weaned" her soul, not from him, but from "yearning" for him. The grave, then, belongs more to her than to him, because her own life has been buried in and with his body. Finally, she dares not think of him, an indulgence in "Memory's rapturous pain." The poem ends with a question: How could she "seek the empty world again," having once experienced him but now absolutely unable to recapture his love? She cannot do so, and thus will languish eternally in a state of lingering.

Forms and Devices

Brontë wrote "Remembrance" in accord with conventions of poetry at the time in that the work itself is mechanically, though masterfully, balanced. The eight stanzas have a neatly observed rhyme scheme of *abab, cdcd, efef*, and so on. Odd-numbered lines usually contain twelve syllables, although some are clipped to eleven. Even-numbered lines consistently have a ten-count rhythm. The poet makes occasional use of alliteration ("forgive if I forget," "No later light has lightened," "while the world's tide,") and assonance ("existence could be cherished," "wish to hasten").

The effectiveness of the poem, however, does not depend upon use of convention. Rather, her evocation of a series of images not only makes impressions but also conveys meanings. The poem starts with "Cold in the earth and the deep snow piled above thee," manifesting at once the most powerful feeling of the work. Not only is the poet mentally and spiritually visiting the grave of her dead lover, but also both she and the reader realize the finality of death and the hopelessness of recovery.

The first two stanzas of the poem record questions, as does the final line. Has she forgotten him, and, having known him, can she now or at any time "seek the empty world again?" The first two questions are true questions; the final one is itself an answer: No, she cannot forget him nor can she "seek the empty world again." Such an effort is pointless, for death is final and her love irreplaceable.

The middle stanzas contain an "if-but-then" structure, which forms the heart of these sentiments. In the fourth stanza, she considers what would happen "if" she succeeded in forgetting him. The seventh stanza expresses the "but," or objection, to her assertion: The "Despair" which could set in was "powerless to destroy" her feelings. The "then" part of the equation shows that she has maintained control over herself and her passion, which she now recognizes to be useless.

The poet maintains balance both in terms of the meter of the lines and in the overall structure of the poem. Images of death pervade both elements and abound throughout: Time is an "all-severing wave"; thoughts can and do "hover"; "brown hills have melted"; the "World's tide" bears her along. Brontë's effort has been to embed her thoughts in a series of images in order to force herself to try once again to be at peace with her love's death.

Themes and Meanings

"Remembrance" is not so much a poem about death as it is about the eternal hopelessness of its acceptance. Death cannot be undone; its repercussions cannot be altered, and its totality cannot be mitigated. Its reality continues to affect her own life to the extent that the poet claims that the tomb of her love is more hers than his. "Remembrance" disputes and denies the common idea that time heals all wounds. Herein, the poet is fixated in a time that shows little if any movement onward, even as she recognizes the irrevocability of its—and her own—passing. Life does not go on: Life has stopped.

The persona of the poem records her fifteen years of effort to accept and live with the death of her love. She cannot forget him; she cannot turn to another. She cannot, consequently, live again meaningfully in the world around her. The only apparent reality is her memory, which still controls and dominates not only her thoughts and feelings but also her actions. Intellectually, the poet knows the error of her ways. She recognizes the futility of worshiping cold snow, and she knows that the distance in time of fifteen years should afford her some relief. One aspect of her nature truly wants to overcome his loss and to redefine her existence as one in which "change and suffering" are not the only constants. Such dreams, though, can only perish. She remains entrapped in a life of union with one dead, and inescapably so.

Arguably, the poet's entrapment is of her own making. There is an intense pleasure on her part derived from knowing that her love for the dead youth is in fact absolute. She prides herself in knowing that she is "Faithful indeed" as a "spirit"—not a person—who "remembers" after all these years. Her "Remembrance" is the vitality of her life blood, a manifest, lamentable treasure.

The poet, then, does not accept death so much as she accepts her own condition: She will remain fixated in her quiet despair, continuing to pay obeisance to a love that can be actualized only in her memory. It is perhaps futile and vainglorious for her to exist in such a state. She protests that she has made every attempt to rid herself of the consequences of his death, yet she would not go on. She is clearly unable to resurrect him bodily; only in memory can she keep him the main part of her being. In this realm, then, "Remembrance" exists not as a futile entrapment but as an honorable tribute in an elegiac fashion. The world is indeed "empty," and she should not seek it again; rather, she should continue to bask in the glory of the grave, inevitably not capable of emotional involvement with another.

It is worthy and honorable for her to keep alive the memory of someone whom she had loved; it is admirable for her to believe that his love has meaning and still defines her after all these years. The poem's meaning, however, can be determined by focusing closely on the last two lines. "Anguish" (at his death) is described as "divinest." The poet loves, finally, not her dead love, but her love of him. She cannot resurrect him, but she can keep alive her love for him, which is exactly what she does. It is because of her love for such "anguish" that she will not move into the "empty world again."

Carl Singleton

REMOVE THE PREDICATE

Author: Clark Coolidge (1939-   )
Type of poem: Lyric
First published: 1987, in *American Poetry Since 1970: Up Late*

The Poem

To the casual glance, this poem reads like an anecdote that someone on quaaludes is trying to tell. While there are enough components to encourage one to make the usual kind of sense, a quick glance shows that these components are at times displaced, distorted, or diffused. Re-readings reveal these first impressions to be accurate but inadequate. The author was anything but language-impaired or addled by drugs. Yet even as one traces symmetries that can scarcely be thought unintended, something of one's early impression remains: One is reminded that any use of language is bound, by the nature of words, to be "language-impaired"—words push back and interfere with those meanings one had intended before trying to formulate them on the page. As trace upon trace of deliberation manifests itself and an intellectual picture begins to form—the way a photograph develops in a dark room—something is still withheld. Words and reality seldom coincide exactly; the effect is like shadowy areas in the snapshot, which throw other parts into bright relief.

First to stand out will probably be the coincidence of the poem's beginning and end each having to do with knowing. While one is not told who "they" (line 1) are, one is invited to equate them with "the old" (as in the phrase "the known is old," in the last line), which leaves for "us" the appellation "new." From the first two, and the final, lines alone, it is easy to construct some such meaning as "the old possess a knowledge that is useless to us; what is known already must belong to the old; what is unknown is what is new, and that is our province." "We," presumably, are the young. When this conclusion is applied to the poem as a whole, considerable evidence appears in its support. For one thing, this soliloquy or meditation takes place in Rome, a very old city, and one that strikes the speaker as being "all built of under"—surely, in one sense, of layers of history. Again, readers are told that "All the vaunted/ spears of time . . . , buried in a . . . heap/ under the cats' mistakes [are] nothing," which also supports the initial conclusion concerning this poem's primary meaning. It is a short step to the formulation "Yank comes to Rome, rubbernecks, says 'So what?,' goes home."

This interpretation, however, while certainly derivable from the poem, is not the poem. In order to derive the message, one must overlook or discard other pieces of the work. When so much has to be omitted, one must consider the likelihood of complications, including the complication of authorial irony. One way to read this poem is as a dramatic monologue; one need only recall the work of Robert Browning to remember the likely gap between speaker and author in this type of poem. Clark Coolidge could well be impersonating an attitude—even possibly one he had himself held. Looking closer, one finds oppositions between old ways and new in which the underlying sympathy seems to lie with the old, as where "that one pure spring" appears to be preferred to "my/ millionth trattoria." Again, the penultimate line might suggest that a coin (as it were) is being "palmed," that the side one had thought was correct might prove to be wrong. The poem is so fraught with baffles, however, that there can be no general agreement as to such speculations.

Forms and Devices

Part of the noted deliberateness of this poem occurs in the regularity of the stanzas, two of five lines and two of six; the lines, too, approximate one another in length, even though the poem has no conventional rhythm or rhyme. The first three lines, for example, each contain ten syllables—the "classic" number, that of the iambic pentameter line. Instructively, however, these lines never become iambic pentameter. It is as if the tension between old and new noted in the content were also embedded in the form: old syllable-count, new meter. Perhaps one should not too quickly dismiss the matter of end rhyme: The first four lines of stanza 2, for example, have identities of assonance.

While the syntax may strike an unprepared reader as extraordinary and difficult, to those familiar with Coolidge's earlier poetry it will, by comparison, seem almost normal. Early in his career, the poet wrote works—*The Maintains* (1974), *Polaroid* (1975)—that were hailed as "nonreferential"; something of his view of his own writing may be obtained by considering the following extract from his piece on a fellow poet, Larry Eigner: "an invisible & steadying 'is' behind everything . . . all particles in the pile soon to reach/ *nounal state* . . . the word 'air' & its immediate prepositioning. . ./ these 'scenes' don't exist, never have . . . the poem is built// each line/ equals/ its own completion// and every next line/ its consequence." The approach, one notices, is by way of the mechanics of language and not the psychology of the individual nor the arrangement of society. While to the tyro "Remove the Predicate" may seem difficult in a quite unaccustomed way, to the reader familiar with Coolidge's work from the outset, this recent poem seems at once fairly predictable (the emphasis is on language; the title focuses on a part of speech) yet surprising, because of the large amount of normative coherence constituting it. Here is no parade of words stripped (apparently, anyway) of syntax, as in "one on below out until within/ through once those even since/ you the what says kinds/ bolt what hence when such both"—to quote from *Polaroid*—but instead something that very nearly fails to draw attention to itself via the difficulty presented by the arrangement of its words.

Yet even though "Remove the Predicate" appears to be a poem interpretable by older methods than would ever serve with his earlier work, if one keeps in mind the history of Coolidge's poetry, one will beware of imposing orders upon the arrangements of a man who has indicated, by precept and example, that words (no matter how juxtaposed) already provide an order to which the shuffles and grunts of syntax are in no way a superior wheeze.

It is true that if one removes "dope," "fault," and "fear weed" from the first stanza, one can feel well on one's way to completing a graspable sense of the sentence; however, the poem inserts and insists on those words. The apparently reachable clarity most prove an *ignis fatuus* if one is required to remove pieces of the poem in order to achieve it. Despite his movement toward the normative between the early and this later work, Coolidge proves reluctant to go the entire distance; for him, the relation of reality to language must always be questionable, and this will always be seen in his writing, whether obviously or subtly. The reader will always, if remaining honest to each word as well as to the composition they suggest overall, be forced to acknowledge that ideas of the real, on the one hand, and of the poem, on the other, should stay open to question.

In this poem, certainly, symmetries are recognizable: There are two stanzas of five lines each and two of six lines each; the first three lines each have ten syllables, enforcing a measure that subsequent lines will be heard as obliging or departing from; and "consistency of place and time" affirm the sentences and much that they contain. Yet there is a point beyond which these assembled symmetries cannot take one, an ideal order to which, despite their promises, they cannot deliver the reader. This surely is the point of the poem's devices.

Themes and Meanings

There are considerable chunks of apparently meaningful syntax in "Remove the Predicate." The poem may lack one single overarching meaning—most of Coolidge's poems do, since he has set his face against such—but to do its dance, the poem needs a number of partners. It needs the initial question, in order for the rest of the poem to have something to catch against, like a flywheel; it also needs those other pieces for the flywheel to drive. There appear to be themes: the theme of the past being of no possible use to the present, and the idea that the opposite of that opinion may also be true.

The clearest statement one can make about this poem is that when in Rome, one finds much "built of under"—of meanings and materials beneath other such items—and will "look under things" while there. Elements of the surreal complicate the plot. "Documents" that are "cut and parcelled/ out of well water" cannot occur in nature. "Hoops of tell" and "fear weed" also exist only in language, although one can surmise metaphorical meanings for them. That will remain a personal and private act. Common agreement can hardly be the hope of the poet when writing those phrases.

Quite the opposite is true. The matter of personal knowledge being largely tacit informs Coolidge's operations, creating poems that defy a unified interpretation. One must replace the predicate with oneself.

David Bromige

RENASCENCE

Author: Edna St. Vincent Millay (1892-1950)
Type of poem: Narrative
First published: 1912; collected in *Renascence and Other Poems*, 1917

The Poem

"Renascence" is a narrative poem of 214 metrical lines split into nine stanzas of varying length. Although it literally means "rebirth," the poem's Latinate title carries different connotations than does its English equivalent. The title "Rebirth" might have led readers to expect a poem with a strongly earthly or physical aspect. Edna St. Vincent Millay's title, in contrast, suggests that the poet is about to speak of more elevated matters, possibly spiritual or cerebral. The poem does start on a purely physical level, although it soon leaves that plane behind. The persona of the poem, or narrator, tells of a moment when she looks around and becomes sharply conscious of the landscape around her: mountains, trees, a bay, and islands. "These were the things that bounded me," she says of them. Seeing them as boundaries, however, sparks a mental crisis. The world suddenly feels disturbingly small. In her heightened and anxious state, even the sky seems near enough to touch. She reaches for it and finds herself swept into a visionary episode.

Initially, she enters a paradoxical state: She becomes all-seeing and all-feeling but does not lose her sense of individual being. She gains a godlike perspective that gives her such a wide view of human suffering that it threatens to overwhelm her merely human reactions: "For my omniscience I paid toll/ In infinite remorse of soul." She experiences the deaths of a thousand people by fire and sympathetically finds herself perishing with each of them even as she simultaneously stands apart as an individual, mourning for all. She similarly experiences the death of another group of unfortunates caught in an accident at sea: "A thousand screams the heavens smote;/ And every scream tore through my throat." The weight of her universal compassion soon grows so great that it presses her into the earth: "Into the earth I sank till I/ Full six feet under ground did lie." In this state of spiritual extinction, she feels the weight leave her. She welcomes the soothing earth: "Deep in the earth I rested now;/ Cool is its hand upon the brow/ And soft its breast beneath the head/ Of one who is so gladly dead." Above her, she then hears the sound of rain, which reminds her of life and its simple joys. She regrets missing not only the rain but also the sun that follows rain: "O God, I cried, give me new birth,/ And put me back upon the earth!" At this outburst, a torrential rain washes her from the grave and restores her: "I know not how such things can be!—/ I breathed my soul back into me." She finds herself back within the world of physical limitations, a return filled with joy: "Ah! Up then from the ground sprang I/ And hailed the earth with such a cry/ As is not heard save from a man/ Who has been dead, and lives again." She also possesses insight she had not been given before:

O God, I cried, no dark disguise
Can e'er hereafter hide from me
Thy radiant identity
. . . .
I know the path that tells Thy way
Through the cool eve of every day;
God, I can push the grass apart
And lay my finger on Thy heart!

The poem concludes with a twelve-line coda in which the narrator affirms her new understanding, which relates the limitations of the outer world to inner dimensions. The world, she says, is as wide as the heart and as tall as the soul. She then issues a caution against weakness in either: "But East and West will pinch the heart/ That cannot keep them pushed apart;/ And he whose soul is flat—the sky/ Will cave in on him by and by."

Forms and Devices

To make this transcendent episode vivid, Millay uses a vocabulary consisting of common, concrete words. She expresses the onset of the vision in terms of touch and hearing: "Infinity// Held up before my eyes a glass/ Through which my shrinking sight did pass" and "Whispered to me a word whose sound/ Deafened the air for worlds around." When her poetic persona then experiences omniscience, Millay describes the visionary's subsequent remorse as a physical burden: "And so beneath the Weight lay I/ And suffered death, but could not die." The weight pushes the visionary into the earth, which Millay describes in starkly contrasting but earthy terms: first as the dusty confines of a grave and then as the calming hands and bosom of a comforting mother. Paradoxes, in fact, help convey the visionary's successive states of disorientation. Her omniscience battles with her individuality, her subsequent "death" becomes a seedbed for a renewed thirst for life, and her final, revivifying vision of the sun leads to her release from the grave by a torrent of rain. Millay's sense of tone and phrasing gives such opposing images and motifs colorful life. Her most musical lines call to mind the lyricism of English poet John Keats ("To catch the freshened, fragrant breeze/ From drenched and dripping apple-trees"). In contrast, her sometimes morbid concerns, bold imagination, and deceptive simplicity suggest the influence of American author Edgar Allan Poe. Her lines contain many elements to be found in the work of her contemporaries, including preoccupations with exoticism and deep sentiment. Yet Millay combines unabashed lyricism with unflinching statements to give to "Renascence" distinct freshness and vivid life.

Millay composed "Renascence" in rhymed couplets of iambic tetrameter: Each line contains four feet, or pairs of syllables, in which the accent generally falls on the second syllable. Although the majority of lines observe this regular pattern, the poet demonstrates flexibility from the outset. Her opening line begins with a trochee: "All I could see from where I stood." The typical reader will place stress on the first syllable of the first foot. In the last three feet of this four-foot line, the stress falls regularly upon each second syllable. She demonstrates another kind of metrical flexibility in the fourth couplet of the first stanza, where she shortens the lines by a syllable: "Straight around till I was come/ Back to where I'd started from." By this removal of the initial foot, Millay achieves a quickening of pace that speeds the reader onto the fifth couplet. Insofar as the next sixteen syllables of the stanza reiterate the first words of the poem, the shortening of that preceding couplet also helps give the repetition a certain weight of inevitability.

Themes and Meanings

"Renascence" is a poem about limits. In the course of the poem, the visionary persona, who may or may not have been Millay herself, moves from experiencing limits as stifling and constricting to experiencing them as liberating and as the measure of one's spiritual being. Despite the extraordinary nature of her experiences, the visionary narrator goes through tribulations common to many: People often grow dissatisfied with their circumstances, wish for more, then become distressed if they receive what they wanted. The visionary in "Renascence" feels constricted by the small scope of her immediate world. She is then given an unlimited viewpoint that distresses her until she begs for relief. She finds this relief in death and burial, a situation that soon makes her yearn for life again. Only then does she realize the value of what she started with: the physical world and its natural limits. Her "renascence," or rebirth, is mental, not physical. She returns to a world identical to the one she initially abandoned but sees it through new eyes.

"Renascence," one of Millay's youthful works, asks the perennial questions of youth: What is the meaning of existence? What does it mean to be an individual? Is there anything special about being "me" as opposed to being anyone else? Millay approaches these questions by imagining an ideal soul who looks around and sees only "normal" reality, which seems confining and unsatisfactory. She then imagines that soul dwarfed through contact with the greatness of a universal soul. In learning insignificance, the individual soul gains the perspective necessary to appreciate significance. The soul then values the world as it is given, even if it is no more than a constricted spot surrounded by mountains, woods, a bay, and islands.

The world is worth living in, Millay seems to say to her readers. However, it is worth living in most for those who understand what the visionary in the poem has come to see: that the limitations that appear to be outside are actually inside. "The heart can push the sea and land/ Farther away on either hand," she says, "The soul can split the sky in two,/ And let the face of God shine through." Moving beyond limitations, especially those imposed from within, constitutes genuine rebirth.

Mark Rich

REPORT FROM THE BESIEGED CITY

Author: Zbigniew Herbert (1924-1998)
Type of poem: Lyric/meditation
First published: 1983, as "Raport z obleżonego miasta," in *Raport z obleżonego miasta i inne wiersze*; English translation collected in *Report from the Besieged City and Other Poems*, 1985

The Poem

"Report from the Besieged City" is a dramatized meditation on aggression, ethics, and civil autonomy. Zbigniew Herbert employs long lines of free verse, in contrast to the rather clipped rhythms of many of his other poems. The poem consists of forty-nine lines, divided irregularly into verse paragraphs that vary from single lines to groups of ten and eleven. The piece is voiced for an imagined persona who is much like Herbert himself, but also a compiled transhistorical witness to the invasions that have taken place in Poland and elsewhere over the last thousand years.

The title makes one think either of a news report from a war zone or of a logbook or military journal. The "Besieged City" does not refer to any particular place—although Herbert makes reference to past events in Warsaw and Gdansk—but stands instead generally for all cities and hometowns that have ever suffered through tyranny or invasion; the city here is a locus, a recurrent figure or image, through which Herbert explores the issues of civil responsibility, community, and social action.

The poem begins with the speaker or persona, a citizen of the Besieged City, recounting how he, unable to participate actively in the defense of his homeland, is given the "inferior role" of recording the events of the struggle. Herbert contrasts the writer or poet to what he sees as a fundamentally better social role, that of the soldier or activist.

Despite his doubts about the significance of his words, the speaker of the poem makes a brief attempt at a journal, marking "the rhythm of interminable weeks" in a list of seven dateless days. He records tortures, humiliations, and diseases alongside the minor victories and defeats that characterize a drawn-out battle. In the face of endless repetitions of terrible events, record-keeping becomes absurd, and its readership, dulled by accounts of atrocity after atrocity, can only be bored, as the speaker realizes: "all of this is monotonous. . . ."

Although the speaker wants to "avoid any commentary" and write only about "the facts," his tactics change in the seventh verse paragraph. He becomes, rather than a characterless transmitter of information, a critical thinker, commenting freely on what he has seen and heard under siege, creating for himself and his readers a widened sense of historical context for the struggle at hand, comparing his own battle to those waged against the invaders and exterminators of other times: "Goths the Tartars Swedes troops of the Emperor regiments of the Transfiguration." All these nations at one time sought to invade, conquer, or partition sovereign Poland. (The "regiments of the Transfiguration" were members of the Russian regular standing army, under Czar Peter I in the late seventeenth century.) The speaker situates himself and his people among those who have been overrun by outsiders, nations which, though resolute in their autonomy, lost their struggles. The names in this list are more contemporary than in that of the invaders: "the defenders of the Dalai Lama the Kurds the Afghan mountaineers." Herbert recalls oppressions and invasions by China, Iraq, and the Soviet Union.

The speaker also allows his own emotions to creep into his account, recalling with bitter irony how, under siege, his countrymen have raised a "new species of children" who know, instead of fairy tales, only stories of war and killing. He resents the hands-off efforts of other countries to send aid and realizes the inherent solitude of the struggle for autonomy anywhere. Responsibility, for Herbert, has an existential basis, rooted always in the insurmountable solitude of human existence.

Herbert concludes his poem by focusing on this solitude. Should the City itself fall and only one citizen escape its swelling cemeteries, that citizen would still carry the City—that is, its sovereignty and its sense of community and civil liberty—within himself. He will, Herbert tells us, "be the City." No matter if the siege ends in physical defeat, all hopes for future justice abide in "our dreams," the one realm to which tyrants and oppressors have no access.

Forms and Devices

Herbert's style is distinctive. Characteristically, he uses little or no punctuation in his poetry. Sentences and rhetorical or grammatical units are demarcated only by line breaks. Often, Herbert compresses two or more sentences into a single unit, yielding a sense of urgency and rhythmic fluidity: "yet the defense continues it will continue to the end." The content of a line is never obscured by such effects, and its meaning may even be enhanced; oppositions and elaborations flow together, creating a shifting web of poetical checks and balances, as the mind of the poem's speaker plays back and forth over the events of "the siege" and his "commentary."

The formal basis of Herbert's poetry is opposition. "Report from the Besieged City," along with other poems from the same volume, is composed of several layers of balanced or embedded contraries. Herbert sometimes uses the rhetorical scheme of antithesis to achieve this balance, placing antonyms in a grammatically parallel relationship, as in "cemeteries grow larger the number of defenders is smaller" or "if the City falls but a single man escapes." The poem's speaker sometimes contradicts himself; he would "avoid any commentary," he asserts, and yet he "would like to inform the world" of his despair and outrage. Countertensions and oppositions permeate the texture of this poetry.

This rhetorical balancing act is matched by a wider, conceptual field of oppositions. The active, fighting life is contrasted sharply by the speaker to the secondhand experience of the chronicler or poet. Activism and criticism, physical struggle and contemplation, and factuality and commentary are all held in tension within the poem. The external conflict between the attackers and the defenders—the tyrannical "barbarians" and the autonomous city dwellers—becomes a correlative of another, internalized conflict, as the speaker struggles to reconcile suffering and righteousness in his "report." His writing, on the one hand, as a record of the tortures of "interminable weeks," provides a means of informing the world and of justifying the struggle, but, on the other hand, his work does little or nothing to alleviate the pain of that struggle or to stop the onslaught of extermination and defeat. The poem may well be only a gesture of futility.

This inherent duplicity leads the speaker to doubt himself: "I record—I don't know for whom—the history of the siege . . . I know it can't move anyone." The only hope the speaker retains comes in the form of a paradox, bodied forth in the figure of the "exile"—one cut off from all community and society—who somehow carries the values of the City, which for Herbert constitute the actual City, within himself. The antithetical structures and contraries of the entire poem have been compressed into this single, contradictory figure at its close, who is at once solitary and all-encompassing.

Themes and Meanings

"Report from the Besieged City" is in many ways a pessimistic poem, predicting only the inevitable defeat and collapse of the City—a bastion of personal freedom, community, and positive social values—and affirming only the insurmountable solitude of human existence. If Herbert holds out any hope in the face of oppression and injustice, it lies in the "dreams" of the last line of the poem, which alone remain unhumiliated and unbetrayed. In the original Polish of that line, the verb *zostały*, which is translated here as "have been," can also have the sense of "remained" or "stayed behind." Herbert writes not so much about success or heroism or a newfound personal liberation as he does about remainders and leftovers. For him, an essential core of values exists within all human beings—the "City" that even exiles still carry inside themselves—that cannot be exterminated. Paradoxically, in terms of this poem, we come to experience the undefeatable quality of that essence only in humiliation and defeat; those who know nothing of siege and struggle at first hand, those full of "comfort and good advice," are, for Herbert, out of touch with the values and the dreams of freedom that motivate the poem's speaker and his fellow citizens.

Herbert's poetry is, then, ruthlessly ironic. Longing for a world of human liberty and productive community, he recognizes the inevitability of degradation, humiliation, and defeat. His humility has some roots in Christianity; the paradoxes of Pauline thought—which glorifies weakness as strength, submission as victory, and finds in death a new life—are remarkably similar to those in Herbert's poetry. For Herbert, however, humankind remains largely unredeemed, and liberation, whether theological, philosophical, or political, is merely the property of "dreams." He finds no new life, but instead buries deep within himself only the faintest glimmer of hope.

Kevin McNeilly

REPRESSION OF WAR EXPERIENCE

Author: Siegfried Sassoon (1886-1967)
Type of poem: Dramatic monologue
First published: 1918, in *Counter-Attack and Other Poems*

The Poem

"Repression of War Experience" is an unrhymed poem in three stanzas. Along with the poem's publication date, the title suggests an unwillingness or inability to recall or accept experiences undergone during World War I. In using the clinical word "repression," Siegfried Sassoon might well be making direct reference to the book *Die Traumdeutung* (1900; *The Interpretation of Dreams*, 1913), in which psychoanalyst Sigmund Freud pointed out that although a person may not fully register traumatic experiences at the time they occur, repressed memories always return to haunt the sufferer. Because Sassoon speaks through the persona of an English soldier rather than in his own voice, "Repression of War Experience" is not a lyric but a dramatic work. As is true of all dramatic monologues, the voice of the persona dominates the poem.

In the first stanza, the soldier is at home in England on a summer night. He lights some candles and watches as moths flutter around the flames, wondering why they seek that which will kill them. Almost immediately, however, he finds that the moths trigger memories of his own wartime terrors, thoughts that he has "gagged all day." In the second stanza, the longest of the three, the mood changes as the soldier gives himself instructions on how to behave: He resolves to maintain control by lighting his pipe and seeks solace in nature by wishing for a rainstorm "to sluice the dark" with "bucketsful of water." Needing a more immediate solution, however, he gazes at the books lining the room but becomes unnerved by the sight of a huge moth bumping against the ceiling, which leads him to think about the garden outside the house; he imagines ghosts in the trees, not of his comrades lost in battle but of an older generation, "old men with ugly souls" who stayed at home to die slow, natural deaths. In a final effort to pull himself together, the young man reassures himself that he is far away from the war. In this last stanza, however, the soldier imagines that he hears the ominous sound of muffled guns on the front lines in France. They are sounds he cannot silence.

Forms and Devices

Since Sassoon describes warfare from the point of view of one who has actually experienced combat, those who have fought in any war or who know somebody who did can easily identify with this poem. Like the war poetry of Edward Thomas, Ivor Gurney, and Wilfred Owen, all of whom fought in World War I, Sassoon's poetry has been widely read. As Patrick Quinn points out in *The Great War and The Missing Muse* (1994), Sassoon, together with these other poets, helped swing the opinion of the literary establishment in England against the war. It is easy to see why Sassoon caught the attention of the English public. Utilizing a technique of documentary realism, the poet uses the slangy language of the barracks: "jabber," "O Christ," and "bloody war." Initially, too, the poem focuses on familiar images that could have been found in any house in England at the time the poem was written: candles, moths, a pipe, roses, and books. However, the poem is more than a factual journalistic record. Sassoon also uses dramatic irony, a device essential to any dramatic monologue: Caught at a critical moment, the soldier unintentionally reveals more to the reader than he realizes.

Unlike most dramatic monologues, which are addressed to an audience, the soldier in this poem is talking to himself. At times, the soldier addresses himself as "you"; at other times, he speaks in the first person. In Freudian terms, the soldier's use of "you" seems to suggest that his superego, his commonsense self, is speaking, whereas the use of "I" implies thoughts emerging from deep inside, the Freudian id, site of the repressed memories of war. Conflict exists between these two parts of the soldier's psyche. Sassoon makes this conflict clear through the device of juxtaposition. In the first line of the poem, for example, he juxtaposes the image of the candles the soldier lights with the moths flying into "liquid flame." Then, to show that the soldier associates these moths with his fallen comrades, Sassoon juxtaposes an image of the war itself. In this way, the poet implies a comparison between the suicidal moths and the soldier's mates who "blunder in" and become engulfed in gunfire at the battlefront in France. A final juxtaposition ends the stanza: The soldier's superego admonishes, "It's bad to think of war," but his id reasserts itself in the young man's fear of losing control of "ugly thoughts" and being driven out "to jabber among the trees."

Sassoon continues this pattern of juxtaposition in the second stanza. Just after the soldier lights his pipe and remarks, "Look, what a steady hand," he must "count fifteen" to regain control. Next, Sassoon juxtaposes the soldier's thoughts of the delights of a possible rainstorm with the possible delights offered by the books lining his shelves, a connection that the soldier himself cannot accept. Instead, he bites his nails and lets his pipe go out, unable or unwilling to read "the wisdom of the world/ . . . waiting on those shelves." Then, as if to show that the soldier's id is winning its struggle against the superego, Sassoon juxtaposes the image of the suicidal moth bumping and fluttering against the ceiling with a second image generated by the id rather than a cautionary admonition from his superego as was the pattern in the first stanza, a nightmare vision of ghosts that the soldier thinks he sees lurking in the trees outside. However, it is the final series of implied comparisons of this stanza that dramatizes the extent of the young man's angst: He first identifies these ghosts as "horrible shapes in shrouds" and then, confusing this nightmare with reality, asserts that the shrouds cannot be those that envelop the bodies of his fallen comrades because his comrades are "in France."

In the final stanza, the soldier's hold on reality snaps completely. Although his superego briefly reasserts itself to reassure the young man that he is "summering safe at home," the remembered sounds of muffled gunfire trigger his primal trauma: the fear of death on the battlefield. Feeling this fear just as intensely as if he were still at the front, he says, "I'm going stark, staring mad because of the guns." By concluding on a characteristic note of savage irony, Sassoon shows that the young soldier, far from achieving a therapeutic, Freudian breakthrough, is succumbing to his posttraumatic stress. The sound of the "whispering guns" cannot be quieted.

Themes and Meanings

"Repression" is a poem about the power of repressed memory. It is also a highly serious, accusatory work. As Erich Maria Remarque wrote in *Im Westen nichts Neues* (1929; *All Quiet on the Western Front*, 1929), it focuses on a soldier who, while he may have escaped physical harm, was "destroyed by the War." By tracing this young man's failure to come to terms with his war experience, Sassoon may be suggesting that the trauma of World War I, mostly fought from muddy, vermin-filled trenches, is so great that it renders any such accommodation impossible.

This poem differs from other war poems written during this period: Thomas describes the way the war violated the natural order of things, Gurney recaptures particular scenes with painful quietness, and Owen mourns the tragedy of young men killed in battle, while "Repression of War Experience" dramatizes in a particularly direct fashion the manner in which the experience of war can inflict permanent psychic damage so painful that is must be repressed. However, the poem also suggests that the young soldier was not the only one to repress the war, implying that others, perhaps military censors, the press, or those who profited from the war—the "old men with ugly souls"—also engaged in repression, preventing the British public from becoming aware of the futility of continuous, massive bombardments by the guns that "never cease." Sassoon's sudden twisting of the reader's expectation at the end of the poem—the soldier's descent into madness, which makes the reader feel uncomfortable or perhaps even responsible for the soldier's breakdown—may suggest that Sassoon saw as his poetic mission the necessity to pierce the dehumanization and complacent patriotism of many people in England during this period. In the end, it is this poem's direct indictment of the brutal consequences of repression for both the soldiers who fought and those who sent them out to "blunder in/ And scorch their wings" that makes it so powerful.

Susan Tetlow Harrington

REQUIEM FOR THE PLANTAGENET KINGS

Author: Geoffrey Hill (1932-   )
Type of poem: Sonnet
First published: 1959, in *For the Unfallen: Poems, 1952-1958*

The Poem

Geoffrey Hill's poem "Requiem for the Plantagenet Kings" is one of a series of lyrics in an elegiac mood which appears in an early group of poems ironically entitled *For the Unfallen* (1959). The requiem focuses on events and figures of the turbulent medieval period dominated by the formidable Plantagenet rulers of England, (1154-1399), and postulates a curious, paradoxical vision of them that questions the one-dimensional view given by history (which is concerned with cause and effect).

The ironic tone of the poem is immediately evident in the title, since the premise that these restless and energetic kings could ever rest in peace seems a contradiction in terms. A requiem (rest), the introit to the service for the burial of the dead, seems almost precipitant, since the Plantagenets' influence extended far beyond their mortal lives.

Nevertheless, the poet does constrain them tightly and succinctly in a sonnet form, although varying the rhythm of the usual iambic pentameter and freely employing half-rhymes. The bonds are burst as well in the opening four-line stanza of general observation, usually reserved for the conclusion of a sonnet. Indeed, the lines might stand as a terse epitaph, but they lack the abstract elegance and formal diction usually associated with such a commemoration. There is no flattering summary of the Plantagenets' lives and deeds as soldiers, lawgivers, or champions of justice; there is, instead, a suggestion of the wild, wasteful prodigality not only of their lives but also of the age in which all victories seemed Pyrrhic. Despite the "Ruinous arms" (line 2), the death, and the blood, there did emerge the concept of the just war (for good or ill) and the idea of an order, called the state, achieving constitutionality. If history is a book read backward and is the final judge, the first stanza suggests a temporal evaluation of the reigns. "Men, in their eloquent fashion, understood," despite the traumas of life and the kinetic frenzy of the period.

The Plantagenets, often given to violent outbursts of temper and rash action, were determined to possess and keep their inherited lands on the continent, but the kings of France were equally determined that they should not. In a contest of wills, the legality of the Plantagenet claims became a spurious excuse for what was essentially a matter of pride, rapacious greed, and the joy of proved arms.

In the second and longer stanza, their temporal roles fulfilled and temporal judgment pronounced, they lie, entombed in the dust and decay of their mortal frames. "Relieved" now of their souls, they await yet another judgment. All the pride of arms and vitality has been translated into a panoply of past glory and the frozen beauty of Gothic chantries where men praise their lives and where monks—whose services have already been recompensed—pray in perpetuity for the repose of their souls. Only doomsday will render the higher judgment of their actions, when "the scouring fires of trial-day/ Alight on men."

Forms and Devices

In a variation of the Shakespearean sonnet, Geoffrey Hill creates a web of diction whose complexity is very like that of William Shakespeare's own. The irony, however, which gives an enigmatic quality to Hill's work, is singularly his own.

Irony, "the act of dissembling," is not intended in this poem to mislead or obscure but to subject the Plantagenets to a prismatic light that catches a fuller portrait than is afforded by a simple reading of historical events or a formal biography. Startling and oblique, the facets of the prism reveal not only a multitude of accepted views of their reigns but also the emotional, psychological, and intellectual response of the poet, thus becoming fused in the experience which is the poem.

The prism is largely, and most frequently, a product of the exactness of the poet's diction. This is not to say that only a single meaning can be read in it, but rather that its precision and compression—so that the ambiguity of the word refracts—allow many meanings to coalesce. In the first line of the poem, for example, the curious image, "the possessed sea," presents not only the primary image of the sea but also the unexpected adjective, "possessed." How so possessed, becomes the question that can be answered only in the hint of at least two diametrically opposed ideas. Certainly the poet means, on the one hand, that the Plantagenet kings thought of themselves as owning the English Channel, which stood between them and their French possessions; on the other hand, the kings were also peculiarly "possessed" by it, in the sense of being obsessed with their rights to the land often denied them. Furthermore, the term "sea" for the English Channel may allude to the Caesars, who thought of the Mediterranean as *mare nostrum* ("our sea"), thus suggesting their grandiose ambitions, even, perhaps, mastery; it may also, possibly, be a reference to the exalted opinions the Plantagenets had of themselves. The irony is most pointed when considered in context of the last lines of the poem, implying that the "sea," after much carnage, really possesses them all—all who were venturous enough to seek to possess the other shore.

This intricate ambiguity of diction is matched only by the poet's agility in the use of the metaphor (implied comparisons). It would seem the height of irony, for example, to refer to the "chantries" as "caved." The very ornateness of the church architecture, however, so surprisingly compared to a cave, elicits the recognition that caves were the first burial chambers of primitive man. To compare them here, therefore, is to impose a dimension of humanity upon the otherwise formal distancing in the deaths of kings. Since the conclusion of the poem is decidedly Christian in tone, it should be remembered that the bloodied body of Christ was placed in something very like a cave; thus, the image links all humanity with the divine. The poem concludes, as it began, with the image of the sea, a traditional symbol of eternality into which the print of the "daubed rock" (blood?) tells of the Plantagenets' passage in the flux of time.

Themes and Meanings

Two themes are interwoven in the text of "Requiem for the Plantagenet Kings." The first of these, a traditional motif, *sic transit gloria mundi* ("thus passes the glory of the world"), is a poignant recognition that all in the material world is subject to the depredations of time, which shows little mercy to man or his works. The Plantagenets lie "secure in the decay/ Of blood," as the poet observes.

The plaint appears in the early doom-laden poetry of the Anglo-Saxons (*The Seafarer, The Wanderer, The Ruin*, c. mid-eighth century) and continues as a familiar theme in English poetry. It is particularly suited to medieval sensitivities, since the bitter contrast of splendor and squalor, of dream and reality, the ideal and the base, was acutely painful. The juxtaposed images in the poem, for example, of the gross reality of war, as in "the sleeked groin, gored head," and the grace of the "well-dressed alabaster" by which the Plantagenets were remembered, harmonize by a strange, subtle metamorphosis which time and art can also mercifully unfold. Geoffrey Hill suggests that the transmutation by art of raw experience preserves something of man and his work.

Inextricably linked with the first theme is an exploration into the paradoxical nature and meaning of history with which Hill struggles and returns to in his later works, *King Log* (1968) and *Mercian Hymns* (1971). Like other poets of the twentieth century, he has been compelled to accommodate to the findings of twentieth century physics, particularly the relationship of space and time and its unsettling implications for reading, writing, and understanding history. It is the tension created when the older views, traditional and religious, form a Gordian knot in "Requiem for the Plantagenet Kings"; the ambiguity of Hill's diction, unresolved and complex, mirrors not only his own, but twentieth century man's bewilderment and uncertainty.

On the one hand, to paraphrase Heraclitus, if you cannot step into the same river twice—that is, you, like the river, are changing from moment to moment—then history can only be history of that moment; hence, the poem, with its simultaneity of presentation. The ultimate reality of the world is change. On the other hand, if humankind is the instrument of a greater transcendental will, it may be part of a larger design whose meaning is obscured in the divine. The question is, then, were the Plantagenets ministers or scourges of the divine will, or were they simply the flotsam and jetsam of the flux of time? Geoffrey Hill's closing of the poem would suggest that only the end of time can possibly reveal the solution to the puzzle.

Maureen W. Mills

THE RESCUED YEAR

Author: William Stafford (1914-1993)
Type of poem: Meditation
First published: 1964; collected in *The Rescued Year*, 1966

The Poem

William Stafford's "The Rescued Year" is a meditative poem comprising eight verse paragraphs ranging in length from seven to eleven lines. The subject of this meditation is human memory and the continuous nature of human knowledge as passed from generation to generation, and because of the way the poet treats his subject the poem borders on the elegiac. The year that looms so large in the poet's mind has been "rescued" from oblivion, or the loss of personal experience from communal memory; precisely because it has been retrieved from such loss, this year out of the poet's past represents for him a kind of ideal: "Time should go the way it went/ that year. . . ."

At the outset the poet asks the reader to imagine a large globe, and on this globe to "press back that area in the west where no one lived,/ the place only your mind explores." He then recalls a family trip by train across Kansas, a trip that ended "against the western boundary/ where my father had a job." This latter reference is to the town of Liberal, one of five Kansas towns in which Stafford spent his adolescence (and probably the most important to him in imaginative terms).

The second verse paragraph outlines some of the characteristics that made this time in the poet's life seem idyllic: America was at peace, and his family's existence "had/ each day a treasured unimportance." The third and fourth verse paragraphs juxtapose three male figures: a local preacher, who mouths abstract catchwords such as "honor"; the poet's father, whose curiosity and openness to experience lead him to knowledge and understanding; and the poet himself, who takes his father as a model in this regard.

In the fifth and sixth verse paragraphs four female figures are similarly brought together: the poet's mother, pictured as making paper presents to bedeck a tumbleweed hung up for a Christmas tree; the poet's sister, who is dating an oil-rich farmer from nearby Hugoton; a girl whom the poet himself is seeing; and the girl's mother. Verse paragraph 7 recalls another family trip across Kansas that spring, with "my father soothing us with stories," one of these about an old man "who spent his life knowing,/ unable to tell how he knew."

The final verse paragraph reiterates the theme of personal experience and communal memory. In the first line the poet says that he "hold[s] that rescued year" in the ways his father showed him. He then concludes the poem with a complicated series of images in which things are either traced to their origins or viewed as results: the smoke from a coal fire turning back into chunks of coal and then into a seam of coal lying in the earth; the quiet after a whistle fades, a circumstance in which the poet feels "no need, no hurry"; and finally a train (presumably the one on which the Stafford family arrived in town) which the poet envisions returning to "our station," where the sound of the cars being coupled "will ripple forward and hold the train." This coupling of the train provides a metaphor of how memory works: individual images and experiences "ripple forward," or present themselves, and "hold the train" in the continuity of remembered and shared human activity.

Forms and Devices

Stafford's verse is deceptively simple. It is based on the rhythms of speech, and its diction for the most part utilizes a plain vocabulary. Yet irony and ambiguity are never far beneath the surface of this apparently straightforward style. In "Near," another poem from the collection in which "The Rescued Year" appears, the poet acknowledges the quirkiness of this style: "Walking along in this not quite prose way/ we both know it is not quite prose we speak." This "not quite prose way" is not quite prose indeed; it is in fact an intricate balance of speech movement and poetic rhythm.

"The Rescued Year" would seem to be written entirely in free verse, for example, but a closer examination reveals that the poem's lines are a mixture of free verse and metrics. The first line of the second verse paragraph, though apparently written in free verse, is actually trochaic ("Time should go the way it went"), and the following line is clearly iambic, its two interior pauses nothwithstanding: "that year: we weren't at war; we had." In fact, given the poem's theme of rescuing experience from oblivion, it is possible to view the occasional use of metrics here as "rescuing" traditional modes of poetic expression from the oblivion of the almost universal contemporary use of free verse.

Stafford resorts to tradition in another way in the poem, and that is through his use of rhyme. Near or full, these rhymes are sometimes in end position, but frequently they are buried within lines. The fourth verse paragraph provides the richest example of rhyming in the poem (the rhymes appear in added italics here; the poet is speaking of his father):

> Like him, I tried. I still *try*,
> send my sight like a million pickpockets
> up rich people's *drives:* it is time
> when I pass for every place I go to be *alive.*
> Around any corner my sight is a *river,*
> and I let it *arrive:* rich by those brooks
> his thought poured for hours
> into my *hand.* His creed: the greatest ownership
> of all is to glance around and *understand.*

Perhaps the most noticeable—but hardest to define—feature of the poet's style is his frequent obliqueness of phrasing, a main component of his ambiguity. This obliqueness is well illustrated by a line and a half from the passage quoted immediately above: "it is time/ when I pass for every place I go to be alive." The curious syntax (something like "Every place I go comes alive when I pass it" might be expected) adds something to the expression of the idea, lifting it from the prosaic, the ordinary. By adding the prepositional phrase "for every place," the poet makes the scene he passes seem to come alive, to participate in his act of seeing, even to greet him. This sort of intimate interaction between the observer and the observed is a characteristic of Stafford's work as a whole, and through its agency that part of the world one ordinarily thinks of as inert becomes active, newly vital, and more whole.

Themes and Meanings

The theme of "The Rescued Year" is human memory and the role it plays in preserving knowledge and experience. This theme, or some aspect of it, recurs quite often in Stafford's work, often in poems about members of his family. The most powerful of these, such as "My Father: October 1942" and "Listening," focus on Stafford's father, and it is he who figures most prominently in "The Rescued Year," who models for the poet an openness— of eye, ear, and heart—to whatever is at hand.

The poem's diction and imagery clearly emphasize the visual, the sort of seeing that leads one to understand; this is shown in such a passage as "Around any corner my sight is a river,/ and I let it arrive." In the fourth verse paragraph the poet says that, more readily than to the preacher's doctrines, he can assent to what he calls his father's "creed": "the greatest ownership/ of all is to glance around and understand."

The poet mentions another figure who is similarly open to experience and who has an intuitive understanding of the world, the old man who "spent his life knowing,/ unable to tell how he knew." This anonymous old man provides a model of self-sufficiency in his happy, almost innocent wisdom and his closeness to the natural world.

What finally sets "The Rescued Year" apart is not incandescent language or scintillating argument but rather the quiet conviction with which it sets out its vignettes of remembered experience. At the end, the poem harks back to its beginning in the image of the returning train, but it is important to note that the poet is not actually remembering here. The train's return is something he merely posits, something that will happen in the future. The poet's imagining of the train is no more substantial than the companion image of "the name carved on the platform" (presumably his own), which he feels will "unfill with rain" as the train pulls in.

Yet in these concluding lines the poem achieves its vision, however brief or tentative. In expressing the idea that the train's being coupled makes a movement both backwards and forwards, the poet suggests that this movement is like memory itself: looking back, then carrying experience forward, producing the ripple of understanding that "hold[s] the train" for those who come after.

Roy Scheele

RESOLUTION AND INDEPENDENCE

Author: William Wordsworth (1770-1850)
Type of poem: Lyric
First published: 1807, in *Poems in Two Vols.*

The Poem

"Resolution and Independence," known in manuscript as "The Leech Gatherer," is a poem of 140 lines divided into twenty stanzas. The published title suggests the thematic moral learned by the speaker from an encounter with the leech gatherer, who supplies the manuscript title.

The poem is written in the first person, the speaker probably being the poet himself (when he was about to be married), who describes a strange experience he had one spring morning when he met an old man while walking across an English moor. The first two stanzas set the scene of an animated landscape filled with sounds of birds and rushing water, sights of bright sunshine reflected from wet grass, and a rabbit kicking up a mist as it runs away. The poet says, in the third stanza, that he was as happy as the scene he surveyed.

Yet unexpectedly, and suddenly, he fell into a deep melancholy, which he describes in the fourth and fifth stanzas. He is perplexed about his strange sorrow, which contrasts so strongly with the scene about him and his former happiness. In stanzas 6 and 7, he considers the plight of persons (perhaps like himself) who have spent their lives without much consideration for anything except their own happiness; two great poets, Thomas Chatterton and Robert Burns, illustrate the fate of those who begin in joy and end in great sadness.

In this meditative mood, the poet sees with surprise, in stanza 8, a very old man. The old man seems as solid as a great stone placed atop a hill; at the same time, he seems mysteriously out of place, the way a sea animal might if it has been found somewhere on land. The poet passes from these comparisons in stanza 9 to observe in stanzas 10 and 11 that the old man is a pathetic example of human suffering, one who searches for leeches in pools of water. These he might collect and sell for medical uses by physicians of the time.

Finally, in stanza 12, the poet speaks to the old man, asking how he makes his living, and hears a reply in stanzas 13 through 15. What strikes the poet, however, is not the substance of the old leech gatherer's remarks, but rather the style of his speaking. In stanza 16, therefore, the poet realizes that he has not understood what the old man has been saying, so he has to repeat his question in stanza 17.

The leech gatherer is patient with the young poet, so he repeats his answer in stanza 18—that he gathers leeches from the pools on this barren moor. The effect of this encounter, produced by both the style and substance of the old man's remarks, is described by the poet's words in the last two stanzas: He is troubled, as if in a vision, with the image of the old man as a rebuke to himself for not being stronger, for not being more resolute and independent. In the future, when he feels again the temptation to fall into melancholy, he will remember the example of this old leech gatherer, whose fortitude will guard the poet against further temptations of despair.

Forms and Devices

The poem acquires its tone of solemnity and ritual encounter from its use of a stanzaic form associated with ceremony and seriousness: the rhyme royal (sometimes called the Chaucerian stanza, because Geoffrey Chaucer used it in several of his poems in the fourteenth century). This is a stanza of seven lines which are arranged to rhyme *ababbcc.* "Resolution and Independence" makes one change from the traditional form, because it adds an extra metrical foot to the seventh line to make a stanza of six iambic pentameter lines, concluding with a line of iambic hexameter (to echo the way the Spenserian stanza concludes). This additional, longer line brings each stanza to a thoughtful, self-reflective conclusion that provides a basis for renewed consideration and progressive self-examination to open each successive stanza.

Self-reflective meditation is dramatized by the encounter between poet and leech gatherer, as each seems puzzled by the strange behavior of the other. Since the form of the poem is controlled by the poet, his own strangeness is objectified by the reflection of his consciousness in the appearance of the other person. The dramatic encounter becomes an occasion for self-awareness for the poet. There is a hint of narrative to the poem, because the poet tells a story with a beginning, middle, and end to outline the plot of a young man's growing up: It is thus a form of initiation and springtime renewal.

The poet's interest in the old man's formal style of speech is a sign of the poet's professional interest in language. The poem is highly metaphorical, creating an inner landscape from the imagery of the external setting, as when the opening stanza describes the brooding stock dove to convey a double sense of "brooding": darkly thinking and warming to create new life. The sounds and signs of spring and morning, with rain and running water, yield to images of shallow pools in which the old man hunts for leeches. Most impressive, at the center of the poem's form is the device of the double simile in stanza 9: Here the psychological impact of the old man's appearance is conveyed by a comparison with a "huge stone" atop "an eminence," and the stone itself is compared with "a sea beast crawled forth." Several qualities of the old man's significance are suggested: his peculiar appearance amid so much solitude, his condition of alienation, his fortitude, and his independence.

By the end of the poem, the old man has been internalized by the speaker, so that the poet's mind becomes haunted by the memory of the leech gatherer as a monument to endurance, integrity, and resolution. The devices whereby this is accomplished are figurative uses of language which are metaphors of substitution, as the old man's voice sounds like water and his very body is turned first into a rock, then a sea beast, a cloud, and finally a dream, as the poet transforms him into a figure of his own mind.

Themes and Meanings

At the heart of the poem is the question of whether the poet will become a responsible human being, independent of others for his own happiness. He realizes that his essential quality of mental or spiritual identity cannot rely upon an external environment for its continuing strength. At first, the speaker feels at one with the happy springtime setting, but when he falls suddenly into despair, he is puzzled into a crisis of confidence in himself. Then, when he has most need, the old man appears as if "by peculiar grace" to serve as an admonishment.

All that occurs in the poem is a consequence of the poet's sense of need, apparently without cause. The powers of mind, as imagination, usurp the poet's consciousness of everything that surrounds him, including the leech gatherer, making it difficult for the poet to keep hold of the external reality through which both he and the leech gatherer move. In this is the theme of mental experience transcending physical limitations. Yet the poet's imagination seizes upon the details of the encounter to nourish itself, to create a self-reflecting image for the poet to study as a lesson in resolution and independence.

The poet needed to feel self-reliant just as he was nearly falling into helpless and mysterious despair. The leech gatherer supplied what the poet needed, because the poet had the imagination to make use of the encounter. The meaning of the poem is that the human mind transcends the natural environment upon which it has been accustomed to depend and from which it can draw spiritual and mental nourishment, even though the lesson of transcendence is not without its mysteries and pains of dislocation. Every human being is, like the old man and, as the poem demonstrates, like the young poet, lonely and alienated from the rest of nature, because a human being is essentially different from natural being. Nevertheless, in a triumphant exercise of imaginative self-reflection, "Resolution and Independence" celebrates the human capacity to make use of the natural and to learn from sympathetic responses to fellow human creatures.

Themes of vocation, maturation, and creativity are embodied in the poem's texture of natural imagery, dramatic awareness of human pathos, and narrative recall of a momentous morning's adventure. Although the poem is not one of those which William Wordsworth called "lyrical ballads," it nevertheless achieves the lyrical shape of those famous poems, because it makes its meaning a song of subjective achievement through a shaping of the objects of circumstance. Mind makes meaning from environment; environment does not make meaning for mind.

Richard D. McGhee

THE RETRIEVAL SYSTEM

Author: Maxine Kumin (1925-   )
Type of poem: Meditation
First published: 1978, in *The Retrieval System*

The Poem

Like so much of the poet's work, Maxine Kumin's "The Retrieval System" focuses on human-animal interactions. In this case, the poet examines the surprising ways that certain animals remind her of the "lost" people in her life and how these correspondences serve to "retrieve" those individuals.

The first line of the poem sets the pattern. "It begins," Kumin writes, "with my dog." The pronoun "it" refers to the system of resemblance that seems to well up from the poet's subconscious when she is alone. In the first of five stanzas, the poet comments on how her late dog's brown eyes reminded her of her father, who is also deceased. The eyes of both dog and man shared certain qualities; both were "keen, loving, accepting, sorrowful."

This linkage leads to another outlined in the second stanza and the first part of the third. Here the poet remarks about how much the "tiny voice" and "terrible breath" of an old goat "who runs free in pasture and stable" remind her of her "former piano teacher// whose bones beat time in [her] dreams."

This resemblance is, in the third stanza, followed by two more examples of how the poet's dead family and friends are linked with the "patient domestic beasts" in her life. Kumin writes of how much her "willful/ intelligent ponies" remind her of her "elderly aunts" and how much her cat in "faint chin," "inscrutable squint," and cry resembles her sister, who died at the age of three.

The fourth stanza continues this pattern of apparently free association. After a brief reference to her sister's funeral and a quote from the twenty-third psalm, *"The Lord is my shepherd,"* a subtle reference to the often symbiotic relationship between man and beast, the stanza occupies itself primarily with one poignant correspondence. The poet focuses on a "yearling colt" whose exuberant energy recalls the "cocksure" quality of a boy that the poet once loved but who died thirty years earlier in World War II.

This temporal reference seems to snap the poet out of her reverie temporarily and to bring readers not only to the poem's present but also to a forecast of what is to come. A television weatherman, who reminds the poet of an owl who has found a home in her barn, outlines current conditions and predicts snow. The weatherman-owl connection, however, leads to another apparently serendipitous linkage. The owl's face that is both "heart-shaped" and "donnish, bifocaled, kind" conjures up memories of the poet's late dentist, who filled in one of the poet's wisdom teeth, just like the snow threatens to fill the "open graves" of memory.

Forms and Devices

Kumin is noted for her formalist approach to poetry, her use of traditional metrical patterns. In the case of "The Retrieval System," however, the poet experiments with something akin to free verse. Yet, underneath the apparent freedom of her poetic line lies Kumin's masterful control. She manipulates stanza length, for example, to underscore her theme. The first three stanzas are six lines each, the fourth is eight, and the fifth is nine. Like the accumulating references to the dead, the basic structure of the poem adds increasing weight to the last two stanzas. In effect, the entire poem offers a verbal equivalent to the final image of the shrouding snow.

Another Kumin strength is her careful use of detail. In the third stanza, for example, the poet makes three references to musical selections associated with her late piano teacher. Each is extraordinarily resonant. "Country Gardens" by twentieth century Australian-born American composer Percy Grainger is a piano duet, a fact that underscores the relationship between poet and teacher. The piece is also a tone poem meant to conjure up country life, an apt parallel to Kumin's bucolic setting. The second musical selection, "Humoresque," by nineteenth century German composer Robert Schumann, is a piece that calls attention to the shifting moods of Kumin's poem. As its title indicates, the piano piece is intended to be lively and funny, just like some of the poet's correspondences, particularly the piano teacher and elderly aunt examples. Yet, at the same time, the reader cannot help but think of the composer's tragic death in an asylum following a failed suicide by drowning, a reference that may foreshadow the burial at sea of the boy-lover in stanza 4. Finally, there is the "unplayable" music of eighteenth century German composer Johann Sebastian Bach, whose work was forgotten for a time only to be resurrected long after his death. This Bach reference underscores the theme of retrieval. The use of the adjective "unplayable" may refer to the fast fingering required of many Baroque keyboard pieces, a tempo at odds with the poet's prevailing mood of reverie.

Throughout this essentially meditative poem, the principal agency of correspondence is synecdoche, a figure of speech in which a part signifies the whole. Thus, a dog's eyes conjure up memories of the poet's father. The power of these correspondences comes from the concrete language that the poet employs to describe the animal "features" that "uncannily" come to the surface of her mind when she is alone and offer her a means by which she can be linked to people lost to death. The goat, for example, has "flecked, agate eyes" with "minus-sign pupils."

Themes and Meanings

From time to time, all people use mnemonic devices to train the memory. There is, for example, the namelike acronym "Roy G. Biv" commonly used by schoolchildren to help them remember the colors of the spectrum: red, orange, yellow, green, blue, indigo, and violet. In the case of "The Retrieval System," Kumin develops a system of resemblance between the familiar animals resident on her New Hampshire farm and the significant human beings in her life, now dead. The second and third lines of the fourth stanza provide the poem's explicit thesis: "it is people who fade,/ it is animals that retrieve them."

"The Retrieval System," the title poem in a 1978 collection by the same name and the poet's sixth separate volume of verse, deals with a recurring theme in Kumin's work, the subject of loss. Most notable in this regard are the poet's many elegies to American confessional poet Anne Sexton, who was Kumin's closest friend and creative collaborator for seventeen years before her sudden suicide in 1974.

Kumin's coping with loss is essentially optimistic. "I don't want to brood," she writes in the second line of the fourth stanza. In much of her poetry on this subject, Kumin contends that one can reconnect to the dead through the agency of the imagination, particularly through the exercise of metaphor. At times, the correspondence is humorous, as when the goat's blat reminds her of her piano teacher; at other times, the correspondence is more poignant, as when the cry of her cat sounds like her little sister in pain. Yet, Kumin does not, in this poem, dwell upon either mood too long, nor does she seem to provide a hierarchy of loss as she moves from father to piano teacher, from aunts to sister, and from boy-lover to dentist. Hers is a democracy of separation and retrieval.

In addition to being part of a long tradition of elegiac verse, "The Retrieval System" is also a good example of what might be termed nature poetry, for it is not just the people who are memorialized in the poem but also the animals. Kumin, who follows in the footsteps of twentieth century American poet Robert Frost in the exploitation of the New England countryside in all seasons, pays as much attention to the animals in her life as she does to the humans that she refers to in her essays as her "tribe." For example, the dog that calls to mind her late father has eyes whose "phosphorescent gleam" is a "separate gift." The yearling colt "runs merely to be." Because of the keenness of the poet's observational skills, these animals can stand on their own. They are not merely physical receptacles for the imaginative reincarnation of lost family and friends.

It is interesting to note that "The Retrieval System" was written around the time of Kumin's personal transformation from weekend and summer visitor to permanent resident of rural New Hampshire. Her thoughts on this change are captured in the "Place Where I Live" section of her 1979 collection of essays entitled *To Make a Prairie: Essays on Poets, Poetry, and Country Living*. These prose pieces are redolent with animal life, particularly in winter, and there are fragments that focus on "beasts" similar to those in the poem, particularly a young horse and a resident owl. Critics have long remarked on the poet's reverence for animals, either because of their capacity to explain people to themselves or because of their own inherent magic.

S. Thomas Mack

RETURN

Author: Czesław Miłosz (1911-   )
Type of poem: Lyric
First published: 1991, as "Powrót," in *Dalsze okolice*; English translation collected in
    Provinces, 1991

The Poem

"Return," with thematic divisions consisting of single sentences or short paragraphs, is a meditative poem whose cadence conforms more to the rhythms of prose than to those of verse. The poem is written in the first person and is autobiographical. Although the poet includes the reader in his musings, there is no doubt that the focus is on the poet's own life experiences. In fact, "Return" can be considered an emotional history of Czesław Miłosz's life in capsule form.

The poet has returned home to the places of his youth. They, like him, are ostensibly the same and yet not the same. The passage of time has changed all the important details. The man and his homeland are now "incomprehensibly the same, incomprehensibly different." Standing on the shore of a lake, the poet remembers the sufferings and despair of his younger self standing on this same shore, but the experience of many years has made him realize that such pain was not his alone but the inevitable result of living in a cruel world. However, he honors the boy and all young people who have not grown "sly," who refuse to acquiesce, and who refuse to "participate for ever."

The middle section of the poem changes in tone as the poet deals briefly with the gifts of the world, a woman's body, and the beauty of a lake, but this mood is fleeting as the poet almost immediately asks if it has all been worthwhile. Many of Miłosz's poems written outside his native Lithuania deal with the experiences and people of his past. At times these past voices threaten to drown out his own living voice, but in "Return," where one might expect the poet to be surrounded by images of the past calling to him, there is, paradoxically, silence. The ghosts of the past have left him; he is the only one standing on the shore.

The last section of the poem carries with it the implicit subtext almost always present in Miłosz's later work. To fully understand a poem, the reader must be familiar with the vicissitudes of the poet's life, such as his boyhood in Lithuania, his life under the Nazi and Stalinist regimes, and his decision to escape to the West in search of artistic freedom. For an appreciation of "Return," this background knowledge is especially important because the conclusion of the poem not only contains Miłosz's philosophical commentary on his life (and on life in general) but also constitutes a type of poetic manifesto or "life" manifesto. Miłosz's life may have been one of "chaos and transience," but poetry is "the changeless garden on the other side of time."

Forms and Devices

At first glance, "Return" seems devoid of any poetic devices or images, but the apparent simplicity of the proselike lines is deceptive. What first attracts the attention is the use of the "I" in the first lines, but as the poet begins to feel the chasm between his younger and older selves, the pronoun shifts to "you" for the boy of his youth and then to "he" and "we" as all are enveloped in the evils of the world. The "I" returns as the poet individually feels the beauty of the world, but the "I" of the older man and the "you" of the boy merge in their appreciation of the gifts of life: "Only for me" and "Only for you." While separate in suffering, they unite in joy. In the last section, only the "I" of the old man remains as he reflects on what has happened to him since he left this place so many years before.

"Return" is very representative of Miłosz's later work in its almost complete rejection of any poetic devices such as metaphor or symbol. Any attempt at versification or rhyming techniques is also absent. The two- and three-line divisions of the poem are meant to correspond to the natural flow of thought. However, also dominant in Miłosz's poetry is nature imagery, and again "Return" is no exception. What is different because of the theme of the poem (Miłosz's return home) is that all the imagery exists in the present. In other poems, similar sounds, smells, and shapes call forth correspondences to the past while the poet strives in vain, at times, to stop this sensorial stream of past consciousness. In "Return," the opposite occurs as the poet vainly tries to use the past to orient himself in the present, but he cannot find the "traces of the lanes."

It is characteristic of Miłosz's poetry that even in the midst of the contemplation of the most beautiful landscape there is always the bitter realization of the evil inherent in the world that beauty covers. Even in "Return," in the contemplation of a beloved, often longed-for sight, the image of the cruel demiurge who created a "pitiless" world of "chaos and transience" appears. The poet sets apart the concept of this horror by twice repeating the question "How can it be?"; it is the only repetition of the poem. For Miłosz, this evil deity is the poetic icon for the dark side, "the imperfect Nature" of his philosophical dualism; the "perfect Nature" that his poetry has tried to find is symbolized by the "changeless garden on the other side of time."

Themes and Meanings

"Return" is a poem about a poet and the meaning of his life and work. Therefore, many of the important themes of Miłosz's poetry are at least touched upon in the poem. Miłosz is a Metaphysical poet. The greater part of his work in the West has been autobiographical, in which the quintessential challenge has been the question of identity. Miłosz has used his own personal experiences as stepping stones in his examination of the value of human existence. In "Return," this exploration of meaning is linked to another recurrent theme: the analysis of one's life as it approaches its conclusion. Miłosz does not aggrandize the episodes of his life or emphasize hardships or problems. If anything, he deprecates his own history: "Somehow I waded through; I am grateful that I was not submitted to tests beyond my strength." His, he ironically states, has been "a blindly accomplished destiny."

Many critics have spoken of the conflict inherent in Miłosz's worldview; the poet himself calls this metaphysical dilemma his "ecstatic pessimism." This seeming contradiction of terms is colored by the Manichaeanism inherent in Miłosz's philosophy. The world can be beautiful; the poet is fascinated by this beauty, but he knows that it is always contaminated by evil. His pessimistic evaluation in "Return" of the importance of his own life is linked to this same duality. As a poet he re-creates beautiful images, but, given the autobiographical nature of his work, a certain disappointment or dissatisfaction, even bitterness, is always present. For example, he condemns those who are trained in "slyness" but then characterizes himself sarcastically as having "grown slyly just" and praises those who have chosen suicide rather than continue participating. The mood of Miłosz's poetry swings constantly from joy to despair, from skepticism to faith, in his search for answers. The world is "horrible," "comic," and "senseless," but through his poetry, which has been both the means and goal of this search, he has validated his belief in its opposite.

Miłosz's poetry has been distinguished by the persistence of memory, by the multitude of voices, and by the different levels of time that meet and diverge in the poet's consciousness. The reader should expect the same poetic layering in "Return," but it is not there, a fact that surprises the poet himself. Always haunted by the past, he has expected it to reach out and grab him on his return; he has even chosen a favorite spot of his youth for this blending of lives. However, in this literal return to the past, he seems to have mysteriously lost the ability to emotionally and figuratively recapture it. Away from his homeland, he has always walked with those he left behind, but here there are no "troubled spirits flying by." The ghosts have brought him here, but now it is as if they have left him alone to answer his questions by himself. The insistent "I" of the poem defines his solitude and the stark loneliness of existence.

In an age that eschews personal responsibility, Miłosz has stood out as an ethical as well as a Metaphysical poet. His own life was dramatically changed by historical forces, and thus he constantly examines the role of the individual in society. To what extent can the individual accept credit for his actions? To what extent must he accept blame? In "Return," a sense of personal guilt is apparent as the poet concedes that his choices have led him away from the real world. Did he have a choice?

Charlene E. Suscavage

RETURN

Author: Octavio Paz (1914-1998)
Type of poem: Lyric
First published: 1976, as "Vuelta," in *Vuelta (1969-1975)*; English translation collected in *The Collected Poems of Octavio Paz: 1957-1987*, 1987

The Poem

The 168 lines of "Return" are divided into 7 stanzas of unequal length. "Return" marks Octavio Paz's return to Mexico City after serving as Mexico's ambassador to India between 1962 and 1968. He resigned this post after the massacre of Mexican students at Tlatelolco in 1968. The Lopez Velarde epigraph, which refers to the destruction of the Catholic provinces during the Mexican Revolution, calling the country "the subverted paradise," mirrors Paz's revulsion at seeing modern Mexico debased by a megalomaniac government and compliant citizens.

The first stanza is an objective rendering of the speaker's walk through the streets of Mexico City and Mixcoac. The speaker's tone is pleasant as he views "bougain-villea/ against the wall's white lime." The setting assumes the qualities of a painting except for the lines "Letters rot/ in the mailboxes," which is the only negative image in the stanza and a reference to a lack of communication. The mention of Mixcoac, the Mexican home of Paz's infancy, and the lines "I am walking back/ back to what I left" connect the reader to the speaker's remembered past, a past that has all but vanished.

In the next stanza, the speaker loses contact with the external world. His objective state turns within as his body and spirit dissolve. He speculates about death in Mexico City under the "pounding fist of light." The speaker wonders what it would be like to die in a city office or hospital or on a city pavement and concludes that such a death "isn't worth the pain." Pedestrians become unimportant, just as the speaker feels himself to be. Existence is nothing more than "mist."

The third and fourth stanzas vividly depict the suffering of an entire population. The educational system, religious institutions, and business enterprises all appear to share the movie theaters' "ghost populations of desire." The people of the city help promote the decay of the culture with their sordid, middle-class desires, which lead only to suffering. The speaker implies that the nature of this suffering leaves the city's citizens with no haven. He denounces several professions, claiming that their members are too selfish to save their culture. People are called "buffoons," "coyotes," and "satraps." Those who should serve, including members of the military and the civil government, do not.

The next stanza examines the result of human corruption. No longer does the speaker focus upon the people but upon the modern wasteland created by them. Decay, poverty, and death are the by-products of the modern dilemma in which gardens "rot," people are "urban nomads," and poverty-ridden districts and shantytowns are laced by "thoroughfares of scars." At the conclusion of the stanza, the speaker states,

"City/ heap of broken words," indicating that all promises and hope for a renewed life have disintegrated.

In the sixth stanza, the fractured society is shown as having lost a common language. "Yesterday's news" becomes "more remote/ than a cuneiform tablet smashed to bits." A shared language (closer to a shared system of belief) becomes an anomaly. Without this language, there can be "no center." The society's recovery depends on a way of communicating that will include all Mexicans. Yet the only reality that the bankrupt culture honors is the dollar sign, which is stamped "on every forehead," a reference to the greed of individuals who have become noncommunicative islands of personal suffering.

The final stanza begins with a feeling of frustration as the speaker comments, "We are surrounded/ I have gone back to where I began." The epigraph had suggested that paradise has been lost, but the speaker is not willing to judge things in terms of "success or failure"; the Chinese sage mentioned by the speaker would answer that it is an error to judge things in this manner. The speaker proclaims that the city "is not a subverted paradise/ it is a pulse-beat of time," implying that his personal reflections and declarations have no actual meaning outside the poem itself.

Forms and Devices

"Return," with its "Time/ stretched to dry on the rooftops," owes much to surrealism. The tone of the poem leaves the reader with several horrific images of modern Mexico City. As the speaker moves from one fantastic observation to the next, using a stream-of-consciousness technique, the reader is rarely allowed a static vision of the speaker's surroundings. At times, memory is mixed with observation, and the result is a blurring of the line between reality and the speaker's imagination and past.

Imagery occupies an important position in "Return." The vividness of this imagery adds to the surreal quality of the poem as well as to the atmosphere of decay. Personification, metaphor, and simile aid Paz in creating this surreal mood. Ash trees and the wind "whistle." The "sun's spread hand" creates "almost liquid/ shadow and light." The sun of midday is a "pounding fist of light." Colleges and temples possess "genitals." Ideas become "swarms of reasons shaped like knives." The buildings of Mexico City are described as "paralytic architecture," and the nation's streets become "thoroughfares of scars/ alleys of living flesh."

Enjambment is used with great success in the poem. Paz employs little punctuation. The ideas of the poem are controlled by the placement of lines on the page. The images, however, are constantly overlapping. The free-flowing pattern created by enjambment adds to the overall dreamlike quality of the work. Nightmarish images are placed in close proximity. Since Paz examines the sometimes enigmatic nature of memory as well as reality, enjambment allows him to blend and distort many of these images. In turn, this blending of images emphasizes the ambiguous nature of memory. Without convenient stopping points, the reader is forced to follow the speaker's observations in rapid succession.

The use of poetic devices to achieve a level of experience that combines the past, present, and even the future adheres to the speaker's desire to reach a point where such divisions are indistinguishable. Paz's methods are directly tied to his thematic intent. Without these poetic devices, the poem would be less effective.

Themes and Meanings

"Return" functions on a variety of thematic levels. The nature of memory, the function of time and self-imposed boundaries, loss of purpose, decay in the modern world, and the power of the imagination all play important roles in the poem.

Ostensibly, the poem appears to focus on the speaker's return to Mexico. His displeasure with what he sees is apparent as he assembles a host of urban wasteland images that are fused with his memory. At one point he comments, "I am in Mixcoac," the place of his infancy. He states, "I am walking back/ back to what I left/ or to what left me." The speaker's memory of his homeland is not distinct from his visions of modern Mexico. He indicates that his past has become part of his present, a present that does not offer the remembered sanctity of childhood.

The speaker's exposure to Mexico City and its corruption greatly disturbs him. He sees that his people, along with their institutions, have failed. Traversing the city, he moves deeper into the very fabric of Mexican culture. His once-objective observations are tinged with infuriation and bitterness. Yet the speaker does not view his people without pity. He sees the common man and woman partially as victims, citizens whose institutions and culture have betrayed them. Nevertheless, the modern Mexican wasteland is a creation of the speaker's compatriots, whether villains or victims. The speaker senses the enormity of their failure as he glides from one image of despair to the next. His surroundings become dehumanized, and the speaker eventually loses his body and spirit to these surroundings. At one point, he exclaims, "We are surrounded." His apprehension for the future of Mexico and his accompanying sense of futility only accentuate modern Mexico's predicament.

The circular nature of the poem is evident when the speaker states, "I have gone back to where I began." In a sense, the title of the poem speaks of a return to the beginning of the poem. The reader as well as the speaker must restart their individual attempts to discover meaning. The speaker bemoans the fact that the Mexican people no longer have a philosophical center upon which to focus. So the reader is locked into a circular pattern that lacks finality. There is no center for the reader. Each person, within a separate sphere of existence, circling without any fix on a center, can do nothing but search for a focal point, something that the speaker has claimed is lost. The cyclical nature of the poem and existence itself prove to be obstacles in reaching any specific end.

The conclusion of the poem presents the reader with a new dilemma. The speaker denies the previous thematic content of the poem by commenting, "It is not a subverted paradise/ It is a pulse-beat of time." The speaker cancels assumptions about theme or meaning by informing the reader that the poem does not signify anything except what the reader brings to the poem. There are questions that the speaker asks about the modern wasteland and the meaning of life in that wasteland; there are, however, no absolute answers. He comments, "I walk without moving forward/ We never arrive/ Never reach where we are/ Not the past/ the present is untouchable," illustrating that he does not know the answers to the questions he himself has posed.

The poem transports the reader beyond the construct of linear time. The past is lost; the present is never the present, because linear time forces it immediately into the past. Divisions become ephemeral. The power of the imagination and the workings of the poet's memory convey to the reader the many possibilities of an existence without boundaries. In a sense, the poem restores the reader by engaging him or her in the creative process. The return of the poem's title becomes representative of a renewal of spirit that the poem brings about as well. The wasteland does exist, but the power of the imagination transcends that wasteland.

Robert Bateman

THE RETURN

Author: Ezra Pound (1885-1972)
Type of poem: Lyric
First published: 1912, in *Ripostes*

The Poem

The apparent simplicity of this twenty-line poem belies its mysterious subject and persona. Its short lines, straightforward diction, and compelling rhythms pull the reader forward through a series of striking images, but at the poem's end, he or she is nowhere nearer to discovering the dramatic situation.

Most scholars agree that "The Return" is about the return of the ancient, pre-Judeo-Christian gods to earth, but others argue that the poem describes the retreat, the "anabasis," of a once-mighty army. Either interpretation fits, although the "Gods of the winged shoe" in the third stanza suggest the former reading. In either case, "The Return" portrays the passage of a group of formerly heroic beings, now weary and worn out by their anxieties. The persona watches them pass and describes their slow, uncertain movement. He seems to be calling others to witness the defeated return of this godlike host.

Line 1 suggests that the persona was present when these hero-gods were at the zenith of their power or that he is at least knowledgeable about their former glory; the fact that they have "returned" implies an earlier journey. If these are indeed the ancient gods who held sway before the advent of modern religions, then the assumption is that monotheism has conquered but not yet destroyed them. The less mysterious interpretation—that these are warriors returning after years of hard campaigning—would also account for the persona's description of the defeated, but still awe-inspiring, host.

The speaker describes the exhausted pace of the returned heroes. Their slow, "wavering" step in stanza 1 is the result not only of their simple physical enervation but also of their moral collapse. Although these beings have not met with formal defeat, their long struggle has drained them of self-confidence and psychological strength. Their uncertainty, moreover, suggests that they have no real destination; in their absence, they have lost their former home.

Stanza 2 continues the description of their march. At one time, they moved forward in confident phalanxes, but now they have been reduced to a mass of stragglers, returning "one by one." The implication is that each being has been reduced to an isolated individual who no longer draws power from their combined might. Once again, the persona stresses the emotional climate that hangs over the returnees: Some nameless fear makes them hesitant. He contrasts their timidity with their original appearance of inviolability.

In stanza 3, the speaker continues his description of the heroes' former strength. They seemed to take flight in their eager movement forward. Supernaturally powerful hunting dogs, their "silver hounds," accompanied them, and in their keenness, the dogs sniffed the air and strained at their leashes. The characterization of this former greatness continues in stanza 4. The persona summons up the full-throated hunting cries of the beings, the swiftness and ruthlessness of their hounds, and the ominous excitement of the hunt. In the final stanza, however, the speaker returns to the present: The dogs lag on their leashes and the beings who hold them are pale and drained.

Forms and Devices

"The Return" is written in free verse, having no set number of beats per line, no recurring rhyme scheme, and no regular stanza pattern. Although it is certainly not the first instance of free verse in Western literature, it has been said that the poem marks the start of the free verse "movement" that has dominated English-language poetry in the twentieth century. Moreover, "The Return" is widely praised as a model of the form, an example of the supple power of free verse when its "freedom" is fully under control.

Yet, despite the poem's label as free verse, individual lines use a variety of complex rhythms, including variations on ancient prosodic patterns. The rhythmic pattern of the final stanza, for example, mimics the classical "adonius" meter, often used in Greek heroic poetry; this same rhythm is similar to that used in older English-language liturgical writing.

The key thing to note, however, is the way that Ezra Pound has wed his theme to his prosody: As the poem describes the straggling return of defeated heroes, its rhythms mirror the hesitant pace of their march. Stanza 1, for example, accomplishes this conjunction of theme and rhythm in two ways: through internal rhythms and through the curtailments at the ends of lines. Line 1 is broken midway by a semi-colon (the line's caesura), causing a pause in the reader's forward movement. Yet the line is also punctuated by strong stresses, beginning with its first word, "See," which is in turn followed by two unstressed beats, "they return." The initial stress acts as an exclamation calling the persona's hearers to witness the heroic column as it passes, but the two succeeding unstressed beats and the following midline break are a kind of letdown, mirroring the disordered step of the returning gods. Immediately, however, the speaker regains his awe and repeats the opening "see," thereby pulling his hearer's attention more strongly to an event that is important to him.

At lines 1 and 3 of this stanza, the syntax is unnaturally broken between an adjective and its modified noun, causing the reader to stop and "stumble," matching the slow, unrhythmic pace of the gods. This break and pause is reinforced by the meaning of the separated words: "Tentative" ends line 1 before it can be joined to "Movements," beginning line 2; "uncertain" cuts short line 3 before it can modify "Wavering" in line 4. The resulting rhythm exactly reproduces the footfalls of defeated men as they step uncertainly forward, pause, look around, and stumble on.

This device is repeated in stanza 2, where the speaker describes the movement of snow blown by shifting winds. In this metaphor comparing the gods to the light, powerless snow, line 3, ending with "hesitate," itself "hesitates" before it continues on to line 4, completing the thought—"And murmur in the wind."

In contrast to the broken, uncertain rhythms of stanzas 1 and 2, stanzas 3 and 4 describe the godlike heroes as they were in the past, full-blooded, keen, and "inviolable." Stanza 4, for example, begins with the repeated hunting cry, "Haie! Haie!," a double stress that underscores the power and unity of the gods as they hunted during their golden age. This line is followed by a series of repetitions in lines 2, 3, and 4 (a parallelism): The speaker is eager to recall the gods' splendor to his hearers, and he does this by underlining their heroic attributes through the repeated "These were . . ./ These . . ./ These were. . . ."

The other crucial formal device in "The Return" is its vivid sensory imagery. In fact, the poem is an example of Imagist method; Imagism was a poetic theory, largely created by Pound himself, that sought to emphasize highly charged visual, tactile, and olfactory impressions instead of distinct subject matter, so that the images themselves would join directly to tell the poem's story. Here, the persona carefully describes the "trouble" of the returnees' "pace," their "pallid" appearance, and their straggling, isolated march. The snow metaphor in stanza 2 reinforces this collection of images. In contrast, the "silver hounds" of stanza 3 and the hounds' keen scent in stanzas 3 and 4 bolster the once-glorious appearance of the gods, while the dogs' slack leashes of the final stanza mirror the enervation of defeat.

Themes and Meanings

Pound was one of many thinkers and writers at the end of the nineteenth and the beginning of the twentieth century who believed that the Judeo-Christian religious tradition had crippled the spiritual and psychological life of many people. He believed that the otherworldly, self-renouncing tendency of monotheistic religions had caused people to ignore the world around them, making them dull and ridden with guilt.

Yet, Pound also believed that, under the surface, modern human beings still retained an older belief in a polytheistic universe where godlike spirits dwelled in springs, trees, mountains, and fields. Throughout his poetic life, Pound reasserted this conviction in an attempt to refresh the minds and senses of twentieth century urbanites cooped up in their cities and penned in by their guilt.

"The Return" is an expression of this belief in the continuing reality of humankind's ancient gods. Although these beings, as the poem portrays them, have been defeated, they are by no means dead. In "The Return," Pound, through his persona, calls out to his readers in an attempt to gain their attention: The gods still exist for those who have eyes to see them.

Generally, this poem has an elegiac tone: Even as Pound reasserts the continued existence of the gods, he acknowledges their lost vitality. Thus, the poem struggles with two contrasting themes: the isolated, forgotten status of the gods in the modern era and the memory of their ancient splendor. Pound acknowledges that the gods at the zenith of their power were neither kindly nor merciful. These were superhuman beings with ferocious, superhuman passions. The gods were hunters, perhaps of human souls, and their strengths were those associated with predators—keen senses, an aptitude for violence, power, and speed. Yet these same attributes, Pound seems to say, are ones that humans have lost in the modern world. For all their faults, the ancient gods lived in close association with humans, imparting to mortals these full-blooded immortal traits. In contrast, contemporary human beings live in a universe remote from their all-seeing, omnipotent, monotheistic God, whose ultimate characteristics humans cannot share.

The poem ends hesitantly, akin to the stumbling pace of the returning gods. Perhaps, the final stanza implies, the gods have fallen so low that a recovery of a polytheistic world view is impossible. In the modern world, both humanity and its ancient heroes have grown weak, pale, and slow.

John Steven Childs

RETURN TO MY NATIVE LAND

Author: Aimé Césaire (1913-   )
Type of poem: Lyric
First published: 1939, as *Cahier d'un retour au pays natal*; translated as *Return to My Native Land*, 1968; English translation collected as *Notebook of a Return to My Native Land*, in *Aimé Césaire: The Collected Poetry,* 1983

The Poem

Return to My Native Land is an extended lyric meditation (1,055 lines in the original French). Aimé Césaire wrote the first version in the late 1930's, having completed his studies in France, upon his return to his native Martinique (revised versions appeared in 1947 and 1956). Although the general mode of the poem is lyric, it mixes modes frequently. It has some epic qualities, especially evidenced by the narrator who, as an epic hero should, is trying to embody in himself the best qualities of his race. Further, about half the poem is written in prose.

The poem can be generally broken down into three parts. The first part is an examination of the poet's native Martinique, and particularly its capital, Fort-de-France. In the second part, he reacts, often negatively, to the people and history of this land. In the third, he learns not only to accept but also to embrace the people and spirit of his native land.

Césaire is often associated with the French Surrealist poets, and even a brief glance at the poem reveals why. In the first full paragraph, he tells a cop to "Beat it"; then, in a quick rush of images, he turns toward paradises that are lost to such people as the cop, nourishes the wind while rocked by a thought, and unlaces monsters—among other things. Such images have the impossible, dreamlike quality characteristic of Surrealism, and this quality keeps up throughout the poem. Overall, the poem does have a narrative shape, which is not characteristic of Surrealism, and as these images in the beginning suggest, the overall thrust of the poem involves the speaker's attempt to unleash the spirit of his native land which has been hidden, and imprisoned, and made to look monstrous by the subjugation of imperialism.

The key phrase in the first section of the poem (most of which is written in prose) is the phrase that begins many paragraphs, and indeed, the poem itself: "At the end of the wee hours." Literally, this phrase refers to the time immediately before sunrise and suggests someone who has been up most of the night, throughout the wee hours. Figuratively, the phrase suggests someone on the edge of an insight that is slowly dawning. Indeed, what the reader finds in this first section is an exploration of the city which focuses on observations of how the land's history of rule by France has twisted and distorted it.

The reference to "Josephine, Empress of the French, dreaming way up there above the nigger scum," is a good example of the type of image to be found in this section. It refers to a statue of Josephine, robed in the manner of the Napoleonic empire, which does in fact stand in the center of the public square of Fort-de-France. The statue seems to pay no attention to the "desolate throng under the sun," meaning the people of African descent who populate Martinique, and the populace feels no connection to her. She is a symbol of the French empire, and a reminder to the people that their culture and ethnicity is considered second class in this city.

Other recurring phrases also provide a clue to what holds the various images of this section together: "this town sprawled flat," "this inert town," the narrator repeats several times, to emphasize the idea that this is a town paralyzed in certain ways by colonialism. Other images of the town crawling, of life lying prostrate, and of dreams aborted also give the sense of a people struggling against a paralyzing burden.

The second section of the poem begins when the narrator thinks about going away and examines the other people he could be. In this section, the poem switches back and forth between free verse and prose. Though not all the possibilities of who he could be are examples of who he would want to be, some are. At one point, for example, he fantasizes himself returning to the "hideousness" of this land's "sores" and presenting himself as a redeemer, someone who can speak of the freedom that the native population has never known.

This leads him to consider the grim despair of the lives of these people he would save. "Who and what are we?" he asks, and tries to give this question as large (rather than as specific) an answer as possible. He identifies with all the Africans in his past, the ones who lived lives his own European sensibilities consider pagan, as well as with a man who was dragged "on a bloodspattered road/ a rope around his neck"—a clear reference to enslavement.

This section is full of lines in which the narrator seems to be shrinking from his heritage. When he exclaims, "So much blood in my memory!" he is genuinely overwhelmed by the violence of this past. Similarly, when he says, "I may as well confess that we were at all times pretty mediocre dishwashers, shoeblacks without ambition," he is truly troubled by how effective the colonial occupation of his land has been in aborting the dreams of his people. This disappointment with his people and his land comes to a focus when he finds himself smiling mockingly at a black whom he sees as "comical and ugly"—because he realizes he is looking at this man through the eyes of the imperialists who have controlled his country.

Recognizing this, he is forced to recognize the extent to which he has been participating in the victimization of his native land simply through accepting the values and customs that the French have imposed on them, and he vows to change. "I will deck my natural obsequiousness with gratitude," he says, meaning that he will no longer bow to the values he has been taught (those values that tell him that the Martinicans of African descent can be viewed as second-class citizens) but will actively embrace his people, happy for who they are.

This last third, with its revolutionary spirit of optimism, contains the lines that were to become central to the artistic and political negritude movement of the 1940's, 1950's, and 1960's: "My negritude is not a stone, its deafness hurled against the clamor of the day . . ./ my negritude is neither tower nor cathedral/ it takes root in the red flesh of the soil/ it takes root in the ardent flesh of the sky." That is to say, his negritude, his blackness, is not a weapon nor a construct to hide behind; rather, it is something organic and alive and a part of the land in which he lives.

From this point on, the tone of the poem is one of almost unbounded acceptance of his land, his people, and his heritage. The pain of "the shackles/ the rack . . ./ the head screw," which is the type of pain that earlier in the poem seemed almost overwhelming, is not denied here, but it is seen as pain that can be accepted. The work of man, he sees, "has only begun," and though this presages more hard work ahead, it is a fundamentally positive thing because it means that the present order, in which blacks in his land feel the need to bow down not only to whites, but to white culture, is a temporary and passing order. "The old negritude," he says several times, "progressively cadavers itself"—meaning the old sense of what it means to be black is dying. The work that the last third of this poem announces as begun, is the work of celebrating all the forms and contradictions of the new negritude (meaning the new way of being a black person) that is being created.

Forms and Devices

One use of form in this poem that a reader cannot help but notice is the way the poem mixes prose and free-verse passages. In the first section, when the narrator is providing a general overview, the dominant mode is prose; in the second, when he is wrestling with his own sensibility, prose and verse are mixed; and in the last section, when he is trying to achieve a new sensibility, the dominant mode is verse.

A closer look at this movement in the poem provides some insight into what the poet is doing. Many of the verse passages, especially early in the poem, are actually lists of images or people. The prose passages also contain such lists, but putting these lists into verse seems to be a way of focusing on each individual item in the list, as if the narrator is trying to clarify his thoughts by examining them closely. As the poem continues, free verse becomes the dominant mode of discourse, as if to call attention not only to what is being talked about, but the language itself. The implication seems to be that this new creative spirit of negritude the narrator is trying to achieve is an inherently poetic spirit, one that will take strength from the rhythms and sounds of language.

A dominant metaphor holding the poem together is the image of an awakening. As already mentioned, the phrase "At the end of the wee hours" implies not only a town that is about to awake but also an artistic sensibility that is on the verge of awakening to the realities of living in an imperialist society. As the poem progresses, he awakens not only to the reality of the history of enslavement, brutality, and cultural subjugation that the people of his native land have endured but also to the vitality of their spirit. While at the beginning of the poem the town is viewed as inert, toward the end the town is viewed as lively and the people as dancing. Not only has the town come awake but the speaker's sensitivity to the life of the town has also awakened.

Although there are passages (especially some of the prose passages) in which the narrator seems to be Césaire himself, it would be a mistake to assume that the narrator of this poem can, in all cases, be identified as Césaire. Rather, it might be more correct to say that this is a narrator who speaks for Césaire. That is to say, Césaire the poet has created a persona that embodies his own sensibility. To complicate this further, one of the ways that he expresses his sensibility is by speaking of the whole history of his people as contained in himself (as Walt Whitman often did in his poetry). This comes through especially in passages such as the one that begins by discussing "tadpoles hatched" by his "prodigious ancestry" and goes on to list the dead places of his soul that have been created by the uprootings and violence suffered by his ancestors.

Themes and Meanings

Although the central thematic concern of the poem is the importance for the person who lives as the subject of a colonized land to decolonize his or her own mind and sensibility, one of the central paradoxes of the poem is that it is written in French, the language of the colonialists, not in the native Creole of the Martinican population. Indeed, in their brief introduction to *Aimé Césaire: The Collected Poetry* (1983), Clayton Eshleman and Annette Smith point out the paradox that Césaire, the spokesperson for decolonizing the mind, who was later to become mayor of Fort-de-France, the city on which he focuses in *Return to My Native Land*, apparently never thought of Creole as a suitable language for his poetry.

Further, the traditions from which the poem seems to borrow are largely the traditions of French literature. Not only does the poem's rush of bizarre and often grotesque images seem to place it in the context of French Surrealist literature, but, as Eshleman and Smith also note, the images of hardship and misery seem to owe much to such images in the works of Victor Hugo, the great French novelist of the nineteenth century, whose works Césaire read as he was growing up.

A partial resolution of this apparent paradox can be seen through an analogy to the writers of the Harlem Renaissance of the 1920's, who were also greatly influential in Césaire's poetry. The images of people from the whole history of the black race that the narrator includes and identifies with, may remind readers of Langston Hughes's early poem, "The Negro Speaks of Rivers"; similarly, the ending of the poem, in which he speaks of transcending the binds and confines that have been placed on his people, bears a similarity in tone and spirit to another Langston Hughes poem, "I, Too, Sing America," which talks of the inevitability of African Americans being included in the mainstream of American life.

Similarly, the type of revolution that Césaire seems to be advocating in this poem is not a revolution that results in the violent overthrow of the past; rather, it is a revolution through inclusion. Toward the end of the poem, the narrator speaks of rallying dances to his side, including the "it-is-beautiful-good-and-legitimate-to-be-a-nigger-dance," as if to say that he wants to celebrate who he and his people are and can be, not dictate who they cannot be or what they should not do.

Shortly thereafter, he says, "bind me with your vast arms to the luminous clay/ bind my black vibration to the very navel of the world/ bind, bind me, bitter brotherhood." The image of being bound, which earlier implied slavery, has been transformed here into an image of connection to the natural world and to other people. He does not want to forget or forsake his connection to the white-dominated French world. Rather, he wants to have the chance to accept his connection to this world on his own terms, and in a life-affirming way, rather than have the terms of this connection dictated by imposed power structures.

To put this more directly, the task this narrator takes on is the task of defining for himself a concept of his own negritude, starting from the realities that have been imposed on the black population of his native land by white, European colonizers. The fiery optimism of the last section of the poem, with its unqualified lines of acceptance such as "I accept . . . I accept . . . totally, without reservation," is the optimism of someone who has learned he can see beauty and create life even from within the ruins of a system that has defiled the life and beauty of his land and people.

Thomas J. Cassidy

RETURNING

Author: Linda Pastan (1932-   )
Type of poem: Lyric
First published: 1981, in *Waiting for My Life*

The Poem

"Returning" is a free-verse poem of twenty-one lines divided into three seven-line stanzas. The title raises some key questions about the poem: Where is the main character of the poem (a woman identified only as "she")? Where is she returning from? Where is she going? On one level the answers are easy. Linda Pastan employs an extended analogy, based on a parachutist returning from the sky to "the coarser atmosphere of earth," to present this returning. It is more difficult to decide to what other process the parachutist's descent provides an analogy. The first stanza sets up this analogy and brings the parachutist from the clouds down to treetop level. The second stanza awakens the subject's eyes and nose to the sensations of this coarser life of earth. She smells the pines, and her husband starts to "swim" into view. In the final stanza, the parachutist lands in her garden and pushes the chute aside, signaling the end of the flight. In the last three lines, the poet likens the discarding of the parachute to the way "she pushed the white sheet/ from her breasts/ just yesterday."

The first line ("She re-enters her life") provides a clue to the nature of the analogy. The subject has been away from her normal life, perhaps in an altered psychological or physical state. In fact, the place she has been seems to suggest a Platonic ideal: Apparently, it has a very fine atmosphere as contrasted with "the coarser atmosphere of earth." In this other reality, she experienced "the sensual shapes of clouds" whereas in her "life" she finds only "cloud-shaped trees." Furthermore, the shapes of the trees are deceptively inviting, for the soft leaves are "transitory" and the branches are "sharp." Indeed, the place where the poet has been is clearly more pleasant than her normal world. Stanza 2 presents a dawning earth consciousness as the smell of pines pierce "the surface of memory" and a vision of the speaker's husband "starts to swim/ back into sight." Stanza 3 identifies both the duration and quality of the poet's flight: "brief but brilliant." All of this suggests that the speaker is "returning" from a sexual climax.

Forms and Devices

The understated effectiveness of Pastan's poem is quite remarkable. She conveys the sexual experience so discreetly that it could be completely missed. Except for the last three lines, it appears only as distantly reflected in the "sensual shapes of clouds" and the "silky" texture of the parachute. The lofty imagery used to describe the ecstatic state, in other words, is quite separate from any hint of the physical mechanisms that play a large part in producing that state. The major device of the poem is an extended analogy between the descent of a parachutist and the experience of a woman after sexual climax. In that sense, this poem is like a miniature allegory with one kind of experience described through the language of another kind of experience. Understanding one thing in terms of another is a traditional technique of poetry, whether in simile, metaphor, analogy, or allegory. The use of an extended and consistent simile or metaphor through the whole poem is less common.

Pastan's choice of imagery is quite interesting. Through most of the poem, the parachutist is pictured against a natural backdrop: clouds, trees, branches, leaves, pine scent, and a dark lake. Against this backdrop, the husband "starts to swim/ back into sight" at the end of stanza 2. In stanza 3, the garden provides an interesting transitional image of nature under human control. It is also described as "their" garden, the woman's and her husband's, and seems to indirectly allude to the mutuality of the sexual act. This leads to the final, completely human image of the white sheet juxtaposed with human breasts. The image of breasts, often associated with fertility and nurture, works well with the garden and the possibility of procreative sex.

Themes and Meanings

"Returning" is a poem about the aftermath of an ecstatic moment, presumably a sexual climax. The experience is so intense and pleasurable that it must be considered otherworldly rather than a part of the poet's ordinary life. It also appears, at least at the climactic moment, to be a solitary experience. It is only as the woman floats down to the harsher realities of the earth that her husband starts to come into view. However, this is also a poem about a meaningful relationship: The woman lands in the garden that she and her husband cultivate, plant, tend, and harvest together. It is a product of partnership with a "brief but brilliant" interlude of solo flight. The poem is not particularly erotic, but it is highly attentive to the senses of the subject as she passes between states of being. The association of sex with flight has been used in poetry before, but Pastan's particular use of a falling parachutist to illustrate the subject's return to her ordinary life is striking. Falling through the air in a parachute must necessarily be an exhilarating but brief experience. The poem is also unusual in being situated around the transitional moments rather than being firmly rooted in one state or the other.

Although the ecstatic experiences are achieved by different means, two other well-known poems provide a comparison to Pastan's passage between the worlds of the ecstatic and the ordinary. In John Keats's "Ode to a Nightingale," the poet, on the "viewless wings of Poesy," flies away to the land of the sweetly sad singing of the nightingale, a fairyland where the Queen-Moon sits on a throne surrounded by "all her starry Fays." He indulges in the "soft incense" of seasonal plants and fruits, but all too quickly he is recalled to his ordinary reality, not sure if his experience was a vision or a "waking dream." Likewise, in Robert Frost's "Birches," the poet escapes the "pathless wood" of his normal life for a brief time by contemplating and then climbing a birch tree. After an ice storm, the birches, sun shining through their "crystal shells" of ice, provide an extraordinary vision of beauty, raising the poet out of his ordinary self. The birches also provide an escape from this life by serving as a ladder "*Toward* heaven." For Keats and Frost, like Pastan, the ecstatic experience is brief but brilliant. They live in the ordinary reality of this life, where branches are "sharp" (Pastan), "one eye is weeping" (Frost), and "men sit and hear each other groan" (Keats). Their brief escapes give them a chance to gain perspective on this life and give them a toehold in another world even as they return to this world.

Scott E. Moncrieff

RHAPSODY ON A WINDY NIGHT

Author: T. S. Eliot (1888-1965)
Type of poem: Lyric
First published: 1915; collected in *Prufrock and Other Observations*, 1917

The Poem

"Rhapsody on a Windy Night" is a lyric poem in free verse. It is divided into six stanzas that vary in length from nine to twenty-three lines each, with a separate closing line at the end of the poem. In one way, the title seems to reflect the poem's form, since in music a rhapsody is an irregular, unstructured piece. The poem at first appears to be an uncontrolled jumble of oddly juxtaposed images in lines and stanzas of irregular length, with no consistent rhyme scheme but with scattered rhymes, repetitions, and variations throughout. "Preludes" and *Four Quartets* (1943) are other poems showing T. S. Eliot's interest in using musical forms.

From another perspective, the title is ironic, since the label "rhapsody" suggests a mood of enthusiasm or frenzy that the poem does not convey. A situation that could be romantic—a midnight stroll in the lamplight and moonlight—is actually dominated by images of sterility, decay, isolation, and despair. Moreover, the only sign of the wind is found in the two lines stating that the street lamps "sputtered," although the wind is emphasized in the title and is an important image associated with decay and spiritual emptiness in other poems, such as "Preludes" and "Gerontion."

"Rhapsody on a Windy Night" is written in the first person, but the reader learns less about the speaker as a distinct personality than he or she does in Eliot's other early monologues, such as "The Love Song of J. Alfred Prufrock." On his nocturnal walk, this speaker does not express his thoughts or emotions directly or effusively, as one would expect in a "rhapsody." As he passes a succession of street lamps, moving in and out of their pools of light, he seems controlled by their commands to consider the sordid images in the streets and the distorted images thrown up by his memory. In the last stanza, he obeys mechanically as the lamp, illuminating the entrance to his apartment, orders him to return to his daily routine and prepare for bed.

The speaker's strange nocturnal visions are unified by some fairly consistent patterns, as the first or second line of each stanza (except the third) marks the time from midnight to four in the morning, and each stanza (except the first and third) quotes the lamps that direct his observations. He notices and remembers a woman with a torn and stained dress lingering in a doorway; the moon appearing as a similar aging, diseased woman; a cat licking up butter; eyes peering through shutters; dry geraniums; and stale smells of chestnuts, females in closed rooms, cigarettes, and cocktail bars. Although the memory interjects other images that seem out of place—such as driftwood, a useless rusted spring, a child grabbing a toy on a quay, and an old crab gripping a stick—the images all are united through the dominant characteristic of twisting or distortion. This "crowd of twisted things" culminates in the speaker's final sensation as he is compelled, at the poem's end, to return to everyday life—"The last twist of the knife."

Forms and Devices

Eliot believed that poetry must be difficult in order to reflect the complexity of modern civilization. He also believed that the poet's first concern should be his language. He wrote that "the only way of expressing emotion in the form of art is by finding an 'objective correlative'; in other words, a set of objects, a situation, a chain of events which shall be the formula of that *particular* emotion" (*The Sacred Wood*, 1920). A poem such as "Rhapsody on a Windy Night," therefore, does not explain feelings or thoughts in any general, conventional way. Readers must work to discover the complex patterns of meaning, sound, and structure underlying the stream of bizarre and banal images that make up the poem.

Metaphors and other figures of speech provide one method for connecting disparate images. The first two stanzas contain the most complex figures of speech, as abstract ideas about the nature of memory give way to the concrete objects that dominate the poem. The memory has floors that can be "dissolved" under the influence of midnight and moonlight, preventing it from dividing perceptions logically or precisely. Time and memory become concrete when the midnight spell on the memory is compared to a madman shaking a dead geranium. As rational memory is destroyed and nonrational forces take control, strange combinations of images are shaken from the depths of the memory.

Other similes connect different sensory experiences. Light and sound are combined when each street lamp "Beats like a fatalistic drum," reinforcing the incantatory rhythm of the poem and anticipating the speaker's realization of his own entrapment in a futile existence. Then the personification of the street lamps, with their ability to order the speaker to observe what they describe throughout the poem, gives him a detached, impersonal perspective that reflects Eliot's determination to break away from the lyrical subjectivity of nineteenth century Romanticism. The speaker receives impressions from the objects lighted in the street and his memory responds with free associations, comparing (in stanza 2) an open door to a grin and the corner of an eye to a crooked pin.

The rest of the poem consists of more fragmentary juxtapositions of images, with fewer explicit connections provided by similes, but with other poetic and linguistic devices helping to make connections. Eliot rejected the label *vers libre* (free verse) when it implied absence of pattern, rhyme, or meter. Although there seems to be something undisciplined or unexpected in the way lines and sentences are developed in this poem (suggesting subconscious or involuntary utterances), there is a complex interplay of syntactic patterns, semantically related words, internal rhymes, intermittent end rhymes, alliteration, and other sound patterns linking the woman in stanza 2, the woman in the moon in stanza 5, the particularly fragmented details of the branch and broken spring in stanza 3, and the glimpses of human and animal actions in stanza 4.

By stanzas 5 and 6, the romantic idea of incantations is replaced by a monotonous effect in these patterns and repetitions. The parallel lists of dry and stale images, the short imperatives, and the rhymes and alliteration that create ironic links in "Cologne" and "alone"; "Mount," "Memory," and "key"; and, finally, "life" and "knife" emphasize the limitations of memory and the mundane, isolated lives of individuals.

Themes and Meanings

Although "Rhapsody on a Windy Night" appears to be organized according to the hours of night, the sequence of impressions in the poem is dictated by psychological connections more than by chronology. The influence of the French philosopher Henri Bergson is evident when the speaker lets his memory synthesize unconsciously and spontaneously (rather than analyze rationally or logically) and when he seems repelled by the idea of blind reflex actions—the kind of automatic and empty motions that unite the cat licking rancid butter, the child with vacant eyes grabbing a toy, the crab gripping a stick, eyes peering through shutters, a woman twisting a paper rose, and his own mechanical preparations for bed.

This creative process of the memory, however, leads to nothing hopeful for the speaker, as the futile action of shaking a dead geranium implies. All the images that are so imaginatively synthesized are twisted or distorted in some way. Some are literally twisted concrete objects—a branch, a broken spring, a torn hem, and a crooked pin—while other objects take on unusual properties or configurations—street lamps beat like drums and speak, sand stains a dress, an eye "twists like a crooked pin," and a cat "flattens itself in the gutter." Some involve twisting motions or sensations, including the smells that "cross and cross across her brain." Still others are distorted by deterioration—the rusted spring has lost its strength, the butter is rancid, and the moon is a woman with infirmities ranging from feeble eyesight and a face cracked with smallpox to a loss of memory. His experience of new kinds of associations with these "twisted things," along with the vacant eyes, the stale smells, and the confinement of "shuttered rooms," only makes the speaker more horrified at the sterility and decay of everyday life by the end of the poem.

Many of these images show the influence of the French Symbolist poets of the late nineteenth century, especially Jules Laforgue, from whom Eliot borrowed the geranium and lunar images, the idea expressed in the line of French, and the poem's cynical attitude. As Gertrude Patterson observed in *T. S. Eliot: Poems in the Making* (1971), this is one of the early poems that deal with a single emotion rather than multiple, conflicting feelings; Eliot's attraction to the slums resulted in the expression of "consistent disgust at the life of the city." "The last twist of the knife" is the speaker's realization that sleep can only prepare him for an existence more empty and monotonous than the observations and memories he has experienced in the streets.

Tina Hanlon

THE RHODORA

Author: Ralph Waldo Emerson (1803-1882)
Type of poem: Lyric
First published: 1839; collected in *Poems*, 1847

The Poem

Ralph Waldo Emerson's "The Rhodora" consists of sixteen lines, the basic rhythm of which is iambic pentameter. Some critics call the poem an "extended sonnet," in part because of its meter, in part because it is a kind of song in praise of the shrub named in the title, and in part because of its having sixteen rather than the fourteen lines of the traditional sonnet.

The rhodora is a shrub found in eastern North America; it has purple or rose-purple flowers that often bloom before the leaves appear. In the poem, Emerson accordingly writes of its "leafless blooms" and "purple petals." However, the poem is not just about the shrub; it is also a philosophical statement about the relationship between the viewer of the shrub, the rhodora, and the "Power" that is the driving force behind the workings of the universe.

At the same time, it is a statement about the superiority of what the poet calls "simple ignorance," which is a kind of instinctual knowledge, to the wisdom of the people Emerson in the poem calls "sages." In Emerson's philosophical vocabulary, "simple ignorance" is equated with what he calls "Reason," a kind of knowledge that comes to people intuitively from the realm of spirit or divinity; the sages' wisdom is connected with what Emerson calls "Understanding," a kind of knowledge that comes from perception of things of this world. Typically for Emerson, Reason is superior to Understanding.

In the poem, the speaker encounters the rhodora in May, the beginning of the New England spring and, according to the poem, the time when "sea-winds" pierce "our solitudes." On the simplest level, these words indicate that in May people leave their winter-imposed seclusion and, like the speaker in the poem, begin to move about.

The speaker finds the rhodora blooming in the woods in an area where no one will see it. Located in a "damp nook," it seems to bloom to please "the desert and the sluggish brook." "Desert" here may be an adjective describing brook, meaning that it runs through an uninhabited region. At any rate, because the area is so moist, "desert" cannot have its common modern meaning of an area barren or almost barren of vegetation. Instead, it most likely has an older meaning indicating that the area is uninhabited by human beings. The rhodora's petals fall into "the pool" and make the "black water . . . gay" with their beauty. Compared to the rhodora, even the redbird or cardinal looks less beautiful.

After describing the rhodora and its location, the poet addresses the plant, telling it that if the sages ask it why it blooms where no one can see it, the shrub should respond, "if eyes were made for seeing,/ Then Beauty is its own excuse for being." The speaker "never thought to ask" why the rhodora should appear where it can be seen only by "earth and sky" rather than by people, but in his "simple ignorance" supposed that the "self-same Power" that brought the speaker to the flower brought the flower to its present location.

Forms and Devices

"The Rhodora" involves a process by which the poet comes to a larger understanding of the workings of the universe. The interaction between poet and flower produces in the speaker a kind of wisdom that transcends that of the sages, people who, at least in this poem, consider themselves wise. Yet the speaker immediately undercuts the idea that they are wise by having them ask a question of the flower, an act that their so-called wisdom would tell them is a waste of time.

The sixteen-line poem is written in fairly regular iambic pentameter. If one reads "flower" in line 8 and "Power" in line 16 as monosyllabic, the exceptions to the pentameter are lines 3, 11, and 12. Lines 11 and 12 form what some critics call a gnomic couplet or an epigram, that is, a pair of rhymed lines that give a concise statement of principle in carefully chosen, effective words. Unlike any other part of the poem, they have feminine rhyme, that is, rhyme involving two words each with two syllables, the first of which is stressed and the second of which is unstressed and identical in both words; in "The Rhodora," the words are "seeing" and "being." Their having eleven rather than the usual ten syllables as well as feminine rhyme adds great emphasis to these two important lines by creating a surprise for the reader, who expects regular iambs with masculine rhymes.

The rhyme scheme of the poem varies from rhymed couplets to alternating rhymed lines. The last four lines involve alternating rhymes. The final line, although itself consisting also of fairly regular iambic pentameter (again, absolutely regular pentameter if "Power" is read as a monosyllabic word), when set in type is visually longer than any of the other lines, giving it a kind of emphasis that coincides with its final position. This emphasis works well with the importance of the statement the lines make, since they indicate that some kind of "Power" directs all things in the universe.

One central technique of the poem is contrast. It is introduced early, in the contrast between the flower and its location: The beautiful flower appears in a deserted, even unattractive place. Another contrast involves that between the cardinal and the flower, with the flower being more beautiful than the red plumage of the bird. The most important contrast is between the sages with their wisdom and the speaker's "simple ignorance." The speaker's acceptance contrasts with the sages' desire to know. The sages think in terms of worldly wisdom, what Emerson elsewhere calls "Understanding." Readings of the poem often connect the sages with utilitarian thinkers, that is, people concerned with practical rather than aesthetic things. For them, beauty that is unseen is "wasted." For the speaker, however, who views things in terms of what Emerson calls "Reason," beauty is never wasted.

Themes and Meanings

Discussions of the central meaning of "The Rhodora" usually point to passages from Emerson's first book, *Nature* (1836). The poem's discussion of the speaker's "simple ignorance" (Reason) versus the sages' wisdom (Understanding) is explained by material from the chapters entitled "Language" and "Idealism" in *Nature*. In the former, Emerson writes, "That which, intellectually considered, we call Reason, considered in relation to nature, we call Spirit. Spirit is the Creator." In the latter chapter he writes, "The understanding adds, divides, combines, measures, and finds everlasting nutriment and room for its activity in this worthy scene." Thus, the understanding deals with things of the material world. Emerson follows this sentence with, "Meantime, Reason transfers all these lessons into its own world of thought, by perceiving the analogy that marries Matter and Mind." Thus, Reason deals with things of the realm of Spirit and connects things of the material world with the realm of the Spirit.

Another important passage from *Nature* is in the chapter entitled "Beauty," in which Emerson writes, "Beauty, in its largest and profoundest sense, is one expression for the universe. God is the all-fair. Truth, and goodness, and beauty, are but different faces of the same All," words that imply that beauty is one of the faces of God. Thus, beauty need not be defended or explained: It is a manifestation of God's presence on earth.

The sages' question about the plant's "charm" being "wasted" becomes ridiculous in light of this idea, and the poet's proposed response, with its surprising logic, becomes appropriate. The poet responds that the flower's response should include the words, "if eyes were made for seeing." The logical extension of this idea is, "Then beauty is made to be seen." However, for Emerson, logic works on the plain of the Understanding. Instead of giving the logical answer, Emerson focuses on the idea that the statement "eyes were made for seeing" implies that there is purpose in the universe, that things happen for a reason. The poet's proposed response, "Beauty is its own excuse for being," implies that beauty is part of the purpose. Whether beauty is seen is beside the point.

Thus, the poem moves from the speaker's perception of a beautiful object—a rhodora—to an intuition about what the speaker calls the "Power" that flows through the universe and that makes itself visible in the rhodora's flower. This "Power," the speaker feels, also directs the speaker's own movements and in extension all people's movements, ending permanently what the speaker in the first line of the poem calls "our solitudes" and connecting humans with the entire universe.

Richard Tuerk

RING OUT YOUR BELLS

Author: Sir Philip Sidney (1554-1586)
Type of poem: Lyric
First published: 1598, in *Certaine Sonnets*

The Poem

"Ring out your bells" is part of a miscellaneous collection of thirty-two sonnets and songs. This song is divided into four stanzas, each composed of six lines of verse and four lines of choral refrain. The speaker's opening request, addressed to his neighborly audience, suggests the ancient custom of tolling church bells to announce a local death. It also establishes the common funereal experience and the solemn tone for this poetic monologue about the death of love. The speaker distances himself from his own abstract emotion, the idea of love, by personifying it (giving love human attributes and treating it as if it were a real person). In this way, the concept of love, separated from himself, becomes a fictive character whose death is cause for his initial request. When love is viewed as a separate individual, the speaker can complain bitterly about his frustration and misery, the causes for love's infection, sickness and death, and his haughty mistress's abusive and capricious cruelty. Thus, there are three characters in this dramatic song: the speaker, his absent mistress, and love.

The idea of death, a universal event, introduces the situation and allows the speaker to appeal to a reader's sympathetic responses. When he urges his listeners to action—to ring the church bells, openly express grief, wail sorrowful songs, and read thirty requiem masses—the speaker clothes another commonplace occurrence, a romantic dispute and separation, with the mental anguish normally associated with death and funerals. Other experiences familiar to some readers are the paradoxical conflicts and frustrations in some love relationships. In the first three stanzas, the speaker elaborates on the misery, scorn, and rejection love endures when honor and loyalty are considered to be worthless virtues. He portrays love dying on a bed built from his mistress's foolish and overweening pride; wrapped in a burial shroud of disgrace; valued, even in her last testament, with false worth and censure; and finally entombed in the lady's cold, stony heart. Ironically, the inscription on love's tombstone will reveal that the lady's glancing eyes once shot arrows of love at the speaker, creating instant love between them. This magical, first-sight love, an old Elizabethan belief, is similar to what William Shakespeare developed with his star-crossed lovers Romeo and Juliet.

The first three choral refrains, identical in their four lines, echo the lover's plaints about his proud mistress's scornful, frenzied behavior. Also, the fourth line repetitively recalls a prayer drawn from church rituals. The fourth stanza abruptly and radically shifts perspective. The speaker announces his error with a phrase similar to a biblical comment, "Love is not dead, but sleepeth" (Matthew 9:24). Actually, love and his mistress are just deliberating on a reward worthy enough for him. With his reversed attitude, the speaker praises his mistress. His reawakened love helps him turn his scathing accusations into self-scorn and mockery for his earlier comments. Despite the speaker's jubilation, the song's final line paradoxically repeats the religious prayer that concludes the first three refrains, "Good lord, deliver us."

Forms and Devices

Sir Philip Sidney was a poetic experimenter, synthesizer, and innovator in poetic theory and forms. He sought new ways to use and revitalize old literary traditions and conventions such as those popularized in Petrarchan and Platonic love poetry. Petrarchan love sonnets featured aristocratic and courtly lovers who complimented and manipulated an idealized mistress with extravagantly flattering metaphors, images that implied parallels between two ostensibly different things. For instance, some facial features of an iconic mistress might be suggestively likened to stars, roses, pearls, or cherries. Platonic love originally described an aristocratic code of chivalrous devotion to a married lady or to one of superior social rank. Through time, the chaste nature of this old bond was sometimes abused. In courtships in which lovers were not given favors or awards, the discontented petitioner agonized, complained, and pleaded repeatedly to the untouchable lady, who refused him. In "Ring out your bells," the speaker's catalog of grievances typifies him as a Platonic lover whose courtship has been soundly rebuffed. In rebellion, his thoughts turn dark when his virtues or lofty aims are not rewarded in some way.

Simple patterns of imagery support the synthesis of Petrarchan and Platonic traditions. The speaker implies an analogy between love's tomb and the mistress's stony heart and suggestively equates love's eyes with the love darts in the epitaph. Even the mistress's unpredictable behavior resembles the manners of the aristocratic coquettes depicted in Petrarchan sonnets. However, one extended metaphor dominates most of the content. Throughout the song, the implied analogies between the banality of a broken romance and the heartbreak of death are determined and reinforced by the funereal and religious wrappings associated with the death metaphor.

Sidney's interest in prosody, the metrical structure of verse, relates to his stylistic strategies to match rhythms and words. Just such a metrical innovation introduces the fourth stanza. Sidney dramatically stops the rhythmical pattern of iambs when his phrasing and meter dictate a pause underscoring his speaker's changed perspective. The startling statement, "Alas, I lie," in iambic meter (one unaccented syllable followed by one accented syllable), is followed by a trochee (one accented syllable followed by one unaccented syllable), "rage hath this error bred." The accentual stress on "rage" also emphasizes and intensifies the trochaic pattern in the ensuing line: "Love is not dead." Repetition of this same trochee, along with "but sleepeth" in the next line, allows Sidney to match sound to the sense of the verse. Although he does not mention this song, William A. Ringler, in the introduction to *The Poems of Sir Philip Sidney* (1962), writes that several of Sidney's sonnets "bring a new rhythm into Elizabethan verse . . . the first regularly sustained accentual trochaics in English" until the 1590's.

Themes and Meanings

"Ring out your bells" is a poem about the subject of love. However, it is the hidden driving force of desire behind the various forms of love that Sidney explores through the filter of his own experiences and feelings. Sidney's personal world included the political arena in Queen Elizabeth I's court. There, he and others sought the monarch's royal favor, which could give them government employment, financial rewards, or honors testifying to their worldly worth and virtue. Additionally, these courtiers courted noble patrons who could help arrange aristocratic marriages for them or help support their political, military, or literary endeavors. Sidney had direct experience with frustrated desires in his attempts to solicit more than temporary governmental or military appointments from Queen Elizabeth.

The flattering compliments of Petrarchan love sonnets aimed at courting a lady's favors arise from the same ambitious urges of desire as the hyperboles (conscious exaggerations) used to court a queen or a noble. There is little difference between practices. Furthermore, when the Platonic lover suffers and rages about his mistress's scorn and rejection of his worth and faithfulness, his misery underlines the desire behind his egoistic self-love. Feelings of worth, honor, and personal identity grow from the self-validation gained from recognition or reward for deeds accomplished. Human courtiers such as Sidney felt equally discouraged and frustrated when their valiant efforts were rejected.

Sidney's literary world evidences another of his own literary desires, an altruistic wish found in his great love for poetry. At the heart of Sidney's book *The Defence of Poesy* (1595) are his defense and definition of what poetry is, what it can or should do, and how to write it to accomplish this lofty goal. Moreover, when he viewed the poetry of his own time, Sidney was not happy with the poetic abuses he saw. As Ringler observes in his introduction to *The Poems of Sir Philip Sidney*, Sidney "set out to be a Daedalus to his countrymen, to teach them rules of right writing, and to provide them with models to follow." This idealistic aim underwrites his effort to achieve an example of good poetry with a deeper level of meaning. In "Ring out your bells," Sidney works within the traditions and conventions of love poetry. However, he rejuvenates them by showing what a few changes can do to hackneyed concepts and images. His double vision, the extended metaphoric comparison of love's trivialities with the solemnity of death, transforms the Petrarchan/Platonic single-vision lyric into a brief model of a mock-heroic romance. This second point of view indirectly points out the comical exaggerations, trivialities, stupidities, and abuses. Ironically, the final prayer might well express the poet's own desire: "Good lord, deliver us" from poets who abuse poetry.

Betsy P. Harfst

THE RIVER-MERCHANT'S WIFE
A Letter

Author: Ezra Pound (1885-1972)
Type of poem: Dramatic monologue
First published: 1915, in *Cathay: Translations by Ezra Pound for the Most Part from the Chinese of Rihaku, from the Notes of the Late Ernest Fenollosa and the Decipherings of the Professors Mori and Ariga*

The Poem

Ezra Pound's adaptation of a poem by Li Bo, an eighth century Chinese poet, is a dramatic monologue spoken by a sixteen-year-old girl. It is written in open verse in the form of a letter from the wife of a river-merchant to her husband, who has been away from their home for five months.

The opening of the poem conveys both immediacy and continuance. The first line begins with the word "while" and presents an image of the wife as a young girl. The second line starts with the word "I" and contains an image of the girl playing at the moment when she met her future husband. The effect that is created is a feeling of recollection which draws time's passage across the consciousness of the present. The focus is shifted from the "I" to a memory of "you." The first stanza concludes with the couple merging into "we"—"small people" who lived in a village in a state of unreflective innocence.

The second stanza begins a triad of quatrains that recapitulate the three years of their marriage. In the first of these, the girl remembers herself at fourteen as severe, contained, and shy at the moment of the ceremony. She seemed to be acting out of obligation. Then, at fifteen, she began to relax and remembers that she "desired" to join her husband in both temporal and etherial realms, recognizing the immediate call of the physical as well as the transcendant appeal of the eternal. Her question that concludes the third stanza is a compression by Pound of a tale of a woman who waited on a tower for her husband's return. In his cryptic reference, he implies that the woman is content to be in her husband's company or to be by herself. The fourth stanza moves to the present, and the wife is now sixteen. Five months ago, the river-merchant had departed on some unexplained journey. He has covered considerable distance in both geographic and temporal terms, and the wife expresses her unhappiness.

The last section of the poem, an extended stanza of ten lines, is located entirely in the immediate present. It is a powerful expression of the wife's feelings and an attempt to demonstrate to the river-merchant how she has grown into a mature and more complete stage of love. Her references to the seasonal changes in the natural world indicate that she no longer entertains a concept of a theoretical love which is "forever and forever and forever" but has realized that nothing can exist outside of time. The image of mosses in an accumulation "too deep to clear them away!" suggests the effect of time's passage, and the image of "paired butterflies" shows that she is aware of love's delicacy and fragility. Her maturity is registered by the extremely powerful use of the only active verb in the poem: Her statement "They hurt me" refers to seasonal changes and their consequences. Her reflective utterance "I grow older" summarizes the range and scope of time that the poem encompasses.

The last part of this stanza contains a reversal of mood. Demonstrating her resiliency and depth of character, the wife now addresses her husband as an equal partner. Adopting an almost businesslike tone but maintaining her care and concern, she expresses her confidence in herself by declaring that she too will leave the protection of their home in order to meet him along the river Kiang. The willingness to travel along the river herself solidifies the relationship, and the reference to Cho-fu-Sa (Pound's version of the Chinese *Ch'ang-feng-sha* or "long wind beach") is a specific commitment to a particular place, rather than the previous nebulous "forever" of the second year of her marriage.

Forms and Devices

Pound wrote that "An 'Image' is that which presents an intellectual and emotional complex in an instant of time." Pound believed that the essence of this method, called Imagism, had been captured by the Chinese ideogram, which fused picture and meaning in one symbol.

The striking opening image of "The River-Merchant's Wife" captures an entire cultural epoch. Pound originally used the American slang "bangs," but the taut language of "hair was still cut straight" is an accurate rendering of the ideogram and of the appearance of young Chinese girls of that era. This image is followed by one of the river-merchant as a boy, his masculine aspects immediately established by his appearance "on bamboo stilts, playing horse" while she follows the traditional feminine activity of "pulling flowers." Their early sensual attraction is implied by the boy parading around her and "playing with blue plums."

The playful imagery of the first stanza is abruptly replaced by images of unease and uncertainty when the couple are actually married in her fourteenth year. She is presented as "scowling," "bashful," and never laughing. The wall is an image of enclosure and her desire to "mingle" their dust forever suggests claustrophobia and internment. The psychological condition of their first year of marriage has been precisely evoked.

When the river-merchant departs during the third year of their marriage, the images show how the girl's sense of herself, her marriage, and the world is evolving. The river imagery ("swirling eddies" and "narrows") indicates the dangers of the outside world. The husband, previously on stilts, now drags his feet under the pressure of responsibility. The wife's sorrow is accentuated by seasonal references, the moss grown "too deep to clear" both a sign of time's passage and a symbol for the weight of loneliness. The "paired butterflies" remind her of her single state, and her vision of them "already yellow with August" is a projection of her sense of accelerated time.

The final image of the poem is a parallel one in which the wife and her husband are both depicted on the river Kiang, its "narrows" demarking it as a place of menace.

They are moving toward each other, their resolve to overcome obstacles a testament to the possibilities of a future in which the separate "I" and "you" of the poem will be joined as an unstated "we"—a union quite different from the separate lives of the "we" in the first stanza. This transference completes the cycle of shifting personal pronouns that functions as a frame for the imagery. From the introduction of the individual "I" and "you," to Pound's brilliant inversion "I married My Lord you" (which combines direct address with continuing personal consciousness), to the series of almost accusatory "you's," to the use of the third-person "they" to indicate fate in the last stanza, the variants anchor the images and reinforce their meanings.

Themes and Meanings

Pound's introduction of poetry by Li Bo into the Western literary canon was a part of his program to increase cultural awareness. Pound viewed "criticism" in the largest sense to include versions of literary creation, such as "criticism by translation" and "criticism in new composition." His adaptation of "The River-Merchant's Wife: A Letter" was designed to open the field of early Chinese civilization to Western eyes, and he succeeded so well that T. S. Eliot remarked on the appearance of *Cathay* (1915) that it "invented Chinese poetry for our time." Some professional sinologists attacked Pound for his lack of accuracy, but he dismissed their inability to appreciate the power of his poetry and his approach to translation.

Pound was interested in innovative uses of familiar forms, and he admired Robert Browning's employment of dramatic monologue to capture the spirit of a moment in historic time. Pound believed that Browning's work permitted a combination of the "human" or distinctly personal and the cultural, or socially resonant. Such crucial elements of "The River-Merchant's Wife" as the correspondence of human emotion to natural setting, the representation of the eternal cycle of the seasons as time's passage and human growth, and the linking of romantic intensity with restraint and composure are products of Pound's fusion of Browning's methods and Li Bo's artistry.

Ford Madox Ford commented that "the poems in *Cathay* are things of supreme beauty. What poetry should be, that they are." Pound took the ultimate vessel for expressing feeling—the lyric—and used its full capacity for transmitting essential human emotions within the mode of the dramatic monologue. Pound's fervent proclamation that "nothing matters but the quality of affection" is the primary principle of his philosophy of composition and is at the heart of the appeal of "The River-Merchant's Wife." Without striking false notes or falling into sentimentality, Pound has shown that what he loved well—language, culture, and art—remains as his poetic legacy in his finest work.

Leon Lewis

RIVERS AND MOUNTAINS

Author: John Ashbery (1927-   )
Type of poem: Narrative
First published: 1966, in *Rivers and Mountains*

The Poem

The opening of John Ashbery's "Rivers and Mountains" ("On the secret map the assassins/ Cloistered,") very well might cause the apprehensive reader to declare, "The map is not the territory." Indeed, that is part of the point, and the reader attempting to comprehend "Rivers and Mountains" from the preconception that it will be either a coherent whole or a representation equivalent solely to the sum of its parts will find the work daunting, if not ultimately frustrating.

"Rivers and Mountains," without self-promotion or celebration, presents a subtle, nuanced perspective on the human consequences of war, both victory and defeat. As the opening image develops, the reader is reminded that this is a poem. Even as the assassins cloister in "the city/ Of humiliation and defeat," Ashbery defines the material used to create the work: "wan ending/ Of the trail among dry, papery leaves" almost lacks subtlety, the dual meaning of "leaves" having been emphasized by the early "Gray-brown quills."

These lines appear initially not to be so much making something as searching for profundity. While a lesser poet might have presented a less ostentatious phrasing, expecting to be praised for subtlety, Ashbery rises to his self-wrought challenge, merging poem and subject into a territory that maps poem-writing to map-reading: "like thoughts/ In the melodious but vast mass of today's/ Writing fields and swamps."

The first verse is notable for its lack of human activity: Even the "rioters"—ostensibly but not definitively human—have been "quelled." Ashbery develops the aura of devastation more from musical imagery than direct description of the landscape. The phrases "Deaf consolation of minor tunes" and "Singing on marble factory walls" evoke sadness or despair even more clearly than "fields and swamps" as "little bunches of weeds." Ashbery uses musical referents to transform the territory into a representation of the map, even as the references to writing tools cause the description of the landscape and the creation of the poem to converge.

Also emphasizing the desolation, while also foreshadowing possibilities of resurrection, is the motif of sleep. Beginning as "dull sleep," the area becomes moderately more active as the rioters are "turned out of sleep in the piece of prisons," and the area finally reaches the relatively active "quiet walking." The sleep imagery may not signal a new day, but it certainly promises one.

The closest the first verse comes to a direct observation of destruction is the shortest sentence in the poem: "The bird flew over and/ Sat—there was nothing else to do." Yet even the apparent naturalness of this image is gradually transformed from the pastoral bird into a powerful waterfall and finally to people, "some with places to go." At the end of the verse, the waterfall is making a "light print" on the stones. The assassins may have started the verse cloistered, but their landscape has been edited, the mountains transformed by the river—and the poet.

The second verse—a single sentence—continues juxtaposing map, territory, and poem but offers more hope. The musical imagery transitions from "minor tunes" to "a melody heard/ As though through trees," the line break serving to emphasize the life of the area. The phrase "The land/ Was made of paper processed/ To look like ferns, mud or other" continues the conflation of map and territory, while the second line's emphasis upon the human concept of "process" indicates the possibility of restoration. The evidence of humanity, though, resembles that found at an archeological excavation. Ashbery elides "homes/ Flung far out," "public/ Places for electric light," a "major tax assessment area," and "formal traffic" throughout the verse. There is no activity showing that people are living there; for all the evidence, no human life is mentioned in the second verse.

The final verse dismisses the consequences of the destruction, completing the history of the episode. Reality and perception merge, and while the testament to destruction of the first two verses is authenticated, it is an entirely different attitude that prevails. Ashbery chooses precisely the correct term: "Fortunately, the war was solved/ In another way." Only by treating the destruction as part of a "solved" riddle can one explain the apparent joy amid the destruction. After all, winners rarely emphasize the details of failed campaigns in their histories. Ultimately, rivers triumph where mountains fail by "isolating the two sections/ Of the enemy's navy."

As the winners selectively emphasize—one might say rewrite—their history, they allow people to "quietly move among the rustic landscape/ Scooping snow off the mountains." As the war ends, the survivors begin to return to the life outlined in the first two verses. This is a life of tax assessments and traffic and "the unassassinated president"— a haunting phrase in 1966 that has lost little of its impact. The leaders will read letters and create stamps to celebrate the victory. By the end of the third verse, the verse that elides the moment of triumph, "love . . . Wetting pillow and petal," appears to have fashioned a "sun-blackened landscape." Ashbery, having tempered desolation with images of pale hope, now turns the brightest moment of celebration into a time of reflection.

Forms and Devices

In *Other Traditions* (2000), Ashbery notes that three lines by composer Franz Schubert offer a "magnificent" definition of poetry: "But the poem is just this/ Speaking of what cannot be said/ To the person I want to say it."

Much of Ashbery's early work—from his exquisitely provocative first volume in 1956, *Some Trees* (W. H. Auden's 1956 selection for the Yale Series of Younger Poets), through the pointillist pieces in *The Tennis Court Oath* (1962) and *Rivers and Mountains*—is more deliberately evocative than provocative. This is not to say that Ashbery does not want readers to contemplate or consider his work so much as react to it. Yet, like a painting by Larry Rivers or Jackson Pollack, contemplation is subsumed by the visceral nature of one's reaction.

Ashbery himself has expressed some reluctance to embrace his early works. This, however, should be viewed in the context of poets such as Auden, who rewrote his early works to fit his later personal and political conceptions. In the context of such remarks as Auden's that his own "The Orators" "must have been written by a madman," Ashbery's statement that "Europe" from *The Tennis Court Oath* "helped me along but I don't value it as much as [later poems]" is positively enthusiastic.

"Rivers and Mountains" follows the free-verse form of poetry popularized by modernist poets, most notably T. S. Eliot. However, Ashbery follows in Auden's tradition of using modernist form while maintaining a distinctly nonmodernist (if not precisely postmodernist) sensibility. Like Auden, Ashbery is more likely to write from the personal and less likely to declare his writing deep or profound. Neither of these in themselves keeps the work from being either universal or profound, though some critics seem to believe that profundity is limited to those who proclaim their work and themselves profound.

Themes and Meanings

"Rivers and Mountains" presents a collage of aspects of life both before and during wartime: Strategy and tactics are intermingled with descriptions of animal life, tax assessments, geography, and the acts of workers trying to maintain normal activities in extraordinary times.

While some critics proclaim Ashbery's immediate progenitor to be Wallace Stevens, or—rather absurdly—T. S. Eliot, it is with the work of Auden that much of Ashbery's early work, and most especially this poem, grapples. Marjorie Perloff's comments that Ashbery's landscape is "like a comic strip version of Auden's" is unfair to both Ashbery and comic strips. Auden's early poetic landscape is rather similar to Ashbery's.

The poem parallels Auden's description of the quotidian activities surrounding the fall of Icarus in his "Musée des Beaux Arts." Similarly, Ashbery limns the area without focusing upon any specific occurrences, reemphasizing the fact that the description of a territory, like a map, may show much while revealing nothing. By the end of the second verse, both the map used by the assassins and the territory described by Ashbery are equally invalid interpretations. Phrases such as "the forest floor/ Fisheries and oyster beds" highlight a narration more concerned with juxtapositions than meaning, more impressionistic than objective. The first two verses of the poem, with more unsaid than said, create a comprehensive image of absence and destruction, leaving only hints of hope.

The poem acknowledges "Musée des Beaux Arts" directly with the phrase "light bounced off the ends/ Of the small gray waves to tell . . . About the great drama." This reflects the reality of a Pieter Bruegel the Elder painting in which the waves from his splash are the evidence of Icarus. Ashbery draws a contrast to Auden's sentiment, continuing the line with "that was being won," surely not the feeling of either Icarus or those receiving the "light."

Kenneth L. Houghton

THE ROAD NOT TAKEN

Author: Robert Frost (1874-1963)
Type of poem: Lyric
First published: 1916, in *Mountain Interval*

The Poem

"The Road Not Taken" is one of Robert Frost's most familiar and most popular poems. It is made up of four stanzas of five lines each, and each line has between eight and ten syllables in a roughly iambic rhythm; the lines in each stanza rhyme in an *abaab* pattern. The popularity of the poem is largely a result of the simplicity of its symbolism: The speaker must choose between diverging paths in a wood, and he sees that choice as a metaphor for choosing between different directions in life. Nevertheless, for such a seemingly simple poem, it has been subject to very different interpretations of how the speaker feels about his situation and how the reader is to view the speaker. In 1961, Frost himself commented that "The Road Not Taken" is "a tricky poem, very tricky."

Frost wrote the poem in the first person, which raises the question of whether the speaker is the poet himself or a persona, a character created for the purposes of the poem. According to the Lawrance Thompson biography, *Robert Frost: The Years of Triumph* (1971), Frost would often introduce the poem in public readings by saying that the speaker was based on his Welsh friend Edward Thomas. In Frost's words, Thomas was "a person who, whichever road he went, would be sorry he didn't go the other."

In the first stanza of the poem, the speaker, while walking on an autumn day in a forest where the leaves have changed to yellow, must choose between two paths that head in different directions. He regrets that he cannot follow both roads, but since that is not possible, he pauses for a long while to consider his choice. In the first stanza and the beginning of the second, one road seems preferable; however, by the beginning of the third stanza he has decided that the paths are roughly equivalent. Later in the third stanza, he tries to cheer himself up by reassuring himself that he will return someday and walk the other road.

At the end of the third stanza and in the fourth, however, the speaker resumes his initial tone of sorrow and regret. He realizes that he probably will never return to walk the alternate path, and in the fourth stanza he considers how the choice he must make now will look to him in the future. The speaker believes that when he looks back years later, he will see that he had actually chosen the "less traveled" road. He also thinks that he will later realize what a large difference this choice has made in his life. Two important details suggest that the speaker believes that he will later regret having followed his chosen road: One is the idea that he will "sigh" as he tells this story, and the other is that the poem is entitled "The Road Not Taken"—implying that he will never stop thinking about the other path he might have followed.

Forms and Devices

In his essay "The Constant Symbol," Frost defined poetry with an interesting series of phrases. Poetry, he wrote, is chiefly "metaphor, saying one thing and meaning another, saying one thing in terms of another, the pleasure of ulteriority." His achievement in the poem "The Road Not Taken" is to bring these different uses of metaphor into play in a delightfully ironic balancing act. That is to say, the speaker solemnly uses the metaphor of the two roads to say one thing, while Frost humorously uses the speaker as a metaphor to say something very different.

The speaker is a solemn person who earnestly believes in metaphor as a way of "saying one thing in terms of another." The speaker uses the details, the "terms," of a situation in nature to "say" something about himself and his life: that he has difficulty making a choice and that he is regretfully certain that he will eventually be unhappy with the choice that he does make. When he first considers the two roads, he sees one as more difficult, perhaps even a bit menacing ("it bent in the undergrowth"), and the other as being more pleasant ("it was grassy and wanted wear"). Even in taking the second path, though, he reconsiders and sees them both as equally worn and equally covered with leaves. Changing his mind again, he believes that in the future he will look back, realize that he did take the "less traveled" road after all, but regret "with a sigh" that that road turned out to have made "all the difference" in making his life unhappy. The speaker believes that in the future he will be haunted by this earlier moment when he made the wrong choice and by the unfulfilled potential of "the road not taken."

In contrast to the speaker, Frost uses metaphor to "say one thing and mean another." That is, Frost presents this speaker's account of his situation with deadpan solemnity, but he uses the speaker as a specific image of a general way of thinking that Frost means to mock. The speaker first grasps at small details in the landscape to help him choose the better path, then seems to have the common sense to see that the two roads are essentially equivalent, but finally allows his overanxious imagination to run away with him. The reader is meant to smile or laugh when the speaker scares himself into believing that this one decision, with its options that seem so indistinguishable, will turn out someday to be so dire as to make him "sigh" at "all the difference" this choice has made. Frost's subtle humor is most likely what Frost was referring to when he described the poem in 1961 as "tricky," for the Thompson biography documents two letters Frost wrote near the time of the poem's publication (one to Edward Thomas and one to the editor Louis Untermeyer) to convince these readers that the poem is meant to be taken as a joke on the speaker and as a parody of his attitudes.

Themes and Meanings

"The Road Not Taken" is an excellent example of what Frost meant by "the pleasure of ulteriority" in his poetry. That is, the poem offers an entertaining double perspective on the theme of making choices, with one perspective fairly obvious and the other more subtle.

Considered through the perspective of the speaker himself, "The Road Not Taken" is an entirely serious, even a sad poem. It expresses both the turmoil of making a choice and the depressing expectation that the choice he makes between seemingly equal options will turn out for the worse—is in fact going to make an even greater difference for the worse than seems possible when he makes the choice.

Considered from Frost's perspective, on the other hand, "The Road Not Taken" is a humorous parody of the speaker's portentous habits of mind. Frost's 1931 essay "Education by Poetry" offers further clarification on this point. In it, he wrote that people need to understand that all metaphors are human constructs that "break down at some point"; people need to "know [a] metaphor in its strength and its weakness . . . [h]ow far [one] may expect to ride it and when it may break down." From this perspective, the main problem of the speaker in "The Road Not Taken" is that he tries to ride his metaphor too far and too hard. Although he sees it break down early in the poem (in that he actually cannot see any real difference between the two roads), the speaker persists in thinking that the road is "less traveled" in some way that he cannot see and that this difference will lead to dire consequences later on.

One other common interpretation of the poem deserves brief consideration: the view that the poem is a celebration of nonconformity, an exhortation to the reader to take the road "less traveled." In this interpretation, the title is seen as referring to the road that the speaker does take (which is "the road not taken" by most other people), and the speaker is seen as ultimately exultant that he took the road "less traveled," because it "has made all the difference" in enhancing his life. To consider the validity of this interpretation, one must put aside Frost's stated intentions for the poem—an act that many critics consider sometimes justified because an author's intentions cannot be seen as fully controlling the impression made by a literary work. Aside from the issue of Frost's intentions, however, this interpretation still conflicts with many salient details in the poem. One problem with this view is that the speaker can hardly be praised as a strong nonconformist if in the middle of the poem he can see little difference between the paths, let alone vigorously choose the road "less traveled." Another problem is that he imagines telling his story in the future with a "sigh," an unlikely gesture for a vigorous champion of nonconformity.

In 1935, Frost wrote on the subject of style that "style is the way [a] man takes himself. . . . If it is with outer seriousness, it must be with inner humor. If it is with outer humor, it must be with inner seriousness. Neither one alone without the other under it will do." "The Road Not Taken" is a notable example of Frost's own sophisticated style, of his ability to create ironic interplay between outer seriousness and inner humor.

Yet the humor of the poem also has its own serious side. This humor conveys more than merely the ridicule found in parody: It also expresses an implied corrective to the condition that it mocks. This condition is that the speaker sees the course and tone of his life as determined by forces beyond his range of vision and control. Frost implies that if the speaker were able to see himself with some humor, and if he were able to take more responsibility for his choices and attitude, he might find that he himself could make "all the difference" in his own life.

Terry L. Andrews

ROCK AND HAWK

Author: Robinson Jeffers (1887-1962)
Type of poem: Meditation
First published: 1935, in *Solstice and Other Poems*

The Poem

"Rock and Hawk," one of Robinson Jeffers's most often reprinted short poems, has been regularly identified as one of his signature pieces—that is, it presents, in simple, direct form, one of his main themes. That theme has been called "Inhumanism." It is based in the concept that humans, far from being the central point of reference in the cosmos, are a minor component of the process, significant only because they are capable of producing damage out of proportion to their importance. The idea is Darwinian, growing out of Jeffers's post-college researches in medicine and biology. It can be considered an early statement of the radical environmental attitude.

The poem accomplishes this by presenting what it calls a "symbol": a falcon perched on an ancient, massive rock high on a headland. In this symbol, the poem states, "Many high tragic thoughts/ Watch their own eyes." This complex allusion draws several ideas together. On one level, thoughts of high tragedy have conventionally been those that best represented the values of human civilization, those qualities that humans prized. Here they "watch their own eyes," as if distrustful of their own motives. Second, in one high tragedy, that of Oedipus, the hero literally pierces his eyes because of the horror he has been forced to discover about himself. Finally, if thoughts of high tragedy are thus suspect, their eyes betray fundamental human hypocrisy. The rock juts out, the single prominent figure in this landscape; nothing else can live there. The implication is that the rock has life of its own, or at least participates in a life. Its survival proves this; earthquake and storm have worn all else down. On this rock rests a falcon.

Jeffers passes then from establishing the scene to meditating upon it. He states that this is the proper emblem of the future, superseding those of Christianity and Mormonism. The image of rock and hawk together demonstrates the polar potentialities of existence: life in hawk, death in rock—both secure and balanced states in the cosmic cycle. Further, both remain remote from human interference and human misinterpretation. Because they incarnate and reflect the values that accept life and death as parts of the span of existence, they teach humans to imitate them to grow into the totality of the cosmos.

The balanced attitudes that rock and hawk illustrate are those of "consciousness" and "disinterestedness." Both are necessary, as both life and death are necessary, and each is dependent on the other. These transcend human values, as this emblem outfaces tragedy. Tragedy may help humans draw success out of partial failure; theoretically, it teaches survival. Jeffers argues that complete survival will come only after incorporation of the union of rock and hawk, the combination of "the falcon's/ Realist eyes and act" with "the massive mysticism of stone."

Forms and Devices

Robinson Jeffers is remarkable among modern poets for his simplicity of presentation. He uses a minimum of effects, preferring, like his biblical models, to rely on basic devices to project his themes. "Rock and Hawk" is no exception. It is one of Jeffers's "short line" poems, in which he forsakes his customary preference for long lines—those with more than five stresses. This poem presents seven three-line stanzas, each with three stresses spaced irregularly.

This stark simplicity serves his subject well. It is doubled by his diction. The poem first announces that it centers on a symbol, thereby spelling out what it is doing. It follows this with an arresting phrase and a classical figure: In this symbol, "high tragic thoughts/ Watch their own eyes." The figure is a double paradox—thoughts cannot literally watch, and things cannot in any case look at their own eyes. The figure reminds one of the celebrated passage in William Shakespeare's *Julius Caesar* (c. 1599-1600) in which Cassius asks Brutus, "Can you see yourself, Brutus?" Jeffers uses the figure to suggest a number of things, chief among which is probably that Western culture's conventional ways—the high tragic ways—of looking at things may not be enough.

The second stanza presents the first part of the symbol, the rock, standing "where the seawind/ Lets no tree grow." This personification is important. It suggests that control resides in the entire natural process rather than in some god or force. The rock is characterized by a double epithet: "Earthquake-proved, and signatured/ By ages of storms." The first suggests not only that it has stood the test of time but also that it incorporates design features that surpass all the works of humans. The second uses back-formation to create the image of impersonal names—again, not human—carved into the surface, a testimony of the controlling natural process.

The persona employed in the poem now asserts itself. It chooses this image for itself, not for humankind. This reminds the reader that humans are the emblem-making animal. This symbol, fashioned by nature, transcends humans, unless they reject their earlier limited symbols to join the entire natural order in this.

The remainder of the poem presents a series of paired abstractions, epithets, and images to reinforce and translate the central symbol. This simple structure underscores Jeffers's simple but daring point. Reiteration drives the point home. Humans must learn from the natural order, but not by simply imposing their will and shortsighted values upon it. To show this, Jeffers inverts personification. He confers "realist" eyes on the falcon, not to suggest that it possesses human rationality, but to say that man needs to relearn the "fierce consciousness of the predator." Similarly, the rock displays "massive mysticism"; it is not the bemused contemplativeness of humans, who assume indifference and superiority, but the total submission of stone.

Themes and Meanings

Jeffers's themes are overt, but this does not mean they are always easy to discern or assess. In part, the reason for this is that the poet's philosophy—the so-called Inhumanism—is so stark, bleak, and uncompromising. It is not entirely novel; Shakespeare certainly anticipated some of his negativism in *Hamlet* (c. 1600-1601), and

Jonathan Swift devastated the notion of the inherent goodness of humankind. Jeffers, however, exceeds both in refusing to find any independent redeeming value in the species. For him, humans are simply another part of an evolved complex. Far from inheriting a right to dominate, humans will be lucky to survive. They will only survive if they recover the vision of the complex itself, to consider with clear-eyed, personal indifference the health of the whole.

This requires accepting the role of either hawk or rock without dissent. Undoubtedly this is difficult. Anyone would rather eat than be eaten. Jeffers feels that it is exactly this egocentric human-first attitude that must be overcome if the entire bio-mass is to survive. Left unchecked, humans will continually inflict damage on the system in order to pursue their private, limited objectives. Over the long term, these repeated injuries will unbalance the system to the point that everything, including humankind, is destroyed. This progressive deterioration is inevitable unless humans learn to change.

Jeffers accepted this theme as his personal poetic mission, developing aspects of it in a series of poems both short and long. Here he is most concerned with demonstrating the shortcomings of the tragic ideal, a prime motivator of human behavior in our civilization, with reference to the universal attitude he espouses. Thus, he begins by promising to reveal "a symbol in which/ Many high tragic thoughts/ Watch their own eyes." Near the end of the poem, he describes "the falcon's/ Realist eyes" as one pole of the new emblem with which humans should replace that of tragedy. Presumably, the contrast will reveal the shortcomings of the old human view.

The final lines of the poem suggest these deficiencies. The two poles, rock and hawk, will be immune to failure and success. Jeffers implies that the view which considers any human participant is ultimately destructive of the whole. Any art or literature that makes the hero of tragedy its ideal figure fosters this view. Aristotle suggests in his *De poetica* (c. 334-323 B.C.E.; *Poetics*) that the lesson of tragedy is double. The first point is that even though the hero fails, one learns from the hero's mistakes. The second is that even the hero can be sacrificed for the good of society. As long as human society is viewed as in twofold competition, with other species and with other societies, such a lesson is probably useful.

Jeffers contends, however, that at this point in evolution, this lesson and view are not only wrong but are dangerously wrong. Take away the central assumption of tragedy, that humans are the central and moral determinant of the universe, and one sees that humans are only one more part. Final survival depends on this recognition.

James Livingston

ROMAN SARCOPHAGI

Author: Rainer Maria Rilke (1875-1926)
Type of poem: Sonnet
First published: 1907, as "Römische Sarkophage," in *Neue Gedichte*; English translation collected in *New Poems [1907]*, 1984

The Poem

"Roman Sarcophagi" is a sonnet consisting of four stanzas broken down into two quatrains followed by two tercets. In the original German, the rhyme scheme follows a pattern that runs *abab, cddc, efe, efe*, and the lines average ten syllables in length. The title refers unambiguously to the poem's subject, ancient stone coffins, often ornamented with carvings, in which the Romans buried the dead.

Two pieces of information are crucial to a proper understanding of this poem. First, the word "sarcophagus" comes from two words in the ancient Greek that together mean "flesh eater." As the *Oxford Universal Dictionary (3d ed.)* notes, "sarcophagus" originally referred to a kind of stone that was supposed to devour decaying flesh. Eventually, it came to refer to coffins made from this stone. Second, in the years preceding the publication of *New Poems*, Rainer Maria Rilke made several visits to Italy. Always attentive to the historical and cultural details of the places he visited, Rilke at one point discovered, as Robert Bly explains in *Selected Poems of Rainer Maria Rilke* (1981), that "In the middle ages, Italian farmers . . . would knock the ends out [of the sarcophagi] and line them up so that they became irrigation canals, carrying water from field to field." Between these two pieces of knowledge, Rilke will weave his poem.

The opening stanza begins abruptly, as though the poet were speaking with some urgency in the midst of an ongoing meditation. Addressing the reader in the first-person-plural "we" form, the poet refers to a general condition that both presumably share. Referring to the ruins of the antique sarcophagi, the poet affirms that, like them, reader and poet alike "are scattered out and set in place." Yet, unlike the sarcophagi, human beings also share common negative emotions that the poet identifies as "thirst," "hatred," and "confusion." All these qualities "dwell in us," and taken together they indicate that being human is somehow to be lacking, is somehow synonymous with being unfinished.

The notion of "dwelling" leads gracefully into the second stanza, in which the poet shifts from describing the shared human qualities of the living to depicting the actual sarcophagi and the contents they once held. The poet names the accoutrements that once accompanied the dead into their coffins, the "rings, glasses, ribbons, and images of gods," which, in their reality as things, strike a vivid counterpoint to the negative, amorphous human qualities described in the first stanza. Among these distinct and definite things a human being once lay, a "slowly loosening something" that in death perhaps acquired a completeness that it lacked in life.

In the third stanza, the poet plays specifically on the etymological origins of "sarcophagus," describing the bodies as "swallowed by those unknown mouths." Rilke further plays on this image by making an imaginative leap from the "mouths" of the coffins to the "brain that one day will make use of them," a reference that perhaps on the most literal level refers to the farmer who eventually will invent a new use for them.

In the concluding stanza, the poem becomes starkly literal as the sarcophagi complete their transformation from ritualistic vessels for the dead to practical vessels for irrigation of the farmers' fields. The poem closes with an image of moving water rendered with a simple and sensuous clarity.

Forms and Devices

Rilke's subject matter is conducive to a rich exposition. In his intertwining of the etymological history of the word "sarcophagus" with the actual history of the sarcophagi, he is able to generate a series of surprising images and transformations. In a certain very real sense, "Roman Sarcophagi" was a poem waiting to be found, and Rilke seems happy to let the inherent poetic richness of his subject reveal itself. As is clear from the first-person-plural "we" of the opening stanza, the poet here, as so often in *New Poems*, gives the reader the impression that he is merely pointing to some meaning already present in the world. For Rilke, it would seem, the task of the poet is not so much to make meaning for the reader as it is to recover and share a communal meaning that is already "out there," waiting to be found.

Yet the reader should not be seduced too easily, for one can argue that Rilke's ability to see the potential buried within his subject, along with his apparently effortless ability to render this shared meaning, is precisely the measure of his mastery as a poet. A close reading of "Roman Sarcophagi" reveals that the poet carries a few selective details and figures through a series of imaginative transformations from stanza to stanza.

Most notably, the etymology of "sarcophagi" suggests to the poet an image of the coffins as mouths. In the first stanza, the one ostensibly least focused on the story of the coffins themselves, the poet describes the "unfinished" nature of human life in terms of "thirst." In the second stanza, he draws a comparison between the confusion or thirst of living humans and the "slowly loosening something" of the Romans in the coffins—it is as though the confusion of life only slowly vanishes after death as the indefiniteness of the human body gradually dissolves among the definite objects placed alongside it. Finally, in the third stanza, the body is completely swallowed by the coffin-mouths, and in the fourth, fresh, shining water runs through the coffins.

Through this developing cluster of images, the poet has shown how "thirst" might "dwell" in people, just as the decaying body dwells in the coffin. With the movement of water through the transformed coffin, the human "thirst" of the first stanza finally has been quenched.

On the surface, it would seem that Rilke is attempting a direct, almost objective presentation of his subject, but further reflection demonstrates that the poem works by means of a chain of details selected from the subject at hand in order to present the reader with a startling, almost miraculously ironic transformation as the human "thirst" of the opening stanza is eventually quenched by the water the farmers use for irrigation. Rilke presents the objective history of the sarcophagi but does so through selective images that emphasize processes of death, decay, and eventual rebirth.

Themes and Meanings

Often in Rilke's *New Poems* it seems as though the poet in observing his subject is attempting to look into a mirror. Yet the thing that is regarded throws back an image not of the poet's self but of all that the self is not. In other words, the striking otherness of the observed subject provides the poet with a way of understanding what it means to be human, precisely because the subject itself is something beyond the human. In "Roman Sarcophagi," the poet describes human life as confused and unfinished. As is clear from Rilke's other work, to be incomplete is a source of both great pain and great joy, for if one is incomplete this means merely that more life is to come; in short, one's very lack of completion is simply the negative side of one's potential for growth. Continually throughout his career, Rilke's poetry explores the ways in which people grow and change over the course of a life. For Rilke, growth is always synonymous with life itself, and failure to grow is a kind of death.

Hence, in Rilkean terms, the Romans buried in the sarcophagi become fully completed human beings only as they gradually dissolve among the artifacts buried with them. Hundreds of years later, when the farmers break the ends out of the coffins and place them end to end as irrigation canals, any trace of the bodies the coffins once may have contained has disappeared as the coffins are transformed from ritualistic vessels for the dead into wholly practical vessels for bringing water and life to the crops. Whereas once the coffins contained the dead, they now bring water—bright, shining, animate—the most elemental of life-giving substances.

In telling the story of the transformation of the sarcophagi, it seems that Rilke has hit upon the perfect image for describing a metamorphosis from life to death to new life again, a new life figured in the image of the flowing water with which the poem closes. Such a passage seems all the more vivid and believable because of the strikingly literal terms in which Rilke renders it.

Vance Crummett

ROMANS ANGRY ABOUT THE INNER WORLD

Author: Robert Bly (1926-   )
Type of poem: Narrative
First published: 1967, in *The Light Around the Body*; revised in *Selected Poems*, 1986

The Poem

"Romans Angry About the Inner World" begins with a question, and the rest of the poem is an attempt to answer this question: "What shall the world do with its children?" It was written during the Vietnam War as one of the blatant antiwar poems Bly collected in *The Light Around the Body*, but the contemporary conflict is placed in the historical context of ancient Rome, which—once the parallels are understood and the distant past conflated with the present—makes the present terror even more horrific.

The poem is built around a series of parallels between "executives" and "executioners." At first these terms seem to suggest a contrast, but the reader quickly realizes that Bly intends to associate them with each other: The "executioners" of ancient Rome have become the "executives" of contemporary society. The present-day executives, like their ancient Roman counterparts, are unaware of the "leaping[s] of the body" or of any of the ways that one can "float/ Joyfully" toward the "dark" positive places in the psyche.

The central section of the poem describes the execution of Drusia by the Romans. The Romans believed that Drusia had "seen our mother/ In the other world"—that is, that she was a member of the mystical cult of the Magna Mater, or Great Mother. This cult appeared in very ancient times, and its members were persecuted by the Romans. Members encouraged the development of the speculative side of consciousness and celebrated the archetype of the feminine. Drusia was therefore regarded as dangerous, and she was tortured and then killed by the Romans.

The other world that Drusia has seen is the "inner world" of the poem's title; the contrast between the "inner" and "outer" worlds is important in terms of Bly's political and psychological theme in this poem. The significance of such contrasts is made clear in the epigraph to the book, which is taken from the writings of Jacob Boehme, the seventeenth century German mystic who based much of his philosophy on the notion of the "two worlds." Part of the epigraph reads: "For according to the outward man, we are in this world, and according to the inner man, we are in the inward world." Bly, following Boehme, develops his dichotomy in terms of the contrasts between the inner and outer worlds and between the masculine and the feminine sides of the psyche. The contrast is between the Romans, who "had put their trust/ In the outer world" and women such as Drusia, who have put their trust in the inner world. The Romans want Drusia to "assure them" that they have put their trust in the right place, and when she refuses to do so they kill her.

After they have tortured and killed Drusia, the Romans dump her body onto the ground. Immediately, and almost miraculously, a light snow begins to fall. It covers

Drusia's "mangled body," and the murderous executives/executioners are "astonished" and withdraw. The poem ends with two vivid and somewhat enigmatic images that attempt to define the significance of the contrast between the inner and outer worlds.

Forms and Devices

"Romans Angry About the Inner World" consists of a single stanza of thirty lines written in free verse. In lieu of more conventional poetic devices such as rhyme and meter, Bly relies on rhythm, juxtaposition, imagery, the dichotomy of the "two languages" (the epigraph from Boehme continues, "Since then we are generated out of both worlds, we speak in two languages, and we must be understood also by two languages"), and especially on the kind of "deep images" for which Bly is famous. These devices control the movement of the narrative and establish a meditative mood complementary to the theme.

In many essays and in various interviews Bly has described and defined what he means by "deep images." They are images that stress feelings and that "trust" emotional states of mind without excluding the intellect. They often "leap" from one thing to another in the same way that the mind "thinks in flashes"; they merge inward "reality" with outward reality; they are filled with spiritual energy and are psychologically accurate even though, when first described, they often seem to be irrational. Bly discusses these deep images in terms of the contrast between "inwardness" and "outwardness" in his essay "Recognizing the Image as a Form of Intelligence" (1981), in which he argues that a deep image can join Boehme's two worlds together. Therefore, "when a poet creates a true image, he is gaining knowledge; he is bringing up into consciousness a connection that has been forgotten."

"Romans Angry About the Inner World" ends with two deep images, both of which are attempts to describe the way in which the inner world relates to the outer world. In the first of these images, Bly compares the inner world to "a thorn/ In the ear of a tiny beast!" that the thick fingers of the executives are unable to pull out. That is, the inner world is something inside themselves that the executives wish to renounce but cannot. In the final image the inner world is called a "jagged stone/ Flying toward us out of the darkness." Putting aside safe, distanced references to the dastardly practices of the ancient Romans or to the anonymous evil-minded executives of the twentieth century, Bly implicates himself and his readers: The inner world, like a premonition of some inevitable cataclysmic event or impending apocalypse, is coming toward *us*.

Themes and Meanings

In his essay "Leaping up into Political Poetry" (1967) Bly writes, "America . . . may become something magnificent and shining, or she may turn, as Rome did, into . . . the enemy of every nation in the world [that] wants to live its own life." "That decision," he says, "has not yet been made." He adds that "a true political poem is a quarrel with ourselves"; it is "a sudden drive by the poet inward" that attempts to "deepen awareness."

Just as the whole of "Romans Angry About the Inner World" depends upon the question posed in the first line, the poem's theme is Bly's attempt to answer this question. It is not a question to which any explicit answer can be given, and for this reason, before he turns to consider it in terms of contemporary time, Bly first establishes a historical context for it. In terms of ancient Rome the context consists of showing what should not have been done—and thus, by way of contrast, suggesting what might be done now. That Bly chooses his historical example from ancient Rome is important. Readers may be reminded of a number of parallels between ancient Rome and twentieth century America: Rome was a major political power, it was prosperous and powerful, and it maintained what was regarded as an "enlightened" empire. Still, Rome fell. Bly seems to suggest that unless Americans learn from Rome's example, they may well be doomed to a similar fate. The poem is a warning against the destruction that the people of the United States face unless they change their ways.

But how is such a change possible? "What shall the world do with its children?" Children are the world's hope for the future. They are innocent. They have not been trained as either "executives" or "executioners." They are still open to the inner world of the psyche, filled with mystery and illumination. There seems to be a hint of a biblical passage in Bly's reference to children. Jesus said, "Suffer the little children to come unto me, and forbid them not: for of such is the kingdom of God. . . . Whosoever shall not receive the kingdom of God as a little child, he shall not enter therein" (Mark 10:14-15, King James Version). Bly's image of the "thorn," combined with the fact that the Romans persecuted Christians, makes it seem as though Bly is developing his theme through a religious thesis, even though he is thinking of it in a universal context.

The "jagged stone/ Flying toward us out of the darkness" at the end of the poem appears to be a harbinger of some imminent destruction about to visit the world and, no doubt, to change it as drastically as the fall of the Roman empire changed the ancient world. The Romans were "angry about the inner world" and sought to suppress it, but one should not be. Rather, people should welcome the inner world as children would. Thereby they may see to their own, and the world's, salvation.

William V. Davis

ROOMING HOUSES ARE OLD WOMEN

Author: Audre Lorde (1934-1992)
Type of poem: Lyric
First published: 1970, in *Cables to Rage*; slightly revised in *Coal*, 1976

The Poem

Audre Lorde's "Rooming Houses Are Old Women" is a thirty-line free-verse lyric that expresses the emotional and spiritual state of impoverished, lonely, old black women. The poem is laid out in three parts, the longest being the first, with fifteen lines, and the shortest being the three-line middle section. At first, these parts seem to be simply demarcations of setting, as it were, slowly moving readers, along with the old women, from the interior of rooming houses to the exterior world and back again, but a closer reading shows that they are intended to lead to inward states after an exploration of external circumstances.

The slow movement is perfectly congruent with the slow shuffle of the women, whose mundane "waiting," "rocking," "shuffling," and "searching" express the essence of their being. However, the poem is more a particularly candid depiction of urban blight and the burdens of isolation, age, and poverty than it is a philosophical inquiry into socioeconomic injustice, alienation, or desolation.

Lorde shows keen insight into the lives of the underprivileged, as she focuses on feelings of disconnection and falterings. The poem offers a sympathetic view, but it does not make any bald accusations against a particular agency. Instead, it gently and sensitively describes the aching vulnerability of the victimized women. The first stanza has substantial physicality because of the setting and the emblems of poverty and isolation, but the emotional impact is undeniable as one follows the old women in their slow, repetitive ambit. Their only movements in this stanza are those of rocking and of going to the rent office, the stoop, or the community bathroom and kitchen. Their lives are ones of waste, the "once useful garbage" under their "bed boxes" emblematic of decay and futility. Age has withered their sensual drive, for they are not carnally aroused by the "loud midnight parties" next door and their suggestions of sex. Their lives are dimming, as illustrated by the light brokenly passing through "jumbled up windows." Their only social consolation appears to be gossip: "who was it who married the widow that Buzzie's son messed with?"

The brief second section carries readers outside the seedy rooming house. However, instead of representing a refreshing break or interlude from deprivation, it reinforces the women's vulnerability by showing how by being dependent on welfare and community charity, they expose themselves to the indignity or "insult" of this dependency.

The final stanza concerns itself with an internalization of the subjects' feelings. The poem carries readers back inside the rooming house, where the old women are observed in small actions that anticipate unclear ends. Are they at "the end or beginning of agony"? The poet captures this uncertainty in the final five lines by groping, herself, toward some understanding of their fate of "not waiting/ but being/ the entrance to somewhere/ unknown and desired/ but not new."

Forms and Devices

The poem begins with a virtually oracular utterance, "Rooming houses are old women," which is glossed by connected images of the women's lot. The rocking chair and dark windows, the shared community facilities, and the domestic limitations are all useful emblems in providing readers with perceptions of the stubborn facts of the situation. The images come out of the materials of daily life and serve as metaphors for states of being. For instance, the dark windows, which are also called "jumbled," speak to the loneliness, confusion, and darkened vision of the old women; the "fishy rings left in the bathtub" mark the loss of the old women's eroticism or sexual desire, for they are perceived as something unpleasant, offensive, or suspect. The bathtub rings link with the gas rings and the " incomplete circles" described by the rocking to comprise a dominant image of repetition, unvarying action, and negative energy on the part of the women, who lack the psychological perfection or inner unity that the geometry of a circle normally indicates.

Lorde employs a remarkable imagistic restraint. Her images are few in number but do not seem overused, and the genius of her poem is its uses of textures of time and place without becoming fruitlessly bound by them. There is no covert reference or complication in the first two stanzas, for this is a poem that shapes its meaning typically through particulars of experience. Avoiding didactic sequences or arguments, Lorde remains true to expressions of thought and feeling.

The poem is free from the norms of "poetic" speech. Its acute verbal simplicity and commonplace diction are moving despite the commonness. Lorde personalizes the idiom by the personas of old women, and the sudden break into oral vernacular ("and who was it who married the widow that Buzzie's son messed with?") seals this device.

The cluster of *o* vowel sounds—some distinct, others submerged by consonants— in the first ten lines produces an assonance that subtly suggests lamentation or grief. The alliterative w's reinforce the repetitive stresses of a poem that depends on its diction, sparse imagery, and deliberate rhythm to project a virtually elegiac tone. The heavy stresses, consonance, and slowly moving lines—where one can almost hear the awkward shuffle of the women—become figurative devices for achieving meaning and effect.

The poem has an external circularity: It moves from interior to exterior and back again; from women at their windows to the same women at the same windows. Yet in the final verse, the diction modulates from the intimately vernacular and concrete to the abstract, as Lorde abandons her clusters of common nouns in favor of participles ("waiting," "searching," "hoping," "being") and abstract nouns ("somewhere/ unknown and desired/ but not new"). The shade of ambiguity in the closing line increases the intensity of the poet's sympathy for her subject. The old women are, perhaps, waiting for nothing more than what all people expect at the end of life.

Despite the oracular opening, the poem has a modernity that is expressed by particulars of imagery and by the open form of the verse, where the line breaks usually occur where commas or periods would normally be used. The absence of rhyme does not affect the lyrical quality, and the poem's import is carried by its rhythm.

Themes and Meanings

Before she reached her poetic apex in the personal vision of *The Black Unicorn* (1978), a collection of poems of elemental wildness and lucidity, Lorde revealed her deep interest in the significance of difference in other peoples' lives. As a young girl, she deliberately lopped off the *y* from her first name—"Audrey"—setting a precedent for her own self-determination. As an urban black wife and mother, she had direct experience with racism and socioeconomic prejudice, and when she asserted her identity as a lesbian feminist, she demonstrated the extent to which her imagination was charged by a sharp sense of racial injustice and cruelty. Her poems give voice to indignant humanity. Late in life, the poet was given the African name Gamba Adisa, meaning "Warrior: She Who Makes Her Meaning Clear," and her poem "Rooming Houses Are Old Women" provides ample evidence of this strength.

Lorde writes not as a seer but as a sympathetic being whose mission is to give voice to these largely silent victims. The women have only one dimly articulated sentence in the first verse, and it is a question that speaks to the breakdown of memory ("who was it who married the widow that Buzzie's son messed with?"). This air of bumbling vagueness or indistinct thought is compounded by other instances of the women's slow, awkward physical movement and by the rocking, which is really an inaction, being momentum without clear gain or purchase.

The old women demonstrate an inherent stoicism as they conduct their lives of poverty, loneliness, and failing energy. There is no visible reaction from them in the first verse, apart from the bewildered memory of Buzzie's son and the adulterous widow, and the "insult" of welfare is marked only by their "slow shuffle" and "leftovers." Feeling steals into the final verse in the phrase "the end or beginning of agony," but this is quickly displaced or reduced by the women's almost becalming "hoping" and "waiting." The ambiguously abstract pitch of the final four lines removes any possible commerce with the heroic. "Rooming Houses Are Old Women" is an emphatic representation of a small segment of disadvantaged humanity whose fate is shrouded in socioeconomic and psychological blight. Its lyricism carries elegiac notes, but this feeling is the product of the poet's recognition of the old women's plight.

Keith Garebian

THE ROSE

Author: George Herbert (1593-1633)
Type of poem: Lyric
First published: 1633, in *The Temple*

The Poem

George Herbert's "The Rose" is a lyric and meditative poem first published as part of his collection *The Temple*, a group of poems written as a record of a man's efforts to recognize and follow God's will; it was also intended to guide and comfort others. "The Rose" has the musical and cyclical qualities typical of many poems in the collection as well as many of Herbert's hymns that appear in the Anglican hymnal. Each of its eight stanzas of four lines has a rhyme scheme of *abab*. Every line begins with a beat and continues in three iambic feet. Three stanzas—1, 5, and 7—include two lines ending in feminine rhyme; that is, the second-to-last syllable receives the beat, and the unaccented syllables rhyme. These three sets of lines come to bear the important message of the poem: The rose offers pleasure, it purges, and it claims repentance.

The poem is also something of a meditation that takes the form of a dialogue with self or an imagined questioner. The speaker explains his reasons, either to a friend or to himself, for adopting the life he has chosen. His decision to give up his life in order to be more useful reflects a submission to God's will. Pressed, in the first line, to take more pleasure in life, the speaker responds that he wants no more pleasure than he has apportioned to his "strict but welcome size." Pleasures, he explains, do not exist. They are only griefs in disguise. He offers the rose as a symbol of all that is beautiful in the world to explain his point. The rose, he notes, is fair and sweet, but its beauty is accompanied by pain: It is thorny, and it pricks. This discomfort must be borne by the admirer of the rose. If the rose symbolizes all "that worldlings prize" and ultimately causes pain, it is clear, by extension, that all other worldly joys also bring suffering. With suffering comes repentance, and, while repentance cleanses, it also rends the spirit, just as "physick" (medicine) rends the body.

The speaker thus prefers health over the cure. He refuses the offer of worldly pleasure, yet he refuses it gently ("fairly"). Surprisingly and paradoxically, however, he ends by accepting the rose. Through analysis of the rose as representative of life's pleasures, he has seen his reason for rejecting it. Yet as he explains his choice, he recognizes more clearly the beauty of his own preference for the simple, godly life. This life now comes to be best represented by the rose. In its simple, incomparable beauty, it is unlike the worldly pleasure of life even if it does provide an instructive metaphor for it. Thus, the rose comes to represent the simple, beautiful, and accessible gift that he accepts.

Forms and Devices

"The Rose," like all of Herbert's poems, has an orderly, clever, and paradoxical form. Using simple words, Herbert constantly invents new forms that appropriately reflect the ideas being explored. His poems use all the repetitive devices (particularly rhyme, alliteration, assonance, consonance, and repetition of words and phrases), as well as meter and form, to convey meaning. The shaping of some poems to reinforce the literal meaning shows the importance he attaches to the form itself. The form also reflects the perception of an orderly universe, which is revealed through close observation, analysis, and a metaphorical habit of mind.

Herbert's poems present an artistic formulation of the analysis of a conflict. The result is often a dialogue. The Socratic dialogue was, for the classically educated person of the seventeenth century, the way to explore a topic in order to understand it. Herbert uses the dialogue repeatedly in his poems, achieving both clarification of an issue and the intimate tone for which his work has been so admired. The participants in the dialogue are sometimes an unnamed questioner (as in "The Rose"), sometimes two aspects of self, and sometimes God and self. Through this technique, readers sometimes hear the voice of the tired, angry, or lonely Christian with whom they identify. At other times, readers hear the voice of Herbert's gentle, loving, and caring God. This intimate voice draws readers into the poem, creating an emotional response that creates, in turn, a tension with the more aesthetic response prompted by the carefully contrived form. While "The Rose" does not create the highly emotional response of some of Herbert's other poems, it does illustrate the technique. The speaker draws the reader into his thought process and his final jubilant celebration of his own choice by offering the rose as a symbol of it.

Herbert also writes from a metaphorical habit of mind. In the tradition inherited from medieval times, sixteenth and seventeenth century writers expected to see correspondences in an orderly world. This way of viewing the world was not unlike the contemporary manner of seeing metaphors, but it differed in degree. For them, metaphor became a symbol or emblem reflecting complex meaning and values. The rose acquires complex meaning: The beauty and the pain that comes from seizing it represent the delight of seizing the pleasures of the world and the attendant pain of this action. Herbert shows, through the rose, that beauty and pleasure do have a cleansing and redemptive effect, but this is an effect that this seeker of the good life does not enjoy and that can be avoided by choosing a path different from the path of pleasure and delight that the rose has come to represent. The rose then accrues a meaning that is similar to the emblematic meaning of Christ's cross.

Themes and Meanings

The theme and meaning of this poem point to Herbert's life, in which poems ultimately became prayers and prayers became poems. His early life of high hopes, high achievements, and thwarted ambitions prepared him to write poems about people's attempts to align themselves with God's will. Born into a good family, Herbert was well-educated and brought up to expect a court position. He served as a tutor and as the University Orator at Trinity College in Cambridge, England, positions meant to prepare him for such a career. However, he saw his plans fail to materialize at the deaths of those influential friends who would have recommended him. He then began, later in life than most, to pursue Holy Orders. This was not a completely new direction for him, for he had been influenced by his mother, who encouraged him to pursue a religious life. However, his decision to become the parson at the country church in Bemerton, England, at age thirty-five did require a change in his life. His poems of the struggle to accept God's will and recognize His love for humanity were written during the four years he was pastor at Bemerton before his death at age thirty-nine.

"The Rose" could serve as an introduction to Herbert's task of describing humankind's inner conflicts. He commits himself to the ascetic life, a life not lacking in its own kind of beauty. In its description of the speaker's resolution to turn away from the inviting pleasures of this world and focus on the "size" of self, it speaks to all humankind. Through the internal conversation explaining the speaker's choice, the poem offers a reaffirmation of a spiritual decision.

While some readers of devotional poets have preferred the more spontaneous verses of Herbert's disciple Henry Vaughan or the more impassioned poems of John Donne, Herbert's admirers appreciate the subtlety of his wit and the sincerity of his voice, both of which are evident in "The Rose." The manipulation of the rose itself to symbolize first what he rejects and then what he accepts shows the nature of his wit and his appreciation for paradox. Indeed, all of his poems are informed by that major paradox of Christian teaching: In order to save one's life, one must lose it for the sake of Christ. The carefully designed artistic form and the clearly realized, particular voice of this ardent pilgrim create poems that express both the universal truth of humanity's relationship with God and each person's struggle to accept God's love and will. Typical of Herbert's work, this poem demonstrates the correspondence between form and meaning. "The Rose" encloses the totality of its meaning through the order, the voice, the dialogue, the symbol, and the paradox.

Bernadette Flynn Low

ROUTE

Author: George Oppen (1908-1984)
Type of poem: Meditation
First published: 1968, in *Of Being Numerous*

The Poem

"Route" is a long poem in free verse consisting of fourteen sections, each structured differently. The title indicates that the poem describes a series of journeys: the narrative of the poet's own life, the process of creating poetry, travel by car and other modern forms of transportation, and the voyage of humankind itself from the promise of human chromosomes to a fast-approaching apocalypse. Although the poem is written in first person and includes autobiographical material from George Oppen's life, most of "Route" is a philosophical meditation that considers multiple points of view and the perspective of "we" rather than "I."

The first section presents a series of ancient, elemental materials ("the beads of the chromosomes," "sources," "crude bone," "the mass of hills," and "the sun") that the speaker tries to link to a contemporary moment of individual perception ("Your elbow on a car-edge/ Incognito as summer"). The speaker says that the motive for writing this kind of poetry, which is made up of separate and distinct images, is to "achieve clarity." The second section describes the importance of this clarity as a "force" that human beings experience as shared rather than "autonomous," despite the fact that even the objective world is discontinuous and constantly changing like a "house in moonlight." Next, the speaker develops the idea that the "thing" should not be reduced to "nothing" and that even the act of looking out a window at the world should be done without egotistical emotions. Then the speaker argues that words themselves are also things and are not "transparent" and have ethical implications for "those in extremity." He also claims that people actually understand reality best in the state of boredom because then they are truly able to experience time.

There is a radical change in tone from the fourth to the fifth section as the poem moves from dreamlike images to a journalistic prose account. It reports a story about the suffering of French people forced to hide in individual holes during much of World War II in order to avoid being drafted into the German army and depicts information Oppen actually received while serving as a soldier and translator. The sixth section returns to lines of verse but continues with a meditation on the nature of war, although, as elsewhere, abstract concepts are presented through concrete relationships. The section concludes with things that are so simple ("there is a mountain, there is a lake") that they are often misunderstood.

The eighth section explores how humanity's view of modern life has been changed by the automobile. Although cars are "filled with speech," it is the man whose car has crashed who "sees in the manner of poetry." In the next section, the speaker compares the countryside that is driven through to a historical context, but he presents history in personal terms, including an allusion to the suicide of Oppen's mother when he was a child. The tenth section continues this roadside perspective as a way to understand a poetic perspective that is composed of scenes rather than symbols and that is, by definition, finite rather than infinite.

The twelfth section views the larger human-made landscape of "sheetmetal," "concrete," and "gravel," which is modern but is haunted by time and related to the fruit of the biblical Tree of Knowledge. In the thirteenth section, it becomes clear that the roadside landscape has already supplanted traditional public urban architecture, which was built so that people could entangle themselves "in the roots of the world" or to provide "shelter in the earth." In the final section, the speaker predicts cataclysm for his culture like that experienced by the American Indians. In the conclusion, however, the speaker refuses to abandon his civilization, even if it is doomed, and affirms the reality of this world as it approaches its end.

Forms and Devices

Oppen is considered to be one of the founding Objectivist poets, and he uses a succession of objective images to achieve the poetic effects of "Route." The Objectivists were a diverse group launched by Ezra Pound, who believed that poetry should rely on images rather than metaphors, and influenced by William Carlos Williams, who asserted that there should be "no ideas but in things." Because Oppen believed in the importance of giving realism to the thing described in his poetry and not merely treating the image as a vehicle for a more abstract or intellectual concept, he avoids relying on metaphors. A careful reading of "Route" shows few metaphoric constructions, even when the logic of the poem would seem to demand it. Sometimes the poem juxtaposes images or words without making the relationship between them completely clear, so that the reader may wonder whether or not a phrase such as "Reality, blind eye" is a metaphor. Sometimes the poem isolates the image from the rest of the text so that it can have greater impact as a moment of perception such as the "sea anemone . . . filtering the sea water through its body." Although the poem opens with a simile comparing chromosomes to a rosary, much of the poem uses association by proximity rather than association by comparison, so that it is not just the images themselves that are poetic, but the sequence of images: "And beyond, culvert, blind curb, there are also names/ For these things, language in the appalling fields."

Oppen defines poetic experience primarily in visual terms with his "moving picture," but "Route" is also a poem that functions on an auditory level, although the speaker would seem to be diminishing the importance of song by saying, "Let it be small enough." In many ways, "Route" is not a poetic poem: It includes a long section of narrative prose, and it is structured more as a meditation than a lyric. Nonetheless, although the poem is in free verse, its music appears in the use of repeated refrains such as "We will produce no sane man again" and "All this is reportage." Oppen also builds rhythm by repeating grammatical constructions ("of invaders, of descendants/ Of invaders"), metrical patterns ("into gravel in the gravel of the shoulders"), and words ("Clarity, clarity, surely clarity is the most beautiful/ thing in the world,/ A limited, limiting clarity"). The most striking lines use simple diction in extraordinarily complex clauses (both grammatically and musically): "These things at the limits of reason, nothing at the limits of dream, the dream merely ends, by this we know it is the real."

Themes and Meanings

Oppen argued that he was trying to bring greater realism into poetry, although his realism was philosophical realism rather than the sociological or psychological realism that most readers would associate with the term. Many of Oppen's ideas about how human beings perceive the world moment by moment were derived from and influenced by the twentieth century German philosopher Martin Heidegger. Other concepts in "Route" that also appear in Heidegger's work include time as a dimension of being, boredom as a way to experience reality, the importance of "things" in themselves rather than just as they relate to ideas, the belief that language is not a transparent medium for ideas, and the conviction that the relation of human beings to the earth is in crisis.

Oppen is also responding to moral questions raised by the historical events of World War II and his personal participation in combat. Although Oppen was a well-known pacifist for most of his life, in "Route" he tries to understand his time as a soldier in Europe. His enlistment could be easily understood in ideological terms: Oppen was a leftist Jew and a confirmed anti-Nazi. "Route," however, presents more complexity. The speaker in the poem sees the war in terms of "madmen" who "have burned thousands/ of men and women alive," but he also realizes that they were "perhaps no madder than most." A series of rhetorical questions about war are raised in the sixth section, but the poet does not presume to answer them. In talking about the war, the speaker suggests that the truth is both "perfectly simple" and "perfectly impenetrable" and suggests that truth is not necessarily moral.

"Route," like the larger book in which the poem appears, *Of Being Numerous*, compares the isolation of people as autonomous individuals with solitary perspectives to communal responsibilities to act ethically toward other people and the world. Perhaps nowhere in the poem is the existential dilemma of isolated individuals more poignant than in the wartime story about men living alone in holes in the French countryside for years, even while snow fell, even at the cost of sacrificing the safety of their families. The men's decision to enter their lonely holes is not presented in idealistic or nationalistic terms, but the story is important because these are men who made an ethical decision not to fight while Oppen made an ethical decision to fight. The abstractions of pacifism, therefore, prove unimportant to both combatants and noncombatants.

Elizabeth Losh

RUBY TELLS ALL

Author: Miller Williams (1930-   )
Type of poem: Dramatic monologue
First published: 1985; collected in *Imperfect Love*, 1986

The Poem

"Ruby Tells All" is a sixty-four-line, five-stanza poem written in blank verse. The title of the poem establishes both the occasion of the poem and the confessional nature of the piece: The speaker in the poem is a woman named Ruby, who recounts some of the major events in her long life and reflects upon what life has taught her. One of the strongest features of the poem is the voice of Ruby, an unwavering and direct voice that characterizes her and establishes her position in society.

"Ruby Tells All" is an appropriate introduction to Miller Williams's work because Williams frequently writes poems that are dramatic monologues: works in which a character directly addresses an audience in such a way as to unintentionally reveal some substantial insight or show some important aspect of his or her personality. As is the case with many of Williams's dramatic monologues, in "Ruby Tells All" the speaker is identified in the poem's title. While there is little interaction between speaker and listener in the poem, some critics have maintained that Ruby is telling her life story to a customer at the coffee shop where she works. Support for the assumption that Ruby is speaking to one of her customers comes in the second stanza, in which Ruby says, "I've poured coffee here too many years/ for men who rolled in in Peterbilts."

In the first stanza Ruby tells about her childhood; in the second she explains how difficult it is as an adult to tell truth from lies. In the third stanza she recounts a major event in her adult life, and in the fourth stanza she discusses old age and sums up her thoughts about what is important in life. Finally, in the final stanza, she considers what she might do to reestablish a connection with her long-lost daughter.

The poem begins with a recollection from Ruby's youth. As a child, she was told that "crops don't grow unless you sweat at night," and she explains that in her childhood she felt as if she were especially important because she thought "that it was my own sweat they meant." This stanza indicates Ruby's connection with life and with the process of growth. However, with the passing of childhood comes the loss of "everything that's grand and foolish." One of the losses brought about by the end of childhood is the ability to discern truth from lies. The second stanza deals specifically with Ruby's inability as an adult to tell truth from falsehood.

The third stanza focuses on the most important event of Ruby's adult life: a love affair with a married man, an affair that produced a daughter. Although Ruby feels that, "Given the limitations of men, he loved me," the man disappears, leaving her to raise her daughter on her own. Ruby has apparently been a good mother; she loves her daughter, and she says that she "raised her carefully and dressed her well." At the time of the poem, however, the daughter has grown up and moved away. Ruby does not know where she is.

The fourth stanza contains Ruby's reflections on old age, especially her growing awareness of the passage of time and the inevitability of her own death, as well as her opinions about men and their natures. She assesses what does and does not matter in life. In the fifth stanza she laments the fact that she has lost touch with her daughter and wonders what she could do or say to bring her daughter, if she is still alive, back into her life.

Forms and Devices

"Ruby Tells All" is an excellent example of Williams's tendency to write about ordinary people in ordinary language. Ruby's diction characterizes her as a working-class person, but even though her language is ordinary, Ruby is able to achieve extraordinary insights about life. The most important formal aspect of the poem is its meter; it is written in blank verse (unrhymed iambic pentameter). Iambic pentameter is the most common pattern in English poetry, and its rhythm appears naturally in English speech and writing. Therefore, iambic pentameter is a suitable meter for a poem that is "spoken" in the voice of one character.

The formal meter of the poem is, however, in juxtaposition to Ruby's diction. Her common diction is especially apparent in stanza 2, in which she says, "I wouldn't take crap off anybody/ if I just knew that I was getting crap/ in time not to take it." In addition to juxtaposing Ruby's common diction with formal meter, Williams uses juxtaposition to close the poem by mixing her philosophical musings with personal ones. When contemplating what she might tell her daughter if they should meet again, Ruby wonders if she should say "that against appearances/ there is love, constancy, and kindness" or that her fingers hurt at night and she has dresses she has never worn. The juxtaposition of philosophical concerns with ordinary ones is indicative of Williams's ability to write powerfully about common people who have uncommon insights about life.

In "Ruby Tells All," Williams employs repetition and metaphor to highlight the poem's essential concerns: an assessment of what matters in life and the notion that life is composed of loss and change. For example, the clause "Everything has its time" appears twice in the poem, once in stanza 3, in which Ruby discusses the loss of the man who fathered her daughter, and again in stanza 4, when she speculates about growing old. Also in stanza 4, the word "don't" is repeatedly used to help characterize the negative natures of men. Moreover, in the final stanza, three lines begin with the words "maybe that"; the repetition of these words introduces a catalog of Ruby's alternatives concerning what she might tell her lost daughter.

The poem is also informed by metaphors that promote its thematic concerns. The first metaphor occurs in stanza 1 when Ruby notes that "We lose everything" and that everything "becomes something else." Reversing a commonplace observation, she says that "one by one,/ butterflies turn into caterpillars." The second important metaphor occurs in the fourth stanza, in which she comments on men and their natures. According to Ruby, "What's a man but a match,/ a little stick to start a fire with?"

The varied line length of the first, third, and fourth stanzas is another formal element in the poem. The first stanza, which deals with Ruby's childhood, is fifteen lines long; the third stanza, which deals with her adult life, is sixteen lines long; and the fifth stanza, which deals with her old age, is seventeen lines long. Each stage of her life is, therefore, marked by a longer stanza.

Themes and Meanings

"Ruby Tells All" is a poem about coming to terms with the nature of life, deciding what matters in life, and dealing with the inevitability of death. Ruby believes that life is characterized by loss and change, and she believes that, in the end, some things matter "slightly" and some things do not. According to Ruby, people "lose everything that's grand and foolish," and everything "has its time." Everything includes Ruby herself, who mentions that she feels "hollow for a little while" when she reads the obituaries in the newspaper and finds that someone younger than herself has died.

Ruby's thoughts about the passage of time and about death and dying lead her to make assessments about what is important in life. For her, dying matters, pain matters, and being old matters, but men do not matter. Indeed, Ruby believes that men have limited natures and that they live by negatives such as "don't give up,/ don't be a coward, don't call me a liar,/ don't ever tell me don't." She assumes that her daughter has learned these lessons about life and men, and at the conclusion of the poem she lists some of the other life lessons she might offer her daughter. Indeed, her thoughts about her lost daughter are evidence of her desire to stay connected with the human community as long as possible given the inevitability of death.

Dave Kuhne

THE RUINED MAID

Author: Thomas Hardy (1840-1928)
Type of poem: Narrative
First published: 1901, in *Poems of the Past and the Present*

The Poem

Thomas Hardy's "The Ruined Maid" is a dialogue between two farm girls in late Victorian England, one of whom has left the farm for city life, and the other of whom has remained in the country. The poem consists of six quatrains, each of which is organized in the same fashion. The first girl—unidentified by name and yet living on a farm—addresses the other girl, named Melia, who answers. In all but one stanza, the last one, the first girl has three lines of the quatrain, and Melia is given a one-line response in which she uses the word "ruin" or some variation of it. Through this conversation, Hardy provides social commentary about his real subject: prostitution and its effects.

The poem is set in "Town," presumably a small rural town to which Melia has returned and near which she previously lived. The two girls have not seen each other for some time, and the chance meeting on the street affords them an opportunity to catch up. It is not clear that, previously, they have been close friends; however, they have been close acquaintances, and hence there is something of an intimate, yet casual, conversation.

In the introductory stanza the first speaker addresses Melia by inquiring, at once, about her "fair garments" and "such prosperi-ty." Melia replies, "'O didn't you know I'd been ruined?'" This establishes the pattern of the poem as well as indicates the characters and personalities of the two young girls. Melia assumes something of a haughty manner and a superior air to her friend, who has not been off to the city to be "ruined." Similarly, the other girl is somewhat naïve about Melia and in awe of her.

In the second stanza, the matter of appearance continues to receive the emphasis. The first girl recalls that Melia used to wear "tatters, without shoes or socks" and points out that she presently is wearing "gay bracelets and bright feathers three." Unknown to the girl who has remained in the country, the bracelets and feathers are signs of Melia's profession, not new wealth or realized culture. Similarly, in the third stanza, the poet draws attention to language: Melia has learned how to talk in a way that fits her "for high compa-ny!"—so the first girl thinks. However, she does not realize that the diction—an absence now of phrases such as "thik onn" and "theäs oon"—does not reveal what could truly be called "polish."

In the fourth and fifth stanzas, Hardy turns to the physical condition of Melia's body and her health. The first girl notices that Melia's hands are no longer "like paws" (from manual labor); nor does she presently have "megrims or melancho-ly" (migraine headaches and depression). The poem concludes with "Melia's assertion that "You ain't ruined," emphasizing the differences between the two girls and the choices they have made.

Forms and Devices

The twenty-four lines of the poem are deliberately written in an uncommon meter of three dactyl feet followed by an iamb. Hence, each line has an unusual count of an odd number of syllables: eleven. All of the verses have an *aabb* rhyme scheme. It is curious that Hardy did not choose iambic pentameter for this poem, since iambs more accurately reflect actual speech in English; however, this peculiar form gives the poem a certain racy, conversational tone which keeps the interchanges moving.

The most important poetic mechanism, however, is not revealed by mere scansion of lines. Rather, the central literary device at play here is that of the pun. While most great poets hold puns in disdain and use them seldom, if ever, in serious poetry, Hardy chooses to organize the entire discourse around the one word "ruin," which appears in the last line of each stanza in Melia's responses to the other girl. Specifically, "ruin" means being destitute of any financial resources or worldly goods; at the same time, it means being void of chastity and purity—that is, Melia, now working as a prostitute, is morally ruined.

The irony of Hardy's punning needs further explanation. Melia is morally ruined, although she now has money and therefore is not financially ruined like her acquaintance. On the other hand, the girl who has no money has her chastity and is not ruined. Both girls are "ruined," but each in a different way. In the last line of each of the first five stanzas, Melia acknowledges her ruin but does so in something of a coy fashion. It is not clear that the other girl realizes what Melia is admitting.

The poet has also painstakingly included assonance, consonance, and alliteration in almost every line. Consider the lines "'Your hands were like paws then, your face blue and bleak/ But now I'm bewitched by your delicate cheek.'" Notice the repetition of the initial *b*-sounds in "blue," "bleak," "but," and "bewitched." Vowel sounds are repeated in "paws" and "face," "bewitched" and "delicate." Also, the word "your" is used three times without creating any poetic offense.

The poem also reveals a special attention to language in other ways. In the third stanza, the first speaker realizes that Melia's speech has changed during her absence from the country. A few of the words have lost their Victorian connotation in the century since the poem was written. "Tatters" are torn clothes; "megrims" is a rustic corruption of the later word "migraine"; and "melancho-ly" is word that fell into disfavor for "depression."

Themes and Meanings

While Victorian England is stereotypically recalled for its extreme antiprurience, the facts often bear out a different matter. Such was the case with prostitution in London in the late 1800's when, according to some estimates, as many as 20 percent of teenage females may have been forced into supporting themselves in this manner. Hardy's purpose in this poem is to focus on and dramatize the plights of young women entering such lives. In so doing, he displays both extreme sympathy and a lack of compassion for both young women. The poet's attitude toward both of them evidences a rather dual attitude.

The first girl is obviously enamoured with Melia's appearance, language, and relative wealth. An air about her indicates admiration, even envy or jealousy, for the new circumstances of her acquaintance from "Town." Melia has returned with what appear to be better possessions, clothes, and speech. However, the first girl does not realize the source of these items; nor does she truly understand, for example, that "gay bracelets and bright feathers" hardly constitute the dress of high society. She does not see these for what they truly are: trade markers and prostitute flags.

Melia herself also has something of an ambiguous regard for her new circumstances. She seems pleased with her dress and diction; she now claims proudly to have "Some polish"; she boasts that she doesn't have to work and also of having a "lively" existence. However, her last utterance is not clearly a boast. The first girl says, "'I wish I had feathers, a fine sweeping gown,/ And a delicate face, and could strut about Town!'" To this Melia replies, "'My dear—a raw country girl, such as you be,/ Cannot quite expect that. You ain't ruined.'" But how does one read Melia's final three words? Perhaps they indicate a wistful confession that she wishes she herself were not morally ruined and had remained financially ruined. Or, perhaps, a certain haughtiness is continued as Melia puts on airs for her companion.

Hardy's own attitude toward his subject seems to be remarkably restrained. The poem does not forthrightly condemn prostitution; yet it does clearly evoke sympathy for both young women. The overriding comment, here, is that both are "ruined," and, perhaps, it doesn't much matter if one is ruined monetarily and the other morally. Hence, the poem is not really so much an attack on the evils of prostitution or the hypocrisy of Victorian society as it is a lament for the plights of both girls. One girl is morally pure but condemned to living in "tatters, without shoes or socks." The other is immoral and living in "gay bracelets and bright feathers"; yet this is hardly an improvement. The real problem is that while morality can be bought and sold, it is not rewarded. Both girls are doomed to miserable existences.

Carl Singleton

SADNESS AND HAPPINESS

Author: Robert Pinsky (1940-   )
Type of poem: Poetic sequence
First published: 1975, in *Sadness and Happiness*

The Poem

"Sadness and Happiness," the title poem of Robert Pinsky's first collection, is divided into thirteen sections, each of which contains five unrhymed quatrains. The title of the poem is, simply, the subject of the poet's meditation: He considers the sadness and happiness in his own life and in the lives of others.

The poem is written in the first person. Pinsky discusses his own life, the career choices he has made, and his family. The poet is not speaking through a persona; part of the poem's success derives from Pinsky's attempt to remove all masks and speak, with wit and candor, from his heart.

The first section is typical of the entire poem. In it, Pinsky addresses large philosophical themes, and he balances them with specific events or memories. He begins the poem by suggesting that, in memory, it often "becomes impossible/ to tell" sadness and happiness from each other. This is a theme to which he will return often in the poem. Sadness and happiness are "Crude, empty" terms, but he uses them because "they do/ organize life." Others, including the "sad American/ house-hunting couples with kids," may use closet space to organize their lives, but Pinsky prefers the abstractions of sadness and happiness for his purposes. Pinsky moves easily somehow from the notion of closet space to "*post coitum triste*," or the sadness following intercourse. This discursiveness is typical of the poem; if the poem follows a pattern at all, it is the mazelike pattern of associative thought.

The second section follows the sexual meditation. Pinsky notes that the "'pain' and 'bliss'ts;'" of early courtly love sonnets were based in part on the speaker's desire "to get more or better" sex, but Pinsky sees that "'Bale' and 'bliss' merge" even in sexual relations. Sadness and happiness cannot be separated, partially because the memories of sexual pleasures are joined by "absurd memories of failure."

Passing through historical allusions to the "muttered babble" of "Korsh, Old Russia's bedlam-sage," and the musical references to the "sex-drowsy saxophones" of the blues, Pinsky arrives, in sections 5 and 6, at his relationship with his wife. The noises in the historical and musical asides give way to the sounds of a particular memory Pinsky has of his wife. While driving with her, everything he sees, apart from his wife, seems ambiguously "full of emotion, and yet empty—/ . . . all empty/ of sadness and happiness." In Central Square in Cambridge, Massachusetts, Pinsky meets the Salvation Army brass band, the "farting, evil-tempered traffic," "young girls begging," and "filth spinning in the wind." Everything seems empty, except for his wife.

Memories of his wife slip into recollections of previous women with whom he was involved. He asks "'some lovely, glorious Nothing,' Susan,/ Patricia, Celia" to forgive him for his "past failures"; he also wishes he had no past. He would like only his wife, without the other "foolish ghosts" of the past, to urge him "to become some redeeming/ Jewish-American Shakespeare."

In section 8, he recalls his romantic, adolescent dreams, his fantasy of becoming "a vomit-stained/ ex-Jazz-Immortal, collapsed/ in a phlegmy Bowery doorway." Instead, he has become a poet with a normal life, a wife and daughters. He then imagines himself as a type of prophet who would like to address the Central Square crowd, "the band,/ the kids, the old ladies awaiting/ buses, the glazed winos." His imagined speech to them is a comic mixture of the hortatory tones of T. S. Eliot and Ezra Pound; his harangue, however, just as it begins to gather steam, trails off. Instead of continuing his attack on the "city of/ undone deathcrotches," he attacks himself, reflecting on his perverse ability to enjoy "air pollution . . ./ even the troubles of friends."

Pinsky stays with the Central Square environment in section 10 and wonders whether the "two bright-faced girls" should win his admiration as they cross the square with their "long legs flashing bravely above/ the grime." He continues the meditation in section 11, concluding that "the senses/ are not visionary, they can tug/ downward."

Recalling with pride a "sandlot home run" leads Pinsky to a recollection also of his errors, the "poor throws awry/ or the ball streaming through,/ between my poor foolish legs." This recollection of the ballfield leads to the final thoughts in the poem, a meditation on the Spanish word *polvo*, or dust, which in the poem comes out of the "reddish gray/ powder of the ballfield" and leads to the dust that bodies turn into in death. Pinsky concludes with a complaint against the impermanence of life. For Pinsky, "It is intolerable/ to think of my daughters, too, dust" or of his wife changed into "*el polvo*." He decides that humans are "desperate to devise anything" to "escape the clasped coffinworm/ truth" of art or nature.

Forms and Devices

Pinsky attempts to name, or at least discuss, some organizing principle for the vagaries of life, and his formal choices reflect the difficulties of this task. It would seem at first glance that this poem, with its division into sections and quatrains, is very regular, or at least predictable in some way, but Pinsky works against the structure he imposes on the poem. The sections are not ironclad divisions; rather, they are permeable boundaries. Pinsky, in fact, ends only one section (the last, section 13) with a complete sentence, while all the others spill over into the section that follows. Stories or digressions do not end because a section ends, but continue and trail off, finally, in a subsequent section.

Images or memories also are not confined to one particular section of the poem. In sections 2 and 3, Pinsky speaks of Petrarchan love poems and chivalric trophies, and admits, in a distanced way, that he

stood
posing amiss while the best prizes

of life bounced off his vague
pate or streamed between his legs.

In section 12, the inflated Petrarchan image becomes appealingly pedestrian when the poet recalls his sandlot baseball days: the "agony of recalled errors . . ./ . . . poor throws awry/ or the ball streaming through,/ between my poor foolish legs." Nothing remains fixed in the poem.

Even words will not hold steady. In the closing sections, Pinsky speaks of "*el polvo,*" which is the "reddish gray/ powder of the ballfield," but also the dust on which a girl dances in the Cervantes poem and the dust that his daughters and his wife will become in death. It is difficult to organize or structure a philosophy when everything seems to be in flux, and nothing—not even the formal structuring device of quatrains and sections—can halt it.

The game that Pinsky's wife uses to organize life, the "invented game,/ Sadness and Happiness," also offers little consolation. Pinsky brings this point home by noting at the start of the poem that it is often "impossible/ to tell one from the other in memory," and then reemphasizing the idea by a formal and unusual device: Pinsky will never allow the words happiness or sadness, or their synonyms, to stand alone in the poem. The two emotions are always joined somehow, usually within a line or two. When discussing "*post coitum triste,*" he says he is happy not to have experienced it often. He says that with no past, he would be happy "or else/ decently sad." When he sees the "gray sad leaves" falling in autumn, he thinks they "can bring/ joy, or fail to." And when crossing the bases after hitting a home run, he conflates the two again by recalling the "happiness/ impure and oddly memorable as the sad/ agony of recalled errors."

The poem emphasizes the inability of humans to fix things in place by showing the slippage possible between concepts, simple words, images, structuring devices like sections and quatrains, or the present and the past.

Themes and Meanings

This typically modern, elliptical poem that in its discursiveness resists precise meaning addresses the oldest theme in literature, present as far back as the *Epic of Gilgamesh* (c. 2000 B.C.E.): humans attempting to deal with their mortality. The poem, in parts, is a verse autobiography, but all the memories of the past lead to the final vision of the future, in which all Pinsky's family—and the poet himself—will be dead. The poet speaks of "that romantic/ fantasy of my future bumhood" that he held in adolescence; in maturity, however, the only fantasy he has of his future is the prospect of an inevitable death.

How does one counter one's impermanence? Pinsky's wife plays the "Sadness and Happiness" game with the children to help them organize and stabilize life, but Pinsky points out the dangers in that generous approach. People are, in Pinsky's words, "desperate to devise anything . . .// to escape" life's transitory nature. Yet Pinsky does not offer the reader much ease from the burden. William Shakespeare in his poems offered his loved ones permanence through art, suggesting, in Sonnet 18, that "So long as men can breathe, or eyes can see,/ So long lives this [poem], and this gives life to thee." Pinsky is not so glib or cocky. His art simply records the anguish and the muted pleasures of living in a world of impermanence. He offers his wife and children his sadness, but he cannot offer them immortality through art.

The poem attempts to ward off the powers of death—the change that "all/ changes breedeth"—by listing with wit all the minute particulars of a man's life, from his baseball days and early failed romances to his dreams of grandeur in addressing and working a Central Square crowd. All the attention to the stuff of life, however, even the two girls' "long legs flashing bravely above/ the grime," brings Pinsky to a philosophical moment that seems akin to Platonism. He believes that

> it takes more than eyes
>
> to see well anything that is worth
> loving; that is the sad part, the senses
> are not visionary, they can tug
> downward, even in pure joy.

Yet Pinsky is wedded to the senses, even while he is perfectly aware of their limitations. The poem does not offer the reader a vision of a Platonic realm; it only critiques the world of the impure senses. Pinsky, in the end, is a poet who sees the world and its transience clearly, mourns appropriately, and continues to make song, attempting, with wit, to fashion sense out of a world that constantly eludes him.

Kevin Boyle

THE SADNESS OF BROTHERS

Author: Galway Kinnell (1927-   )
Type of poem: Elegy
First published: 1980, in *Mortal Acts, Mortal Words*

The Poem

In seven stanzas of free verse, Galway Kinnell, the first-person narrator, remembers his lost brother, who died twenty-one years before. Kinnell creates an imaginary reunion he and his black-sheep brother might have in their fifties if they could meet. His brother had run off years ago, after his dream of being a pilot failed; he wandered around and eventually died as an exile from his family. Kinnell imagines that they meet and hug, and that his splintered family is momentarily reunited.

The poem is divided onto five sections, beginning with the surfacing of a subconscious memory of the brother that Kinnell experiences as "a mouth/ speaking from under several inches of water." This resurrected corpse of a memory brings an ugly image of the lost one as "wastreled down" with "ratty" eyes. In part 2, old photographs of World War II airplanes and of a tractor left by his brother trigger Kinnell's memories. He remembers that his brother's soaring dream of being a pilot was shattered when he "washed out" of pilot training in 1943. Kinnell's brother, broken by this failure, became a wanderer for twelve years until he died in an automobile crash in the Wyoming desert. In part 3, the poet sees himself and his lost brother as both possessing traits of their unsuccessful father, Scotty. He remembers his father's walk and "jiggling" knees, his beliefs in "divine capitalist law" even though he was starving, and his half-failures both in war and in civilian life. Also, he remembers, with some nostalgia and gentle humor, the whole family sleeping in one bed because of the cold and their poverty; when one turned, they all had to turn. This reminder of unity and warmth ends when the poet states that Scotty's life "revealed not much/ of cowardice or courage: only medium mal." The father, even though he shared his wife's dreams and "bourgeois illusion," remained only a "medium" man with some evils and weaknesses who, like the lost brother, was not successful.

At the beginning of part 4, the narrator shifts to the present tense and imagines his dead brother with him at his present home. Kinnell describes the fears he might experience in reuniting with the prodigal brother, who had become a stranger. He fears that his brother might be obnoxious, want "beer for breakfast," or criticize his family's "loose ways/ of raising children." Kinnell then recalls the rebellious, snarling, and gangsterlike behavior of the black-sheep brother as a teen. Then, in contrast to the snarling teenage image, Kinnell remembers his brother being six years old and innocent, ecstatically waving to the family from the "rear cockpit" of a "Waco biplane" as his dream of being a pilot began.

The last part starts with Kinnell rejecting the fears and, in his imagination, lovingly embracing the lost brother. The brothers stand together in the doorway reunited; both are humanized as Kinnell ends by saying, "we hold each other, friends to reality,/ knowing the ordinary sadness of brothers."

Forms and Devices

Kinnell is a confessionalist poet—that is, he writes about his own personal experience and tries to transmute it and depict it as universal human experience. True to his Whitmanesque roots, he writes in free verse and creates vivid, emotive images through repetition, analogies, irony, and poetic catalogs as he weaves his elegiac "reunion" in this poem.

In the second section, for example, Kinnell moves from the outside world of physical memorabilia—photos left by his brother—inward to the mental images formed in his own memory. Such inward motion may represent one step toward the mental reunion found at the poem's end. Kinnell begins and ends this part of the poem by mentioning the odd photograph in the box, one of a farmer sitting on a tractor and gazing at his fields. The poet repeats the words "photograph" or "photographs" three times and implies a whole cluster of images of planes when he catalogs and lists names of World War II airplanes: "Heinkel HE70's, Dewoitine D333/ "Antares," Loire-et-Olivier H24-2—." Each plane presumably had a photograph, so many photographs are implied. By listing the plane names and exact model numbers, Kinnell reveals his brother's expert knowledge of World War II aircraft. The repetition of names also underscores the brother's obsession with flying.

Ironically, the brother's flying dream was dashed at the point it possibly could have been actualized in life—he went to flight school only to find that "original fear/ washed out/ all the flyingness in him." Apparently, the lost dream destroyed the brother, who was unable to create another viable dream and "only wandered/ from then on" until he died twelve years later in 1955. At the end of this section, Kinnell transforms the snapshot of the farmer on a tractor from a physical image into mental images within "the memory of a dead man's brother." In this very personal stanza, the poet "confesses" his struggle with memories of his sad and unfulfilled brother's death and imaginatively gathers his lost brother into his living memory through repetition and the catalog of old photographs.

Kinnell creates complex and affecting images. The opening simile reads, "He comes to me like a mouth/ speaking from under several inches of water." The image is complex partly because it operates on both visual and aural (hearing) levels and partly because it generates several different associations. On a visual level, the image functions as a form of synecdoche (the use of a single part to stand for the whole or to evoke a more complex whole). Since a mouth is closely associated with a face as a whole, the image can be of a whole face, perhaps a corpse's face, emerging from the deep. If the face is underwater, it is not quite clear and is wavering in appearance, perhaps a whitish blur in dark water. On the aural dimension, a mouth speaking from underneath water produces indistinct or burbling sounds—one imagines something just below hearing trying to bubble through to the surface. The sound is not yet understandable but becomes audible. The complex images of stifled talk and indistinct sounds linked to a bleary image of a humanlike entity striving to surface are evocative and apt representations of a repressed memory trying to break through to a person's consciousness. It also is a memorable and somewhat frightening way to begin a poem about the power of memory to both recall and re-create the dead brother.

Themes and Meanings

Kinnell's "The Sadness of Brothers" is part of a series of long confessional poems about both mortality and different members of his original family. He writes about his mother's death and its effect on him in "The Last Hiding Place of Snow," also published in the volume *Mortal Acts, Mortal Words*. Even though he writes of death in "The Sadness of Brothers," he does not seem particularly morbid. Instead, he seeks to overcome death, at least for a moment, by using the power of language to re-create a reunion with the dead brought to life in a poem. By writing such poems, Kinnell seems to believe that he can existentially protest seeing the dead as wholly separate from the living, since those who are gone can be brought back and immortalized in a work of art. The dead can regain life in the memory of the living.

Kinnell is by no means a unidimensional or wholly dark poet; he also writes well about human joys and about life in a family. Even in *Mortal Acts, Mortal Words*, he pens lighter poems; one is about his own son, Fergus, and is entitled "Fergus Falling." Kinnell also talks about his relationship with his first wife in "After Making Love We Hear Footsteps" and "Flying Home." Earlier in his career, he wrote political poems protesting the savagery of the Vietnam War, and his most famous early poem, "The Bear," apparently was conceived in a southern sharecropper's house while Kinnell was working for a civil rights group. Kinnell is deeply humanistic and a poet of many parts and moods.

David J. Amante

SAILING TO BYZANTIUM

Author: William Butler Yeats (1865-1939)
Type of poem: Lyric
First published: 1928, in *The Tower*

The Poem

"Sailing to Byzantium" is a short poem of thirty-two lines divided into four numbered stanzas. The title suggests an escape to a distant, imaginary land where the speaker achieves mystical union with beautiful, eternal works of art.

"Byzantium" is a loaded word for William Butler Yeats, a word rich with meaning. "Byzantium" refers to an earlier Yeats poem by that title and to the ancient name for Istanbul, capital of the Byzantine empire of the fifth and sixth centuries. In his prose work *A Vision* (1925), Yeats wrote that Byzantium represents for him a world of artistic energy and timelessness, a place of highly developed intellectual and artistic cultures. It represents a perfect union of aesthetic and spiritual energies; Yeats wrote, "I think that in early Byzantium, maybe never before or since in recorded history, religious, aesthetic, and practical life were one." To historians of art, Byzantium is famous for its multicolored mosaics inlaid with marble and gold. Often the mosaics depict Christ or other religious figures in symmetrical arrangements with two-dimensional, impersonal facial expressions.

The first stanza describes a country of "sensual music," presumably Ireland, but representing any place dominated by living for today. As an old man, the poet at once celebrates the fertility and joyful images of teeming fish, birds, and people but despairs of their temporal ignorance. Caught in the endless cycle of birth and death, these living beings overlook certain "monuments of unageing intellect" that the poet seeks to explore.

The old man reflects on himself in the second stanza, calling himself a scarecrow on a stick without much physical vigor. What he lacks in body he compensates for in desire to express himself through singing. Singing (his poetry) will allow him to transcend old age. The spirit of his poetry will carry him to Byzantium, a magnificent and holy city.

The third stanza presents the speaker standing before a golden mosaic, pleading for the Byzantine sages and "God's holy fire" to illuminate his soul. He realizes that his heart is trapped inside a fleshly creature that will soon die; the poet wants to leave this world and enter the world of timeless art through his song—poetry.

The fourth stanza develops the contradiction that a human being cannot leave this world while occupying a body. The poet desires to merge with the elaborate, gold-inlaid Byzantine mosaics and become like a bird perched on a bough, serenading sleepy emperors and nobles for all eternity. Preserved in this mythic form, the poet can observe past, present, and future, rejoicing in his artistic immortality.

Forms and Devices

"Sailing to Byzantium" follows an ottava rima stanza pattern, which usually consists of eight eleven-syllable lines rhyming *abababcc*. Italian poet Giovanni Boccaccio is credited with inventing the form. Sir Thomas Wyatt and George Gordon, Lord Byron, popularized it in England. Yeats, however, modifies the form to suit his own purposes, using ten syllables instead of the original eleven and using slant rhymes instead of exact ones. In lines 1 and 3, for example, different vowel sounds prevent "young" from rhyming exactly with "song."

Yeats constructs his poem around one major opposition: the mortal world of the flesh versus the golden world of eternal art. One of Yeats's major themes in poetry is that no one can make a choice of absolute certainty between precise opposites. The two realms depend on each other for what they mean, as in the case of Ireland with its teeming animal life and the medieval imperial city of Byzantium. Yeats juxtaposes a natural, mortal world driven by the cycle of life and death, with an impersonal, immortal world of art. The speaker yearns to detach himself from the temporal world of his body to find himself inside "the artifice of eternity."

Two metaphors running throughout the poem—birds and singing—point to the differences between Ireland and Byzantium. The bird has long been a spiritual symbol, as in the dove from scripture. The birds in the trees in stanza 1, references to a bird's flight in stanza 2, and the bird "set upon a golden bough to sing" in stanza 4 emphasize the difference between a sensual, physical world of spiritual ignorance and a timeless world of spiritual revelation. The image of the bird in flight in stanza 3 is a pervasive gyre symbol appearing in many of Yeats's later poems. The whirling, coiling motion and the use of the verb "perne" are Yeats's adaptations of the noun "pirn," a small cylinder originally made of a hollow reed or quill on which thread or yarn was wound. Yeats means to imply the merger of his soul with the spiraling bird's flight, just as the poet wishes to lose his soul in the eternal world of art.

The metaphor of music-making and song as poetry establishes Yeats's desire to make his own Byzantine mosaic in verse, where his spirit might be preserved for all eternity. The poet looks at one gold mosaic in stanza 3 and pleads for the sages to "be the singing-masters of my soul," to teach the poet how he might be similarly able to step out of his aging body.

Elements of song pervade Yeats's poem. The old man dreams of the songs he will make if, by merging with voices of sages and Byzantine art, he can transcend the restrictions of mind and body. The reader should note the alliteration of *g, s, l,* and *p* consonants and the assonance or recurring vowel sounds in stanza 4 that reflect the music of language.

References to folk legend, myth, and symbol abound in "Sailing to Byzantium." Throughout his career, Yeats worked symbols into his poetry, giving a universality to ostensibly topical poems. The bird images stand for transcendence, immortality, and the spirit. As another example, the "golden bough" of stanza 4 may refer both to Sir James George Frazer's work in comparative mythology, *The Golden Bough* (1890), and to classical Roman poet Vergil's *Aeneid* (c. 29-19 B.C.E.), in which Aeneas plucks a golden bough in order to descend into Hades.

Themes and Meanings

Yeats's poem offers fertile ground for inquiry into the realms of language, structure, imagination, myth, and symbol. Many critics have written about "Sailing to Byzantium," and the poem seems almost inexhaustible in its supply of ideas. Yeats published "Sailing to Byzantium" when he was sixty-three, so the theme of the life cycle and the differences between youthful exuberance and sterile old age certainly inform the poem. Yet to suggest that Yeats's only concern is his approaching death seriously undervalues the richness of the poem's symbols.

The poem's major theme is the transformative power of art: the ability of art to express the ineffable and to step outside the boundaries of self. Some concrete details of the poem might be read autobiographically, such as the speaker's desire to leave his country, references to himself as an old man, "a tattered coat upon a stick," and having a heart "sick with desire/ And fastened to a dying animal." Although an old man, the speaker still feels the desire to sail to Byzantium and metaphorically to transcend the sensual music of Ireland. He wants to transform his own consciousness and find mystical union with the golden mosaics of a medieval empire.

The poet pleads with the sages in the mosaic to open the door and allow him entry into their world, where he might reflect on past, present, and future. With his body discarded, the poet's concept of time changes. He is no longer the victim of a biological cycle but has liberated himself into a new world, capable of reaching over all eras. The poet leaves behind a temporal world of ignorant lust and physical celebration to gain the perspective of eternity.

Another of the poem's broader meanings is the paradox of consciousness and the body. Yeats entertains the idea that consciousness might continue outside the restrictions of mind and body. The poet's body falls apart, yet his faculties of imagination, soul, and spirit are still passionate and alive. Individuality fades away as the body dissolves in old age, and the poet finds himself reincarnated as a golden bird. This new form exceeds the realms of individuality because it merges with eternal art, the Byzantine mosaic.

While one may be tempted to read "Sailing to Byzantium" as only about the division between mind and body, Yeats's theme of transformation goes far beyond this simple dichotomy. The poem also represents the idea that art supersedes nature. The poet avoids the necessary return to dust by joining "the artifice of eternity." Great works of art, poetry, and song whose spirit expresses great desire have the power to overcome nature. In another poem, "Byzantium," Yeats discusses the relationship between transcendent art and the human hands that made it. "Sailing to Byzantium" explores many levels of aesthetic, spiritual, and intellectual transformation through which the poet journeys far beyond his native land.

Jonathan L. Thorndike

SAINT JUDAS

Author: James Wright (1927-1980)
Type of poem: Sonnet
First published: 1959, in *Saint Judas*

The Poem

"Saint Judas" is a nearly Petrarchan sonnet, in nearly regular iambic pentameter, with an unusual rhyme scheme. Its title suggests that its contents, as well as its form, will represent a modification of tradition, since anyone familiar with the story of Judas Iscariot, apostle and betrayer of Christ, will be surprised to see him canonized in the title of the poem as "Saint Judas." The title simultaneously stimulates curiosity and encourages an open mind for the unorthodox interpretation of character that follows.

The sonnet is written in the first person. Readers of James Wright's later, more confessional poetry will expect the speaker of the poem to be Wright himself, but "Saint Judas" instead takes the point of view of the infamous traitor of the title. It is important to note that the persona of this poem is not to be confused with Saint Jude, another of Christ's apostles, who is known by the Catholic church as the patron saint of desperate cases. The Judas referred to here is the apostle Judas Iscariot, whose story, as it is traditionally told, appears in the Bible in Matthew 27:3-5. Like Robert Browning's murderer in "Porphyria's Lover," or Vladimir Nabokov's child molester in *Lolita* (1955), James Wright's "Saint Judas" is a character who could only arouse sympathy by being seen from the inside.

The narrative of the poem begins in the octave, where the reader finds Judas on his way to commit suicide. He has been momentarily sidetracked by the suffering of a man who has been beaten by a "pack of hoodlums." In his rush to help and give comfort, he forgets himself and his problems. He even forgets the sordid bargain in which he had earlier betrayed Christ to the Roman soldiers in the Garden of Gethsemane for thirty pieces of silver. Most important, he forgets his overwhelming despair.

In the sestet of the sonnet, Judas rushes to the recent victim of brutality, drops his rope and his suicidal intent, ignores the soldiers for whom he had so recently committed the highest treason, and succors the unfortunate man in his arms. It is then that he remembers the last supper that he had with Christ and the traitorous kiss with which he turned Christ over to the Romans. Even though he is haunted by these damning memories, even though he sees himself as "Banished from heaven" and "without hope," he still "held the man for nothing" in his arms. The poem ends with a poignant image of selfless humanity and absolute generosity of spirit.

Forms and Devices

"Saint Judas" is a pivotal poem in James Wright's canon. It is a stylistic bridge between the 1950's formalism of his first two books, *The Green Wall* (1957) and *Saint*

Judas (1959), and the freer, more colloquial verse of his later volumes, *The Branch Will Not Break* (1963) and *Shall We Gather at the River* (1968). This sonnet, which is both the title and the last poem of *Saint Judas*, is a powerful farewell to the traditional rhyme and meter of his early mentors, Edwin Arlington Robinson and Robert Frost, and a tentative welcome to the stark, unadorned diction and powerful imagery of his contemporaries, Robert Bly and William Carlos Williams.

"Saint Judas" relies heavily on the traditional poetic strategy of literary, historical, and religious allusion. Many of Wright's later poems deal with society's outcasts—the drunks, the murderers, the lonely, the alienated, and the discarded—but in "Saint Judas," Wright has taken on the Herculean task of vindicating the archetypical villain and outcast of Western culture: Judas Iscariot. Poets who use allusions know that they risk losing the attention of readers who do not have the requisite cultural background. "Saint Judas" will mean very little to the person who is unfamiliar with the life of Christ and his mercenary betrayal by one of his own disciples with a hypocritical gesture of affection. Traditional poets have always been willing to take the risk that using allusions entails in order to bring even stronger pleasure to those readers who are prepared for the intellectual challenge. It is a risk of which modern poets have become increasingly wary. "Saint Judas" is the last of Wright's poems in which he is willing to rely so completely on the power of archetypical material to inform his verse. It is the last of his poems that would inspire a critic to compare his work with Wordsworth's.

In "Saint Judas," Wright mixes a traditional use of allusion to older literature with the colloquial language of contemporary America. Despite its two-thousand-year-old subject, there is nothing archaic about this poem. Wright refers to the men who brutalize the "victim" of the poem as "hoodlums." He says that Judas forgot his "name," his "number." These simple, direct words force the reader to see the plight of Judas in modern terms. It is not enough, the diction suggests, to have compassion for the historical "Saint Judas"; it might also be necessary to reassess one's opinion of the downtrodden and the condemned of this time.

Themes and Meanings

"Saint Judas" is fundamentally a moral poem that deals with two of Wright's favorite themes: alienation and despair. Judas is alienated from the rest of humanity because of his despicable crime; the reader knows that he despairs, because at the opening of the poem, he is on his way to kill himself. Is there any hope? That is the unusual question that Wright thinks to ask, and it is the kind of question that distinguishes him from so many of the fashionably nihilistic poets of the 1960's. The poem seems to answer: Where there is life, there is hope.

Wright chooses to imagine a Judas who is outside the traditional theological context, who faces his life and death like any other man, and who makes moral choices right up to the moment when he must inevitably swing upon the ash tree. This Judas, confronted with another's suffering, does not play the role of the predictable villain of melodrama, but instead is envisioned as caught up in an act of humanity so complete that he loses himself entirely. If Judas Iscariot is capable of this, what acts might the man on death row be capable of performing? What might anyone be capable of doing?

"Saint Judas" is not only a reassessment of common notions of "the good man" but also a cautionary tale. It warns one not to judge others too harshly. Many people do not doubt that Judas Iscariot must be burning in hell; religion and common sense both seem to confirm this easy verdict. Wright, however, wants his readers to question what anyone can really know about the state of another's soul. One must wonder whether one fatal act condemns a man forever and whether there can be redemption through human kindness. Can even the worst criminal have a moment of goodness? The answer to all of these questions, from Wright's point of view, is made clear in the title, in which he sees Judas as an essentially good man, frail and prone to error like so many others. He made a terrible mistake, but he need not despair, because God, unlike man, is merciful in his judgments.

Cynthia Lee Katona

SAINTS IN THEIR OX-HIDE BOAT

Author: Brendan Galvin (1938-   )
Type of poem: Dramatic monologue
First published: 1992

The Poem

Saints in Their Ox-Hide Boat is a book-length dramatic monologue that owes much
to both the traditions of epic poetry and the traditions of hagiography, or the study of
saints' lives. The speaker of the poem is Saint Brendan the Navigator, who is relating
the tale of his famous voyage that may have taken him as far as North America.
Brendan tells his story to a young scribe, who sets down his words. The interplay between Brendan's story and his discursive comments to the scribe constitutes an ironic
commentary on the poem itself, which is both the history of a voyage and the history
of the poem's composition. The title of the poem refers to the voyage made by a group
of Irish monks led by Brendan on a type of pilgrimage called, alternately, "white martyrdom" or "blue martyrdom," as Galvin explains in his introduction to the poem. A
"white martyrdom" was a pilgrimage by a monk in the general sense, while a "blue
martyrdom" was specifically a pilgrimage by sea. Abandoning their monastic lives
and "every heart-softening face," the monks in the poem embark on a sea voyage in an
ox-hide boat called a curragh. The title, with its plural "saints" and singular "boat,"
suggests a substitution of the smaller community on the boat for the larger monastic
community in Ireland.

Although the characters in the poem are monks, the poem is in many respects a
poem of sailors and the sea. It begins with Brendan relating sailorly advice: how
to embark safely on a sea voyage, what time of year is fortuitous for sailing, and
what kind of sailors to take along. The last is of particular importance, and Brendan
includes a long list of the different sorts of people one ought not to select. He wants,
instead, "a few with sense/ long on muscle." He tells the young scribe this, Brendan
says, because he knows the boy was raised "among fields and hills." Galvin really
is conditioning the reader, however, to understand the demands of the sea and to
illustrate Brendan's thought process as he begins to assemble his crew. Most of
Galvin's readers, like the young scribe, are not familiar with the nautical concerns Brendan describes. Galvin wants to make clear, as he said of the monks in
his poem, that "these men were both religious contemplatives and hardy sailors." Like
all good poets, Galvin creates his own ideal readers by educating them about his
subject.

Preparations for the voyage, the "blue martyrdom," occupy a significant portion
of the poem and provide many comic moments. The sailors are a superstitious lot
and are quick to interpret natural occurrences as good or bad signs that will affect
when they depart. For example, on the first attempt to leave, Owen, the most superstitious of the sailor-monks, interprets a dream about a flock of sheep on a hill.

He questions Martin, the monk who had the dream, about whether the sheep were going up the hill or down, since the former—according to Owen—would mean good luck for a journey, while the latter would spell bad luck. Brendan mordantly observes that "next he'd be interpreting our sneezes." After discussing several other omens, including the crow of a rooster and an upset chair, Owen announces, "—No good will come of our dipping a single oar"; the trip is postponed. The next day, one of the sailors, Diarmuid, sees a hopping raven, considered a good omen. Brendan is hopeful, but then Conor tells of hearing a wren, which Owen believes cancels the good omen. After much discussion, the trip is again postponed. On the third day, one of the monks boards the boat from the left side, an act that Owen believes will bring terribly bad luck, but Brendan insists that they leave and even threatens them with physical violence.

The actual journey, when it finally begins, is decidedly not like other great epic sea journeys, and it contrasts particularly with the *Odyssey*. Homer's epic is filled with mythical creatures: Circe, Cyclops, Scylla, Charybdis, and gods and goddesses in human form. By contrast, Brendan's description of his voyage is pointedly realistic, and he seems more interested in relating the practical concerns of embarking on such a voyage than he is in relating the spiritual dimension of it. Once again, Galvin uses the character Owen and his superstition to contrast with Brendan's common sense. When the monks hear seals barking in the fog one day, Owen wrings his hands, crying that it is the "howling and slobbering" of damned souls. Brendan's realistic attitude is an important counter to Owen's superstition, because the latter's ideas often "found soft nests in his brothers'/ minds." Through contrast to Owen, it is clear why Brendan has become the leader of a growing group of monks. Owen is more closely allied to the pagan era fast receding into the past, while Brendan is helping to found the Christian future of Ireland.

Throughout the journey, natural phenomena undercut the supernatural. The monks witness an island floating in the air, for example, but Brendan correctly interprets it as "another trick of the sea." (Galvin provides a few explanatory notes to his poem, and he explains this natural phenomenon as an atmospheric disturbance called the Hillingar effect.) Often, the conflict between natural and supernatural explanations leads to comedy. For example, Owen tells the other monks about the magical clay on the island of Inishdhugan that has the ability to drive away the lice that have been plaguing them. The monks land and barter with Dhugan, the island's chief. They sprinkle the clay about the boat liberally, only to discover that it does not work at all; indeed, Brendan suspects that the clay made the lice "double their coupling." Similarly, Owen sees yellow eyes glaring at them from an iceberg and screams that Brendan has brought them "where souls/ are conducted after death." Brendan considers joking ("I hadn't recalled dying"), but instead responds with the measured explanation that the yellow eyes are those of an owl.

Along with the humor, Galvin provides realistic descriptions of what such a voyage must have been like. Even as readers laugh at the monks with their lice or at Owen's superstitions, they realize the discomfort and fear the sailors must experience. Galvin provides some graphic details about their life on the curragh: The monks eat their meals in the dark so they will not see "what's already eating what we're supposed to eat." More often, they do not even have food and must subsist on very small rations. Brendan prefers the days when the sea is rough, because only then do the seasick monks not complain of their hunger. Sickness runs rampant. One monk, Diarmuid, is swept overboard, and even Brendan finally succumbs to a feverish vision. Along with these obvious stresses on the monks is the stress of the mundane "memorizing the same/ five faces over and over" as they float day after day on the sea.

Forms and Devices

Saints in Their Ox-Hide Boat has two main antecedents, one of which was the book *The Brendan Voyage* (1978), written by Tim Severin about his re-creation of Saint Brendan's journey in the curragh. Some of the realistic details of Galvin's poem come from this source. The more important of the sources was a historical document, the *Voyage of St. Brendan*, which contains the legends, written in Latin, that the Brendan of the poem dismisses as exaggeration. That text gave Galvin material that his more realistic Brendan could deride and caution his young scribe to avoid. The Latin text probably also provided Galvin with inspiration for the many figures of speech he includes that are typical of writings about saints' lives and of epic poetry. He uses hyphenated epithets that are nearly Homeric in their intensity; warriors are "iron-chested ones," for example, and the sea is a "seal pasture where every angel-haunted/ abbey stone sinks out of memory."

Galvin's poetic imagery is likewise rich, and his use of metaphor noteworthy. Within the space of a few lines, Brendan describes humans as no more than a "clutch of fish bones," describes the Irish islands as a "stone beehive," and discusses his monastic vows as a forgoing of the "lit/ eye of a woman and the poured-milk/ turn of her neck." In just these few metaphors, Galvin illuminates Brendan's theology, the Irish geography, and the devotion required when one takes monastic vows.

Although the poem is nominally a dramatic monologue, and the entire poem is related by Brendan to the young scribe at the monastery, Galvin energizes his poem with exchanges between Brendan and others. At several points Brendan directly addresses the young scribe, giving his narrative a conversational tone. He reminds the scribe repeatedly to write the story down just as he tells it, with no embellishment. When commenting on the younger monks who accompanied him on the voyage, Brendan takes a moment to comment on the scribe's youth as well. On other occasions, Brendan relates dialogue and disputes between the various monks, particularly his ongoing dispute with Owen. Galvin indicates reported language without quotation marks, instead using dashes to distinguish them from Brendan's other description. The trip to the island of Inishdhugan is one such extended passage. The description of the monks' interaction with the canny old pagan, Dhugan, is notable for the amount of reported language given by Brendan. The passage has Dhugan asking riddles of the monks, followed by their often comic responses:

> —Well, riddle me this then. I move
> what cannot move itself. Though none can
> see me, all bow down to me. What am I?
>
> —God! One of the brothers whispered behind me.
>
> —Yes, God! the others encouraged.
>
> —Almighty God, I answered smiling at
> the thought I'd cornered him now.
>
> —The wind, he answered with a smirk.

By having Brendan quote the other characters, as in this passage, Galvin is able to give his poem a sense of immediacy without violating the rules of the dramatic monologue form.

Similarly, the poem culminates in a conversation just as Saint Brendan has arrived off the coast of North America. In the only truly supernatural moment of the poem, an angel appears to Brendan, and Galvin intersperses the monk's words with those of the heavenly visitor. The angel, though Brendan fears he may be a devil, provides a vision of the future. He forecasts Irish warfare and division, the potato famine, and the great emigration of the Irish to North America. They will need "the sanctuary of places like this," the angel says. This section of the poem is the most technically complex, for Brendan relates the conversation with the angel but also tells the reader what his thoughts were at the time. Because Brendan did not know if the angel could "listen inside as well as out," the scene is very tense, and the interspersing of the dialogue with Brendan's thoughts dramatizes his inner conflicts, particularly at the conclusion of the poem when the angel shakes him, shouting "—Say it, man! Out with it!" This suggests that the Angel *does* know what Brendan is thinking. Galvin indents Brendan's response both to draw attention to the great statement of faith that follows and to provide a fitting sense of closure to the poem:

> O Lord
> I have loved
> the Glory of
> Your house

The poem ends with no punctuation, as if to say that Brendan's hymn of praise to God does not cease but rises upward forever.

Themes and Meanings

Saints in Their Ox-Hide Boat has as a major theme the conflict between Christianity and paganism. Galvin, in his introduction to the poem, observes that during Saint Brendan's life there existed "no clear distinction between early Christian and late pagan." Brendan is clearly conscious of the way the "old persuasion" of pagan beliefs has lasted well into the early Christian era. This persistence is particularly obvious in the early part of the poem, as the monks are stalled by the numerous bad omens. While Brendan is part of his culture and is not immune to superstition, he grows frustrated with Owen, the exemplar of the superstitious sailor. Likewise, Brendan criticizes the tendency of scribes to populate their records of saints' lives with fantastic creatures. At several points, he addresses the young monk who is recording his story, and admonishes him to write it just as he tells it, "whether you consider it/ fantastical, or not fantastical enough."

Indeed, though Brendan reminds the boy not to create things or to exaggerate the difficulties, there is much in the monk's story that is fantastic, not the least of which is the journey itself. The idea of a group of monks traveling in a curragh and reaching the shores of North America seems unbelievable, though it is a journey that has been re-created in modern times.

Perhaps most difficult to understand is why Brendan went on the voyage at all. Indeed, Brendan himself questions his motives, wondering if it was pride that led him to embark on the "blue martyrdom" or if it was an honest attempt to find God. Brendan recognizes, too, it might partly be to escape the "hammering and dust" that accompanies the monastic community that has grown around his personality. Galvin, in his introduction to the poem, explains that abbots often found their desire to "maintain a small community" subverted by their own charisma. The society on land has become oppressive to Brendan, and he believes that he must "break from that abbey's yoke" to contemplate and come closer to God. It is ironic that so many retreat from society to Brendan's monastery in order to find God while the leader himself needs still more seclusion. Brendan mulls over the question of his own motives, as he says, "without arriving at a solid answer." After Diarmuid is swept overboard, he labels himself a "gambler with souls not my own." It is in part this sort of honesty and self-effacing criticism that makes Galvin's Brendan so sympathetic a character. When he describes "fishing/ for Diarmuid's soul with my prayers," the reader feels the sense of loss and culpability that Brendan feels. Similarly, when Brendan orders the scribe to "make me no miracles. I am no saint," his honesty is so convincing and so appealing that he seems a saint in spite of himself.

Finally, then, the poem is about exactly what it says it is about: a pilgrimage to find God. Because Galvin has presented Brendan throughout the poem as a realist, not prone to exaggeration or to flights of fancy, the most fantastic element of the poem, Brendan's vision of the future, seems believable. The scribe need not fabricate a miracle: Brendan provides him with one by describing the appearance of the angel, who says that North America will one day be a "sanctuary" for the Irish. Fittingly, the poem ends with words of Brendan that affirm his faith and, ironically, his sainthood.

Joe B. Fulton

THE SALUTATION

Author: Thomas Traherne (c. 1637-1674)
Type of poem: Lyric
First published: 1903, in *The Poetical Works of Thomas Traherne*

The Poem

In the contemplative lyric "The Salutation," Thomas Traherne celebrates the wonder of life through the eyes of a first-person speaker who has only recently become aware of life's gifts. The lyric consists of seven regular six-line stanzas, forty-two lines total. What begins as a celebration of existence becomes by the end a religious poem in praise of the Creator.

In the first stanza, the speaker addresses parts of his physical body—limbs, eyes, hands, and cheeks—to inquire why they were originally hidden from him. Where, he asks rhetorically, was his speaking tongue? The questions imply a common theme in Traherne's poetry: the pre-existence of the soul. He implies that the parts of his body have also been hidden from consciousness, that they too have been in existence. Thus what is celebrated is in one sense not pre-existence but a newly acquired mental awareness of existence.

In the second stanza, the speaker acknowledges that his pre-existence was unconscious, that he remained thousands of years beneath the dust in "Chaos" and now welcomes his lips, hands, eyes, and ears as newly discovered treasures. Acknowledging in the third stanza that he has been nothing, the speaker also welcomes sensory pleasures as joys he has discovered and experienced. Stanza 4 lauds the richness of these joys, comparing them metaphorically to gold and pearls. To the speaker it appears that human joints and veins contain more wealth than all the rest of the world.

Stanza 5 represents a major change of emphasis, a pivotal point in the lyric, for the speaker who has celebrated his sensory pleasures now reflects upon them as gifts from God. From nothingness, the speaker has arisen into a world of greater objects and substances—earth, seas, sky, day, sun, and stars. All of these, he declares, become his—presumably because he celebrates them, reflects upon them, and admires them.

In stanza 6, the speaker expresses his conviction that God has prepared all the wonders of the world for his existence and that all creation serves him. Mythically like an Eden, wide and bright, the world created for the speaker brings with it an assurance that God has adopted the speaker as his son and heir, that he has received title to a great legacy.

In the final stanza, the speaker rejoices in the novelty of his existence, the strangeness of all things outside himself that were created for him. The world is "fair," its contents "Treasures" and "Glories." The greatest wonder is that all was created for one who once was nothing. The speaker thus celebrates the Creator through praise of the creation and through his understanding of its purpose.

Forms and Devices

Among the poem's most creative conventions is the introduction of the first-person speaker. In the first stanza, reference to his "Speaking Tongue" suggests that he has just begun speaking, like an infant who has become aware of his own body and senses and is struck with wonder at their power. The speaker does not remain at that stage, however; he quickly develops a sense of his being and of mental categories (abstractions) such as time. He is able to admire the universe outside himself and to discern the purpose of its creation. Optimistically finding everything created pleasant and good, he celebrates the Creator through celebrating creation. Throughout his development, the speaker maintains a tone of naïve and innocent wonder as he celebrates himself, the world, its purposes, and the Creator. Thus, Traherne presents a developing intellect from childhood to maturity, but the speaker retains the child's sense of wonder and optimism throughout. In his Eden there is neither a serpent nor a Fall; the fictive speaker's mind develops and expands without any awareness of guilt and sin.

Each of the poem's six-line stanzas, rhyming *ababcc*, exhibits an unusual metrical pattern: two iambic feet in line 1, four in line 2, five in line 3, three in line 4, and five in lines 5 and 6. Traherne also uses repetition to create emphasis and conviction. In the final stanza, the word "strange," or one of its variants, occurs six times, employing the schemes of repetition called "ploce" and "polyptoton." The device creates a tone of incantation that urges acceptance of the poem's message.

The poem's diction is simple, even plain, reminiscent of the Puritan plain style of the seventeenth century. Adjectives such as little, fair, bright, glorious, and wide are typical of the poem's simple and basic vocabulary. Nouns, on the other hand, suggest biblical origins of the plain style and add to the religious and elemental emphasis created by the poem: God, Eden, dust, gold, glories, joys, eternity, chaos, abyss. The rich imagery is dominated by sight images, some quite general, others specific and vivid. Earth, seas, light, and day contrast with the more specific gold, pearl, cheeks, and limbs.

Figures of speech seem conventionally chosen in order to make abstract ideas more concrete or to heighten the reader's sense of value. The limbs of boys, for example, become sacred treasures, and the world as prepared by God becomes a glorious store.

Themes and Meanings

Although Traherne belongs among the Metaphysical poets, he is among those Metaphysicals more accurately termed meditative or contemplative poets. "The Salutation" best fits the contemplative poem designation, for its speaker does not engage in a disciplined, structured meditation for the purpose of self-improvement. Instead, he turns his attention to objects outside himself in order to cultivate a sense of wonder and praise their existence. For its effect, the poem depends upon the reader's ability to share his profound sense of naïve wonder when viewing his own existence and that of the external world.

Although the speaker assumes a kind of quiescent pre-existence of the soul, this theme is more subdued than in other Traherne poems, such as "Wonder" and

"Shadows in the Water." The speaker views himself as having existed beneath dust and chaos for thousands of years, as having been nothing. Such a minimal conception of pre-existence heightens the wonder by contrasting the speaker's state with the richness and diversity of life on earth. Through identifying himself with dust and nothingness, the speaker magnifies his existence.

Like many lyrics, this one belongs among those that praise external nature and contemplate Dame Kind, with a view toward belonging or uniting with nature, as the more conventional mystic seeks unity with God. The poem attempts to portray all being as miraculous—a source of contemplation—and it conveys Traherne's own sense of wonder at the mystery of life. It follows his assumption that to praise and celebrate creation, to unite with it, is somehow to possess it. Contemplation, an individual act, enables him to view the world as created for man the individual, and the speaker seems to realize that only through contemplation can he experience a truth of this kind: "The Sun and Stars are mine; if those I prize."

The wonder and mystery that the speaker celebrates are made partially understandable through his grasp of divine purpose, a canon of faith with the speaker. The speaker can believe that everything was created by God not merely for man as a species but also for himself as an individual. Thus one finds in the poem a mystical version of Protestant individualism. Instead of the more common Puritan version in which the anxiety-ridden individual considers himself the center of a powerful drama of God and Satan struggling for his soul, with the outcome in doubt, Traherne presents the drama of the individual celebrating and seeking union with a totally benign creation, serenely assured that all is directed by God.

In an anthropocentric perspective, he views all of creation as a preparation for his own existence. Resorting to the myth of creation, the speaker depicts the world as an Eden prepared by God for a single soul and as evidence that he has been chosen as God's heir. In this Eden one finds no trace of the Fall, no evidence of fallen nature, only a fair creation prepared by God for man's benefit. The speaker naïvely expresses his own response to the strangeness in the form of a concluding paradox:

> But that they mine should be, who nothing was,
> That Strangest is of all, yet brought to pass.

In addition to celebrating the wonders of creation, the poem focuses on the drama of the individual soul. Just as he perceives no evidence of the pain and suffering of life, the speaker feels little unease regarding his own salvation. Yet as God's heir he must play his part in the mythic Eden of creation. Salvation is an individual matter, and the speaker appears to find a key element as one involving optimistic praise and identification of the self with creation.

Stanley Archer

SAME TIME

Author: Octavio Paz (1914-1998)
Type of poem: Meditation
First published: 1962, as "El Mismo Tiempo," in *Salamandra*; English translation
collected in *The Collected Poems of Octavio Paz: 1957-1987*

The Poem

"Same Time" is a long poem of 184 lines in free verse. Its format represents a break with Octavio Paz's early practice; under the influence of Stéphane Mallarmé, he had begun to think of a poem as a visual object. Accordingly, he emphasized white space through the use of short lines, occasionally allowing a single word to suffice for the line. Except for question marks, the poem has no punctuation. The title introduces one of the poem's chief themes: time's movement in relation to the individual and to poetry.

The first-person narrator inhabits a city of ceaseless flux, an impersonal flow of traffic in which glimpses may be had of people, for example, the couple by the iron railing and the nameless old man talking to himself. The city has alternately fascinated and repelled poets since Charles Baudelaire (1821-1867). Paz was captivated by T. S. Eliot's use of the theme in *The Waste Land* (1922). Poets are intrigued by the phenomenon of an individual consciousness boxed in by millions of other individuals with whom there is no communication: "To walk among people/ with the open secret of being alive." The poem was written in Paris, but memory takes the narrator to Mexico City, where the cars become trolleys carrying passengers from the Zócalo, Mexico City's main square, to the suburbs.

The narrator invokes the memory of walking Mexico City's pitted streets during the rainy season, June to September. His eyes lift to the clouds racing through the Mexican night sky, and their shape enraptures him; they become "Mistresses of eyes." Unbidden, a word comes to mind: "alabaster." The moment represents a transition from passive onlooker to user of words: The poet will make "castles of syllables." Writing—the creation of poetry—supplies an identity to this single person surrounded by millions.

Today, in the flow of the city, the poet still writes, shuttling words back and forth across the page, but with a newfound perspective: The world exists independently of him. The lyrical "I" is only one pulse beat in the throbbing river of humanity. Advice given by two philosophers, Mexico's José Vasconcelos and Spain's José Ortega y Gasset, reinforces the need for thinking and meditation in order to give meaning to life. Writing is a solution. To record the beauty of the world, the sun sinking into the river, the feminine cluster of grapes, revives the poet.

In these moments of beauty, time may be preempted. Images return, even though time does not, and their recurrence supplies a sense of continuity. When the words for poetry appear, there takes place a fullness of presence, of time within time that is a moment of transparency.

Forms and Devices

To show that there may be another kind of time within the chronological time that defines all living creatures, Paz resorted to a spiral-like poetic form. The poem's lack of punctuation means that the conventional grammatical signposts (commas, periods, semicolons) will not be present to convey a linear approach. Less circular than *Piedra de sol* (1957; *Sun Stone*, 1963), which opens and closes with the same lines, "Same Time" nevertheless begins and ends in a way that suggests a movement from a point—the stillness outside the city—to a similar point at a higher level of consciousness: "time within time/ still/ with no hours no weight no shadow/ without past or future." The effect is reminiscent of a spiral whose movement is accentuated by the abundance of empty spaces facing the readers' eyes. One also can note how the negation of the first line, "It is not the wind," is echoed in the closure, "It is not memory."

A single-word line provides special emphasis. "Lit," "bird," and "clouds" suggest the lightness that is pointing toward "alabaster" and, ultimately, "transparency." "Alabaster" occurs at the midpoint of the poem. On one level, it is an allusion occasioned by Paz's reading of Rubén Darío's *Prosas profanas* (1896; *Profane Hymns and Other Poems*, 1922): "Heavenly alabaster inhabited by stars:/ God is reflected in such sweet alabaster." This is the reason for the word's favored position, for it is such sweet whiteness that prepares the way for the evocation of transparency. "Alabaster" appears alone twice, and it represents an axis in the poem, after which the narrator discovers an identity through poetry and heightened perception.

Effective images are scattered throughout: Some are clearly based on a real or remembered moment, such as the "blackbird on a gray stone," and some are ambiguous, such as "three leaves fall from a tree." The memory of the streetcars stimulates a cluster of metaphors. The "trolley-poles" call to mind "Black rays," their sparks are "small tongues of fire," and the noise they make on the way to the suburbs is compared to crashing towers. Other isolated metaphors sparkle throughout this long poem: The sweep and grandeur of poetry (or music) is captured in "castles of syllables"; the roundness of grapes suggests "feminine clusters."

As the narrator walks mentally through the cities of his life, he remembers many objects: trees, cars, houses, a dog, a bird, the fig tree. For the most part, these objects exist as images in the poet's memory, but occasionally they acquire the status of symbols. The sky is omnipresent, clear (without "a wrinkle"), filling up with clouds that hint of gestation and prepare for the near-miraculous appearance of the word "alabaster." Paz has prepared the reader for the various symbolic meanings of this word: purity, lightness, beauty, softness, celestial presence. This symbol, in turn, converts into the "word," which for Paz means poetry, music, art, and creativity.

Anaphora, the repetition of words or phrases at the beginning of a line, is used at the beginning and end of the poem. "It is not the wind," it is not the sea, but "It is the city," and at the conclusion, one reads that "It is not memory," but "It is transparency."

Themes and Meanings

"Same Time" is a showpiece for several of Paz's favorite motifs: seeing, writing, and time. The tradition of the poet-seer, an individual with special ways of seeing, goes back to the European Romantics. Paz's version of it is shaped by his experiences in Mexico and India and his vast knowledge of Western literature.

The recurring moment of transparency in Paz's poetry refers to those seconds in which his vision allows him to see beauty in great detail and glimpse extraordinary relationships between words and objects. It is unsummoned, as he says, but perhaps triggered by another word ("alabaster") or object ("cloud"). With this opened eye, the poet explores beauty, his gaze "sustains loveliness" and seems to effect a change upon his notion of time. Moments of transparency for Paz are not unlike those moments of epiphany mentioned by James Joyce and explored in loving detail by Spanish poet Juan Ramón Jiménez.

Transparency provides the optimum moment in which poetry can crystallize. The "thin unsummoned transparency" that appears in the middle of the poem facilitates creativity, a fact that the poet has long recognized ("You said") but not always adhered to ("You made nothing"). In these states of lucidity in which light (and here one must think of the strong sunlight of his native Mexico) passes through all barriers, the poet can build castles out of syllables.

The heightened sense of awareness that Paz calls transparency bestows on the moment a sense of presence. This intuition of otherness is not memory, the poet carefully notes, but rather it is as if time had acquired a new dimension. Within the relentless chronological nature of the time that defines people may be another time in which the phenomena of the world are weightless (like the bee that does not cast a shadow in the Jorge Luis Borges story "The Secret Miracle"), and the time neatly divided into past, present, and future melds into something indivisible. In such an instant, one is spared the need to talk about time passing: "Perhaps time doesn't pass/ images of time pass." T. S. Eliot, whose poetry deeply impressed Paz, begins "Burnt Norton," the first of the *Four Quartets* (1943), with a similar meditation on the nature of time that includes the lines: "If all time is eternally present/ All time is unredeemable."

There is no need to reclaim time if such visions can be granted to poets and their readers. "Same Time" points to this moment: "It is not the wind . . . it is not memory . . . it is transparency."

Howard Young

SAN ILDEFONSO NOCTURNE

Author: Octavio Paz (1914-1998)
Type of poem: Lyric
First published: 1976, as "Nocturno de San Ildefonso," in *Vuelta (1969-1975)*; English translation collected in *The Collected Poems of Octavio Paz: 1957-1987*, 1987

The Poem

"San Ildefonso Nocturne," written in free verse, is divided into four stanzas of unequal length. Octavio Paz once again uses punctuation, a practice that he had abandoned in previous books. He also returns to the circular form he introduced so successfully in 1957 in *Piedra de sol (Sun Stone*, 1963). "San Ildefonso Nocturne" begins with the poet viewing through the window of his room a garish display of neon advertising in an unnamed city. Parts 2 and 3 move into the narrator's past as a boy in Mexico City, and part 4 closes with the poet once again in his room watching the neon advertisements flashing in the night. In *Sun Stone*, the same six lines open and close the poem; in "San Ildefonso Nocturne," a similar effect is achieved through the repetition of a scene—the poet at the window.

In his hotel room, the narrator sees the neon lights of advertisements spray the blackness of his window. Preoccupied as always by communication, he connects the advertising signs with the syllable clusters he is putting down on his page. The words turn into ants; there is a tunnel that will lead him somewhere. "What does it [the night] want?" he asks at the conclusion of part 1.

The night wishes to summon him to Mexico City in the year 1931, when he would have been seventeen. Squinting lights contrast with the neon glare of part 1. Pockets of characteristic poverty greet his eyes; children cover themselves with unsold newspapers. A lascivious clatter of heels, metonymy for a woman of the night, provokes two allusions explained by the poet. The lines *"a sky of soot/ the flash of a skirt"* are taken from the Mexican poet Ramón López Velarde, and the French phrase *"C'est la mort—ou la morte"* ("It is death—or the dead woman") comes from Gérard de Nerval's sonnet about Artemis, the huntress. Both allusions suggest prostitution.

The poet now refers specifically to San Ildefonso, a college built by the Jesuits in the seventeenth century, and his memory evokes the buried idols and canals of the Aztec city of Tenochtitlán covered by present-day Mexico City and its vast central plaza, the Zócalo. He recalls two novels he read as a boy, Fyodor Dostoevski's *Bratya Karamazovy* (1879-1880; *The Brothers Karamazov*, 1912)—thus the reference to Alyosha K (Karamazov), the saintly one of the brothers—and Stendhal's *Le Rouge et le noir* (1830; *The Red and the Black*, 1898), whose hero was Julien Sorel.

Part 3 recognizes that the man who writes is the small boy, and the narrator bemoans the failure of his generation to have any positive effect upon the world. Part 4 stresses the power of language, as Paz is seen again writing at the window, and introduces a new personage, his sleeping wife; she represents nature, and with her he can lose his fear of death as he flows with her body.

Forms and Devices

Paz achieves his circular structure by means of many devices. Not only does the scene remain the same, but also the vocabulary duplicates itself. The poem commences with an unusual use of the verb "to invent": "In my window night/ invents another night." A few lines later, the city "invents" the lights, and in part 4, the sleeping wife "invents herself." This motif contributes to the circular motion of the poem. Paz also reprises metaphors and sometimes translates them. What were "Sign-seeds" in the city's night window are flatly stated at the closure of the poem to be part of the "commercial sky." The "high-voltage calligraphy" of the first scene goes through the stage of "squinting lights" in the evocation of the poet's adolescence to the straightforward description of reality's "commercial sky."

From his reading of T. S. Eliot's *The Waste Land* (1922), Paz learned about allusions and the practice of footnoting them, which he does in the case of the quotations from López Velarde and Nerval. He takes it for granted, however, that his readers will understand the references to Alyosha Karamazov and Julien Sorel. Part 2 contains buried allusions to Eliot's "Burnt Norton" ("galleries of echoes") and *The Waste Land* ("broken images").

The metaphors that describe the neon lights are especially arresting. Their profusion suggests a convulsed carnival; the endless flickering contained within forms "nomadic geometries." They represent a tension in the poet's mind ("false heaven/ hell of industry") and beckon with the promise of the benefits of progress and the predicament it brings.

Movement between various points of time is one of the poem's most intriguing aspects. The poem is about a series of returns, and it is significant that it appeared in a collection that Paz called *Vuelta* (*Return*, 1987), an account of his coming back to Mexico after years of living in the Far East and Europe. The first point in time is the present of the narrator, and the city whose lights he contemplates, although unnamed, is probably Mexico City. The tunnel at the end of part 1 will lead him to a point in adolescence, and the space is the Zócalo, Mexico's huge main square ("vast as the earth"). The Zócalo is rich in reminders of his country's colonial past (the cathedral's façade is a petrified garden), but it also sits upon the site of the ancient Aztec capital Tenochtitlán in an area once covered by canals. The transfer made by the reader and narrator is expressed in the line "sun turned to time,/ time turned to stone," in which the elements of life (sun), time, and history (stone) blend together.

The nocturne is haunted by history—that of the narrator and his friends—full of friendly ghosts that in his memory become flesh.

Themes and Meanings

One of the resonant words of this poem is the verb "invent." The night invents another night, the city invents signs, streetlights invent yellow pools of light, and the sleeping woman invents herself. More than an example of personification, Paz's use of *inventar* underlines the sense of magic and heightened awareness that has always concerned him as a poet. He intends the verb to carry its basic meaning, "to come across suddenly" (like the moments of transparency in his other poems), which implies the use of the imagination, another faculty that fascinates him.

The poem affords its author a chance to take stock of himself and to compare the present-day author, halfway through his life, with the seventeen-year-old crossing the Zócalo. The literary heroes he remembers bear special significance. Alyosha Karamazov and Julien Sorel assisted him in the invention of bolts of lightning to hurl against the century, and they stand for two sides of the poet himself: Alyosha, the pure in heart, stands as a buffer between his family and the world; and Julien, the ambitious hero from the provinces, has an enormous drive to succeed.

The "we" in this section refers to Paz and his cohorts, who, like all young idealists, made up in virtue what they were lacking in humility. As is usually the case, however, their desires for reform were betrayed by their own weaknesses as well as, in the case of Mexico, the entrenched strength of the system. Paz carries denouncement to the level of hyperbole, a zigzag of reconciliations, apostasies, recantations, and bewitchments.

He refuses to accept the possibility of blame. History itself, he writes, is the error. This assertion presumes that outside the accumulation of failures generally recorded by history there is an intimate sort of history—"everyone's anonymous heartbeat"—which is unrepeatable and identical. This core of personal human experience allows the poet to assert that "Truth/ is the base of a time without history."

It is such moments that the poet Octavio Paz has tirelessly sought and described. That is why he writes. Faced with the Hamlet-like dilemma of thought versus action, he chooses "the act of words." In the making of poetry, he enters once again into history, but neither as a direct participant nor as a mere bystander. He sees poetry as a "suspension bridge between history and truth" (events and intimacy), a way of coming and going—slightly frightening, as are all suspension bridges over the canyon between thought and action.

At the conclusion of part 4, Paz introduces one of his most important themes: the glory of the female body and the love that it represents. The union of individuals in love (the "truth of two," as he calls it in *Sun Stone*) redeems the individual from oblivion. Gazing at the form of his sleeping wife, he believes her to be copying nature, its islands and lagoons (such was Tenochtitlán when the Spaniards came). He knows that truth does perhaps lie outside of history: It is "the palpable mystery of the person."

Howard Young

SAPPHICS AGAINST ANGER

Author: Timothy Steele (1948-   )
Type of poem: Lyric
First published: 1986, in *Sapphics Against Anger and Other Poems*

The Poem

Timothy Steele's "Sapphics Against Anger" is composed of seven stanzas written in the sapphic form of four unrhymed lines. Sapphic verse is organized around a special strophe form. A poem in sapphic strophes always appears in four-line stanzas with a short fourth line. The title of this poem has to do with seven sapphic strophes written against, or in opposition to, feelings of anger. As the title poem of the collection, the piece reflects some of the themes of the whole book, especially in its apparently autobiographical first-person speaker, which in this instance is also true to the first-person voice of Sappho's own poetry.

The general theme of "Sapphics Against Anger" is the need to control anger, one of the strongest of human emotions. The poem serves as a caution and a reflection for the speaker, who exorcises his anger through the writing of this disciplined form. The tone of the poem becomes lighthearted as it progresses, and a secondary theme, of not taking oneself too seriously, is established. The first stanza sets up the conflict between perspective and impulse, which governs the entire poem. The speaker wishes when angered to be "near a glass of water" to douse the flames of his temper. He longs to remember the importance of silence as a means of controlling what might be an ill-considered reaction. The poem plays off the interrelations of the temper, temperament, and temptation.

Continuing in a meditative manner, the speaker attempts to learn a lesson from the philosophers and poets who have written previously about controlling the passions, especially anger. He first invokes Aristotle, the Greek philosopher, who believed that giving in to anger only made one respond with anger more readily. The speaker then places himself in a scene from Dante's *La divina commedia* (c. 1320; *The Divine Comedy*, 1802) in the *Inferno* section of the poem. He imagines himself being talked about by Vergil and Dante. Vergil, in stanza 4, says to Dante, that the speaker of "Sapphics Against Anger" is suffering now because he "at the slightest provocation,/ Slammed phone receivers down, and waved his arms like/ A madman." Vergil compares the destructive power of the speaker's uncontrolled outburst with that of invaders, such as Attila the Hun, known as the Scourge of God, who invaded Europe in the fifth century, and Genghis Khan, the Mongol conquerer of the thirteenth century. The speaker realizes, while overhearing the two poets' fictional conversation, how easily he can and will ruin his own marriage by persisting in being angry about everything.

The balance of stanza 5 leads to the poem's conclusion in stanzas 6 and 7. First, the speaker wants to resist giving in to self-pity. Then he concludes that he should let the anger wash over him as easily as the soap runs off the dishes and down into the sink drain. Finally in stanza 7, the speaker decides that all emotions, including anger, might have places in a balanced and well-ordered life. He reconciles himself to the idea that strong feelings can be a motivator to live better as much as they can be destructive elements in personal relationships.

Forms and Devices

Steele's facility with traditional poetic devices and forms enlivens his poetry on the themes of nature and human nature. In "Sapphics Against Anger," he re-creates both the formal and the tonal qualities of grace and force associated with the Greek poet Sappho's own verse of the seventh or sixth century B.C.E. Her "Homage to Aphrodite" is a hymn of invocation in which the poet describes Aphrodite's qualities and her previous acts of goodness toward the speaker, and states the aim of the speaker—to ask a new favor based on their past relationship. Sappho's first-person narrator in this poem probably refers to herself, and the development of her request is presented over three distinct periods of time. The structure of the poem encompasses past and present with an offer of a plan for the future. Likewise, Steele uses a first-person, apparently autobiographical speaker and moves the anger he experiences across three time periods, from the present to the past and then to future implications.

The sapphic stanza, characterized by three sapphic lines and a fourth called the adonic, was probably adapted by the Latin poet Catallus from his reading of Sappho's odes. Through Horace, the sapphic form became popular with first Roman poets, then later European poets who studied Latin poetry for models of expression and for poetic forms. Steele's sapphic stanzas follow the tradition of four unrhymed lines per strophe. The metrical structure of the three sapphic lines is two trochees (one long followed by one short syllable) and a dactyl (one long and two short syllables) completed by two more trochees. The adonic line features one dactyl and one trochee, which highlights the rhythm. Following Horace, there are substitutions in the first, second, and third lines among the stanzas to enhance the flow. While the meter is intricate, the use of it is subtle and unobtrusive. Steele's facility with the form may be favorably compared with that of Robert Frost or Philip Larkin.

The poem presents a problem, which it sets about to solve. The hypothesis, revealed in the initial stanza, is that anger is a problem for human nature. This issue is more fully studied in stanzas 2-6. The conclusion, found in stanza 7, is optimistic, stressing how impulses can be controlled through reason. The syllogism runs thus: If anger controls people, then people only make trouble for themselves by giving in to it; therefore, self-control allows people to master what might ruin them and those whom they love.

In the repetition of the invocational phrase "May I," located in stanzas 1-3 and stanza 5, Steele employs the rhetorical device known as anaphora. Steele advances his desires by degrees from wanting to stop being angry, to looking for proof that anger is wrong, to finally putting his feelings to "good purpose" by learning from his errors in judgment. When Vergil cites the examples of Attila and Genghis Khan in stanza 4, he uses an obsolete form of anaphora, known as asphaleia, in which examples are cited in support of an idea, not to make the claim or to confirm its validity.

The language of the poem, like its descriptive qualities, is clear and direct. Steele does not use extended metaphors, the symbolism is easily interpreted, and the use of allusions is not exceptionally complex. From textual clues, the reader knows that Attila and Genghis Khan were destructive forces, not to mention spoilers among the people they conquered. The allusion to *The Divine Comedy* is also general enough not to elude most readers.

Finally, Steele uses enjambment in both of its meanings. First, he completes ideas introduced in the first or second lines in the third or fourth lines of the stanza. Second, he blends the middle of the poem, stanzas 3-5, together, carrying over the narrative of literary and historical proofs of the destructive power of anger, from one stanza to the next. Stanzas 1, 2, 6, and 7 are complete as sentences and individual thoughts. The balancing between enjambment and end-stopped stanzas gives the speaker a certain decisiveness and creates a pace of hurry and rest.

Themes and Meanings

In "Sapphics Against Anger," the speaker, who seems inclined to rush to judgments and jump to conclusions, is forced to pause and reflect on the harm of yielding to negative emotions. He envisions ruining his marriage with his angry reactions and his capacity to exaggerate common situations into warlike moments. In the poem, the speaker develops a strategy for understanding and controlling his anger, which builds with each stanza.

The setting of the poem suggests an argument occurring over dinner and a simmering down as the speaker washes the dishes. Through this ordinary act of cleaning up, the speaker realizes the degree of his own mess and gains a clear perspective. The rising and falling patterns of the sapphic stanzas imitate the emotional ebb and flow of the speaker's thoughts as they reflect the pitch of the poem and its rhythm.

The speaker, at the beginning of the poem, does not possess any special insight into human nature, but by stanza 7, he is more aware that he must be responsible for the intended as well as the unintended consequences of his anger. Vergil's observation that anger caused the "poor dope" to ruin his marriage is the turning point in the poem. From that point on, the elements of the poem join to enable speaker to realize he must change.

Steele writes about the complexity of human nature in "Sapphics Against Anger." He makes the speaker neither a hero nor a villain; rather, he is an ordinary man, expressing a common failure, who sees a need to mend his ways before it is too late. The speaker finds his hope in the metaphoric cleaning of the dishes, as his old self swirls away with the soap and the dirt from the plates. In the end, the speaker is aware of his powers, both intellectual and emotional, to lead with compassion, not to be led by his anger.

Beverly Schneller

A SATIRE AGAINST MANKIND

Author: John Wilmot, earl of Rochester (1647-1680)
Type of poem: Satire
First published: 1679; collected in *Poems on Several Occasions*, 1680

The Poem

"A Satire Against Mankind," sometimes called "A Satire Against Reason and Man-kind" or simply "Satire," is one of John Wilmot, earl of Rochester's best-known po-ems. Written in iambic pentameter with a slightly irregular rhyme scheme (rhyming couplets occasionally give way to triplets), it is a humorous but bitter denunciation of human nature and all its vain pretensions to wisdom and virtue. The first forty-five lines of the poem form a general reflection on the failings of reason, which misleads and deceives people. People believe themselves to be eminently wise, but they are in fact the greatest of fools. Reason is compared to an *ignis fatuus* (literally a "false fire," or will-o'-the-wisp) that leads people through the treacherous landscapes of their own minds. Clever people who profess to be "wits" are singled out for particular criticism, wit being decried as "vain frivolous pretence."

Rochester then introduces an interlocutor, a "formal Band, and Beard," or conven-tional, venerable clergyman, who agrees with the speaker in the poem that wit is ab-horrent, but who takes issue with him for railing against humankind and reason in general. This interlocutor praises humankind as being made in God's image and pos-sessing souls, which, he says, raise people above the beasts by allowing them to com-prehend the universe, Heaven, and Hell.

The speaker retorts that people are mites who presume to compare their brief lives to the infinite. Humanity makes up its own cosmic mysteries and then solves them. The speaker is contemptuous of philosophers who prefer their cloisters to the wide world, and who spend their time thinking because they are incapable of doing.

The speaker distinguishes between false reason and right reason, which exists only insofar as it governs action and helps people enjoy life. This "right" reason comes from the senses; for example, the speaker's right reason tells him to eat when he is hungry, whereas humankind's more common false reason says to wait until the clock indicates that it is the hour to dine. The speaker will allow that there is some value in reason if it is this right reason, but that humankind, in general, is still contemptible. People, he says, are worse than beasts who act on instinct. Beasts prey on other beasts for food, but humans prey on other humans by betraying them wantonly, out of hypoc-risy and fear. Humans lust for power to protect themselves from other people. The concept of honesty is laughable, because an honest person will be cheated and de-spised. Politicians, he says, are venal and corrupt, and raise their friends and family rather than promote the good of the country. Church leaders are sinful hypocrites who preach heartily against sin but are really grasping and adulterous.

In the final stanza, the speaker claims that there may exist a humble, pious, honest person, and if he were to meet such a person he would be glad to recant this whole diatribe and pay homage to honesty; yet if there is such a person it would only prove that "Man differs more from man, than man from beast."

Forms and Devices

Rochester supports his satire with vivid and sometimes fanciful images and metaphors, many of which extend for line after line. His images are often deliberately ridiculous, so as to point out the ridiculousness of human pretensions. When he describes reason as "an *ignis fatuus* of the mind," for example, he describes how it leads the stumbling follower through "fenny bogs, and thorny brakes," over "Mountains of whimseys" to a "boundless sea" where he tries desperately to stay afloat on books and to "swim with bladders of philosophy." Some of the humorous comparisons are more barbed; wits, he says "are treated just like common whores,/ First they're enjoyed, and then kicked out of doors." Combining his criticism with humor makes it more palatable to the reader, and ensures that the poem will be taken more as a clever satire than as a vicious diatribe.

Rochester's intent is not entirely to amuse, though. Many of his images are wickedly persuasive as they expose the darker side of human nature. He compares people to beasts who are armed by nature with teeth and claws, and says, "Man, with smiles, embraces, friendships, praise,/ Unhumanely, his fellow's life betrays." He chooses as his examples of humankind the types who are supposed to be the most just and least self-interested of men. The statesman, he says, should "his needful flattery direct,/ Not to oppress, and ruin, but to protect." Instead, the statesman is proud and corrupt, receives bribes, and advances his family's interests over the country's. Clergymen receive the same satirical treatment. Rochester asks, "Is there a churchman who on God relys?/ Whose life, his faith, and doctrine justifies?" Rochester's answer is an emphatic no. The clergyman, he says, "from his pulpit, vents more peevish lies,/ More bitter railing scandals, calumnies,/ Than at a gossiping are thrown about." The clergymen is, moreover, proud, licentious, and greedy. By choosing as his particular subjects figures who should be examples of virtue in the community, Rochester broadens his satire from the individual to society.

Themes and Meanings

Rochester lived at the dawn of the Enlightenment, a time when new scientific discoveries and new ways of thinking were sweeping aside long-held traditional beliefs. Rochester was probably very familiar with Thomas Hobbes's *Leviathan* (1651), and much of his poetry seems to reflect a Hobbesian influence. It was in Rochester's era that the traditional notion of humanity being at the center of a divinely ordained universe, in which God took an active and pervasive interest, was replaced by a new vision of the cosmos as a vast, impersonal world, in which the role of humankind was minor. God was still a presence in this new vision, but He was seen as being like a clockmaker; He created the world, set it in motion, and sat back to watch impartially as it operates.

In such an intellectual environment, doubt of human's importance and distrust of, or contempt for, older ideas of people's divine nature as common in literature. "A Satire Against Mankind" is a compelling and particularly dark enunciation of these doubts. Rochester mocks humankind for thinking that the gift of reason raises them to a status close to the divine: "This supernatural gift, that makes a mite,/ Think he is the image of the Infinite:/ Comparing his short life, void of all rest,/ To the Eternal, and the ever blest." He sneers at human intellectual pretensions: "This busy, puzzling, stirrer up of doubt,/ That frames deep mysteries, then finds 'em out."

Rochester does not reject humankind and its pretensions to reason as completely worthless, however; he expresses a firm belief in human ability to know the immediate environment, via the senses. In this sense, he is a true product of the Enlightenment, in that he trusts empirical evidence and observable experience above all metaphysical speculations. He says: "Our sphere of action, is life's happiness,/ And he who thinks beyond, thinks like an ass." Rochester objects to human presumption in believing that one can understand cosmic mysteries and the nature of the universe simply because, as a human, one is capable of thought.

Rochester's satire seems to spring as much from pain at human weakness as from contempt for human follies. The final stanza is a kind of apology (in some early texts it is shown as a separate addendum to the main part of the satire) in which Rochester says that meeting a truly virtuous, modest, and pious man would readily convince him to revise his views on humankind. One senses that he truly wishes to discover such a good person and would be glad to "adore those shrines of virtue" if he could. Yet even such a paragon would not entirely convince him of humankind's redeemability; if such a person did exist, it would only prove that there is more difference among individual people than there is between human and beast. The whole poem, despite its stinging criticism of human vice and weakness, is tinged with sadness at human imperfections and inability to make sense of anything beyond one's immediate sensory perceptions. At the end of one's life, Rochester says, "Old age, and experience, hand in hand,/ Lead him to death, and make him understand,/ After a search so painful, and so long,/ That all his life he has been in the wrong." It is this heartfelt undertone of pain and sorrow at the human condition that tempers the vitriolic condemnation of humanity and makes "A Satire Against Mankind" both a classic statement of the ethos of Rochester's era and a timeless meditation on the nature of humanity.

Catherine Swanson

SCENTED HERBAGE OF MY BREAST

Author: Walt Whitman (1819-1892)
Type of poem: Lyric
First published: 1860, in *Leaves of Grass*, third edition

The Poem

In "Scented Herbage of My Breast," as in the other poems in the collection entitled *Leaves of Grass*, the poet Walt Whitman adopts a mask or persona through whom he speaks. The voice of this persona assumes various tones, usually ones that suggest a robust, celebratory, all-embracing stance toward life. In this particular lyric poem, the persona addresses himself to herbage, or grass, a symbol that is at the heart of the volume of poetry in which this poem appears.

The speaker begins by noting the timelessness of the grass, whose perennial roots are not frozen in the winter and whose blooms reappear every year. Looking at this grass, the persona says that he is reminded of both death and love, two realities that are, for him, beautiful and reminders of still another reality, life. As he muses on the relationship among beauty, death, and life, he observes that he is unable to prefer death or life, for he sees them as intricately connected by the cycle of life-death-life that pervades Whitman's poetic vision.

His reflections on this cycle compel him to announce his role as a spokesperson for himself and his comrades. As if he is blowing a bugle, initiating a drum roll, and raising a flag, the persona announces his intention: "I will say what I have to say by itself,/ I will sound myself and comrades only, I will never again utter a call only their call,/ . . . I will give an example to lovers to take permanent shape."

Following this announcement, the persona makes a subtle shift in the "you" whom he addresses. Up to this point, he is addressing the grass, but now he speaks to death, stating that he sees death as "the real reality." Additionally, he sees that the cycle of life-death-life has a special time frame, one in which life "does not last so very long" and death lasts "very long"—these two words being the final words of the poem.

This lyric thus moves from a specific symbol—"Scented herbage"—toward the abstraction that is death. The speaker begins his song by singing to this specific symbol, and he concludes by addressing the general, abstract notion of death. Whitman's poetic mask expands his vision from material to spiritual reality, from the particular to the universal, from the individual to the universal.

Forms and Devices

In the center section of "Scented Herbage of My Breast," the speaker refers to the grass as being "Emblematic and capricious blades." Those two adjectives suggest the ways in which the poet views both symbolism and voice, two aspects of this poem and other poems that are critical to Whitman's techniques.

Like many of his nineteenth-century contemporaries, including Ralph Waldo Emerson, Whitman was interested in objects as emblems or symbols. Grass, and what Whitman described as the "leaves" of grass, became his emblem, or visible sign, of an invisible reality. By describing this emblem as a part of the natural world and a part of his own physical being—the "Scented herbage of his breast"—he was able to emphasize the way in which grass symbolizes the cyclic quality of nature and the persona's similarly cyclic quality. Life yields to death, which contributes to new life.

The voice that sings of this cyclic quality is as capricious as the grass that is described in that way. If capriciousness suggests qualities of unpredictability and fickleness, then the voice in Whitman's poem does indeed possess those qualities. It begins with the gentle observation about grass and the reflective comment that the speaker will think later about the meanings of this "Scented herbage." Repeating the phrase "I do not know," the speaker suggests an exploratory approach, a thoughtful posture.

This reflective voice yields to a much bolder stance when the speaker issues an order to the grass: "Grow up taller sweet leaves that I may see! grow up out of my breast!/ Spring away from the conceal'd heart there!" As a result of getting a clearer view, the poet sees his role of singing, on behalf of the human community, a song of death and life, and so he announces his role of singer/spokesperson for all.

The poetic voice then assumes still another tone, this one different from the original exploratory stance and the subsequent commanding and announcing tones. In the final lines of the poem, the persona seems to have become one who has made meaning out of the symbol he was examining. Despite words that suggest tentativeness in the last lines—"perhaps" and "may-be"—the speaker sounds certain: He knows that death lasts as long as immortality, for death is a part of the cycle in which life and death, one and the same, last forever.

Themes and Meanings

One of the best ways to approach the many meanings of this lyric poem is to see where it fits in the collection in which it appears, *Leaves of Grass*. It is one of approximately fifty poems that appear in a section entitled *Calamus*. Whitman explained the reason he entitled his section as he did: "Calamus is the very large and aromatic grass, or rush, growing about water ponds in the valleys—spears about three feet high; often called Sweet Flag; grows all over the Northern and Middle States. The recherché or ethereal sense of the term, as used in my book, arises probably from the actual Calamus presenting the biggest and hardiest kind of spears of grass, and their fresh, aquatic, pungent bouquet."

This notion of aromatic grass explains why Whitman would describe his major symbol as "Scented herbage," and it suggests why he would add the reference to his breast. For Whitman was, in many ways, a poet of the physical, physiological body, and his poetry is replete with references to the human anatomy and to songs celebrating the beauty and strength of the body. In this poem, the persona is indeed rhapsodizing over the aroma, the hardiness, the life that is symbolized by the grass and that is inherent in the human body.

The persona is also singing of comradeship, a theme that connects the cluster of poems in the *Calamus* section of *Leaves of Grass*. Many critics have analyzed this section as suggesting ideas about relationships among male lovers, and this may, perhaps, be the focus of the persona's attention. Yet the more universal focus is also clear: a call to connections between the visible and invisible worlds, between the individual and community, between the self and the other, between death and life.

Marjorie Smelstor

THE SCHOLAR-GYPSY

Author: Matthew Arnold (1822-1888)
Type of poem: Pastoral
First published: 1853, in *Poems*

The Poem

"The Scholar-Gypsy" is a pastoral poem, in twenty-five ten-line stanzas, based on a legend recounted by Joseph Glanvill in *The Vanity of Dogmatizing* (1661). Matthew Arnold supplies the essential elements of the legend in lines 31 through 56 of the poem.

The poem opens on a pleasant August afternoon, with the poet-shepherd dismissing his companion shepherd to take care of his usual pastoral chores, bidding him to return at evening when the two will renew their quest. Meanwhile, the poet waits in a pleasant corner of a field filled with colorful flowers, lulled by the distant sounds of sheep and workmen; trees shield him from the sun as he looks down on the university town of Oxford.

The poet picks up Glanvill's book and rereads the tale of the talented but poor scholar who left his studies at seventeenth century Oxford to learn the mystic secrets of the gypsies. Rumors persisted that the scholar was seen occasionally; in stanzas 7 through 13, the poet imagines that the scholar is still glimpsed by shepherds, by country boys, by Oxford riders returning on the ferry, by young girls, by reapers, by a housewife darning clothes at the open doorway of a lonely cottage, by the blackbird, even by the poet himself. These seven stanzas primarily evoke the pastoral countryside around Oxford.

Making a quick turn at stanza 14, the poet ceases to daydream and realizes that it has been two hundred years since Glanvill's story and that the scholar is certainly dead and buried. The poem then turns again, at the beginning of stanza 15, where, by his imaginative leap, the poet realizes that the scholar still lives in spirit and imagination. From here until the last two stanzas, the poet contrasts images of the life of the still-living scholar, free to pursue his quest, against the lives of ordinary mortals. These contrasts are present in almost every stanza of this section, usually with the scholar presented first, and modern humans second. The scholar possesses an "immortal lot" because he has not wasted his spiritual and psychic energy on the changes and schemes of mortals. He left the world young and fresh, firm in his resolve, secure in his vision, self-sufficient; he still seeks his one goal, the spark from heaven. Humanity also seeks the spark, but it fails to appear; even the wisest sage can tell only of wretched days and misery. Modern life is a disease, and the poet repeatedly urges the scholar to fly from all contact with ordinary mortals and to continue to nurse his unconquerable hope that someday the spark will fall.

In the final two stanzas, which act as a sort of parable, the poet compares the urgent necessity for the scholar to flee to the action taken by a Tyrian trader who finds his usual territory increasingly overrun by lighthearted Greek traders. Recognizing the Greeks as invaders of his native city, Tyre, the trader turns his ship about, sails west from the Peloponnesus, through the Mediterranean, to beaches outside the Straits of Gibraltar, where he finds new customers among the dark Iberians who come to examine his wares.

Forms and Devices

With its formal language and stanza form, "The Scholar-Gypsy" displays many of the characteristics of an ode. This stanza form may well have been suggested to Arnold by that employed by John Keats in "Ode to a Nightingale" and "Ode on a Grecian Urn." In addition, the lush imagery of the more pastoral parts of the poem may owe something to the example of Keats.

There are important dichotomies in the poem which influence the overall structure. The poem tends to fall into two separate but related parts, reflecting the two quests documented in the poem. The first part, the first thirteen stanzas, deals primarily with the quest of the poet for the scholar; the second part, the remaining stanzas with the exception of the final two, deals with the quest of the scholar (and of Arnold) for the spark from heaven, the mystical moment of insight. The first part, along with the two final stanzas, contains most of the pastoral language in the poem, while the second part is marked more by poetry of statement as well as by a different tone.

As in much of Arnold's best poetry, it is the imagery that carries the burden of meaning and emotion. There is the contrast in the language of the two parts mentioned above; but in the second part itself, there is an even more important division, one that leads to the expression of one of the poem's major themes. One finds, in almost every stanza, language that characterizes the life of the scholar: "immortal," "fresh," "undiverted," "firm," "unclouded joy," "gaily," "unconquerable," "enchanted," set off against language used to describe the modern intellectual plight: "exhaust," "numb," "sick," "doubt," "half-believers," "casual creeds," "vague," "wretched," "misery," "sick," "palsied," and others. This contrast adds up to convey to the reader a powerful emotional understanding of the intellectual life of Arnold's day, with its uncertainty and strife.

The effect of the imagery is probably most concentrated in the final two stanzas. Here Arnold intends the extended image of the Tyrian trader to sum up the poet's advice to the scholar to flee all contact with ordinary mortals. This final summarizing extended image is a hallmark of many of Arnold's poems and clearly a common poetic practice for him. Similar images may be seen in "Dover Beach," "Sohrab and Rustum," "Tristram and Iseult," "Rugby Chapel," and others. In "The Scholar-Gypsy" the closing image is probably also intended, with its return to lush pastoral imagery, to calm the reader after the vigorous and biting denunciation of the modern world.

The pastoralism of the poem is perhaps its most noticeable aspect. Unlike so many poets who return to the traditional Arcadia or to a generalized sort of rural serenity, Arnold has naturalized, or domesticated, his pastoral. Arnold uses a very specific countryside, that around Oxford, as the locus for his poem. All the places mentioned in the poem are real places, well-known to Arnold and to many Oxford students. Arnold often walked the countryside described and often returned to it for refreshment. In his days at Oxford, Arnold was frequently accompanied on his walks by his close friend, the poet Arthur Hugh Clough; for the two of them, many of the local places, as well as the legend of the scholar-gypsy itself, acquired special, personal meanings.

Themes and Meanings

The pastoralism of the poem leads immediately to several themes. Most generally it represents, as it does for many poets, an escape from the intolerable world of court or affairs. Arnold certainly romanticizes the Oxford countryside, attributing to it his happiest days. Against this romantic background, then, Arnold places the quest for and of the scholar-gypsy, which gives added significance to the background. As a broad generalization, the scholar (and Arnold) seek the meaning of life. Since for Arnold Christianity was dead, and there seemed nothing to take its place giving meaning to life, the result is a constant search and intense loneliness and emptiness in life. Another general way of phrasing all this is that it presents the wisdom of the heart against the wisdom of the head. The head sees the true condition of the modern world, but the heart is drawn to the simpler, more unified life represented by the scholar and Oxford.

The poem itself is much more specific. The countryside is a specific one, well-known and loved by Arnold; the legend of the scholar-gypsy had special meaning for him. The scholar represents a side of Arnold that was at odds with the way in which he had to live his life. Arnold felt himself tugged to and fro by the demands of the world. He believed sincerely that his need to function in the modern world had killed him as a poet. His status as a family man, as an inspector of schools, and as the self-dedicated instructor of the middle-class obliged him to live and work in the world of hurry, change, and debate, while he desired calm and singleness of purpose. It is worthy of note that the only italicized words in the whole poem are in line 152, "Thou hadst *one* aim, *one* business, *one* desire"—emphasizing the poet's desire for singleness of purpose.

While Arnold certainly seeks something that will supply meaning for life, what the poem specifically emphasizes is that the poet seeks a *way* of life analogous to that of the scholar. The scholar is free, dedicated, not pulled about by the daily concerns of modern life—and thus he has a kind of immortality. In this connection, it is to be noted that Arnold is hardly concerned at all, in the images of the poem, with the physical side of modern life, with commerce and trade, with large cities and bustling crowds, with mass culture and the cheap and tawdry. The poet's concern is with the intellectual life, with having something secure onto which to hold, with being in command of one's own soul and intellect. The poem clearly suggests that dedication to the quest is even more important than its resolution.

Finally, for a full appreciation of how seriously Arnold took these issues and this quest, "The Scholar-Gypsy" must be read in conjunction with his later poem "Thyrsis," a pastoral elegy for the death of his friend and fellow poet, Arthur Hugh

Clough. The poem is deliberately connected to "The Scholar-Gypsy" by being only one stanza shorter, by the use of exactly the same rhyme scheme and stanza form, and, most important, by being set in exactly the same landscape and using again the figure of the scholar, which clearly meant so much to both Arnold and Clough.

Gordon N. Bergquist

SCHUBERTIANA

Author: Tomas Tranströmer (1931-   )
Type of poem: Lyric
First published: 1979, as "Schubertiana," in *Sanningsbarriären*; English translation
  collected in *Tomas Tranströmer: Selected Poems, 1954-1986,* 1987

The Poem

"Schubertiana," a poem whose title refers to nineteenth century Austrian composer Franz Schubert, consists of five numbered stanzas of varying length. Stanzas 1, 2, 4, and 5 contain from six to ten lines each; the central stanza, stanza 3, is conspicuously shorter, having only two lines. The poem is written in free verse, but, with the exception of the last two, the lines are extraordinarily long.

The poem begins with an evocation of New York City: its skyscrapers, teeming crowds, fast-paced life, squalor, and occasional violence. The poet, speaking in the first person, moves without transition to an intuitive observation: "I know too— without statistics—that right now Schubert is being played." Not only is Schubert's music being played somewhere, but it is more real to someone, the poet asserts, than anything else—more real than the giant city, its masses, or its misery. The musical performance is certain, even without empirical evidence.

The second stanza abruptly shifts the scene and focus. The biological foundation of all life is evoked in a reference to the physiological structure of the human brain and the swallows' return from South Africa (Transvaal) to Europe, or, perhaps more specifically, to Sweden, to precisely the spot where they had nested the year before. Against the background of the wonderfully intricate structure of the human brain and the seeming miracle of swallow navigation, Schubert, "a fat young man from Vienna, called 'the little mushroom,'" is described as such a consummate musician that he could encompass the signals of an entire life in a few ordinary chords of a string quintet and get a river to flow through the eye of a needle.

This string quintet is the bridge to the third and fourth stanzas. While the quintet plays, the poet walks home through a humid forest, falls asleep, passes weightlessly into the future, and knows that plants have thoughts, that the mind permeates all life. The fourth stanza describes the various kinds of trust that are necessary in the contemporary world: trust in the natural world, in social institutions, and in the equipment of daily life. Yet none of these merits the trust universally placed in it. The quintet, though, testifies that something, though never clearly and directly identified, is worthy of human trust.

Only the fifth and final stanza deals entirely and specifically with music. While a Schubert piano duet plays, its true heroic character is noted. This, however, is not the music for people who are not true to themselves or try to set a price on everything. The long, sinuous melodies in all their developments and varying modulations do not reflect or accompany those who forsake, betray, or compromise themselves or human nature.

Forms and Devices

Although the poem is about Schubert's music, it does not make use of devices that traditionally have been associated with lyric musicality. Even in the original Swedish, there are no strong rhythmic patterns, concentrated repetitions of sounds, or especially euphonious combinations of sounds. The language is, in fact, rather colloquial. One way of looking at the poem's musicality is, however, in terms of the description of Schubert's music in the last stanza. There his melodies are described as long—as opposed, for example, to the short and concentrated rhythmic motifs often found in the music of Ludwig van Beethoven—and as remaining themselves through all changes, modulations, and developments.

The same could be said of the structure of the poem. The lines of "Schubertiana" are extraordinarily long, resembling the long melodic lines in Schubert's work. They have, moreover, no parallel in Tomas Tranströmer's other poems, except his well-known collection *östersjöar* (1974; *Baltics*, 1975), which was published shortly before "Schubertiana." The underlying structure of each stanza is also similar to Tranströmer's description of music that remains fundamentally itself even though undergoing many changes. In each stanza, the poet speaking personally describes an experience or perception—New York City, the physiological structure of the brain and the swallows' miraculous return, the walk through the forest, the question of trust, and the playing of the piano duet—followed by his understanding of the remarkable way in which Schubert's music relates to these extremely diverse situations. Although the situations change, the basic pattern remains the same: Personal experience or insight is juxtaposed to an important aspect of Schubert's music. Since the musicality of this poem is not strongly linked to the sounds of the original Swedish—although there are, to be sure, connections—the musicality can well be seen and understood in translation.

Another reason the poem works so well in English is that its basic strategy is one of comparison, particularly unexpected, even surprising, comparisons. After emphasizing the massive size, the frenetic lifestyle, the chaos, and the brutality of New York City, the poet, without preparation or transition, makes the startling observation that he knows intuitively that someone is performing Schubert. It should be noted that Schubert is best remembered for his extraordinary gift of melody and his rich, evocative harmonies embodied in his songs (*Lieder*, in German) and works for small ensembles or solo instruments. These small-scale chamber works, which are so melodically and harmonically rich, are abruptly juxtaposed to and astoundingly encompass in their own way the sprawling, chaotic city. Similarly, the incomprehensible complexity of the brain and the swallows' astounding migration over thousands of miles are contrasted to a few simple chords of the string quintet into which the signals of an entire life are distilled. It is the string quintet that, in the shortest and most contracted stanza of the poem, accompanies and stands in stark relief against the disquieting yet seminal insight that mind is not unique to humankind but pervades all the natural world. In the fourth stanza, Tranströmer points out that in order to live daily life without sinking through the earth, great trust must be placed in many aspects of the ambient world. Yet, this trust that is so necessary is unmerited in comparison to the trust that the music of a Schubert quintet invites—trust that is compared to the banister that leads through the dark. In the last stanza, the playing of a simple Schubert duet is juxtaposed to the awareness and understanding of the integrity of the music and the personal integrity that it demands.

Themes and Meanings

"Schubertiana" is only one of Tranströmer's many poems that, either directly or indirectly, refer to music and reveal his intense interest in music. Although Tranströmer is a psychologist by profession, he is also an accomplished pianist, and Schubert is one of his favorite composers. His other poems dealing with musical themes include "C Major," "Allegro," "Nocturne," "Slow Music," "Brief Pause in the Organ Recital," and "Carillon." The purpose of "Schubertiana" is not to imitate music or to attempt to re-create a musical experience in words, as many other poets have done; rather, Tranströmer explores the role of Schubert's music, particularly in human existence, but at the same time explores the role of music more generally.

Tranströmer argues that music is not merely an embellishment or adornment of life. Schubert's music is, on the contrary, something that lies at the foundation of human existence. It has to do with the ground of all being and the way in which human beings extend their understanding beyond empirical experience toward this ground that ultimately must remain unknown. It has often been pointed out that Tranströmer maintains a remarkable openness to the unknown. He does not allow his mind to be enclosed by systems, ideologies, or dogma. In the last lines of his poem "Vermeer," for example, a prayer is addressed to cosmic emptiness, but the response that is whispered is "I am not empty, I am open."

"Schubertiana" juxtaposes Schubert's music to a sampling of the most extreme aspects of modern life, and, in so doing, the true nature of the music reveals itself. Schubert's music in its own mysterious way is more real than the physical and social reality of New York City, the hard realities of life in that city notwithstanding; it is more marvelous and awe-inspiring than the complexities of the human brain or than the swallows' ability to return home. This music, though, is more than heightened reality or the object of marvel and wonder: It is revelatory. It breaks down the boundary of time, allowing the arresting insight that plants are rational beings, that they have thoughts, and minds, and thus, is infused throughout the natural universe. Schubert's music, moreover, is such that it more fully deserves human trust than do any of the institutions or conventions of modern life. The music, though, makes ethical demands. In order for any individual to experience these remarkable qualities, music requires absolute personal integrity; it cannot tolerate duplicity or dissemblance. When its demands are met, however, Schubert's music partakes of the fundamental essence of human existence to the extent that it can accompany the individual from the depths of existence upward toward destiny.

Steven P. Sondrup

THE SEAFARER

Author: Ezra Pound (1885-1972)
Type of poem: Lyric
First published: 1912, in *Ripostes*

The Poem

"The Seafarer" is a poem in free verse consisting of some one hundred lines or half-lines, as dictated by the fragmentary nature of the original Anglo-Saxon poem (c. 800). Since the poem is a nearly literal translation, it cannot be analyzed in terms of modern prosody, such as stanzas, rhymes, and meter. Indeed, in the original, spellings vary and punctuation is nonexistent. The poem has, however, a well-modulated movement that derives from a central feeling of isolation, fearfulness, and somber reflection on the human condition and man's fate.

Writing in the first person, Ezra Pound assumes the persona of the anonymous original poet, and therefore, as translator, achieves an immediacy of mood that transcends time and place and speaks with immediacy to his present-day reader.

Pound begins as does the original poet, with an address to the reader: "May I for my own self song's truth reckon." This directness bears witness to the oral tradition of the poem and the poet's intimate approach to his reader, and earlier, his audience. I shall tell you the truth, he says, as I have known it. He continues with a descriptive scene of chilling bitterness, both figurative and literal, in which he pictures the harsh realities of the seafaring life. He dramatically elicits the terror evoked on "Narrow nightwatch nigh the ship's head/ While she tossed close to cliffs." The passage—of some considerable length, and indicating the importance that the seafarer places upon such a harrowing recollection—concludes with a vivid image of the miserable cold in which the air "hung with hard ice-flakes," and indicates his own isolation. The staccato cries of the birds of the sea and air offer but a meager companionship, and prove a poor substitute, with their "sea-fowls' loudness," for the laughter he has once known; the "gannet's clamour" serves for his games, the "mews' singing," for the comradeship of the hall. Above this desolate scene, the seafarer relates, "the eagle screamed/ With spray on his pinion."

In the stream of consciousness that follows, other memories provide a wrenching contrast to the seafarer's present situation. He envies the life of the land-dweller, who will never know his hardship but will also never appreciate the beauties of the earth as does he: the joys of spring when "Bosque taketh blossom," and even the homelier joys of a "winsome wife." The call of the sea, however, is strong. The "lone-flyer," the very bird whose scream he found distressing, becomes the bird who calls him back, and "Whets for the whale-path the heart irresistibly."

The final movements of the poem are, in both style and content, traditional elegiac passages such as those found in many Anglo-Saxon poems. Within these lines are expressed the universal fears and griefs of all people—the passage of time, the loss of old friends, and the futility of life, which must end with death. The world shall be as if the seafarer had never been; even the deeds of warrior and poet cannot forestall death.

Forms and Devices

Although Pound does not adhere strictly to the accentual pattern (four strong beats to the line) that was obligatory for an Anglo-Saxon poet, he does maintain, since it is "from the Anglo-Saxon," many features and characteristics of the earlier prosody. The sea dominates the Anglo-Saxon worldview, and nowhere is it more vivid than in the imagery of "The Seafarer," where it is shown in all its turbulence and power to inspire terror in those who dare to venture into its unknown regions. Despite the sea's omnipresence in the Anglo-Saxon consciousness, the poet is constricted by the limitations of the language. His vocabulary is spare (there are only two denotative words for sea: *see* and *meres*), and he must therefore contrive, for the sake of variety, metaphors and similes—that is, comparisons that will adequately express his mood. The earlier poet uses kennings, which are combinations of familiar words. The skill of the poet is judged by his imaginative use of this device. In "The Seafarer," for example, the technique is richly evident in such substitutions for sea as "the whale's acre," "the whale-path," and "the salt-wavy tumult." Similarly, ice is transformed into "ice-flakes," hail into "corn of the coldest."

If Pound fully utilizes the vitality of the diction of the earlier poet, he also fully employs another of the conventions of the original, the use of alliteration (the repetition of initial consonant sounds within a given line). For example, "Bosque taketh blossom, cometh beauty of berries" fairly bursts with the ripeness of the season, whereas the contrary mood of old age is echoed in "Grey-haired he groaneth, knows gone companions." The line nearly creaks and wobbles under the burden of its message.

Although these prosodic features are common in the verse of the anonymous Anglo-Saxon poet, and in Pound's translation they are not the only features. The commonality is also struck in the recurrent motifs—that is, the recurrent patterns of events or moods and feelings. The traditional *ubi sunt* and *sic transit* motifs are used with great effectiveness to close the poem. In the first of these (*ubi sunt*, or "Where are?") passages, lyric in character, the poet looks about him, remembers the joys of the past with his companions, and, in a desolate tone, realizes that not only has all changed, but he has also been deprived by death of many he has loved. This theme is frequently followed, as it is in "The Seafarer," by a related theme—the *sic transit gloria mundi* ("thus passes the glory of the world") theme—in which the poet notes the brief span allotted to humankind from eternity's store of time. Whether by misadventure or old age, everyone, rich or poor, king or peasant, must meet death at the end of the final voyage.

Themes and Meanings

In the concluding lines of this very personal elegy, the seafarer of the poem becomes an Everyman figure. As he journeys far from his home into the unknown, he is alternately filled with the exhilaration of Ulysses and the despair of Job, as he ponders the dangers of life and the finality of its conclusion. The seafarer is all men who do not understand their beginnings, whose purpose remains obscure, and whose immortality exists only in the memories of those who come after. The warrior seeks fame in great deeds, the poet perhaps in his own song, but—as the poet suggests—all may be vanity.

In the Anglo-Saxon world, the cruel hand of fate, amoral and rigid in its law, oppresses and finally sweeps everyone away into the void of nothingness. The anguish inspired by inescapable death is still felt strongly in the modern world, where many have abandoned faith. Modern humanity, the product of a technological and scientific society, searches just as anxiously for meaning in life as did any ancient counterpart. Within months of the first publication of this poem (in 1912), Pound was to question human fate still further as World War I began. A dark foreboding colors the work of many poets and writers of the early twentieth century, as diverse in character as Pound and Thomas Hardy, as T. S. Eliot and Wallace Stevens.

Ezra Pound, as one of the founders of the Imagist movement, rejected the staid metrical patterns that had dominated Victorian and early twentieth century poetry. It is clear from "The Seafarer" that he had broken the bonds of this dominance by turning to other criteria by which poetry might be judged. In rejecting rhyme and stanza and creating a line whose length was determined by the breath unit or by natural colloquial speech patterns, Pound facilitated the entry of free verse into the lexicon of poetry. The powerful sound devices and the striking imagery inherent in the original "The Seafarer" became a hallmark and technique found not only in Pound's later work, but in twentieth century free verse generally.

Maureen W. Mills

THE SEAFARER

Author: Unknown

Type of poem: Meditation

First published: 960-980 C.E. in the Exeter Book; collected in *Seven Old English Poems*, 1966; lines 1-99a translated into English by Ezra Pound, in *Selected Poems*, 1957

The Poem

The unique copy of "The Seafarer" is found in the Exeter Book, a manuscript anthology of Old English poetry assembled about 975 C.E., although many of the poems, including "The Seafarer," may have circulated in oral versions before being written down in the form in which they now exist. The poem's Christian message would seem to rule out any date earlier than the seventh century, when the Anglo-Saxons were converted; at the other extreme, it may have been composed, at least in the form in which it survives, around the time that the scribe copied it into the book in the second half of the tenth century. The 124-line poem is untitled in the manuscript, and its author is unknown. The best-known translation is that of Ezra Pound, whose rendering of the first ninety-nine lines has been widely admired on its own merits by readers with no knowledge of the original.

"The Seafarer," like most Old English poetry, is characterized by textual problems, abrupt transitions, and apparent inconsistencies in tone and structure that combine to render any modern interpretation tentative and subject to revision. Earlier scholars frequently read the poem as a dialogue between an experienced sailor and a young man who has not yet been to sea, dividing the text into alternating speeches (though with little agreement as to where these speeches begin and end). More recently, the critical consensus has come around to the view that the poem is a monologue by a single speaker, a religious man who has spent a life on the sea and is now meditating on his experience of life on Earth and contemplating the afterlife in Heaven.

The poem begins with the speaker's remembrance of the hardships of his past life on the sea, focusing especially on scenes of solitary voyages undertaken in harsh winter weather. He contrasts his lonely and difficult seafaring existence with that of the dwellers on land, who enjoy the comforts and pleasures of social life. At about line 33 of the poem, the seafarer resolves to return to the sea for another voyage, evidently to a distant land. He then shifts from personal experience to more general remarks in the third person about how seafaring men are different from landsmen, drawn more strongly to wander than to share in an admitted prosperity and the beauty of the land, especially in spring and summer. The seafarer then briefly returns to his personal thoughts about the voyage he is planning.

At about the midpoint of the poem, he explicitly makes the point that life on the land is sterile, fleeting, and insubstantial. In the second half of the poem, he moves away from the autobiographical discussion of his experiences and concentrates on the revelation to which they have led him. He develops at length the argument that worldly goods and honors are transient and insubstantial and that wise people will therefore turn their minds entirely to the eternal life in the heavenly kingdom, considering not how to enjoy themselves on Earth but how to prepare themselves for Heaven, which offers the only true home for humankind.

Forms and Devices

Old English poetry is alliterative, relying on repetition of the initial sounds of stressed syllables rather than on rhymes at the ends of lines as its structural principle. The details of this alliterative practice can be quite complicated, but the most typical form is illustrated by lines 31-32 of "The Seafarer," which appear thus in the original Old English: "Nap niht-scua, nor an sniwde,/ hrim hrusan band, hægl feoll on eor an" ("Neareth nightshade, snoweth from north,/ Frost froze the land, hail fell on earth then"). Each line is divided into two half lines (separated by editorially provided commas in these examples), and the alliterating letters for each line (*n* and *h*) must occur in both halves. Each half line usually has two stressed syllables, and while either or (more often) both may alliterate in the first half line (the "a" line), in the second half line (the "b" line), the first stressed syllable must alliterate and the second must not.

While there are many threads of imagery throughout the poem, including those of cold, barrenness, and the progression of the seasons, the central metaphor is surely that of the ship at sea, which was used throughout classical and medieval literature in a variety of permutations to symbolize human life. The specifically Christian version of the image used in this poem typically identifies the waves and salinity of the sea with the uncertainty and bitterness of postlapsarian life on Earth and the sailor as the Christian tossed about by its various storms and waves. Perhaps the best-known example of this symbolic system is Noah's ark, which was read as a parable of the power of the ship of the Church to save Christians from the floodwaters of sin. Depending upon the nuances of individual interpretation, the seafarer's ship can thus be seen as the Church or his religious faith, which protects him from drowning in the sea of a fallen and sinful world, or as the ship of his soul journeying over temptation (and potential shipwreck at the hands of Satan) toward a heavenly destination. In such readings, the chaos represented by the sea of sin is contrasted with the stability of Heaven.

Other readers have suggested that the sea may also reflect a Christian baptismal image whereby the water represents the possibility of rebirth into faith, thus explaining the seafarer's decision to return to the sea. The ship motif provides a number of possibilities for further elaboration; in "The Seafarer," for example, commentators find that the sea bird in flight represents the seafarer's soul in contemplation of God, that his night-watches represent his earlier spiritual darkness, and that the sea journey represents a religious pilgrimage. These various interpretations are not necessarily contradictory and may merely reflect the poet's sophisticated handling of a complex symbol by developing more than one significance for it.

Themes and Meanings

Early scholars of Anglo-Saxon literature believed that "The Seafarer" represented an early pagan poem that had been adapted for Christian audiences by the insertion of pious formulas throughout and a moral at the end; accordingly, these scholars expended considerable ingenuity in attempting to excise the Christian elements to discover the "real poem" hidden beneath these composite overlays. Pound's famous translation, in line with this emphasis, systematically removes or downplays many explicitly Christian elements of the poem and stops before the overtly homiletic conclusion, which features some dozen direct references to God and the heavens in the last twenty-five lines.

Now, however, critics seem generally to agree that the two halves of the poem are unified by a movement from earthly chaos to heavenly order and that its coherent thematic thrust is the Christian message that the afterlife is more important than life on Earth. The poem is frequently discussed in conjunction with "The Wanderer," another Exeter Book poem that shares many themes and motifs with "The Seafarer," including the structure in which a specific treatment of biographical subject matter—the plight of a wanderer or seafarer—is followed by a more general homiletic section that draws a religious meaning from the earlier material.

The sailor, as a man required to travel over a hostile and dangerous environment, had always seemed to Christian poets to be a naturally apt image of the believer's life on Earth, which should be viewed as a hazardous journey to the true homeland of Heaven rather than as a destination to be valued in itself. In this poem, the speaker seems to be a religious man (or reformed sinner) who has chosen the seafaring life as much for its efficacy as a means of spiritual discipline as for any commercial gain to be derived from it. The original opposition in the poem between landsmen and seafarers gives way to the insight that all men are, or ought to think of themselves as, seafarers, in the sense that they are all exiles from their true home in Heaven. As lines 31-32 (previously quoted) establish, the land can be just as cold and forbidding as the sea, and the virtuous, at least, should hope that they will be sojourning in this harsh world for only a brief time.

True Christian "seafarers" must psychologically distance themselves from secular life, as the seafarer of this poem has done both literally and figuratively. The poet appears to encapsulate his theme at the pivotal midpoint of the poem: "therefore the joys of the Lord seem warmer to me than this dead life, fleeting on land." This recommended ascetic withdrawal from worldly interests should enable the Christian to properly reject the comforts of life on the land as transient and seek spiritual rather than physical comforts.

William Nelles

THE SEARCH

Author: George Herbert (1593-1633)
Type of poem: Meditation
First published: 1633, in *The Temple*

The Poem

"The Search" is a personal meditation in which the author wonders why God appears to have forsaken him. The poem is structured into fifteen four-line stanzas. The rhythm of the poem is terse and staccato because each stanza's first and third lines consist of eight syllables, set off by four-syllable second and fourth lines. The first and third lines rhyme with each other, as do the second and fourth. Each stanza comes to a full stop. This structure lends a tone of driving restlessness, consonant with the searching theme.

The poem is written in the first person; George Herbert speaks directly to and asks questions of God. "The Search" is one in a long collection of Herbert's poems called *The Temple*. All of the poems in *The Temple* are religious in theme, although many have less mournful tones than that found in "The Search." The religious feeling Herbert speaks of in his poetry is considered to be personal and genuine to his actual experience. The reader can assume that Herbert actually felt at some time the longing described in "The Search." This fact is significant to Christian readers of Herbert, who are able to find solace and guidance in his works. Many non-Christian readers also admire Herbert's poetry, in part because of its honesty.

Herbert begins the poem by asking, "whither art thou fled,/ My Lord, my Love?" One can assume that the speaker in the poem at one time enjoyed a closeness with a personal god. His voice is not that of a first-time searcher, questioning the existence of God. At one point in the poem he begs God to "Turn, and restore me." He prays often, does not feel God's presence, yet observes how elements of nature seem to be oblivious to God's absence. The author asks if perhaps God has not created another race of humans, now favored with God's attention, "leaving th' old/ Unto their sinnes?" Of particular pain to the searcher is the possibility that it is God's desire to remain distant, as opposed to this distance being the just wages of faulty individuals. Perhaps God is distant because it is his will.

Partway through the poem, the writer's tone changes from descriptions of his pain and pining to descriptions of God's magnificence and direct entreaties to God to make himself felt. Finally, Herbert reasons that once God does choose to return, despite the once-felt huge distance, he will be as one with God because God, in his awesome power, is the only one capable of creating the distance and of closing it.

Forms and Devices

In agreement with the religious nature of "The Search," Herbert makes use of language familiar to many Christians through biblical allusions. The first stanza contains the line, "My searches are my daily bread," which directly reflects the New Testament's Lord's Prayer, "Give us this day our daily bread." The poet implies here that his daily sustenance consists of looking for the warmth of God's presence, which does not, for him, materialize. Later in the poem, Herbert speaks of a distance so huge that "East and West touch, the poles do kisse." Personification of this nature, such as having two inanimate and completely separate objects, the Earth's north and south poles, kiss each other, is a poetic device used frequently in the Bible's Old Testament. For example, in Psalms 85:10, "righteousness and peace have kissed each other."

While Herbert is considered by most critics to be one of the premier Metaphysical poets in English, his use of Metaphysical conceits is not as pronounced in "The Search" as it is in some of his other works. In his poem "Love (III)," for example, he successfully compares divine love with a waiter in a tavern. This type of imaginative and unlikely comparison is peculiar to Metaphysical conceits, and Herbert excels at it. The metaphors found in "The Search" are not as single-minded or fully developed as the example from "Love (III)," but there are intriguing images of space and distance that appear and reappear through the stanzas almost like a song's refrain. Line 5 describes the searcher's physical attitude of prayer: "My knees pierce th' earth, mine eies the skie." An arc of space is created by the line from the searcher's knees on the ground to the sky as he throws back his head in a prayerful plea. The next two stanzas reinforce the same picture of distance between the earth and sky. The poet looks to the green herbs "below" and the stars "above" to observe that God's other creations, unlike him, are cognizant of God's closeness. The next two stanzas again portray arcs of space, as the searcher is like an archer who "sent a sigh to seek thee out/ . . . Wing'd like an arrow; but my scout/ Returns in vain." Later the poet laments, "Thy will such a strange distance is,/ As that to it// . . . parallels meet." The last two stanzas resolve the poet's grief by closing the painful distance.

The poem's last images are those of the precise movements of two fencers and of the movement of space between them. The poet asks when God "dost turn, and wilt be neare;/ What edge so keen/ What point so piercing can appeare/ To come between?" These lines bring to mind the thin, narrow fencer's rapier that for all its sharpness is too dull to be able to separate God from his chosen. In contrast to the huge expanses God is capable of creating, and about which the poet has talked at length, so can God's "nearenesse bear the bell,/ Making two one." The phrase "bear the bell" is truly enigmatic; it may refer to an unknown Elizabethan expression. It is also possible that it refers to the two fencers' bodies coming together against the "bellegarde," or protective hand covering, of a fencing sword, thereby resulting in their nearness bearing "the bell," making two one.

Themes and Meanings

Like a genuine search, "The Search" is a journey: The poem begins at one place and ends somewhere else. The poet's thinking moves from painful lament to a search for an explanation and finally to a kind of peace. The first part of the poem is a passive description of the grief of separation and the searcher's attempt to rejoin his God. Close to the middle of the poem, one can see the writer's mind shift to ask the source of the separation. The searcher's pain climaxes midway through the poem when he asks if his suffering might be God's will. The faithful searcher wins a final comforting reward, when, as expressed in the last third of the poem, he acknowledges God's greatness. The end of the poem definitely strikes a different tone from the beginning.

"The Search" reinforces a basic concept in Christianity—that when one is suffering and needful, one's immediate response should be to give thanks to and celebrate God. "The Search" is the story of one pilgrim's obedience to this directive and his resulting reward. One of the primary strengths of this poem is the sumptuous and celebratory description of God's greatness. While the language is simple, the images are sophisticated. It has been suggested that even the distance felt from such a magnificent God is in itself a type of relationship with him, and the searcher does find solace in descriptions of God's greatness.

Coupled with the description of one pilgrim's personal journey toward his god can be found the image of the state of Christians as a group in relation to their God. It has been suggested that the poem describes the existential situation of humankind in relation to God—that of an unnatural and evil loneliness and grief after the exile from the Garden of Eden. The distance spoken of in the poem represents the difference between true man and woman as inhabitants of the Garden versus their faulty counterparts after the fall from grace. Thus when the poet begs of God, "Turn, and restore me," he seeks restoration to a place where the poet and humankind once were, in God's presence.

Valerie C. Snyder

THE SEARCHERS

Author: Tomás Rivera (1935-1984)
Type of poem: Meditation
First published: 1976, in *Ethnic Literatures Since 1776: The Many Voices of America*

The Poem

"The Searchers" is a long free-verse poem in seven sections. The title refers to the central theme of the poem: the constant movement of migrant workers as they seek not only work but also truth and dignity. Tomás Rivera presents them as embodying the questing spirit of the Americas, though they are often denied their legal and monetary due. Because the poem deals with the abuse of and discrimination against the migrant workers (Chicanos), the injurious effects of prejudice are a central concern. Though the poem does present the Chicanos as expressing the elemental identity of the Americas, the poem indicates that rejection of the people and their culture has turned them inward, searchers for a truth that can sustain one during adversity and misfortune.

Section I introduces the images of the earth in which the workers search for their history and their humanity, as well as for their livelihood. Throughout the rest of the poem, Rivera draws on the experience of the migrant worker to illustrate his belief that the earth and those who work it will endure. They will find within themselves "the passion to create/of every clod and stone/a new life/a new dream." Their search is based on the perfection of the seed of the newborn child, which is the beginning of all life. Only bigotry and repression can, temporarily, negate the promise of the beginning.

Sections II and III extend the meaning of the word "searcher" to those who look for the past from which they have been separated by oppression and, equally important, to those who look into the face of the inevitable, death, a mystery that is suggested in loneliness and desire. The will to endure is questioned and tested.

Section IV begins the delineation of social repression and injustice that continues through Sections V and VI, in which the poet introduces the names and experiences of some of those who died. These passages poignantly celebrate the survival, the conquest, of these people. They are never alone—in life, in death, or in memory. That they belong to the greater experience of the Chicano is the final assertion of the poem.

Sections V and VI proclaim the solidarity of the people and their culture. The individuals who died (such as Chona, who died giving birth in a sugar-beet field, or Kiko, who died in Italy in World War II) are the martyrs. In their struggles for freedom and dignity, they were destroyed and became points of reference for those who lived after them. Section VII ends the poem with the assertions that people—and race—are greater than death and that the Chicano will continue to search. It is the search for truth and personal dignity that is central to humanity itself.

The movement of the poem from lyric to narrative and back to lyric occurs as Rivera develops his idea of passion: the celebration and acceptance of life. The passion includes pain, but the pain nurtures and deepens the passion as the individual is recalled as someone whose life was never solitary. The experience of the migrant worker necessitated that many people live and travel together. Rivera presents this as closeness, not as crowding. From the closeness came sharing and understanding.

Forms and Devices

The poem is written in both English and Spanish, indicating the bilingual nature of the Chicano. Rivera leaves in Spanish songs and sayings that belong to the community. In them, as well as in the English segments, images of food and relatives, frightening and abusive experiences become metaphors for the human experience. The simplicity of image and language is consciously intended by the poet to relate his subject to the most fundamental conditions of human life. Yet by giving the central word of the poem ("searchers") a value that grows from those who search for work and bodily sustenance to those who search for history, dignity, and religious meaning, he gives great value to even the most common of words, such as "bread" or "kiss." They become a way of searching. He avoids similes and symbols that would take the reader's attention away from the experience of the people. In addition, he uses the work, food, and love necessary for life to give sacred value to such objects as bread and milk. When he mentions items indigenous to the workers—novenas, rosaries, *pan dulce* ("sweet bread"), trucks—he does so to indicate that even the most commonplace of objects and events can tell the story of a people. These objects are significant to the Catholic Chicano workers. He also mentions people with whom he himself worked. They, too, are expressive of their people, though they are never symbolic—they never stand for anything other than themselves.

The poem is generally a lyric; yet it exceeds the intent and tradition of the lyric; "The Searchers" has the sweep of an epic, even though it is much shorter. It tells the history of a people—their trials and conquests; it describes their travels and their way of life. In doing all this, the poem resembles the fiction written by Rivera. His fiction told of the lives of the migrant workers, but it included songs and strong visual images that allowed the reader to experience the spirit of the people. The poem accomplishes the opposite by telling of spirit in image and song, yet forcing the reader to confront the actual experience of the migrant worker through the examples that are presented narratively.

Themes and Meanings

The poem has its origins, perhaps, in the ballad, from which come the lyrical line and the repetition of sounds that combine music and words to make poetry. The ballad also provides the subject: the tale of death and struggle. It resembles contemporary versions of the Mexican *corrido*, a traditional song telling of love and passion, struggle and death. In "The Searchers," Tomás Rivera relates his poem and the lives of migrant workers in the United States to the cultural traditions of Mexico, yet his poem and its characters belong to the United States. His poem, in form, language, allusion, and theme relates a bicultural society that is distinct from the two societies that served as its progenitors.

Though echoing the themes of hope and compassion that occur in so many of Rivera's poems, "The Searchers" places them in the broader context of the Chicano and of Rivera's own philosophical inquiry. By combining meditation with narrative, Rivera extended the poetic resonance of images of workers and the Chicano that are found in many other poems. In "The Searchers," however, he achieves a form that combines the facts of a particular group with the eternal poetic quest for the meaning of life. The elements of danger and death, the struggles to remain alive and to retain dignity, provide an unusual force and poignancy.

This poem is a meditation on the necessities of life by a poet who had struggled to live, who had fought prejudice and ignorance, yet a poet who has not become embittered. As author of the poem, he is the essential searcher, and his poem charts his search from fields and migrant worker camps to the spirit.

Frank L. Kersnowski

THE SECOND COMING

Author: William Butler Yeats (1865-1939)
Type of poem: Lyric
First published: 1920, in *Michael Robartes and the Dancer*

The Poem

"The Second Coming," an intense, lyrical poem of twenty-two lines, addresses a listener prepared to expect useful insight into the meaning of history. Instead, the poet offers a disturbing prophecy of cultural dissolution. The homey, commonplace images of everyday life are merged with an apocalyptic revelation about a new order that portends instability and chaos among humankind. By the poem's last line, the reader senses the impending arrival of something hideous and devastating to human freedom and harmony, an effect wrought by the poet's skillful inversion of familiar symbols and the promise of catastrophe delayed.

The poem can be conveniently divided into three movements: lines 1 through 8, 9 through 17, and 18 through 22. The reader is led progressively through a series of ever more ominous prophecies of upheaval and social discord. Each image is derivative of common religious sentiment of the poet's time, expressed in familiar biblical cadences yet riven with sinister import.

William Butler Yeats begins the first movement with the mysterious image of a falcon turning and turning in a "widening gyre," a radiating spiral, increasingly beyond the reach of its falconer/guide. Outside his command and direction, the falcon can be neither controlled nor diverted in its motion.

As a result of the falcon's centripetal break from both instinct and training, "things fall apart" in the observer's sensory world, and "the center cannot hold"; hence, the poet declares, "mere anarchy" will be "loosed upon the world." The ones who might have stood against social deconstruction "lack conviction," while the ones who will share the spoils of this moral collapse "are full of passionate intensity." "The blood-dimmed tide" slaughters "the ceremony of innocence," and the reader faces the prospect of nightmarish violence. To relieve temporarily the tension of this dire forecast, at line 9 the poet issues a plea for deliverance from the nameless evil about to occur: "Surely some revelation is at hand." His repetitive cry, however, serves only to register the inevitability that no deliverer will arise to defeat the foe: "Surely the Second Coming is at hand!" There Yeats parodies the New Testament doctrine of Christ's return from heaven to Earth to judge the wicked and save the redeemed. Offered up is a much different "second coming" that proffers no element of worthy anticipation for faithful earthly inhabitants.

The "*Spiritus Mundi*," or spirit of the world, cannot quite envision the grotesque shape forming with "lion body and the head of a man" in the desert, its presence noted only by "indignant desert birds" who cannot fathom its significance. Its sphinxlike inscrutability will either surprise or destroy those who seek to resolve its mystery.

In the final movement, lines 18 through 22, "The Second Coming" turns expectation into fearful dread as the poet adorns his prophecy with the portent of disaster and universal human suffering. "The darkness drops again," and "Twenty centuries of stony sleep" are interrupted by the newly awakened monster. A "rocking cradle" has nurtured the "rough beast," whose identity is shrouded in ambiguity in the poem's last line. The beast "Slouches toward Bethlehem to be born," inexorably creeping toward its destiny as the genesis of civilization's ultimate nemesis.

Forms and Devices

The key image in the first movement of the poem is the "gyre," a device used by Yeats to exemplify his theory of history. The falcon's orbit away from the falconer suggests a conelike, ever-widening spiral, as the poet establishes his cyclical view of civilizations passing through growth, maturation, and eventual overthrow by the forces of history. The image is left intact, however, only until line 3, when, in one of the poem's more powerful and memorable lines, Yeats announces history's demise: "things fall apart; the center cannot hold." Poetic image melts into prosaic exposition as history, and the conventional ways in which it may be understood are rendered impotent by the violence wrought by the "mere anarchy" that is unleashed.

"The Second Coming" works as a series of nightmarish images presented sequentially and then summarily upended by the poet's mournful, deliberate commentary on their significance. Rhythm and pacing merge to create a breathlessness in the reader that approximates that of one seeking to escape a nightmare only to discover that one is already awake. Carefully chosen verbs such as "drowned," "vexed," and "reel" carry the tone of impending doom while pushing the reader forward to the poem's climax.

Crucial to the success of this effect is Yeats's skillful juxtaposition of biblical metaphor, inverted in its meaning, and pagan history. The first and second advents of Christ were familiar and benevolent landmarks in the historical mindset of Yeats's original readers—perhaps in a way that they no longer are to many Westerners. The poet's decision to link this Christian commonplace with the ancient riddle of the sphinx creates an unbearable tension in the poem's second movement. Notably, it is the *Spiritus Mundi* and not the *Spiritus Sanctus* (Holy Spirit) who is unable to discern the significance of the lion-man forming in the desert. The spirit of Judeo-Christian faith is absent or banished from the landscape, unable to assist in recovering the vision necessary to countermand this invasion by an alien consciousness.

The poet thus subtly paints the portrait of a secularized humankind no longer in tune with the purposes of God, its respect for the wisdom of the ancient world waning. Emptied thus of interpretive as well as recuperative powers, the reader faces the blank canvas of history, left only to wonder aloud "what rough beast . . . slouches toward Bethlehem," the birthplace of Christ, "to be born?" This ironic counterpose of knowledge and ignorance, discernment and blindness, gives the poem its lasting power to challenge and amaze later generations of readers who still seek illumination of history's meaning in the work of poets.

Themes and Meanings

Yeats believed that human history could be marked in twenty-century intervals. As the birth of Christ ended the reign of Greco-Roman culture, Yeats prophesies in the poem the end of Christianity's dominance over human philosophy and the Western social order in the twentieth century. Clearly, then, he uses the second-coming motif as a reference to a new incarnation other than Christ's that will displace Christian civilization with something less beneficent and conducive to human progress.

Like many turn-of-the-century artists, Yeats felt some ambivalence toward this apparent change in the human order. Ostensibly restricting the artistic imagination with its legalism and fixed moral code, Christianity also provided the metaphors of creator, creativity, freedom, and order that allowed the poet the sense of power to shape the world through words. In the aftermath of Christianity's reduction to mere theology or, worse, mere politics, the poet is forced to become simply one more observer, disarmed by social forces of his authority to address the issues of his times.

Though eccentric in his views of history, especially as set forth in the obscure and perplexing prose work *A Vision* (1925), Yeats was troubled by the overthrow of Czar Nicholas in Russia by the Marxist-Leninists and the apparent rise of Fascism in Europe. These events all portended to him a new "dark ages." Thus, many commentators view the poem as Yeats's prediction of the rise and triumph of totalitarianism in the early stages of the twentieth century.

Understood in this way, the "rough beast" of the poem embodies the lurking authoritarianism of governments and movements that place ideology above individual freedom and dignity as the basis for polity and social order. Often seen as messianic by their followers and supporters—hence the apocalyptic associations with Christ and his Second Coming—such political parties exploit the yearnings of oppressed or disenfranchised peoples for "self-government" ("the ceremony of innocence is drowned"). Their rhetorical hold on the public imagination is aided by the faithless and the feckless ("the best lack all conviction, while the worst/ are full of passionate intensity"); by calculated redefinition of what the "self" means, the people's aspirations are thwarted once the new regime is in power.

In "The Second Coming," the self is exemplified in the falcon that can no longer "hear the falconer"; no "revelation" is forthcoming except that of anarchy unbound. In the poet's view, the absence of either the inward sense of destiny and purpose (the falcon's instincts) or the outward witness of history and civilization (the falconer's call) unleashes a "blood-dimmed tide" of human misery that awaits despotic exploitation. At this symbolic Bethlehem, Westerners thus await a new incarnation whose interest will not be humankind's salvation but rather its subjugation.

Bruce L. Edwards

SEEING THINGS

Author: Seamus Heaney (1939-   )
Type of poem: Lyric
First published: 1991, in *Seeing Things*

The Poem

"Seeing Things" contains two sections. In the first, as the poem begins, the speaker is being helped into a small boat that will carry him and other passengers from Inishbofin, a small island off the coast of northwestern Ireland, to the mainland. He mentions what he sees, smells, and hears as they are helped into the shifting boat that is sitting low in the water. They sit together in "nervous twos and threes," obeying the boatmen's commands. Although the sea is calm, the speaker suddenly becomes anxious because of the motion of the boat as the diesel engine is started. As the boat proceeds over the water, he has the experience of mentally looking down from above at the boat and passengers—as if he were in "another boat/ Sailing through air"—as they fare "riskily" to their destination.

The second section begins with a single Latin word, *claritas*, which means "clearness" or "brightness," a splendor of objects affecting the sight; it also means "clearness to the mind." The speaker, having just experienced the literal waves of the sea, now looks at water carved in stone on a cathedral facade. He describes the sculptor's lines as "Hard and thin and sinuous"; playful fish are cavorting about. The main image in the stone carving is a figure of Jesus being baptized by his cousin John the Baptist, an event which prompts the speaker to write, "The stone's alive with what's invisible." The "invisible" may refer to another occurrence in that same biblical scene. The gospel writer records that a voice from a cloud was heard proclaiming, "This is my beloved son in whom I am well pleased." After the baptism, Jesus took decisive action and embarked on his public life.

The poem concludes with a reference to an atmospheric condition. The heat of the afternoon creates wavy, visible lines of heat in the air. These waves, like the waves of the sea and the water on the cathedral carving, prompt the speaker to reflect on life. He sees life as something dynamic, significant, and capable of sharp changes: The wavering air is "Like the zig-zag hieroglyph for life itself."

Forms and Devices

Although the poem is unrhymed, its cadences carry a lilting Irish rhythm in phrases such as "shilly-shallied," "nobody speaking," "but even so," "Swayed for balance," and "hurrying off." The poet uses devices such as alliteration, assonance, and consonance to approximate the quiet sounds of water on a Sunday morning—a repetition of *s*, *l*, and the short *u* sound in the lines "Inishbofin on a Sunday morning./ Sunlight, turfsmoke, seagulls, boatslip, diesel."

Seamus Heaney's use of unusual adjectives or epithets extends the meaning of the poem. He refers to *claritas* as a "dry-eyed Latin word," signifying a literal, physical condition for seeing things clearly. Then he describes the carving of Jesus as having "unwet knees," an observation that indicates how closely the poet studied the image and, consequently, why he was able to make some original associations with the water image. The "zig-zag hieroglyph" of the poem's last line unifies the poem, since it refers to all the water images and relates the zig-zag image to life's low and high points, to life's shilly-shallying (indecisive) moments, and to positive commitments.

"Seeing Things," as its title implies, is a poem about vision. The fusion of abstract and concrete, of natural and supernatural, is central to Heaney's visionary enthusiasm. Through the use of the image of waves and moving water in different contexts, the poet shares his vision with the reader: First, there are the literal waves of the Atlantic Ocean on which he and the other passengers—possibly schoolchildren, as the scene is based on a memory of Heaney's childhood—were gently tossed by the rocking of the boat. Because of Heaney's Catholic background and education, scriptural images remain an integral part of his work. The passengers also recall Jesus's disciples, frightened in a boat while Jesus slept. Heaney's use of mythology, or more precisely, his Dantesque vision, offers another angle of vision for the same scene: Because the passengers are sitting quietly, obeying the boatmen's commands, the reader is reminded of the mythological Charon, who ferried the dead across the River Styx to Hades.

The next image of moving water in the poem centers on a carving on the front of a medieval cathedral; there is both a "flowing river" and the movement of water as John pours water over Jesus's head. The water image here implies the exact opposite of the ferryman section, because the baptismal waters signify a rebirth, a beginning of Jesus's public life, a looking forward. The final reference to waves concerns waves of heat on a sultry afternoon, which affect vision. The poet presents an abstract pattern, a zig-zag, as symbolic of high and low points in a person's life. In "Seeing Things," the poet looks beyond the thing itself to see or understand the splendor that the thing (waves) represents.

Themes and Meanings

Heaney has commented, regarding this poem, that it is he himself as a child who fears crossing the water on a boat ride to church. He has the same fear of crossing those waves as did the ancient characters of mythology. He does not rid himself of his fear and anxiety until he is safely onshore looking back at the experience.

When he arrives at the church, the story pictured on the church's facade reminds him of the water he has just crossed, but this time, instead of seeing himself as the focus, he looks at the figure of Christ being baptized. The poet meditates on this immersion in water as a deliberate choice—no fear is evident here. Moreover, this event, this baptism, separates the hidden life of Jesus up to this time from the very public life which he sees as his mission or vocation. Heaney may have in mind the differing demands of his own private and public lives. Many of Heaney's poems refer to the struggles he had after deciding to pursue poetry as his vocation, so it is understandable that this baptism makes such an impression on him.

In the last poetic sentence (the last three lines), Heaney pictures the children, himself among them, feeling the intense heat of the day. As the figure of Jesus stands up to his knees in water, he and the children are "up to our eyes" in heat waves, putting the poet in the position of "seeing things" in both a literal and metaphorical way.

Rita M. Scully

THE SEEKERS OF LICE

Author: Arthur Rimbaud (1854-1891)
Type of poem: Lyric
First published: 1891, as "Les Chercheuses de poux," in *Reliquaire*; English translation collected in *Complete Works, Selected Letters*, 1966

The Poem

"The Seekers of Lice" is a twenty-line poem divided into five quatrains of Alexandrines with a rhyme scheme of *abab*. The title suggests an unpleasant topic, playing against the beauty of the poet's words. Sensory images are everywhere in the poem. In the first line, "the child" is introduced; his forehead is covered with "the red torment" caused by the lice. Two "tall gracious sisters" appear "with delicate hands and silvery fingernails." In the second quatrain, these sisters remove the child from his bed and seat him by an "open window." The child is bombarded by the visual sensations of the outside natural world and the sensual fingers of the sisters running through his infested hair.

The child is experiencing more than the removal of the lice, however; he is being tenderly loved by these "tall gracious sisters." In the third quatrain, the child hears the sisters singing through their breathing and whistling as they suck in their saliva. The images and the very words used express the child's heightened auditory experience. The images from the third quatrain are surreal; the child is almost in a trance. He is under the spell of the sisters as they caress his predicament away. The last line of the third quatrain includes "the desire for kisses." The child's experience has taken on an erotic quality. The fourth quatrain describes how he hears the sound of the sisters' black eyelashes "blinking." He smells a "perfumed stillness" while "royal nails" squash "the gray and lazy lice." In this quatrain, the child continues to be overpowered by sensual experiences. He not only inhales the perfume, but he also hears the "crackling" of the lice being squashed. The child is baffled and confused about how to respond to what is happening to him.

Whereas the first quatrain began with "When," the fifth and last quatrain begins with "Then." The situation presented at the beginning of "The Seekers of Lice" finds its resolution in this last quatrain. The first line speaks of the "wine of Idleness." The child is moving ever closer to the realm of rapturous delight. In addition to the wine, there is "the delirium of a mouth-organ's sigh" in the second line, which, combined with the first line, tips the scales beyond self-control. Pain and pleasure are intertwined, and the child cannot help but feel, in the last line of the poem, "an endless need to cry."

Forms and Devices

The power of "The Seekers of Lice" is generated by its musical quality, which plays against the unpleasant reality of the poem's subject. The poet walks a fine line without ever making the poem seem morbid. The rhyme scheme enhances the elegant quality of the poem; the *abab* rhyming makes the poem seem songlike. The reader is swept up in the rhythm as the sensual images weave their spell. The poem begins with "When," almost as a fairy tale would begin with "Once upon a time." As in some fairy tales, the inviting language disguises gruesome happenings.

The child in "The Seekers of Lice" is confronted with a sensual experience that almost overwhelms him. The "tall gracious sisters" have "delicate hands and silvery fingernails" which will move through his hair in search of the "lazy lice." The poem is much more than the mere squashing of lice. Arthur Rimbaud begins the poem by adding surreal touches, as when the child hears the sisters breathe and makes it out to be singing; when they draw in their saliva, it becomes whistling. The poet takes great care in the progression of his images. In the opening lines of the first and second quatrains the child is identified by the genderless term "child," whereas in the opening lines of the third and fourth quatrains, the child is identified as "he." The sisters of the first quatrain become "They" in the second.

Sound, smell, and sight are everywhere in the poem, creating sharp contrasts that show the poet's skill at dramatizing, at setting up finely woven scenes. The experience for the child is one of total sensual release, and Rimbaud employs alliteration to add to the trancelike quality of the poem. "The Seekers of Lice" moves to its emotional conclusion in which "Then" is the first word of the last quatrain, signifying that there will be a resolution. "Wine of Idleness," "delirium," and "slow caresses" bring the child to a heightened sense of happiness that leads to "an endless need to cry." The subject of the poem is all but lost in the delicacy of the ending. "The Seekers of Lice" is a song that sings both sweetly and sadly.

Themes and Meanings

In 1870, Arthur Rimbaud had become tired of living in Charleville, France, with his domineering mother. He wished to set off for Paris and taste a new life that he could only imagine. He was merely sixteen at the time, yet his poetic genius was on the verge of full flower. A teacher by the name of Georges Izambard had become a friend and adviser of young Rimbaud when Izambard was teaching in Charleville. Izambard encouraged Rimbaud by being sympathetic to his situation and his poetic need to expand his horizons beyond the provincial life of his hometown. Rimbaud did escape to Paris, but there he was arrested, since he did not have enough money to pay the full fare. Izambard was contacted, and he sent money to bail Rimbaud out of prison. It was arranged that the young rebel would travel to Douai, which was northwest of Charleville, and stay with Izambard's aunts. He spent two enjoyable weeks with the Gindre sisters before he was forced to return home to Madame Rimbaud.

This episode is important in relation to "The Seekers of Lice," which Rimbaud wrote when he was no older than eighteen. The "tall gracious sisters" introduced in the poem are the Gindre sisters, and—almost certainly—the child is Rimbaud himself. The sisters most likely gave the runaway child tender care that probably both excited and confused him. His experience with his own mother was not of the same kind.

The child came to these two women in need of being rid of the lice that had infested him at his previous location. At sixteen, Rimbaud was in the throes of being awakened erotically. The world of the senses is both intriguing and frightening, and the adolescent wishes to recapture the innocence of childhood even as he yearns to explore the sensual world. Because of the Franco-Prussian War, the schools in Charleville had to be closed down, so Rimbaud's formal education came to a halt. The Gindre sisters served to educate the young poet, in a different way, in the fresh-air world of Douai.

It speaks to the genius of Rimbaud that he was able to encapsulate his experience with these two older women in such an intriguing fashion. The reality of why the child is being caressed never quite disappears totally, but the surreal and sensual images almost win the day. The poem is particularly effective because of the emotional power of its contrasting images. The subtlety of the tenderness expressed speaks to the young Rimbaud's realization of how wonderful it can be to be under the care of concerned females. Inspired by his two weeks in Douai, he wrote a delicately beautiful poem on a distasteful subject. In so doing, Rimbaud harkened back to the beautiful and disturbing poems of Charles Baudelaire.

Michael Jeffrys

SELF-PORTRAIT IN A CONVEX MIRROR

Author: John Ashbery (1927-   )
Type of poem: Meditation
First published: 1975, in *Self-Portrait in a Convex Mirror*

The Poem

"Self-Portrait in a Convex Mirror" is a long poem in free verse, its 552 lines divided into six verse paragraphs of unequal length. The title refers to a 1524 painting by the Italian artist Francesco Mazzola, also known as Il Parmigianino. "Self-Portrait in a Convex Mirror" makes the poet's thoughts about Parmigianino's painting the focus for a different kind of self-portrait, a self-portrait in words.

Although a poet may use the first person as the voice of a persona, a character whose outlook and experience are quite different from the poet's, in "Self-Portrait in a Convex Mirror," the voice is John Ashbery's own. The poem represents the poet thinking out loud, revealing the processes of his own mind as he considers Parmigianino's self-portrait.

In the first verse paragraph, Ashbery quotes from Giorgio Vasari's *Lives of the Most Eminent Painters, Sculptors, and Architects* (1550). Vasari describes how Parmigianino painted his self-portrait on half of a ball of wood as if his face were reflected in the surface of a convex mirror. In the resulting painting, Parmigianino's right hand appears to be thrust forward "as though to protect/ What it advertises." Describing the painting, the poet is also interpreting it, finding in it several paradoxes: a surface which appears to have depth, a "soul [that] is not a soul," and "Affirmation that doesn't affirm anything."

The second verse paragraph suggests an interruption in Ashbery's meditation. In fact, each verse paragraph represents a break in the poet's attention as his thoughts move toward and away from the painting. As Ashbery's attention draws away from the painting, he makes more comparisons between Parmigianino's self-portrait and the poet's own mind. The painting becomes a "mirror" for the poet's thoughts. By painting a picture of himself, Parmigianino has captured for the future the illusion of the present moment, an illusion which the poet tries to duplicate in words.

In the third verse paragraph, the poet meditates on the present depicted in the painting, until his experience of the painting becomes like a dream. The poet awakens from this "dream" into his own present, less fixed and idealized than the present in Parmigianino's painting. It is easier, the poet says, to imagine the future or to remember the past than to gain perspective on the chaotic and elusive present.

As the poet's thoughts drift away from the painting, in the fourth verse paragraph—the poem's shortest—he calls the painting to mind again, thinking of it as a surprising concept, "the first mirror portrait." At first the painting appears to be an optical illusion, a mirror reflecting the poet's own face rather than Parmigianino's. Recognizing that illusion, the poet imagines that he has surprised the painter at his work. As the poet looks into the painting, he is looking into Parmigianino's world and therefore into the past.

In the fifth verse paragraph, the poet wonders if the painting will survive into the future and still be in style, as it has already survived the time since Parmigianino painted it. Ashbery sees Parmigianino's self-portrait as a metaphorical mirror in which each viewer, including those in the future, may find things that are as much in the viewer as in the painting.

The sixth and last verse paragraph, by far the poem's longest, turns back to the painting. Questioning the role that love plays in Parmigianino's painting, Ashbery comes back to the present. The "explosion" of details here and now is "so precise, so fine," that "We don't need paintings or/ Doggerel written by mature poets." Yet the present, with "no margins," seems not to exist when contrasted with "the portrait's will to endure."

The self-portrait was "a life-obstructing task" because it forced Parmigianino away from the pleasures of the present to paint a picture that looked into the future. As a result, however, "This past/ Is now here," in "the painter's/ Reflected face." The poet's present in "April sunlight" in a room in New York City is mingled with the painter's present in the past and in memory.

Forms and Devices

Ashbery's poetry is often regarded as difficult. Written in free verse, "Self-Portrait in a Convex Mirror" represents what is sometimes called the stream of consciousness. Ashbery's free verse challenges accepted notions of poetry. One of his earlier books, *Three Poems* (1972), is actually written in prose, partly to question the boundaries between poetry and prose. The spontaneous and open style of "Self-Portrait in a Convex Mirror" permits Ashbery to imitate both the precision and the vagueness of what flows through his mind. Because it represents the processes of his mind reflecting on the painting, Ashbery's poem is often allusive and ambiguous.

For many years, Ashbery worked as a writer and art critic for *Art News*. "Self-Portrait in a Convex Mirror" includes allusions to art and art criticism as well as to music (composer Alban Berg's comment on "a phrase in Mahler's Ninth" symphony) and to literature (William Shakespeare's *Cymbeline*, c. 1609-1610). When Ashbery incorporates direct quotations from prose works in his poem, he is scrupulous about mentioning the sources of quotes. As the poet transcribes the processes of his own mind, however, he draws upon what he knows, without stopping to explain every reference.

By permitting paradoxes and ambiguities, the poem's inclusiveness adds to its difficulty. When Ashbery says that Parmigianino's picture is "life-obstructing," that statement challenges its context in the poem. Works of art in general, including the poem, are more often thought of as life-enhancing. In order to capture the present, Parmigianino's "obstruction" must stop it. Paradoxically, when it is stopped in a work of art, the present becomes the past, but it also looks into the future. The poet's self-consciousness about the processes of his mind allows him to question his own preoccupations as he holds up the mirror to his consciousness.

When Ashbery ambiguously mentions "The shadow of the city" in the fifth verse paragraph, the city is Rome, where Ashbery says Parmigianino was painting (but not the self-portrait) while the city was being sacked by the imperial forces of Charles V of Spain in 1527. The city is also Vienna, where the poet says he saw the painting with a friend in 1959. Finally, the city is New York, where the poet is now writing the poem. That the sack of Rome was still in the future when Parmigianino was painting the self-portrait is an example of the subtlety of the poet's concern with time.

A key pun in the poem is Ashbery's reference to speculation, which comes "From the Latin *speculum*, mirror." In a sense the poem is all speculation, as Ashbery holds Parmigianino's painting to the mirror of the poet's own mind. Speculation leads to ambiguity. Because the painting explains nothing, it permits contradictory interpretations. The poet wonders, for example, if Parmigianino's hand in the painting is held forth as a shield or as a greeting.

Ashbery heightens the ambiguity of certain sentences by using unclear pronoun references. The poet begins, "As Parmigianino did it," leaving the reader to figure out that "it" refers to the self-portrait in the poem's title. Here, as elsewhere in the poem, the pronoun "it" implicitly includes both self-portraits, Parmigianino's painting and Ashbery's poem. The poet avoids saying "I" until the second verse paragraph (preferring, for example, "the attention turns" to "my attention turns"), when he says "I think of the friends." "Self-Portrait in a Convex Mirror" uses these oblique references to imitate the evasions of the painted self-portrait.

Like the painting, the poem at once identifies and does not identify. How does the poet know that the face in the painting is Parmigianino's? How does the reader know that the identity behind the poem's is Ashbery's? Parmigianino's painting is not identical with Parmigianino any more than writing is identical with thinking. In "Self-Portrait in a Convex Mirror," the phrase "As though to protect/ What it advertises" seems to describe Ashbery's style as much as Parmigianino's painted hand.

Themes and Meanings

"Self-Portrait in a Convex Mirror" is a poem about identity and time, especially about the elusiveness of the present. The differences between Parmigianino's self-portrait in paint and Ashbery's self-portrait in words cause the poet to question art's distortions. Because works of art attempt to make time stand still, they inevitably distort the reality they seek to portray. Perhaps the simplest statement one can make about the poem is that it works out the differences between a painted self-portrait and a poetic one. If Parmigianino's self-portrait is a "snapshot" of his face at a given moment, Ashbery's self-portrait is a moving picture of his mind working in time. Parmigianino's portrait circumscribes the painter's identity more straightforwardly than the poem does. By describing, imitating, and challenging the painting, Ashbery's poem questions the limitations and ambitions of art.

Both the painter and the poet try to capture the elusive present. To do so, both must ignore the details around them which multiply into infinity. Instead of trying to describe everything he sees, the painter focuses on something in particular—in this case, his own reflection. A painting such as Parmigianino's has a central figure, the subject of the painting, but also at least a minimal background of incidental details. Instead of describing his own face, however, the poet describes the painting. Because it takes more time to read Ashbery's self-portrait than it does to look at Parmigianino's, the present in the poem seems more fluid than it does in the painting.

Even when the poet's mind seems to wander, the subject of the poem is still Parmigianino's painting; the poet, however, has more difficulty knowing what to exclude than the painter did. In the sense that the poet could go on responding to the painting, Parmigianino's painted self-portrait is closed and Ashbery's verbal one is open. In Ashbery's self-portrait, the central subject is the poet's mind, or what fills his mind as he thinks about Parmigianino's painting. The incidental details—the poet's speculations about the painting—are the central figure. Nevertheless, Ashbery's returning again and again to the painting gives "Self-Portrait in a Convex Mirror" an anchor that some of his other poems seem to lack.

The poem is an interior rather than an exterior self-portrait. The poet can see with perfect clarity in Parmigianino's picture what the painter looked like on a certain day. Yet the poet has no explanation of the painter's inner being, his thoughts, except what the poet can "read" in the painting. Where the painting is circumscribed and fixed, the poem is loose and fluid.

Ashbery's self-portrait has several vagaries. The poem assumes familiarity with Parmigianino's painting, so it includes no concrete description of the face in the convex mirror. It also never describes Ashbery's own face. Nor does it make clear whether Ashbery has a copy of Parmigianino's painting before him as he writes. He quotes two art critics without explaining whether he is quoting from memory or open books. Words referring to time appear throughout the poem, but the poet never states explicitly the time of the poem's composition. These vagaries suggest the flow of memory and the uncertainty of identity.

The limitations of Parmigianino's invented convention both create and frustrate the inclusive identity Ashbery tries to portray in the poem, which is itself an attempt to see both Parmigianino's and Ashbery's identities in Parmigianino's faked mirror. Art is illusion, giving apparent permanence to something that does not exist except in the work of art. In another sense, the picture exists only when one looks at it, "its room, our moments of attention." "Self-Portrait in a Convex Mirror" moves into "the distance between us," between Ashbery and Parmigianino, between perception and interpretation, between art and audience, and therefore between Ashbery and the reader.

Thomas Lisk

SEPTEMBER 1, 1939

Author: W. H. Auden (1907-1973)
Type of poem: Lyric/meditation
First published: 1939; collected in *Another Time*, 1940

The Poem

"September 1, 1939" consists of nine stanzas of eleven lines each. The title refers to the beginning of World War II, the day that Adolf Hitler invaded Poland. W. H. Auden uses the occasion to write a farewell to the 1930's and to meditate on the social and psychological causes of war.

The poem is written in the first person, with the poet addressing the reader directly. Auden claims to be writing the poem in a bar in midtown Manhattan. While the setting may seem, at first, inappropriate for a serious subject, it is typical of Auden, as well as of many other modern poets, to take a detached point of view—even when their subjects are profoundly important to them. The mood or tone of the entire poem is established in the first stanza. The poet reports directly his feelings of uncertainty and fear for the future, as well as his distrust of the socialist schemes of the 1930's that failed to prevent the recurrence of war.

In the following three stanzas (2 through 4), Auden characteristically gives an intellectual analysis of the causes of the war. Two years earlier, in "Spain 1937," he had used the occasion of the Spanish civil struggle to treat war as a psychological rather than a political phenomenon. Similarly, in "September 1, 1939," he observes that European cultural history is a madness that erupts repeatedly in war. The second stanza affirms the historical and psychological explanations: the emphasis, beginning with Protestantism, on man as an economic being, and the belief that psychopaths like Hitler are created by abuses they suffer in childhood.

Auden next shows how impervious each historical age is to others and how each fails to learn from its predecessors. In the third stanza, the poet refers to the ancient Greek historian Thucydides, who wrote the first history of a war, the Peloponnesian. Thucydides believed that because human nature did not change, such conflicts would be repeated in every age. Auden not only affirms Thucydides' belief, but he also gives the recurrence of war a psychological motive: Humans actually want to experience pain, not avoid it. In the fourth stanza, Auden refers to statesmen who, in all ages, foolishly rationalize war until they are ultimately forced to admit what Thucydides knew: All war reduces to motives of imperialism.

The next three stanzas (5 through 7) become more personal in tone as the poet describes the inhabitants of the bar. Like him, they are typical urbanites who huddle, build defenses against reality, and share a "normal" desire that is impossible to gratify: to be loved exclusively by another human being. Average citizens commit themselves to this impossible goal as determinedly as governments pursue the game of war.

In the eighth stanza, the poet portrays himself not as a common bar patron but as a higher voice of authority. In a poem ("In Memory of W. B. Yeats") commemorating the Irish poet William Butler Yeats, published just six months previously, Auden had asked whether poets could ever, through their verse, alter a course of events. In that poem and in this one, he reaches the same conclusion: All the poet can do is state truths. The truth Auden offers in the eighth stanza was to cause him great difficulty and lead him to remove first this stanza and then the entire poem from his collected works. The last line of the stanza—"We must love one another or die"—Auden changed once to "and die" (for Oscar Williams's reprinting in *The New Pocket Anthology of American Verse from Colonial Days to the Present*, 1955). Yet then Auden decided that both versions were dishonest, since all die anyway.

The last stanza offers a humane and hopeful tone that is absent from the rest of the poem. The poet becomes not a seer but merely one of many citizens who desire a just society. He offers not a sweeping truth but a modest prayer: to reject the prevalent mood of despair and thereby affirm that life is purposeful.

Forms and Devices

Auden is regarded, because of his style, as a poet of logic rather than emotion. He was one of the first modern poets to reject the nineteenth century Romantic concept that reading poetry should be a sensuous experience and a way to reach emotions that could not be explained by reason. Auden argued that images in poetry could show a "one to one correspondence . . . grasped by the reader's reason"; poets did not have to use symbols that suggested multiple meanings or relationships (*The Enchafèd Flood*, 1950).

One feature of Auden's poems, especially in the 1930's and early 1940's, is his frequent use of adjectives to modify neutral or abstract nouns. Another device is to attach an active or colorful verb to a flat or prosaic subject noun. For example, the 1930's are "a low dishonest decade," pain is "habit-forming," and skyscrapers, like tall people, "use Their full height" to impress.

Another way that Auden makes his lines poetic is to transfer adjectives from the words they logically modify to other words in the sentence. It is the readers' job to unscramble the sentence and make it prosaic. For example, New York's rush-hour morning commuters, who give the city its dense workaday population, are described as "dense." Tall buildings that blindly, or unwittingly, "proclaim" are "blind."

In "September 1, 1939," Auden was influenced by Yeats's poem about the Irish rebellion, "Easter 1916." The diction and rhythm of Yeats's poem are echoed, for example, in lines 6 through 11 of Auden's first stanza. The short lines of Auden's poem, usually of six or seven syllables, echo Yeats's of seven or eight.

Though Auden came to regret Yeats's influence on his poems, he never slavishly followed him. Auden's use of rhyme, for example, is subtler and much less regular. Auden is fond of slant (or half) rhymes: life/leaf, grave/grief, fear/expire. Seldom does a pattern of end rhyme last throughout a stanza. Auden frequently uses half-rhymes within lines, as in stanza 5, where the *f-r-t-m* sound pattern of the phrase "fort assume" is answered in the next line by "furniture of home." The incremental repetition of words or phrases, used infrequently, helps Auden to make transitions. At the end of the fourth stanza, a metaphor—the "face" of Imperialism—is transferred to human "Faces along the bar." "Face" is the only word repeated in the entire poem.

Themes and Meanings

"September 1, 1939" records Auden's rejection of some of the ideologies of the 1930's, most notably Marxist socialism. His direct statement in stanza 8, "There is no such thing as the State," sums up what the poem has been building to from its beginning. The "clever hopes" of stanza 1 refer mainly to socialist economic schemes that most of the British intelligentsia espoused after World War I. Such schemes had not diminished the growth of a capitalist economy nor improved the lot of the working class but, worse yet, merely aggravated the social conditions under which totalitarianism flourished.

Auden, however, blames more than one decade. From the time of the Reformation ("Luther until now"), the humanity of man has been diminished. The fascist despair of the 1930's was also the accumulation of such Western philosophical views as Thomas Hobbes', for example, that human life was nasty and brutish.

In "September 1, 1939," Auden's early interest in Sigmund Freud begins to combine with an emergent affirmation of Christianity. Explaining how to account for modern monsters such as Hitler, Auden offers not simply a reductive Freudian approach but a Christian precept. Exploring Hitler's childhood ("what occurred at Linz") is a Freudian tactic to prove scientifically the simple Christian truism of the Golden Rule given at the end of stanza 2.

"September 1, 1939" also expresses themes developed in other works of the period by Auden. In *Letter to Lord Byron* (1937), Auden argues the Freudian/Marxist determinism that behavior is determined unconsciously by instinctive needs, such as hunger and love. In "September 1, 1939," the poet affirms that belief in the problematic eighth stanza: "Hunger allows no choice." The biological need for love is the "error bred in the bone," a desire that can never be fulfilled.

In a later work, "The Prolific and the Devourer," Auden wrote that while a "change of heart," a turning away from Fascism, would not save the world, historical development would nevertheless produce a change of heart. Both failure and success increase human understanding. It is this moderate optimism—which has become known as liberal humanism—that emerges at the end of "September 1, 1939." From the humanist E. M. Forster's essay, "What I Believe," Auden borrows the image of "points of light," noting that their appearance is "Ironic." These points are the "Just," a category very close to the Christian righteous, who emerge out of nowhere (some vast darkness) to "exchange . . . messages" of hope and affirmation. The ending becomes a description, then, of exactly what Auden has done in "September 1, 1939": One of the Just, he has shared his "message" with the reader.

Alvin Sullivan

SERPENT KNOWLEDGE

Author: Robert Pinsky (1940-   )
Type of poem: Meditation
First published: 1979, in *An Explanation of America*

The Poem

Robert Pinsky's "Serpent Knowledge" is a subsection of a book-length meditation, *An Explanation of America*, addressed to his daughter Nicole. In the larger, extended poem, Pinsky both describes and teaches about the past: his own personal past, the past of his generation, and the past particular to Americans in the mid-twentieth century. "Serpent Knowledge" is section 2 of "Part Three: Its Everlasting Possibility" and concentrates on gathering images, ideas, and events that define for Pinsky what evil means in the United States: random violence and war, with their resultant confusion, ambivalence, and distortion.

The poem opens with Pinsky's observation of something his daughter has written in school about snakes. She has found a textbook somewhere that suggests snakes are born "already knowing/ Everything they will ever need to know," and her father, the poet, simply does not believe it. Pinsky's insistence that humans are "Not born already knowing all we need" reinforces the impossibility of knowing fully even oneself, much less the wider world containing evils of humanity's own devising and of "some new stage of life."

The poem engages the reader (and Pinsky's daughter) in a kind of earnest, lucid conversation in which explanations from the past illuminate the meaning of the present. In the first and second stanzas Pinsky introduces a snake, loaded with biblical allusions and sinister aspects, along with his own memories of the Vietnam War, where twists and threads of American political and social history appear as labyrinthine, mysterious, and contorted as a snake's body and the path it follows. Here readers can see distinctly Pinsky's debt to older poet-critics, since it was Samuel Taylor Coleridge who first thought of lyric poetry as a snake doubling back on itself.

In succeeding stanzas Pinsky uses the juxtaposition of personal and universal images from television as well as from documented history, with their similarly odd side-by-side presentation of simple and complex events, to identify spots along "different overlapping stretches/ Of the same highway" that everyone travels through life. He points out, in a tone both pedagogical and fatherly, scenes of past and present encountered on the shared highway: "A family graveyard on an Indian mound" dignifies the past, while "trashy lake-towns, and the tourist-pits" exemplify the present. An extended description of a terrible event where a "teenaged girl/ From down the street" becomes the victim of random and inexplicable violence opens a digression on the forces of evil that could account for this particular horror and others like it. Pinsky is forced to admit that facts confirm a "serpent knowledge"—of evil—in the history of humankind and "in whose [serpent] body they must live."

The final stanzas of the poem turn again to Vietnam, where "Americans descending in machines/ With wasted bravery and blood" carry out orders from unseen commanders. An elaborate analogy to ancient Saguntum, the infamous site of the Second Punic War's near-annihilation of that Roman-occupied town in Spain, sustains Pinsky's blistering indictment of the holocaust produced by every war in history.

Forms and Devices

The division of *An Explanation of America* into three parts, and those parts into subsections, permits the illusion of teaching from a text. This strategy, because it is universally familiar, comforts the reader through the appalling revelations that Pinsky makes about evil in the United States: its erotic urges, its political shrewdness, its spiritual malaise. Pinsky's elegant conversational style in the long, discursive, blank-verse narrative of "Serpent Knowledge" contrasts dramatically with the subject matter he presents.

The poem seems to be loosely organized around graphic particulars of war and violence, but Pinsky's rational, temperate, and civilized tone controls both the pace and presentation of these images to organize the poem structurally beyond vivid particulars. His use of the ordinary enhances the power of his moral authority. In much the same way, his choice of iambic blank verse cools, with its natural rhythm, the prose of conversation. A scene may be real or ideal, "the highway" concrete or abstract: Explicit images compress and illuminate the knowledge that Pinsky wishes to share with his daughter.

"Serpent Knowledge" exemplifies a structural device characteristic of Pinsky's extended meditation: Opening with a dense pattern of recollection composed of vivid and often painful memories, the poem unfolds into complex analogies that produce observations of great insight. Pinsky uses the colon liberally, for its access to long, languid sentences that digress and amplify, so that the poem's structure is serpentine in its progress, snaking through analogy and image. His "snake's-back" is a gentle reminder to the reader that a word or phrase may represent both action and object, just as history is both an event and its arrangement.

Throughout the poem, as historical images and ideas of Vietnam fuse with the casual events and encounters of Pinsky's individual experience, a complex pattern of emotions and connections composes an idiosyncratic explanation of America. Because the tone is conscientious and truthful, the reader concludes that Pinsky's version—or vision—of America is neither sentimental nor satiric.

Pinsky uses the syncopation of jazz in "Serpent Knowledge " to produce a colloquial discourse and rhythmic variation of the regular beat. An avid saxophone player, he loosens up traditional poetic language with offbeat slang that conveys the twang of "goofy," "grisly" America. The poem's humor is punctuated with an irony that assumes the reader's intelligent and patient willingness to appreciate Pinsky's efforts to adapt the traditions of poetic form to reflect the modern American appetite for the awful and for the entertaining. Like the idea of "foreign soil"—for Pinsky, Vietnam, for his daughter, "Oregon" (where the neighbor's child was attacked)—America is transformed "In a time when the country aged itself" into an alien landscape where the inhabitants are unable to profit from their own bitter experiences and are utterly unconscious of repeating a sad and bloody history.

Themes and Meanings

In an interview in 1997 at Northwestern University, Pinsky explained that "the only protection against copying the past is intimate knowledge of the past." His America in "Serpent Knowledge" is young but not innocent; his America is inexperienced but not ignorant. Pinsky represents the United States as a dynamic jumble of mistakes in fact—the serpent in the textbook—and judgment—the Vietnam War—that are transformed into what people call history. Recollections of evil, ancient or modern, are part of that assimilation. Pinsky's thematic development in "Serpent Knowledge" balances the frank, immediate, and animated with the contemplative, cautious, and philosophical dimensions. He is always cognizant of the snake being there. He is keeping an eye on it, as on Nicole, because that is an important human responsibility.

Pinsky is not afraid of the truth, but it is also essential to "Serpent Knowledge" that he is not afraid of his poetic responsibility to speak of truth and of evil. The war in Vietnam is Pinsky's personal choice of an evil, in fact and in imagination, so "threatening to gape and swallow and enclose the poem" that it could devour his work as descriptions of earlier conflicts have dominated history. Knowledge of evil, whether brought by a serpent or by a newspaper, is not intended to make people afraid, but to make them aware.

When all the complexities of modern life are played out against a rich and varied historical panorama, Pinsky expects that his daughter and the reader will grasp at once the universality of the human condition and the unique possibilities of each individual position in the world. If humans are forced to repeat history, Pinsky seems to be saying in the poem, let them at least do better. If Pinsky asks his daughter to take nothing for granted in history, the alternative lesson requires that she accept his tentative moral authority—his story—in order to shape her own future.

Several distinct universal themes merge and emerge in *An Explanation of America* and as part of the texture of "Serpent Knowledge." These themes include evil, in all its forms, which may be beautiful as well as brutal; childhood, in Pinsky's own recollection and that of the daughter to whom he directs his wisdom and common sense in the poem; and the enormous power of language to change, to comfort, to inspire, and to gratify. The "different lacks, and visions" that divide Pinsky from his daughter, and his daughters from each other, are "the words" by which they define and describe their own unique experiences. In that devotion to language Pinsky concentrates his energy as poet, as teacher, and as father. The medium of words, with its tradition grounded in oral poetry and storytelling, is a vital form of communication and of passing on memory from one generation to the next. The redemptive quality of human language is more important than almost any other human ability. However, people can never escape from the truth it tells about the human condition.

Kathleen Bonann Marshall

SESTINA

Author: Elizabeth Bishop (1911-1979)
Type of poem: Narrative
First published: 1956; collected in *Questions of Travel*, 1965

The Poem

In "Sestina," Elizabeth Bishop tells a painful story of a grandmother and a child living with loss. The story, set in a kitchen on a rainy late afternoon in September, features two actions: having tea and drawing. Although the woman tries to remain cheerful and thus protect the child, her tears give away her sadness. The child, meanwhile, not only observes these troubling signs but also draws a house that makes her proud. By the final nine lines of the poem, a surprising thing happens, unnoticed by the grandmother. The buttons in the drawing become "little moons" and "fall down like tears/ . . . into the flower bed the child/ has carefully placed" in the drawing. Thus, while the characters are very close to one another, there is a contrast—even an opposition—between them. The grandmother tries to make the desolate day pleasant, while the child imagines and draws a world preoccupied with tears.

Read aloud, "Sestina" assumes a wondering, storybook tone, especially as the more fanciful details emerge. The teakettle produces "tears" that "dance." The almanac, which both provides the grandmother with jokes and reinforces her sense of doom, "hovers" in a "Birdlike" fashion. Both the almanac and the stove speak.

These details distinguish the child's perspective from the grandmother's. In the opening lines, the grandmother devotes considerable effort to amusing the child. However, as the poem continues, the child's role comes to the fore, first through his or her perceptions and then through his or her drawing. The result is subversive, the child's intuition undercutting the will of the woman. The locus of the struggle is revealed in adjectives: "small hard," "mad," "hot black," "clever," "Birdlike," "rigid," and "inscrutable." Reading such words, one senses greater vibrancy than in the lines depicting the grandmother—the child's developing independence, perhaps, or anger, whether it be directed at the grandmother or elsewhere, that the child's pain spawns.

"Sestina" never states the cause of the characters' sadness. The fact that it is a man whom the child draws "with buttons like tears" may suggest that someone—the grandfather or perhaps the child's father—has died or left. Certainly, the grief is serious, for the final three lines indicate that the problem will persist. A study of Bishop's life reveals her father died when she was one year old, but the absence that may have troubled her more was that of her mother, whom Bishop never saw after she was institutionalized for serious mental illness. The loss of both parents resulted in the young Bishop spending time with her grandmother in Nova Scotia as well as having to move unwillingly to Massachusetts to attend school. Bishop never outgrew the specter of her mother and the terrible feeling of not belonging.

Forms and Devices

Bishop grouped "Sestina" with several other poems about her childhood in Nova Scotia in her 1965 book *Questions of Travel*. Living in Brazil, she found, brought back vivid memories of life in Great Village, along the Bay of Fundy. In "Sestina," as well as "Manners" and "First Death in Nova Scotia," a child figures prominently, providing a persona through which the mature poet presents the past.

The latter two poems use first-person point of view, the child's voice telling the story, but "Sestina" uses the third person. This device blends the poet's adult perspective with the child's. It also permits Bishop to control the emotional distance between the reader and the character. The first stanzas focus on the grandmother, but when Bishop presents the child's perception of the teakettle in the third stanza, the language becomes more urgent. The choice of the third person may have helped Bishop treat highly charged memories, may have allowed her, in other words, to steady herself emotionally and use the characters—human and not—to reenact a persisting trauma.

The setting—both atmosphere and place—is also vital to the story. The chilly, rainy weather, as mentioned earlier, mirrors the unhappiness in the kitchen. Bishop set the poem at a turning point—a liminal moment. The season, as the month and the word "equinoctial" signal, is changing. It is likely, given the fact that Nova Scotia sits halfway between the equator and the North Pole, that "the failing light" is also seasonal. On the other hand, the kitchen, particularly the stove, permits Bishop to emphasize the grandmother's desire for warmth and comfort. The stove, in fact, is reminiscent of fairy tales, especially those in which security and nurturing prepare for a child's maturing.

The poetic form Bishop chose, the sestina, imparts a sense of suspension. This form, which originated in Provençal verse of the Middle Ages, requires the repetition of six words at the ends of lines. The order changes in a prescribed way through six stanzas of six lines, then the six words appear, two per line, in a three-line envoy. Using letters to represent the key words, one finds that the *abcdef* order of the first stanza becomes *faebdc* in the second, then *cfdabe* in the third, and so on. That these words happen to be nouns emphasizes the symbolic, or iconic, nature of the story. The envoy compresses the repetition into three lines, providing finality. This elaborate, regular remixing can have impressive emotional impact; perhaps one should say that this artistry highlights the poet's patterns of thought.

In "Sestina," the repetition seems obsessive, emphasizing the isolation of the scene and the way it encloses the characters. It is particularly easy to feel the repetition as the first line of a stanza ends with the last word of the previous stanza. Regardless of the number of arrangements of the final words, the sense of loss persists. The envoy makes it clear that the trauma has not been resolved.

As much as one examines devices, there remains a feature—tone—that might best be called pure Bishop style. Labels such as "bemused," "knowing," "detached," "ironic," and "whimsical" catch elements of it. The emphasis upon tears, and the artificial way they are portrayed, is one trademark, as is the precise sense of visual detail (Bishop herself sketched and did watercolors). In addition, this poem often sounds like prose: the use of dialogue, for example, and the long, careful sentence comprising the sixth stanza.

"Sestina," in other words, is not personal confession, as the lack of personal names indicates, but representative in the way that a tale is. Along with the persona, the point of view, and the poetic form, the language creates a complex experience for the reader. One sympathizes with both the grandmother and the child, sensing sorrow, yearning, and the tensing of the child's effort to be an individual within the sheltering, suffocating domestic scene. Yet one also hears a wariness in Bishop's telling of their story.

Themes and Meanings

Read within the context of fairy tales, "Sestina" speaks not only of profound sorrow but also of personal growth. The grandmother may pretend to be happy in order to maintain stability and provide shelter, but the child recognizes the difficult emotions of their predicament. Moreover, the play of the child's mind, which turns the almanac into a bird, lets the stove and the almanac speak, and draws its own version of the child's world, provides a distinctive way of being effectual—of, as some might say, "dealing with things." Like many a young protagonist, the child is a hero, or at least a hero-in-waiting, exerting himself or herself to transform the world. Yet, one must not entertain Romantic delusions that art might offer salvation. After all, the child's drawing depicts a "rigid house" and tears falling into a flower bed; in its final speech, the almanac—that voice of the inevitable—interprets: "Time to plant tears."

Going a step further, the voice of the author, with its considerable emotional distance, ensures that this story does not become maudlin. Indeed, when listened to, when one takes the author's playfulness into account, "Sestina" is a very busy story that features not only the woman and the child but also the stove, the almanac, and the images in the drawing, defiant little antagonists or symbols of what can never be said directly.

Geography played a central role in Bishop's life and imagination. Geography and travel stimulated her. She traveled often but made her home in Florida and Brazil long enough to absorb those settings and write of them repeatedly. She wrote both stories and poems about Nova Scotia, where she spent part of her earliest years. Throughout her work, there is the sense of the power of "the interior"—often a region, but in "Sestina" a domestic scene. Bishop could write of places as though looking from afar, like a tourist, but she rewarded—and surprised—her readers with affecting insights that the places yielded. As she writes in "The Map," the poem that opens her first book, "Mapped waters are more quiet than the land is."

Jay Paul

SESTINA: ALTAFORTE

Author: Ezra Pound (1885-1972)
Type of poem: Dramatic monologue
First published: 1909, in *Exultations*

The Poem

In some respects, this poem is not only old-fashioned but archaic—quite different from the modern free-verse poetry for which Ezra Pound is famous. For one thing, as the poem's title indicates, the verse structure is that of the sestina, a form invented by the Provençal poets of the early Middle Ages. For another, the speaker is Bertran De Born, a medieval warlord.

The sestina is a complex seven-stanza verse form: The first six stanzas are six lines long, and the seventh stanza, the "envoy," is three lines long. The first six stanzas all use the same set of concluding words in their six lines, but these recurrent words shift position as the stanzas progress so that the word that ended line 1 in stanza 1, for example, ends line 2 in stanza 2, line 4 in stanza 3, and thus the pattern continues. In a sense, these recurrent ending words take the place of rhyme in giving structure to the stanzas. In this sestina, the ending words are "peace," "music," "clash," "opposing," "crimson," and "rejoicing."

In the lines appearing before the first stanza, Pound provides some background information to help the reader make his or her way through this difficult verse form. "Loquitur" means "speaker," in this case "En" (Sir) Bertrans De Born. In *La divina commedia* (c. 1320; *The Divine Comedy*) Dante portrays De Born as a "stirrer up of strife," a characterization that fits his remarks in the poem that follows. "Eccovi!" is Italian for "here you are," which is addressed to the reader, as is the following line, "Judge ye!"; Pound is inviting the reader to make his or her own judgment about whether Dante's condemnation of De Born was fair. Finally, Pound provides three key background facts: The setting for the poem is De Born's castle Altaforte; the person to whom De Born is speaking, "Papiols," is De Born's "jongleur," or court singer/poet; and "The Leopard" is an emblem of Richard the Lionhearted.

In stanza 1, De Born rages at Papiols, who evidently is his confidant, that the "South" (of France) is too peaceful: He is a warrior, only happy in battle. In fact, during De Born's lifetime the many small fiefdoms of France were often at war with one another and with the forces of Richard of England, who was also lord of much of France. For noblemen such as De Born, warfare was the only honorable occupation (winning a war with a neighboring fiefdom was also the principal source of income). So although the peace that has fallen on Provençe at the opening of the poem is probably only temporary, De Born chafes at being kept from the exercise of his profession.

De Born is so warlike that, as he says in stanza 2, even summer thunderstorms make him happy. Tempests and lightning remind him of war in that such storms disturb the tranquillity of sunny summer days. He imagines that the thunderclouds are engaged in combat and that heavenly beings clash their swords.

The reference to heavenly war in stanza 2 leads naturally to the reference to hell in stanza 3. De Born petitions the hellish powers to grant him strife; he longs to hear the neighing of war-horses and the clang of armor. As far as he is concerned, the concentrated experience of an hour of battle is worth a whole year of peaceful pleasures.

In stanza 4, he returns to the theme of warring nature. The crimson dawn sky reminds him of blood, and the rays of the rising sun appear to be spears in combat against the night. In stanza 5, De Born turns to cursing peace-lovers. Such men, according to him, are weak-blooded and "womanish," and he relegates them to rotting in inactivity. Only in battle, he claims, does a man prove his worth: Peaceful men are not men at all, and he "rejoices" in their deaths.

Once again, in stanza 6, De Born summons Papiols to accompany him to war, specifically against the forces of "the Leopard," King Richard of England—and once again, he damns those who would try to make peace between De Born and his enemies. Stanza 7 acts as a reprise of the preceding themes: De Born yearns for the "music" of battle, prays for combat, and condemns peaceful living.

Forms and Devices

The sestina's highly structured pattern of end words dominates other aspects of this poem's form. Imagery is especially affected by the connotations surrounding the words "peace," "music," "clash," "opposing," "crimson," and "rejoicing."

In fact, clusters of imagery may be grouped about a division of the six words into two sets or about oppositions between individual couplings of the words. "Peace, music, rejoicing," then, serve as one cluster, suggesting obvious associations with joy and art, while "clash, opposing, crimson" clearly suggest strife. Similarly, "clash" contrasts with "music" and "peace" with "opposing."

Each of the "image centers" created by the end words plays on strong sensory description. The poem particularly exploits hearing, smell, and sight in its use of clanging armor and clashing spears, stinking and rotting peace, enflamed and bloody crimson. Yet, just as complex as the end-word structuring of the sestina form is the ironic use to which the image centers are put. "Music" is a good example. In this poem, "music" can mean the delightful songs sung by the jongleur, Papiols; the "frail" tunes of peace; or the sounds of battle. "Peace," too, holds this sort of ironic implication: For the "weak" and "lily-livered," peace means food, women, and wine; De Born, conversely, is only at peace when he is in the middle of combat. Thus, the major challenge of the sestina form—using each end word in a different sense with different associated imagery each time the word changes position—is clearly met in this poem.

Although the sestina is usually associated with Romance-language poetry of the Middle Ages, Pound here employs a kind of mock medieval English to place his poem in the English-language tradition. He does it in at least two ways: First, frequent alliteration, a major structural feature of Middle English poetry, is prominent in "Sestina: Altaforte"; second, archaic words are scattered throughout the work.

Stanza 1 offers a good example of Pound's use of alliteration and other sound repetitions. In line 1, for example, alliteration occurs in "this our South stinks peace" and in the repetition "all! All"; in line 3, "save/ sword,"; in line 4, "purple, opposing"; and in line 5, "broad fields beneath." Most readers will immediately note the use of archaic, Middle English words such as "vair" (the bluish-white color of squirrel's fur) in stanza 1, "destriers" (war-horses) in stanza 3, and "stour" (battle) in stanza 5. Finally, the syntax of the poem also mimics Middle English poetry. Reversal of parts of speech, for example, is common: "have I great rejoicing" in stanza 2 and "howl I my heart nigh mad" in stanza 1. In addition, a number of other archaic syntactic patterns appear, such as "Let's to music" in stanza 1 and "fierce thunders roar me their music" in stanza 2.

Themes and Meanings

The historically specific persona and setting, the medieval verse form, and the archaic word use of "Sestina: Altaforte" combine to suggest one of the poem's major themes: the culturally specific consciousness of a warrior during the Middle Ages. At this period in his poetic development, Pound was very much under the influence of the English poet Robert Browning, part of whose fame rests on his dramatic monologues, poems whose speaker is a real or fictional character usually drawn from past history. Pound was fascinated with this use of "personae" (the word originally meant "masks"), through which a poet could enter into a sensibility utterly different from his own: The challenge of creating another kind of awareness—remote in time and preoccupations from his own—excited him.

Indeed, De Born's personality, as the reader sees it in "Sestina: Altaforte" is in conflict with most modern assumptions about the value of peace over war, of nonviolence over violence. The poem turns ironically about the reversal the persona places on these assumptions: For him, war and death are paradoxically life-giving, and art and joy are to be found in the cries and noisy clamor of battle. Similarly, De Born's view of nature contrasts strongly with contemporary perceptions. The modern person, conditioned in part by the Romantics to see nature as benign and serene, may well be shocked by De Born's glorification of the violence of natural phenomena—the bloodiness of a sunrise or the way a storm "kills" a peaceful afternoon.

Ultimately, the irony in "Sestina: Altaforte" is twofold: First, there is the irony arising from the contrast between De Born's sensibility and that of the modern reader; second, there is the narrative irony existing between Pound's warlord persona and Pound himself.

The period during which this poem was written has often been viewed as a golden age in Europe, whose nations were then at the height of their imperial power. No significant conflict had disturbed European peace since the Franco-Prussian war of 1870, and no real continent-wide war had occurred since the battle of Waterloo in 1815. European commerce was thriving, and the general standard of living had never been higher. Curiously, though, many people, as De Born did, chafed at the complacency and dullness of this time of plenty; they longed for the "excitement" of struggle, which they would experience all too soon in the tragedy of World War I.

Thus, although "Sestina: Altaforte" concerns the warlike impatience of a petty ruler nearly eight centuries in the past, the sort of rage De Born felt over the stagnation of peace was beginning to rise to the surface in early twentieth century Europe. Pound captures this impatience while producing a masterful illusion of the past, both in the vivid re-creation of a medieval warrior and in the crafting of a difficult and archaic verse form.

John Steven Childs

SEVEN LAMENTS FOR THE WAR-DEAD

Author: Yehuda Amichai (1924-2000)
Type of poem: Elegy
First published: 1974, as "Kinot," in *Me-ahorei kol zeh mistater osher gadol*; English translation collected in *The Selected Poetry of Yehuda Amichai*, 1986

The Poem

"Seven Laments for the War-Dead" is composed of seven brief poems, which may be read independently and indeed have been published separately. All are united, nevertheless, by theme, subject, attitude, and continuity of imagery. Together they form one of Yehuda Amichai's ardent protests against war. Lament 1 describes a fragile old man, "[floating] so lightly" through the alleyways of Old Jerusalem, bereft of his son. Lament 2 shifts to a domestic scene, where a happy child is beating his food into "golden mush," while the shadow of his destined death in warfare hovers over the room. In lament 3, two monuments to the fallen in battle are described ironically. One is now a target for enemy soldiers across the battle line, whereas the other resembles a festive wedding cake, concocted by a master chef.

Most poignant of all, lament 4 recalls a comforting childhood experience in long-ago Germany, a land not yet corrupted by wolf emblems and swastikas. Sweet phrases from a zoology textbook are remembered, though the description of "robin redbreast" merges all too quickly into the memory of a fallen comrade, whose blood flowing from his human breast replaces the bird's benign natural pattern. The personal tone of the laments becomes more evident in the fifth lament. The poet's friend Dicky is mentioned by name, and readers of Amichai's short stories will have encountered him before. Here he is compared both in dignity and in agony to the water tower at Yad Mordekhai, before both are hit in the belly by enemy fire.

The last two laments give special focus and emphasis to those who have gone before. Lament 6 demands response to a rhetorical and ironic question: What consolation does formalized commemoration of the dead really provide? Finally, in lament 7 the poet returns to the forlorn image that begins the sequence, the frail old man, without living offspring, lingering at Jaffa Gate. Appropriately, this last is the longest and most passionate of the lamentations, rejecting all the easy consolation that clichés of patriotism and piety have commonly served up to the bereaved.

Forms and Devices

Amichai's poems are written in modern, colloquial Hebrew, which was not his native tongue (German was). However, the poet's orthodox Jewish family provided him from early childhood with a religious education of which rabbinical Hebrew was a significant part. The family left Germany before the Holocaust and settled in Palestine, where Hebrew as a vernacular language was being resurrected. Amichai's Israeli readers enjoy his playfulness with their speech, his ability to employ puns both humorously and seriously, and his command of the connotative strata of a language both ancient and modern, which bears within it over three thousand years of recorded history. Renouncing religious dogmas in his early teens, Amichai has also rejected the hawkish chauvinism of some factions of Israeli society. Yet he always clearly identified himself as both a Jewish and an Israeli poet. His preeminence in Israeli poetry is confirmed by consensus, and it is said that soldiers called into service pack his poems along with their gear. Not only do his images and phrases echo the Bible, but also his verse reflects the influence of Hebrew medieval and modern Diaspora poets. Some of this resonance, occasionally arcane, is lost on the general reader, just as his wordplay translates only imperfectly into the over thirty languages in which his poetry now appears. Yet his acclaim throughout the world attests to remaining features that do survive cultural and linguistic transposition.

Amichai likes to bounce biblical phrases and traditional adages against the clichés, advertising slogans, and political platitudes of his own society. Many of his images come simply from everyday life and at first glance appear to have little poetic resonance until the reader discerns their ironic usage.

"Seven Laments for the War-Dead" employs free verse, though the best English translators have maintained appropriate cadences that reinforce the somber and ironic tone of the stanzas. The most important observations are often made by the juxtapositions of the solemn or grotesque with the ordinary and even festive. Amichai searches for the precise image that, though commonplace, forces his readers to acknowledge the ironies and imponderables of their lives.

In the first lament, the sad old man, no longer just another anonymous statistic, is significantly given a name. His name, Beringer, reveals him to be a Middle European Jew, though perhaps one whose family migrated from Spain or Portugal in the fifteenth century. After long years in the Diaspora, he has reached the Holy Land, only to lose his family and be forever a displaced person, drifting down ancient alleys. Did his son perish for some lofty humanitarian cause or noble religious principle? The poem simply says that he "fell at the Canal that strangers dug/ so ships could cross the desert." Beringer is no Father Abraham, to whom God will grant progeny in old age. His line will vanish from the human race, having perished in the Promised Land. To describe him, Amichai employs his most desolate simile; Beringer is "like a woman with a dead fetus in her womb."

Other laments offer up scenes of homey comfort, pleasant nostalgic remembrance, and even festivity, which are then ironically contrasted with the realities of warfare and its aftermath, never far away. The child eating his potatoes, whose mouth will be gently wiped by his parents, is destined to fall in the desert where only the earth and sand will wash him and purify his lonely body forever. An old zoology textbook is specifically identified as the second volume of zoologist Alfred Brehm's *Birds*, published in the Germany of 1913, a land of philosophers, poets, and gentle scientists who speak of "our feathered friends" and of robins as "harbingers of spring." Yet soon Germany will embark on a war which will be the "harbinger" of all the atrocities of the bloody twentieth century; the Holocaust and the deadly wars of Israeli liberation will follow.

The laments also offer vignettes of anonymous people trying to distance them-selves from grief by objectifying it. Comforting gravestones are erected, elaborate and expensive monuments are commissioned, and festival days of remembrance are designated. However, this idealization of bitter experience is always a lie. Flags fly, and store windows are decked out in a tempting array of dresses. In London's Hyde Park Corner, a marble monument reigns like a magnificent wedding cake, composed of whipped cream and candied cherries. Instead of bride and groom at the top, there is a soldier "lifting head and rifle," a cannon and angel beside him.

Even in a war cemetery, pain is made conveniently manageable. Small wastebas-kets are ready to receive tissue paper torn from store-bought flowers—no need to grow them with the mourner's own hands. A ceramic plaque in French, the ultimate language of euphemism, proclaims "'I shall never forget you.'" Both deceased and bereaved are now equally anonymous. Even Yad Mordekhai, whose water tower re-minds the poet so much of his friend Dicky, is a kibbutz founded by Polish Holocaust refugees now known chiefly for its yearly dramatic reenactment, certainly for instruc-tion but perhaps also for entertainment, of an especially bloody battle of the Israeli War of Independence.

Themes and Meanings

Amichai bore arms in two wars and lived most of his life on threatened ground. Yet his hatred of warfare permeates his writing. Descendants of the patriarch Abraham, both Arab and Jew, inhabit a broken land where every street sign, Amichai says, must be in three languages: "Hebrew, Arabic, and Death." Yet he refuses to accept the spiri-tual and patriotic consolations so frequently offered. Do paltry monuments, with their promises of eternal rest and undying love, merely provide a brief emotional respite before the resumption of hostilities? Is the pain of loss assuaged by pretty children, military bands, new clothes, and garish parades? This "sweet world" seems fit only to be "soaked like bread/ in sweet milk for a terrible/ toothless God." All that may be dis-cerned of the divine presence is indifference or senility. No heavenly harmony is likely to emerge from this chaos; God seems incapable or unwilling to make straight the crooked path.

In other poems, such as "I Want to Die in My Bed," Amichai emphasized his impatience with platitudinous sentiments about heroic death. His countrymen have been too often told, "'May ye find consolation in the building/ of the homeland.'" Yet what good is a homeland filled only with corpses? Amichai rejects that lie writ-ten long ago by the Roman poet Horace: How noble and sweet it is to die for one's country.

For more than two thousand years, Jews throughout the Diaspora have longed for the Holy Land. Yet Amichai, privileged to live in the Holy City, never conquered his yearning for the lost paradise of his childhood, the Germany of his first remembrance. He remains as significant a spokesman for the malaise of the twentieth century as are the celebrated French existentialist novelists and playwrights. He is a wandering Jew, a displaced person in a land not of his birth and in an indifferent universe. Like the postwar existentialists, however, he maintains compassion and a small ray of hope. The lamentation is one of the oldest and most hallowed genres of Hebrew literature. It demands accountability from God Himself, and its very presence in sacred scripture suggests that even from the depths there is always the possibility of gaining the divine ear.

Allene Phy-Olsen

THE SEVEN-YEAR-OLD POETS

Author: Arthur Rimbaud (1854-1891)
Type of poem: Narrative
First published: 1895, as "Les Poètes de sept ans," in *Poésies complètes*; English
translation collected in *Complete Works, Selected Letters*, 1966

The Poem

"The Seven-Year-Old Poets" is a narrative poem composed of sixty-four Alexandrines (the classical French line of verse containing twelve syllables) arranged in
rhymed couplets and in four loosely formed stanzas of four, twelve, fourteen, and
thirty-four lines respectively. Written in 1871, when Rimbaud was sixteen, it exemplifies the poet's unique vision of reality, one that depicts a young boy's yearning for creative and sensual freedom through the written word.

The first stanza expresses the child's relief as his Bible lesson comes to an end, the
book being closed by "the Mother," his own, who has been reading aloud. She is self-
satisfied in her religious devotion but fails to read in her son's blue eyes that his soul is
"filled with revulsions."

The second stanza reveals the secrets of the child's intimate life. Obedient all day,
he sometimes shows nasty habits that are symptomatic of his inability to repress his
true desires. Passing through the halls at school, he sticks out his tongue, his fists
clenched, ready for revolt. In the summer, he locks himself up "in the coolness of latrines," where he reflects and revels in the smells.

The third stanza continues the description of the child's activities, now in winter. In
the garden, the poet lies in the dirt at the foot of a wall, squeezing his eyes until he sees
visions. His only friends are raggedy children, "stinking of diarrhea" and conversing
"with the gentleness of idiots." The mother, presented in the first stanza as pious,
duty-bound, and blind to the rebellious nature of her son, is frightened at the sight of
these children and feigns appreciation of her son's compassion for their state.

The last stanza, the longest, portrays the images that the child describes in the novels he writes, the dreams that oppress him at night, and his delight in solitude. At the
age of seven, he is inspired by exotic images of "Forests, suns, banks, savannas" and
reads illustrated papers depicting Spanish and Italian women laughing. He engages in
sexual antics with the daughter of the workers next door, under whose skirts he sits to
"bite her buttocks." He takes back to his room "the savors of her skin." On Sundays,
"all spruced up," he reads the Bible, and, at night, dreams oppress him because he
does not love God but rather the workers whom he watches returning home at the end
of the day. As an escape from the harshness of reality, he dreams of "the amorous
meadow" and "luminous" and "healthy perfumes." Finally, he seeks solitude in a bare
room with closed shutters, damp and dank, where he rereads his novels filled with exotic and bizarre images of "flesh-flowers," "celestial woods," and "drowned forests."
Lying on pieces of unbleached canvas, the young poet reads and dreams of sails.

The poem ends with an ellipsis, or three suspension points, indicating that the young poet's life continues, following the chronology and development indicated thus far. "The Seven-Year-Old Poets" foreshadows Rimbaud's unique aesthetics, his attempts to create innovative and shocking imagery that acts as a liberating force, as well as one that deflates the smugness of bourgeois taste and morality.

Forms and Devices

"The Seven-Year-Old Poets" is beautiful and spellbinding in its depiction of a child who is already keenly aware of his vocation as a writer. More important, it reveals, through striking ironic juxtaposition, those secret and forbidden pleasures derived by the child in an austere atmosphere dominated by a puritanical mother. The poem begins with "And," indicating that the reader is entering a context that has already begun and that continues to develop. The mother is conveyed by "Mother," the capital letter suggesting her importance, symbolic nature, and forceful presence in the child's life. Not only is she symbolic of adult authority, but she is also the image of pious spirituality, and she is blind to her child's true soul, which is drawn powerlessly to the obscene and forbidden. She is the example of bourgeois respectability and moral rigidity against which Rimbaud revolted in his poetry as well as in his personal life.

To counter the stifling atmosphere created by "the Mother," the young child lives, at times, in another world. Hence, the juxtaposition, in the second stanza, of his actions in the school, where one would normally expect obedience and respectable behavior ("All day he sweated obedience"), and his private activities in the latrines, where he seems to relish the foulness of the air, serves to underline his rebellious nature, a nature that seeks solitude, and of which his mother seems unaware. This attempt to escape from the stifling atmosphere created by his mother is evident also in his choice of friends. He is drawn to children who are "Feeble, with blank foreheads, eyes fading on their cheeks," with dirty, sickly fingers and soiled clothing. He is attracted, therefore, to the underprivileged, downtrodden, and unintelligent; that is to say, to the opposite of the image of the perfect child nurtured by his mother. This is made all the more clear through the image of the young boy "all spruced up" and reading the Bible on those "pale Sundays of December" that he dreads. On these days, ironically, he is aware of his love not of God but of the workmen he watches return home, a love that is forbidden by his mother's religious beliefs and that echoes Rimbaud's own homosexuality.

Ultimately, the use of juxtaposition underlines the dichotomy that makes up the boy's life. He must live in the reality of Puritanism, conservative religion, and oppressive order created and reinforced by his mother but finds solace in his own reality, which is the opposite of the former. His world is one of foul smells, young sexuality, poetic inspiration, and ultimate freedom. The poem closes by evoking the cycle of his life, for he is delighted temporarily in his dreams of sails, symbolic of his quest for freedom of expression, which he achieves in his writing. The suspension points at the end serve to communicate the continuation of the context introduced by the "And" of the first line. Once the dream of sails is extinguished, the child will return to the stifling atmosphere created by "the Mother."

Themes and Meanings

"The Seven-Year-Old Poets" is a metaphor underlining the importance of freedom, in all its varied manifestations, in the life of a child who lives in an oppressive, puritanical, and hypocritical atmosphere dominated by a mother who is symbolic of such a way of life. The title, although in the plural, depicts one young boy who writes novels about his life and dreams of far-off lands, and who, in his private moments, rereads the novels he is writing while lying on pieces of blank canvas, a symbol of his life yet to be lived and the potential for the complete freedom for which he yearns.

The intolerance and hypocrisy of the bourgeois world that he witnesses are portrayed through the oppressive nature of school and church as well as his mother's feigned attempt to support her son's interest in lower-class and underprivileged children. The son's silent rebellion is further accentuated by his awakening sensuality and sexuality, which are translated by images that are both scatological ("in the coolness of the latrines/ . . . dilating his nostrils") and somewhat sadistic ("he would bite her buttocks") in nature.

It is, however, the metaphor of writing that is most fascinating, both as a symbol of the child's quest for freedom (an important theme) and as a reference point for Rimbaud's own life. Written when he was sixteen, "The Seven-Year-Old Poets" foresees the attainment of freedom in all its fullness by the adult Rimbaud in his affair with the poet Paul Verlaine (1844-1896), as well as in the revolutionary aesthetics of his more mature poetry. "The Seven-Year-Old Poets" is an eloquent introduction to his poetry and to his innovative, and, some would say, shocking imagery. More important, however, it foreshadows the breathtaking innovation practiced in his famous poem "Le Bateau ivre" ("The Drunken Boat"), a metaphor for poetic discovery in which the exotic lands and fabulous creatures remind the reader of the "flesh-flowers opened in the depths of the celestial woods" in "The Seven-Year-Old Poets." In the latter, the freeness of the form, combined with the elegance of the Alexandrine verse, are masterfully used by Rimbaud in order to create a refined and yet innovative poetic use of language.

"The Seven-Year-Old Poets" carries the reader through the intricacies of a child's perception of the world, splendid and, at times, full of despair, and ends on an uplifting note: The final image of sails, created by the canvas on which the child lies, will continue to carry him, through his imagination and writing, to foreign lands, unknown sensations, and experiences, and, ultimately, will offer the liberation from reality that he seeks.

Kenneth W. Meadwell

THE SEVENTH ECLOGUE

Author: Miklós Radnóti (Miklós Glatter, 1909-1944)
Type of poem: Meditation
First published: 1946, as "Hetedik ecloga," in *Tajtékos ég*; English translation collected in *Foamy Sky: The Major Poems of Miklós Radnóti*, 1992

The Poem

"The Seventh Eclogue" is a poem in seven stanzas, written in the classical form of the eclogue. The poem begins at twilight, in a military encampment. It soon becomes clear that the poet is a captive, confined in a stockade enclosed by "cruel wire." With the fading of sunlight, the wire becomes physically invisible. The poet knows that the constraining wires are still there even though it is night. Yet the fact that he cannot see them fills him with a visionary hope, a fantasy of escape and liberation.

The second stanza presents the imagined escape of the prisoners. References to Serbia, where the Hungarian Army was engaged fighting on the German side during World War II, make clear the poem's setting and wartime milieu. The poet glimpses a release to "the hidden heartland of home" that is actually so far away. He wonders whether his homeland, or perhaps literally his home itself, is as it once was. Might not the terrible bombing and carnage of the war have destroyed it? The stanza ends with perhaps the most striking line of the poem, "Say, is there a country where someone still knows the hexameter?" The hexameter is a six-beat poetic meter traditionally used in classical Greek and Latin verse, also used in this Hungarian poem in which the poet is deliberately evoking classical forms. By asking if the hexameter is still known in his homeland, the poet is wondering about the survival of civilization itself. Have the expressions of higher culture such as music, art, and poetry survived in war-torn Hungary, or have they been reduced to rubble in the wartime carnage?

In the third stanza, the poet describes the process of writing this very poem in the prison camp, or *lager*, the German term found in the poem. He must write when the guards do not see him, at night, and without a flashlight or book, lacking the ability even to put the correct accents (important in the Hungarian language) on the individual words. He is cut off from the outside world, receiving no mail; the camp itself is shrouded by fog.

People of many nationalities are in the camp, all imprisoned by the Germans, all wanting desperately to go home to their families. Even though they are all aware that death is nearly certain, they hope for a last-minute reprieve, a miracle. The poet compares his condition to that of an animal infested by fleas. The degrading conditions in the camp cannot last much longer, but, as the poet grimly concedes, neither can his life. The moon rises, making the wire once again visible, ending any possible fantasy of escape. The poet sees the armed guards, whose job it is to make sure none of the prisoners will get away.

In the last stanza, the poet addresses his beloved, who is back in his homeland. Despite all his dreams, he feels in his heart his separation from the woman he loves. Her absence, as signified by the bitter image of a cigarette-end replacing her kiss, renders any continuing hope impossible, as the horrible conditions surrounding him bring the poet to a state of final, resigned despair.

Forms and Devices

An "eclogue" refers to a classical poetic form most commonly associated with the Roman poet Vergil. Eclogues sometimes involve dialogue between two characters (as in Radnóti's own "Fourth Eclogue" (1943), but they can also be a monologue such as this one. Eclogues are written in hexameter, or six-beat meter, and traditionally describe a pleasant natural scene that may then suffer calamity or deprivation. Radnóti's prison-camp setting is a particularly dire enactment of the traditional idea of the fallen or violated landscape. The first line might suggest a traditional pastoral scene, with its brooding twilight mood. But the sudden introduction of the "cruel wire" in the second line conveys the agony and emotional directness characterizing the rest of the poem. This is in obvious contrast to the conventionality and formal mood of the classical eclogue, though Radnóti is really extending the classical form, not overturning it. Indeed, Radnóti's combination of emotional power and classicism, rare in twentieth century poetry in any language, is strikingly in evidence in this poem. The classical meter and precedent help contain the suffering and thwarted hope of the poem; they explain it and give it meaning.

Radnóti uses the eclogue form not only to frame the poem but also to contribute to its meaning. In the almost inconceivable barbarism of World War II, classicism—in times of peace merely a way of expressing kinship with literary tradition—becomes an eloquent counterpoint to the barbarism and horror in which the poet is immersed. The poem's most crucial line, "Say, is there a country where someone still knows the hexameter?" exemplifies this protest against barbarism, this sense that what might seem a mere literary form is in fact the saving grace of a world otherwise lost to evil. In the original Hungarian, the line is "Mondd, van-e ott haza még, ahol értik a hexametert?" All the other words in the sentence are terse, ordinary one- or two-syllable words, and the abrupt appearance of the lofty "hexameter" shows how out of place the word is in the prison-camp milieu—and therefore how much the values it connotes are desperately needed.

The poet has difficulty even getting the poem on paper: Not only are the circumstances harrowing, but also the material necessities of writing—light, pen and paper, time, and freedom to write—are fundamentally lacking. That the poem was written at all, much less that it emerged as such an eloquent, accomplished, and fundamentally finished work, is a testimony both to the poet's talent and to the strength of his character. A sense of poetry as an earned if limited victory over barbarism is at the heart of the poem's classicism and its investment in classical forms and meters.

Themes and Meanings

As a Hungarian, Radnóti was not necessarily vulnerable to German imprisonment: after all, Hungary was Germany's ally in the war. However, Radnóti was an independent, left-wing thinker; in addition, he was a Jew. A prime target of Nazi persecution, he lived nearly the entire wartime period anticipating his own death. Although "The Seventh Eclogue" gives voice to rapturous visions of freedom, liberation, and release, the poet knew all the while that, in the real world, he would never be free to return to his home, that his life was to end shortly under the grim conditions of imprisonment. "The Seventh Eclogue" was written in the Haidenau prison camp in the mountains above the Serbian town of Zagubica, where Radnóti was imprisoned by the Germans in July of 1944. Radnóti survived countless ordeals in the following months but was finally shot by the Germans and buried in a mass grave in Hungary in the autumn of 1944.

Yet Radnóti, though recording his torment, does not surrender to it. He attempts to remain a thinker, a poet, a human being; insofar as possible, he goes on as before. This is illustrated by the fact that he had begun writing eclogues before the war, his first being written in 1938, when his own personal heartbreak and his questions about the nature of his poetry seemed far more important than external world events. Thus Radnóti displays an extraordinary consistency, persistence, and courage. He bears witness to the war and, tacitly, his own death, yet produces a poem that stands against all the suffering that he and millions of others had to endure at the hands of the Nazis.

The dialectic between imprisonment and freedom is the central motif of the poem. The poet, imprisoned, is able to attain imaginative freedom; even if the literal redemption of the captives in never achieved in life, a victory of the imagination has been won. But the poem is not credulous in its utopianism. It ends on a note of practical disappointment that the poet is still far from his beloved, who cannot be brought back to him by all the visions in the world. The poem ends on a touchingly personal note, as the presence of absence of the beloved takes precedence over the carnage and torture of the war. Yet this interior focus is part of Radnóti's overall message. The individual, he makes clear, cannot be lost amid a tumult of wars and ideologies. The maintenance of individual feelings and individual consciences, far from being a personal whim, is a prerequisite if civilization—the beauty, mystery, and classical rigor that the poem has been trying to evoke against the darkness—is to be preserved.

Nicholas Birns

SHAME

Author: Arthur Rimbaud (1854-1891)
Type of poem: Lyric
First published: 1891, as "Honte," in *Reliquaire*; English translation collected in
   Complete Works, Selected Letters, 1966

The Poem
   "Shame" is a short poem of twenty lines whose five stanzas are presented (in the original French) in a standard *abab* rhyme scheme. The poet makes use of an anonymous first-person voice to speak about his enmity for an anonymous other, referred to simply as "him." Alluding to a rift that has occurred between the poet and his enemy, the poem expresses vividly the poet's hostile feelings after the separation. Many critics familiar with Arthur Rimbaud's biography believe that the poem communicates Rimbaud's angry reaction after his falling out with his close friend and fellow poet Paul Verlaine.
   The title of the poem "Shame" obviously refers to a feeling the poet wishes to express or evoke, but it is not immediately clear which persona ("I" or "he") feels the shame or why it is felt. By his spiteful tone, the poet would have his reader assume that his enemy, "he," should be feeling shame—presumably because of an injustice the poet has suffered at his enemy's hand. In any case, if the poet feels shame, it is well concealed behind the exaggerated and almost childish violence he would like to inflict on his enemy.
   The poem begins in a grotesque and violent mood, making graphic reference to corporeal mutilation: "As long as the blade has not/ Cut off that brain/ That white green fatty package . . . ." The reader can presume that the poet here is making reference to himself, saying that as long as nobody has committed such violence against the poet, he will be thinking about taking revenge against his enemy. In the second stanza, the poet makes a direct appeal to his opponent to mutilate himself, implying that such a self-mutilation would satisfy the poet's desire for justice. The poet lists in stark, clinical detail the various body parts he believes his opponent should cut off, appearing to take joy in spinning out his sadistic fantasy ("O miracle!").
   In the third and fourth stanzas the poet recognizes the futility of his appeal; he knows that his opponent will not commit such acts, that there will be no justice. In response, the poet declares that he will continue to cause trouble for his enemy as long as "he" is alive: Like a child, the poet will constantly pester "him"; like a skunk, the poet will foul "his" territory. In the last two lines of the fifth stanza, the poet seems to pull back from his vengeful mood when he summons God to have prayers said for his enemy once "he" has died. Rimbaud seems here to hearken back to his early religious instruction, rejecting finally the sin of vengeance and invoking the Christian principle of forgiveness. Perhaps, in the end, the shame is Rimbaud's for harboring sinful feelings. Then again, since Rimbaud is famous for his frequent use of irony, he may not be pulling back at all.

Forms and Devices

Rimbaud is associated with the French Symbolist movement, whose reputation for opaque language and formal complexity is well known. Since Symbolist poets tend to suggest their referents rather than openly naming them, readers should be cautious about pulling meaning too quickly from Rimbaud's deceptively simple poem. The first thing to emphasize in this light is that while the poem's visual appearance and fairly rigid rhyme scheme suggest a strict adherence to poetic tradition, the poem reads as if Rimbaud has simply strung together three more or less prosaic sentences. Unlike some of his more obviously difficult and elegant poetry, this poem seems facile, almost overly accessible. In that sense, the poem embodies a highly wrought tension between tradition and modernity, between complex poetry and accessible prose.

On a first reading, the reader is certain that the central opposition is between the poet and an "other" (perhaps Verlaine). That certainty occurs because the poem's prosaic quality and conventional grammar make this opposition so blatant. For example, the reader readily assumes from Rimbaud's grammatical distinction between "I" and "he" that these pronouns refer to two different people. To further emphasize this opposition between "I" and "other," Rimbaud brackets his appeal to his enemy within parentheses and he repeats in an exaggerated fashion the third-person possessive pronoun "his" in the second and third stanzas: "his nose," "his lips," "his ears," "his belly," "his legs," "his head," "his side," "his guts," "his death." The excessive repetition of "his" convinces the reader that Rimbaud must be referring to the body of an "other." Yet such obvious repetition suggests an indirect appeal to look for deeper poetic meaning.

Indeed, upon closer inspection, the reader begins to notice that the poem's tightly structured rhythm and its frequent uses of enjambment strategically interrupt the poem's linear syntax; they jar the natural flow of prosaic meaning and throw the reader off balance: "He should cut off his/ Nose," "his ears/ His belly! and give up/ His legs!" Whatever Rimbaud's intent, the effect of this strategic positioning of enjambment is to mark a formal division between grammatical subject and object and thus perhaps between "self" and "other" as well.

Rimbaud also strategically undercuts the opposition between "I" and "he" by subtly replacing the demonstrative adjectives in the first stanza ("that brain," "that . . . package") with possessive adjectives ("his") in the second and third. As mentioned above, the reader assumes from the sharp opposition between the first and second stanzas that the two stanzas refer to two different people and assumes, from the continued use of the possessive "his" from the second to the third stanza, that the second and third stanzas refer to the enemy, not to the poet himself. Upon closer inspection, however, the reader notices that the theme of cutting a head from the third stanza actually circles back to the idea of cutting "that brain" from the first stanza. Logically, this would suggest that the subject of the first and third stanzas are the same and thus that the poet is imagining this violence inflicted upon himself. The parentheses around the second stanza, in this case, would seem to indicate formally that the "other" actually lies within the poet.

Such a blurring between self and other is further reinforced by the poet's refusal to name the personas that figure in the poem. Rimbaud restricts himself to a highly ambiguous use of pronouns and he also relies on metonymy and simile to make reference to the poet ("the troublesome child," "the so stupid animal," "like a Rocky Mountain cat"). This poetic device of suggesting and partially naming serves to withhold the poem's concrete referents from the reader's view. In the end, Rimbaud's ambiguity undercuts the reader's initial certainty about precisely who is doing what to whom.

Themes and Meanings

The point of interpreting should never be to make a poem unnecessarily difficult; one should not look for ambiguity where there is none. In this case, however, the poetic ambiguity is clear, and it appears to point to a deeper meaning beyond the prosaic one. One could argue, for example, that Rimbaud's soul is divided against itself and that the poem is a dramatization of Rimbaud's inner psychological turmoil. On the one hand, Rimbaud expresses his sadistic fantasy for revenge, and on the other, he expresses the punishment he should receive for entertaining such sinful thoughts. The formal strategies insisting on opposition noted above would thus serve to punctuate Rimbaud's internal conflict between his asocial desire for vengeance and the moral stricture that prohibits such a desire. "He" in this case would not refer to another person (such as Verlaine) but to the poet's alter ego, to an unconscious self-aggression outside Rimbaud's rational control. According to this scenario, the numerous references to violent acts may be an expression of a guilt complex, a masochistic fantasy whereby Rimbaud irrationally desires punishment for his errors or sins. In that case, the final lines calling for prayer more clearly point to Rimbaud's own expression of shame.

This all may seem wildly speculative unless the reader is familiar with Rimbaud's famous dictum: "I am an other." What Rimbaud means by this is that his psyche is self-divided, one half against the other. The "other," the part outside his rational and linguistic control, speaks through him in spite of himself; it expresses desires and fantasies that reason or morality cannot easily impede. Such an internal division between passion and rationality, between individual desire and morality is a traditional one that goes back as far as the Greeks. Rimbaud radicalizes the opposition by giving this "other" a name, "he," as well as by granting it supremacy. This idea of the divided psyche or the "other within" anticipates Sigmund Freud's idea of the unconscious, and it makes Rimbaud one of the first truly modern poets.

Scott M. Sprenger

THE SHAPE OF THE FIRE

Author: Theodore Roethke (1908-1963)
Type of poem: Lyric
First published: 1947; collected in *The Lost Son and Other Poems*, 1948

The Poem

In 1948 Theodore Roethke published *The Lost Son and Other Poems*, introducing the greenhouse and sequential poems that have come to define his unique style. "The Shape of the Fire" is the last poem in "The Lost Son" sequence. Roethke's long poems are explorations of psychic states, and they progress cyclically rather than in a logical linear narrative. "The Shape of the Fire" begins by returning psychologically to the awakening of consciousness in the womb. The images follow the sensory world of a child, a primordial, animistic, natural world characteristic of "The Lost Son" poems.

Roethke does not depict a comforting landscape. Images are surreal and incoherent, as shapes in a fire are. Knowledge comes from "a nameless stranger." The images of receding water and a beached boat symbolize the stagnation of the spirit. The landscape is unpleasant and threatening; even the flowers "are all fangs." However, it is a time of transition. The speaker envisions the water returning and calls, "spirit, come near." The hour of ripeness, which can result in his release from this sterile landscape, approaches. He calls for his mother to "stir" and "mother me out of here." At the end of section 1, he bids farewell to the elemental forms of nature as he is [re]born.

Part 2 begins with the child's discovery of his body. As in the beginning of part 1, the language is a childlike combination of questions and nursery-rhyme cadences. After this short, playful section, however, comes another nightmare vision, first of an adult figure, "a varicose horror," and then of another wintery landscape characterized by snakes, sticks, sharp winds, and howls. These images represent the problematic time of adolescence, with the primeval ooze and slime of sexuality. Now "the uneasy man" "must pull off clothes/ To jerk like a frog/ On belly and nose/ From the sucking bog." "Words writhe," and the light speaks in a "lewd whisper." He seems betrayed by his own body as he observes, "My meat eats me."

Part 3 provides a short hiatus in the form of enigmatic aphorisms. It provides a transition from "the journey from flesh," which "is longest," to the image of the rose, which "sways least." For Roethke, the movement and journeys that make up the events of life are difficult and frightening. The end he seeks is stasis; the rose, which is a mystical symbol of finished perfection, serves as a guide.

In part 4, when the protagonist again regresses to a primordial natural landscape, full spiritual progress begins. This landscape is supportive and lifegiving. "Death was not" in this environment. Now the cave is not sorrowful, but sweetened with fertile rain and the sustenance of apples. Flowers are everywhere, moving into fullness, "buds at their first trembling," "wakening blossoms," a profusion of flowers, associated with love. The last section of "The Shape of the Fire" is replete with images and symbols of spiritual wholeness and fulfillment: the flowers, "the whole air!/ The light, the full sun" of illumination, and the boat, the symbol of his spirit, which is drifting effortlessly now. The final image compares the light, which enriches the spirit, with the water in a vase, filled to surfeit so that it holds the flower in an invisible yet nourishing and supportive embrace.

Forms and Devices

Roethke's poetry is most innovative in its use of animistic natural imagery and symbolism, its use of the tone and language of childhood, and its intense psychological explorations. Poems such as "The Shape of the Fire" move convincingly from preconscious lack of self-awareness to mature mystical spirituality. *The Lost Son and Other Poems* volume was critically acclaimed for the poet's immediate identification with nature. Nature is anthropomorphized: the cracked pod "calls"; the worm is "fond"; the spiders "cry." It also reflects the protagonist's moods, being frightening and menacing or loving and beckoning as he progresses and regresses on his spiritual journey.

Certain images become symbols, either universal ones, such as light, which brings spiritual illumination, and water, which brings fertility and birth, or personal symbols, such as flowers, which are identified with Roethke's childhood in his father's greenhouse and represent the instinctive urge to struggle into life. Roethke's poems are intensely subjective; few critics separate the protagonist or speaker from the poet himself. The landscape of "The Shape of the Fire" is drawn from his childhood in Michigan, "the marsh, the mire, the Void." It is "a splendid place for schooling the spirit. It is America," he wrote to Louise Bogan in an "Open Letter" (printed in *Mid-Century American Poets*, edited by John Ciardi, 1950).

Yet however personally conceived, Roethke's symbols are also universal, from the dreamlike landscapes, which are night journeys of self-discovery, to the roses, which are symbols of mystical wholeness. No matter how personal or egocentric a poet, Roethke also insisted that his poems represent a racial memory, and his imagery bears this out.

In addition, the startling language of the first segments of the poem attempts to capture the nonsense rhymes and associational, nonlinear narrative of a young child. Roethke says that "rhythmically, it's the spring and rush of the child I'm after . . . if necessary, without relying on the obvious connectives: to speak in a kind of psychic shorthand when his protagonist is under great stress" (from "Open Letter").

Roethke presents landscape as emotion, perception, memory, and dream in direct, almost abrupt, statements that give his poetry the power of immediate perception and thought. His catalogs of proverbs in section 3, like those of his mentor, William Blake, bombard one with strong images that imply a mystical knowing, which becomes more clearly delineated in the final passage. The long, descriptive lines of spiritual illumination one finds here are developed more fully in Roethke's later "North American Sequence."

The cumulative result of this poem, with its experimental childlike rhythms interspersed with adult reflection, its varying line lengths of free verse, and its enigmatic, often disconnected narrative, is to approximate a spiritual journey. The overall form of this stream-of-consciousness technique re-creates his "history of the psyche (or allegorical journey) . . . a succession of experiences, similar yet dissimilar. There is a perpetual slipping-back, then a going-forward; but there is *some* progress" ("Open Letter").

Themes and Meanings

The journey that "The Lost Son" poems represent is the universal experience of individuation. According to psychologist Carl Jung, who formulated this theory, individuation is a process of development arising from the conflict of the conscious and unconscious psychic states. A person can never be whole until both states are given equal attention and exist in equilibrium.

"The Shape of the Fire" illustrates Roethke's attempt to achieve this psychological balance by exploring both psychic states. The regression to childhood, where the line between the conscious and unconscious is blurred, is Roethke's starting point in his search for himself. His use of preconscious imagery as signposts for his own identity is what characterizes his poetry.

The dreamlike imagery represents a night journey; an exploration of the interior of the country also represents a descent into his unconscious. The water, the cave, the elemental natural images are indicative of birth, rebirth, and the depths of the mind all at once. Thus, the poem moves between consciousness and unconscious states in order to achieve this archetypal spiritual wholeness.

"The Lost Son" poems often contain initiation rituals. Parts 1-3 of "The Shape of the Fire" use the elements of initiation rites: the natural signposts; the frightening adults who guide him (the witch, the flat-headed man); the sexual rite, during which he becomes an "uneasy man"; and finally, the mysterious wisdom he receives in part 3. Initiation is an important part of the individuation process for Roethke, whose poetry is obsessed with finding himself and his place in the world.

The last two parts of "The Shape of the Fire" begin Roethke's quest for mature mystical illumination, which comes to fruition with "The Rose" in "The North American Sequence." Here he looks for a sacred time of origins, a time out of time, "further back" when he was part of nature, "mov[ing] through a dream of wakening blossoms." This part of the poem harkens back to another of Roethke's mentors, William Wordsworth, who sees the child as coming from the universal truth of God into the corrupt world of civilization. Roethke is very much a Romantic poet in his association of mystical truths with nature and his fear of the frantic pace and despoiling aspects of urban life.

Thus, for all his personal imagery and subjectivity, Roethke is primarily a poet of archetypal themes. He said of his poems, "I can feel very impersonal about them for they seem to come from a tapping of an older memory—something that dribbled out of the unconscious, as it were, the racial memory" (*The Selected Letters of Theodore*

Roethke, 1968). The evocative power of a poem such as "The Shape of the Fire" resides in the transformation of personal experience through images and symbols into universal experience. If originality marks these poems, it is the originality of the great poet who can see through his experience to the collective memory of all.

Sandra J. Holstein

SHE HAD SOME HORSES

Author: Joy Harjo (1951-   )
Type of poem: Lyric
First published: 1983, in *She Had Some Horses*

The Poem

Joy Harjo's "She Had Some Horses" consists of eight stanzas punctuated by a common refrain with a coda at the end of the work. The poem, written in the form of an American Indian chant, explores a woman's struggle to shape her identity as a modern Native American living in the alien environment of Euro-American culture. The mythic image of the horse, repeated at the beginning of and between every stanza, is juxtaposed with paradoxical images and events from the speaker's life in twentieth century America. These juxtapositions not only sharply define the psychological, spiritual, and cultural conflicts at war in the woman's conscious and subconscious minds, but also build toward the speaker's self-recognition. At the end of the poem, the speaker achieves psychological and spiritual unity by accepting the contradictory sides of her psyche, thereby giving birth to a new and complete being.

The speaker's search for wholeness is rooted in the physical world of contemporary life as well as in the mystical realm of Native American myth and legend. The first line of the poem, "She had some horses," calls upon one of the most powerful and enduring symbols in Native American culture. Every line in the succeeding stanzas begins with, "She had horses . . .," reinforcing the speaker's American Indian identity. The poem explores all facets of the woman's existence, from the elements that make up her physical being to the components of her mind and spirit.

In the first stanza, the woman acknowledges her intimate connection to the created order. Her physical being is made up of fundamental components of the natural world: "bodies of sand," "maps drawn of blood," "skins of ocean water," and "blue air of sky." In the second stanza, the collection of natural elements coalesces into a flesh and blood woman who has "long, pointed breasts" and "full, brown thighs." Violent images in the following lines—"She had some horses who threw rocks at glass houses/ She had some horses who licked razor blades"—clash with the sensual description of the woman's body and reveal the anger and fear that lie beneath the surface of her consciousness.

By the third stanza, fear becomes a dominant force, moving the poem forward. The speaker reveals that she is "much too shy" and retreats into "stalls" of her "own making." Her fear and anger deeply fragment the landscape of her inner life. In the next three stanzas, contradictory images reveal her confusion: "She had horses who lied./ She had horses who told the truth"; "She had horses who had no names./ She had horses who had books of names"; "She had horses who waited for destruction./ She had horses who waited for resurrection."

In the last stanza of the poem, the speaker searches for someone to save her from the anger, fear, and oppression that entrap her. Yet by the end of the poem, she discovers that she is her own savior. Throughout her journey, she has been in the process of attaining wholeness by naming her "horses." The naming ritual gives her power over all aspects of her spiritual and physical life. As she accepts each "horse" as a part of herself, she ceases to experience a splintering of her soul and can finally accept that "She had some horses she loved./ She had some horses she hated.// These were the same horses."

Forms and Devices

As a Native American writer, Harjo follows a different aesthetic from her Western counterparts. The oral traditions of her Muscogee Creek heritage are central to her poetic vision and expression. Although she is acquainted with classic European forms, she chooses not to use them. Her use of the chant form in "She Had Some Horses" is an example of her commitment to her Native American heritage, as well as her defiance of the dominant Anglo culture and its traditions.

The horse was an important spiritual icon to the Plains Indians and symbolizes power, strength, and survival. The speaker views the horse in these culture-specific terms but appropriates the horse as her own personal spirit animal who breaches the boundaries between American Indian myth and tradition and mainstream Anglo society. The refrain and the rhythmic repetition of "She had some horses" and "She had horses" act as a mystical incantation invoking healing and wholeness. The syntactical linkage connects each line to the next, leading the reader through the work and providing an underlying continuity that unites the disparate images of violence, fear, and anger that permeate the poem.

The horse is especially significant as a symbol of survival. The speaker's mind is a spiritual and psychological battleground where conflicting points of view threaten to overcome and extinguish the woman's spirit. The various horses in the poem represent the fractured spiritual condition of the woman: Some horses are positive influences, some negative, and some neutral. In order to survive with her ego intact, the woman must tame the horses of her psyche by accepting them as they are.

It is important to remember that Native American authors often have a different perspective on animal imagery than do European writers. In the case of Harjo's poem, the horses are kin to humans, as well as living spirits who exist regardless of the dictates of Western logic and scientific reasoning.

The Western perspective views the modern world as split between the sacred and the secular. From the Native American point of view, there is no division. In "She Had Some Horses," the spirit animal transcends time and place, bridging the divide between the past, where American Indians lived as a free people, and the twentieth century, where minorities are oppressed by the dominant white culture. Although there is a dichotomy between American Indian and Anglo culture, there is also an underlying reality where unity is possible. This is the domain in which fear meets courage, anger meets peace, and weakness meets strength. It is a realm where contradictory views of the world can become one, and it is a place where the spirit and material universes embrace each other. The horse, a creature of both worlds, makes the meeting and resultant union possible.

Themes and Meanings

As a member of an oppressed minority that has been victimized and nearly destroyed, Harjo is concerned with personal, cultural, and spiritual survival. One of the ways a culture can survive is through storytelling. Commenting on her own calling as a poet and storyteller, Harjo remarked: "In a strange kind of sense [writing] frees me to believe in myself, to be able to speak, to have a voice, because I have to: it is my survival." "She Had Some Horses" is somewhat autobiographical and reflects Harjo's own struggle to survive as a mixed-blood woman in a hostile society. The poem gives a voiceless woman the opportunity to tell her story and, by doing so, make her mark in the world as a person of significance and worth.

The use of memory is another way Native Americans can ensure their survival. Tales of people past and present, ties to ancestral lands, family and tribal histories, and myths provide a deep well of cultural memories from which present and future generations can draw strength to combat racial prejudice and oppression. In her poem, Harjo seamlessly fuses American Indian myths with the speaker's experiences in contemporary American life. The resulting dialogue between the two distinctive worldviews is strained and violent. Yet there is hope. Memory brings perspective, and perspective helps each new generation see old truths in new ways. The woman in "She Had Some Horses" is eventually able to harness the energy of a new vision brought about by her reliance on the archetypes that have lived in the collective mind of her tribe for thousands of years.

Although Native American writers such as Harjo tend to focus on the themes of memory, survival, and tradition, these concepts are universal. For generations, immigrant and minority groups have fought to keep their traditions and myths alive in order to preserve their identity as individuals and as a people. Ultimately, "She Had Some Horses" takes readers on a journey of self-discovery, helping them to know themselves better and to understand their place and purpose within creation.

Pegge Bochynski

SHE WALKS IN BEAUTY

Author: George Gordon, Lord Byron (1788-1824)
Type of poem: Lyric
First published: 1815, in *Hebrew Melodies Ancient and Modern*

The Poem

"She Walks in Beauty" is a short poem, consisting of three six-line stanzas. On the surface it is a fairly conventional description of a beautiful woman, evidently some-one with whom Byron is acquainted. The poet does not identify her by name, indicate his relationship to her, or hint as to the occasion that brought them together. (Scholars have ferreted out these matters.) Even if such information is not essential to under-standing the poem, it is surprising that Byron provides so little concrete detail about the actual appearance of the woman he is describing. He does not speak of her as tall or short, slender or statuesque; he does not tell his readers the color of her dress or the color of her eyes. In fact, at the end of the poem the only specific fact the reader knows is that she has black hair.

Nevertheless, there is no doubt that the lady has made a definite impression on the poet. To him, she is beautiful in the same way that "night" is beautiful, and, as he has-tens to add, he means a particular kind of night, one of "cloudless climes and starry skies." There is no threat of a storm in this imagined landscape; there are no clouds to produce even a shower. Such a night is not really dark, for, as readers are told, the sky is filled with stars. Their light is soft and subdued; similarly, the dark lady has "ten-der" eyes, as unlike those of less subtle women as the light of a "starry" night is from that of "gaudy day."

Byron proceeds to amplify his earlier suggestion that a perfect combination of "dark and bright" is the secret of his subject's beauty. The second stanza of the poem begins with an explicit statement to this effect: either more or less light, he insists, would have at least to some degree "impair'd" her "grace." At this point, the poet fi-nally gives his readers a clue as to what may have triggered his response, for it appears that the lady does have "raven" hair. However, Byron does not have so specific an ex-planation for the brightness of "her face." He does not seem to mean that she has a rosy complexion; instead, it is her "thoughts serenely sweet," so evident in her facial expressions, that account for the impression she makes on all those who observe her.

In the final stanza, Byron continues to explore the relationship between inner and outer beauty. The blushes that appear on the lady's "cheek," her "smiles," everything on her "brow," or countenance, all reveal her sterling virtue. In the last lines of the poem, Byron sums up what he surmises: that the lady spends much of her time doing good deeds, that her "mind" harbors no animosity toward anyone, and that when love enters her heart, it is an "innocent" emotion. Byron's description of a dark-haired lady thus becomes much more: It is also his definition of the ideal woman.

Forms and Devices

Though Byron may have rebelled against tradition in other ways, his poems are generally conventional in form. "She Walks in Beauty" is no exception. It is written in standard iambic tetrameter, with alternating rhymes, a new set in each stanza. Metrically, the poem is quite predictable; there are none of the lilting anapestic variations so familiar in Byron's other works, but stately measures are appropriate for a woman who is herself so decorous. The masculine line endings and the use of end-stopped lines, alternating with lines which necessitate a pause, recall the neoclassical heroic couplet, a form Byron much admired. However, here there is no satire nor epigrammatic wit; instead, the purpose of the form is to ensure the slow progress of the poem, thus emphasizing the lady's dignity, her steadiness, and her self-control.

The poem is also interesting in the degree to which it is dominated by a single simile. Although after the first stanza the poet abandons explicit references to the night, throughout the poem he emphasizes the idea of perfect balance, not only between dark and light but also between thought and action, mind and heart.

Nevertheless, though "She Walks in Beauty" praises harmony, it has other implications as well, reminding one that, for all his neoclassical dedication to form and balance, Byron was, after all, a Romantic. To a degree, the images work to deny the poet's explicit statements, for although the pace of the poem is in keeping with its praise of tranquillity, its images stress movement and therefore the inevitability of change. Byron's lady is not posing, but walking. She is shown in motion, her hair waving, her "eloquent" face expressive as she responds to the world around her and to her own thoughts—sometimes with smiles, sometimes with blushes. These small alterations imply that just as the stars will move in the night sky and night itself turn to day, the lady will change. Only in the poem will she remain forever lovely and innocent.

Themes and Meanings

Byron's biographers agree about the occasion that inspired the poem. On June 11, 1814, Byron is said to have attended a party, perhaps a ball, at the home of a Lady Sitwell, and there to have seen for the first time his young cousin by marriage, Mrs. Robert John Wilmot, dressed in a black mourning dress adorned with spangles. Supposedly Byron wrote "She Walks in Beauty" either the same night or early the next morning.

If the account of Mrs. Wilmot's gown is accurate, it is easy to see why Byron thought of a starry night when he looked at the young beauty. Moreover, though death is not actually mentioned in "She Walks in Beauty," the fact that the lady's dark clothing was a token of mourning makes it likely that the conventional association of night and death was in Byron's mind as he wrote the poem.

This interpretation also helps to explain why Byron included the poem in the volume *Hebrew Melodies*. One of Byron's friends had suggested that the poet and a young composer, Isaac Nathan, collaborate in producing a volume of songs in the Hebrew folk tradition, and Byron agreed to work with Nathan on the collection. For that reason, a great many of the lyrics that Byron wrote take as their subject matter characters and stories from the Old Testament. Byron not only included "She Walks in Beauty" in the volume but also made a point of asking Nathan to have it appear first in every edition of *Hebrew Melodies*. The most obvious explanation is that Byron usually placed what he considered his best poem in a collection first. Since "She Walks in Beauty" is one of Byron's most anthologized poems, evidently in this case the poet's judgment was accurate.

There may also be a thematic justification for Byron's using "She Walks in Beauty" to introduce *Hebrew Melodies*. Certainly it is the depiction of an ideal woman. One has only to look at the modifiers to see why this woman would be so easy to live with: "tender," "softly," "serenely," "sweet," "pure," "soft," and "calm." It is, however, significant that the final word of the poem is "innocent." Byron's ideal may be viewed as a portrait of Eve before the Fall, appropriately placed first here, as it is in the Old Testament.

"She Walks in Beauty" is one of the few optimistic lyrics in *Hebrew Melodies*. The later poems show human beings as fallen creatures in a fallen world. What scant hope there is may come through art. For example, in the second poem in the collection, "The Harp the Monarch Minstrel Swept," King David's songs elevate humanity above its fallen condition. However, generally life is shown as essentially tragic and probably meaningless. In "Jephtha's Daughter," an innocent young woman is forced into martyrdom. In "All Is Vanity, Saith the Preacher," it is asserted that even poetry is helpless against despair.

Any discussion of the meaning of "She Walks in Beauty" should also point out how inconsistent Byron's admiration of the woman is with his own Romantic tendencies. This ideal woman has the neoclassical virtues of reason, moderation, and self-control. By contrast, Romantics value feeling above reason. Byron usually shows rebellion as proof of intellectual independence, excess as a road to truth, and passion as an indication that one is truly alive. Considering the rest of his works, as well as his life, it is ironic that Byron was so drawn to the virtuous lady he describes in "She Walks in Beauty." On the other hand, it is only human to value that which one has lost and which, unfortunately, will probably not long survive in this fallen world.

Rosemary M. Canfield Reisman

THE SHEPHERD'S WEEK

Author: John Gay (1685-1732)
Type of poem: Mock pastoral
First published: 1714

The Poem

The Shepherd's Week is a series of six poems, each representing one of the days of the week; Sunday has been omitted, ostensibly for religious reasons. The title establishes these poems as pastorals, and they do derive from the pastoral tradition. Five of the six are based on the *Eclogues* of the Roman poet Vergil, dated between 43 and 37 B.C.E (English translation, 1575), which in turn were influenced by the idylls of Greek poet Theocritus, written about 270 B.C.E. However, though Gay acknowledges his debt to his predecessors, *The Shepherd's Week* is not a conventional pastoral. Gay substitutes the unlettered, realistic characters of his own English countryside for the usual elegant, artificial shepherds and shepherdesses who use the rural scene only as a backdrop. For this reason and because of its comic tone, *The Shepherd's Week* is customarily described not as a pastoral but as a mock pastoral.

In his prose introduction to *The Shepherd's Week* entitled "The Proeme to the Courteous Reader," Gay announces his intention: to write a "simple Eclogue" in the Theocritan mode, thus demonstrating to the poets of his age what a pastoral should be. Gay comments at length on the influence of "maister Spencer" (Edmund Spenser) and the *Shepheardes Calendar* (1579) on his own work in terms of structure and even the names of his characters. "The Proeme" ends with an explanation of his choice of language. The "Prologue," which follows, is addressed to Henry St. John, First Viscount Bolingbroke, the great Tory leader and a member of the poet's circle. Gay describes the shepherds' grief upon hearing a rumor that their monarch, Queen Anne, has died and their relief when they find that she is alive and well, having been saved by her physician, Dr. John Arbuthnot, another of Gay's friends. Arriving at court to see Arbuthnot, though he does happen to have with him the poems for Bolingbroke, Gay notes how different this world is from the one he left. Then he performs as expected. He praises the most prominent courtiers present, lauds the Tory leadership, and modestly presents his completed "Eclogues" to Bolingbroke, assuring him that if there were any possibility that his verse would interfere with statecraft, he would gladly "burn book, preface, notes and all."

Each of the six poems in *The Shepherd's Week* has its own cast of characters and its own drama. "Monday; or, The Squabble" begins with two lovesick shepherds discussing their miseries. Lobbin Clout is enamored of Blouzelinda, while Cuddy cannot sleep for thinking of his Buxoma. They decide to have a contest to see which of them can best praise his mistress in song, with the sage Cloddipole serving as a judge. Before long, Cloddipole's patience wears thin. He stops the competition without declaring a winner and sends the two shepherds off to water the neglected livestock. In

"Tuesday; or, The Ditty," Marian bemoans the fact that she has lost her beloved Colin to Cic'ly. Her error, she thinks, may be in having given Colin a knife, for superstition teaches that knives *"always sever love."* These speculations are cut short, however, when Goody Dobbins arrives to have her cow serviced, for Marian must bring out the necessary bull.

"Wednesday; or, The Dumps" is about Sparabella's abandonment by Bumkinet, who is so blind that he prefers Clumsilis to her. Remembering how her love for Bumkinet enabled her to resist the advances of the local squire, Sparabella waxes bitter about love and finally resolves to kill herself. However, she cannot find a satisfactory method of committing suicide, and, since night has fallen, she decides to postpone any drastic action until the next day. In "Thursday; or, The Spell," another maiden is faced with the loss of her lover, but Hobnelia is a practical person who always has a remedy at hand. Throughout her relationship with Lubberkin, Hobnelia has routinely used spells to keep him in line. She explains these spells in detail, ending with a description of how she obtained a love potion for use in this present crisis. Fortunately, this time nature, not the supernatural, comes to her rescue. Suddenly Lubberkin turns up in an amorous mood, and Hobnelia, who dreads the thought of dying a virgin, is more than willing to cooperate with him.

The subject of "Friday; or, The Dirge" is not love but death. Bumkinet returns from an absence ready to "quaff a cheary bowl" with his friends, only to learn that their Blouzelinda has died. Sadly, he recalls happier days. As in traditional pastorals, nature itself is urged to grieve for the lost maiden, and Grubbinol insists that all living creatures seem aware of her death. He then proceeds to a poignant account of the scene at Blouzelinda's deathbed during which she expressed her wishes concerning both the disposition of her small treasures and her simple funeral. The shepherds do not think that they will ever cease to grieve for Blouzelinda. Then they see "bonny *Susan*" and transport her to the ale house where, with "ale and kisses," they manage to "forget their cares."

The central character of "Saturday; or, The Flights" is Bowzybeus, who, though a drunkard, is acknowledged to be the Muse's darling. Roused from his stupor by the local lasses, he pulls himself together and, obviously inspired, puts on an impressive performance. Bowzybeus sings about nature and the supernatural; he transports his listeners to a fair like the one he has just attended, with its peddlers and mountebanks; he recites the old, familiar ballads; and at one point he even intones a psalm. Then the music stops. After receiving the kisses that will be his only reward, Bowzybeus again falls asleep. Thus both the day and *The Shepherd's Week* come to an end.

Forms and Devices

Even if, as he insists, Gay intended to avoid the usual artifice in his pastoral, *The Shepherd's Week* is clearly the work of a highly self-conscious artist. For example, at the end of "The Proeme," the poet identifies the language used by his characters as his own invention. He explains that though it is certainly not what one would hear at court, neither is it any identifiable rural dialect. Some of the characters' expressions are very modern, but a good many of them are archaic. In case some future "lover of Simplicity" should arise to translate *The Shepherd's Week* into a "modern dialect," Gay has helpfully included "glosses and explications of uncouth pastoral terms." This machinery is part of the joke, for any writer knowledgeable enough to provide it would have been able to make his language as consistent as he wished.

It is also important to note that this supposedly artless work is highly allusive. It has been pointed out, for example, that all but one of the poems are based on specific Vergilian eclogues. "Tuesday," the exception, has a contemporary model, for it was designed to fulfill the criteria for a "Pastoral Ballad" set forth by Gay's fellow poet Alexander Pope in *The Guardian*. There are also many allusions to classical mythology in *The Shepherd's Week*. For instance, the drunken Bowzybeus is clearly drawn from Silenus, one-time tutor and thereafter follower of Bacchus, the Greek god of wine. There is more to the resemblance, however, than the enthusiasm for strong drink: When he is inspired, Bowzybeus appears almost godlike. Gay does not draw his allusions only from classical sources. His characters have an ancient oral culture of their own. They quote old proverbs, as Lobbin Clout does in "Monday" when he insists that "Love is blind"; like Hobnelia, they live by spells and superstitions; and they respond enthusiastically when Bowzybeus sings the ballads they know so well. The fact that Gay does not aid his reader by footnoting his allusions while he spends so much effort on the language is still another indication of his tongue-in-cheek attitude toward his subject matter, his readers, and the work itself.

The verse form used for *The Shepherd's Week* is particularly effective for comic and satirical purposes. Consisting of a pair of rhymed end-stopped lines, the eighteenth century heroic couplet not only has the classical virtue of symmetry but also lends itself beautifully to epigram, antithesis, and comic reversals. "Tuesday," for instance, contains numerous examples of artistically satisfying parallelism, such as "In ev'ry wood his carrols sweet were known,/ At ev'ry wake his nimble feats were shown." After giving examples of Marian's inability to continue her usual tasks, Gay sums up the situation with an epigrammatic comment: "For yearning love the witless maid employs,/ and *Love*, say swains, *all busie heed destroys*." In "Monday," Lobbin Clout calls to his sweetheart in well-crafted antitheses: "Come *Blouzelinda*, ease thy swain's desire,/ My summer's shadow and my winter's fire." The funniest passages in the poems, however, are those in which the poet or his characters indulge in sentiment and then, within the space of a couplet or two, reverse the mood with a reminder of reality. Thus in the last four lines of "Tuesday," Marian stops weeping when a cow is brought to be bred. Not only does she "dry her tears," but she also takes care of business and makes sure that she is paid.

Gay's imagery, too, reflects the frequent changes of mood and tone that are meant to keep the reader off balance. For example, in "Friday," Bumkinet's "doleful dirge" provides a generalized and idealized version of grieving nature, with its "dewy sorrow," its "ev'ning tears," and its "rolling streams" with their "watry grief." On the other hand, the hogs "wallowing mid a feast of acorns" and the detailed description of the butter-churning process are highly realistic, as are the elements of the dying girl's will. Generally, the poet moves from idealized images to realistic ones rather than the converse. Thus in the final two verse paragraphs of "Friday," he first presents some conventional scenes in conventional language. His bulls standing with "curled brow" and his maidens at their milking might have come from any bucolic landscape. However, Gay's images soon become much less picturesque. His hogs in "sinking mire" and his moles at work thus prepare for the realistic conclusion of the poem. The description of "bonny *Susan*" in flight, pursued and captured by the shepherds, is not only more vivid than the earlier conventional imagery, but it also emphasizes the difference between literature and life. Thus, with consummate skill, Gay utilizes various poetic techniques to underscore his ideas.

Themes and Meanings

Because satire cuts two ways, sometimes three or four, it is always subject to misinterpretation. However, even the most prominent scholars of eighteenth century literature admit that they are uncertain as to the purpose and meaning of *The Shepherd's Week*. There are a number of theories. It is sometimes argued that Gay's work is in large part merely a burlesque of the pastoral pattern. On the other hand, English writer Samuel Johnson and others have believed it to be a worthy example of what a pastoral should be. The moving account of Blouzelinda's death would certainly support this view. Some critics believe that *The Shepherd's Week* was intended to parody the Vergilian eclogues on which five of Gay's poems are based; others believe that it was written in order to ridicule the poet's contemporary Ambrose Philips, who had fallen out with Gay's friend Pope. It has even been argued that references to the popular songwriter Thomas D'Urfey are in fact an oblique attack on Philips.

Some resolve these critical difficulties by saying that perhaps *The Shepherd's Week* has no single target but is, in essence, just one *jeu d'esprit* after another, united in that they all reflect the poet's perception of the absurd in human conduct. Thus in "The Proeme," first Gay plays himself as he attacks the literary establishment with its "critical gallimawfry"; then he assumes the mask of unctuous piety, insisting that only "great clerks" should comment on religion and explaining that he omits Sunday from his week for religious reasons; finally, with his explanation of the language and with his footnotes, he pretends to be pedantic. By the end of "The Proeme," Gay has satirized at least three kinds of absurdity, and a careful examination of the comments addressed to the reader leads one to suspect that there is probably a fourth because anyone who would take such obsequious flattery at face value would, without question, qualify as a fool.

The contrast between rural and urban life, which is a standard theme of pastoral poems, is basic to *The Shepherd's Week*. In the traditional pastoral, however, worldly people such as those in the "Prologue" are simply transported to the country, where they spend their time brandishing their crooks, observing sheep, and composing poetry. Gay's characters, on the other hand, are country bred and naïvely unaware of the outside world. Often they are very funny, as when, in "Monday," the two lovers descend from high-flown sentiments to descriptions of food. Whenever he appears to mock his rural folk, however, Gay is once again setting a trap for his readers. If they laugh at real shepherds and shepherdesses because they think of them as a different breed from themselves, it is the urban sophisticates, not the rural innocents, who are the real fools.

Nowhere is the thematic complexity of *The Shepherd's Week* more evident than in the treatment of sex. In his "Prologue," Gay points to the gathering of wealth as the primary motivation of England's ruling classes. Indeed, their only interest in the rural population is in what they produce. Gay does not have to remind readers that among such people marriages are matters of contract and that what they call love is, like poetry, a mere diversion from "affairs of States and Kings." By contrast, Gay's shepherds and shepherdesses are refreshingly sincere. They fall passionately in love; they are miserable when the object of their affection is absent or indifferent or, worst of all, enamored of another; and when, as at the end of "Thursday," mutual desire and opportunity coincide, they couple ecstatically, without thought of the consequences. Eventually these young lovers will marry, settle down, and work toward the wisdom of the old. At the moment, however, they are simply responding to the urgings of nature.

In implicitly contrasting the artificial existences of city dwellers with the natural lives of country folk, Gay is doing what the best pastoral poems have always done. Even though he sometimes mocks the excesses of the pastoral convention and even light-heartedly laughs at his simple characters, Gay's mock pastoral was not written either as an attack on the form itself or as a satire of rural life. Indeed, the materialistic courtiers could learn much from the shepherds and shepherdesses in Gay's poem. There is much about them to admire. They are compassionate, capable of honest joy and grief, and highly practical. After their flights of fancy, they always get back to work, for whatever one's emotional condition, the cattle must be watered and the cream must be churned. They may seem ignorant, even foolish, but they know secrets that cosmopolitan readers could never comprehend: how to adjust to the rhythms of nature and how to keep their balance in success and failure, happiness and frustration, life and death. Unlike at least some of Gay's readers, they have no inflated sense of their own importance but are, instead, keenly aware of their participation in the great cycle of death and rebirth. After Blouzelinda, Susan may bring her own kind of joy, but eventually, when the songs are over and "the sun descends," one has no choice but to succumb to sleep.

Rosemary M. Canfield Reisman

THE SHIELD OF ACHILLES

Author: W. H. Auden (1907-1973)
Type of poem: Meditation
First published: 1955, in *The Shield of Achilles*

The Poem

W. H. Auden's "The Shield of Achilles" is a nine-stanza poem that uses an episode from Homer's ancient Greek epic *Iliad* (c. 800 B.C.E; Eng. trans., 1616) to meditate on the violence and brutality of the modern world. The poem begins with an unnamed woman looking over the shoulder of an unnamed man; the two are named in the last stanza, but those who know the *Iliad* well will immediately recognize from the poem's title that the woman is the goddess Thetis, the mother of the Greek hero Achilles. The man over whose shoulder she looks is Hephaestos, the god of fire and metal-working, who is commissioned by Thetis in book 18 of the *Iliad* to make a shield for Achilles to carry into battle. In the first stanza, Thetis looks to see how Hephaestos is decorating the shield. Expecting to see conventional symbols of victory and power, she sees instead that Hephaestos has used images of "an artificial wilderness" and a "sky like lead."

The next two stanzas depict in sharper detail the images engraved or embossed on the shield: a barren plain filled with expressionless people standing in line, "waiting for a sign." As they stand, a voice comes from above declaring the justice of "some cause." Without discussion or reflection, the people march away in lines to serve that cause, which eventually brings them to grief.

In the fourth stanza, the poem returns to Thetis. Where she expects to see "ritual pieties" in the forms of sacrificial cows and ceremonial offerings, she finds instead "Quite another scene." Again, the following two stanzas describe the scenes depicted on the shield. This time, she sees a barbed-wire enclosure, where bored sentries and a crowd of detached observers watch as three figures are crucified. "They" have no hope, no pride, and the lines are written so that "they" might be the crucified figures— the crowd, or the sentries, or all three. They have lost their humanity, and "died as men before their bodies died."

The seventh stanza returns to Thetis and Hephaestos. Thetis looks this time for athletes and dancers, symbols of strength and agility. Instead of a playing field or dance floor, she finds a "weed-choked field." The only person in that field, as described in stanza 8, is a poor and dirty boy with nowhere to go and nothing to do but idly throw a stone at a bird. The only world he knows is one of rape and murder and betrayal; he knows nothing of tenderness or compassion.

As the poem ends, Hephaestos finishes his work and limps away and Thetis has her first full look at the shield. She is horrified by what she sees, and by the thought that her son will carry representations of violence and cruelty into battle. In the last line of the poem, the narrator points out something that neither Thetis nor Hephaestos knows: that Achilles himself will soon die in the war against Troy.

Forms and Devices

The most important rhetorical device in "The Shield of Achilles" is contrast, between what Thetis expects to see on the shield and what she does see, and between the ancient world and the modern world. Three times, Thetis looks over Hephaestos's shoulder, expecting to see idyllic and pastoral scenes of civilizations enjoying peace and prosperity. The images she expects—olive branches, sacrificial animals ornamented with flowers—are from the classical world, and the language of these stanzas invokes an earlier time, with phrases such as "untamed seas," "ritual pieties," "Libation and sacrifice," and "flickering forge-light."

The people in Thetis's imagined scenes are strong, adventurous, pious, and happy. The actual images on the shield, however, are quite different. The landscape is bleak and infertile, and the people are without emotion or hope. Far from dancing and competing in athletic games, they stand silently, blankly, or they march in columns without passion or reason. Instead of "well-governed cities" she sees an "unintelligible multitude"; instead of "ritual pieties" she sees a crucifixion that clearly echoes Christ's, with an audience of uncaring observers; instead of athletes and dancers gathered in celebration, she sees one lone boy. The plain language and imagery of barbed wire and statistics in these passages set them in the modern world.

Auden emphasizes these contrasts by using two different stanza forms. Stanzas 1, 4, 7, and 9 are set squarely in ancient Greece, and the reader's gaze is directed toward Thetis and Hephaestos. These stanzas are composed of eight three-stress lines; the second and fourth lines rhyme, as do the sixth and eighth. The other stanzas, in which the scenes of modern life are presented in detail, are quite different. These stanzas are in the seven-line form known as rime royal. The lines are in iambic pentameter, with the rhyme scheme *ababbcc*. The contrast is striking, both visually and aurally, and it is impossible not to notice the movement between stanzas focused on Thetis's innocent expectations and those focused on the harsh realities depicted on the shield.

Irony is another important device used in the poem. Thetis does not see it, but it is ironic that she would expect a shield, an instrument of war, to be decorated with images of pastoral beauty. Her son is a soldier, an "iron-hearted man-slaying" hero, yet she is dismayed at the idea that Hephaestos would create images of desolation and ruin to please him. By commissioning a weapon she becomes complicit in acts of war and aggression, yet she responds with horror to the physical, social, and spiritual destruction that is the only possible result.

Themes and Meanings

Throughout a long career as a poet, Auden returned again and again to three themes that appear in "The Shield of Achilles": the spiritual emptiness that arises from oppressive government, the essential loneliness of modern individuals, and the ultimate hope of redemption provided by the Christian God. As a child in England during the Great Depression and then as a young man in the United States during World War II, Auden saw many examples of the mindless acts and hopeless figures that he places on Achilles's shield, but he found in Christianity a way to escape the despair that arises from life on Earth. In much of his poetry, Auden attempted to speak universal truths that might change the world. He rejected grand but ultimately artificial language and wrote about the world outside rather than about his interior life and personal struggles.

Auden worked for a short time as a political propagandist in Spain during that country's civil war, and he saw at first hand that modern totalitarian governments are capable of stripping away the humanity of their citizens. During the 1930's, much of Auden's writing was overtly political, concerned directly with the rise of fascism and the possibilities for justice offered by socialism and Marxism. Over time, however, he came to see that fighting oppression with oppression, or fighting violence with violence, destroyed everyone involved. Unlike Thetis, he came to see that even a just cause can be corrupted when those who support it use evil means.

The modern figures in "The Shield of Achilles" are faceless and voiceless. They are not individuals, but rather packs or multitudes, and they have no ideas of their own; they wait for orders and follow them, without thinking or arguing, reduced to nothing but "a million eyes, a million boots." The only person who is seen individually in the modern sections of the poem is the "ragged urchin," who is not a part of a multitude but completely alone. He has nothing particular to do, and no one to wonder where he is; seeing a bird, a thing of beauty in a desolate landscape, his first impulse is to throw a stone at it. This is what the modern world has created: a child who has never known love, who has no reason to expect loyalty or compassion. He is the product of Thetis, who even as she watches the creation of a weapon expects to see images of beauty and peace.

Auden was not hopeless, in spite of the bleak picture he presents of the world. He believed that meaning and purpose could be found in Christianity, and he placed a reminder of that hope within the poem. Although the guards and the "ordinary decent folk" watching the three figures being crucified are unmoved by what they see, the figures are clearly representations of Christ and the two men crucified with him. Christ's ultimate sacrifice brought hope back to a despairing world and demonstrated the eternal presence of God's love. Though the culture of violence and oppression may crush the spirit, for Auden the possibility of redemption offered by God is always present. The lone bird can still fly "up to safety," and the poet can induce the reader to "weep because another wept."

Cynthia A. Bily

THE SHIP OF DEATH

Author: D. H. Lawrence (1885-1930)
Type of poem: Lyric
First published: 1932, in *Last Poems*

The Poem

"The Ship of Death" is composed of 107 lines, divided into ten sections of varying lengths (section 4 has four lines, section 7 twenty-five lines). The title refers to the ancient burial practice of placing a model ship in the tomb with the corpse to carry the soul to heaven.

Section 1 describes the time of death as autumn, when apples fall and their seeds are dropped into the earth through the rotting fruit. Each person passes through such a period of autumn, as the person undergoes a separation of self from self. Each must prepare for such a separation. Thus, section 2 calls upon all ("you," the readers) to build a ship of death, because the season of frost has arrived and apples are ready to fall. The smell of death is in the air, and the soul cowers within the cold body.

Section 3 questions the success of suicide, refusing to believe that the murder of one's self could be rewarded with the desired tranquillity of death. Instead, section 4 asserts, one should rely upon one's experience of the peace that comes from "a strong heart." This is the kind of quiet that one hopes for, and it cannot be had through suicide.

The task of all is, therefore, to begin to prepare for the death that is a part of natural process, for the fall from life that is like the fall of the ripe apple in autumn. Each should build a ship of death for the long journey into "oblivion." Each can experience in the body the decline of nature as a bruising of being, as a passage of the soul from the weakening body. Time and space are experienced by the aging body as the buffeting of ocean waves against the beach; it is upon that limitless ocean, whose sources come from beyond time and space, that the ship of death will be launched.

The body breaks up and falls into pieces in section 6, where the soul discovers that it cannot find anything solid outside its body. The flood waters are death-waters, now within as well as without the body. The soul is increasingly frightened, huddling in terror as it waits the final annihilating waves of destruction.

"We are dying, we are dying," the poem says; since we are dying all the time, we can only resign ourselves to the inevitability of the end. We must help the soul by building a ship for it to cross the ocean of death; we must put aboard it the implements of life, "food/ and little dishes," for comfort of the frightened soul. One departs the body as a soul launched upon a ship that has no destiny, no charts to guide it, and no means to steer it upon the dark waters of death. In the deepening darkness, both the soul and the ship disappear as they drift without direction and fall into nothing, toward "nowhere."

Section 8 is a surrender, an absolute resignation to the disappearance of all: Both body and ship are "gone, entirely gone." The end has been reached, and the end "is oblivion." When all has sunk into nothing, something occurs. Section 9 is a break in the plane of oblivion, as "a thread" of light stretches itself out to make a horizon, to open a space for new consciousness. The stunned speaker is uncertain of what can be believed: "Is it illusion?" Then the thread of light "fumes" into a broader, dawn-like light. Suddenly, the ship is sighted, drifting beneath the gray light. Then the light turns yellow, and finally it is rose-colored; "The whole thing starts again."

The flooding waters of death subside to open section 10. A "frail soul," beaten and disoriented by the darksome voyage, leaves the ship and steps into a shell-like body waiting for its return. The ship returns upon the sea as the soul reenters its body. The soul now finds the peace of oblivion in its bodily being. This is what awaits the person who builds the ship of death, so each should begin to build what each will need to cross waters of death for the peace of oblivion.

Forms and Devices

"The Ship of Death" is an irregular form of lyric with elegiac material in free verse. Each section is made up of verses grouped into stanzalike units of independent clauses: These may be one line, or they may be as many as nine lines (as in section 7). The effect is a tone suggesting talk, solemn but intimate and ordinary. The intimacy is a product of bringing together the speaker and audience/readers at the opening of section 4: "O let us talk."

The main devices of this poem are symbolic images, literary allusions, and rhetorical questions. The poem moves in an undulating, shifting way from the declarative statements of section 1 to the interrogatives of 2, 3, and 4. Then there is an increase in the imperative, commanding tone: "Build then, . . . you must." With little exception, this is the tone sustained to the end, with its "oh build it!" The form of biblical prophecy or pastoral sermon helps shape the poem.

Literary allusions range from obvious to subtle, as Lawrence draws upon his rich literary heritage to help create the themes of his poem. The most obvious is in section 3, with its echoes of William Shakespeare's *Hamlet* (c. 1600-1601) "can a man his own quietus make/ with a bare bodkin?" Hamlet's soliloquy on suicide is invoked to put the issue of the poem on a line of courage that confronts death in a positive and heroic way. While this may be slightly ironic, indicating that modern souls are more timid than Hamlet, it still works to align the modern soul with the heroic Hamlet in a more subtle way. When Hamlet is sent to England, he makes a strange voyage by ship, from which he returns a changed person, resigned to providence. Lawrence's poem also aims for this. There are other, important allusions as well. The poem opens with strong references, through the imagery of the "falling fruit" of autumn, to John Keats's "To Autumn," as well as to Shakespeare's *King Lear* (c. 1605-1606), with its line, "the ripeness is all."

The imagery of falling fruit as a symbol for the fallen body, from which a "soul" exits like a seed from rotting pulp, is a way to keep the process of death and dying in a natural dimension; therefore, when the soul returns from its journey at the end, it is more credible, because the soul is like the seed which sprouts into new life after a period of germination in earth's darkness. The action of the fall is itself likened to a journey, and this is made to be a journey by water. References to the "ark" and "flood" make the journey an individual experience of the biblical narrative of Noah, so that the natural process is lifted into a spiritual and religious dimension as well.

Themes and Meanings

The meaning of "The Ship of Death" is religious, because it draws upon traditional beliefs to shape its expression. Invoking Hamlet's soliloquy puts the religious question of suicide in a Western, Judeo-Christian setting that rejects suicide. To allude to the building of the ark by Noah is to solicit the power of divine commandment for the preparation to die as a preparation to survive death; destruction is divinely determined, but obedience to God delivers one from the annihilation of that destruction.

There is ambiguity in the meaning of the ship as an ark, however, because there is quite clearly a connection between the "ship of death" and the model ships placed with corpses in the tombs of ancient Egyptians. This connection raises the possibility that the little ship may be less effective in its voyage than the story of Noah suggests. Those Egyptian ships have gone nowhere, have indeed sometimes lain ironically less preserved beside the better preserved bodies whose souls they were to protect.

Finally, "The Ship of Death" is less confidently a statement of certainty about religious hope for life eternal than it is about the stern necessity of psychological renewal in every person's natural life. Perhaps each night's sleep is a passage over the flood of death-darkness, so each morning is a survival of spirit from the death of the body in sleep's oblivion. More clearly, though subtly, the poem's meaning is limited to the search for self-identity: "to bid farewell/ to one's own self, and find an exit/ from the fallen self." This is a familiar theme of Lawrence's writing, in fiction as well as in poetry, and it produces a meaning of self-discovery through self-renewal in "The Ship of Death."

Richard D. McGhee

SICILY

Author: Roland Flint (1934-2001)
Type of poem: Narrative
First published: 1987, in *Sicily*

The Poem

Roland Flint's twenty-stanza poem "Sicily" tells the story of the poet's visit to the town of Nicosia, Sicily, an island off the southern coast of Italy. Far from the life of suburban America, the poet meets people who trigger memories of his late mother and son. The Sicilians the narrator meets believe in their futures, but because they live in the shadow of the largest active volcano in Europe, they realize that life is subject to sudden catastrophe. In this foreign locale, the poet discovers he can behave as the Sicilians; he finally grieves for the losses he has suffered and comes to terms with his life.

The poem begins with a reference to the narrator having reread novelist and short-story writer "John Cheever for months" before accepting an invitation to visit Sicily. The "quick decision" to travel to remote Sicily and the "changes" in his environment have left the narrator "bewildered," but by the close of the poem, bewilderment gives way to understanding.

In the poem's first stanza the narrator writes that author John Cheever sees life as "confusing" yet "absorbing and dull, pained and sweet,/ Addictive and merciless— vexed, like laughter in grief." The following stanzas describe the landscape of Nicosia, the hotel where the poet narrator stays, and a dinner given by his Sicilian hosts. The narrator comments on the atmosphere of Sicily, with its "invisible hints of the shot-gun/ and a prohibition of women." After hearing breaking glass ("crystal splintering"), the narrator likens the subsequent "furious male shouting" to "Bandy Polyphemo," the most famous of the Cyclops who, in the ancient Greek poet Homer's *Odyssey* (c. 800 B.C.E.; Eng. trans., 1616), lived in a cave not far from Nicosia.

Next, the poet participates in a multilingual poetry reading where he notices a "girl of seven or so" who "understood more in her way" than the poet did. The poet narrator moves on to reflect on the nearby volcano, Etna, which has remained active since the time of the ancient Greek playwright Aeschylus and the ancient Greek poet Pindar, both of whom wrote about it. The narrator notices that he can see the volcano from everywhere he is. Antonio, a bus driver, explains some of Etna's history and sings the part of the doomed lover from the Italian opera *Cavalleria Rusticana*. The narrator meets Grazia Martinez, a young woman translator who, because "Etna has been out her window forever," also knows her future is not "separate from molten grime and catastrophe." The translator reminds the poet of his late mother.

In the succeeding stanzas, the narrator recalls the sudden death of his mother, who was buried on the anniversary of the death of his child. Only now, in Sicily, does the narrator realize that the coincidence of the date of his child's death with that of his mother's burial, which had seemed "the worst season's worst addition," has become a "symmetry of dates. . . ./. . . to salve or line/ The permanent crack" in his heart. In the last stanzas of the poem, the poet is perplexed yet thankful to grieve again, having learned through his travel and his encounters with Grazia and Antonio that life lived in the shadow of catastrophe is not at all unusual, and that the "after-life" of the dead may be "in our remembering."

Forms and Devices

"Sicily" is not written in formal meter; it is a free-verse poem. The poem is in open form, with stanzas varying in length from four to thirteen lines. The lines are generally end-stopped; that is, the poet's thought is completed in each line, causing the reader to pause, or punctuation marks require the reader to pause at the end of the line. End-stopped lines slow down the movement of a poem, and Flint's use of them contributes to the meditative sense of "Sicily." While the poem's lines are fairly uniform, the poet uses one hemistich, or half line, in the third-to-last stanza, when he writes "'and left her there,'" quoting what his sister said about their buried mother.

The poet's language is not formal but rather conversational. However, while Flint uses casual speech, he is writing for a sophisticated audience, one familiar with the work of John Cheever and Cheever's tendency to place his characters in rainy environments where they are washed clean of their sense of isolation and confinement. Further, the poet alludes to Homer and is specific in his mention of the Sicilian writers Massimo Ganci, Franco Grasso, and Luigi Pirandello, as well as the classical writers Aeschylus and Pindar and the well-known opera *Cavalleria Rusticana*, which is set in Sicily. In addition, Flint makes a direct allusion to Robert Hayden's tribute poem "Those Winter Sundays" by recalling Hayden's description of his father's service to his family ("love's austere and lonely offices"). Flint writes that his mother "taught love's offices as gifts."

The most unusual aspect of Flint's use of language is his consistent use of the second-person singular tense throughout his narrative. By using the word "you," Flint includes his reader in his very personal return to his grief. The impact of Flint's word choice is doubled when the poet identifies the reader as himself: "You consider," "you are in a hotel," "You are in a small party of writers," for example. Flint repeats words crucial to the idea of his personal redemption, including different forms of the verb "bewilder" and the nouns "rain" and "belief." The poet's repetition and variations of words in "Sicily" deepens the reader's emotional involvement in the narrative.

"Sicily" has one overarching symbol, Etna, the volcano surrounded by the towns of Nicosia, Catania, Acireale, and Nicolosi, all mentioned in the poem. Not only do the people who live in the towns beneath Etna know that they live "in the permanent radius of risk," but also do Flint's readers understand that they are "not separate from molten grime and catastrophe." The volcano, active at least since the beginning of Western literature, symbolizes the capricious natural forces that Sicilians have always accepted as a part of their daily lives, but that the poet-narrator has lost touch with. Only by journeying to the land of the volcano does the poet realize that loss and hope are "the tangled core" of life.

Themes and Meanings

Flint's poems are generally contemplative, concerning themselves with how human beings find balance in the midst of anguish and loss. Often relying on anecdotal material, Flint's poems examine the depths of human endurance and despair. "Sicily" is typical of Flint's work. The poet uses his trip from Washington, D.C., to the Italian island for a poetry reading as a catalyst for his long poem. Just as Flint chooses simple, direct language to express a sophisticated perspective, he chooses the simplest of images from his trip to explain the most complex of human emotions.

A bus driver named Antonio explains the impact of one of Etna's earlier eruptions and "What the earthquakes hit and missed" and then sings from an opera based on a Sicilian novella. The reader sees that Antonio can celebrate his country in spite of its randomly destructive history. When "one of the foreigners" offers a young translator "a marzipan" (a sweet cake), she in turn presents the "sea at Acireale today—and the sky." The translator cherishes the natural world in which she lives, so much so that she can offer it as a gift. These accessible images are a direct connection to the poet narrator's philosophy that life is beautiful because it is so fragile.

Flint uses two specific narrative techniques in his poem, foreshadowing and making use of the rhetorical device of quoting certain characters. When the poet mentions that he has become bewildered by the changes in his environment (in stanza 2), he prepares the reader to realize the other changes in his environment that have left him bewildered, the death of his child and the death of his mother. In stanza 7, the poet mentions how a young girl appears to understand "more" than the poet does. The mention prepares readers to see how, in stanza 11, the woman translator also understands more than the poet does.

Instead of restating what his characters have said, Flint reports their speech. Reporting speech is more direct than paraphrasing speech. Most writers use quotations when the authority of the source being quoted is relevant to advancing a thesis. Flint is no exception. He quotes John Cheever's view of life, the translator who is grateful for a small courtesy, his mother who had a premonition of her sudden death, and his sister who says "I can't stop thinking we just put her in the ground/ and left her there." The quotations illuminate the concepts central to Flint's vision of life: bewilderment, gratitude, foreknowledge, and grief. Underlying these concepts is Flint's acceptance of life, with its "harsh surface beauty" that is nonetheless worth opening oneself to.

Ginger Jones

A SIGHT IN CAMP IN THE DAYBREAK GRAY AND DIM

Author: Walt Whitman (1819-1892)
Type of poem: Narrative
First published: 1865, in *Drum-Taps*

The Poem

Walt Whitman's "A Sight in Camp in the Daybreak Gray and Dim" is a fifteen-line poem written in the free verse that is characteristic of much of Whitman's work. The poem is broken into four uneven stanzas, ranging from one line to six lines in length. Although ostensibly a narrative influenced by the poet's experiences as a nurse during the Civil War, the poem is also a meditation upon humanity's inability to learn the lessons of the past.

Much of Whitman's work, particularly his lengthy meditative poem "Song of Myself" (1855), is profoundly influenced by Transcendentalist philosophers such as Ralph Waldo Emerson. In the vein of Emerson's "Self-Reliance," Whitman's early poetry promises to provide the "original energy" of "nature without check" and is ultimately optimistic and vital. However, after an 1862 visit with his wounded brother, Whitman became a wartime nurse, serving both Union and Confederate wounded in a hospital encampment in Washington, D.C. The optimism and hopefulness of romantic Transcendentalism suddenly seemed out of place at such a time and in such an environment.

Like many of Whitman's selections from *Drum-Taps*, a collection of poems written about the American Civil War, the title of "A Sight in Camp in the Daybreak Gray and Dim" is taken from the first line of the poem. The narrator has emerged from his tent "sleepless," and walking near "the hospital tent" he sees "three forms" on "stretchers lying," beneath a "Gray and heavy blanket, folding, covering all." The narrator's mindset at this discovery is made clear from his description of the "daybreak gray and dim." This is not a glorious new day full of promise and potential, but rather the dawn of a day that will bring lessons somber and sad in the forms of the three war casualties.

"Curious" and "silent," the narrator lifts the blanket "from the face of the nearest . . . first," finding an elderly man with "well-gray'd hair, and flesh all sunken about the eyes." The narrator asks the dead man "Who are you," naming the corpse "my dear comrade." Although one may quickly suppose the narrator speaks to a fallen Union soldier whose cause is sympathetic to the narrator's (and Whitman's) own, to do so is to miss the point. The dead man is the narrator's comrade because each is a human being, a member of a wartorn and beleaguered people. Uncovering the face of the second blanket-shrouded form, the narrator finds a young man, a "sweet boy with cheeks yet blooming," and again asks him, "who are you my child and darling?"

Finally, the narrator inspects the third victim, a man whose age is neither "child nor old," his face colored a "beautiful yellow-white ivory." Examining this last casualty, the narrator does not ask "who are you" but instead states, "Young man I think I know you." The face of this final victim, he realizes, is the "face of the Christ himself,/ Dead and divine and brother of all, and here again he lies."

Forms and Devices

It is almost impossible for a reader to overestimate the influence of Whitman's verse on the poets that followed him. Although Whitman was not the first poet to write in free verse, the poems included in *Leaves of Grass* (1855-1892), like "Song of Myself," so demonstrated his mastery of free verse that this form of poetic expression became inextricably linked with his name. Detractors of free verse are far less common now given the prevalence of the style throughout much of the twentieth century; what was rebellious during Whitman's life is now commonplace.

The lack of formal line lengths, meter, and rhyme schemes in much of Whitman's poetry does not mean that form was not an important tool to the poet. The long, breathless lines of "Song of Myself" seem to convey that the poet truly is energized by his understanding of nature, and that his powers of creativity are bursting at the seams; he cannot write quickly enough to place his impressions upon the page. The more somber subject matter of "A Sight in Camp in the Daybreak Gray and Dim," however, is also served by Whitman's use of free verse.

The poem begins with its longest stanza as the narrator describes his early rising and discovery of the three dead men. The entire first stanza is a series of inverted subordinate and appositive clauses that finally culminate in the lines, "Over each the blanket spread, ample brownish woolen blanket,/ Gray and heavy blanket, folding, covering all." The breathlessness of the stanza-long, six-line sentence with its clauses that trip on and on until stopped by the blanket—just as death has stopped the three soldiers—demonstrates to the reader the troubled and questioning state of the narrator's mind.

The second stanza contains shorter sentences but longer lines. The narrator's query to the body of the "elderly man"—"Who are you my dear comrade?"—forms its own line. The question is emphasized even further when it is asked again. "Who are you sweet boy with cheeks yet blooming?" forms its own separate single-line stanza and further demonstrates the passionate sorrow of the narrator's question.

Whitman not only uses repetition to reveal the importance of the narrator's query but also repeats words and phrases to make his point clear to the reader. The fourth line states twice that the "three forms" spied by the narrator are "lying" on their stretchers; it is clear that they are dead and that they shall never rise again. This is again emphasized with the repetition of "blanket" along with the reiterated fact that the single blanket is covering all three men. Whatever their possible differences in life, the three are all now covered by the casually indifferent blanket of death.

Themes and Meanings

The first key to understanding Whitman's point in "A Sight in Camp in the Daybreak Gray and Dim" is to remember the context and physical setting of the poem. In placing a poem that tells of a "hospital tent" in a cycle of poems about the United

States Civil War, Whitman expected that his readers would understand that the poem is on some level about the war and that the three dead men are victims of the great conflict. As stated earlier, the same blanket covers all three casualties of the war; the sides they fought for in life are insignificant in the shadow of their shared fates. Union and Confederate soldiers alike are victims to the human tendency to kill other humans.

The ages of the fallen men are also significant. The first man uncovered, the "elderly man so gaunt and grim, with well-gray'd hair," is old, and the reader is to understand that war destroys the old. The next unveiled is a "child and darling," a "sweet boy with cheeks yet blooming." War, and all that it stands for—violence, lack of compassion, vengeance—also destroys the young. The third member of the deceased soldiers, with a face neither "child nor old," shows that war destroys those in the full bloom of life.

In the face of this destruction, the narrator asks the first two casualties, "who are you?" In part this signifies the loss of identity that violent death results in; the corpse's hopes, dreams, and beliefs are all lost. Perhaps the repetition and vehemence of the questions, however, must cause the reader to ask "Who am I?" Who are humans, that they could perpetuate such violence upon one another again and again over the ages? Who are these Americans of the Civil War era, who, while considering themselves enlightened and civilized, feel justified in holding others slaves and are content to destroy each other in a war?

The number of forms on the stretcher is made important by the narrator's assertion that the third man is "Christ himself." The number three has Christian significance; in this case, the number not only calls to mind the Holy Trinity of Father, Son, and Holy Ghost, but also recalls the fact that two other men were crucified on Calvary with Christ. Although Whitman was not religious according to the conventional notion of the term, he was spiritual, and here he is concerned with what Christ represents: all that is possible and all that is good in humankind and the potential that humanity, as a race, must strive for. Nonetheless, states the narrator, "Dead and divine and brother of all, and here again he lies." The declaration seems to announce that although nearly two thousand years have passed since Christ's life, humans are still killing each other in wars and falling sorrowfully short of the potential that Christ represented. Humans are still destroying all that is Christ-like in each other and themselves.

Like many of the other *Drum-Taps* poems, "A Sight in Camp in the Daybreak Gray and Dim" is more somber and questioning than is typical of Whitman's work. In some ways, its preoccupation with the poet's firsthand encounter with war prefigures the emergence of realism in American literature. After the Civil War, the bombast, optimism, and love of self that characterized Romantics and Transcendentalists failed to adequately reflect the American mood; in "A Sight in Camp in the Daybreak Gray and Dim," Whitman provides a bridge to the literary future in both form and theme.

Scott Yarbrough

THE SIGNATURE OF ALL THINGS

Author: Kenneth Rexroth (1905-1982)
Type of poem: Lyric
First published: 1949, in *The Signature of All Things*

The Poem

"The Signature of All Things" is divided into three parts: The first comprises thirty-two-lines; the second, twenty-five; and the third, twenty. The title of the poem derives from a book by the seventeenth century mystic Jakob Böhme, the reading of which initiates the poem. Written in the first person, the poem relates the visionary, intensely spiritual experience of the poet.

True to Böhme's teaching that the "outward visible world with all its beings is a signature, or figure, of the inward spiritual world," the poet begins with the image of his body "stretched bathed in the sun"; from his own physical being, the poet's awareness radiates to his surroundings, progressively more animate: water, laurel tree, and creatures.

These creatures perform the endless cycle of birth and death: The wren "broods in her moss-domed nest"; a newt "struggles with a white moth/ Drowning in the pool." Such observations lead the poet to recall his relationships, whether with humans— "those who have loved me"—or his natural environment—the "mountains I have climbed," the "seas I have swum in." These reminiscences prove redemptive; his "sin and trouble fall away/ Like Christian's bundle." This reference to John Bunyan's *Pilgrim's Progress* (1678, 1684) reinforces the sense of the poet's life as a pilgrimage of love. Böhme, as the poet describes, "saw the world as streaming/ In the electrolysis of love." Electrolysis, a chemical transformation involving dynamic currents, can serve as a purification process.

The second part of the poem finds the recumbent poet now standing "at the wood's edge." Following the mystic way, he has emptied himself of all preconceptions: "Watching the darkness, listening/ To the stillness." His humility is rewarded; an owl—a symbol of wisdom—arrives and awakens him to a world brimming with light. He proceeds to an oak grove, formerly the site of an Indian village. There he comes upon a group of heifers, "Black and white, all lying down/ Quietly together." Opposites—life and death, black and white—resolve in a tranquil scene of fruitfulness and communion.

In the final part of the poem, the poet recovers a rotten log from the bottom of a pool. Once it dries in the sun for a month—a full cycle of the moon—he chops it for kindling. Emerging late that night, after reading "saints" and "philosophers" on "the destiney of man," the poet looks up at the "swaying island of stars," then down at his feet, where all about him are "scattered chips/ Of pale cold light" that are "alive." Witness to and finally active participant in the cycle of renewal, the poet forms the nexus of living worlds of light—experiencing his destiny.

Forms and Devices

In keeping with its sacramental vision, the poem abounds in natural imagery. Flora and fauna; elements of earth, air, fire, and water; senses of sight, sound, and smell—all direct the poet's inner journey toward the epiphany that climaxes the work. A visionary poet in the tradition of William Blake, Kenneth Rexroth has stated, "Poetry is vision, the pure act of sensual communion and contemplation."

Adhering to the doctrine of correspondences taught by the mystic Böhme, the poet evokes nature as emblematic of spiritual realities. The laurel tree symbolizes expiation and eternity as well as victory and triumph. The oak, rooted in the graves of Indians, connotes endurance; sacred to Zeus, it represents the essence of divine power. Such imagery infuses the poem with a sense of rebirth. The clearest metaphor of renewal is left for last: the rotten log that the poet transforms into kindling fuel.

The setting of July, the height of summer, implies growth and maturity. The poet, at "forty summers," is ripe for the mystical rebirth of his sensual awareness and creative power, which he experiences in the course of the poem. The context of these awakenings is described in the imagery of illumination: the owl's eyes "glow"; the meadow is "bright as snow"; creatures appear in the "blur of brightness" and "cobwebbed light"; scattered wood chips are "ingots/ Of quivering phosphorescence."

The poet conjures these sacramental images in familiar language. The unrhymed measured lines—ranging from eight syllables each in the first part of the poem to seven in the last two—convey the intimacy of conversation. Rexroth called this syllabic form "natural numbers," saying that it allowed him to emphasize the "natural cadences of speech."

Themes and Meanings

The central meaning of the poem, a celebration of personal transcendence, lies in spiritual illumination. Rexroth has said that "our experience of reality begins and ends in illumination."

Rexroth was a proponent of Personalism—identified with the work of Dylan Thomas and Walt Whitman, among others—which defines poetry as personal vision, communion, and communal sacrament. For the poet, meaning evolved from spiritual community, from Martin Buber's "I-Thou" communion. The poem's organic vision reconciles self and other, life and death in the eternal process of creation.

A student of Böhme, Rexroth took to heart the mystic's teaching that the light of divine love streams through the universe and that humankind is the signature of God in the world. In his introduction to the book for which "The Signature of All Things" is the title poem, Rexroth wrote: "These are simple, personal poems, as close as I can make them to integral experiences. Perhaps the integral person is more revolutionary than any program, party or social conflict."

With luminous faith, the poet sought to reassert the powers of spiritual communion against the anomie promoted by urbanization and industrialization in the twentieth century. As critic Morgan Gibson has commented, the experience of the "integral person" in communion is Adamic: The individual becomes universal, and the universal, paradisal. From his wide reading as well as his translation of foreign verse, Rexroth evidenced an aesthetic that transcended space and time. According to Victor Howes, in *The Christian Science Monitor,* Rexroth was looking for a "sort of day-to-day mysticism"—that is, a direct and universal one. As Rexroth himself put it, "that sense of exaltation, that feeling of being on the brink of the coming of the absolute, is really a habit of living."

Amy Adelstein

SILENCE

Author: Robert Bly (1926-   )
Type of poem: Pastoral
First published: 1962, in *Silence in the Snowy Fields*

The Poem

The eighteen free-verse lines of Robert Bly's "Silence" serve as an introduction to his beginning as a poet actively attempting to explain the symbiotic relationship between humans and nature, of which he became vividly aware during his youth in rural Minnesota. Bly was also intrigued by nature as the source of poetry. In "Silence," eventually collected in his first gathering of poems, *Silence in the Snowy Fields*, Bly demonstrates his movement toward a canon of poetry focusing upon deeply hidden images that must be dredged up by the poet from what psychologist Carl Jung called the "collective unconscious," the source of all memories and ideas. Bly was certain that the source of all poetry, or the inspiration at least, was to be found deep in this repository of an individual's inspiration.

Like most of Bly's nature poems, "Silence" depicts a nature that is active, not something just to be admired or rationalized as many earlier nature poets, such as William Cullen Bryant, treated it. The narrator of "Silence," a rural writer "Cradling a pen, or walking down a stair/ Holding a cup," is thrust into both the real and the metaphysical nature that surrounds him and tries to explain the nature-human dynamic to himself and to the reader.

The first stanza establishes an archetypal chronology for the poem. The reader is witnessing the end of one point in the speaker's understanding and the beginning of another when he laments, "The fall has come, clear as the eyes of chickens." The controlling reality of this stanza is dramatized through the auditory impact of "Strange muffled sounds [that] come from the sea," which are amplified through such adjectives as "muffled" and " crashing." The introduction of sea sounds as deep images for the sounds of life or for the psyche of a poet writing from rural Minnesota produces a surreal moment into which the narrator is thrown. Once the primacy of nature is established, Bly introduces a human into the equation. It is morning, for the narrator tells readers that he is "walking down a stair/ Holding a cup in [his] hand." The narrator is not just a component of the world in which he finds himself; he is one who observes and interprets his surroundings "among these doorposts and cars" because as he enters this world he is "Cradling a pen," as a poet would. However, he does not completely immerse himself into the real world of "the pastures that lie in the sunlight." He is "the man inside the body" whose charge is to understand how what he perceives through his intellect relates to the natural world around him and the primal instincts it produces in him.

In the third and last stanza, the surreal world of stanza 1 and the mental world in stanza 2 are brought into alignment. The individual element of the collective unconscious found in the narrator seeks an outlet or explanation. However, Bly presents his narrator in his quest for understanding of his place as "Something homeless . . . looking on the long roads." Like "A dog lost since midnight," the narrator must search out the source of his cravings or a refuge from his interpretations.

Forms and Devices

Bly uses three stanzas of six free-verse lines each for his poem "Silence." Free verse permits Bly to escape the highly stylized poetry of which he is often critical. In addition, each stanza forms syntactical units rather than poetic lines, possessing two sentences each and creating a conversational rather than lecturing tone. For example, stanza 1 opens with the declaration that "The fall has come, clear as the eyes of chickens." The speaker then begins a more complex sentence to develop the underlying idea of the first. The second sentence describes the effect of this coming autumn through the continuous mention of sounds that are constant reminders to the narrator of this date, much as Whitman's "hermit thrush" does in "When Lilacs Last in the Dooryard Bloom'd." Stanzas 2 and 3 follow this statement-development construction.

Bly freely utilizes sight and sound imagery to produce the physical aspects of nature that trigger the narrator's contemplation. In stanzas 2 and 3, Bly moves from the reminders set off by the ocean sounds to images that must be pursued, each representing the acquisition of knowledge or understanding, "sunlight" and "window pane" being the most prominent. The "sunlight" is the sought-after objective that is most readily confronted by the narrator, who is hindered by "The sloth of the body" but who strives to enter the ultimate understanding through the mirror of the soul, "the window pane."

Bly opens "Silence" with near onomatopoeic sound references to moving water to draw the reader's attention to the archetypal significance of water as the source of life and intellect (another Jungian concept). The narrator, in the second stanza, is also in action "Cradling a pen, or walking down a stair/ Holding a cup in [his] hand." However, this movement is not permitted to proceed "into the pastures that lie in the sunlight" because of "the sloth of the man inside the body"; rather, the narrator must allow his imagination to move into the surrounding nature. The picture that is conjured up is of an individual whose main involvement in the nature/human consideration is one of intellect, not of physicality.

The narrator's imagination is given form when Bly compares it to "A dog lost since midnight," "a small duck/ Among the odorous reeds," and "a tiny box-elder bug searching for the window pane," all sentient beings "homeless [and] looking on the long roads" for meaning. Their quest, "the young sunlight," must be pursued if it is to be understood. This has direct bearing upon Bly's attempt to understand how and why a poet must pursue the inspiration for his poetry hidden deep in his collective unconscious and triggered by natural influences.

This pursuit of connecting human intellect and creativity to natural surroundings finds an appropriate vehicle in the pastoral quality of "Silence." As do other poets who are concerned with the influence of nature upon humanity, Bly realizes that nature is most appropriately studied in nature itself.

Themes and Meanings

The primary theme expressed in "Silence" is humans' need to fit into the natural surroundings by coming to terms with who they really are, "Something homeless . . . looking on the long roads," as in Robert Frost's "The Road Not Taken," looking for direction for their psychological and artistic quests. Being a place poet, Bly understands the influence and pull that place has upon an individual, especially one "Cradling a pen" and ready to record interpretations and reactions that the natural surroundings trigger.

Lying beneath this most obvious theme is one that could be elusive to the superficial reader. The constant movement toward the source of life and inspiration represented by "Strange muffled sounds [that] come from the sea" joins Bly, in attitude at least, to Carl Jung, whose work is concerned with the source of intellect and psychology, the collective unconscious. Bly's narrator's attempt to find understanding is represented as being like "a tiny box-elder bug searching for the window pane" that will allow it to glimpse the world in which it belongs, delineating the role of nature poets such as Bly.

The thematic tie among all the stanzas and levels of discussion in "Silence" is the concept that artists must create their own realities out of the world around them. As did many early and late modernist poets, Bly utilizes surrealism to present his personal reality. His "box-elder bug searching for the window pane" is reminiscent of T. S. Eliot's yellow, catlike fog in "The Love Song of J. Alfred Prufrock." In both instances, the poet does not rely upon mere object poetry; rather, each puts a particular spin or personal vision upon it, a right granted by the poet's personally confronting nature.

"Silence," like Bly's other nature poems, investigates the human relationship with nature by delving into the poet's contest with the deep imagery that nature brings to the forefront of his imagination. Bly's narrators are most often perceptive individuals who move through life understanding, at least for themselves, what life is all about or at least what one must do in order to produce such an understanding.

Tom Frazier

THE SILKEN TENT

Author: Robert Frost (1874-1963)
Type of poem: Sonnet
First published: 1939; collected in *A Witness Tree*, 1942

The Poem

Robert Frost's "The Silken Tent" is both a love poem and a metaphor describing the poet's relationship to his beloved as well as to his poetry. "The Silken Tent" is a sonnet written in the Shakespearean style, yet with Frost's uniquely American twist on form. It is a simple sentence written in fourteen lines of rhymed iambic pentameter. Frost makes use of his ties to nature in general, and New England in particular, to address the universality of human relationships and love. This is also a poem about people's individual relationships within the wider universe. At once simple and complex, "The Silken Tent" serves as a compelling metaphor for poetry within the context of lives and relationships.

Frost opens with the line "She is as in a field a silken tent" and immediately creates an image for the reader. The vision is of a tent in a field at midday, standing firm against the summer sun, sturdy and sure, supported by a strong "central cedar pole" which serves both to support and to point the pinnacle of the tent heavenward, toward the sun. Yet this tent is not set up for a rustic outing within the elements. Rather, it stands tall as Frost's symbol of the complexities of love and the connections of relationships, which "owe naught to any single cord" and are "strictly held by none" but are always "loosely bound/ By countless silken ties of love and thought."

Frost completes the sentence by noting that although life and love may be capricious, they are serious business; they are often filled with conflicts or choices that may be invisible to the human eye but pose a heavy burden for the heart and soul. At the same time, it is at those very moments when people most need the support of love that the strength of the cedar pole and the importance of the gentle but resilient "silken ties" that are so fundamental to meaningful relationships are most apparent.

Frost clearly writes this as a love poem. Originally titled "In Praise of Your Poise," it opens the love sequence in *A Witness Tree*, for which Frost received a Pulitzer Prize in 1943. It is a love poem written in the traditional sonnet form, but it is much more. Frost, always one to delight in the importance of sound and sense and the natural rhythms of speech, uses the sentence, one of the simplest units of meaning, to address the universal themes most important to him.

"The Silken Tent" is a masterful metaphor on life, love, and poetry. The tent stands alone in nature, pointing toward the sun at midday. Similarly, the poet seeks the courage to stand so firmly in the field of his dreams, all the while being tested and pulled in many directions by the numerous ties or connections in his life. Most ties are as unseen as the invisible silken threads, yet they are no less real. Some pull the poet off-center, while others serve as support against that force. The poem describes the internal and external conflicts faced in life, as well as the conflicts faced by every poet who struggles to put the invisible realities of the soul into print without betraying the form that makes poetry what it is.

Forms and Devices

Frost used a modern twist on a very traditional form in "The Silken Tent." Clearly a sonnet in the English tradition, he keeps his New England perspective as he puts his emotions to paper. In the ancient tradition of the biblical Song of Songs and following also in the tradition of John Donne, this is a lusty poem about passion and the forces being exerted upon the relationship. It is both capricious and restrained. The verse is honest, yet measured and controlled.

"The Silken Tent" is a true Shakespearean sonnet. Frost uses fourteen lines of iambic pentameter in measured rhyme. The rhyme scheme is the traditional *abab cdcd efef gg*. This is a break from Frost's many monologues written in blank verse. In this poem the rhyme is clear ("tent" and "relent"; "breeze" and "ease"; "pole" and "soul"), but it is never forced or predictable. The poem is masterfully crafted, allowing for the natural flow of typical New England speech patterns within the traditional constraints of the sonnet form, using iambic pentameter.

The "she" in the poem is not like a tent; Frost does not use simple simile. Rather, he uses an extended metaphor. The woman is "as in a field a silken tent." She stands as a poetic symbol. The woman, the tent, the poem, all seem to be as one. Each stands alone seeking to find its place in the sun, each in a field, be it a green space in nature, the field of human relationships, or the field of language the poet navigates in search of words to bring the intimacies and intricacies of life to fruition on the printed page.

In this poem, images are essential elements. The cedar pole and the silken threads signify strength. A cedar pole is lasting and connects the modern world of nature to the ancients. People are connected to traditions and to one another through the power of lasting love and words. Human connections to nature and to one another are strong, and yet they must be willing to sway in the breeze, to "relent" when the time is right. People must allow themselves the freedom to seek and enjoy the "sureness of the soul" that comes when they are confident in their place in the world, when they have a true and lasting love, or in Frost's case, when the innermost thoughts of the poet can take form in such a way as to surprise and delight the poet or the reader with a revelation for which neither was completely prepared. Like the woman and the tent, individuals stand alone, each in his or her own world, supported by unseen connections. Each person stands open to the perils and the capricious joys of nature, seeking the sunlight of happiness.

Themes and Meanings

In his poems, Frost almost always reveals the connectedness of nature to humanity, and of all humans to one another. Poems such as "Design" stress the organized nature of the universe. Others, such as "Tree at My Window" and "Stopping by Woods on a Snowy Evening" explore the inner and outer aspects of nature in relation to the internal and external struggles of the poet. Human beings must exist within and deal with the external forces of nature. At the same time, the connections that individuals share with one another are at times all-consuming within that wider frame. Together, people learn to deal with the elements and with their natural yearnings, including love, in life. However, personal relationships are rarely as clear-cut as the lines drawn between humans and the natural forces of the environment.

"The Silken Tent" succinctly draws the forces of nature and relationships into focus in a few remarkably well-chosen words. Those words, in the form of a sonnet, present a vivid image on a number of levels and thus speak to the reader in a number of different ways. Frost has a gift for making the truly complex appear simple. "The Silken Tent" can be read on a literal level, as a poem that uses the image of a tent to symbolize lust or love. One may also see it as a love poem. It is, however, much more.

This poem is a commentary on love through the ages as well as in modern times. Frost speaks of love as the eternal challenge of the ages, as an all-encompassing force that pulls readers in a number of directions at once. It both throws one off balance and supports innermost needs. It challenges and sustains the soul at the same time. Yet love can be elusive and ephemeral. Even when one knows that it is there, love is not always easy to see. It is always changing, as one is changed by the progression of natural forces in life. Love requires freedom of movement, but the "bondage" of which true lovers are acutely aware is a positive connection that is self-sustaining for both parties. It is this connection that brings about the "sureness of the soul" which is the pinnacle of love made manifest between two people.

It is that sureness, that contentment, that Frost seeks through the metaphor of the tent. As with human relationships, a poem must sway and move, be able to sustain the varied threads of thought the poet and the reader bring to the verse. A poem must therefore have the strength to sustain the thought and the resilience to speak to an ever-changing audience without sacrificing its sense of form. The poet must maintain his sense of self and, like the central cedar pole, support his thoughts and ideas, always aware that he is, like the silken tent, subject to the forces of the natural world. Yet the poet must also always be true to the metaphor waiting to take form from deep within when the time is right. In "The Silken Tent" Frost gives form to the aspects of human nature that are often overlooked by the purely objective eye.

Kathleen Schongar

SINCERELY

Author: Naomi Shihab Nye (1952-   )
Type of poem: Epistle/letter in verse
First published: 1994, in *Red Suitcase*

The Poem

"Sincerely" is a cleverly constructed seventy-nine-line poem about the art and craft of letter writing. Its author, inspired by her Palestinian American heritage and extensive travels to Asia, the Middle East, and Central America, considers correspondence from friends, family, and strangers a fascinating subject. She begins the six-part poem by describing envelopes as "usually white and slim,/ bleached as a shell we might press to our ears." Letters, she suggests, are full of mystery, humor, pathos, and joy. Within the first few lines, Naomi Shihab Nye poses several thought-provoking questions about letters: What are their unique shapes and sizes? Where do they travel in their long journey from one place to another? What do they bring us? Most important, what do they demand from us?

As if to illustrate the answers, Nye shares brief portions of five letters, each presumably a response to an earlier epistle. The first begins "Thank you. The articles about raising children/ arrived when my child was being very difficult." Sometimes letters come with much needed advice. Unfortunately, in this particular case the narrator lost the parenting articles before she could put their helpful hints to use. Nevertheless, because she is grateful for the kind gesture, in return she encloses a brochure listing places to buy Hawaiian clothing in Texas, "should you have a need." With this exchange Nye humorously illustrates that letters provide an avenue for reciprocal sharing of a wealth of information, some useful, some fanciful.

The poem's second section opens with a letter writer's familiar apology: "I am sorry I did not answer for so long." As if to explain, the writer describes an important professional project that has consumed all her time; it involves writing to poets in sixty-eight countries asking for permission to publish their poems. This daunting letter-writing task, which costs 95 cents per letter, has prevented the speaker from penning personal letters to friends. She attempts to correct this situation in part 3 by responding to a woman who has lived on an island her entire life but who is now leaving. Ironically, the narrator longs to revisit the island, whose beauty has stayed with her since her visit many years before: "your island/ stays lodged inside me, a mint/ I turn over and over with my tongue for its endless/ flavor." It is apparent that the two writers would like to change places, just as their letters do, but they cannot.

In section 4 the speaker marvels at how the mail system permits individuals who barely met, "barely brushed one another" in the rush of life, to become friends and to share ideas, books, and cherished possessions that link their diverse communities. The final section appropriately celebrates the wonder and richness of new acquaintances who arrive by mail with a hello "so long and wide/ whole countries live inside it." These enlightening and welcome missives bring descriptions of each tree and corner in another part of the world. Ending the poem with a return to shape and size, Nye symbolically suggests that letters should be made in the shape of kites to ride "the ache of breeze" that lies between the correspondents.

Forms and Devices

Figurative language abounds in Nye's lively poem about the power of the written word. Engaging the reader's fancy, she employs personification to explore the human qualities of letters. She calls them "travelers" who journey through "slots and chutes and shelves and bags" and then, because often it is a very long and tiring journey, fall asleep in the narrator's black mailbox. When she slices open the letters with the blade of a small knife taken from "a case carved like a fish," this simple gesture "opens a far world" as news from friends and family pours forth, "cranking the creaky door of the heart." Sometimes, visited by an "impudent question," she wonders if she is equal to the task of responding. Like the words of the letters she receives, Nye's words touch and enlighten readers. Poet William Stafford has praised Nye's poetry for combining "transcendent liveliness and sparkle along with warmth and human insight." He calls her "a champion of encouragement and heart."

One reason for Naomi Shihab Nye's appeal is her skillful use of metaphor to examine gently the interplay of countries and cultures. In the third section, the letter to her island friend, the speaker compares her memory of the island to a mint, rolling around on her tongue as she absorbs and savors the flavor. This sweetness sharply contrasts with the other woman's aching desire to leave the same island. Her friend wears "the colors of the horizon inside [her] bruise," suggesting that the reality of her life is surely nothing like the speaker's delicious island memory. One of the ways readers come to understand the complexity of other cultures is by sharing stories. Nye introduces this intimacy through juxtaposed events, images, and bits of dialogue, which in a sense become for the reader an overheard long-distance conversation.

The poetic discourse of "Sincerely" consists of a series of questions, of the sort one typically asks friends in correspondence, such as "Yes, I am fine. . . . What about you?" and, in reference to a long lapse between letters, "Can you be patient?" Later in the poem, as she ponders sending a woolen doll from Chiapas to a new friend, she asks, "Do you want her?" The questioning draws readers into the epistolary exchange, and although they hear only half the conversation, they may occasionally be tempted to answer, to slip into a new role, thereby better understanding cultures outside their own experience. Nye elicits this reader response so subtly that the effect may be overlooked.

Themes and Meanings

The collection from which this poem comes, *Red Suitcase*, is filled with global travels and the curiosity and richness engendered by life's journeys. Poet and literary critic Alicia Ostriker has written that "Naomi Shihab Nye is at home in this world . . . a world that includes the Middle East and Texas, men and women, childhood, parenthood and old age, the pain of war and exile." She brings a particularly accepting and peaceful vision to her poetry that transcends political difference and transforms singular lives into global communities. "Sincerely," as its title suggests, offers an epistolary method and a truth-seeking heart for this important undertaking. Nye's favorite motif of travel is explored in new ways. As the speaker reflects upon the entire letter-writing phenomenon, she says, "Think of the waves and wires/ this envelope must cross. The mountains and muddles." It seems almost a miracle that people worldwide can connect in this way.

An important consideration for Naomi Shihab Nye is that letters (and her poem about letters) can be used to enhance global and personal understanding. Often people are consumed by their own lives—their children, their jobs, or as Nye says, "the flood of comings-and-goings." While they may not think they have the time or interest to learn about other cultures, letters provide the perfect opportunity. While letter writing may appear to be a simple act, there exists another layer of meaning beneath the words. One of Nye's earlier collections of poetry about ethnic diversity, acceptance, and peace is entitled *Words Under the Words* (1995), and "Sincerely," too, shows an emphasis on subtext, on the lives behind the words. These range from the speaker's busy professional literary life to the lonely life of her friend living "on the cliff so long,/ staring off to sea dreaming what lies/ on the other side." The island dweller believes that big U.S. cities are "what is happening." The poet's vision, however, casts doubt on the assumption that Western ways are the "right" or only ways. Never one to coerce her readers, Nye considerately packs a suitcase big enough for everyone and says, "Come along." If readers welcome new vistas and experiences, they will find her a sensitive and compassionate guide.

Carol F. Bender

SIR PATRICK SPENS

Author: Unknown
Type of poem: Ballad
First published: 1765, in *Reliques of Ancient English Poetry*

The Poem

"Sir Patrick Spens" is a well-known and popular ballad of unknown origin. The poem has many versions, with considerable variation in length and detail, as indicated in Francis James Child's five-volume collection, *The English and Scottish Popular Ballads* (1882-1898), which includes eighteen versions under the title "Sir Patrick Spence." The most widely known version is a composite one with modernized spelling which appears in volume 1 of *The Norton Anthology of English Literature*, starting with the first edition in 1962. In the most common version, the poem has eleven stanzas, each consisting of four lines, with the second and fourth lines rhyming. Even in the modernized version, the language suggests a long-ago Scots dialect that is more easily understood when the words are said aloud than when they are seen printed on the page. This is entirely appropriate and in keeping with the history of ballads, anonymous narrative songs that were preserved by oral transmission long before they were written down.

It is also typical of ballads that the historical events which might have led to the creation of the ballad are unclear. It is not known which king might be referred to in the poem or if there ever was an actual Sir Patrick Spens. Connecting details, such as why the king ordered Sir Patrick Spens to sea, where he was headed, or why the Scots lords were aboard the ship, are not given, but the stark tragedy is clear.

"Sir Patrick Spens," like most traditional ballads, relates a sad and tragic story of danger and death. The Scottish king, in Dumferline, wants a sailor to sail his ship. An old knight says that Sir Patrick Spens is the best sailor; the king writes and signs a letter, which is delivered to him as he is walking along the seacoast. At first Sir Patrick laughs at the order, then a tear blinds his eye and he asks who has done this "ill deed" to send him to sea at this time of the year (presumably winter, when the sea is at its roughest).

Sir Patrick Spens tells his men that they will sail in the morning. One man expresses the fear that there will be a deadly storm and that they will "come to harm," because he has seen an omen of danger, a circle rounding out the new moon. A group of Scots noblemen are aboard the ship when it sinks. The ladies on the shore will wait in vain for their return. They will never see Sir Patrick Spens or his passengers again. Instead, deep in the sea, halfway between somewhere and Aberdour, Scotland, there lies Sir Patrick Spens, with the Scots lords at his feet.

Forms and Devices

"Sir Patrick Spens" consists of quatrains (stanzas of four lines), with the second and fourth lines rhyming, a rhyme scheme commonly signified as *abcb*. The lines alternate between tetrameter (four metrical feet, or stressed syllables, per line) and trimeter (three feet per line). Such quatrains are called ballad stanzas. The basic meter is iambic, an unstressed syllable followed by a stressed (accented) syllable, the most commonly used poetic foot in English-language poetry. "Sir Patrick Spens" is virtually a model of the form of the traditional English ballad.

The regular meter, or beat, of the ballad is typical in that ballads were originally songs. The simplicity of the music to which they were sung not only influenced the distinctive verse form but also promoted a simplicity in the narrative itself. In addition, because they were oral, rather than written, over time stanzas were lost or forgotten, phrases altered, and details changed. Further changes were made as editors from the eighteenth through the twentieth century collated versions and selected phrases and lines they deemed most poetic or appropriate. Thus the narrative has an intense compression, a spareness that concentrates on the culmination of the action, on the heart of the tragedy.

The poem opens with an image: "The king sits . . ./ Drinking the blude-reid wine." That blood-red wine is foreboding and immediately raises disturbing questions. Is the king capable of making sound judgments? Does he revel in asserting his authority? Does he understand the risk to all those he sends to sea? Imagery carries much of the drama of the story. After the king sends his letter, the fourth stanza shows Sir Patrick reading the orders. At first he laughs in disbelief, but he quickly understands its mortal import, and "a tear blinded his ee" (his eye). Nonetheless, he summons his crew. As so often occurs in ballads, some omen of death emphasizes the danger and psychologically increases the fear. An unnamed crew member laments that late the night before, "I saw the new moon/ Wi' the auld moon in her arm,/ And I fear./ That we will come to harm." The image of the crescent moon with the outline of the fully rounded moon was often believed to be an indication of severe storms to come, but in the poem there are no details of storms, winter seas, or a ship floundering and sinking. Juxtaposed with the image of the ominous moon, however, is an image of death by drowning. Here the poetic device is synecdoche, using a word that substitutes a part for the whole: The lords had worried about their cork-heeled shoes getting wet; now their hats float above the water.

The women will wait in vain for any of the lords or for Sir Patrick Spens, for they will "see thame na mair" (no more). The use of the age-old Scots dialect makes the entire poem, including the ending, seem more authentic; the words seem to come from the voice of the bard singer or a common person dolefully considering the inexorable workings of destiny. Deep under the water, "there lies guid Sir Patrick Spens."

Themes and Meanings

No historical Sir Patrick Spens or Spence is known. "Sir Patrick Spens" may be based on a thirteenth century historical event, or combination of events, involving a Scottish king's daughter or granddaughter being taken to or brought home from Norway. It may be a conflation of several different shipwrecks, focusing on the dangers of sailing and the supernatural omens that forewarn the doomed. It may simply be a story of suffering and loss that has no specific historical reference but is common to the human condition. Indeed, the ballad has a hauntingly universal appeal.

Many questions and themes emerge. The drowning seems needless, senseless. Yet there is at least a grudging admiration for Sir Patrick's prompt acquiescence to the king's unavoidable order and an even clearer sense that Sir Patrick's men go with him to sea because they are personally loyal and willing followers. One might wonder whether treachery was involved in the old knight's telling the king that Sir Patrick Spens was the best sailor. One might ask whether the king had an overwhelming reason to risk sending a ship to sea at a bad time of year and thought Sir Patrick was his only hope. Such concerns about human motivation have remained problematic throughout the centuries. The supernatural also continues to intrigue. Is there some unknown power that seeks to warn individuals about their actions? Is there some intuition, or some external projection of inner knowledge, that enables people to make optimal choices?

There are sociopolitical implications in the inclusion of the Scots lords, who appear in the numerous versions of the poem but are never explained. Although as in most ballads there is no editorial commentary, it is clear that Sir Patrick Spens is more admirable than the lords, particularly in the depiction of the lords as being so fussy that they did not want to get their fancy cork-heeled shoes wet even while aboard a ship and in the wry finality of their hats floating on the water. They themselves are not merely drowned with Sir Patrick but are "at his feet" in the watery grave.

A similar attitude is taken toward the ladies who sit with their fans in their hands and stand with their gold combs in their hair, waiting fruitlessly for their lords to return. These are not hardworking peasant women longing for the return of their husbands or sons. These ladies, like their lords, are pictured as the idle rich, perhaps as insensitive and demanding of others as the king may be.

These motifs do not lessen the impact of the narrative. Rather, everything adds to the impact of the loss of good Sir Patrick, to the finality of the loss of the ship and all aboard, and to the sense of events often being the result of forces beyond any individual control. At some level, the human spirit often finds itself crying out, with Sir Patrick Spens, "O wha is this has done this deed,/ This ill deed done to me"—and yet, the poem suggests, the individual continues to act, and at best proceeds with courage in the face of whatever storms may blow.

Lois A. Marchino

SIR WALTER RALEGH TO THE QUEEN

Author: Sir Walter Ralegh (c. 1552-1618)
Type of poem: Lyric
First published: 1655, in *Wits Interpreter*; collected in *The Poems of Sir Walter Raleigh, with a Biographical and Critical Introduction*, 1813

The Poem

Written sometime between 1581 and 1587, "Sir Walter Ralegh to the Queen," a thirty-eight-line lyrical poem in five stanzas, directly addresses Queen Elizabeth I of England. The queen has perhaps criticized Ralegh's failure to write love poems for her recently as indicative of his lack of affection or passion. His poem is meant to refute such criticism and to explain that his love is indeed true and unwavering despite his poetic silence. His organizing idea is the difference between true love and false love—with his love being true and others' love false.

His initial image compares human passions to "floods and streams" to argue that shallow passions, like shallow streams, "murmur," while deep passions, like deep floods of water, remain silent because of their natures. His conclusion on the basis of this analogy is that those who speak or write much about their inner feelings of affection in reality feel no such affection. If they are very verbal and outspoken about their emotions ("rich in words"), they will be lacking in the deeper affections characteristic of a lover and will be incompetent in the true art of love ("poor in that which makes a lover"). The second stanza applies the general rule to the particular case and asks the Queen, whom Ralegh praises as the "dear Empress" or ruler of his heart, not to misunderstand the value and nature of true passion. He asks her not to think that he feels no pain at her silence or their separation just because he does not beg her to be more compassionate and to take pity on his sad state. Instead, his silence is indicative of the depths of his genuine regard. Furthermore, if he does not write love poems complaining that she misunderstands how deeply her beauty has conquered his heart, the cause is not from any absence of love on his part but from "excess of duty" or a sense of obligation to her as queen.

The third stanza explains further. Ralegh says that because he knows that he seeks to serve a perfect saint, whose returned affection all desire but none deserve, he chooses to endure pain and grief rather than reveal his feelings. His strong, passionate feelings would compel him to write love poems to her, but because she is too high above him in rank, status, and perfection, and in fact too high above all other potential human lovers, discretion, reason, and devotion make him choose to be her suitor from afar, to love in silence. This silence, he argues, betokens a deeper sorrow at the distance that separates them than words could. Though words might be wittier, they would be more superficial. As a "beggar" who cannot speak, he argues that he deserves more pity than those who openly complain about their lovelorn state. His final appeal is for the queen, his "dearest heart," not to misread his secret passion, a passion he swears is true. Ultimately, he asks for her compassion for the deep pain he hides at the same time that he asserts that he asks for no compassion. (The psychological game is like that employed in William Shakespeare's Sonnet 130, claiming not to be doing something while doing something.) Thus, in a poem that is a love complaint, Ralegh claims not to be writing love complaints out of courtesy and love for his queen. He claims that silent suffering is more indicative of love than writing a poem in which he presents himself as the silent sufferer.

Forms and Devices

Scholarly debate has questioned whether "Sir Walter Ralegh to the Queen" (sometimes called "The Silent Lover" or "To the Queen") is truly a five-stanza poem or two poems merged: "Sir Walter to the Queen" (one stanza) and "Wrong not, Dear Empress of my Heart" (four stanzas). Certainly, the first stanza differs in form from the last four. It contains four lines with alternating end rhyme (*abab*) and then a concluding couplet (*cc*), all in iambic pentameter. The remaining four stanzas have eight lines each, an alternating rhyme that changes sound sets after the first four lines (*ababcdcd*), and iambic tetrameter. However, the stanzas are unified by imagery and argument, and major Ralegh specialists argue that they belong together. Lines 1, 3, and 5 of the first stanza have variations on the iambic meter, lines 3 and 4 are enjambed, and the couplet has a feminine rhyme; such variations recur throughout the remaining stanzas.

Ralegh rhymes "prove" with "love" and "utter" with "suitor," sounds that no longer rhyme in English but that did in Renaissance England. The word "Plaints" is a shortened form of "Complaints" and refers to a special convention of love poetry—the love complaint, in which the lover complains about ill treatment at the hands of an indifferent or uncaring lover, all to win her pity and compassion and perhaps an admission of returned affection. Ralegh must be cautious here because his audience is not a real lover or even a would-be lover but the queen, on whom his fortune depends, and his poem, though privately passed around a limited court circle, was nonetheless a public statement, not an intimate, private communication.

As a literate and unmarried queen, Elizabeth enjoyed playing the witty game of love through poetry as a way to bind her courtiers to her. As a court favorite who had many enemies, Ralegh had to move between flattery and witty gamesmanship—he had to flatter, entertain, and win the queen's favor and support. The poem depends on a central image to make its argument: passions compared to floods and streams that can sweep one up in their power. Shallow, noisy streams of little force are contrasted with deep, silent channels of force and power. This comparison was a standard Renaissance image. Sir Edward Dyer's "The lowest trees have tops," for example, similarly asserts, "Where waters smoothest run, deep are the fords," and "True hearts have ears and eyes, no tongues to speak," while Sir Philip Sidney's *Arcadia* (I,127) notes, "Shallow brooks murmur most, deep silent slide away." The watery nature of the image would be connected with the Renaissance idea of the four humors that control human behavior—in this case emphasizing blood, which would motivate the lover and cause passion to overwhelm reason. It would also wittily play with the queen's nickname for Ralegh. Others called him simply "Wat," but she called him her "Water," since he sailed the seas winning booty and new lands for her. Ralegh plays his own variations on the water image and theme, managing to have things two ways: He asserts his passion in the image of deep, powerful waters but also his reason, which makes him do what duty and discretion demand rather than yield to personal feelings of love that would be presumptuous, given the difference in status between his beloved and himself.

Themes and Meanings

"Sir Walter Ralegh to the Queen" is an anatomy of love—its central theme is the difference between true love and false love: False love is hidden in a swirl of superficial verbiage; true love is painfully silent. Ralegh's argument follows traditional Renaissance themes and conventions. For instance, he emphasizes the traditional Elizabethan view of humankind as torn between passion and reason, emphasizing that his passion would lead him to write love poems (complaints), and praise the queen's saintly perfection, beauty, and glory in order to win her affection or at least to entertain her. In contrast to despairing lovelorn poetic narrators (such as Sir Thomas Wyatt in "Whoso list to hunt"), he has let reason dominate for the queen's sake. Revealing his affection openly would not only be indiscreet and subject to misinterpretation, given her high rank and the fact that so many others are also charmed by her, but would also be a denial of the depth of his true affection, which, like deep waters, is so strong that he must be silent. Another poetic convention of courtiers is exaggerated praise of the beloved, who here is acknowledged to be beyond the reach of mortals.

The poem's themes of secret love, of the despairing, agonizing lover, and of a potential for misunderstanding or public injury recur in Ralegh's poetry. They seem in keeping with Ralegh's ongoing poetic dialogue with his queen, although some modern commentators have attempted to attribute this poem to Sir Robert Ayton rather than to Ralegh. Inevitably, in such a poem, private meaning related to the daily personal conversations between the queen and her favorite would lie behind the public utterance, especially given Ralegh and the queen's love of theatrics and their long history of public performance of their interacting life roles. In "See those sweet eyes," for example, Ralegh expresses a similar sentiment and situation—the lover gazing on the "sweetest eyes" is unable to plead his case and praise his beloved's beauty because her greatness, her inexpressible merit, and his sense of duty force him into silence.

The uncertain chronology of the poem in terms of Ralegh's relationship with the queen leaves critics uncertain about the precise vicissitudes of Ralegh's career—whether he was in or out of favor—at the time this poem was written. What is known is that the poem was written to serve the needs of Ralegh's career and it fuses personal feeling with conventional arguments. Ralegh thus turns his life into art.

Gina Macdonald

SIREN

Author: Christopher Ifekandu Okigbo (1932-1967)
Type of poem: Lyric
First published: 1964, in *Limits*; collected as "Siren Limits" in *Labyrinths, with Path of Thunder*, 1971

The Poem

The work of Christopher Okigbo, a Nigerian poet, is extremely difficult to approach, because it incorporates both the African and European traditions. This blending is evident in the imagery and allusions that rely interchangeably on the two heritages. It also distinguishes the technique, which not only reflects the indigenous literature and religious incantations of the Igbo people in Nigeria but includes as well the ritualistic language of Roman Catholicism and Western poets ranging from Gerard Manley Hopkins to T. S. Eliot.

The four numbered parts of "Siren" constitute what might be called Okigbo's artistic credo. Here the poet—noted for his reluctance to discuss his own work—is "Suddenly becoming talkative." Part 1 of "Siren" employs an essential ingredient of the Igbo religious ceremony, the incantation, as the poet invokes the goddess with her traditional trappings, "A tiger mask and nude spear." Having undergone his "cleansing" through this quasi-religious ceremony, he is ready to express his Africanness through poetry.

In the second part, Okigbo draws an elaborate metaphor in which he traces the development of a poet's career, starting as "a shrub among the poplars"—that is, an aspiring writer among those already established. He sees writers as "Horsemen of the apocalypse," which is a typical reaction in Africa where the writer considers himself and is considered by others to be the conscience and voice of a people battling to overcome the tragic aftermath of colonialism. Finally, he imagines fame displaying "its foliage" and hanging like "A green cloud" over the world.

The third part elaborates on the struggle of the artist, who creates in adverse circumstances amid "Banks of reed./ Mountains of broken bottles." The introduction of a line that will be repeated several times, "*& the mortar is not yet dry. . . .,*" suggests the poet should not rush into the exercise of his craft until he is ready and until his audience is receptive: he must wait until the mortar, or the inspiration and receptiveness, has set firmly. Otherwise, "the voice fades . . ./ Not leaving a mark."

Okigbo often borrows lines from other poets, and such is the case with the refrain, "*& the mortar is not yet dry. . . .*" It comes from Canto 8 by Ezra Pound (1885-1972). The only change Okigbo made was to replace Pound's opening word "As" with "&." In its original context, the line stands as a warning to a painter not to paint the chapels until they are ready; as Pound says in the next line, "it w'd be merely work chucked away." Okigbo uses this quotation to clarify the stages of the poet's development and in so doing lends the rather mundane statement a fullness and richness lacking in its original presentation.

The account of the poet's plight continues in the fourth part, a series of abstract images representing the trials the artist faces in a hostile world. Once the difficulties have been overcome, though, the poet may be awakened from his dream of creativity and his "poem will be finished."

Forms and Devices

The lyricism, economy of expression, stark imagery, and emotional intensity of "Siren" draw not only from the indigenous forms of Igbo poetry but also from modernist European poetry, with which Okigbo was familiar. Such allusions as "weaverbird," "palm grove," "he-goat-on-heat," and "My lioness" are very African. At the same time, lines such as "So we must go,/ Wearing evemist against the shoulders," bring to mind the opening of T. S. Eliot's "The Love Song of J. Alfred Prufrock." Yet the poetry is not derivative; rather, it makes striking use for its own purposes of the poet's divided heritage by echoing African and European texts.

Some readers of Okigbo's work have observed that it does not really matter whether every line of the poems can be grasped intellectually and their exact meaning explained. The imagery, so much of it drawn from the African experience, both traditional and contemporary, may at times mystify the Western reader. Yet even when the density seems overwhelming, pure lyricism dominates and provides a poetic experience more emotional and aesthetic than cerebral. The fourth part of "Siren," for example, while undeniably obscure in its allusions and abbreviated expression, still brims with a poetic intensity that succeeds in itself.

A passage from the third part of "Siren," exemplifies Okigbo's technical virtuosity at its best. Five lines consist simply of "Hurry on down," each followed by an indented line; two of the lines describe actual places: the gate and the market. The other two admonitions to "Hurry on down" move from reality into "the wake of the dream"; this juxtaposition of the concrete and the abstract is a recurrent phenomenon in Okigbo's poetry. The final invitation to "Hurry on down" has as its destination the "rockpoint of CABLE." Cable Point is a real location in Nigeria, a sacred waterfront with a rocky promontory and the place where traditional religious pilgrimages end. The repetition and the rhythms established suggest the movement of a procession through the gate and the market; this section might well stand as a description of a pilgrimage. Then the glimmer of reality vanishes, as is always the case in Okigbo's poetry. And the pilgrimage becomes the poetic quest.

Another section in the third part shows how the poem gains emotional intensity through devices both dense and stark. Saying that the poet "must sing/ Tongue-tied without name or audience," Okigbo calls this moment "the crisis-point." Yet the voice survives and speaks, "Not thro' pores in the flesh/ but the soul's backbone." That metaphor, "the soul's backbone," so simple, yet so brimming with suggestiveness, is an altogether original way to describe the indefinable quality that directs the poetic process.

Although Okigbo expresses the fear at the end of the third part of "Siren" that his poetry, "Like a shadow," would fade, "Not leaving a mark," the misgiving was unfounded. His work is striking in its technique, both dense and spare, richly allusive, full of imagery coming "from the flag-pole of the heart." Admittedly, at times the very imagery that distinguishes the poetry sometimes distracts from its clear and concise meaning. Yet, like the oral African tradition from which Okigbo drew, a poem such as "Siren" more often sounds than means.

Themes and Meanings

Reared in the Catholicism brought to Africa by missionaries and educated in mission schools, Okigbo revolted against the imported theology and like a prodigal son returned to the religion of his ancestors. This rejection and return form the basis of much of his poetry, as does the plight of the artist caught in a chasm between two conflicting traditions, the indigenous and the borrowed. "Siren" gains resonance when read in the context of Okigbo's other poetry, but even alone it turns into an important document illustrating the way African poetry in English has usurped the colonial language and transformed it into that which is undeniably African.

On one level, "Siren" expresses Okigbo's dedication to the art of poetry. The poem's name, "Siren," suggests that he has no choice but to follow this path, for he has been bewitched. The title, drawing from Greek mythology, brings to mind those insidiously seductive creatures who by their singing lured mariners to destruction. Yet as Okigbo so often does with allusions, he reverses the destructive element of the Siren and turns her into the goddess of poetry whom he invokes in part 1. Thus the Siren of poetry, addressed as a kind of African goddess in spite of her Greek origins, retains the ability to bewitch and seduce, but sheds her pernicious qualities for creative ones.

On another level, "Siren" expresses the dilemma of many an African writer in English, not just that of Okigbo. After all, they are writing in the language of the former colonizer; and African writers and critics, well aware of this irony, often question how the African experience can be expressed in a borrowed language, especially that of a conqueror who had derided all things African. These writers also find themselves far from the "center" of English language literature, that is British and American writing. As Okigbo says, they are "shrub[s] among the poplars." Who will listen to them or read them? Many of their countrymen do not know English, so the writers are sometimes accused of pandering to the West, where readers may think "the mortar is not yet dry" on what has come to be called "postcolonial literature." This writing from the former colonies, then, is at "the crisis-point" and may be in danger of "Not leaving a mark." Even as the poem concludes, Okigbo says "*& this poem will be finished*," thus implying that he—and the others—will continue the pursuit of the impossible, "To pull by the rope/ The big white elephant."

Robert L. Ross

THE SKATERS

Author: John Ashbery (1927-   )
Type of poem: Meditation
First published: 1964; collected in *Rivers and Mountains*, 1966

The Poem

The Skaters is an extensive meditation, its 739 lines divided into four sections of unequal lengths. The title, taken from the Giacomo Meyerbeer ballet *Les Patineurs*, introduces the controlling metaphor of the poem, figures gliding swiftly over opaque surfaces, and rightly suggests that the poem's technique will be one of actions rather than of statements and conclusions.

The poem is written in the first person, yet as with many of John Ashbery's poems, the identity of the speaker is in constant, restless metamorphosis. One can never at any moment claim to know exactly who the "I" is, and one must not assume that it is always the poet speaking as himself.

The Skaters is a poem of perceptions unrestricted by framing devices, and it presents the reader with an almost overwhelming panorama of details and incidents. It prefers experience to understanding and confounds any attempts to summarize it by ordinary means. As a meditation on the vast subject of uncertainty, that unseen region over whose mere surface the skaters move, it must be elusive in order to be true to its subject. Nevertheless, the intimacy and playfulness of its tone permit the reader, once the usual critical faculties are relaxed, to follow the poem through its distinctive movements into an understanding of its intentions.

Section 1 introduces the problem around which the poem conducts its meditations: How can one for certain assume that life is good when nothing in life is certain? This problem is embodied in the skaters whose "swift blades" glide gracefully but unknowingly, quickly but circuitously, leaving no permanent record of their passage behind them. The first section continues through many variations of this thematic imagery—"water surface ripples," "gestures half-sketched against woodsmoke," drifting balloons, soap bubbles—each of which intensifies the poet's awareness of his dilemma. If everything is merely transient, it is easy to conclude that "Everything is trash."

Section 2 describes the poet's attempts to escape his dilemma through numerous dreams in the form of imaginary voyages similar to those in Charles Baudelaire's "The Invitation to the Voyage" and Arthur Rimbaud's "The Drunken Boat." Being only imaginary, however, none of these voyages can ever be completed, so the speaker is thrown back upon his original problem, one which may now be thought of as a life of infinite departures and no arrivals.

Section 3 explores the harshness of reality after a long dream. The most naturalistic and autobiographical of the poem's sections (recalling details from the poet's childhood on a New York farm and from his years of voluntary exile in Paris), it discovers the one and only arrival of which the speaker can be certain: death. This certainty is quickly judged to be of little comfort and no practical use. Rejecting death, the speaker hurries to reaffirm dreaming as his "most important activity," his greatest freedom in an incomprehensible world.

In a parade of fragmentary scenarios, the final section reinforces the futility of attempting to contain reality with patterns and philosophies. Ashbery chooses to celebrate what he cannot refute: the arbitrariness of everything. The poem ends, therefore, with the constellations of Taurus, Leo, and Gemini rising in a "perfect order" which is neither astronomically nor astrologically valid, but which instead is the order of pure accident.

Forms and Devices

In a poem as turbulent and extensive as *The Skaters*, nearly all the devices of English poetry are employed, wholly or partially, literally or allusively, as the language of the work proliferates through the poet's various intentions. Indeed, it may well be said of Ashbery that he has constantly attempted to write a kind of poetry that cannot be captured by any conventional definition.

Still, there are clearly a number of key devices that propel *The Skaters* toward its thematic ends. Chief among these is the metaphor which gives the poem its title. A skater trusts his life to surfaces alone and so embraces in his activity the notion of experience without understanding, movement without depth. Were he to pause in his gliding, for reflection, he would fall and be none the wiser for having reflected. The skater accepts the circuitousness of his sport, not as a vapid sequence of repetitions, but as a series of infinitely unique variations on the theme of movement. Thus the skater is the perfect metaphorical representative of both the poem's rhetorical technique and of its closing affirmation.

The most memorable imagery in *The Skaters* serves to reinforce the effect of its principal metaphor. In nearly every passage, images of drift, of careless motion, appear. Balloons, soap bubbles, smoke, and sudden storms all arise in their turns and as quickly disappear, only to reappear at later moments, as if to proclaim the durability of their waywardness, the permanence of their transient natures.

Mirroring this waywardness at the level of language itself is Ashbery's propensity to combine vulgar phrases (such as "I'd like to bugger you" and "all your old suck-ass notions") with high poetic diction, passages of triviality ("Any more golfing hints, Charlie?") with those of profound seriousness. The effect is to make the poem's voice as elusive as its imagery and its central metaphor. The words of the poem are thus as restless as its subject matter and so emulate in verse the techniques of the American "action painters" (such as Jackson Pollock and Franz Kline), whose canvases Ashbery, himself a noted art critic, so fervently admires. As the action painters regard their pictures as pure surfaces across which paint is literally pushed and pulled by the various energies of the artist, so Ashbery thinks of his page as a white surface (like a frozen pond) over which his imagination crosses and recrosses in the form of words. In literature, this method hearkens back to the aleatory (that is, intentionally accidental) devices of the French Surrealist movement founded by the poet/philosopher André Breton. Since *The Skaters* was written in Paris, Ashbery's affinity for Breton and his followers seems all the more serendipitous. Thus, one might say that all the devices of *The Skaters* work paradoxically to expose rather than to conceal their verbal trickery, just as it is the poem's paradoxical intention to celebrate intentionlessness.

Themes and Meanings

The Skaters unfolds its theme as a series of potential solutions to the problem of affirming life in the midst of countless uncertainties. Most philosophies console their adherents with at least the possibility of an absolute truth, a fixed point at the center of a changing world. Ashbery permits himself no such consolation, so he restlessly pursues the virtue of restlessness. The poem's very existence is the poem's theme (echoing the poet Archibald MacLeish's dictum that poems should not mean, but be), with the pursuit of affirmation substituting for affirmation itself.

Ashbery's theme has two distinct components. The first is essentially negative and expresses the futility of any search for certainty conducted among the chaotic surfaces of human life. The poem accumulates supporting evidence, not on behalf of Plato's harmonious world of eternal forms, but on behalf of the constant flux of Heraclitus, whose primary principle is expressed in the saying that no man steps into the same river twice. For the urban, twentieth century Ashbery (considered the chief figure of the New York School of poets), the ever-changing river becomes a city street: "We step out into the street, not realizing that the street is different." The world is entirely mutable; moreover, humans are not always even capable of perceiving its mutability. Such bleak considerations lead Ashbery to the expression of his theme's darkest component—"Only one thing exists: the fear of death." A person continues to live, not because any particular aspect of life is valuable or worthwhile, but because one would rather inhabit the unmeaning flux of being than achieve the fearful certainty of nonexistence.

Yet the lyrical profusion of *The Skaters* quickly evokes the brighter component of the poet's theme. There is, after all, a pleasure in uncertainty, the pleasure of anticipation, the ecstasy of the skater who seems to move effortlessly through an ever-accelerating panorama. While anticipation does not guarantee satisfaction, it does indeed vividly animate the days and years through which it transpires. If all experience is arbitrary, deprived of any ideal pattern, is there not possibly then a perfect arbitrariness, an accident entirely liberated from the disappointing constraints of hopeless intentionality? Thus Ashbery chooses to close *The Skaters* with those constellations rising in accordance with no mythological or scientific order whatsoever. One cannot fail to find certainty if one does not seek it, but instead rejoices in the infinite possibilities created by its absence. In the universe of *The Skaters*, the sheer abundance of dizzying perceptions available to anyone more than compensates for the poverty of human understanding. The meaning of life is in the mere living of it.

Donald Revell

SKETCH FOR AN AESTHETIC PROJECT

Author: Jay Wright (1935-   )
Type of poem: Narrative
First published: 1971, in *The Homecoming Singer*

The Poem

"Sketch for an Aesthetic Project" is a long narrative poem in four sections totaling ninety lines. Jay Wright employs the first-person voice to lend immediacy to the spontaneity of experience and thought. Three lines from Thomas Kinsella's "Nightwalker" introduce the poem: "I believe now that love is half persistence,/ A medium in which, from change to change,/ Understanding may be gathered." Wright's narrator achieves this understanding by equating aesthetics with the natural changes of love. The poem's first section contains three stanzas; the remaining three sections contain one stanza each.

In the first section's five-line stanza, the narrator describes his restlessness with his "stomp[ing] about these rooms in an old overcoat." Anxiety seldom compels him to leave his enclosure "even on sunny days," and his cold rooms suggest a dormant foundry.

One night, when he does leave, he finds emptiness, and this suggested locale corresponds to Wright's native Albuquerque, New Mexico, or the Mexico that he deeply enjoys. In the second and longest of this section's stanzas, the speaker discovers in the vacant environs a few persons, a burro, the sounds of his own footsteps, and the furtive "unthinking walkers" cursed by the arcane. The soul he hopes to meet "tugging a burro up the street/ loaded with wet wood" would be his alter ego, laden with fuel to ignite a beauteous aesthetic response, but this figure only beseeches him for alms. In this section, the poet establishes the searching artist who must tramp about in rain that soaks his sensibility and that, although he does not know it, becomes directly responsible for his sketch.

In his home place, the poet reconstructs his travels, "recalling the miracle of being there"—namely, in Harlem, New York—where he walked summers innocently while he breathed the city's smells, listened to its voices, and while his thoughts lingered on its religious and spiritual life, centered momentarily on the old deacon who is "a rabbi of the unscrupulous" to the women who watch him pass. The speaker identifies with this man who abides among the maddening voices of the people. Despite his physical distance from Harlem at this point in the poem, the aesthetic proximity unnerves him.

In section three, the narrator and "ingenuous sailors" experience the dullness of waiting near or on the sea. The speaker says, as if to himself, "Wake" to open the section to the artless but toiling sailors transporting their "bloody cargo" of slaves "up the shoreline." Keeping "a log for passage" enables him to record his emotional response to his project. The "parchments of blood" constituting this log happen to be "sunk where I cannot walk" because they are in his subconscious and racial memory. After the sailors have been "intensely buoyed by the sight of land/ and the fervent release of cankered bodies," the narrator remembers that even in the silence there prevails a "mythic shriek."

In the final and briefest section, the poet returns to the coldness, understanding the shriek as a metaphor for music. He realizes that his aesthetic solitude was an illusion, and that aesthetic beauty is undeniably alive and is "swift and mad as I am/ dark in its act/ [and] light" in the way it softens his irresolute notions about what an artist must do.

Forms and Devices

Because Jay Wright's poems are both deeply spiritual and profoundly experiential, his figurative language encompasses regions such as his native southwestern United States, Harlem, and other African American communities, and the richness of their languages, idioms, and rhythms. Many of his poems reflect his appreciation of African culture and history and its dissemination in the western hemisphere, and his readers also encounter Mesoamerican allusions and images.

Wright's narrative technique utilizes subtle musical qualities. He quickly creates staccato effect in "Sketch for an Aesthetic Project" with *st* sounds, often referring to action, in section 1—"I stomp," "I step," "staggering," "streets," and "a dimeyed student." He achieves a similar effect with "I clatter over cobbled streets. . . . I pretend not to be afraid of witches." The tensions that assist and sustain creativity are reflected in this section's hard consonants, but these hard sounds yield to softer sounds as the poem proceeds until they return in section 3. The effective repetition of words and sounds, another musical quality, can be found in the phrase "only, perhaps" in line 8, restated in line 11 of the first section, and near the close of sections 1 and 3, where those whose presence the narrator needs would either "pluck my pity" or "pluck my bones."

The narrative style of section 2 is less figurative and more direct, its language denotative, although the poet finds vitality in the streets of Harlem. Yet Wright freely relies on hard verbs and active adverbs to heighten the subtheme of the suppression of ideas and actions. The narrator may walk his home streets, but he does not fear the witches who reside there "or any forces/ ground down under the years here,/ carping and praying under stones." These do not intimidate him. The burro tugged by one he hopes to meet carries a burden, and in front of the Harlem store-front church the speaker feels weighted down beneath the deacon's scrutinizing gaze, admitting that, later in the poem, he can neither "grovel under the deacon's eyes" nor remain on his stairs. These images culminate in his depiction of the reality of the sea upon which he cannot perform the miracle of walking.

In addition, the second section of the poem contains sibilant sounds, especially in the passage "I walk in summer, innocently,/ . . . down Seventh, . . ./ twisting." This sibilance continues into the third section, where Wright skillfully deploys *ss* words such as "blessed" and the "less" suffix.

Themes and Meanings

Cooped up in his rooms, the artist-narrator cannot create. He must depart to see emptiness, to remember a vibrant and colorful life, and to fashion his aesthetic from both conditions.

Aesthetics has to do with the artful and beautiful qualities of an artifact or an expression. The arts are characterized by intangibles that tend to defy descriptive analysis, and a precise meaning of aesthetics and aesthetic qualities may be relative to the individual artist and perceiver. Everyone, however, whether creative artist, inventor, layperson, or devotee, responds emotionally and intellectually to aesthetic qualities of harmony, symmetry, motion or rhythm, perception, sonority and tone, and the effects these and related elements have on the senses.

In "Sketch for an Aesthetic Project," Wright associates the restless search for the moment of creation with memory, history, and immediate reality. His speaker relates the total experience of intimate awareness about his surroundings, and this intellectual totality cannot be divorced from what he knows experientially. Wright does not quote Kinsella spuriously, for love is the principle of the artist's desire to create something beautiful. An artistic person cannot function without love, just as the tension love produces must be recognized as being stifled should he remain pensive in his cold rooms, avoiding the world outside.

The speaker loves his tranquil home and he loves Harlem. He comes to recognize and accept his ability to assimilate both places just as he can assimilate place and history. Slavers and "ingenuous slavers" can make no art; their anticipations of landfall are fruitless. Their cargo means more to him because he can connect the descendants of the cargo to something wonderful even if it is maddening. The sickly images of "cankered bodies" and the "bloody parchments" are the stuff of creation.

The music of the last section culminates the gathering process of his understanding, for the aesthetic gesture springs from those balances described by the "mythic shriek" of awareness, the "illusion of solitude," the "swift and mad," the dark and light. Wright has found that aesthetic principles make for a delicate balance of these images to one who resorts to understanding history, the spirituality offered by the mundane, and the divinely inspired perceptions of one's own self-worth.

Ron Welburn